ECONOMIC AND FINANCIAL SANCTIONS OF THE UNITED STATES

From the Cold War era to the current century, the US has wielded substantial authority in imposing sanctions. This book delves into the intricate and multifaceted landscape of US economic and financial sanctions, unraveling their historical development, legal foundations, and geopolitical motivations. Case studies on five of the most-sanctioned countries in the world – Russia, Iran, Iraq, Cuba, and Venezuela – provide a deeper understanding of how the sanctioning measures allow the US to extend its reach beyond its national boundaries through extraterritorial laws, sophisticated enforcement mechanisms, and the pervasive dollar-denominated global economic structure. Meticulous and nuanced, this book is a go-to resource for understanding sanctions regimes from both multilateral and unilateral perspectives and the relevant international laws and jurisprudence.

Caf Dowlah is a visiting scholar at the University of Miami Law School. Dr. Dowlah has published more than 30 scholarly papers and authored over a dozen books, including *Foundations of Modern Slavery* (2021) and *Cross-Border Labor Mobility* (2020).

Economic and Financial Sanctions of the United States

LEGAL PERSPECTIVES

CAF DOWLAH

University of Miami Law School

CAMBRIDGE
UNIVERSITY PRESS

CAMBRIDGE
UNIVERSITY PRESS

Shaftesbury Road, Cambridge CB2 8EA, United Kingdom

One Liberty Plaza, 20th Floor, New York, NY 10006, USA

477 Williamstown Road, Port Melbourne, VIC 3207, Australia

314–321, 3rd Floor, Plot 3, Splendor Forum, Jasola District Centre, New Delhi – 110025, India

103 Penang Road, #05–06/07, Visioncrest Commercial, Singapore 238467

Cambridge University Press is part of Cambridge University Press & Assessment, a department of the University of Cambridge.

We share the University's mission to contribute to society through the pursuit of education, learning and research at the highest international levels of excellence.

www.cambridge.org
Information on this title: www.cambridge.org/9781009471343

DOI: 10.1017/9781009471381

When citing this work, please include a reference to the DOI 10.1017/9781009471381

First published 2025

A catalogue record for this publication is available from the British Library

Library of Congress Cataloging-in-Publication Data
NAMES: Dowlah, Caf, 1958– author.
TITLE: Economic and financial sanctions of the United States : legal perspectives / Caf Dowlah, University of Miami Law School.
DESCRIPTION: Cambridge, United Kingdom ; New York, NY : Cambridge University Press, 2025. | Includes bibliographical references and index.
IDENTIFIERS: LCCN 2023052222 | ISBN 9781009471343 (hardback) | ISBN 9781009471381 (ebook)
SUBJECTS: LCSH: Sanctions (Law) – United States. | Economic sanctions – United States.
CLASSIFICATION: LCC KF9225 .D69 2025 | DDC 341.5/820973–dc23/eng/20231120
LC record available at https://lccn.loc.gov/2023052222

ISBN 978-1-009-47134-3 Hardback
ISBN 978-1-009-47135-0 Paperback

Dedicated to the countless Iraqi infants and children whose lives were tragically cut short as a result of a global deception masked by Iraq's alleged possession of weapons of mass destruction.

Contents

Figures

Tables

Preface

This book explores the intricate and multifaceted nature of the economic and financial sanctions of the United States, unraveling their historical evolution, legal foundations, enforcement mechanisms, geopolitical underpinnings, and tangible impacts on targeted nations, entities, and individuals around the world. Few studies provide such a comprehensive understanding of US sanctions regimes, rooted in meticulous research and scholarly interpretations.

The US has been a central force in imposing sanctions, especially during the Cold War, continuing into the twenty-first century. Presently, over two dozen countries and countless entities and individuals navigate inescapable US sanctions, extending beyond borders through extraterritorial laws, sophisticated enforcement, and the dollar-dominated global economic system. Unlike previous empires, that of the US defies geographical constraints.

In the pages that follow, we invite readers on a journey that delves into intricate queries surrounding breaches of international law, casting light on both the intentional and unintended outcomes of these measures from the vantage points of the principles of international law, state sovereignty, and fundamental human rights. We navigate the terrain that questions the validity and effectiveness of sanctions as tools to deter globally wrongful actions.

To facilitate a more profound comprehension of the sanctions regimes, this book undertakes in-depth analyses of two Latin American countries, two Asian countries, and a Eurasian nation that have been subject to US sanctions since World War II: the Russian Federation, the Islamic Republic of Iran, the Republic of Iraq, the Republic of Cuba, and the Bolivarian Republic of Venezuela. Through these case studies, the historical contexts, geopolitical landscapes, legal foundations, and the repercussions of the sanctions regimes on the economies and populations of these nations are unveiled.

The meticulous research and legal analyses presented in this book draw upon secondary sources from around the globe – both Western and non-Western literature has been extensively studied to offer a well-rounded viewpoint on the US sanctions regimes. The intention is to foster a more comprehensive grasp of this pivotal aspect of modern global affairs, its influence on shaping norms and principles in the global legal order, and the concurrent challenges and prospects it introduces to the contemporary world.

Grateful acknowledgments are owed to numerous scholars and researchers whose works have been consulted and referenced throughout this book. This project has received contributions from numerous individuals in various capacities, although it is not feasible to acknowledge each contribution individually. However, I would like to extend my sincere gratitude to Professor Gillian Lester, dean of Columbia Law School, and Professor David Yellen, dean of the University of Miami Law School, for granting me the position of visiting scholar in 2022 and 2023, respectively. Such opportunities facilitated my access to their extensive library resources, enabling thorough research for this project. I also thank Irina Kandarasheva of Columbia Law School Library and Carolina Morris of the University of Miami Law School for their valuable assistance in my research endeavors.

I hold special appreciation for Professors Caroline Bradley from the University of Miami Law School, Sergio Campos from Boston College Law School, and Lori Damrosch from Columbia Law School. Their review of multiple chapters of the book, along with their perceptive and constructive insights, comments, and feedback, has been invaluable. Additionally, I extend my gratitude to the anonymous reviewers at Cambridge University Press for their thorough and constructive evaluation of the manuscript, which has significantly contributed to its intellectual rigor.

Furthermore, I would like to extend my sincere gratitude to Professor Gary Hufbauer of the Peterson Institute of International Economics in Washington, DC, a distinguished expert in the domain of economic sanctions, who has served as my mentor over a considerable period. The unwavering guidance he has generously offered has proven to be of exceptional significance in the course of this academic pursuit.

Finally, my sincere gratitude goes to Matt Gallaway, publisher of Law at Cambridge University Press, for his enthusiastic engagement in the project and adept management of the editorial review and approval process. I also extend special thanks to Jadyn Fauconier-Herry, the editorial assistant, and the production editor Jessica Norman at Cambridge University Press, project manager Swati Kumari, and copy-editor Judith Everard for their adroit navigation of the book through the production process.

It has been a remarkable intellectual odyssey into the US and international legal frameworks and discourses on economic and financial sanctions from both historical and contemporary perspectives. While I have borrowed extensively from the contributions of scholars, authors, and contributors worldwide, any factual inaccuracies or omissions within this manuscript are exclusively my responsibility. I rely on readers to critically evaluate its worth and scholarly merit.

August 27, 2023
Coral Gables, Miami.

Caf Dowlah, Ph.D., LLM.
Visiting Scholar
University of Miami Law School

Table of Cases

Table of Statutes and Regulations

STATUTES

REGULATIONS

Conventions, Treaties, and Resolutions

CONVENTIONS/TREATIES

Additional Protocol Relative to Non-Intervention, 1936
Charter of Economic Rights and Duties of States, 1970
Charter of the Organization of African Unity, 1963
Covenant of the League of Nations, 1919
Declaration on the Enhancement of the Effectiveness of the Principle of Refraining from the Threat or Use of Force in International Relations, 1987
European Convention on Human Rights, 2010
EU–Russia Cooperation and Partnership Agreement (CPA), 1997
Final Act Embodying the Results of the Uruguay Round, 1994
First Geneva Convention (Convention for the Amelioration of the Condition of the Wounded in Armies in the Field), 1864
First Hague International Peace Conference (the Hague Convention on the Laws and Customs of War on Land), 1899
Geneva Conventions Additional Protocols, 1977
Helsinki Final Act, 1975
Intermediate-Range Nuclear Forces Treaty (INF Treaty), 1988
International Covenant on Economic, Social and Cultural Rights (ICESCR), 1966
Iran–United States Claims Settlement Declaration, 1981
Maastricht Principles on Extraterritorial Obligations in the Area of Economic, Social, and Cultural Rights (Maastricht ETO Principles), 2012
Rome Statute of the International Criminal Court, 1998
Treaty of Versailles, 1918
United Nations Charter, 1945
United Nations Convention on the Law of the Sea (UNCLOS), 1994
United Nations Declaration on the Right to Development, 1986
United Nations Convention on Jurisdictional Immunities of States and Their Property, 2004
United Nations General Assembly Resolution Mandating Special Rapporteur, 1999

United Nations Resolution on Violations of International Human Rights Laws, 2014
United States–Iran Treaty of Amity, 1955
Universal Declaration of Human Rights (UDHR), 1948
Vienna Convention on the Law of Treaties (VCLT), 1969
Westphalian Peace Treaties, 1648

UNITED NATIONS SECURITY COUNCIL (UNSC) RESOLUTIONS

UNSC Resolution 660 (August 2, 1990)
UNSC Resolution 661 (August 9, 1990)
UNSC Resolution 665 (August 18, 1990)
UNSC Resolution 666 (September 13, 1990)
UNSC Resolution 678 (November 29, 1990)
UNSC Resolution 686 (March 2, 1991)
UNSC Resolution 687 (April 3, 1991)
UNSC Resolution 688 (April 5, 1991)
UNSC Resolution 706 (August 15, 1991)
UNSC Resolution 712 (September 19, 1991)
UNSC Resolution 715 (October 11, 1991)
UNSC Resolution 778 (October 2, 1992)
UNSC Resolution 986 (April 14, 1995)
UNSC Resolution 1051 (March 27, 1996)
UNSC Resolution 1137 (November 12, 1997)
UNSC Resolution 1284 (December 17, 1999)
UNSC Resolution 1302 (June 8, 2000)
UNSC Resolution 1441 (November 8, 2002)
UNSC Resolution 1443 (November 2002)
UNSC Resolution 1483 (May 22, 2003)
UNSC Resolution 1518 (November 24, 2003)
UNSC Resolution 457 (December 4, 1979)
UNSC Resolution 461 (December 31, 1979)
UNSC Resolution 2321 (November 30, 2016)
UNSC Resolution 2356 (June 2, 2017)
UNSC Resolution 2371 (August 5, 2017)
UNSC Resolution 2375 (September 11, 2017)
UNSC Resolution 1696 (July 31, 2006)
UNSC Resolution 1737 (December 2006)
UNSC Resolution 1747 (March 2007)
UNSC Resolution 1929 (June 2010)
UNSC Resolution 2231 (July 20, 2015)
UNSC Resolution 1919 (April 29, 2010)

UNITED NATIONS GENERAL ASSEMBLY (UNGA) RESOLUTIONS

UNGA Resolution 59/38 (December 2, 2004)
UNGA resolution 2131 (XX) (December 21, 1965)
UNGA Resolution 3281 (XXIX) (December 19, 1972)
UNGA Resolution 2625 (A/RES/25/2625) (October 24, 1970)
UNGA Resolution 42/22 (November 18, 1987)
UNGA Resolution 68/262 (March 17, 2014)
UNGA Resolution GA/12492 (February 23, 2023)
UNGA Resolution GA/12341 (June 23, 2021)
UNGA Resolution 48/121 (December 20, 1993)
United Nations Commission on Human Rights Resolution (E/CN.4/1992/84) (March 6, 1992)
United Nations Human Rights Council Resolution 27/21 (A/HRC/RES/27/21) (October 3, 2014)

Presidential Executive Orders

EO 10348 (April 26, 1952)
EO 10896 (November 29, 1960)
EO 3347 (February 3, 1962)
EO 11037 (July 20, 1962)
EO 11387 (January 1, 1968)
EO 11677 (August 1, 1972)
EO 11683 (August 29, 1972)
EO 11796 (July 30, 1974)
EO 11798 (August 14, 1974)
EO 11810 (September 30, 1974)
EO 11818 (November 5, 1974)
EO 11940 (September 30, 1976)
EO 12170 (November 14, 1979)
EO 12170 (November 14, 1979)
EO 12205 (April 7, 1980)
EO 12211 (April 17, 1980)
EO 12283 (January 23, 1981)
EO 12722 (August 2, 1990)
EO 12938 (November 1994)
EO 12938 (November 14, 1994)
EO 12957 (March 15, 1995)
EO 12959 (May 6, 1995)
EO 13224 (September 23, 2001)
EO 13224 (September 23, 2001)
EO 13224 (September 23, 2001)
EO 13224 (September 23, 2001)
EO 13224 (September 23, 2001)
EO 13290 (March 20, 2003)
13290 (March 20, 2003)
13303 (May 22, 2003)
13315 (August 29, 2003)
EO 13328 (February 6, 2004)
EO 13338 (May 11, 2004)
EO 13350 (July 30, 2004)
EO 13350 (July 30, 2004)
EO 13364 (November 29, 2004)
EO 13382 (June 2005)
EO 13382 (June 29, 2005)
EO 13382 (June 29, 2005)
EO 13382 (June 29, 2005)
EO 13438 (July 17, 2007)
EO 13533 (March 1, 2010)
EO 13572 (April 29, 2011)
EO 13573 (May 18, 2011)
EO 13582 (August 17, 2011)
EO 13660 (March 6, 2014)
EO 13660 (March 6, 2014)
EO 13661 (March 16, 2014)
EO 13661 (March 16, 2014)
EO 13662 (March 20, 2014)
EO 13662 (March 20, 2014)
EO 13668 (May 27, 2014)
EO 13685 (December 19, 2014)
EO 13685 (December 19, 2014)
EO 13685 (December 19, 2014)
EO 13694 (April 1, 2015)
EO 13694 (April 1, 2015)
EO 13757 (December 28, 2016)
EO 13808 (August 2017)
EO 13810 (September 21, 2017)

EO 13818 (December 20, 2017)
EO 13827 (March 19, 2018)
EO 13835 (May 21, 2018)
EO 13848 (September 12, 2018)
EO 13849 (September 20, 2018)
EO 13849 (September 20, 2018)
EO 13850 (November 1, 2018)
EO 13857 (January 25, 2019)
EO 13850 (April 2019)
EO 13871 (May 8, 2019)
EO 13873 (May 14, 2019)
EO 13876 (June 24, 2019)
EO 13883 (August 1, 2019)
EO 13883 (August 2019)
EO 13884 (August 5, 2019)
EO 13902 (January 10, 2020)
EO 13949 (September 21, 2020)
EO 13949 (September 21, 2020)
EO 14024 (April 5, 2021)
EO 14024 (April 15, 2021)
EO 14039 (August 20, 2021)
EO 14039 (August 20, 2021)
EO 14065 (February 21, 2022)
EO 14066 (March 2022)
EO 14066 (March 8, 2022)
EO 14068 (March 11, 2022)

Abbreviations

AAWH	American Association for World Health
ACH	Automated Clearing Houses
ADB	Asian Development Bank
AEOI	Atomic Energy Organization of Iran
AES	Automated Export System
AFDB	African Development Bank
AGOA	African Growth and Opportunity Act
AIA	Afghan Interim Authority
AIIS	American Institute for International Steel
AML	Anti-Money Laundering
ANPRM	Advanced Notice of Proposed Rule-Making
ARIO	Articles of Responsibility of International Organizations
ARSIWA	Articles on Responsibility of States for Internationally Wrongful Acts
BCM	billion cubic meters
BCV	Central Bank of Venezuela
BDCs	Beneficiary Developing Countries
BIS	Bureau of Industry and Security
CACR	Cuban Assets Control Regulations
CANF	Cuban American National Foundation
CAPTA	Correspondent Account or Payable-Through Account Sanctions
CAR	Central African Republic
CBDC	Central Bank Digital Currency
CBI	Caribbean Basin Initiative
CBR	Central Bank of Russia
CCL	Commerce Control List
CEIEC	China National Electronics Import and Export Corporation
CESCR	International Covenant on Economic, Social, and Cultural Rights
CFIUS	Committee of Foreign Investment in the United States
CFSP	Common Foreign and Security Policy (of EU)
CFT	Countering the Financing of Terrorism

CHIPS	Clearing House Interbank Payments System
CIA	Central Intelligence Agency
CIPS	Cross-Border Interbank Payment System
CIT	Court of International Trade
CNL	Competitive Need Limit
COMECON	Council for Mutual Economic Assistance
CPA	Coalition Provisional Authority of Iraq
CPA	EU–Russia Cooperation and Partnership Agreement
CPI	Consumer Price Index
CRE	Commercial Real Estate
CRS	Congressional Research Service (of USA)
CSCE	Conference on Security and Cooperation in Europe
CSL	Consolidated Screening List
CTR	Currency Transaction Report
DCS	Direct Commercial Sales
DDTC	Directorate of Defense Trade Controls
DFI	Development Fund for Iraq (of UN)
DIA	Defense Intelligence Agency
DNR	Donetsk People's Republic
DPAs	Deferred Prosecution Agreements
DPL	Denied Persons List
DPRK	Democratic Republic of Korea
DRC	Democratic Republic of Congo
DSB	Dispute Settlement Body
EACU	Eurasian Customs Union
EAR	Export Administration Regulations
EBRD	European Bank for Reconstruction and Development
ECCN	Export Control Classification Number
ECHR	European Court of Human Rights
ECJ	European Court of Justice
ECLAC	Economic Commission on Latin American Countries
ECOSOC	United Nations Economic and Social Council
ECR	Export Control Reform
EIU	Economist Intelligence Unit
EO	Executive Order
EU	European Union
FAO	Food and Agricultural Organization of the United Nations
FARC	Revolutionary Armed Forces of Colombia
FATF	Financial Action Task Force
FBAR	Foreign Bank and Financial Accounts
FBI	Federal Bureau of Investigation
FED	US Federal Reserve System

FEMA	Foreign Extraterritorial Measures Act of Canada
FinCEN	Financial Crimes Enforcement Network
FMS	Foreign Military Sales
FRBNY	Federal Reserve Bank of New York
FRWN	Federal Reserve Wire Network
FSB	Federal Security Service (of Russia)
FTA	Free Trade Agreement
FTO	Foreign Terrorist Organization
FTOs	Foreign Terrorist Organizations
GAO	Government Accountability Office
GATS	General Agreement on Trading in Services
GATT	General Agreement on Tariff and Trade
GDP	Gross Domestic Product
GRU	Military Intelligence Agency (of Russia)
GSP	Generalized System of Preferences
HRC	United Nations Human Rights Council
IAEA	International Atomic Energy Agency
IAEA	International Atomic Energy Authority
IAMB	International Advisory and Monitoring Board (for Iraq)
IBC	Iraq Body Count
IBRD	International Bank for Reconstruction and Development
ICAO	International Civil Aviation Organization
ICC	International Criminal Court
ICCPR	International Covenant on Civil and Political Rights
ICJ	International Court of Justice
ICRC	International Committee of the Red Cross
IDA	International Development Association
IDB	Inter-American Development Bank
IFIs	International Financial Institutions
IHL	International Humanitarian Law
IHRL	International Human Rights Law
IIN	Interbank Information Network
IJC	International Court of Justice
ILC	International Law Commission
ILO	International Labor Organization
INF	Intermediate-Range Nuclear Forces Treaty
INFU	International Nuclear Fuel Authority
INSTEX	Instrument in Support of Trade Exchanges
IPR	Intellectual Property Rights
IRA	Internet Research Agency (of Russia)
IRGC	Islamic Revolutionary Guard Corps (of Iran)
ISAF	International Security Assistance Force (for Afghanistan)

ISN	International Security and Non-proliferation
ITAR	International Traffic in Arms Regulations
ITC	International Trade Commission
JCPOA	Joint Comprehensive Plan of Action
LAS	League of Arab States
LDBDCs	Least-Developed Beneficiary Developing Countries
LNR	Luhansk People's Republic
MDBs	Multilateral Development Banks
MFN	Most-Favored-Nation
MIF	Multinational Interception Force (for Iraq)
NAFTA	North American Free Trade Agreement
NATO	North Atlantic Treaty Organization
NGO	Non-Governmental Organization
NITC	National Iranian Tanker Company
NPT	Nuclear Nonproliferation Treaty
NRC	Nuclear Regulatory Commission
NSA	National Security Agency
NSC	National Security Council
NSG	Nuclear Suppliers Group
NSPC	National System of Payment of Cards
NSPM	National Security Policy Memorandum (of USA)
NTR	Normal Trade Relations
OAC	Office of Antiboycott Compliance
OAS	Organization of American States
OEA	Office of Enforcement Analysis
OFAC	Office of Foreign Assets Control
OFCs	Offshore Financial Centers
OFE	Office of Export Enforcement
OFFP	Oil for Food Program (of Iraq)
OHCHR	Office of High Commissioner for Human Rights (of UN)
OIP	Office of Iraq Program
OPEC	Organization of Petroleum Exporting Countries
ORHA	Office of Reconstruction and Humanitarian Assistance (for Iraq)
PBOC	People's Bank of China
PdVSA	Petróleos de Venezuela, S.A.
PEPFAR	President's Emergency Plan for AIDs Relief
PNTR	Permanent Normal Trade Relations
QRS	Quantitative Restrictions
RTGS	Real-Time Gross Settlement
SAR	Suspicious Activity Report
SCT	SEPA Instant Credit Transfers
SDGTs	Specially Designated Global Terrorists

SDN List	Specially Designated Nationals and Blocked Persons List
SDT	Special and Differential Treatment
SDTs	Specially Designated Terrorists
SEC	Securities and Exchange Commission
SEPA	Single Euro Payments Area
SFMS	Structured Financial Messaging System
SPFS	System for Transfer of Financial Messages
SSI	Sectoral Sanctions Identification List
SWIFT	Society for Worldwide Interbank Financial Transactions.
TARGET	Trans-European Automated Real-Time Gross Settlement Express Transfer
TCOs	Transnational Criminal Organizations
TDO	Temporary Denial Order
TFTP	Terrorist Finance Tracking Program
TIPS	TARGET Instant Payment Settlement
TJN	Tax Justice Network
TRIPS	Agreement on Trade-Related Aspects of Intellectual Property Rights
TRQ	Tariff-Rate Quota
TSC	Targeted Sanctions Consortium
UAE	United Arab Emirates
UAVs	Unmanned Aerial Vehicles
UCC	Uniform Commercial Code
UCM	Unilateral Coercive Measures
UNCITRAL	United Nations Commission on International Trade Law
UNCLOS	United Nations Convention on the Law of the Sea
UNESCO	United Nations Educational, Scientific and Cultural Organization
UNGA	UN General Assembly
UNHRC	United Nations Human Rights Committee
UNHRC	United Nations Human Rights Council
UNICEF	United Nations Children's Emergency Fund
UNMOVIC	United Nations Monitoring, Verification and Inspection Commission for Iraq
UNSC	United Nations Security Council
UNSCOM	United Nations Special Commission for Iraq
USAID	United States Agency for International Development
USITC	United States International Trade Commission
USMCA	United States–Mexico–Canada Agreement
USML	United States Munitions List
USSR	Union of Soviet Socialist Republics
USTR	Office of the US Trade Representative
UVL	Unverified List
VCLT	Vienna Convention of the Law of Treaties

WAML	Wassenaar Arrangement Munitions List
WFP	World Food Program of United Nations
WHO	World Health Organization
WMD	Weapons of Mass Destruction
WTO	World Trade Organization

1

Overview of Economic and Financial Sanctions

I INTRODUCTION

The existing legal literature does not provide any universally accepted definition of the term "sanctions." The term itself also does not appear in any major international legal instruments – neither the covenants of the League of Nations nor the United Nations (UN) Charter mention "sanctions" anywhere (Asada, 2020, 4).[1] The International Law Commission (ILC) coined the term for the first time in 2001 but deemed it "controversial" and "imprecise" (ILC, 2001).[2] Legal scholars broadly agree that defining the concept of "sanctions" from legal perspectives is "notoriously difficult" (Hovell, 2019, 140) because of its "slippery and imprecise" legal character (Ronzitti, 2016, 9; see also Gordon et al., 2019, 1–3).

Over the course of time, however, a deluge of interpretations of the term "sanctions" has emerged from multiple academic disciplines – encompassing political science, international relations, and economics, as well as law – which has resulted in an impressive literature that provides a divergent but highly intersecting understanding of the term.

Political scientists (including foreign affairs specialists) typically understand the term "sanctions" as an exercise in influence and power in international relations and foreign policy. To them, sanctions are foreign policy tools to deter, punish, or signal displeasure at other states' acts and threats, as a middle ground between

[1] Article 16 of the Covenant of the League of Nations (1919), however, uses the term "military sanctions" as a means to exercise pressure and punish acts of war. The Covenant also provides for economic and financial measures when a state resorts to war in violation of Articles 12, 13, or 15. Article 41 of the UN Charter (1945) also refers to such actions but describes them as "measures," not as "sanctions." Currently, the UN uses the term "sanctions" to indicate measures taken by the UN Security Council (UNSC) under Article 41 against a member state to remedy a situation falling under Article 39 that implies a threat to or a violation of international peace (Herik, 2017; O'Connell, 2002).

[2] The ILC, a UN body established by the UN General Assembly in 1947, promotes the progressive development of international law and its codification. Composed of thirty-four members, the ILC collectively represents the world's principal legal systems, but its members serve as experts in their individual capacity, not as representatives of their governments. For greater detail, see www.un.org/en/global-issues/international-law-and-justice, accessed on December 15, 2022.

"business as usual" and the "use of force" or a declaration of war (Gordon et al., 2019, 2; see also Lowenfeld, 2003, 2). Such sanctions generally include diplomatic and political measures, such as the interruption of diplomatic relations, registering protests and condemnation, political disengagement, and so on, against a target state (Doxey, 1996, 10; Drury, 2001, 486).

To economists, sanctions are the "deliberate, government-inspired withdrawal, or threat of withdrawal" of customary levels of economic and financial activity to achieve foreign policy or national security goals that would have occurred in the absence of such sanctions (Hufbauer, 2007, 3). Such sanctioning measures include restricting imports or exports, freezing assets, the annulment of foreign assistance, restrictions on credit and banking facilities, and so on. To economists, sanctions provide a broad set of tools that can be imposed on a target state as well as entities and individuals within the state (Drezner, 2003, 643–645; Lektzian, 2013).

In legal literature, on the other hand, the term "sanctions" refers to actions and measures aimed at the suspension or interruption of normal interactions between states in order to demand a change in a particular behavior of a targeted state that breaches international law (Gordon et al., 2019, 2). The objective is to compel the target, without using military warfare, to abide by international law and correct its objectionable behavior (Ronzitti, 2016). From a legal standpoint, the term, thus, envisages both negative and positive connotations – it implies a penalty or punishment for illegal behavior or non-conformity with international law and at the same time confers legitimacy and the dignity of law on such coercive measures (Beucillon, 2021, 9).

In legal literature, the term "sanctions" is also applied in a much narrower sense than in other disciplines. In *stricto sensu*, "sanctions" in legal studies refers to "coercive measures" taken in the execution of a decision of "a competent social organ … legally empowered to act in the name of the society or community that is governed by the legal system" (Asada, 2020, 4; see also Crawford, 2001, 57). Thus, sanctions must be imposed by a competent social or community organ, such as a state, or a collective body, such as the UN, and can be legally undertaken without the will or consent of the target, and must be aimed at constraining the target's access to the resources needed to engage in prohibited activities in order to restore conduct that is acceptable from international law perspectives (Reisman and Stevick, 1998).

Legal studies on sanctions are more concerned with whether a state has actually committed an internationally wrongful act from international law perspectives; whether the sanctioner state is actually an "injured state" in relation to the wrongful act, in accordance with the ILC; whether the sanctioning measures aimed at a target are lawful, necessary, appropriate, and proportionate; whether they conform with international treaties and conventions, such as the UN Charter and international human rights laws, and international humanitarian laws; whether the sanctioning measures involve the exterritorial application of domestic legislation; and whether they violate the principles of state sovereignty or non-intervention in the internal and external affairs of a state (Dawidowicz, 2017; Dupont, 2012, 41–42).

From a practical standpoint, a sanctions regime is usually characterized by a dual-agent model composed of a "sender" or "sanctioner" – a sanctioning state or authority – and a "target," or "sanctioned," state, entity, or individual (Farrall, 2007, 10). It typically incorporates three essential elements: (a) the nature of the measures enacted by a competent organ as a reaction to the alleged unlawful behavior of the target; (b) the type of actors (sanctioners) involved in the performance of the measure; and (c) the objectives of the sanctioning measures (Bothe, 2016, 33; deLauro, 2020).

A sanctions regime also depends on the approach that underpins it. For example, a purpose-oriented approach emphasizes sanctions as a tool to enforce international legal norms to respond to a breach of a legal norm. An identity-oriented approach focuses on the identity of the sanctioner, that is, whether sanctions have been adopted by a state, a group of states, or an international organization, and whether the sanctions constitute retorsions or countermeasures, and so on.[3] A measures-based approach envisages the nature of sanctions undertaken, whether they are economic, political, diplomatic, and so on (Ruys, 2017, 19).

The applicability of these approaches depends on the objectives of the sanctioners. For example, a purpose-oriented approach would generally envisage sanctioning tools that constitute threats for the target's failure to observe international standards or obligations by serving as a deterrent to internationally undesirable or unacceptable behavior, albeit "without attempting to unseat its regime, occupy its territory, or destroy its infrastructure" (Murphy, 2000, 8). Boutros-Ghali (1995, 26), a former UN Secretary General, puts the approach succinctly when he describes sanctions as "blunt instruments" but limits their purpose "to modify the behavior of a party that is threatening international peace and security and not to punish or otherwise exact retribution."

On the other hand, an identity-oriented approach would emphasize the identity of the sanctioner. For example, a multilateral sanctions regime imposed by the UN Security Council (UNSC) would carry greater significance than an autonomous sanctions regime imposed by a state or a regional body of states, such as the Organization of American States (OAS). Similarly, a measures-based approach would emphasize the types of sanctions adopted. For example, a diplomatic sanction

[3] The concepts of retorsions and countermeasures will be explained in detail in Chapter 2. Broadly, under international law, policy measures described as countermeasures involve a form of self-help which can be resorted to only if the target state has actually committed an internationally wrongful act. Retorsion, on the other hand, refers to internationally lawful measures undertaken by a state in response to prior injuries by another state. Retorsion is largely unregulated by international law, need not necessarily be temporary or reversible, and may contain a punitive element, while countermeasures may not contain the punitive elements. For greater detail, see Dawidowicz (2017), Dupont (2012, 41–42), and Kamto (2010, 1174–1176).

may involve an interruption in diplomatic relations, a cultural sanction may involve nonparticipation in a sports competition, an economic sanction may involve export restrictions, and a financial sanction may involve restrictions on banking and credit flows (Ruys, 2017, 19–22; Gordon et al., 2019, 1–3).

Obviously, the legality and legitimacy of sanctions will depend on the nature and purpose of the sanctions regimes, the identity of the sanctioner, and the specific sanctioning measures adopted. For example, the EU uses the concept of "restrictive measures," instead of sanctions, to bring about "a change in policy or activity by the target country, part of country, government entities or individuals."[4] Noticeably, such a conception of sanctions lacks any punitive element – they are rather aimed at achieving a concrete goal of changing a policy by restricting some behavior of a target (Ronzitti, 2016, 9). On the other hand, the US has adopted sanctioning measures numerous times, aiming at regime change in foreign countries (Hufbauer, 2007, 116–119).

The rest of the chapter is organized as follows: Section II explores the origin and evolution of sanctions; Section III sets out the broad typologies of sanctions episodes; Section IV sheds light on the objectives of sanctions; Section V describes the overall effectiveness of sanctions; Section VI explores the effectiveness of US sanctions regimes; and Section VII provides a road map of the book.

II THE EVOLUTION OF SANCTIONS

The earliest recorded incidence of sanctions can be traced to ancient Greece, specifically to the Megarian decree of Pericles, issued in 432–433 BC.[5] Historically, until World War I, sanctions were instruments of war, and countries deployed them during wartime as a punitive measure. Some of the pre–WWI sanctions episodes include: the American colonies boycotting British goods in the 1760s to compel the British Crown to change its taxation and trade laws, notably the Stamp Act (1765) and the Townsend Act (1767); the French and the British sanctioning each other during the Napoleonic Wars (1793–1815); the US embargo against British goods in response to the British Navy limiting US trade with France (1812–1814); Britain and France blockading the Danube to block arms supplies to Russia during the Crimean War (1853–1856); US sanctions against the Confederacy during the Civil War to cut off the South from foreign imports (1861–1865); and the US blockade of Cuba and the Philippines during the Spanish-American War (1898).[6]

4 The EU describes sanctions as "restrictive measures." See Council of the European Union, "Guidelines on Implementation and Evaluation of Restrictive Measures (Sanctions) in the Framework of the EU Common Foreign and Security Policy." 15579/03, Brussels, December 3, 2003.

5 Apparently, Pericles imposed the sanctions to avenge the theft of female attendants of his partner Aspasia, which eventually led to the Peloponnesian War (431–404 BC). For greater detail, see Baldwin (1985, 150–152), Hufbauer (2007, 3), Gottemoeller (2007, 100), Mulder (2022, 5–7), and Watson (2004, 24).

6 For greater detail on pre–WWI instances of economic sanctions, see Hufbauer (2007, 29–32, Table 1.2), Mulder (2022, 1–22), Rathbone (2013, 1063), and Gordon (1999, 325–331).

As Hufbauer (2007, 3) points out, however, most of the pre-WWI sanctions episodes were not well documented and were either foreshadowed or accompanied by warfare; thus, they may not be relevant to the post–WWI period, when most of the sanctions episodes have been standalone economic actions.[7] Of 11 sanctions episodes that occurred between 1914 and 1940, nine were linked to disrupting military adventures or complementing a broader war effort;[8] four were imposed by the League of Nations,[9] one of which succeeded in inducing Greece to back down from its incursion into Bulgaria in 1925; and another failed to persuade Italy to withdraw from Abyssinia (current Ethiopia) in the mid 1930s.[10] During WWII, the US-led allies imposed two sanctions regimes against Germany and Japan, both without the approval of the League of Nations.[11]

The futility of the League of Nations in enforcing sanctions did not discourage sanctioners from deploying such instruments, however. This is because, by then, sanctioning measures aimed at quarantining target countries from global trade and finance, subjecting them to "an unbearable form of imprisonment," had already been found to be a great antidote to war (Mulder, 2022, 5). Of the three major weapons used during the interwar period – air power, gas warfare, and economic blockade – blockade was found to be the deadliest: During WWI, 300,000–400,000 people died of blockade-induced starvation and illness in Central Europe alone (Offer, 1989, 33–34). It was indeed clear that while "war is barbarous … the boycott is an infinitely more terrible instrument of war" (Wilson, 1923, 71).

Sanctions episodes have also accelerated since WWII because they are easier to enforce, and evading sanctions may be difficult and expensive (Hufbauer,

7 For a list of sanctions episodes between WWI and 2000, see Hufbauer (2007, 20–33, Appendix 1A). The list also provides the names of sanctioners, sanction targets, and the duration and goals of these sanctions. It is, however, notable that Mulder (2022, 14) maintains that during the nineteenth century, when the international system was ruled hierarchically by a group of great powers and governed by European principles of law, most of the sanctions episodes were conceived as punitive measures to uphold "civilization" against "barbarism."

8 The sanctions episodes that occurred between WWI and WWII include: UK versus Russia (1918–1920: anti-Bolshevism); League of Nations versus Yugoslavia (1921: border dispute); League of Nations versus Greece (1925: border skirmish); League of Nations versus Paraguay and Bolivia (1932–1935: Chaco war); UK versus USSR (1933: release of British citizens); UK and US versus Mexico (1938–1947: expropriation); Alliance Powers versus Germany and Japan (1939–1945: WWII); US versus Japan (1940–1941: withdrawal from Southeast Asia); US versus Argentina (1944–1947: destabilize the regime of Juan Perón). Based on Appendix 1.A of Hufbauer (2007, 20–33).

9 As mentioned above, the Covenant of the League of Nations granted member countries the right to resort to "military sanctions" as a means to exercise pressure and punish acts of war.

10 With respect to Greece, in 1925 the League of Nations warned of a possible naval blockade and economic sanctions unless Greece desisted from border skirmishes with Bulgaria, to which Greece ultimately agreed. With respect to Italy, the League imposed a limited trade embargo and restrictions on loans and credit to Italy – the sanctions were not applied by non-League member countries, however, including the US.

11 The sanctions episodes were Alliance Powers versus Germany and Japan (1939–1945) and the US versus Japan (1940–1941).

2007, 97–98). They also provide a great political advantage to unilateral sanctioners – they "do not generate somber processions of body bags bringing home the mortal remains of the sons and daughters of the constituents" (Reisman and Stevick, 1998, 94).

Since WWII, however, sanctions have been applied more frequently in peacetime, largely as a tool for law enforcement, rather than as a tool for punishment during wartime, and they have increasingly been deployed to uphold "standards of behavior expected by custom or required by law" prior to the use of force as a last resort (Joyner, 2016, 46). Since 1945, the goals of both multilateral and unilateral sanctions have also increasingly been geared to address human rights violations, promote democratization, prevent nuclear proliferation, end military conflicts, and fight international terrorism, money laundering, drug trafficking, and so on (Schwab, 1999; Mulder, 2022, 294).

The number of unilateral and multilateral sanctions has also increased phenomenally since the end of WWII. For example, Hufbauer (2007, 20–23) chronicles 204 episodes of economic and financial sanctions on state and non-state entities between 1945 and 2007; Felbermayr (2020) identifies 729 multilateral and unilateral sanctions episodes between 1950 and 2016; and the EUSANCT Dataset identifies 325 sanctions imposed or threatened by the EU, the US, and the UN during the period 1989–2015.[12]

Since WWII, the US has emerged as the most prolific enforcer of unilateral sanctions in the world. Equipped with unique military dominance, nuclear weapons, and strategic air power, and a preeminent role in global economic and financial markets (Mulder, 2022, 293), the US has increasingly been using sanctions to sustain its hegemonic power around the world (Davis and Ness, 2021). For example: In 1953,

[12] This all depends on how different databases define the concept of sanctions, the methodologies they employ, and the scope of their investigation. The Global Sanctions Data Base, which Felbermayr (2020) relies on, defines sanctions as binding restrictive measures – no matter whether they are applied by the UN, other international organizations, groups of countries, or individual nations – and they include all types of such measures, such as trade, financial, travel, arms, and other forms of sanctions. For greater detail, see cepr.org/voxeu/columns/global-sanctions-data-base. On the other hand, Hufbauer (2007, 2–3), on which this study heavily depends, uses a case study approach, covering only sovereign states and how they use sanctions to achieve foreign policy goals to gain leverage over others, and defines sanctions strictly as the "deliberate government inspired withdrawal, or threat of withdrawal, of customary trade or financial relations." The EUSANCT Dataset covers sanctions threats and sanctions imposed by the EU, the US, and the UN during 1989–2015, and identifies 325 sanctions threats. For details, see www.polver.uni-konstanz.de/gschneider/research/archive/eusanct/, and Weber and Schneider (2022). Yet another prominent sanctions database – the Targeted Sanctions Consortium database, which focuses only on the UN-targeted sanctions since the end of the Cold War – has identified sixty-three sanctions episodes against twenty-three country regimes (Biersteker, 2018). For a current list of UN sanctions, see www.un.org/securitycouncil/sanctions, and for a list of US sanctions see www.treasury.gov/resource-center/sanctions. The UN and the US are not the only sanctions enforcers, however; the EU, the UK, China, Russia, and many other nations also impose sanctions.

the US overthrew the Mosaddeq regime of Iran to reinstall Reza Shah Pahlavi; in 1956, it forced French and British forces to withdraw from the Suez region; in the 1960s, it forced Egypt to stop supporting rebels in Yemen; in the 1970s, it overthrew the Allende regime in Chile; and in the 1980s, it overthrew a number of political regimes in Latin America.[13]

The pace, force, and extensiveness of economic and financial sanctions have, however, intensified greatly since the end of the Cold War in 1991. While only two sanctions episodes were imposed by the UN during the entire period of the Cold War – against Rhodesia (now Zimbabwe) (1965–1979), and against apartheid South Africa (1977) (Renwick, 1981; Reisman and Stevick, 1998) – in the 1990s, the UN imposed more than thirty sanctions regimes targeting twenty-four countries, including Iraq, former Yugoslavia, Libya, Liberia, Somalia, Haiti, Rwanda, Sierra Leone, Sudan, Eritrea, Ethiopia, the UNITA (Angola), and Afghanistan (LaRae-Perez, 2002).

The phenomenal rise in multilateral sanctions since the 1990s has largely been possible due to the end of the Cold War, which catapulted the US to the position of the sole superpower in the world. Since then, the US has been deploying its unprecedented economic and political might actively and strategically to influence the UN to adopt sanctions against nations hostile to it, to reward its allies, and to punish its rivals and enemies through alliances and defense pacts, using its vast economic and financial networks and mechanisms to subdue the economies of those countries who stand in its way (Rahmat, 2015; Davis and Ness, 2021). As a result, according to UN estimates, in 2015, one-third of the world's population lived in countries that were under some form of economic sanctions (Felbermayr, 2020).[14]

III TYPOLOGY OF SANCTIONS EPISODES

Sanctions episodes have been categorized variously, reflecting changes in the evolution of international law, institutional settings for the adoption and enforcement of sanctions, sanctions objectives and outcomes, and other pragmatic matters. Based on institutional settings (sanctioning organs), sanctions episodes can be categorized as: (a) unilateral – those imposed autonomously by a state; (b) multilateral – those imposed by multilateral institutions like the UN; (c) regional – those imposed by a group of states, such as the EU and the OAS; and (d) non-governmental – those imposed by non-governmental organizations (NGOs), such as sanctions episodes against apartheid South Africa in the 1980s or military-ruled Myanmar in the 2010s.

[13] For other such instances, see Appendix 1A of Hufbauer (2007, 20–33).

[14] It is however notable that in the last decade the US's preeminent superpower position has increasingly been challenged, especially because of the rise of China as a formidable economic and military power.

Based on their nature and objectives, sanctions can also be viewed as political and diplomatic measures, cultural and communication measures, and economic and financial measures; based on their scope, sanctions can be categorized as comprehensive sanctions, targeted/smart sanctions, issue-based sanctions, and secondary or extraterritorial sanctions. Some of the sanctions regimes also may fit into more than one category.[15]

A *Sanctions Episodes Based on Their Nature and Objectives*

Political and Diplomatic Sanctions

Such sanctions are aimed at coercing a target state in a measured way, to encourage it to refrain from international wrongful acts and oblige it to respect international law and norms. Generally, such sanctioning measures include the interruption of diplomatic relations, protests and condemnations of the target state's policies and behavior, the recall of diplomatic representatives, severance of diplomatic relations, the suspension of high-level political visits, the refusal of a negotiated settlement of the dispute, the demand for a regime change, and so on. Such measures and tools are often viewed as "less feeble than scolding an ambassador and less bloody than sending in the marines."[16]

Historically such sanctions have been found to be more useful and effective than the outright severance of diplomatic relations as they often signal the potential for imposing further restrictions to prohibit internationally wrongful policy or behavior. As described in Chapter 2, international law allows individual states to take such political and diplomatic measures unilaterally without UN approval. Obviously, only relatively powerful states, such as the US and the EU, can effectively pursue such sanctioning measures, although even smaller states may also adopt such sanctions with a measure of success.[17]

Cultural and Communications Sanctions

Cultural and communication instruments of sanctions generally include measures such as the cancellation of or restrictions on cultural exchanges, scientific cooperation, and educational ties; landing and overflight or transit privileges; telephone, cable, and postal links; land and water transit, docking and port privileges; tourism and visa privileges for target nationals; and so on (Doxey, 1996, 10). For example, the US and many other countries boycotted the Moscow Summer Olympics in 1980 in protest against Russia's invasion of Afghanistan.

[15] For example, collective sanctions implemented by a group of states can be referred to as unilateral, regional, as well as multilateral sanctions, while the same sanctions episodes can be described as secondary and/or extraterritorial sanctions. More on this below.

[16] See, "Sanctions: History Lessons," *The Economist*, October 19, 2006.

[17] Some of the relevant examples include: Indonesia versus Malaysia in the mid- 1960s, Spain versus the UK over Gibraltar in the mid 1950s through mid 1980s, India versus Nepal in the late 1980s, and Greece versus Albania in the mid 1990s (Hufbauer, 2007, 60–62).

Human Rights Sanctions

The use of sanctions on the grounds of human rights violations is a relatively new phenomenon – it may well be traced to the late 1970s and early 1980s when the US imposed a series of sanctions against repressive regimes in Latin American countries such as Nicaragua, Paraguay, Argentina, El Salvador, Panama, and Cuba. In the 1990s, the US imposed similar sanctions against scores of African countries. Since the 2000s US sanctions against states responsible for human rights violations have assumed almost a common pattern. As discussed in Chapter 2, the Sergei Magnitsky Rule of Law Accountability Act of 2012 (P.L. 112–208) and the Global Magnitsky Human Rights Accountability Act of 2016 (P.L. 114–328) empower the US president with broad authority to impose targeted sanctions against individuals responsible for gross violations of internationally recognized human rights.

Such sanctions, however, often draw criticism for targeting countries whose leaders might not be well disposed to the US, often for failing to serve the cause of peace, and even for further aggravating the already existing poor human rights situation in the target countries. For example, sanctions imposed on Sudan on the grounds of the ongoing genocide in Darfur (2001–2009) hindered the transportation of necessary supplies and goods, further increasing the conflict and the local production of small arms, and, thus, what started as a genocide soon turned into a tragic civil war, causing a much greater humanitarian disaster. Similarly, comprehensive sanctions imposed on Iraq and Haiti in the 1990s resulted in massive humanitarian disasters, and even in genocides, according to some observers.[18]

Economic and Financial Sanctions

Such sanctions incorporate wide-ranging measures, including embargoes and boycotts, cancellation of development or technical assistance, restrictions on credit and bank facilities, restricting access to international financial institutions, and freezing or seizing of assets. Among the 208 sanctions episodes studied by Hufbauer (2007), the US either alone or in concert with its allies had deployed economic and financial sanctions in 109 cases, the UN in 20 cases, the United Kingdom (UK) in 16 cases, the EU in 14 cases, the former Soviet Union (Russia since 1990) in 13 cases, and the Arab League and its members in four cases.[19]

In recent decades, especially since the debacle of comprehensive sanctions on Iraq in the 1990s, economic and financial sanctions have emerged as the preferred tools for targeted sanctions (Brzoska, 2003, 1345–1346; Drezner, 2011). And between

[18] For greater detail on the adverse effects of sanctions imposed on the grounds of human rights violations, see LaRae-Perez (2002) and Albal (2021); for greater detail on the effects of sanctions on Sudan, see Elliott (2016), Larsen (2009), and Milanovic (2011); and for greater detail on the effects of sanctions on Iraq, see Chapter 7 of this volume, and Cortright and Lopez (1999), Drezner (2011), Garfield (1999), and Gordon (2010).

[19] Based on Appendix Table 1A in Hufbauer (2007).

economic and financial sanctions, financial sanctions have been emphasized more because: (a) they are relatively easier to enforce because governments and international financial institutions are important providers of financial flows; (b) private financial markets tend to be relatively more regulated than goods markets; (c) as fewer larger players are involved in international finance markets, it is easier to enforce and monitor financial sanctions; and (d) evading financial sanctions may be more difficult and more expensive than evading economic (trade) sanctions (Hufbauer, 2007, 97–98).[20]

Financial sanctions have also been a dominant part of US unilateral sanctions WWII the world. As discussed in Chapter 4, despite major structural shifts in the international monetary system since WWII – such as the emergence of digital currencies and new payment ecosystems, and the emergence of new reserve currencies such as the euro and renminbi – for all practical purposes, the US dollar still reigns supreme in global economic and financial transactions. The dollar still commands over a 60-percent share in global reserves currency and over a 50-percent share in global trade invoicing, cross-border bank claims, and outstanding international debt securities.[21]

Thus the "weaponized interdependence" (Farrell and Newman, 2019) created by the dollar not only thrives, but also attempts made by several countries, such as China, Iran, and Russia, to avoid transactions in US dollars have so far achieved little progress. The benefits of staying connected to US financial institutions for any sanctions breaker still outweigh any potential gains in violating US sanctions (Rosenberg, 2019, 11).

Financial sanctions, such as the freezing of assets, have also been found to be a very effective sanctions tool. For example, the US freeze on Iranian assets following the Iranian hostage crisis in 1979 led to the eventual freeing of the diplomats; the UK's freeze of Argentine assets in 1982 led to the British victory in the Falklands; and the freezing of Kuwait's assets during the Gulf Crisis in 1990 prevented Saddam Hossain from plundering them. There have, however, been many instances where the measure of freezing assets has had very little effect, such as freezing the assets of Panama's Manual Noriega, Haiti's Raul Cédras, Iraq's Saddam Hossain, Syria's Assad, drug cartels in Colombia and Mexico, and Russia's President Putin and Russian oligarchs.[22]

[20] Among 204 sanctions episodes listed in Hufbauer (2007), financial sanctions were imposed in combination with trade sanctions in 100 cases.

[21] For greater detail on the US dollar's dominance over the global financial system, see Chapter 4 of this volume, IMF (2020 and 2021), McDowell (2023), and Mulder (2022).

[22] The interruption of foreign assistance can also be viewed as a form of financial sanction. Historically, such tools have proved to be effective when they were imposed on less developed countries or countries that depended heavily on such assistance. Among the 204 sanctions episodes studied by Hufbauer (2007), such restrictions were imposed alone or in combination with other sanctions in 153 instances, and the overall effects have been found to be mixed. More on this below.

B Sanctions Episodes Based on Institutional Settings

Multilateral Sanctions

This study considers sanctions regimes as collective and multilateral when they are imposed by the UNSC, which, backed by the authority and credibility vested in the UN system, legally and legitimately represents the collective will of the global community.[23] Article 41 of the UN Charter (Chapter VII) vests the UNSC with monopoly powers to impose multilateral sanctions in order to maintain international peace and security. The UNSC is viewed as the most appropriate institution for imposing such sanctions because it can induce cooperation among its member states to exert greater coercive power on the target (Drezner, 2011, 75). Moreover, the UNSC-mandated sanctions regimes provide well-specified descriptions of alleged wrongful acts and clearly lay out objectives,[24] and it is mandatory for all UN member states to implement all UNSC-mandated sanctions domestically.[25] The targets, thus, have little scope to evade sanctions (Bapat and Morgan, 2009, 1081).

Multilateral sanctions, adopted and imposed in pursuance of Chapter VII of the UN Charter, are considered third-party sanctions, as the UN cannot claim to be an "injured state," and their implementation is left to member states. The deliberative process of the adoption of sanctions is, however, restricted to the five permanent members, and 10 nonpermanent members of the UNSC elected for a two-year term. All UNSC resolutions, including sanctioning measures, require a simple majority, but no UNSC resolution can be passed without the approval of all five permanent members, and any of the five members can exercise their veto power to block any UNSC resolution.

The UNSC adopted its first sanctions regime in 1966, against Rhodesia. Since then, as of February 2023, the UNSC has established 30 multilateral sanctions regimes, of which 14 are still in force.[26] The UN sanctions are subject to the

23 Thus, sanctions imposed autonomously by a group of states – such as the EU, the OAS, or the US and its allies – without the authorization of the UN, are not considered multilateral. For example, the sanctions regimes imposed on Iran under the Joint Comprehensive Plan of Action (JCPOA) by the US and its allies in 2015 were indeed collective and multilateral in character, but they are not considered multilateral in this study as they were not sanctioned by the UNSC.

24 Notably, Article 2(4) of the UN Charter bans the use of force by any state outside of self-defense, but it does not prohibit sanctions by actors other than the UNSC. Moreover, Chapter VIII of the UN Charter allows the UNSC to delegate its sanctioning power to regional organizations and even to encourage them to adopt sanctions, provided that such bodies share the same concerns to maintain international peace and security as the UNSC and the sanctions imposed are consistent with the core purpose and principles of the UN and are based on prior authorization from the UNSC (Brzoska, 2003, 1345–1346).

25 Not all UNSC sanctions carry the same weight or force, however. Only sanctions imposed by the UNSC under Chapter VII of the UN Charter are binding for all UN member states, the others are mere recommendations (Ronzitti, 2016).

26 UNSC sanctions have targeted countries such as: Southern Rhodesia, South Africa, the former Yugoslavia (2), Haiti, Iraq (2), Angola, Rwanda, Sierra Leone, Somalia and Eritrea, Eritrea and Ethiopia, Liberia (3), Democratic Republic of the Congo, Côte d'Ivoire, Sudan, Lebanon, DPRK (North Korea), Iran, Libya (2), Guinea-Bissau, Central African Republic, Yemen, South Sudan

fundamental principles and norms of international law, known as *jus cogens*, and other limits prescribed by human rights laws and humanitarian laws. Article 41 of the UN Charter provides a nonexhaustive list of areas of sanctions that includes: the complete or partial interruption of economic relations and of rail, sea, air, postal, telegraphic, radio, and other means of communication, and the severance of diplomatic relations.[27] The targets of UNSC sanctions can be state and non-state actors and individuals. More often than not, leading countries play an important role in drafting and adopting UNSC sanctions.[28]

Unilateral Sanctions

This study considers sanctions episodes imposed by a state, a group of states, or a regional body of states as autonomous unilateral sanctions because they are imposed in accordance with their own foreign policy interests and objectives. Most unilateral sanctions are imposed by a handful of powerful states such as the US and the EU, which are capable of exerting considerable hegemonic powers on the global stage.[29] Apparently, powerful nations find unilateral sanctions more attractive than other foreign policy tools at their disposal. Gordon et al. (2019, 3–5) identify four major advantages of unilateral sanctions in the context of the US – the most prolific unilateral sanctioner in the world.

First, unilateral sanctions are easier to implement. The US ordinarily adopts its unilateral sanctions under the International Emergency Economic Powers Act of 1977 (IEEPA: P.L. 95-223), which authorizes the US president to impose sanctions when the US faces an "unusual and extraordinary threat" against its national security. But the determination of such threats has always been a political exercise – presidents have invoked the IEEPA to impose sanctions for issues as important as nuclear proliferation, but also as inconsequential as the mistreatment of some opposition leaders in a foreign country (Casey et al., 2020).

Second, most of the other tools available for coercive diplomacy are usually expensive and unattractive compared with unilateral economic and financial sanctions. For example, deploying military force is monetarily expensive and politically costly as it puts lives on the line, and other tools, such as covert action or diplomatic pressure, are also either very risky or ineffective (Reisman and Stevick, 1998;

and Mali, as well as organizations: ISIL (Da'esh), Al-Qaeda, and the Taliban. The subject areas of UNSC sanctions have included: supporting the political settlement of conflicts, nuclear nonproliferation, and counter-terrorism. For greater detail, see www.un.org/securitycouncil/sanctions/information#:~:text=Today, accessed February 3, 2023.

27 For greater detail, see legal.un.org/repertory/art41.shtml, accessed February 3, 2023.

28 For example, as discussed in Chapters 6 and 7, the US played a crucial role in intensifying UNSC sanctions regimes against Iran and Iraq.

29 For example, since the Russian invasion of Ukraine and occupation of Crimea in 2014, Western powers – primarily the US, the UK, and the EU – have imposed a total of 11,073 sanctions on Russia: 8,667 on individuals, 2,273 on entities, 116 on vessels, and 17 on aircraft. For greater detail, see www.atlanticcouncil.org/blogs/econographics/russia-sanctions-database/, accessed January 27, 2023.

Reinisch, 2001). Contrastingly, economic and financial sanctions not only impact the intended targets but also function as a means of levying substantial fines for violations of the sanctions (Goldman and Lindblom, 2021; Nephew, 2020).[30]

Third, there are few legal constraints or doctrines that dictate how, when, and for how long unilateral sanctions can be imposed, whereas there are numerous bodies of international law and jurisprudence governing the use of force, on top of domestic legal constraints. Moreover, even if sanctions episodes are designed poorly, and even if they may cause harm and injury to innocent parties, there remain not many legal bars to the use such tools. And finally, unilateral sanctions are flexible in design and calibration – they can be precisely targeted at states, entities, and individuals depending on political expediency and circumscribed to US jurisdictions only.

Secondary and Extraterritorial Sanctions

Unilateral sanctions, however, come with much narrower reach compared with multilateral sanctions – they only bind persons and entities within the jurisdictions of their own countries. To overcome this narrow reach of primary sanctions, powerful sanctioning states, such as the US and the EU, often seek to enlarge the effect of sanctions by adopting extraterritorial legislation, or making formal and informal arrangements or diplomatic alignments with other states or entities, and establishing a nexus between territorial reach and personal jurisdiction.[31] Such measures, aimed at bolstering the enforcement of primary sanctions, are often described generally as "secondary sanctions."

Powerful states tend to justify such actions on the grounds that target states, entities, and individuals often attempt to evade the effects of sanctions by utilizing alternative sources, and they thus often lack coercive power to ensure effective enforcement of their sanctions (Beucillon, 2021). Although only a handful of powerful states, such as the US and the EU, are capable of extending primary sanctions through secondary sanctions, they often blur the typical distinction between unilateral and multilateral sanctions (Drezner, 2011, 77; Franco, 2015).

Such secondary sanctions, that extend to third states, entities, and individuals, are also often described as extraterritorial sanctions. They are not interchangeable terms, however, because extraterritorial sanctions can be implemented through both primary and secondary sanctions (Dawidowicz, 2017). For example, in recent years the US has imposed sanctions on Iran, Russia, and Venezuela, targeting non-US persons and financial entities who engage in business activities with persons and entities

[30] As discussed in greater detail in Chapter 4, in recent years, many foreign banks have paid billions of dollars in penalties for violations of US economic and financial sanctions.

[31] For example, as explained in Chapters 3 and 4, the US uses the definition of "US persons" to include all US citizens, all aliens – legal or illegal, all tourists, and almost anybody on US territory. Similarly, for the purposes of sanctions, any transactions made with US dollars – no matter in US territory or in a foreign land, no matter such transactions are made by US persons or foreign persons – fall under the purview of US jurisdictions.

within these countries. These secondary sanctions prohibit third-country individuals and entities from engaging in business with the sanctioned countries, and thus the reach of both US primary, as well as secondary, sanctions apply extraterritorially to third-country nationals or entities (Chercheneff, 2021; Hirschhorn, 2022, 209–216).

Criticisms of Unilateral Sanctions

While unilateral sanctions provide certain advantages to powerful nations, their legitimacy is often questioned on the grounds that they are essentially based on the sanctioners' own views and interpretation of the foreign situation to which they seek to react; they undermine the UN's monopoly right and authority to adopt and impose sanctions in the maintenance of international peace and security; they impose the sanctioners' own interpretation of international law on the targets and the global community; and they are mostly directed at less developed countries (Davis and Ness, 2021; Marossi and Bassett, 2015, 71–80).[32]

Unilateral sanctions have also been criticized for contradicting the basic principles of the multilateral trading system (Ashley, 2021; Ilieva et al., 2018); for coercing a change in the conduct of a target state, which may result in significant collateral damage to the socioeconomic status and basic human rights of the broader population (Joyner, 2017; Owen, 2012, 103); for disrupting and destabilizing the supply chains for essential goods and services and limiting the access to basic medicine and healthcare needs (OHCHR, 2012); and for leaving durable collateral injuries which may persist long after the conclusion of the sanctions campaign (Reisman and Stevick, 1998).

Extraterritorial application of unilateral sanctions has also been criticized on the grounds of their scope, legitimacy, and lawfulness, as they often affect wide ranges of people across countries, and potentially encroach upon diverse branches of international law and international relations (Beucillon, 2021, 8). Many also view some unilateral sanctions as "economic warfare" against the entire population of a target state (Lowe and Tzanakopoulos, 2012; Mulder, 2022), which often causes massive human rights and humanitarian law violations on the broader population (Garfield and Santana, 1997, 15; OHCHR, 2012) while inflicting little or no pain on the political elites (Albal, 2021; Peksen 2009, 2011; Drury et al. 2014).

C *Sanctions Episodes Based on Scope*

Issue-Based Sanctions

Since the 1970s, there has been prolific growth of issue-based sanctions which envisage relatively modest foreign policy goals, such as expropriation claims, combating

[32] By the end of 2022, the US had unilateral sanctions on Belarus, Burundi, Central African Republic, Cuba, Democratic Republic of the Congo, Iran, Iraq, Lebanon, Libya, Mali, Nicaragua, North Korea, Russia, Somalia, Serbia, Sudan, South Sudan, Syria, Venezuela, Yemen, and Zimbabwe. Most of these are among the poorest countries in the world. For the list of US unilateral sanctions, see www.treasury.gov/resource-center/sanctions, accessed on December 4, 2022.

terrorism, drug trafficking, money laundering, and so on. The US has been at the forefront of adopting such measures – most often it does so alone, but occasionally it enlists some allies as well. Such sanctions episodes proliferated with international plane hijacking incidents, such as that following the massacre at the Munich Olympics in 1972 and the downing of Pan Am flight 103 in 1988;[33] and the cocaine epidemic in the 1980s when the US sanctioned several drug trafficking countries to compel them to cooperate with the US antidrug efforts.[34]

In the 1990s, as global attention shifted to non-state actors of terrorism with the emergence of Osama bin Laden's al Qaeda network on the world stage, the US began imposing financial sanctions, such as asset freezes and prohibitions on fund transfers by individuals and entities designated under the Specially Designated Terrorists (SDTs) and the Foreign Terrorist Organizations (FTOs) lists maintained by the Treasury Department. The scopes of the SDTs and the FTOs were further widened to include international money-laundering activities under the Patriot Act of 2001 (P.L. 107–156),[35] which also authorized the establishment of the Terrorist Finance Tracking Program (TFTP) to identify and investigate the financial infrastructure of the international terrorist networks.[36]

Comprehensive Sanctions

Comprehensive sanctions regimes are generally understood as a combination of economic measures that prevent exports (embargo) and restrict imports (boycott) of goods and services; financial measures to prevent the target state from accessing capital and credit systems; and monetary restrictions aimed at destabilizing the currency values of a target country. Comprehensive sanctions that require such a cumulative set of measures are thus plausible under the auspices of a global entity like the UN. Apparently, the global community once believed that such a course of

33 Although the sanctions succeeded in reducing plane hijacking incidents, the broader problem with international terrorism remained for a long time. During the 1980s through the 1990s, the US branded scores of countries, such as Libya, Syria, Iraq, Iran, South Yemen, North Korea, and Cuba, as state sponsors of terrorism.

34 US Congress passed several statutes addressing such issues, including the Comprehensive Drug Abuse Prevention and Control Act of 1970 (CDAPCA: P.L. 91-513). The Controlled Substances Act (CSA), Title II of the CDAPCA, provides the legal basis for the War on Drugs by authorizing federal jurisdiction over possession, trafficking, and manufacturing of drugs. The War on Drugs still continues – the CDAPCA was last amended in 2022. Over the years, the US has sanctioned scores of countries for drug trafficking, including Iran, Syria, Afghanistan, Nigeria, Mexico, Colombia, and Venezuela.

35 The official title of the Act, passed on October 26, 2001 by the 107th US Congress, is: Uniting and Strengthening America by Providing Appropriate Tools Required to Intercept and Obstruct Terrorism Act of 2001 (USA PATRIOT Act).

36 The TFTP, established under the Department of the Treasury, draws its statutory authority, among others, from the IEEPA (1977) and the United Nations Participation Act of 1945 (UNPA). For greater detail, see home.treasury.gov/policy-issues/terrorism-and-illicit-finance/terrorist-finance-tracking-program-tftp, accessed on December 14, 2022.

action was the best way, apart from direct warfare, to exert pressure on a country that flouts international law (Brzoska, 2003; Drezner, 2011; Gordon, 2010).

Historically, such considerations guided the UNSC to impose comprehensive sanctions regimes against Iraq, Haiti, and former Yugoslavia in the 1990s. Obviously, the facts that comprehensive sanctions may cause excessive and indiscriminate civilian harm and suffering, may violate social and economic human rights of the civilian population, and deprive them of basic foods, necessities, and medicines hardly bothered the sanctioners (Garfield, 1999, 124–126; Reisman and Stevick, 1998).

The devastating effects of comprehensive sanctions on Iraq, however, brought forth a decisive change in the global mindset. As discussed in Chapter 7, comprehensive sanctions regimes literally demolished the country's entire infrastructure, caused over one million deaths, and by all means turned Iraq, an economically advanced country outside the Western world, into one of the poorest nations in the world (Cordesman and Hashim, 1997; Gordon, 2010). The humanitarian cost of comprehensive sanctions on the Iraqi population was so severe that many observers described it as a "genocide" mandated by the global community.[37]

Worse still, all comprehensive sanctions regimes imposed by the UNSC in the 1990s – against Iraq, Haiti, and former Yugoslavia – largely failed to achieve their stated goals of reaching a political compromise with the targeted regimes, while a more carefully crafted combination of economic and financial sanctions, with clear objectives, imposed against Iran, succeeded in bringing the country to the negotiating table, which paved the way for the Joint Comprehensive Plan of Action (JCPOA) in 2015 (Farrall, 2007, 107).

Targeted Sanctions

Well-documented humanitarian crises that resulted from the comprehensive sanctions regimes against Iraq and Haiti forced the UN and leading unilateral sanctioners to switch to more precise or targeted sanctions, in order to avoid indiscriminate effects of sanctions on civilian populations in target countries (Reinisch, 2001, 852).[38] The resultant targeted sanctions regime, also known as smart sanctions, envisages two major forms of sanctions: sectoral and individual sanctions. While sectoral sanctions are aimed at impacting a target state's core economic sectors, such as arms and

[37] The UN Human Rights Committee, for example, described the devastating effects of the comprehensive sanctions regime against Iraq as a violation of Article 25 of the Universal Declaration of Human Rights, and Articles 11 and 12 of the International Covenant on Economic, Social and Cultural Rights (Ferrara, 2017).

[38] The transition toward targeted sanctions resulted from three major initiatives undertaken under the auspices of the UN following the Iraq debacle: (a) the Interlaken Process, convened by Switzerland in 1998, explored ways of optimizing targeted financial sanctions; (b) the Bonn–Berlin Process, convened by Germany in 1999, focused on optimizing the use of travel bans, aviation sanctions, and arms embargoes; and (c) the Stockholm Process, initiated by Sweden, focused on the practicality of implementation and monitoring of the targeted sanctions (Brzoska, 2003).

oil, manufacturing or banking, and so on, financial sanctions are aimed at freezing of assets, cutting-off from global banking and credit systems, blocking money-laundering and terrorism-financing instruments, and so on (Hawkins and Lloyd, 2003, 441).

Targeted sanctions also aim at specific persons and entities who have the power to influence the state's unacceptable behavior, and they target not only government officials but also business people and elites. Targeted sanctions also may take thematic and horizontal forms, which focus on individuals or entities related to specific targets, such as human rights violations, cyberattacks, terrorism, money laundering, and so on (Drezner, 2011, 97). All unilateral and multilateral sanctions are now directed at such specific targets, and the UN, the US, and the EU, as well as several other nations, now maintain their own blacklists of such targets.[39]

Theoretically, targeted sanctions are expected to impose costs on the elite and their core supporters so that pressure points and incentives are created in a society in order to push the target government to initiate a bargaining process as a way of mitigating the target's defiance strategies (Cortright and Lopez, 2000, 168; Giumelli, 2016, 38–40). But targeted sanctions have also generated controversies of their own with respect to the procedural rights of sanctioned individuals and entities, as they receive no warning prior to the imposition of sanctions (deLauro, 2020; Ferrara, 2017). Moreover, as discussed in Chapter 5, recent sanctions episodes, imposed on Russia since its second invasion of Ukraine in February 2023, largely resemble comprehensive or near-comprehensive sanctions.

IV OBJECTIVES OF SANCTIONS

A primary objective of a sanctions regime is to condemn or confront a violation of international law and force compliance with international law without resorting to lethal force. The underlying assumption is that such non-lethal coercion will exert sufficient bite on the civic population of a target state that they will exert political pressure on the political leadership to change its objectionable behavior. Sanctioners also use sanctions for stigmatization of the target state before the international community, to gain bargaining power, to express their own policy preferences, to deter similar behavior by other states, or just to send a signal to the population of a target country to take action against their leaders to stay away from internationally acknowledged wrongful policy or behavior (Giumelli, 2016, 38–40; Joyner, 2016, 3).

39 The US, for example, regularly updates a list of sanctioned individuals and entities under the Treasury Department's Specially Designated Nationals (SDN) list. On June 1, 2023, the SDN list was 2,184 pages long. Available at www.treasury.gov/ofac/downloads/sdnlist.pdf. More on the SDN list in Chapters 3–5.

Based on a study of 729 publicly traceable sanctions cases over the period 1950–2016, the Global Sanctions Data Base found that the stated policy objective of sanctions often relates to human rights issues and democratization, while the second most popular group of objectives includes: policy change, preventing wars, ending wars, and regime destabilization, territorial conflict-related issues. And, while in the early period of the survey, the objectives of policy change and regime destabilization were dominant, the pattern changed dramatically after the mid 1990s, when sanctions predominantly aimed at improving human rights, ending wars, and solving territorial conflicts. In more recent years, the survey found democracy-related policy objectives became more dominant.[40]

The stated objectives of sanctions may well be quite different at times from their actual objectives, however. There have been many instances where sanctions regimes were driven by hidden political objectives, such as the long-lasting US trade embargo against Cuba, the US-instigated comprehensive UN economic sanctions against Iraq, and the US sanctions against Iran and several Latin American countries. Sanctions may well also be aimed at serving domestic political purposes rather than changing the behavior of a target state.[41]

Many US presidents have imposed sanctions largely to demonstrate leadership, react forcefully against outrages abroad, answer domestic outrage, or galvanize public support. For example, US sanctions against China in the wake of the Tiananmen Square massacre (1989), the Helms–Burton sanctions against Cuba (1996), the Iran and Libya Sanctions (1996), and Myanmar sanctions (2003) were principally designed to assuage domestic constituencies and to make moral and historical statements (Hufbauer, 2007, 54). Time-series cross-section data from 50 countries between 1966 and 1992 also indicate that US presidents consider US relations with the target state and American domestic politics before initiating any economic sanctions regime (Drury, 2001).

Some studies suggest that the underlying political motivations of developed countries to impose sanctions targeting less developed countries may lie with lack of democracy and civil liberties in those countries. Based on sanctions data for the period 1978–2000, Cox and Drury (2006), for example, conclude that democracies target non-democratic regimes mostly as a substitute for military conflict, and the increased frequency of civil conflicts in developing countries as well as the demand for promotion of democratization in the post–Cold War era have created more opportunities and incentives for developed countries to use economic coercion against non-democratic regimes.[42]

[40] For greater details, see cepr.org/voxeu/columns/global-sanctions-data-base, accessed on February 23, 2023.

[41] David Lloyd George, a British opposition leader, famously remarked on the League of Nations sanctions against Italy in 1935: "They came too late to save Abyssinia from subjugation by Italy, but they are just in the nick of time to save the British Government" (cited in Hufbauer, 2007, 6).

[42] These authors also found that democracies have sanctioned other democracies, citing issues of democracy or human rights, only 18 percent of the time, while they did so 37 percent of the time with respect to nondemocracies.

V EFFECTIVENESS OF SANCTIONS

There has been an avalanche of studies on the effectiveness of sanctions, beginning from those imposed by the League of Nations, and the results have been anything but mixed. Numerous studies suggest that, no matter whether sanctions are comprehensive or targeted, they often violate the human rights of the general populations in the targeted states in many shapes and forms. For example, studies suggest that sanctions impose significant hardship on innocent populations (Shagabutdinova and Berejikian, 2007); erode government respect for human rights (Adam and Tsarsitalidou, 2019; Peksen, 2009; Wood, 2008); result in the contraction of the target economy and thus cause economic and financial distress to the population (Hatipoglu and Peksen, 2018; Hufbauer, 2007; Neuenkirch and Neumeier, 2015); result in widespread poverty, greater income inequality, and worsening of public health (Afesorgbor and Mahadevan, 2016; Allen and Lektzian, 2012; Neuenkirch and Neumeier, 2016; UNHRC, 2014); enable targeted regimes to pass on the lion's share of the sanctions-induced economic pain and suffering to the general population (Gordon, 2010; Neuenkirch and Neumeier, 2016; Weiss et al., 1997); and increase hardship for the general population through rationing of supplies, smuggling, and other black-market channels (Helleiner and Andreas, 2005; Early, 2015; UNHRC, 2014).[43]

Studies also suggest that all the suffering and human rights violations caused by sanctions have taken place when it has been well known to the world community that sanctions hardly work, or do not work at all.[44] Based on an analysis of 11 UN sanctions regimes adopted between 1990 and 1999, Cortright and Lopez (2000) concluded that three of them were moderately to highly successful in gaining compliance; five had very limited, although notable, effects; and three ended up in complete failure. Among the partially successful cases, Iraq and Yugoslavia were under comprehensive sanctions, and Libya was under limited sanctions. Also, based on a survey of sanctions imposed between 1900 and 1990, Hufbauer and Schott (1985) found a success rate of 34 percent, while for sanctions imposed after 1973, the success rate was 24 percent.

Similarly, in a study of twenty-three targeted sanctions regimes imposed by the UN, Biersteker (2018) found no strong evidence to the effect that targeted sanctions were more successful than conventional sanctions. The study also found that targeted measures attained their primary goals in only 22 percent of the cases. With

[43] For an excellent summary of the relevant studies and their findings, see Liou et al (2021) and Peksen (2011 and 2019).

[44] Some studies, however, conclude that sanctions actually do not work. See, for example: Galtung (1967), Bienen and Gilpin (1980), Amerongen (1980), Doxey (1996), Pape (1997), and Haass (1998). Some studies see the theoretical impossibility of sanctions resulting in bringing about changes in target states' policies. See, for example: Barber (1979), Baldwin (1985), Lindsay (1986), Wagner (1988), Nossal (1989), and Tsebelis (1990). Some point out the dismal record of success of sanctions. See, for example: Hoffman (1967), Nincic and Wallensteen (1983), and Wallensteen (1968).

regard to the effectiveness of sanctions in constraining access to resources to the targeted leaders and regimes, the study found targeted sanctions succeeded only 27 percent of the time.[45] Arguing that only 5 percent of all sanctions regimes indeed succeeded, Pape (1997, 76) asserts, "at the end of the day, there is little empirical evidence that sanctions can achieve ambitious foreign policy goals."

VI EFFECTIVENESS OF US SANCTIONS

Apparently, many unilateral sanctions regimes imposed by the US have been quite successful in achieving their stated objectives. For example, in 1953, US sanctions succeeded in overthrowing the Mosaddeq government of Iran to restore the pro-American Reza Shah Pahlavi to power; in the early 1960s, US sanctions forced Egypt to stop its support of rebels in Yemen and the Democratic Republic of Congo; in 1956, US sanctions forced French and British troops to withdraw from the Suez region; in the early 1960s, US sanctions resulted in the overthrow of Rafael Trujillo in the Dominican Republic, and Brazilian President João Goulart; in 1973, US sanctions played a key role in the overthrow of Salvador Allende in Chile; in the 1980s, US sanctions succeeded in overthrowing the regime of Anastasio Somoza in Nicaragua; and in the 1990s, US sanctions succeeded in defeating the Sandinistas.

Not all US unilateral sanctions succeeded, however. For example, US sanctions largely failed in overthrowing Alfredo Stroessner of Paraguay, military regimes in Argentina and El Salvador, and Raul Cédras of Haiti. Also, decades of US embargo against Cuba failed – Fidel Castro survived the sanctions, and his communist regime still survives.[46] Also, US sanctions targeted at African countries in the 1990s – aimed at regime change and democratization – as Hufbauer (2007, 14–15) maintains, achieved a mixed success. They succeeded in bringing about multiparty elections in Malawi and restored democratic government in Niger, but failed in Togo, Equatorial Guinea, Cameroon, Burundi, Gambia, and Ivory Coast. Also, US sanctions against Iraq resulted in humanitarian disaster.

In the most recent phase, US sanctions, directed at Russia, Iran, and Venezuela, which are discussed in great detail in this volume, have been much more sweeping, comprehensive, and rapid compared with previous US sanctions regimes, and they have apparently caused massive disruptions in the targeted countries. So far, however, they have not succeeded in achieving the stated goals of the US – the Iranian regime is still in place, the Maduro government of Venezuela is still in power, and Russia has not yet changed its policy toward Ukraine.

[45] Earlier, a study by Shagabutdinova and Berejikian (2007), based on a large number of smart sanctions, however, found that smart sanctions had been more effective compared with traditional sanctions.

[46] The US sanctions regimes against Cuba are discussed in Chapter 8.

VII ROAD MAP OF THE BOOK

Beginning from the commercial ban against merchants from the Greek port city of Megara in 432 BC, the concepts and constructs, and the scopes and focuses, of sanctions regimes have undergone numerous transformations over the course of more than 2,500 years, responding to the needs of international legal and economic orders. Sanctions have restricted the free flow of trade, investment, capital, and credit around the world, along the way, affecting countless governments and populations, both rightly and wrongly, all in the name of restoring customary international legal norms, espoused both rightly as well as wrongly.

This book examines the unfolding of the latest chapter of this incredible journey since WWII, focusing on a comprehensive understanding of the legal frameworks and executive infrastructures of the US – the most prolific enforcer of economic and financial sanctions in the world. The study analyzes how sanctions regimes have been adopted and enforced across the globe in the light of US legislation, customary international law, international human rights law, international humanitarian law, and the international trading system. The effects of both primary and secondary sanctions, as well as their extraterritorial application, on individuals, entities, and governments are explored in the context of five of the most-sanctioned countries in the world: Russia, Iran, Iraq, Cuba, and Venezuela.

Based on the broad sketch of sanctions regimes outlined in this chapter, Chapter 2 explores unilateral and multilateral economic and financial sanctions from the perspective of public international law. Chapter 3 focuses on the highly sophisticated legal frameworks under which the US adopts and enforces its sanctions regimes. Chapter 4 focuses on US sanctions enforcement infrastructures and mechanisms – the long arms of sanctions enforcement that link domestic and international financial institutions, as well as global networks, to enforce US sanctions across the globe.

The second part of the book – Chapters 5 through 9 – focuses on case studies of five of the most-sanctioned countries in the world to provide an account of how sanctions have affected their governments, economies, and populations. Chapter 5 focuses on Russia – the largest and the most-sanctioned country in the world – where sanctions are apparently aimed at prevention of aggression toward neighboring Ukraine. Chapter 6 focuses on Iran – one of the longest-sanctioned countries in the world – apparently aimed at preventing nuclear proliferation. Chapter 7 covers Iraq, which experienced the most disastrous consequences of comprehensive sanctions in modern times – a reaction to weapons of mass destruction that never existed. Chapter 8 focuses on Cuba, a country that has been subjected to US sanctions longer than any other country in the world, largely because of the country's commitment to communism. Finally, Chapter 9 focuses on Venezuela, a country that had longstanding sound relationships with the US, but incurred the wrath of the US in recent decades due to its socialist agenda.

REFERENCES

Adam, A., and S. Tsarsitalidou. 2019. Do Sanctions Lead to a Decline in Civil Liberties? *Public Choice*, 180(3–4):191–215.

Afesorgbor, S., and R. Mahadevan. 2016. The Impact of Economic Sanctions on Income Inequality of Target States. *World Development*, 83:1–11.

Albal, E. 2021. Evaluating Sanctions in the Context of International Law. *Peace Review*, 33(1):131–139.

Allen, S., and Lektzian, D. 2012. Economic Sanctions: A Blunt Instrument? *Journal of Peace Research*, 50(1):121–135.

Amerongen, O. 1980. Economic Sanctions as a Foreign Policy Tool? *International Security*, 5(2):159–167.

Asada, M. 2020. Definition and Legal Justification of Sanctions. In M. Asada (ed.), *Economic Sanctions in International Law and Practice*, pp. 3–23. London: Routledge.

Ashley, L. 2021. Unilateral Coercive Measures: Towards International Humanitarian Law and International Human Rights. In S. Subedi (ed.), *Unilateral Sanctions in International Law*, pp. 233–254. Oxford: Hart Publishing.

Baldwin, D. 1985. *Economic Statecraft*. Princeton, NJ: Princeton University Press.

Bapat, N., and T. Morgan. 2009. Multilateral Versus Unilateral Sanctions Reconsidered: A Test Using New Data. *International Studies Quarterly*, 53:1075–1094.

Barber, J. 1979. Economic Sanctions as a Policy Instrument. *International Affairs*, 55:367–384.

Beucillon, C. 2021. Introduction. In C. Beucillon (ed.), *Research Handbook on Unilateral and Extraterritorial Sanctions*, pp. 1–18. Cheltenham, London: Edward Elgar.

Bienen, H., and R. Gilpin. 1980. Economic Sanctions as a Response to Terrorism. *Strategic Studies*, 3(1):89–98.

Biersteker, T. et al. 2018. UN Targeted Sanctions Datasets (1991–2013). *Journal of Peace Research*, 55(3):404–412.

Bothe, M. 2016. Compatibility and Legitimacy of Sanctions Regimes. In N. Ronzitti (ed.), *Coercive Diplomacy, Sanctions and International Law*, pp. 33–42. Leiden: Brill.

Boutros-Ghali, B. 1995. *An Agenda for Peace*. New York: United Nations.

Brzoska, M. 2003. From Dumb to Smart? Recent Reforms of UN Sanctions. *Global Governance*, 9(2003):519–535.

Casey, C. et al. 2020. The International Emergency Economic Powers Act: Origins, Evolution, and Use. Washington, DC: Congressional Research Service. R45618.

Chercheneff, L. 2021. Challenging Unilateral and Extraterritorial Sanctions under International Economic Law: Exploring Leads at the WTO and the OECD. In C. Beucillon (ed.), *Research Handbook on Unilateral and Extraterritorial Sanctions*, pp. 239–256. Cheltenham, UK: Edward Elgar.

Cordesman, A., and A. Hashim. 1997. *Iraq: Sanctions and Beyond*. Boulder, CO: Westview Press.

Cortright, D., and G. Lopez. 1999. Are Sanctions Just? The Problematic Case of Iraq. *Journal of International Affairs*, 52(2):735–755.

Cortright, D., and G. Lopez. 2000. *The Sanctions Decade: Assessing UN Strategies in the 1990s*. Boulder, CO: Lynne Reiner.

Cox, D., and A. Drury. 2006. Democratic Sanctions: Connecting the Democratic Peace and Economic Sanctions. *Journal of Peace Research*, 43(6):709–722.

Crawford, J. 2001. The Relationship between Sanctions and Countermeasures. In V. Gowlland-Debbas, and M. Rubio (eds.), *United Nations Sanctions and International Law*, pp. 57–68. The Hague: Kluwer Law International.

Davis, S., and I. Ness. 2021. Introduction: Why Are Economic Sanctions a Form of War? In S. Davis, and I. Ness (eds.), *Sanctions as War: Anti-imperialist Perspectives on American Geo-economic Strategy*. Leiden and Boston: Brill.

Dawidowicz, M. 2017. Third-Party Countermeasures and the ICJ. In M. Dawidowicz (ed.), *Third Party Countermeasures in International Law*, pp. 36–71. Cambridge: Cambridge University Press.

deLauro, A. 2020. The UN Sanctions Regime. LUISS Academy, Working paper no 9/2018–2019.

Doxey, M. 1996. *International Sanctions in Contemporary Perspective*. 2nd ed. Houndmills: Macmillan.

Doxey, M. 2009. Reflections on the Sanctions Decade and Beyond. *International Journal*, 64(2):539–549.

Drezner, D. 2003. The Hidden Hand of Economic Coercion. *International Organization*, 57:643–659.

Drezner, D. 2011. Sanctions Sometimes Smart: Targeted Sanctions in Theory and Practice. *International Studies Review*, 13(1):96–108.

Drury, A. 2001. Sanctions as Coercive Diplomacy: The U.S. President's Decision to Initiate Economic Sanctions. *Political Research Quarterly*, 54(3):485–508.

Drury, A., P. James, and D. Peksen. 2014. Neo-Kantianism and Coercive Diplomacy: The Complex Case of Economic Sanctions. *International Interactions*, 40:25–51.

Dupont, P. 2012. Countermeasures and Collective Security. The Case of EU Sanctions against Iran. *Journal of Conflict and Security Law*, 17(3):301–336.

Early, B. 2015. Introduction: Why Busted Sanctions Lead to Broken Sanctions Policies. In B. Early, and B. Early (eds.), *Busted Sanctions: Explaining Why Economic Sanctions Fail*, pp. 1–16. Stanford, CA: Stanford University Press.

Elliott, K. 2016. The Impacts of United Nations Targeted Sanctions. In T. Biersteker, S. Eckert, and M. Tourinho (eds.), *Targeted Sanctions: The Impacts and Effectiveness of United Nations Action*, pp. 172–189. Cambridge: Cambridge University Press.

Farrell, H., and A. Newman. 2019. Weaponized Interdependence. *International Security* 44(1):42–79.

Farrall, J. 2007. *United Nations Sanctions and the Rule of Law*. 1st ed. London: Cambridge University Press.

Felbermayr, G. et al. 2020. The Global Sanctions Database. *European Economic Review*, 129 (October 2020):1–23.

Ferrara, F. 2017. Striking a balance in the United Nations: The Need for Safeguarding Human Rights against Economic Sanctions. LUISS thesis. Available at: tesi.luiss.it/19800/

Franco, C. 2015. Remarks by Marco Roscini at the IAI Conference of 13 February 2015 on *Coercive Diplomacy, Sanctions and International Law*, book edited by N. Ronzitti. Available on the website of the Istituto Affari Internazionali.

Galtung, J. 1967. On the Effects of International Economic Sanctions: With Examples from the Case of Rhodesia. *World Politics*, 19(3):378–416.

Gardner, R. 1980. *Sterling–Dollar Diplomacy*. New York: Columbia University Press.

Garfield, R. 1999. Morbidity and Mortality among Iraqi Children from 1990 through 1998: Assessing the Impact of the Gulf War and Economic Sanctions. Available at: www.casi.org .uk/info/garfield/dr-garfield.html.

Garfield, R., and S. Santana. 1997. The Impact of the Economic Crisis and the US Embargo on Health in Cuba. *American Journal of Public Health*, 87(1):15–20.

Giumelli, F. 2016. The Purposes of Targeted Sanctions. In T. Biersteker et al. (eds.), *Targeted Sanctions: The Impacts and Effectiveness of United Nations Action*, pp. 38–40. Cambridge: Cambridge University Press.

Goldman, Z., and A. Lindblom. 2021. The US Position and Practice with Regards to Unilateral and Extraterritorial Sanctions: Reimagining the US Sanctions Regime in a World of Advanced Technology. In C. Beucillon (ed.), *Research Handbook on Unilateral and Extraterritorial Sanctions*, pp. 130–148. Cheltenham, UK: Edward Elgar.

Gordon, J. 1999. Sanctions as Siege Warfare. *The Nation*. March 22, 1999. Available at: archive.globalpolicy.org/component/content/article/170-sanctions/42074.html.

Gordon, J. 2010. *Invisible War: The United States and the Iraq Sanctions*. Cambridge, MA: Harvard University Press.

Gordon, R., M. Smyth, and T. Cornell. 2019. *Sanctions Law*. EBSCO Publishing: eBook Comprehensive Academic Collection (EBSCOhost).

Gottemoeller, R. 2007. The Evolution of Sanctions in Practice and Theory. *Survival*, 49(4):99–110.

Haass, R. (Ed.). 1998. *Economic Sanctions and American Foreign Policy*. New York: Council on Foreign Relations.

Hatipoglu, E., and D. Peksen, 2018. Economic Sanctions and Banking Crises in Target Economies. *Defense and Peace Economics*, 29(2):171–189.

Hawkins, D., and J. Lloyd. 2003. Questioning Comprehensive Sanctions: The Birth of a Norm. *Journal of Human Rights*, 2(3):443–465.

Helleiner, E., and P. Andreas (Eds.). 2005. *Economic Nationalism in a Globalizing World*. Ithaca, NY: Cornell University Press.

Herik, L. 2017. *Research Handbook on UN Sanctions and International Law*. Cheltenham, UK and Northampton, MA: Edward Elgar.

Hirschhorn, E. et al. 2022. *U.S. Export Controls and Economic Sanctions*. New York: Oxford University Press.

Hoffman, F. 1967. The Function of Economic Sanctions: A Comparative Analysis. *Journal of Peace Research*, 2:140–159.

Hovell, D. 2019. Symposium on Unilateral Targeted Sanctions. Unfinished Business of International Law: The Questionable Legality of Autonomous Sanctions. *American Journal of International Law*, 113:140–145.

Hufbauer, G. and J. Schott. 1985. *Economic Sanctions Reconsidered. History and Current Policy*. Washington, DC: Patterson Institute for International Economics.

Hufbauer, G. et al. 2007. *Economic Sanctions Reconsidered: History and Current Policy*. Washington, DC: Patterson Institute for International Economics.

ILC (International Law Commission). 2001. *Articles on the Responsibility of States for Internationally Wrongful Acts (ARSIWA)*. New York: United Nations.

Ilieva, J., A. Dashtevski, and F. Kokotovic. 2018. Economic Sanctions in International Law. *UTMS Journal of Economics*, 9(2):201–211.

IMF (International Monetary Fund). 2020. *Reserve Currencies in an Evolving International Monetary System*. Washington, DC: International Monetary Fund.

IMF (International Monetary Fund). 2021. *Reserve Currencies in an Evolving International Monetary System*. Washington, DC: International Monetary Fund.

Joyner, D. 2016. International Legal Limits on the Ability of States to Lawfully Impose International Economic/Financial Sanctions. In A. Marossi, and M. Bassett (eds.), *Economic Sanctions under International Law: Unilateralism, Multilateralism, Legitimacy and Consequences*, pp. 83–93. London: Springer.

Joyner, D. 2017. UN Counter-Proliferation Sanctions and International Law. In L. Herik (ed.), *Research Handbook on UN Sanctions and International Law*, pp. 110–121. Cheltenham, UK: Edward Elgar.

Kamto, M. 2010. The Time Factor in the Application of Countermeasures. In J. Crawford et al. (eds.), *Law of International Responsibility*, pp. 1174–1176. Oxford: Oxford University Press.

LaRae-Perez, C. 2002. Economic Sanctions as Use of Force: Re-evaluating the Legality of Sanctions from an Effects-based Perspective. *Boston University International Law Journal*, 20(1):161–188.

Larsen, K. 2009. "Territorial Non-Application" of the European Convention on Human Rights. *Nordic Journal of International Law*, 78:56–73.

Lektzian, D. 2013. *Making Sanctions Smarter: Are Humanitarian Costs an Essential Element in the Success of Sanctions?* Oslo: International Peace Research Institute and Norges Rode Kors.

Lindsay, J. 1986. Trade Sanctions as Policy Instruments: A Re-examination. *International Studies Quarterly*, 30(2):153–173.

Liou, R., M. Amanda, and D. Peksen. 2021. Revisiting the Causal Links between Economic Sanctions and Human Rights Violations. *Political Research Quarterly*, 74(4):808–821.

Lowe, A., and A. Tzanakopoulos. 2012. Economic Warfare. In R. Wolfrum (ed.), *Max Planck Encyclopedia of Public International Law*. Oxford: Oxford University Press. Available at: opil.ouplaw.com/display/10.1093/law:epil/9780199231690/law-9780199231690-e292.

Lowenfeld, A. 2003. Trade Controls for Political Ends: Four Perspectives. *Chicago Journal of International Law*, 4(2):354–369.

Marossi, A., and M. Bassett (Eds.). 2015. *Economic Sanctions under International Law: Unilateralism, Multilateralism, Legitimacy and Consequences*. London: Springer.

McDowell, D. 2023. *Bucking the Buck: US Financial Sanctions and the International Backlash against the Dollar*. New York: Oxford Academic.

Milanovic, M. 2011. *Extraterritorial Application of Human Rights Treaties*. Oxford: Oxford University Press.

Morgan, C. et al. 2014. Threat and Imposition of Economic Sanctions 1945–2005: Updating the TIES dataset. *Conflict Management and Peace Science*, 31(5):541–558.

Mulder, N. 2022. *The Economic Weapon*. New Haven, CT: Yale University Press.

Murphy, J. 2000. *Sanctions in Transition*. London: The David Davies Memorial Institute of International Studies.

Nephew, R. 2020. Implementation of Sanctions: United States. In M. Asada (ed.), *Economic Sanctions in International Law and Practice*, pp. 93–115. London: Routledge.

Neuenkirch, M., and F. Neumeier. 2015. The Impact of UN and U.S. Economic Sanctions on GDP Growth. *European Journal of Political Economy*, 40:110–125.

Neuenkirch, M., and F. Neumeier. 2016. The Impact of U.S. Sanctions on Poverty. *Journal of Development Economics* 121:110–119.

Nincic, M., and P. Wallensteen. (Eds.). 1983. *Dilemmas of Economic Coercion: Sanctions in World Politics*. New York: Praeger.

Nossal, K. 1989. International Sanctions as International Punishment. *International Organization*, 43:301–322.

O'Connell, M. 2002. Debating the Law of Sanctions. *European Journal of International Law*, 13:63–79.

Offer, A. 1989. *The First World War: An Agrarian Interpretation*. Oxford: Clarendon Press.

OHCHR (UN Office of the High Commissioner of Human Rights). 2012. Thematic Study of the Office of the United Nations High Commissioner for Human Rights on the Impact of Unilateral Coercive Measures on the Enjoyment of Human Rights, Including Recommendations on Actions Aimed at Ending such Measures. (2012) A/HRC/19/33.

Owen, M. 2012. The Limits of Economic Sanctions under International Humanitarian Law: The Case of the Congo. *Texas International Law Journal*, 48:103–112.

Pape, R. 1997. Why Economic Sanctions Do Not Work. *International Security*, 22(2):90–136.
Peksen, D. 2009. Better or Worse? The Effect of Economic Sanctions on Human Rights. *Journal of Peace Research*, 46(1):59–77.
Peksen, D. 2011. Economic Sanctions and Human Security: The Public Health Effect of Economic Sanctions. *Foreign Policy Analysis*, 7(3):237–251.
Peksen, D. 2019. When Do Imposed Economic Sanctions Work? A Critical Review of the Sanctions Effectiveness Literature. *Defense and Peace Economics*, 30(6):635–647.
Rahmat, M. 2015. Unilateral Sanctions in International Law: A Quest for Legality. In A. Marossi, and M. Bassett (eds.), *Economic Sanctions under International Law: Unilateralism, Multilateralism, Legitimacy and Consequences*, pp. 71–81. London: Springer.
Rathbone, M. et al. 2013. Sanctions, Sanctions Everywhere: Forging a Path through Complex Transnational Sanctions Laws. *Georgetown Journal of Law*, 44:1056–1094.
Reinisch, W. 2001. Developing Human Rights and Humanitarian Law Accountability of the Security Council for the Imposition of Economic Sanctions. *American Journal of International Law*, 95(4):851–872.
Reisman, W., and D. Stevick. 1998. The Applicability of International Law Standards to United Nations Economic Sanctions Programs. *European Journal of International law* 9:86–141.
Renwick, R. 1981. *Economic Sanctions*. Harvard Studies in International Affairs. Issue 45. Cambridge: Harvard University Center for International Affairs.
Ronzitti, N. 2016. Sanctions as Instruments of Coercive Diplomacy: An International Law Perspective. In N. Ronzitti (ed.), *Coercive Diplomacy, Sanctions and International Law*, pp. 1–32. Leiden: Brill.
Rosenberg, E. 2019. *Assessing the Use of Sanctions in Addressing National Security and Foreign Policy Challenges*. Washington, DC: Center for a New American Security.
Ruys, T. 2017. Sanctions, Retortions and Countermeasures: Concepts and International Legal Framework. In L. Herik (ed.), *Research Handbook on UN Sanctions and International Law*, pp. 19–51. Cheltenham, UK: Edward Elgar.
Schwab, P. 1999. *Cuba: Confronting the U.S. Embargo*. New York: Macmillan.
Shagabutdinova, E., and J. Berejikian. 2007. Deploying Sanctions while Protecting Human Rights: Are Humanitarian "Smart" Sanctions Effective? *Journal of Human Rights*, 6(1):59–74.
Tsebelis, G. 1990. Are Sanctions Effective? A Game-Theoretic Analysis. *Journal of Conflict Resolution*, 34:3–28.
UNHRC (United Nations Human Rights Council). 2014. Human Rights and Unilateral Coercive Measures. UNHRC Res (03 October 2014). A/HRC/RES/27/21.
Wagner, R. 1988. Economic Interdependence, Bargaining Power and Political Influence. *International Organization*, 42:461–482.
Wallensteen, P. 1968. Characteristics of Economic Sanctions. *Journal of Peace Research*, 3:248–267.
Wallensteen, P. 1983. Economic Sanctions: Ten Modern Cases and Three Important Lessons. In M. Nincic, and P. Wallensteen (eds.), *Dilemmas of Economic Coercion: Sanctions in World Politics*, pp. 87–130. New York: Praeger.
Watson, A. 2004. *An Introduction to International Political Economy*. London: A&C Black.
Weber, P., and G. Schneider. 2022. Post-Cold War Sanctioning by the EU, the UN, and the US: Introducing the EUSANCT Dataset. *Conflict Management and Peace Science*, 39(1):97–114.

Weiss, T. et al. (Eds.). 1997. *Political Gain and Civilian Pain*. Lanham, MD: Rowman & Littlefield.

Wilson, W. 1923. *Woodrow Wilson's Case for the League of Nations*. Princeton, NJ: Princeton University Press.

Wood, R. 2008. A Hand upon the Throat of the Nation: Economic Sanctions and State Repression, 1976–2001. *International Studies Quarterly*, 52(3):489–513.

2

Economic and Financial Sanctions under International Law

I INTRODUCTION

The legality and legitimacy of economic and financial sanctioning measures[1] depend on multiple factors, such as whether the sanctioning measures are imposed by a particular state, a group of states like the European Union (EU), a regional body of states like the OAS, or a multilateral body like the UN. Other factors include whether the sanctions are imposed as countermeasures, countersanctions, or retorsions; whether they are targeted at states, entities, or individuals, or all of those; whether they are primary, secondary, or extraterritorial sanctions; whether they are punitive or peaceful coercive measures; whether they are compatible with the principles of non-intervention and equality of sovereign states; whether they are compatible with the fundamental human rights and extraterritorial human rights obligations of sanctioners; and whether they are necessary, appropriate, and proportional to the alleged injuries, and whether the sanctioner is an actually an "injured state" in respect of an international wrongful act.

This chapter examines the legality and legitimacy of sanctioning measures from the perspectives of international laws and regulations, customs, and conventions. Section II explores international legal frameworks of unilateral and multilateral sanctions; Section III examines sanctioning measures in the context of international trade laws as envisaged by the World Trade Organization (WTO); Section IV focuses on both unilateral and multilateral sanctions from the perspectives of international human rights laws and international humanitarian laws; and Section V concludes the chapter.

1 The UN usually designates its sanctioning measures as "sanctions regimes"; the EU designates its sanctions as "restrictive measures"; and the US describes them as "sanctions programs." For a particular package of sanctioning measures adopted in relation to a particular state or situation, the UN usually uses the number of the UNSC resolution. For example, the 2006 UNSC sanctions on North Korea in relation to its proliferation of nuclear, biological, and chemical weapons is known as the "1718 regime." The EU also uses the term "sanctions regime" for a package of sanctions, but designates them by the name of the country, such as "Syrian sanctions regime" (Gordon, 2019, 6–7).

II INTERNATIONAL LEGAL FRAMEWORK OF SANCTIONS

As discussed in Chapter 1, the existing legal literature provides no widely accepted definition of the term "sanctions." Generally, sanctions paradigms are characterized by a dual-agent model composed of a sender or sanctioner and a target state, and broadly involve a suspension or interruption of normal relations in response to a change in policy or behavior on the part of a target state that breaches international law. Most importantly, sanctions are viewed as a non-lethal option to force a target state to abide by international law and correct its objectionable behavior without involving military warfare (Boutros-Ghali, 1995).[2]

From the international law perspective, a sanctions regime not only envisages a penalty or punishment for nonconformity with international law, or failure to observe international standards or obligations by a target state, it also confers legitimacy and the dignity of law to such coercive measures (Beucillon, 2021, 1–9; Doxey, 1996, 4; Kuyper, 1990) as long as they are undertaken by a competent social organ legally empowered to act in the name of the society or community that is governed by the legal system (Asada, 2020, 4; Crawford, 2001, 57).

Legal literature also distinguishes sanctions from other concepts, such as "retorsions" – internationally lawful measures undertaken by a state in response to a prior injury to another state;[3] "reprisals" – measures taken in response to a previous breach of international humanitarian law;[4] and "countermeasures" – measures that a nation can lawfully take in response to sanctions.

The legal frameworks of sanctions have also undergone major changes in recent decades due to the proliferation of sanctioning measures aimed at internationally wrongful behavior by non-state entities and individuals, for example, in fights against terrorism, money laundering, drug trafficking, human trafficking, and so on. Similarly, in recent decades there has been extraordinary expansion in legally

[2] The EU, for example, describes the aim of such measures as "to bring about a change in policy or activity by the target country, part of country, government entities or individuals." See "Guidelines on Implementation and Evaluation of Restrictive Measures (Sanctions) in the Framework of the EU Common Foreign and Security Policy." 15579/03, Brussels, 3 December 2003.

[3] The term "retorsion" refers to the suspension and termination of treaties under Article 60 of the Vienna Convention on the Law of Treaties (VCLT) and the right to adopt unilateral trade restrictions based on the national security exception in Article XXI of the General Agreement on Tariffs and Trade (GATT) or Article XIV of the General Agreement on Trading in Services (GATS). Thus, retorsion may constitute a response to a prior internationally wrongful act, but this need not necessarily be the case. Also, retorsion is largely unregulated by international law and need not necessarily be temporary or reversible, and may contain a punitive element, while sanctions are supposed to be temporary and reversible (Dawidowicz, 2017a; Ruys, 2017, 24–25; Dupont, 2012, 41–42).

[4] The term "reprisal" refers to acts in retaliation for acts contrary to international law on the part of the offending state, which have remained unredressed after a demand for amends. Reprisal may also comprise use of force and other non-forcible measures, and may involve self-defense, temporarily sanctioning the use of force, but contingent on the occurrence of an "armed attack." Countermeasures may be triggered by any internationally wrongful conduct, but must be non-forcible in nature, and necessary and proportional (Crawford, 2013, 677; Dawidowicz, 2017b; White, 2017).

permissible extraterritorial sanctions which target third countries, individuals, and entities. While the "first generation" sanctioning measures of the 1980s through 1990s were relatively precise in their stated scopes and enforcements, the "second generation" extraterritorial sanctioning measures of recent decades often produce a "chilling effect" on third countries, individuals, and entities.[5]

In understanding the legal standpoints of sanctions, it is also important to note that the sanctions laws originate with decisions made by states or international organizations, such as the US, the UN, and the EU. Each of these sanctioning authorities inhabits a separate legal sphere, and they adopt and implement sanctioning measures in different ways depending on their respective sources of authority. At the same time, these legal systems by no means are hermetically sealed from one another, they often involve overlapping sources and jurisdictions of law, and rather reflect the multiplicity and confluence of sanctions laws (Gordon, 2019, 4–6).

Multilateral Sanctions

Multilateral sanctions[6] are imposed collectively by the UNSC pursuant to Chapter VII of the UN Charter (Articles 39 and 41) in the interest of maintaining international peace and security.[7] Article 39 requires the UNSC to adopt sanctioning measures based on a prior determination that "a threat to the peace, breach of the peace, or act of aggression" exists, and that it requires all UN member states to enforce such measures.[8] Article 41 of the Charter empowers the UNSC to impose "complete or partial interruption of economic relations," ranging from individualized asset freezes to trade embargoes to restore international peace.

Article 25 of the UN Charter makes it mandatory for all UN member states to implement UNSC-mandated sanctions on private individuals and companies on the domestic front, and Article 103 of the Charter makes it obligatory for all UN members to grant precedence to UNSC-imposed resolutions over any other obligations they may have pursuant to any other international treaties. Such prima facie supremacy of the UN obligations vis-à-vis other international obligations plays a crucial role in the implementation of UN sanctions regimes by the member states (Gordon, 2019, 5–6; Herrik, 2017).

Multilateral sanctions imposed by the UNSC have emerged as the central instrument for maintaining global peace and security, especially since the end of the Cold

5 Some of the relevant studies include: Sossai (2020), Gibney (2022), Goldman and Lindblom (2021), Carter and Farha (2013), and Mallard and Hanson (2021).

6 As explained in Chapter 1, in this study, only those sanctions imposed by the UNSC are considered multilateral sanctions. Those imposed by an individual state or a group of states, such as the EU, or a regional body like the OAS, are considered unilateral sanctions.

7 The UNSC has the mandate to maintain international peace and security pursuant to Chapters VI, VII, VIII, and XII of the UN Charter, but the UNSC's sanctioning decisions are governed by Article 27 of the UN Charter and Rule 40 of the Provisional Rules of Procedure of the UNSC.

8 Article 6 of the UN Charter empowers the UNSC even to expel a member state from the UN on the grounds of persistent violation of UN principles.

War. Prior to that, between 1945 and 1990, the UNSC used Article 41 of UN Charter only twice – against Rhodesia in 1966 and against apartheid South Africa in 1987 – and both of these sanctions regimes were comprehensive in character.[9] However, at the end of the Cold War, with the apparent ceasing of adversarial relations between the two superpowers – the US and the former Soviet Union (current Russia) – the 1990s came to be the "sanctions decade" for the UNSC (Asada, 2020, 5), when a series of partial or comprehensive sanctions were imposed on scores of countries, including Iraq, former Yugoslavia, Libya, Liberia, Somalia, Haiti, Rwanda, Sierra Leone, Sudan, Eritrea, Ethiopia, the UNITA forces in Angola, and Afghanistan. Since 1990, UNSC has imposed 30 sanctions regimes targeting 22 countries.[10]

Following the humanitarian disaster of the comprehensive sanctions regime imposed on Iraq in the 1990s,[11] however, the UNSC abandoned the traditional measures of comprehensive sanctions. It adopted targeted sanctions, which are directed at the leaders, decision-makers, specific sectors, or geographic regions, and so on, instead of targeting the entire population of a country indiscriminately.[12] Since then, the UNSC has also adopted elaborate sanctions monitoring structures, such as overseeing committees, panels of experts, monitoring teams, and more sophisticated sanctioning tools (Gordon, 2019, 11–12).

Legal Boundaries of Multilateral Sanctions

The sweeping and binding nature of the UNSC resolutions with respect to economic and financial sanctions has been upheld by the International Court of Justice (IJC), although whether the UNSC can also adopt armed intervention for restoring international peace and security remains controversial (Gordon, 2019, 5–6). Although it remains controversial whether the UNSC is permitted to use armed force, Articles 41 and 42 of the UN Charter indicate that if economic sanctions prove to be ineffective or inadequate to deter internationally wrongful acts, then it may be within the powers of the UNSC to resort to military offensive as well to implement its resolutions.[13] Some scholars even argue that these choices may not

[9] During the same period the US imposed sanctions more than 40 times (LaRae-Perez, 2002).

[10] Currently, the UNSC has 14 ongoing sanctions regimes focused on supporting political settlement of conflicts, nuclear non-proliferation, and counter-terrorism, and its consolidated list of sanctions designates 704 individuals and 254 groups or organizations. For greater detail, see www.un.org/securitycouncil/content/un-sc-consolidated-list, accessed on February 5, 2023.

[11] As explained in Chapter 7, comprehensive sanctions imposed on Iraq in the 1990s caused the deaths of at least half a million infants and children, while overall deaths exceeded one million.

[12] Since the Iraq debacle, targeted sanctions have been adopted for both unilateral and multilateral sanctions in order to eliminate or reduce unintended consequences. Some scholars, however, are skeptical that even targeted sanctions can eliminate all unintended consequences, especially humanitarian costs to the broader population in a target country. See, for example, Moiseienko (2021), Mohamad (2015), and Lopez and Cortright (1995).

[13] Notably, Article 41 of the UN Charter grants the UNSC the right to decide "measures not involving the use of armed force" to give effect to its decisions, but it also provides that it may "call upon the Members of the United Nations to apply such measures." Article 42 of the Charter grants the UNSC

be mutually exclusive – they rather should be viewed as primary means of action by which the UNSC can address a breach of international peace and security (LaRae-Perez, 2002, 180).[14]

Thus, there exists little dispute that the UNSC is specially mandated to articulate, operationalize, and monitor multilateral sanctions. It is also a fact that, over the decades, multilateral sanctions imposed by the UNSC have become well institutionalized in international law and *jus cogens* norms (Crawford, 2013; Tomuschat and Thouvenin, 2005). At the same time, neither the UNSC as the sole organ with the responsibility for maintaining international peace and security, nor its actions and inactions in maintaining universal standards in the conduct of sanctions, are viewed as immune from the test of institutional and legal integrity (Schechla, 2022, 258–259). In other words, questions are being raised whether UNSC sanctions regimes are unbound by law, that is, whether they can legally be challenged in a court of law.

This very issue came to the front and center in *Yassin Abdullah Kadi and Al Barakaat International Foundation v. Council and Commission* (2008), decided by the European Court of Justice (ECJ).[15] *Kadi* brought forth three broad arguments before the ECJ against UNSC sanctions imposed in pursuance of Article 41 of the UN Charter: (a) the legality of the sanctions measures by reference to the Charter (the *ultra vires* argument); (b) the legality of the sanctions measures by reference to *jus cogens* norms of customary international law (the *jus cogens* argument); and (c) the legality of the sanctions measures by reference to the state responsibility on countermeasures (the *countermeasures* argument) (Gordon, 2019, 15; Hovell, 2019).

The first issue centered on whether UNSC acted in compliance with the UN Charter, whether it violated the stated purposes of the Charter to promote and encourage respect for human rights and fundamental freedoms, and whether the UNSC sanctions were *ultra vires* to the Charter and breached its internationally recognized human rights obligations. The ECJ ruled that: (a) the applicant's right

power to take action "by air, sea, or land forces as may be necessary to maintain or restore international peace and security," and also specifies that such "action may include demonstrations, blockade, and other operations by air, sea, or land forces of Members of the United Nations."

14 As discussed in Chapter 7, both Presidents George H. W. Bush and George W. Bush used UN resolutions to attack Iraq in 1990 during the first Gulf War and in 2003 to topple Saddam Hossain from power, respectively. Also, as mentioned in Chapter 1, the League of Nations provided for the use of economic and military sanctions when a member state went to war in violation of Article 12, 13, or 15 of its Covenants. But unlike the UN Charter, the League's Covenants did not make it binding for all its members to implement its resolutions.

15 The case matter relates to Yassin Abdullah Kadi, a Saudi Arabian resident who established the Al Barakaat International Foundation in Spånga, Sweden. The European Council froze his assets in accordance with the 1267 Taliban/Al Qaida sanctions regime of the EU's Common Foreign and Security Policy (CFSP) involving persons and entities associated with Usama bin Laden, the Al-Qaeda network, and the Taliban, in accordance with UNSC Resolutions (Common Position 2002/402/CFSP –Regulation (EC) No. 881/2002). For details, see Joined Cases C-402/05 P and C-415/05 P, *Kadi & Al Barakaat International Foundation v. Council and Commission*, Judgment, 3 September 2008.

of defense as well as their right to an effective legal remedy was infringed and (b) the EU legal system was independent of international law and the UNSC resolutions on terrorist sanctions were unable to penetrate this independent system, and thus could not prevail over the EU's fundamental rights guaranteed by Article 103 of the Charter (Farrall, 2007, 72–73; Milanovic, 2011, 241).

The second issue was whether the UNSC resolutions were subject to the customary rules of international law having *jus cogens* status. The ECJ Court of First Instance ruled that UNSC sanctions could not take precedence over peremptory norms of international law as set by *jus cogens*, and the court was empowered to scrutinize the lawfulness of the UNSC resolutions under the EU legal system. The court thus set a unique precedent as to the legality of UNSC sanctions regimes, which had never been successfully invoked before in any court, whether international, domestic, or regional (Hovell, 2019).

The *Kadi* rulings drew considerable controversy, however. Article 53 of the Vienna Convention on the Law of Treaties (VCLT), for example, defines *jus cogens* as "a norm accepted and recognized by the international community of States as a whole as a norm from which no derogation is permitted and which can be modified only by a subsequent norm of general international law having the same character" (cited in Crawford, 2013, 83). Some scholars believe that as the *jus cogens* doctrine enjoys the highest status in customary international law, the UNSC resolutions should also be subject to the doctrine. Reinisch (2001, 859–860), for example, opines that the UNSC "must respect peremptory norms of international law because the core values protected by the concept of *jus cogens* are simply not derogable." On the other hand, Crawford (2013) argues that although derogation of *jus cogens* is prohibited, and may even carry legal consequence, no state has been held criminally liable for violating *jus cogens*.[16]

On the third issue of *Kadi*, with respect to "countermeasures," that is, non-performance of international obligations by a state in response to internationally wrongful acts committed by another state, the ECJ deferred the matter to Article 51 of ARSIWA (Articles on the Responsibility of States for Internationally Wrongful Acts) by the International Law Commission (ILC), which provides that countermeasures must be proportionate to the injury suffered and must take into account the gravity of the internationally wrongful act and the rights in question.[17] The ECJ ruled that, although ILC's law on countermeasures did not apply *prima facie* to sanctions adopted by the UNSC because the UN could not be an "injured state" for the purpose of taking action against other states or individuals, the UN sanctions

[16] Article 5 of VCLT (1969), which entered into force on 27 January 1980, states: "The present Convention applies to any treaty which is the constituent instrument of an international organization and to any treaty adopted within an international organization without prejudice to any relevant rules of the organization."

[17] Article 51 of ILC (2001) states: "Countermeasures must be commensurate with the injury suffered, taking into account the gravity of the internationally wrongful act and the rights in question."

were functionally analogous to countermeasures and thus the limitations set out in ARSIWA should apply to the UN as well (Gordon, 2019, 15–16).

The ECJ ruling in *Kadi* thus sets a powerful precedent that, although there exists no recognized judicial forum for the review of sanctions regimes adopted or enforced by the UNSC, some courts may be willing to assert jurisdiction over challenges to some specific measures imposed by such resolutions.[18] The ILC's position on the applicability of *jus cogens* to the UNSC resolutions is not so clear, however. Although it provides clear legal understanding of *jus cogens* norms with respect to the prohibitions on critical issues, such as genocide, the unlawful use of force, piracy, and torture, it provides no such clear-cut ruling with respect to the applicability of *jus cogens* norms to the UNSC resolutions.[19] Apparently, the UN Ombudsperson Office has the responsibility of reviewing certain UN decisions, including those of the UNSC, but the office does not serve as a court (deWet, 2013).

Unilateral Sanctions

Unilateral sanctions are those autonomously adopted and imposed by a state or a group of states, or a regional body of states, without the approval of the UNSC (Happold, 2016, 1).[20] In most cases, such unilateral sanctions have been adopted by powerful states like the US and the EU. Among the 174 instances of unilateral sanctions between 1945 and 2000, the US either alone or in concert with its allies deployed such sanctions 109 times (Hufbauer et al., 2007, 17), and the EU, the "trailblazer in unilateral sanctions," was a close second with 48 instances to its credit (Herrik, 2017; Ilieva et al., 2018).[21] By June 2023, the US had 32 active sanctions programs aimed at more than 20,000 individuals and entities strewn across more than 20 countries on the grounds of terrorism, narcotics trafficking, weapons proliferation, human rights abuses, invasion of another state, and so on.[22]

Unilateral sanctions are adopted autonomously, and thus are essentially based on the domestic laws of the sanctioning countries. The economic, financial, and

18 Some specialized courts, such as the European Court of Human Rights (ECHR) also appear to be willing to assert jurisdiction over UNSC resolutions. More on this below.

19 See the ILC's "Analytical Guide to the Work of the International Law Commission," adopted at its 69th session in 2017. The session also decided to change the title of the topic from "jus cogens" to "peremptory norms of general international law (jus cogens)." Available at: legal.un.org/ilc/guide/1_14.shtml.

20 In the legal literature, unilateral sanctions have often been described interchangeably as "autonomous sanctions," "unilateral coercive measures," "unilateral economic measures," "coercive economic measures," and so on (Ashley, 2021; Dupont, 2021). A consensus seems to be emerging in recent years, however, to describe them as "unilateral coercive measures" (UCM), following the UN Human Rights Council's coinage of the term (HRC 2015, 74). This study, however, refers to autonomous unilateral sanctions as "unilateral sanctions."

21 As of 2016, 25 of 43 restrictive measures imposed by the EU on non-EU member states were adopted without the authorization of the UN (Gestri, 2016).

22 The most recent list of US unilateral sanctions is available at: www.treasury.gov/resource-center/sanctions, accessed on February 5, 2023.

political tools and instruments deployed to achieve sanction objectives are also their own, and based on their own conception of the target's alleged misconduct and international wrongful act (Giumelli, 2016, 38–40).[23] Under the UN Charter, every state has the freedom and liberty to revise its relations with other states as it pleases, provided that the measures are not contrary to international law, or in breach of any specific legal obligations of the state to other states. There are no customary obligations for a state to maintain any particular relations with other states (Happold, 2016).

At the same time, under the UN Charter, UN General Assembly (UNGA) resolutions, and other international treaties and conventions, states have certain duties to maintain international peace and security, respect the principles of sovereign equality of states and non-intervention in the internal and external affairs of other states, and uphold the rights of development and human rights of the peoples of other states. But numerous instances suggest that unilateral sanctions often violate international law, contravene the General Agreement on Tariffs and Trade (GATT)/WTO trading system, or are based on questionable legality (Hovell, 2019, 140; Joyner, 2017). Also, in most cases, especially with respect to those imposed by the US, unilateral sanctions have largely been targeted at less developed countries, often involving strategic deployment of vast economic and financial networks and mechanisms to subdue targets that stand in the sanctioner's way (Davis and Ness, 2021).

Unilateral sanctions are thus largely unregulated, but some of the international customary laws, conventions, and principles that are often used for their legal interpretation are explained below.

The Principle of State Sovereignty

Article 2(1) of the UN Charter grants sovereign equality to all member states – no matter whether a country is socialist or capitalist, a theocracy, democracy, or autocracy. The Charter also prohibits any armed attacks on a foreign country except on the ground of self-defense, and grants the UN the right to impose collective sanctions in order to maintain international peace and security. Article 2(1) also requires all member states to refrain from giving assistance to any state against which the UN takes any preventive or enforcement action. The concept of "sovereignty," ingrained in Article 2, thus distinguishes a state from other territorial entities, and provides legal standing in both domestic and international affairs.[24]

[23] This study also considers sanctions imposed by a regional body of states – such as those imposed by the OAS – as unilateral sanctions. Such sanctions, as Happold (2017) explains, may not be even be considered as "sanctions," however, because a regional body imposes sanctions in reaction to unconstitutional changes by a member state, and the target state, as a member of the body, has agreed to be bound by its rules.

[24] The UN Charter, under Chapter 1, Article 2(1)–(5), states:

> 1. The Organization is based on the principle of the sovereign equality of all its Members; 2. All Members, in order to ensure to all of them the rights and benefits resulting from membership, shall fulfil in good faith the obligations assumed by them in accordance with the present Charter; 3. All Members shall settle their international disputes by peaceful means in such a

From the international law perspective, the principle of sovereignty implies that a state possesses the supreme legal power to command the subordination of all individuals and entities within the state. In the international arena, a state is not subject to any higher authority – it has no obligation to any authority to which it has not consented, and it embodies the freedom to exercise its rights as it sees fit given the powers and authority at its disposal (Fabri, 2008).

The principle of state sovereignty is also firmly rooted in historical developments over the centuries. Under the classic Westphalian principles,[25] the rights and duties of a "sovereign" state were subject to customary international law, while the fundamental rights and duties of individuals within a state were subject to the constitutional, administrative, and criminal norms of domestic public law. Such a conception of state sovereignty had indeed propelled the emergence of strong sovereign and authoritarian states in seventeenth-century Europe (Danchin, 2009).

In the eighteenth century, such a "horizontal legal setting" of sovereign equality (Tanzi, 2010, 307), which resulted in Westphalian systems of "absolute sovereignty" and "authoritarian states"(Lopez and Cortright, 1995, 68), gradually embraced the concepts of modern states that embody liberal democratic values, such as citizenship, freedom, democracy, and the rule of law. By the nineteenth century, many of these modern states embraced concerns for the environment and social equality; and by the mid twentieth century, they also codified broad civil, political, social, and economic rights of citizens internationally through international charters and conventions, principally by the UN Charter. Such processes gradually imposed greater limits on the powers of sovereign states while expanding those of the ordinary citizens (Dunchin, 2009; Fabri, 2008).

Eventually, such expansion of the rights of individuals vis-à-vis sovereign powers brought a significant shift in international public law. Sovereign equality of states emerged as the basic axiom of *par in parem non habet imperium* (equals have no sovereignty over each other) (Albal, 2021), but did so in the context of a community of equals, where the sovereignty of each finds its limit in that of the others, signifying

manner that international peace and security, and justice, are not endangered; 4. All Members shall refrain in their international relations from the threat or use of force against the territorial integrity or political independence of any state, or in any other manner inconsistent with the Purposes of the United Nations; 5. All Members shall give the United Nations every assistance in any action it takes in accordance with the present Charter, and shall refrain from giving assistance to any state against which the United Nations is taking preventive or enforcement action.

25 Notably, the Westphalian Peace Treaties of 1648, which followed the breakdown of medieval imperial and clerical universalism in Europe, led to the emergence of the modern international system of territorial and sovereign states, a system whereby states could maximize their own interests, while at the same time striving for a balance of power. Following the Treaty, some nation states, city states, and principalities perceived themselves as parts of a European collective bound together by an emerging law of nations (*jus inter gentes*), largely replacing the traditional Roman international law known as *jus gentium*. For further details, see Bring (2000), Sampford (2010), and Tanzi (2010).

the "reversibility of sovereignty" as well as the principle of equality simultaneously (Bring, 2000).[26]

Since the 1980s, however, with the waves of economic and political globalization, fundamental human rights emerged as an essential feature of both international and domestic public law as the "sovereignty" of states came under the purview of "supranational" or "global" laws.[27] With the resultant growth in cosmopolitan norms of universal justice and human rights, public international law no longer regulates relations between states only, but also extends its reach to the rights and duties of individuals within states. As the walls between the states broke down, so did the walls between public law and public international law (Sampford, 1995, 50), resulting in the "triumph of human rights over sovereignty," under which, as former UN Secretary General Kofi Annan asserts, "the concept of national sovereignty is itself conceived in order to protect the individual rights, and not the inverse, it is the raison d'etre of the State" (Fabri, 2008, 33).[28]

In the contemporary world, thus, there exists no affair that is necessarily internal or domestic by nature – states no longer have the absolute right or power to determine the fate of their own nationals. Not only that, the more a state concedes to human rights, the more it gains legitimacy in the world. The consequent erosion of sovereignty now blurs the boundaries between public international law and domestic public law because the limitations on state power caused by the internationalization of human rights, the pace of globalization and interdependence, and the increasing domestic reach of treaties infuse international doctrines and methodology in domestic law in all forms (Danchin, 2009; Fabri, 2008).

Some scholars even argue that, just like the Drago Doctrine,[29] which states that a state cannot use force against another state to collect its debts, the use of economic

[26] As Menkes and Kociołek-Pęksa (2019, 15–16) explain, the principle of *par in parem non habet imperium* also implies that a sovereign state is not legally entitled to extend its jurisdiction over another sovereign state, and a sovereign state is immune from sanctions imposed by another sovereign state. A sovereign state thus enjoys immunity with reference to acts of *iure imperii* (by the right of the sovereign) in international law, which also grants a sovereign state a "monopoly" right to determine the grounds for the effectiveness of international norms on its internal order.

[27] Human rights came to assume legal standing with the first Geneva Convention of 1864, which sought to protect human rights in times of war under international humanitarian laws. International protection of human rights, both in war and outside war, began to take off more robustly, however, after WWI, more precisely, with the Treaty of Versailles (1918), which introduced a system of protection of human rights of minorities, and established the International Labor Organization (ILO) to protect the rights of workers. It was not until after the end of WWII in 1945, however, that the idea of general and more comprehensive global human rights protections appeared under the Universal Declaration of Human Rights (Fabri, 2008, 34–35).

[28] For greater detail on the transformation of the political and legal concept of sovereignty of states, see Chopra and Weiss (1992), Damrosch and Scheffer (1991), Fabri (2008), Lopez and Cortright (1995), Sampford (1995), Tanzi (2010), and Walker and Mendlovitz (1990).

[29] Espoused by Argentinian foreign minister Luis Drago in 1902 in protest against the so-called gun-boat diplomacy, the Drago Doctrine stipulates that it is repugnant to international law for a foreign power to intervene forcibly in the affairs of another state to secure the repayment of public debt obligations.

coercion against another state, or coercing a sovereign state to change its behavior in areas which are within its sovereign right, should be considered a violation of the customary international law principles of non-intervention and non-coercion (Albal, 2021; Dupont, 2012, 316).

The Principle of Non-Intervention

Political intervention, direct or indirect, for whatever reason, in the internal or external affairs of a state is ordinarily prohibited under international law. At the same time, offering of good offices for mediation or dispute settlement among nations; demands for implementation of human rights and fair treatment of minorities; proposals for judicial or arbitral settlement; protests or requests to abide by international law; and criticisms of the form of government or certain policies of a state may not be considered actionable interventions under international law. A state crosses the line, however, when political pressure or threat to use force accompanies such diplomatic gestures, or when it engages in hostile propaganda against another state, finances opposition parties in another state, or bribes foreign officials in order to change policies or political regimes in another state (Ronzitti, 2016, 3).

The principle of non-intervention can be traced to the early nineteenth century, when the US frequently intervened in the internal affairs of Latin American countries under the Monroe Doctrine,[30] but the Additional Protocol on Non-Intervention, signed by the continental American states in 1936, is often cited as the first such written agreement. The Agreement reads: "The High Contracting Parties declare inadmissible the intervention of any one of them directly or indirectly, and for whatever reason, in the internal or external affairs of the Parties."[31]

Article 2(4) of the UN Charter, cited above, emphasizes settlement of international disputes among states through peaceful means, and requires states to refrain from use of threat or force against the territorial integrity or political independence of any state. Thus, any use of economic, political, or other type of measures to coerce another state with a view to influencing its foreign or domestic policy in an unjustifiable manner constitutes a violation of the principle of non-intervention, and is incompatible with the duty of a UN member state pursuant to Article 2(3–4) of the UN Charter (Blum, 1977; Subedi, 2021).

Some scholars argue, however, that the UN Charter provides rather inadequate guidance to the principle of non-intervention, and for a legal understanding of the

Although this view has not yet evolved into a normative international law, over the course of time, it has been incorporated into several international treaties and conventions as well as ILC documents.

30 In the early nineteenth century, the US intervened in Latin American countries dozens of times under the so-called the Monroe Doctrine. Named after the fifth president of the US (1817–1825), the doctrine turned into a central part of US foreign policy later, under the so-called "Big Stick" policy of Theodore Roosevelt (1901–1909). Under the doctrine, the US justified its interventions in Latin American countries on the grounds of intervention by the then imperial European powers to recover debts. The Drago Doctrine, mentioned above, was a response to such intervention.

31 The original source in Offut (1928) is cited in Ronzitti (2016, 9).

principle, one should rather look into the UNGA resolutions as well as regional treaties and declarations, and more specifically to UNGA resolutions 2131 (XX) and 2625 (XXV), which are geared to the principle (Ronzitti, 2016, 3–4).[32] UNGA Resolution 2625 (XXV),[33] for example, states:

> No state or group of states has the right to intervene, directly or indirectly, for any reason whatever, in the internal or external affairs of any other state. Consequently, armed intervention and all other forms of interference or attempted threats against the personality of the state or against its political, economic and cultural elements, are in violation of international law.

The Resolution thus designates the following actions as specific violations of the principle of non-intervention: (a) armed intervention and other forms of interference against a state or against its political, economic and cultural elements; (b) organize and incite subversive activities toward the violent overthrow of the regime of another state; (c) interfere in civil strife in another state and the use of force to deprive peoples of their national identity; and (d) use of economic, political, or any other type of measures to coerce another state in order to obtain from it the subordination of the exercise of its sovereign rights. The linchpin of non-intervention thus lies with acts that qualify as "coercive," or intended to force a policy change in the target state (Jamnejad and Wood, 2009; Ruys, 2017, 25).

Among the regional instruments of non-intervention, Article 19 of the OAS Charter provides that no state or group of states has the right to intervene, directly or indirectly, in the internal or external affairs of any other state; and Article 20 of the same Charter provides that no state may use coercive measures of an economic or political character in order to force the sovereign will of another state, and obtain from it any advantages of any kind. The OAS regulations thus prohibit not only armed force but also any other form of interference against the personality of a state or its internal and external affairs (Ronzitti, 2016, 16–17).

The Helsinki Final Act, signed in 1975 by 35 countries, including the US, the former Soviet Union, Canada, and most of the European nations, as a part of the Conference on Security and Cooperation in Europe (CSCE) – came as another milestone agreement with respect to the principle of non-intervention. In its Declaration, the Helsinki Act states: "The participating States will refrain from any intervention, direct or indirect, individual or collective, in the internal or external affairs falling within the domestic jurisdiction of another participating State,

[32] Ronzitti (2016, 3–4) also refers to Article 32 of UNGA Resolution 3281 (XXIX) on the Charter of Economic Rights and Duties of States; and UNGA Resolution 42/22 on the Declaration on the Enhancement of the Effectiveness of the Principle of Refraining from the Threat or Use of Force in International Relations, adopted in 1987.

[33] UNGA Resolution 2625, passed in 1970, affirms the importance of progressive development and codification of the principles of international law concerning friendly relations and co-operation among states. For greater detail, see A/RES/25/2625.

regardless of their mutual relations."[34] Similar statements can also be found in many subsequent regional agreements (Cabernes, 1967; Nasu, 2013).

Court Proceedings

The International Court of Justice (ICJ)[35] has adjudicated several cases involving the principle of non-intervention, some of the notables cases include *The Corfu Channel Case (1946), Nicaragua v. United States of America (1986), DRC v. Uganda (2005),* and *Bosnia v. Serbia (2007)*. Two of these cases are discussed below in greater detail.[36]

In *Nicaragua* v. United States, Nicaragua filed a suit against the US in April 1984 alleging that the US had imposed an economic embargo and commenced a series of military and paramilitary activities against the country in the form of aiding counterrevolutionaries and conducting airspace overflights and harbor mining after the Nicaraguan socialist party – the Sandinistas – took power in 1979, and had begun assisting neighboring Honduras and El Salvador.[37] The US, in response, cited collective self-defense as a justification for its actions, although neither El Salvador nor Honduras had requested such help from the US.

The ICJ ruled that "[a] State is not bound to continue particular trade relations longer than it sees fit to do so in the absence of a treaty commitment or other specific legal obligation."[38] Addressing the US argument of collective self-defense, however, the ICJ ruled that unless the aggrieved state requires aid, collective self-defense did

[34] For greater detail, see history.state.gov/milestones/1969-1976/helsinki, accessed on February 8, 2023.

[35] Notably, Article 38 of the Statute of the ICJ identifies three main sources of international law to decide disputes submitted before it: (a) international conventions, whether general or particular, establishing rules expressly recognized by the contesting states; (b) international custom, as evidence of a general practice accepted as law; (c) the general principles of law recognized by civilized nations. These sources are also subject to "subsidiary means for the determination of rules of law," which include Article 59 of the same statute, which qualifies that the ICJ decisions have no binding force except between the parties and with respect to that particular case, and also of "judicial decisions and the teachings of the most highly qualified publicists of the various nations." For greater detail see: www.icj-cij.org/statute.

[36] Of the other two cases not discussed in detail, the *Corfu Channel Case* (UK and Northern Ireland against Albania) arose from incidents that occurred on October 22, 1946, in the Corfu Strait, when two British destroyers struck mines in Albanian waters and suffered damage, including serious loss of life. *DRC v. Uganda* (2005) involved a case brought before the ICJ on June 23, 1999 by the Democratic Republic of the Congo (DRC) against the Republic of Uganda involving a dispute concerning alleged acts of armed aggression perpetrated by Uganda on the territory of the DRC in violation of the UN Charter and of the Charter of the Organization of African Unity.

[37] The Sandinistas belonged to the political party called the Sandinista National Liberation Front (FSLN), founded in the early 1960s with the goals of rooting out US dominance over the country and establishing a socialist society modeled after the Cuban Revolution. In 1979, the Sandinistas succeeded in taking power by overthrowing Anastasio Somoza after 42 years of military dictatorship. The Sandinistas, under the leadership of Daniel Ortega, governed Nicaragua between 1979 and 1990. Ortega, however, was subsequently re-elected in 2006, 2011, and 2016.

[38] See *Nicaragua v. United States of America* [1986] ICJ Rep 392 [205]; Carter (1987, 1167), Gibney (2022), Happold (2017), and Henderson (1986, 196).

not justify hostile behavior. The court directed the US immediately to cease and refrain from all acts constituting breaches of its legal obligations, and make reparation for all injury caused to Nicaragua by the breaches of obligations under customary international law and the Treaty of Friendship, Commerce and Navigation, that the US and Nicaragua had signed at Managua on January 21, 1956.[39]

Interestingly, the ICJ adjudged that the US economic sanctions against Nicaragua could not be deemed as a breach of the customary law principle of non-intervention, while ascertaining that the "element of coercion" formed the very essence of prohibited intervention, and that the US violated customary international law by training and arming anti-Sandinista forces ("Contras"). The ICJ, however, ruled that the US was not responsible for any of the widespread atrocities carried out by the Contra rebel forces, notwithstanding the substantial levels of military, political, and economic support provided by the US, because it was not established that the US had exercised "effective control" over the Contras (Gibney, 2022, 17).[40]

In *Bosnia* v. Serbia, the first issue was whether Serbia was responsible for the genocide carried out by various Bosnian Serb paramilitary forces that it was allied with. In its judgment, the ICJ relied on the ILC guidelines for determining whether the Bosnian Serb forces acted as "state agents" for the Serbian state, and held that they were neither *de jure* nor *de facto* state agents of Serbia as the paramilitary forces had no "complete dependence" on the Serbian government.

A second issue was whether the Serbian government had "directed and controlled" the actions of the Bosnian Serb forces at the time of the genocide. In adjudging the issue, the ICJ invoked the "effective control" test from its Nicaragua decision, holding that in order to achieve this standard it must be shown that the Serbian government exercised "effective control." Then, referring to the perceived "differences" between the Bosnian Serbs and the Serbian government following the overthrow of Srebrenica, when most of the acts of genocide took place, the court ruled that this requisite level of "effective control" was not achieved.

The final issue before the ICJ was whether Serbia was responsible for being complicit in genocide. The ICJ applied the ILC Article 16 on state responsibility[41] to reject the claim on the grounds that it had not been established "beyond any doubt"

39 The amount of the reparations, however, was left to subsequent proceedings in case the parties were unable to reach an agreement. The US refused to take part in the proceedings and in September 1991, Nicaragua informed the ICJ that it did not wish to continue the proceedings. On September 26, 1991, the case was removed from the court's list. For greater detail, see *Nicaragua v. United States of America* [1986] ICJ Rep 392 [205].

40 The Court ruled: "In light of the evidence and material available to it, the Court is not satisfied that *all* the operations launched by the contra force, at *every* stage of the conflict, reflected strategy and tactics *wholly* devised by the United States" (ICJ, 1986, para 6).

41 Article 16 of ARSIWA (2001) states: "A state which aids or assists another state in the commission of an internationally wrongful act by the latter is internationally responsible for doing so if: (a) That state does so with knowledge of the circumstances of the internationally wrongful act; and (b) The act would be internationally wrongful if committed by that state."

that Serbia possessed the specific intent (*dolus specialis*) required by the Genocide Convention. Despite the exceptionally high number of victims, it was not clear that, at the crucial time, the Serbian government supplied aid to the perpetrators of the genocide in full awareness that the aid supplied would be used to commit genocide. The court, however, ruled that Serbia had failed to meet its obligations to "prevent" genocide and to "punish" those who had engaged in it because it had the apparent ability to "influence" the actions of its Bosnian Serb allies (Gibney, 2022, 17–19).

The Principle of Countermeasures

International law permits a state to use coercion against another state, but does so "only for prescribed contingencies and under prescribed conditions." Such contingencies for a state, no matter whether acting unilaterally or in association with others, stem from the customary law of self-defense and the law of countermeasures, and unilateral sanctions, imposed without UNSC mandate, draw their legal standing primarily from the law on countermeasures (Reisman and Stevick, 1998).

Article 22 of ARSIWA (ILC, 2001, 75–77) defines countermeasures as non-forcible, but coercive, measures taken in response to an internationally wrongful act to induce an aggressor state to cease its wrongful act, and, if applicable, to demand reparations. According to the Article, an internationally wrongful act of a state constitutes "a breach of an international obligation by a State when an act of that State is not in conformity with what is required of it by that obligation, regardless of its origin or character" (Damrosch, 2019, 105), and "Countermeasures may only preclude wrongfulness in the relations between an injured State and the State which has committed the internationally wrongful act" (ILC, 2001, 76–77). Article 12 of ARSIWA (ILC, 2001, 54–55) identifies two elements of internationally wrongful act: (1) conduct consisting of an action or omission that is attributable to the state under international law and (2) the action constitutes a breach of an international obligation of the state.

Countermeasures are thus rooted in very complex legal parameters. In simple words, however, to adopt countermeasures, a sanctioning state must establish that: (a) the targeted state committed an internationally wrongful act; (b) the sanctioning state is an "injured state"; (c) the measures are aimed at inducing the targeted state to comply with its obligations; (d) the measures are proportionate to the injury suffered; (e) the measures may not affect fundamental human rights or *jus cogens* norms, such as due process rights of individuals or entities targeted by sanctions measures; and (f) the measures will be terminated when the wrongful act has ceased (Hovell, 2016).

Thus, a key condition for adopting countermeasures is that a sanctioning state must be an injured state. This condition is less stringent, or less controversial, however, when a group of states adopts such measures. For example, when a state violates an obligation that protects the collective interest of a group of states, such as a multilateral disarmament regime or nuclear proliferation treaty, as in the case of Iran or North Korea, or an *erga omnes* violation occurs, or grave human rights violations as in the case of Syria or Myanmar, sanctions adopted by a regional body of states as countermeasures generate less controversy than, for example, a state, such as the US, imposing such sanctions unilaterally.

Countermeasures, in accordance with ARISWA, may also be viewed on a spectrum, with non-forcible measures at one end, forcible measures at the opposite end, and in-between a gray area where regulations may be rudimentary or non-existent (White and Abass, 2018, 524). Some scholars believe that unilateral countermeasures usually fall in the "gray area," as establishing the conditions of an "injured state" by a sanctioning state may often be controversial, and even ARSIWA leaves the "resolution of the matter to the further development of international law" (Hovell, 2019).

Moreover, unilateral economic coercion, so far as it is a violation of international law, alone cannot lawfully give rise to the exercise of (armed) self-defense because economic coercion alone is not prohibited under Article 2(4) of the UN Charter, and Article 51 of the Charter allows self-defense only if an armed attack has occurred (Ronzitti, 2016, 14–15). Thus, considerable uncertainty exists with respect to the imposition of autonomous sanctions by a state on the ground of being an "injured state" or as self-defense. Moreover, for countries like the US and organizations like the EU, the most prolific enforcers of unilateral sanctions, establishing that they are actually "injured states," or that their sanctions were actually in self-defense, may be questionable.[42]

The relationship between economic sanctions and countermeasures also remains contentious because of international laws pertaining to human rights and humanitarian laws, and several UNGA resolutions that recognize the inalienable right to development of all nations. UNGA Resolution 41/128, "Declaration on the Right to Development," for example, prohibits the use of economic, political, or any other type of measure to coerce a state in violation of the principles of the sovereign equality of states and of the right to development.[43] Second, although international humanitarian laws apply exclusively to armed conflict, international human rights laws apply at all times, during both peacetime and armed conflict. And, third, as

[42] As mentioned above, in *Nicaragua v. USA (1986)*, the ICJ questioned the US defense of collective self-defense. Also, the US reliance on self-defense against Afghanistan following the September 11, 2001 attack has often been questioned, on the ground that the conditions for the implementation of self-defense might not have been met as the US was not actually attacked by Afghanistan. The US was rather attacked by a terrorist group called Al-Qaeda, which enjoyed the support of Afghanistan's Taliban regime (Asada, 2020, 36).

[43] UNGA Resolution 41/128, adopted in December 1986, states:

> Article 1.1: The right to development is an inalienable human right by virtue of which every human person and all peoples are entitled to participate in, contribute to, and enjoy economic, social, cultural and political development, in which all human rights and fundamental freedoms can be fully realized. Article 1.2: The human right to development also implies the full realization of the right of peoples to self-determination, which includes, subject to the relevant provisions of both International Covenants on Human Rights, the exercise of their inalienable right to full sovereignty over all their natural wealth and resources.

ruled by the ICJ in *Nicaragua v. United States* (1986), if economic sanctions resemble a state of conflict and the situation turns into a state of economic warfare, then economic sanctions can legally be deemed armed conflict.

Countermeasures by Third Parties

Countermeasures can also be adopted by a third party – a state or a group of states not directly injured by a wrongful act of a target state – when serious violations of human rights or the territorial integrity of a state occur. Article 48 of ARSIWA allows any state other than an injured state to adopt countermeasures, provided: (a) the obligation breached is owed to a group of states including that state, and is established for the protection of a collective interest of the group; or (b) the obligation breached is owed to the international community as a whole. A third-party invocation of countermeasures thus must be in the collective interest, and the sanctioning state must not act in its individual capacity by reason of having suffered injury, but in its capacity as a member of a group of states to which the obligation is owed, or indeed as a member of the international community as a whole (ILC, 2001, 127).

Article 42 of ARSIWA, however, does not distinguish between different sources of international law for establishing the protection of collective interest of the group or determining a breach of obligation to the international community as a whole. The obligations protecting a collective interest of the group thus may be derived from multilateral treaties or customary international law, such as "obligations *erga omnes partes*" (ILC, 2001, 126). Thus, the UNSC, for example, can legitimately adopt such measures pursuant to Article 41 of UN Charter. Numerous other instances also exist in which a third state or a group of states, not directly affected by internationally wrongful act, have adopted and enforced countermeasures based on other agreements or treaties (Dawidowicz, 2017a; ILC, 2001, 126–127; Tomuschat and Thouvenin, 2005, 218–219).

The UN, however, cannot claim to be an "injured state," and it adopts countermeasures under the authority vested in the UN Charter. A state or a regional body of states may adopt countermeasures only when there is a serious violation of obligations of a state owed to the international community, such as acts of genocide, major human rights violations, or violations of the Covenant on Civil and Political Rights. In such situations, Article 48 of ARSIWA entitles a state or a regional group of states, to take "lawful measures" against the alleged wrongdoer.

Article 54 of ARSIWA also provides that, by virtue of Article 48, such "lawful measures" can also be taken to ensure cessation of the breach and demand reparation in the interest of the injured state or of the beneficiaries of the obligation breached (ILC, 2001, 137–139). The question remains, however, to what extent these states may legitimately assert a right to react against unremedied breaches. The ILC Commentary on Article 54 cautions that a distinction must be made between individual measures, whether taken by one state or by a group of states each acting in its individual capacity, and the institutional reactions in the framework of international organizations, such as under the authority of Chapter VII of the UN Charter.

There have also been instances when states reacted against what were alleged to be breaches of the obligations referred to in Article 48 without claiming to be individually injured, and such reactions have taken the form of economic sanctions or other measures, such as breaking off air links or other contacts, which can be "lawful measures" rather than "countermeasures" as the measures are taken as "injured state," not for the protection of the collective interest or those owed to the international community as a whole. The ILC Commentary #3 on Article 54 cites several such instances (ILC, 2001, 138–139).

At the same time, the ILC Commentary #4 on Article 54 provides that, in some other cases, certain states similarly suspended treaty rights in order to exercise pressure on states violating collective obligations. However, they did not rely on a right to take countermeasures, but asserted a right to suspend the treaty because of a fundamental change of circumstances.[44] Article 54 of ARSIWA thus leaves it open whether and in which circumstances a state or a group of states may adopt third-party countermeasures (Dawidowicz, 2017b).

Countersanctions by a Target State

Target states rarely adopt countersanctions simply because in most cases they are less powerful countries, while major unilateral sanctioners are the most powerful countries in the world. As discussed in Chapter 5, in recent years, Russia, the largest and the most sanctioned country in the world, has adopted countersanctions several times, targeting sanctioning measures imposed by the US and the EU, describing them as contrary to international law and the WTO trading rules. Also, as discussed before, during the period of the Trump Administration (2016–2020), Mexico, Canada, the EU, and China adopted countersanctions in retaliation to US tariffs on their exports to the US.[45]

A target state, however, has no recourse to adopt countersanctions against multilateral sanctions imposed by the UNSC – Article 48 of UN Charter makes it mandatory for all UN members to implement UNSC sanctions, and that mandate includes the targeted state as well. Also, adopting countersanctions against sanctions is tantamount to unlawful non-compliance with the UNSC resolutions. A target state is

44 For example, in *Collective Measures against the Federal Republic of Yugoslavia* (1998), adopted in response to the humanitarian crisis in Kosovo, the European Community adopted legislation providing for the freezing of Yugoslav funds and an immediate flight ban. For some member countries, such as France, Germany, and the UK, the latter measure implied the non-performance of bilateral aviation agreements. Because of doubts about the legitimacy of the action, the British Government initially opted for the one-year denunciation procedure provided for in Article 17 of its agreement with Yugoslavia. However, it later changed its position and denounced flights with immediate effect. Justifying the measure, it stated that "President Milosevic's … worsening record on human rights means that, on moral and political grounds, he has forfeited the right of his Government to insist upon the 12 months-notice which would normally apply" (ILC, 2001, 138–139).

45 There are, however, numerous examples of diplomatic countersanctions. There has been a series of diplomatic expulsions and counter-expulsions in recent years involving countries like the US, the EU, Russia, Venezuela, Iran, and Cuba.

entitled to adopt countersanctions against unilateral sanctions imposed by a state or group of states. The question here, however, should be whether the sanctions were imposed lawfully, abiding by international law, and if the target state resorts to countersanctions against a lawfully imposed sanction, then it commits an international wrong. On the other hand, if the sanctions were imposed unlawfully, then the countersanctions of the target state would amount to countermeasures, since they are taken in reaction to an international wrong (Ronzitti, 2016, 30–31).

With respect to trade disputes, such as restrictions on imports or exports, a target state can place the matter before the Dispute Settlement Body of the WTO, which provides a legitimate dispute resolution mechanism to verify whether an economic sanction violates international law, and whether the content of the countermeasures is lawful or not.

Judicial Proceedings in Third-Party Countermeasures

Two major cases that illustrate the ICJ's interpretation of third-party countermeasures are explained below: *Barcelona Traction* (1970) and the *Tehran Hostages* case from the Iran hostage crisis (1979).

The dispute in the *Barcelona Traction* case involved a Belgian claim to a right of diplomatic protection of Belgian shareholders in a Canadian company, named the Barcelona Traction, Light and Power Company, which was incorporated in Spain. Belgium claimed that the Belgian shareholders in the company were victimized by a series of actions taken by certain administrative and judicial organs of Spain in relation to the company, and demanded reparation for internationally wrongful acts which led to the bankruptcy and total spoliation of the company (Briggs, 1971).

The key issues before the ICJ were to determine the admissibility of the claim – whether Belgium had standing (*jus standi*) to exercise diplomatic protection of the shareholders in a Canadian company, which in essence also involved determination of the nationality of a corporation; and to determine as an *obiter dictum* whether some international legal obligations are so important that all states must have an interest in their protection.

The ICJ ruled that: (a) the alleged injury was done to the company itself; (b) it did not cause any direct injury to the rights of Belgian shareholders; (c) the nationality of a corporation is determined by national incorporation rules; and (d) under the law of diplomatic protection, the espousal of a claim of a Canadian company was a matter within the rights of Canada, not of Belgium, or any other state. The court also noted that the protection of investors – like Belgian shareholders in the Barcelona Traction company– is rather regulated through bilateral investment treaties, which called for investor–state dispute settlement through arbitration based on treaty stipulations or other special agreements (Tams and Tzanakopoulos, 2010).

To many observers, the rulings in *Barcelona Traction* came as a "classic judicial text" for modern analytical debate on the formulation and enforcement of the *erga omnes* concept for communitarian norms as third-party countermeasures

(Dawidowicz, 2017b, 52). Crawford (2013, 77), for example, argues that in *Barcelona Traction* the ICJ rather took a very reserved view in dealing with the subject of injury to aliens, by holding the view that the law of state responsibility for injury to aliens was limited, and also by adopting a strictly formal view of the corporate veil and a traditional and narrow approach to diplomatic protection. Crawford acknowledges, however, that *Barcelona* marks the emergence of the important idea that states can have obligations that are owed not individually to other states, but in some sense collectively.

Arguing largely in the same vein, Ruys (2017, 45) also maintains that the ICJ judgment in *Barcelona Traction*, distinguishing between the obligations of a state vis-à-vis another state in the field of diplomatic protection and the obligations of a state toward the international community as a whole, has made it accepted that states (and entities) other than the injured state (or entities) are entitled to invoke the responsibility of another state in the case of a breach of an obligation that protects a collective interest of the group (*erga omnes partes*), or an obligation that is owed to the international community as a whole (*erga omnes*).[46]

The *Tehran Hostages* case (1979)[47] was brought before the ICJ by the US in November 1979 against Iran, alleging grave violations of diplomatic and consular law arising from the seizure and holding as hostages of US diplomatic and consular staff in Tehran, and demanding reparations.[48] In its judgment delivered in May 1980, the ICJ ruled that a fundamental prerequisite for relations between states lies with the inviolability of diplomatic envoys and embassies, but that Iran had violated such obligations owed to the US under the conventions in force between the two countries and the rules of general international law. The court also pointed out that while the conduct of militants, who took the hostages, could not be directly attributed to the Iranian state, the state had however done nothing to prevent the attack or release the hostages, and instead, certain organs of the Iranian state had indeed endorsed those acts and decided to perpetuate them, and thus Iran had breached the cardinal principles of international law governing diplomatic and consular relations.[49]

In its ruling, the ICJ also referred to the measures that the US took prior to bringing proceedings before the court, such as placing the matter before the UNSC, and enforcing several unilateral countermeasures against Iran, such as freezing Iranian

46 Ruys (2017, 45) also maintains that such understandings have also been confirmed in recent ICJ judgments in *tBelgium v. Senegal* (2012) and *Whaling in the Antarctic (Australia v. Japan: New Zealand intervening)* (2014).

47 The discussion on this case is brief here as it is explained in greater detail in Chapter 6, in the context of US sanctions against Iran.

48 For the background of the proceedings, see *United States Diplomatic and Consular Staff in Tehran* (*U.S. v. Iran*), Merits, 1980 I.C.J. 3 (May 24).

49 The ICJ ruling was made in the absence of the Iran's participation and upon rejection of Iran's communications to the Court that it lacked jurisdiction in the matter. The case was removed from the ICJ List on May 12, 1981.

assets held in the US. The court ruled that such countermeasures were lawful and justified on the ground of Iran's prior wrongful acts (Damrosch, 2019, 106), and that the adoption of third-party countermeasures could not be excluded per se simply by virtue of the existence of a competing treaty-based enforcement mechanism (Dawidowicz, 2017b, 52–63).

III UNILATERAL SANCTIONS AND INTERNATIONAL TRADING SYSTEM

Unilateral economic sanctions – restrictions on exports and imports – typically contravene the basic principles of the multilateral trading system as enshrined in the GATT–WTO agreements. The WTO prohibits any restrictions on trade except on the grounds of GATT Article XXI, known as the "Security Exceptions,"[50] and provides rules for settlement of a dispute when trade is prohibited or restricted between or among its members. The Dispute Settlement Body (DSB) of the WTO provides a mechanism to verify the legality of the alleged trade dispute measures among the members – no matter whether they are imposed in the form of sanctions, countermeasures, or countersanctions. The central issue is whether they violate the commitments made under the WTO agreements.[51] Under the WTO, trade disputes are treated as disputes, not as sanctions or countermeasures, however, and the dispute has to be raised and settled within the orbits of the WTO rules.[52]

A *The WTO Trade Regime*

All WTO rules are mandatory for all its members – no matter whether a country is large or small, developed or developing – and any restriction on trade of commodities or services may only be imposed by a member on another member to the extent permitted by the exception clauses as enunciated in Article XXI of GATT (1994),[53]

[50] Almost all trade agreements – no matter whether multilateral, regional, or bilateral – generally include some provisions of national security exception which allow the signatories to impose sanctions on the grounds of furthering or protecting national security interests without violating such agreements, or international trade law (Gordon, 2019, 2–3).

[51] Not all trade or sanction disputes in the world, however, can be settled under the auspices of the WTO as not all countries in the world are WTO members. Currently, there are 195 countries in the world, of which 193 are UN members, while the Holy See and the State of Palestine are non-member observer states. But as of February 2023, the WTO had 164 members. Some of the major targets of unilateral sanctions, such as Iran and North Korea, are not yet members of the WTO. China became a member of the WTO in 2002, while Russia joined only in 2012.

[52] Since its inception in 1995, resolving trade disputes has been one of the core activities of the WTO. By May 2022, as many as 614 trade disputes were placed before the WTO, and the organization had issued over 350 rulings.

[53] For greater detail, see "The Final Act Embodying the Results of the Uruguay Round," signed by 125 member countries of GATT in Marrakesh in April 1994, which replaced the GATT, established in 1947, with the WTO, with effect from January 1, 1995. For greater detail, see Dowlah (2004, 30–37).

and any such actions must also take into consideration the rights of private individuals if they are also affected by restrictions (Bothe, 2016).[54] The national security exception, along with similar exceptions incorporated in Article XIV of the General Agreement on Trade in Services (GATS) and Article 73 of the Agreement on Trade-Related Aspects of Intellectual Property Rights (TRIPS), provide that "nothing in this [WTO] Agreement shall be construed to prevent any contracting party from taking any action which it considers necessary for the protection of its essential security interests."[55]

The WTO also prohibits discriminatory trade restrictions, and thus, if such measures are targeted at a particular WTO member, it presents a prima facie conflict with a member's GATT obligations. Depending on their design and scope, sanctions may conflict with GATT: Article I(1) – most-favored nation (MFN) treatment; Article III(4) – the national treatment provision; and Article XI(1) – general elimination of quantitative restrictions. Such conflicts may be avoided, however, if sanctions fall within the terms of GATT Article XX (general exceptions) or GATT Article XXI (national security exceptions) (Mitchell, 2017).

Any trade restrictions – on imports or exports, or both, and on goods or services, or both – inevitably imply a limiting effect on free trade, and thus are incompatible with GATT Article XI(1). They also violate various obligations and commitments under GATS and each of the four modes of supply enunciated under GATS Articles II:1 and XVI:1. Also, when a WTO member imposes a complete ban on trade in services with sanctioned persons and entities owned by them, those restrictions breach that member's obligations in various service sectors governed by the GATS.[56]

54 WTO rules however apply only to trade restrictions. Remedies to financial sanctions, that may affect individual rights, such as freezing of investment funds and/or bank deposits, are generally provided under bilateral investment or trade agreements (Dolzer and Schreuer, 2012, 1–19). Also, in *Barcelona Traction*, as noted above, the ICJ ruled that investment disputes should be settled on the basis of bilateral treaty stipulations or other special agreements (Tams and Tzanakopoulos, 2010).

55 Article XXI of GATT states:

> Nothing in this Agreement shall be construed: (a) to require any Member to furnish any information the disclosure of which it considers contrary to its essential security interests; or (b) to prevent any Member from taking any action which it considers necessary for the protection of its essential security interests; (i) relating to fissionable materials or the materials from which they are derived; (ii) relating to the traffic in arms, ammunition and implements of war and to such traffic in other goods and materials as is carried on directly or indirectly for the purpose of supplying a military establishment; (iii) taken in time of war or other emergency in international relations; or (c) to prevent any Member from taking any action in pursuance of its obligations under the United Nations Charter for the maintenance of international peace and security.

56 Article I of GATS states:

> For the purposes of this Agreement, trade in services is defined as the supply of a service: (a) from the territory of one Member into the territory of any other Member; (b) in the territory of one Member to the service consumer of any other Member; (c) by a service supplier of one Member, through commercial presence in the territory of any other Member; (d) by a service supplier of one Member, through presence of natural persons of a Member in the territory of any other Member.

Article XXI of GATT (1994), under "security exceptions," however, grants the contracting parties freedom to avoid trade rules to protect national security, but it does so without defining what constitutes "essential security interests," leaving its interpretation to the contracting parties (Smeets, 2000, 11). Some scholars argue that these concepts were negotiated during the protracted Uruguay Round of GATT (1987–1994), at a time when the Cold War ended and the US triumphed as the only global superpower, and as a result, they were deliberately coated in ambiguous political language favoring powerful nations to impose sanctions for political purposes (Bogdanova, 2021; Murrill, 2018). Article XXI thus provides "the greatest potential for future use and abuse" (Hestermeyer, 2011, 586), and poses "a latent, lingering threat" to the entire WTO system (Browne, 1997, 86).

Lowenfeld (2003, 916–918) also argues that GATT Article XXI has never been invoked to gain commercial advantage, and it has always been invoked for adopting restrictive measures in pursuance of foreign policy objectives. The "sovereignty safeguard principle" just permits a state to impose unilateral sanctions on national security prerogatives, and while it accords considerable latitude for states to impose unilateral sanctions, the latitude is neither "total" nor entirely "self-judging," as such sanctions may prompt WTO Panel Review (Mitchell, 2017, 284).

The defenders of the GATT "security exceptions" also maintain that, despite apparent incompatibility at first blush, unilateral sanctions and fair trade in the long run can be viewed as not only compatible but also facilitatory to free trade. To them, historically sanctions enforced on the grounds of national security concerns to combat Nazism, Communism, terrorism, and other threats, not only thwarted such threats, but also contributed to the creation of conditions favorable to liberalization of trade around the world (Baldwin, 2003; Gordon, 2019, 3–31; Lowenfeld, 2003, 916–918).

B *The WTO Dispute Settlement Mechanism*

Any unilateral sanction,[57] adopted without a UNSC mandate, that falls within the ambit of Article XXI must be justified under GATT Article XXI(b), which excuses a WTO contracting party from such measures if it considers it *necessary* for the

Article II:1 of GATS states:

> With respect to any measure covered by this Agreement, each Member shall accord immediately and unconditionally to services and service suppliers of any other Member treatment no less favorable than that it accords to like services and service suppliers of any other country.

Article XVI:1 of GATS states:

> With respect to market access through the modes of supply identified in Art. I, each Member shall accord services and service suppliers of any other Member treatment no less favorable than that provided for under the terms, limitations and conditions agreed and specified in its Schedule.

[57] Notably, the WTO Article XXI exception covers all multilateral sanctions authorized by UNSC resolutions, but not those authorized by UNGA resolutions.

protection of "essential security interests" of the country that relate to: (i) fissionable materials; (ii) traffic in arms; or (iii) time of war or other emergency in international relations. Over the years, however, Article XXI(b) has drawn serious controversies over the interpretation of what a country "considers necessary," what constitutes "essential security interests," and what can be deemed as "emergency in international relations," pursuant to the Article.

The debate over the issue has been quite intense over the decades. Some argue that the requirement of "necessity" is a matter of "self-judging," that is, a WTO member can determine the "necessity" for itself by citing any one of three grounds stipulated in Article XXI(b). Some argue that the Article does not accord unfettered discretion to a member state – it rather accords considerable deference to the opinions of other WTO members, and any invocation of such a defense should be subject to substantive review by a WTO Panel (Alford, 2011, 697; Mitchell, 2017, 284).

Moreover, Article 3(2) of the WTO dispute settlement procedures requires that GATT rules be interpreted in light of the "customary rules of interpretation of public international law." The WTO Appellate Body has held that such customary rules include certain provisions of the VCLT, such as a treaty must be interpreted in "good faith" in accordance with the ordinary meaning to be given to the terms of the treaty in their context and in light of its object and purpose, and the preparatory work may also be used as a supplementary means of interpretation (Bogdanova, 2021).

The US, a country which was involved with the preparatory work of Article XXI(b), has been the foremost proponent of the view that the WTO leaves Article XXI(b) (in the GATT 1947 context) to the judgment of each contracting party of any action which it considers necessary for the protection of its essential security interests. The US has also raised objection to the competence of the WTO Panel in matters of national security multiple times – in reference to its measures against Czechoslovakia (1949), Nicaragua (1985), and Cuba (1996), and US–Iran/Libya (1996) (Hestermeyer, 2011).[58]

C *WTO Panel Reviews*

While what constitutes an "emergency in international relations" or "national security exception," or what a country may consider "necessary" measures pursuant to Article XXI (b) remains unsettled, it is well established that the Article affords some degree of latitude and some margins of deference to the judgment of a WTO member while also subjecting it to WTO review. During

58 The European Council also took a similar view with respect to measures against Argentina (1982). The Council however abandoned its position that Article XXI(b) is self-judging and non-justiciable in 1991 when it recognized Yugoslavia's right to request the establishment of a WTO Panel. The European Council also reiterated its revised position when it itself brought a complaint against the US Helms–Burton Act in 1996 before the WTO Panel (Mitchell, 2017, 297: Schloemann and Ohlhoff, 1999, 436). See also Chapter 8 of this volume.

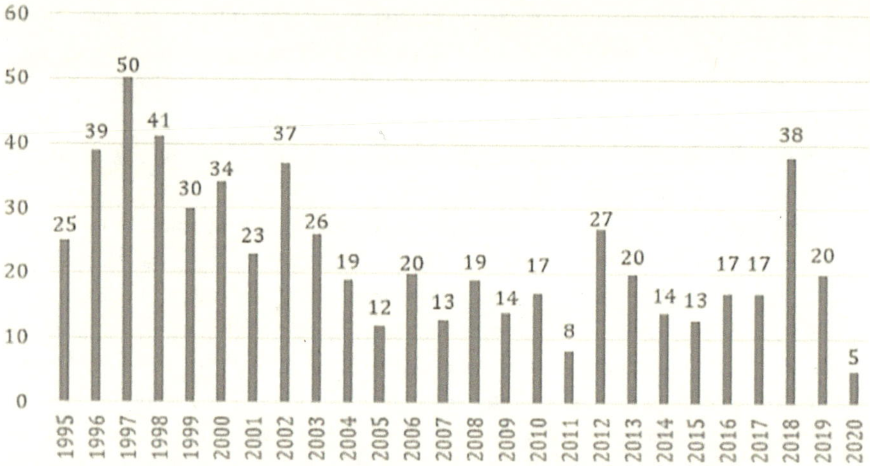

FIGURE 2.1 Requests for WTO consultations on trade disputes (1995–2020)
Source: WTO website: "Dispute Settlement Activity – Some Figures," available at www.wto.org/english/tratop_e/dispu_e/dispustats_e.htm. accessed on February 23, 2023.

the GATT period (1947–1994), economic sanctions were hardly subjected to trade adjudications,[59] but since GATT was replaced by the WTO in 1995, such disputes have increased phenomenally. In fact, several hundred trade disputes have been brought to the WTO system for adjudication since 1995 (see Figure 2.1). Some of those cases are elaborated below as examples.

In *Ecuador and the European Commission* (2000), the dispute arose when, relying on GATT Article XXI(b), Ecuador suspended its concessions under the TRIPS Agreement to the European Community, arguing that the words "party considers" of the Article entitled the country to interpret it as entirely self-judging and non-justiciable. Ecuador also raised DSU Article 22(3)(c) of DSU (WTO Understanding on Rules and Procedures Governing the Settlement of Disputes), which permits a complainant to suspend concessions under another agreement if that "party considers" that it is not practicable or effective to suspend concessions under the WTO agreement.

The WTO Panel rejected Ecuador's claim that GATT Article XXI(b) was self-judging and non-justiciable, and concluded that the language of DSU Article 22(3)(c) afforded a "certain margin of appreciation" to the party relying on them, but that a "margin of review" by the Panel nonetheless remained, and that DSU Article 22(3)

[59] Only five trade disputes involving GATT Article XXI were placed before the GATT between 1947 and 1994: Sweden–Import Restrictions on Certain Footwear (1975: L/4250); US–Nicaraguan Trade (1986: L/6053); Trade Measures Taken by the European Community against the Socialist Federal Republic of Yugoslavia (1991: L/6948); United States–The Cuban Liberty and Democratic Solidarity Act: Request for the Establishment of Panel by the European Communities (1996: WT/DS38/2). For further details, see Mitchell (2017).

was not directly parallel with GATT Article XXI(b), although both contained the same self-defining language implying a similar meaning (Balan, 2013).

In *Russia–Traffic in Transit*,[60] Russia invoked GATT Article XXI(b)(iii) – emergency in international relations – to justify its unilateral economic sanctions against Ukraine in the context of the Crimean crisis. The WTO Panel upheld the invocation, acknowledging that the conflict between Ukraine and Russia constituted an "emergency in international relations," and that trade-restrictive measures implemented by Russia were "taken in time" of such emergency. The Panel, however, rejected Russia's claim that the invocation of Article XXI(b)(iii) by a WTO member renders its actions immune from scrutiny by a WTO Panel due to its self-judging nature (Chercheneff, 2021; Hofer, 2021).

In *Russia–Traffic in Transit*, the WTO Panel also distinguished between the objective and the subjective elements of the national security clause of Article XXI(b). The Panel interpreted the prerequisite for taking actions "in time of war or other emergency in international relations" as an objective element, as a "limitative qualifying clause." In ascertaining the subjective elements for determination of "essential security interests" and the "necessity of such measures" against the background of the principle of "good faith," the Panel stressed that the element of "essential security interests" should be articulated "sufficiently enough to demonstrate their veracity," and the element "necessary for the protection" should require a minimum degree of plausibility between trade-restrictive measures and their ability to contribute to the protection of declared security interests (Bogdanova, 2021, 176).

In *Saudi Arabia–Measures concerning the Protection of Intellectual Property* (2020),[61] in a matter involving a dispute over a Qatar-based broadcasting company's alleged pirate broadcasting in Saudi Arabia, the WTO Panel, relying on the same analytic framework as in *Russia–Traffic in Transit*, adjudicated that the tension between Qatar and Saudi Arabia met the threshold of being "emergency in international relations," and with the added violations of Articles 41.1 and 42 of the TRIPS Agreement, the invocation of "national security exception" was justified. The Panel decided, however, that although the broadcasting company concerned (beoutQ) was engaged in pirate broadcasting in Saudi Arabia and thus violated Article 61 of the TRIPS Agreement, a national security exception could not be justified on this ground alone (Bogdanova, 2021).[62]

60 See WTO Panel Report, *Russia –Measures Concerning Traffic in Transit [Russia –Traffic in Transit]*, WT/DS512/R and WT/DS512/R/Add.1, adopted 26 April 2019. The case is revisited in Chapter 5 in greater detail.

61 See WTO Panel Report, *Saudi Arabia–Measures concerning the Protection of Intellectual Property Rights [Saudi Arabia–Protection of IPRs]*, WT/DS567/R.

62 Notably, in *Case Concerning Certain Questions of Mutual Assistance in Criminal Matters* (2008), the ICJ also affirmed that GATT Article XXI(b) provided a WTO member with a "very considerable," but not "total discretion" in the exercise of the Article (Mitchell, 2017, 298).

D *The WTO and Secondary Sanctions*

GATT Article XXI(b) – essential security interests – has also been invoked to justify secondary sanctions on several occasions. For example, Egypt invoked it during the Arab League Boycott (involving both primary and secondary sanctions against Israel) in 1969–1970; Saudi Arabia invoked it to participate in the Arab League Boycott during 1995–1996; and the US invoked it to justify its sanctions against Nicaragua in 1985, and against Cuba and Iran in 1996. However, the legal standing of the use of this Article for justifying secondary sanctions is far from clear (Mitchell, 2017, 300) as any invocation of "essential security interests" requires the presence of two cumulative elements: (a) the existence of a credible security threat; and (b) the threatened security interest is so "essential" that the imposition of restrictive trade measures in response would be proportional (Balan, 2013).

This issue was tested in *Nicaragua v. USA* (1986), in which the US invoked "collective security interest" to impose secondary sanctions on the neighbors of Nicaragua by restricting economic dealings between the target and third parties. But during the proceedings, Nicaragua's neighboring country Peru argued that "it was implausible that a small country [Nicaragua] with modest resources could constitute an extraordinary threat to the national security of the US" (Mitchell, 2017, 299). As noted above, the ICJ rejected the US argument by asserting that unless the aggrieved state requires aid, collective self-defense did not justify economic sanctions or other hostile behavior. Some scholars argue that the secondary sanctions must fail the "essential security interests" test even where primary sanctions might satisfy it, especially when the threat posed by that target's trading partners is too "attenuated and remote" to satisfy the requirement (Meyer, 2009, 905).

E *The WTO and Human Rights*

Since the UN Human Rights Council (UNHRC) adopted its Resolution 27/21 in 2014, mandating evaluation of the negative impacts of unilateral coercive measures on the enjoyment of human rights, and appointed a UN Rapporteur to carry out the mission,[63] the human rights perspective has been catapulted into the debate on the legality of unilateral sanctions at the UN level with a renewed focus on whether such sanctions violate the prohibition on the use of force enshrined in Article 2(4) of the UN Charter. Since then, the possibility of applying the same human rights standards with respect to use of WTO Article XXI – national security exception – has also gained renewed attention around the world (Bogdanova, 2021).

The 2014 UNHRC resolution also called upon the UN member states not to adopt unilateral coercive actions with extraterritorial effects, with a tacit reference to the Sergei Magnitsky Rule of Law Accountability Act, 2012 (P.L. No. 112–208),

[63] Prior to that, in 1999 a position of Special Rapporteur on the Human Rights of Migrants was created pursuant to UNGA Resolution 1999/44. The mandate has been extended every three years since then. See

under which the US Congress authorized the US president to impose targeted sanctions against individuals involved in grave human rights violations in Russia. But in 2014, following the cyber-attack on Sony Pictures Entertainment, the US imposed several extraterritorial economic sanctions on individuals or entities responsible for the cyber-attack on information and communications technology and services on the grounds of the WTO's national security exception. Some scholars argue that such actions of the US not only show "a troubling tendency to overstretch the traditional jurisdictional principles" (Emmenegger, 2016), but also may well be unjustified under GATT Article XXI(b)(iii) (Bogdanova, 2021).

The US, however, doubled-down on its indifference to 2014 UNHRC resolution when it adopted the Global Magnitsky Human Rights Accountability Act, 2016 (P.L. No. 114–328), which authorized the president to impose sanctions against targeted foreign persons responsible for violations of internationally recognized human rights worldwide. Also, in 2020, the US imposed unilateral economic sanctions against several Chinese companies on the grounds of human rights violations.[64]

IV SANCTIONS AND INTERNATIONAL HUMAN RIGHTS LAW

The remarkable proliferation of economic sanctions regimes since the end of the Cold War has been underpinned by the presumption that economic sanctions, as opposed to military tools, are less destructive means to deter internationally unlawful acts, and that such sanctions may induce civilian populations in target states to create pressures on their governments and leaders to change the policy or behavior that the sanctioners detest (Drury, 2006; Giumelli, 2016, 38–40). But such presumptions vanished in thin air in the 1990s when the horrifying details of the human rights violations of comprehensive sanctions on the civilian population in Iraq came to light.[65]

www.ohchr.org/en/special-procedures/sr-migrants/about-mandate. But in 2014 the UNGA expanded the role of the special rapporteur to cover violations of international human rights law under UNHRC Resolution 27/21 (UN Doc. A/HRC/RES/27/21. 3 Oct. 2014), which called upon all member states:

> [To] stop adopting, maintaining or implementing unilateral coercive measures not in accordance with international law, international humanitarian law, the Charter of the United Nations and the norms and principles governing peaceful relations among States, in particular those of a coercive nature with extraterritorial effects, which create obstacles to trade relations among States, thus impeding the full realization of the rights set forth in the Universal Declaration of Human Rights and other international human rights instruments, in particular the right of individuals and peoples to development.

64 See US Department of the Treasury Press release: "Treasury Sanctions Chinese Entity and Officials Pursuant to Global Magnitsky Human Rights Accountability Act." July 9, 2020. These sanctions specifically targeted a Chinese company named the Xinjiang Production and Construction Corps (XPCC), which harvests a third of China's cotton and has a significant share in tomato exports, and allegedly has long been engaged in forced labor.

65 As discussed in detail in Chapter 7, many observers noted that the comprehensive sanctions on Iraq resulted in a "genocide," which caused more deaths than the total death from all weapons of mass destruction throughout history.

Based on the findings, a UN Sub-Commission on the Promotion and Protection of Human Rights declared the sanctions on Iraq "unequivocally illegal under existing international humanitarian law and human rights law" (Reinisch, 2001), and eventually, the UN and other sanctioners opted for targeted sanctions from the late 1990s.[66]

While the rationale and the effectiveness of sanctions regimes – no matter whether comprehensive or targeted, unilateral or multilateral – have widely been questioned (discussed in Chapter 1), a near universal consensus has emerged in recent decades that they impose significant hardship on the civilian populations in targeted countries by causing massive human rights violations (Joyner, 2015; Peksen, 2009). Some UN agencies have also pointed out that economic sanctions, including targeted ones, adversely affect many of the most basic human rights of the affected population including "the right to life, the rights to health and medical care, the right to freedom from hunger and the right to an adequate standard of living, food, education, work and housing" (UNHRC, 2014).

Given such a preponderance of evidence of adverse effects of economic sanctions on civilian populations, especially pertaining to human rights, numerous studies have scrutinized existing legal frameworks and case law from the standpoints of international human rights laws, international humanitarian law, the UN Charter, as well as other international conventions and treaties. The discussion below first analyses the broad international legal framework on human rights, and then explores it in the contexts of both multinational and unilateral sanctions.

A *International Legal Infrastructures of Human Rights*

Until the early nineteenth century, states enforced their international rights through diplomatic interventions, trade wars, countermeasures, and ultimately by using military force. Wars were not illegal but were subject to customary norms of necessity and proportionality. No law obligated states to respect the human rights of their own nationals – customary international law rather insulated states from any international criticisms about the way they treated their own nationals. As mentioned before, in the seventeenth century, the Westphalian doctrine strengthened the powers of sovereigns at the expense of citizens.

By the late nineteenth century, the world began to witness the first rudiments of international humanitarian law with the signing of the First Geneva Convention (1864). A series of subsequent conventions, organized in response to changes in the nature of warfare and with the aim of protecting human rights in times of war, and their ratification by a number of states, gradually gave rise to a quasi-form of international human rights laws by the end of the nineteenth century. In the twentieth century, the parameters of international human rights law, as well as international humanitarian law, changed dramatically. Among others, the atrocities that occurred

[66] The switch from comprehensive sanctions to targeted/smart sanctions is discussed in detail in Chapter 1.

during WWII convinced the world that a state's treatment of its own nationals was within the concerns of the international community (Vazquez, 2003). The resultant edifice of international legal frameworks stands on several pillars.

First, the Treaty of Versailles (1918) paved the way for international institutionalization of human rights law. The treaty established a system of protection of human rights for minorities in order to ensure both non-discrimination and respect for difference. It also founded the International Labor Organization (ILO) with the aim to protect the human rights of workers, and empowered it to frame binding labor laws subject to the consent of the signatories.

Second, following WWII, several multilateral human rights instruments, such as the UN Charter (1945), the Universal Declaration of Human Rights (UDHR, 1948), the International Covenant on Civil and Political Rights (ICCPR) (1966), and the International Covenant on Economic, Social and Cultural Rights (ICESCR) (1966), came to form a legal edifice of international human rights norms and obligations for all states. While some of these instruments are not legally binding on all states, the covenants of the ICCPR, and the ICESCR, which is also known as the Universal Bill of Human Rights, have been ratified by most countries, and thus are legally binding instruments.[67] Although some states are not signatories to some of these legal instruments, by now these covenants have already attained the status of *jus cogens* from which no state can opt out.[68]

Third, many declarations/resolutions of the UNGA set acceptable standards with respect to lawfulness of sanctions and their impacts on human rights. For example, the UNGA Declaration on the Right to Development (1986) provides that, in imposing sanctions, sanctioning states must adhere to the right to development of target states. UNGA Resolution A/RES/60/251 (2006), which established the UNHRC, requires international cooperation to achieve full realization of human rights incorporated in international human rights treaties. The UNGA Resolution, which mandated a special rapporteur in 1999, and its subsequent amendment in 2014, envisages international human rights law and standards, and provides advisory opinions to the UN on the impact of sanctions on human rights and the extraterritorial jurisdiction of unilateral sanctions of states (Skogly, 2022, 28).[69]

67 These covenants taken together guarantee the rights to self-determination, free disposition of natural wealth, and non-deprivation of means of sustenance. The ICCPR guarantees the rights to life; freedom from torture, cruel, inhuman or degrading treatment or punishment; liberty and security of persons; and the ICESCR guarantees equal rights of men and women; the right to work, social security, and education; and adequate standards of living and enjoyment of highest attainable standard of physical and mental health (Shagabutdinova and Berejikian, 2007).

68 For example, no matter whether it is a signatory or not, no state can opt out of its legal obligations as envisaged by these legal frameworks with respect to torture, slavery, human trafficking, and so on, including in times of war or other public emergencies.

69 The Special Rapporteur's office is also responsible for establishment of a centralized register at the UN Secretariat level to recapitulate the list of all the unilateral sanctions in force.

Fourth, there has been considerable development of legal frameworks on extraterritorial obligations of states and international organizations with respect to human rights.[70] For example, Article 2 of ARSIWA and Article 4 of ILC's Articles of Responsibility of International Organizations (ARIO) provide guidance on any action or omission that can be attributable to a state or an international organization that is in breach of international human rights obligations. Turkelli (2022) identifies three such obligations of states and international organizations as: (a) responsibility for their own acts or omissions resulting in human rights violations, including the acts of state agents, or a failure to abide by their global obligations; (b) human rights violations originating from the acts or omissions of international organizations to which they are members; and (c) the entities or bodies that have obligations to regulate, or engage in, acts or omissions resulting in human rights violations.

Pursuant to the ILC ARSIWA (2011), conduct of human rights violations can be attributed to state organs when persons or entities exercise elements of governmental authority, to organs and persons of third states even when those organs, persons, or entities are acting in contravention of instructions or excess of the authority they possess, as well as the conduct of person(s) that act on the instructions, direction or control of the states, or conduct acknowledged by a state as its own. The wrongfulness of a state's conduct can be determined when the said conduct is not in conformity with what is required of the state by way of obligation, or a responsibility triggered by an act of breach of an obligation, or a state is engaged in gross or systematic breach of the peremptory norms of the ILC.[71] The law on state responsibility also extends to aiding and assisting in the commission of an internationally wrongful act with the knowledge of the circumstances of that wrongful act (ILC, 2001, Article 16 and Article 14).[72]

Finally, although the rules of international humanitarian law, as codified in the Geneva Conventions (1949) and Additional Protocols (1977), apply only to cases of declared war or of any other international armed conflict (Reinisch, 2001, 860), concerns are being expressed to expand the scope of such laws to conflicts in peacetime as well, especially in cases when the severity of economic sanctions resembles

[70] The discussion on extraterritorial human rights obligations is primarily based on Turkelli (2022), which provides detailed guidelines, as well as relevant articles of ARSIWA and ARIO, as to what constitutes human rights violations and how to determine wrongfulness of such conduct of a state or states, their organs, and agencies.

[71] Under the provisions of Articles 20–24 of ARSIWA, however, wrongfulness may be precluded by valid consent, lawful self-defense, countermeasures, force majeure, distress, necessity and compliance with an obligation arising from *jus cogens*.

[72] In *Bosnia and Herzegovina v. Serbia and Montenegro*, for example, the IJC (2007) noted that Article 16 of ARSIWA on aid and assistance reflected customary international law on a state's responsibility for complicity. Some, however, maintain that the complicity of a state does not need to be limited to the ARSIWA definition, as obligations can also be established under the non-refoulement obligations under international refugee regimes, or positive obligations under other human rights conventions (Lanovoy, 2016; Turkelli, 2022).

a state of economic warfare.[73] Proponents of this strand of thought, including the ICJ as discussed below, argue that as economic sanctions imposed during peacetime may unlawfully infringe upon the human rights of civilians in target states, and as most human rights treaties allow derogation from human rights obligations in public emergencies, such an expansion may prevent human rights violations under sanctions regimes (Joyner, 2015, 14; Albal, 2021).[74]

B *Human Rights Obligations of Multilateral Sanctions*

As the devasting humanitarian crisis of Iraq showed, multilateral sanctions imposed by the UNSC, in the name of the global community and restoring international peace and security, may well cause massive human rights violations when the civilian population is indiscriminately subjected to sanctions aimed at changing the behavior/policy of the political leaders. At the same time, considerable controversy exists whether the derogation clauses of international human rights and humanitarian laws and conventions also apply to UNSC actions.

Some scholars argue that making human rights a binding obligation on the UNSC would be a daunting task, as the UN is not a party to any such laws or conventions.[75] They emphasize that the UNSC's peace-preserving and peace-restoring functions can be carried out best when it can freely decide "if, when, against whom, and how to react to threats to and breaches of world peace and security," and it is not treated merely as "a law enforcement organ" of the UN (Reinisch, 2001, 856).

An opposing strand of thought argues that the UNSC has the obligation to exercise its sanctioning powers in accordance with the purposes of the UN, as enshrined in the UN Charter, which is to promote and encourage respect for human rights, and it cannot possibly do so if it itself violates human rights law in its application of sanctions (Joyner, 2015, 14). Exponents of this thought also point out that Article 24(2) of the UN Charter provides that the UNSC acts "in accordance with the Purposes and Principles of the United Nations," and Article 1(1) of the Charter emphasizes

73 For example, the ICJ applied such a rationale in *Nicaragua v. United States* (1986) by stipulating that:

> [T]he general principles of humanitarian law cannot be limited solely to armed conflict: … the obligation to provide essential goods and foodstuffs contained in the Geneva Conventions and Additional Protocols applicable in time of war applies also in peacetime since the obligations do not derive only from the Conventions themselves but from the general principles of humanitarian law to which the Conventions merely give specific expression.
>
> (Cited in Reinish, 2001, 860–861).

74 Some argue, however, that despite a "growing convergence" of human rights and humanitarian laws, the applicability of humanitarian laws should be limited to situations constituting some sort of armed conflict (Rienish, 2001, 860; Reisman and Stevick, 1998, 95).

75 Some other scholars who may be grouped in this category include: Provost (1992), Reisman and Stevick (1998), Segall (1999), Swindells (1996), Reinisch (2001), and Michaelsen (2014).

that the UNSC maintains world peace and security "in conformity with the principles of justice and international law."[76]

Controversy also exists with respect to the UN's own obligations and commitments to human rights. For example, the UN Charter emphasizes protection of human rights and fundamental freedoms across the world, while also requiring a commitment from the member states to refrain from interference in the domestic affairs of other states (Article 2(7)). To some scholars, such an ambiguity indicates that the human rights provisions of the UN may not enjoy firm legal standing when it comes to the sovereign rights of states in their internal affairs (Kelsen, 1950; Skogly, 2022, 27).

As the UNSC is not a signatory to any international treaty or conventions, Michaelson (2014), for example, argues that the principle of proportionality may provide a useful procedural tool to check the powers of the UNSC. The principle of proportionality, according to Michaelson, comprises of two tests: a necessity test and a proportionality test. While the necessity test requires weighing and balancing of the sanctioning measures to determine whether it can reasonably be expected that they would achieve the professed objectives (Geiss, 2005, 175), the proportionality test evaluates the immediate or prospective consequences of sanctions in terms of their necessity for the objectives (Owen, 2012, 18).[77]

C *Human Rights Obligations of Unilateral Sanctioners*

Under the hierarchy of the norms of international law envisaged by the UN Charter, establishing the peace and territorial integrity of states stands at the apex of the international legal system, to which the other norms, including those related to human rights, are subordinated. Also, under the legal regime of the UN Charter, states are permitted to use force only in response to armed attacks against their territorial integrity, and thus, they are left with the option of employing countermeasures/sanctions not involving the use of force in foreign relations in the absence of an armed conflict.

At the same time, studies suggest that: (a) the assumption that the use of economic sanctions presents "non-lethal" and "non-destructive" solutions to foreign policy options is utterly exaggerated (Reisman and Stevick, 1998, 86); (b) economic sanctions may indeed cause long-term damage to human rights and humanitarian violations in target states (Ashley, 2021; Gordon 2010; Joyner, 2015); and (c)

[76] Apparently, the International Criminal Tribunal for the Former Yugoslavia also held similar reasoning about the accountability of the UNSC (Oosthuizen, 1999). Reinisch (2001, 856) also admits that such UN Charter-based interpretive discourse considerably weakens the position of those who espouse that that UNSC should not be subjected to human rights obligations.

[77] Some studies suggest that economic sanctions, whether multilateral or unilateral, fail the legal necessity test when the purpose of the sanctions was to improve the human rights situation but they result in deterioration of human rights (Gutmann, 2018).

sanctioning states themselves breach international legal norms and commit internationally wrongful acts when the sanctions that they impose to protect human rights result in human rights violations (Gutmann, 2018; Mohamad, 2015).

Studies also suggest that there may be an inherent trade-off between the obligations of states to the rules of conduct mandated by international laws and conventions, and the mechanisms available for enforcement of sanctions against international wrongful acts (Albal, 2021). That is, there may be a sanctions–repression nexus – as sanctions trigger domestic dissent, and such instability induces the target government to employ repression, sanctions may further foment the sanctions–repression link (Liou et al., 2021).

An international legal framework with respect to human rights violations by unilateral sanctions has been rather slow to emerge. For example, the UN Charter does not provide any specific legal framework for sanctions-related human rights violations.[78] The scholarship on the humanitarian and human rights implications of unilateral sanctions has generally been addressed by a plethora of instruments, such as the fundamental principles of international humanitarian law, international human rights law, the law of countermeasures as encapsulated by ARSIWA, the UN Charter, the UN Declaration of Human Rights, UNGA resolutions, and such other international treaties, declarations, and soft law instruments (Hofer, 2017, 175).

But due to such international agreements and conventions and so on, studies suggest that four major forms of human rights have now been addressed and protected both at global and regional levels, which each state is required to abide by. These rights are: (a) basic human rights – the right to life (political imprisonment, disappearance, torture); (b) economic rights (property rights, freedom to trade); (c) emancipatory rights (women's economic and political rights); and (d) political rights and civil liberties (freedom of assembly and speech) (Gutmann, 2018; Reinisch, 2001).

Moreover, the determination of legality and legitimacy of unilateral sanctions has increasingly been subjected to fundamental norms of international humanitarian and human rights law, as well as the tests of necessity, proportionality, and discrimination standards with respect to their goals and objectives, social and economic costs, as well as consequences (O'Connell, 2002; Reisman and Stevick, 1998).

More recently, the Maastricht Principles on Extraterritorial Obligations in the Area of Economic, Social, and Cultural Rights (Maastricht ETO Principles) has proposed another set of legal standards on extraterritorial human rights obligations of sanctioners (Gibney, 2022). While international law regulates the (horizontal) relationship between sovereign states, and international human rights law regulates the (vertical) relationship between a state and its own citizens, the ETOs are

[78] As mentioned above, the UN Charter, however, moved the issue of human rights protection from being a national issue to a matter of legitimate international concern, apparently to recognize the fact that certain human values may not be left with individual states alone, and the international community should have a role in ensuring such rights.

concerned with the "diagonal" relationship between a state and individuals living in other countries. In other words, these principles address the human rights obligations of states to individuals who are outside their territorial borders (Skogly and Gibney, 2022).[79]

D *Judicial Interventions*

Some ICJ adjudications provide interesting perspectives on human rights violations caused by unilateral coercive actions. For example, the ICJ rulings in *Nicaragua v. United States* (1986) involved massive human rights violations by Nicaraguan paramilitary forces, who received military and economic assistance from the US. The court agreed that the Contras were essentially creatures of the US government and the relationship between the two entities was extraordinarily close, but still ruled that in order for the US to be held liable for human rights violations carried out by the Contras, the US would have to be in control of virtually every activity of the paramilitary forces engaged in Nicaragua (Gibney, 2022, 17).

Similarly, in *Bosnia v. Serbia* (2007), the Serbian Republic was involved in a widely acknowledged genocide in Bosnia, and the question before the ICJ was whether the Serbian Republic, by providing assistance to Bosnian Serb forces, had acted in violation of international human rights law. The court ruled that notwithstanding the widespread atrocities suffered by the Bosnian Muslim population and despite the extraordinarily close ties between the Bosnian Serb forces and the Serbian government, the Serbian Republic was not "responsible" in any manner for the acts of genocide that occurred following the fall of Srebrenica.

A great judicial triumph with respect to international human rights law, however, came in 1998 when a British court issued an arrest warrant against the Chilean dictator Augusto Pinochet. It was the first time in history that foreign judges had applied the principle of universal jurisdiction by declaring themselves competent to judge crimes committed in a foreign country by a former head of state. After the arrest of Pinochet in London, former UN Secretary General Kofi Annan described the event as a "triumph of human rights over sovereignty," and proclaimed, "It is no longer acceptable to see governments flouting their citizens' rights under the pretext of sovereignty" (cited in Fabri, 2008, 33).[80]

V CONCLUDING REMARKS

Sanctions in international law, from a *sensu largo* perspective, may encompass all forms of coercive measures, including countermeasures, retorsions, reprisals, and

[79] Studies suggest that the ETO principles are being accepted by UN treaty bodies as well as other international law venues (Gibney, 2022).

[80] Pinochet was extradited to Chile in 2000 and died in prison there, in 2006, without being convicted.

use of force, while a *sensu stricto* meaning of sanctions would imply coercive measures, adopted and imposed by a competent legal authority to restrain a wrongdoer from breaching of international legal norms, and penalizing the wrongful act with appropriate and proportional corrective measures. There is, however, no supranational body to determine and enforce the legality or legitimacy of sanctions. Internationally, sanctions are rather governed by a plethora of public or customary international laws, the UN Charter, UNSC and UNGA resolutions, international humanitarian laws, international human rights laws, the law of countermeasures, international treaties, conventions, and declarations, and other soft law instruments, such as the ILC ARSIWA, judicial decisions and interpretations of competent international judicial bodies, and "the teachings of the most highly qualified publicists of the various nations."

All sources of international law are not equally binding on all nations, however. The doctrine of state sovereignty limits the jurisdiction of international laws and conventions to the consent of the nations. While UNSC resolutions are binding on all UN members, the UNGA resolutions or the provisions of the UN Charter are not; while the mandates of the Geneva Conventions and those of the ICCPR, and the ICESCR, are considered mandatory as most of the nations have ratified those, neither the provisions of the ARSIWA, nor are the judicial decisions of the ICJ, or international human rights laws binding on all nations around the world.

It is therefore not surprising that the legality and legitimacy of both multilateral and unilateral sanctions are increasingly being questioned. The legality of the UNSC sanctions has been challenged on the grounds of whether they are *ultra vires* to the UN Charter, whether they violate the *jus cogens* norms of customary international law, and whether they conform to the law of countermeasures. The legality of unilateral sanctions has been questioned on the grounds of whether the target state has actually committed an internationally wrongful act; whether the sanctioner is actually an "injured state"; whether the sanctioning measures are proportionate to the alleged injury; whether the sanctions affect fundamental human rights norms or *jus cogens* norms; and whether they are terminated when the alleged wrongful act ceases.

The legality and legitimacy of unilateral sanctions have also been questioned in the context of the WTO trading system – whether discriminatory trade restrictions conflict with the sanctioning country's GATT obligations; whether the national security exceptions clauses are being misused without the existence of a credible security threat; whether the imposition of restrictive trade measures is proportional to the alleged threat; and whether the WTO dispute settlement system is actually equipped to handle such trade disputes.

In the context of the US, the most prolific enforcer of unilateral sanctions, questions have also been raised with regard to the extraordinary expansion in its extraterritorial sanctions that increasingly target third countries, individuals, and entities. Controversies exist whether such sanctioning measures violate the principles of sovereign equality of states and non-intervention in the internal and external affairs of another state, and whether they violate the extraterritorial human rights obligations of the US.

REFERENCES

Albal, E. 2021. Evaluating Sanctions in the Context of International Law. *Peace Review*, 33 (1):131–139.

Alford, R. 2011. The Self-Judging WTO Security Exception. *Utah Law Review*, 2011:697–698.

Asada, M. 2020. Definition and Legal Justification of Sanctions. In M. Asada (ed.), *Economic Sanctions in International Law and Practice*, pp. 3–23. London: Routledge.

Ashley, L. 2021. Unilateral Coercive Measures: Towards International Humanitarian Law and International Human Rights. In S. Subedi (ed.), *Unilateral Sanctions in International Law*, pp. 233–254. Oxford: Hart Publishing.

Balan, G. 2013. The Latest United States Sanctions against Iran: What Role to the WTO Security Exceptions. *Journal of Conflict and Security Law*, 18(3):365–393.

Baldwin, D. 2003. Prologomena to Thinking about Economic Sanctions and Free Trade. *Chicago Journal of International Law*, 4(2):272–281.

Beucillon, C. 2021. Introduction. In C. Beucillon (ed.), *Research Handbook on Unilateral and Extraterritorial Sanctions*, pp. 1–18. Cheltenham, UK: Edward Elgar.

Blum, Y. 1977. Economic Boycotts in International Law. *Texas International Law Journal*, 12:5–15.

Bogdanova, I. 2021. Targeted Economic Sanctions and WTO Law: Examining the Adequacy of the National Security Exception. *Legal Issues of Economic Integration*, 48(2):171–200.

Bothe, M. 2016. Compatibility and Legitimacy of Sanctions Regimes. In N. Ronzitti (ed.), *Coercive Diplomacy, Sanctions and International Law*, pp. 33–42. Leiden: Brill.

Boutros-Ghali, B. 1995. *An Agenda for Peace*. New York: United Nations.

Briggs, H. 1971. Barcelona Traction: The *Jus Standi* of Belgium. *American Journal of International Law*, 65(2):327–345.

Bring, O. 2000. The Westphalian Peace Tradition in International Law – From Jus ad Bellum to Jus contra Bellum. *International Law Studies*, 75:57–80.

Browne, R. 1997. Revisiting "National Security" in an Interdependent World: The GATT Article XXI Defense after Helms-Burton. *Georgetown Law Journal*, 86(2):405–433.

Carter, B. 1987. International Economic Sanctions: Improving the Haphazard U.S. Legal Regime. *California Law Review*, 75:1159–1276.

Carter, B., and Farha, R. 2013. Overview and Operation of U.S. Financial Sanctions, Including the Example of Iran. *Georgetown Journal of International Law*, 44(3):903–914.

Chercheneff, L. 2021. Challenging Unilateral and Extraterritorial Sanctions under International Economic Law: Exploring Leads at the WTO and the OECD. In C. Beucillon (ed.), *Research Handbook on Unilateral and Extraterritorial Sanctions*, pp. 239–256. Cheltenham, UK: Edward Elgar.

Chopra, J., and T. Weiss. 1992. Sovereignty Is No Longer Sacrosanct: Codifying Humanitarian Intervention. *Ethics and International Affairs*, 6:95–118.

Crawford, J. 2001. *The International Law Commission's Articles of State Responsibility: Introduction, Text and Commentary*. Cambridge: Cambridge University Press.

Crawford, J. 2013. *State Responsibility – The General Part*. Cambridge: Cambridge University Press.

Damrosch, L. 2019. The Legitimacy of Economic Sanctions as Countermeasures for Wrongful Acts. *Ecology Law Quarterly*, 46:95–111.

Damrosch, L., and D. Scheffer (Eds.). (1991). *Law and Force in the New International Order*. Boulder, CO: Westview Press.

Danchin, P. 2009. Whose Public? Which Law? Mapping the Internal/External Distinction in International Law. In J. Farrell, and K. Rubenstein (eds.), *Sanctions, Accountability and Governance in a Globalized World*, pp. 27–52. Cambridge: Cambridge University Press.

Davis, S., and I. Ness. 2021. Introduction: Why Are Economic Sanctions a Form of War? In S. Davis, and I. Ness (eds.), *Sanctions as War: Anti-imperialist Perspectives on American Geo-economic Strategy*, pp. 1–24. Leiden and Boston: Brill.

Dawidowicz, M. 2017a. *Third-Party Countermeasures in International Law*. Cambridge: Cambridge University Press.

Dawidowicz, M. 2017b. Third-Party Countermeasures and the ICJ. In M. Dawidowicz, *Third Party Countermeasures in International Law*, pp. 36–71. Cambridge: Cambridge University Press.

deWet, E. 2013. From Kadi to Nada: Judicial Techniques Favoring Human Rights over United Nations Security Council Sanctions. *Chinese Journal of International Law*, 12:787–807.

Dolzer, R., and C. Schreuer. 2012. *Principles of International Investment Law*. 2nd ed. London: Oxford University Press.

Dowlah, C. 2004. *Backwaters of Global Prosperity: How Globalization and the GATT/WTO Trade Regimes Marginalize the World's Poorest Nations*. New York: Praeger.

Doxey, M. 1996. *International Sanctions in Contemporary Perspective*. 2nd ed. New York: St. Martin's Press.

Dupont, P. 2012. Countermeasures and Collective Security. The Case of EU Sanctions against Iran. *Journal of Conflict and Security Law*, 17(3):301–336.

Emmenegger, S. 2016. Extraterritorial Economic Sanctions and Their Foundation in International Law. *Arizona Journal of International and Comparative Law*, 33(3):632–660.

Fabri, H. 2008. Human Rights and State Sovereignty: Have the Boundaries Been Significantly Redrawn? In P. Alston, and E. Macdonald (eds.), *Human Rights, Intervention, and the Use of Force*, pp. 33–86. Oxford: Oxford University Press.

Farrall J. 2007. *United Nations Sanctions and the Rule of Law*. 1st ed. London: Cambridge University Press.

Geiss, R. 2005. Humanitarian Safeguards in Economic Sanctions Regimes: A Call for Automatic Suspension Clauses, Periodic Monitoring, and Follow-Up Assessment of Long-Term Effects. *Harvard Human Rights Journal*, 18(2005):167–200.

Gestri, M. 2016. Sanctions Imposed by the European Union: Legal and Institutional Aspects. In N. Ronzitti (ed.), *Coercive Diplomacy, Sanctions and International Law*, pp. 70–102. Leiden: Brill.

Gibney, M. 2022. The Historical Development of Extraterritorial Obligations. In M. Gibney et al. (eds.), *The Routledge Handbook on Extraterritorial Human Rights Obligations*, pp. 13–25. London: Routledge.

Giumelli. F. 2016. From Effective to Useful Sanctions: Lessons Learned from the Experience of the European Union. Coercive Diplomacy, Sanctions and International Law. In N. Ronzitti (ed.), *Coercive Diplomacy, Sanctions and International Law*, pp. 246–269. Leiden: Brill.

Goldman, Z., and A. Lindblom. 2021. The US Position and Practice with regards to Unilateral and Extraterritorial Sanctions: Reimagining the US Sanctions Regime in a World of Advanced Technology. In C. Beucillon (ed.), *Research Handbook on Unilateral and Extraterritorial Sanctions*, pp. 130–148. Cheltenham, UK: Edward Elgar.

Gordon, J. 2010. *Invisible War: The United states and the Iraq Sanctions*. Cambridge, MA: Harvard University Press.

Gordon, J. 2019. The Not So Targeted Instrument of Asset Freezes. *Ethics and International Affairs*, 33(3):303–314.

Gutmann, J. et al. 2018. Economic Sanctions and Human Rights: Quantifying the Legal Proportionality Principle. *Research Papers in Economics*, No. 2/18. Universität Trier, Germany.

Happold, M. 2017. UN Sanctions as Human Rights and Humanitarian Law Devices. In L. Herrick (ed.), *Research Handbook on UN Sanctions and International Law*, pp. 122–140. Cheltenham, UK and Northampton, MA: Edward Elgar.

Happold, M., and P. Eden. 2016. Economic Sanctions and International Law: An Introduction. In M. Happold, and P. Eden (eds.), *Economic Sanctions and International Law*, pp. 1–12. University of Luxemburg.

Henderson, J. 1986. Legality of Economic Sanctions under International Law: The Case of Nicaragua. *Washington and Lee Law Review*, 986(43):167–196.

Hestermeyer, H. 2011. Art XXI: Security Exceptions. In R. Wolfrum et al. (eds.), *WTO – Trade in Goods*, pp. 571–686. Leiden and Boston: Martinus Nijhoff.

Hofer, A. 2017. The Developed/Developing Divide on Unilateral Coercive Measures: Legitimate Enforcement or Illegitimate Intervention. *Chinese Journal of International Law*, 16(2):175–214.

Hofer, A. 2021. Unilateral Sanctions as a Challenge to the Law of State Responsibility. In C. Beucillon (ed.), *Research Handbook on Unilateral and Extraterritorial Sanctions*, pp. 186–204. Cheltenham, UK: Edward Elgar.

Hovell, D. 2016. Due Process in the United Nations. *American Journal of International Law*, 110(1):1–48.

Hovell, D. 2019. Symposium on Unilateral Targeted Sanctions. Unfinished Business of International Law: The Questionable Legality of Autonomous Sanctions. *American Journal of International Law*, 113:140–145.

Hufbauer, G. et al. 2007. *Economic Sanctions Reconsidered: History and Current Policy*. Washington, DC: Patterson Institute for International Economics.

ICJ (International Court of Justice). 1986. *Case Concerning Military and Paramilitary Activities in and against Nicaragua (Nicaragua v United States of America)* [1986] ICJ Rep 14 [222].

ILC (International Law Commission). 2001. *Articles on the Responsibility of States for Internationally Wrongful Acts (ARSIWA)*. New York: United Nations.

Ilieva, J., A. Dashtevski., and F. Kokotovic. 2018. Economic Sanctions in International Law. *UTMS Journal of Economics*, 9(2):201–211.

Jamnejad, M., and M. Wood. 2009. The Principle of Non-intervention. *Leiden Journal of International Law*, 22(2):345–381.

Joyner, D. 2015. International Legal Limits on the Ability of States to Lawfully Impose International Economic/Financial Sanctions. In A. Marossi, and M. Bassett (eds.), *Economic Sanctions under International Law: Unilateralism, Multilateralism, Legitimacy and Consequences*, pp. 83–93. London: Springer.

Joyner, D. 2017. UN Counter-Proliferation Sanctions and International Law. In L. Herik (ed.), *Research Handbook on UN Sanctions and International Law*, pp. 110–121. Cheltenham, UK: Edward Elgar.

Kelsen, H. 1950. *The Law of the United Nations: A Critical Analysis of Its Fundamental Problems*. New York: Praeger.

Kuyper, P. 1990. International Legal Aspects of Economic Sanctions. In P. Sarcevic, and H. Houtte (eds.), *Legal Issues in International Trade*. London: Graham & Trotman.

Lanovoy, V. 2016. *Complicity and Its Limits in the Law of International Responsibility*. London: Hart Publishing.

LaRae-Perez, C. 2002. Economic Sanctions as Use of Force: Re-evaluating the Legality of Sanctions from an Effects-Based Perspective. *Boston University International Law Journal*, 20(1):161–188.

Liou, R., M. Amanda, and D. Peksen. 2021. Revisiting the Causal Links between Economic Sanctions and Human Rights Violations. *Political Research Quarterly*, 74(4):808–821.

Lopez, G, and D. Cortright. 1995. The Sanctions Era: An Alternative to Military Intervention. *Fletcher Forum of World Affairs*, 19(2):65–86.

Lowenfeld, A. 2003. Trade Controls for Political Ends: Four Perspectives. *Chicago Journal of International Law*, 4(2):354–369.

Mallard, G., and A. Hanson. 2021. Embedded Extraterritoriality: US Judicial Litigation and the Global Banking Surveillance of Digital Money Flows. In C. Beucillon (ed.), *Research Handbook on Unilateral and Extraterritorial Sanctions*, pp. 270–287. Cheltenham, UK: Edward Elgar.

Menkes, J., and A. Kociołek-Pęksa. 2019. Heterogeneity, Compliance and Enforcement of Public International Law Remarks on Sanctions and Countermeasures. *Politeja*, 63:7–25.

Meyer, J. 2009. Second Thoughts on Secondary Sanctions. *University of Pennsylvania Journal of International Economic Law*, 30(3):905–934.

Michaelsen, C. 2014. Human Rights as Limits for the Security Council: A Matter of Substantive Law or Defining the Application of Proportionality? *Journal of Conflict & Security Law*, 19(3):451–469.

Milanovic, M. 2011. *Extraterritorial Application of Human Rights Treaties*. Oxford: Oxford University Press.

Mitchell, A. 2017. Sanctions and the World Trade Organization. In L. Herik (ed.), *Research Handbook on UN Sanctions and International Law*, pp. 283–303. Cheltenham UK and Northampton MA: Edward Elgar.

Mohamad, R. 2015. Unilateral Sanctions in International Law: A Quest for Legality. In A. Marossi, and M. Bassett (eds.), *Economic Sanctions under International Law: Unilateralism, Multilateralism, Legitimacy and Consequences*, pp. 71–81. London: Springer.

Moiseienko, A. 2021. Due Process and Unilateral Targeted Sanctions. In C. Beucillon (ed.), *Research Handbook on Unilateral and Extraterritorial Sanctions*, pp. 405–423. Cheltenham, UK: Edward Elgar.

Murrill, B. 2018. The National Security Exception and the World Trade Organization. Congressional Research Services. LSB10223. Washington, DC.

Nasu, H. (2013). Revisiting the Principle of Non-Intervention: A Structural Principle of International Law or a Political Obstacle to Regional Security in Asia? *Asian Journal of International Law*, 3(1):25–50.

O'Connell, M. 2002. Debating the Law of Sanctions. *European Journal of International Law*, 13:63–79.

Offut, M. 1928. *The Protection of Citizens Abroad by the United States*. Baltimore, MD: John Hopkins Press.

Oosthuizen, G. 1999. Playing the Devil's Advocate: The United Nations Security Council Is Unbound by Law. *Leiden Journal of International law*, 12(3):549–563.

Owen, M. 2012. The Limits of Economic Sanctions under International Humanitarian Law: The Case of the Congo. *Texas International Law Journal*, 48:103–112.

Peksen, D. 2009. Better or Worse? The Effect of Economic Sanctions on Human Rights. *Journal of Peace Research*, 46(1):59–77.

Provost, R. 1992. Starvation as a Weapon: Legal Implications of the United Nations Food Blockade against Iraq and Kuwait. *Columbia Journal of Transnational Law*, 30:577–616.

Reinisch, W. 2001. Developing Human Rights and Humanitarian Law Accountability of the Security Council for the Imposition of Economic Sanctions. *American Journal of International Law*, 95(4):851–872.

Reisman, W., and D. Stevick. 1998. The Applicability of International Law Standards to United Nations Economic Sanctions Programs. *European Journal of International Law* 9:86–141.

Ronzitti, N. 2016. Sanctions as Instruments of Coercive Diplomacy: An International Law Perspective. In N. Ronzitti (ed.), *Coercive Diplomacy, Sanctions and International Law*, pp. 1–32. Leiden: Brill.

Ruys, T. 2017. Sanctions, Retortions and Countermeasures: Concepts and International Legal Framework. In L. Herik (ed.), *Research Handbook on UN Sanctions and International Law*, pp. 19–51. Cheltenham, UK: Edward Elgar.

Sampford, C. 2010. The Potential for a Post-Westphalian Convergence of "Public Law" and "Public International Law." In J. Farrall, and K. Rubenstein (eds.), *Sanctions, Accountability and Governance in a Globalized World*, pp. 53–72. Cambridge: Cambridge University Press.

Sampford, C., and C. Parker. 1995. Legal Ethics: Legal Regulation, Ethical Standard Setting and Institutional Design. In C. Parker, and C. Sampford (eds.), *Legal Ethics and Legal Practice: Contemporary Issues*. Oxford: Oxford University Press.

Schechla, J. 2022. Extraterritorial Human Rights Obligations in the Context of Economic Sanctions. In M. Gibney, ed., *The Routledge Handbook on Extraterritorial Human Rights Obligations*. London: Routledge.

Schloemann, H., and S. Ohlhoff. 1999. "Constitutionalization" and Dispute Settlement in the WTO: National Security as an Issue of Competence. *American Journal of International Law*, 93(2):424–451.

Segall, A. 1999. Economic Sanctions: Legal and Policy Constraints. *International Review of the Red Cross*, No. 836.

Shagabutdinova, E., and J. Berejikian. 2007. Deploying Sanctions while Protecting Human Rights: Are Humanitarian "Smart" Sanctions Effective? *Journal of Human Rights*, 6(1):59–74.

Skogly, S., and M. Gibney. 2022. Global Human Rights Obligations. In M. Gibney et al. (eds.), *Routledge Handbook on Extraterritorial Human Rights Obligations*, pp. 25–39. London: Routledge.

Smeets, M. 2000. Conflicting Goals: Economic Sanctions and the WTO. *Global Dialogue*, 2(3):119–128.

Sossai, M. 2020. Legality of Extraterritorial Sanctions. In M. Asada (ed.), *Economic Sanctions in International Law and Practice*, pp. 62–80. London: Routledge.

Subedi, S. 2021. The Status of Unilateral Sanctions in International Law. In S. Subedi (ed.), *Unilateral Sanctions in International Law*, pp. 19–60. Oxford: Hart Publishing.

Swindells, F. 1996. UN Sanctions in Haiti: A Contradiction under Articles 41 and 55 of the UN Charter. *Fordham International Law Journal*, 20(5):1880–1959.

Tams, C., and A. Tzanakopoulos. 2010. Barcelona Traction at 40: The ICJ as an Agent of Legal Development. *Leiden Journal of International Law*, 23(4):781–800.

Tanzi, A. 2010. Remarks on Sovereignty in the Evolving Constitutional Features of the International Community. In M. Arsanjani et al. (eds.), *Looking to the Future: Essays on International Law in Honor of W. Michael Reisman*, pp. 299–322. Leiden: Koninklijke Brill.

Tomuschat, C., and J. Thouvenin (Eds.). 2005. *The Fundamental Rules of the International Legal Order. Jus Cogens and Obligations Erga Omnes*. Boston, MA: Martinus Nijhoff.

Turkelli, G. 2022. Extraterritorial Human Rights Obligations and Responsibility under International Law. In M. Gibney et al. (eds.), *Routledge Handbook on Extraterritorial Human Rights Obligations*, pp. 40–51. London: Routledge.

UNHRC (United Nations Human Rights Council). 2014. Human Rights and Unilateral Coercive Measures. UNHRC Resolution (03 October 2014). A/HRC/RES/27/21.

Vazquez, C. 2003. Trade Sanctions and Human Rights – Past, Present, and Future. *Journal of International Economic Law*, 6(4):797–839.

Walker, R., and S. Mendlovitz (Eds.). 1990. *Contending Sovereignties: Redefining Political Communities*. Boulder, CO: Lynne Rienner.

White, N. 2017. Autonomous and Collective Sanctions in the International Legal Order. *Italian Year Book of International Law*, 27(2017):3–24.

White, N., and A. Abass. 2018. Countermeasures and Sanctions. In M. Evans (ed.), *International Law*. 5th ed., pp. 521–547. Oxford: Oxford University Press.

3

Legal Frameworks of US Economic and Financial Sanctions

I INTRODUCTION

The fierce force and sweeping reach of economic and financial sanctions adopted and imposed by the US have been underpinned by two highly formidable tools: (a) an exceedingly intricate and vastly sophisticated legal framework equipped with the necessary powers and authority granted to the president by the US Congress to adopt and enforce sanctioning measures during emergencies as well as non-emergencies; and (b) a massive infrastructure of economic and financial regulations, mechanisms, and networks capable of enforcing the proposed sanctions almost instantaneously, both domestically and internationally. Over the course of time, the US has not only made substantial investments in such legal frameworks and administrative mechanisms, but also perfected the system so meticulously that it provides "real value and options to presidents and congressional representatives alike" (Nephew, 2020, 112).

This chapter focuses on the first instrument – the legal frameworks for adopting and enforcing US economic and financial sanctions that prohibit US nationals as well as non-US nationals and non-US companies from engaging in economic and financial transactions with countries, entities, and individuals sanctioned by the US. The second instrument – the administrative and financial frameworks used for sanctions enforcement – is discussed in Chapter 4.

Apparently, the US adopted its first sanctioning statute in 1806 under President Thomas Jefferson (1801–1809). The statute – the Non-Importation Act of 1806 – banned certain imports from Great Britain in order to coerce the country to respect American sovereignty and neutrality during the Napoleonic Wars (1803–1815). The next year, the US enacted the Embargo Act of 1807 in response to attacks and harassment of US merchant vessels by some European colonial powers, primarily by the British Navy. Over the centuries, the US enforced numerous sanctions regimes, targeting numerous countries, entities, and individuals. As of June 2023, the US maintained more than 30 sanctions regimes targeting countries,[1] and designating

[1] In June 2023, lists of countries under the Office of Foreign Assets Control (OFAC) of the US Treasury Department included: Belarus, Burundi, Central African Republic, Cuba, Democratic Republic of

over 12,000 individuals and entities around the world in its Specially Designated Nationals and Blocked Persons (SDN) List.[2]

The US Constitution grants shared authority to the president and Congress with respect to foreign affairs. Article II of the Constitution grants the president the power to make treaties and appoint ambassadors "with the Advice and Consent of the Senate." Article I of the Constitution, however, grants power to the Congress to "regulate commerce with foreign nations." Over the course of time, events like the world wars, the Great Depression, and the Cold War, have propelled Congress to grant significantly more authority to the president in foreign affairs. As a result, the president can now exert nearly unfettered authority to limit bilateral programs, such as cutting off economic assistance to a foreign country, and ban exports. The president's authority to restrict imports and control foreign loans by private US banks and international financial institutions is somewhat restrained, however, although the president can bypass such limitations by declaring a national emergency.[3]

Thus, US presidents derive their authority to adopt and impose economic and financial sanctions against other countries from both emergency and non-emergency powers granted to them by the Constitution and Congressional statutes. Aside from the Constitution, as of 2021, the president had more than 120 statutes at their disposal to invoke such authorities (Boyle and Lau, 2021). Scholars agree, however, that no coherent and comprehensive analysis of the laws and regulations that govern such sanctions regimes currently exists. Also, the existing laws, as Barry Carter (1999) rightly pointed out in his seminal work, are at best "haphazard" in nature.[4]

the Congo, Iran, Iraq, Lebanon, Libya, Mali, Nicaragua, North Korea, Somalia, South Sudan, Sudan, Syria, Ukraine, Russia, Venezuela, Yemen, and Zimbabwe. For greater detail, see: www.treasury.gov/ofac/downloads/sdnlist.pdf.

2 On June 1, 2023, OFAC's SDN List was 2,184 pages long. Designation in the SDN List means the assets of such persons and entities are blocked and US persons (defined below) are generally prohibited from dealing with them. In addition to the SDN List, the OFAC also maintains: (a) the Sectoral Sanctions Identification List (SSI List), which restricts certain transactions with entities; (b) the List of Foreign Financial Institutions Subject to Correspondent Account or Payable-Through Account Sanctions (the CAPTA List), which includes foreign financial institutions that are subject to Correspondent Account sanctions; and (c) the OFAC Consolidated Sanctions List, which incorporates all US economic sanctions lists administered by OFAC. See www.treasury.gov/ofac/downloads/sdnlist.pdf.

3 National emergency generally refers to a situation in which a government is empowered to perform certain actions that are not normally permitted. In the context of the US, a declaration of national emergency is guided by 50 *U.S. Code § 1621: Declaration of National Emergency by President*, which states: "With respect to Acts of Congress authorizing the exercise, during the period of a national emergency, of any special or extraordinary power, the President is authorized to declare such national emergency. Such proclamation shall immediately be transmitted to the Congress and published in the Federal Register." Also see *the National Emergencies Act of* 1976 (NEA: P.L. 94-412, title II, §201; 90 Stat. 1255).

4 Some recent works on US sanctions laws, such as Gordon et al. (2019) and Hirschhorn et al. (2022), provide excellent updates on some areas of the US sanctions laws and regulations. They are, however, focused more on legal practice rather than scholarly interpretations of the US sanctions laws.

Some of the major statutes that govern the adoption and enforcement of US economic and financial sanctions can be identified as follows: (a) the Trading with the Enemy Act (TWEA: P.L. 65-91), which permits the president to declare a foreign country an enemy of the US and then preclude a range of economic activities with the associated government and its companies; (b) the Immigration and Nationality Act of 1952 (INA: 8 U.S.C. 1158), which grants the president the authority to refuse or nullify visas for individuals deemed a security risk to the US; (c) the Foreign Assistance Act of 1961 (FAA: P.L. 87-195), which grants the president the power to regulate foreign aid and assistance programs; (d) the National Emergencies Act of 1976 (NEA: P.L. 94-412), which terminated all authorities possessed by the president as a result of any past declaration of a national emergency with a few exceptions; (e) the Arms Export Control Act of 1976 (AECA: P.L. 94-329), which grants the president the power to control export and trade in arms; (f) the International Emergency Economic Powers Act of 1977 (IEEPA: P.L. 95-223), which grants the president authority to impose sanctions at any time by invoking emergency in the national interest; and (g) the Export Administration Act of 1979 (EAA: P.L. 96-72) which allows the president to control exports from sanctioned countries and entities.

Some other statutes that have powerful bearings on the presidential authority over sanctions, either in general or with respect to a particular target, include the following: (a) the United Nations Participation Act of 1945 (UNPA: P.L. 89-474), which authorizes the president to act in compliance with sanctions adopted by the UNSC; (b) the Cuban Democracy Act of 1992 (CDA: H.R. 4168) and Cuban Liberty and Democratic Solidarity Act of 1996 (the Helms–Burton Act: P.L. 104-114), which require the president to maintain sanctions against Cuba until certain requirements are met; (c) the Iran Sanctions Act of 1996 (ISA: P.L. 104-172), which requires the president to impose sanctions in certain circumstances on third-country companies that do business with Iran; (d) the Trade Sanctions Reform and Export Enhancement Act of 2012 (TSRA: 22 U.S.C. § 7207), which imposed strict payment requirements with regard to Cuba; (e) the Sergei Magnitsky Rule of Law Accountability Act of 2012 (Magnitsky Act: P.L. 112-208), which requires the president to impose sanctions on those who commit human rights abuses against individuals fighting to expose illegal activity by the Russian government or to defend human rights; (f) the Global Magnitsky Human Rights Accountability Act of 2016 (P.L. 114-328), which expands the president's power to apply similar sanctions on government officials and to protect human rights defenders around the world; (g) the Countering America's Adversaries through Sanctions Act of 2017 (CAATSA: P. L. 115-44), which tightened sanctions against Iran, North Korea, and Russia, and limited the president's ability to end or even liberalize the sanctions against Russia without Congressional approval.

The US sanctions regimes, thus, draw their authority from both emergency and non-emergency statutes. The discussion of US legal frameworks on sanctions is organized as follows: The next section explains the emergency statutes; Section

III discusses the non-emergency statutes; Section IV explains the statutes that govern trade-related sanctions; Section V explains the statutes that relate to sanctions against private financial transactions and international financial institutions; and Section VI concludes the chapter.

II SANCTIONS UNDER EMERGENCY LAWS

US presidents draw their emergency powers to adopt and impose sanctions regimes from three major Congressional statutes: (a) the TWEA (1917); (b) the NEA (1976), and (c) the IEEPA (1977). On top of that, Article II of the US Constitution grants the president nearly unlimited authority to declare a national emergency. To make such a declaration, all a president needs to do is to issue an Executive Order (EO) stating what constitutes the emergency, which powers are being used to deal with the emergency, which of the Congressional statutes is being invoked, and whether any other laws may be invoked. Neither the Congress nor the courts provide any practical oversight on presidential emergency declarations.[5]

A *The Trading with the Enemy Act, 1917*

The TWEA was the first major Congressional statute that granted US presidents sweeping emergency powers. Congress passed as many as 22 statutes during WWI empowering the president to take control of private property for public use during the war – the TWEA was a part of the package. The Act granted the president extraordinary authority over international trade and investment, and communications between the US and its enemies, encompassing railroads and shipyards; telegraph, telephone, and water systems; as well as many other sectors of the economy. Most importantly, the Act essentially left such unfettered authority to presidential discretion, over both domestic and international economic arenas, without any Congressional review (Gordon et al., 2019, 2–3; Rathbone et al., 2013, 1063–1064).

The TWEA defined the legal concept of "enemy" in an extraordinary context; the definition included "any individual, partnership, or other body of individuals [including corporations], of any nationality, resident within the territory … of any nation with which the United States is at war, or resident outside of the United States and doing business within such a territory" (cited in Casey, 2020, 3). The Act thus established its jurisdiction over all US persons anywhere in the world, as well as

5 As of 2020, Congress had delegated at least 136 distinct statutory emergency powers to the president, each available upon the declaration of an emergency through an EO, and only 13 of those required a declaration from Congress. Since 1976, US presidents have declared national emergencies more than 60 times – as many as 31 of them are being renewed annually. Prior to the enactment of NEA (1976), which streamlined the process, there were only eight instances of presidential national emergency declarations. For greater detail, see "A Guide to Emergency Powers and Their Use," December 5, 2018, last updated April 24, 2020, Brennan Center for Justice, New York University School of Law: www.brennancenter.org/our-work/research-reports/guide-emergency-powers-and-their-use.

any foreign entities and foreign subsidiaries of US companies owned or controlled by US persons.[6]

The TWEA's grant of expansive powers to the president was, however, limited to times of war, and the transactions covered by the Act had to be executed wholly within the US. The Act also did not include any provision for the president to use it to declare a national emergency in peacetime. After WWI, in 1921, Congress terminated many of the wartime powers granted to the president, but specifically exempted the TWEA to allow the president to dispose of a large amount of alien property then in government custody.

During the Great Depression, however, Congress reversed course by dramatically expanding the scope of the TWEA to empower the president to declare a state of emergency in peacetime as well. The expansion came following President Franklin Roosevelt's proclamation of a bank holiday in 1933, which suspended all transactions of banking institutions located in the US and its territories for four days, pursuant to Section 5(b) of the TWEA, although this provision at the time was applicable only during wartime.

Congress ratified Roosevelt's actions retroactively three days after his proclamation by enacting the Emergency Banking Relief Act of 1933 (P.L. 73-1, 48) and by amending the TWEA to allow the president to use the Act by declaring a national emergency.[7] Presidents were thus empowered to use the TWEA for both wartime as well peacetime sanctions and, up to the early 1970s, presidents used such powers as the central means to impose sanctions as a part of the Cold War strategy (Carter, 1999, 1230–1231).

President Truman, for example, invoked the TWEA's national emergency powers in 1950 to impose economic sanctions on North Korea and China, and President Nixon used it in 1970 and 1971 to impose sanctions on Vietnam, Cuba, and Cambodia. President Ford invoked the TWEA to continue export controls when the EAA (1976) expired. Overall, the TWEA was used numerous times to issue presidential EOs for imposing sanctions to block international financial transactions, seize US-based assets held by foreign nationals, restrict exports, deter the hoarding of gold, limit foreign direct investment of US companies, impose tariffs on US imports, and so on.[8]

[6] Subsequently, however, confronting resistance from US allies over such a broad jurisdiction of the Act over foreign-incorporated entities, in the 1970s the US adopted an administrative policy of enforcing such jurisdictions narrowly. The statutory reach of "US person" still reached foreign branches of US companies, although separately incorporated subsidiaries were spared (Beckhy, 2018).

[7] The amended Section 5(b) of TWEA reads: "During time of war or during any other period of national emergency declared by the President, the President may, through any agency that he may designate, or otherwise, investigate, regulate, or prohibit" (cited in Casey, 2020, 5).

[8] Presidential EOs issued to declare national emergencies under the TWEA include: 10348 (Apr. 26, 1952); 11677 (Aug. 1, 1972); 11683 (Aug. 29, 1972); 11796 (July 30, 1974); 11798 (Aug. 14, 1974); 11810 (Sept. 30, 1974); 11818 (Nov. 5, 1974); 11940 (Sept. 30, 1976); 10896 (Nov. 29, 1960); 11037 (July 20, 1962); and 11387 (Jan. 1, 1968). See the chronicles of the EOs in Casey (2020, 5–6).

Major concerns with the TWEA have been that: The Act granted nearly unlimited powers to the president (Gordon et al., 2019, 2–3); the powers were not subject to Congressional review (Rathbone et al., 2013, 1063–1064); and presidents often used such powers for actions unrelated to the declared national emergencies (Carter, 1999, 1231). President Roosevelt, as explained above, invoked the TWEA to declare a bank holiday in 1933, when the Act granted the president no such powers. Then, during the 1950s through the early 1970s, several presidents restricted trade and other financial transactions with unfriendly countries, such as China, North Korea, Cuba, Vietnam, and Cambodia, by using the national emergency powers of the TWEA. President Nixon even used it in 1971 to impose a 10-percent surcharge on US imports.

Such concerns over the overuse and overreach of the TWEA led Congress to enact the NEA in 1976, which terminated all authority possessed by the president as a result of past declarations of national emergencies, except certain emergency statutes deemed necessary for the continued functioning of the government (Carter, 1999, 1232). The next year, in 1977, Congress amended the TWEA to limit its application to during wartime only and for declared emergencies. As a result, only the previously declared economic sanctions imposed against Cuba, North Korea, Vietnam, and Cambodia continued under the amended TWEA.[9]

B *The International Emergency Economic Powers Act, 1977*

Congressional reform of the president's emergency powers under the TWEA came in two separate Acts. The first was the NEA (1976), which not only provided for the termination of all existing emergencies under the TWEA, albeit except those based on Section 5(b) of the TWEA, but also imposed new restrictions on the president concerning the manner and duration of national emergency declarations and empowered Congress to conduct a biannual review of such declarations, and termination of moot emergencies through privileged concurrent resolutions (Casey, 2020, 8).

Second, Congress in 1977 enacted the IEEPA to impose strict procedural limits on presidential powers in enforcing economic sanctions for foreign policy purposes during a declared national emergency only, as opposed to the TWEA which provided a statutory basis for the president to impose sanctions during a war as well as

[9] The extraterritorial provisions of the TWEA were, however, vehemently opposed by US allies during the 1982 natural gas pipeline dispute, when President Ronald Reagan threatened to ban the use of American technology for the gas pipeline, demanding the then Soviet Union's withdrawal of martial law in Poland (Lowenfeld, 2002, 91–105). As Congress had never declared war since 1941, and presidents had not invoked the TWEA even in times of armed conflict, Congress grandfathered pre-existing TWEA sanctions by retaining the programs that were already ongoing under the TWEA. Over time, however, such programs dwindled only to the sanctions programs pertaining to Cuba (Beckhy, 2018; Carter, 1999, 1231).

a national emergency. But in the end, Congress left the presidential powers "sufficiently broad and flexible" to enable the president to respond "as appropriate and necessary" to address unforeseen contingencies (Carter, 1999, 1232).

The IEEPA thus enables the president to take a broad array of actions in the name of threats to national security, foreign policy, or the economy, and such actions may include cutting off exports or imports, freezing assets, or restricting private financial transactions during peacetime, and in times of armed hostilities, confiscation of property subject to US jurisdiction of any foreign person, entity, or country.[10] The IEEPA requires the president to submit a report to Congress about the nature of the emergency and the actions taken, but there is no requirement on the president to provide any assessment of the probable consequences of the actions taken (Nephew, 2020).

Although the IEEPA provides certain procedural improvements over the TWEA, it also contains some built-in flaws. For example, while the TWEA provides no definition of "national emergency," §1701 of IEEPA (50 U.S.C. 1982) defines national emergency as an "unusual and extraordinary threat, which has its source in whole or substantial part outside the United States, to the national security, foreign policy, or economy of the United States." But the determination of such threats is left completely to the discretion of the president. As the criteria for determining an "unusual and extraordinary threat" are very broad, the president can invoke the statute to declare a national emergency even in minor disputes, and as declaring a national emergency requires only a brief EO, the president can do so on dubious grounds as well (Carter, 1999, 1234–1235).

Moreover, the reliance of the president on classified information to declare a national emergency requires only a modest standard of proof ("a reasonable basis to believe"), and the president is not required to provide prior notification to potential designations. Over the decades, such loopholes have allowed both Democratic and Republican presidents to use the IEEPA for political expediency – they have invoked the statute for issues that merited sanctions, such as the proliferation of weapons of mass destruction in the case of North Korea or Iran, and some issues that "may be troubling but objectively unlikely to be actually threatening," like the suppression of human rights in Venezuela (Gordon et al., 2019, 1–5 & 3–89).

Second, the IEEPA requires the president to deal with any new threat with a new declaration of national emergency, but it does not bar the president from using the same EO for imposing or adding new designations.[11] For example, EO 12170 was issued by President Jimmy Carter in 1979, more than four decades ago, to declare a national emergency in response to the Iranian Hostage Crisis and to initiate

[10] The IEEPA's grant of powers to the president, however, excludes the power to take title to foreign property, regulate purely domestic transactions, regulate gold or bullion, seize records, and interfere with the international flow of mail or other communications (Carter, 1999, 1239).

[11] See §1702 of IEEPA (50 U.S.C. 1982).

sanctions against Iran. It has been renewed by every president every year ever since,[12] and as explained below, many other EOs have also been renewed many times.

Third, the IEEPA directs the president to consult "in every possible instance" with Congress and "immediately report" to Congress any actions taken under the statute.[13] Also, while enacting the IEEPA, the Congressional leadership emphasized that the use of the statute should be "rare and brief," and it should not be used for "normal, ongoing problems" (Casey, 2020, 8). But the statute only encourages the president to consult Congress; Such consultations are not mandatory, and such a provision hardly deters presidents from using the statute at their discretion (Carter, 1999, 1234–1235).

Finally, the IEEPA delineates three mechanisms for the cessation of a formally declared national emergency: (a) the president possesses the authority to terminate it at their discretion; (b) an automatic termination ensues unless the president opts to renew the emergency within a one-year timeframe; and (c) Congress retains the prerogative to conclude a declared emergency through a joint resolution at any juncture. In the event of a presidential veto, Congress can override it by securing a two-thirds majority in both chambers.[14]

Amendments to the IEEPA

The IEEPA was amended eight times between 1977 and 2007.[15] Five of the amendments altered civil and criminal penalties for violations of orders issued under the Act.[16] Others excluded certain informational materials and expanded the IEEPA's scope following the terrorist attacks of September 11, 2001 (9/11), as part of the Patriot Act,[17] which, among other things, empowered the president to vest frozen assets under certain circumstances and block assets during the pendency of an investigation. The Patriot Act also clarified the types of interest in property subject to the IEEPA, emphasized targeted sanctions aimed at individuals and entities engaged in terrorism-related activities and the proliferation of weapons of mass destruction, and provided for judicial review of sanctions designations (Casey, 2020, 14–16).[18]

12 Most recently the EO was renewed by President Joe Biden in November 2023.

13 See §1703 of IEEPA (50 U.S.C. 1982).

14 Originally, the IEEPA provided for a concurrent resolution of Congress for termination of a declared emergency, but following the Supreme Court's ruling in *INS v. Chadha* (462 U.S. at 954–955), it replaced the provision in 1986 by a joint resolution. More on this case below.

15 In the years 1992 (twice), 1994, 1996, 2001, 2006, and 2007. See Table 1 in Casey (2020) for greater detail.

16 In the original IEEPA, §1705 provided a civil penalty of a maximum of $250,000 or twice the amount of the transaction that was the basis of the IEEPA violation. The amended IEEPA raised the civil penalty to a maximum of $300,000, or twice the amount of the transaction that was the basis of the violation. The maximum criminal penalty for a willful violation of the IEEPA now stands at $1 million, 20 years imprisonment, or both (Gordon et al., 2019, 3–14).

17 See The Uniting and Strengthening America by Providing Appropriate Tools Required to Intercept and Obstruct Terrorism (USA Patriot Act) of 2001 (P.L. 107-56: 115 Stat. 272).

18 For greater detail, see P.L. 107-56 §106, 115 Stat. 277 (2001); P.L. 107-56 §106, codified at 50 U.S.C. §1702(a)(1)(B) (2018); P.L. 107-56 §106, codified at 50 U.S.C. §1702(a) (2018); and P.L. 107-56 §106, codified at 50 U.S.C. §1702(c) (2018).

Title III of the Patriot Act – the International Money Laundering Abatement and Anti-Terrorist Financing Act of 2001 – has been especially instrumental in criminalizing the financing of terrorism around the world. The Act not only allows the Treasury Department to leverage the entire US financial system to persuade foreign banks to stop transactions with terrorism-related financing, it also allows the Treasury Department to impose "special measures" against foreign jurisdictions or foreign financial institutions determined to be money laundering concerns and to freeze monetary assets anywhere in the world that the Treasury deems threatening to US national security interests (Gottemoeller, 2007; Nephew, 2020).

In 2018, Congress passed the Export Control Reform Act (ECRA: P.L. 115-232), repealing the expired AEA of 1979, which, among others, required the president to continue to use the IEEPA to implement not-repealed sections of the AEA (Hirschhorn, 2022, 2–25).[19]

Application of the IEEPA Emergencies

Although the IEEPA was apparently designed to limit presidential authority, albeit in comparison with the TWEA, the proliferation of sanctions regulations since its enactment in 1977 and Congressional concerns raised over the decades suggest that the statute may have actually boosted presidential authority rather than limiting it (Gordon et al., 2019, 3–14). Presidents have used this as the primary statutory authority for imposing economic and financial sanctions in 65 of the 71 emergency declarations made since 1977 (Boyle and Lau, 2021), and most of them did so without major Congressional opposition (Goldsmith, 2019).[20]

Such declarations have proliferated in recent decades as the IEEPA requires the president to make a new declaration for each independent use of the statute. Records suggest that, on average, national emergencies invoked under the IEEPA lasted for more than nine years, but the longest has been President Carter's declaration in response to the Iranian Hostage Crisis of 1979.[21] Six successive presidents have renewed that emergency annually for nearly 40 years, and it is still in effect.[22]

Prior to 1990, the IEEPA was used to target a country or a government, but in 1990 President George H. W. Bush invoked the statute for the first time to direct

[19] As explained below, the not-repealed sections of the AEA (1979) are Sections 11A, 11B, and 11C of the Act. Also see Hirschhorn (2022, 2–25) for an elaborate discussion on the regulations affected by the enactment of the ECRA (2018).

[20] In 2015, however, Congress raised a serious concern when it passed the Iran Nuclear Agreement Review Act (INARA), imposing several conditions on President Obama for implementing the JCPOA that his administration negotiated with Iran and requiring the president to satisfy those conditions before implementing the JCPOA the next year. In another recent instance, in 2017, Congress barred President Trump from lifting sanctions imposed on the Russian Federation. More on this in Chapter 5.

[21] President Carter was also the first president to use the IEEPA – he used the emergency powers of the statute in 1979 to freeze around $12 billion of Iranian assets, to cut off US trade with Iran, and to ban travel to Iran. President Reagan invoked the IEEPA three times between 1985 and 1987 – against Nicaragua in 1985, South Africa in 1985, and Libya in 1986 (Carter, 1999, 1233–1234).

[22] See Casey (2020, 16) for the timeline of applications of the IEEPA between 1979 and 2020.

it to a targeted sanction – his EO 12735 targeted threats posed by the proliferation of chemical and biological weapons. Since then, especially since 9/11, the IEEPA has increasingly been used to target groups and individuals associated with scores of issues, such as terrorism, money laundering, drug trafficking, malicious cyber activities, and so on.[23]

The IEEPA's Jurisdiction over US Persons

One of the far-reaching elements of the IEEPA statute has been that, in contrast to the TWEA, the IEEPA's jurisdiction over "US persons" includes all US citizens and permanent residents, all persons physically located in the US, and all entities organized under the laws of the US.[24] Title 50 of IEEPA – War and National Defense – states, "The term 'United States person' means any United States citizen, permanent resident alien, entity organized under the laws of the United States (including foreign branches), or any person in the United States."[25]

The last part of the definition, "Any person in the United States," implies that anybody physically on the soil of US territories will be subject to US sanctions. That also implies that the IEEPA's jurisdiction of "US persons" not only includes all people in the US – citizens, green card holders, and so on – but also any foreign citizen and corporate person who happens to be in the US territories. Thus, tourists and corporate persons who happen to be in the US also cannot do any business with individuals and entities who are designated by US sanctions, and that what is designated as "US persons" by the statute, in practice, is not limited to the ordinary understanding of who is actually a US person (Breen, 2018, 258–259).

The 2007 IEEPA amendment –the International Emergency Economic Powers Enhancement Act of 2007 (P.L. 110-96) – further expanded the definition of "US persons" by adding the notion of "causing." The amendment makes it "unlawful" "for a person to violate, attempt to violate, conspire to violate or cause a violation of

[23] For example, President George W. Bush issued EO 13224 (Blocking Property and Prohibiting Transactions With Persons Who Commit, Threaten to Commit, or Support Terrorism) on September 23, 2001 in response to the threat posed by terrorism; President Obama issued EO 13694 (Blocking the Property of Certain Persons Engaging in Significant Malicious Cyber-Enabled Activities) on April 1, 2015 to address threats from persons engaged in malicious cyber-enabled activities; and President Trump issued EO 13873 (Securing the Information and Communications Technology and Services Supply Chain) on May 14, 2019 targeting foreign individuals and entities involved in exploiting vulnerabilities in information and communications technologies and services. President Trump also used the IEEPA to sanction members of the prosecutors at the International Criminal Court who investigated potential war crimes in Afghanistan and in the Israel–Palestine conflict. The Biden Administration, however, reversed those sanctions in 2021. For greater detail, see Boyle and Lau (2021).

[24] Title 50 of IEEPA – War and National Defense (50 USC Ch. 35, Section 4 (7)) states:

> The term "United States person" means any United States citizen, permanent resident alien, entity organized under the laws of the United States (including foreign branches), or any person in the United States. … "Any person in the United States," implies anybody physically on the soil of US territories, but diplomats would be excluded under diplomatic protection treaties.

[25] 50 USC Ch. 35, Section 4 (7).

the Act." The amended IEEPA thus spills over to non-US persons who may *cause* a US person to violate the Act, no matter whether deliberately or inadvertently.[26]

As mentioned above, the expanded jurisdiction of the IEEPA drew considerable criticism, especially from allies of the US, since the very beginning, as many foreign subsidiaries of US companies are registered in foreign countries under the laws of those countries, with which they must abide. As early as 1987, the IEEPA's extraterritorial reach of "US persons" encountered such a legal challenge in a London court.[27] Also, as discussed below, many US allies, including the EU and Canada, have enacted blocking statutes to shelter US subsidiaries registered in their countries from the jurisdiction of US sanctions regimes.

The IEEPA's expansive interpretation of "US persons" has also been criticized on the grounds of "due process" of law. Although sanctions targets are overwhelmingly foreign, the Office of Foreign Assets Control (OFAC) never gives any notice of a "wrongful act"; the targets are not even entitled to see the evidence against them before they are designated under any sanctions regime; and any attempts to seek relief in US courts are also futile as the statutes require the courts to grant substantial deference to the executive branch.[28]

Judicial Interventions

The IEEFA has confronted few legal challenges over the decades, mainly because the legal basis for sanctions under the statute has been tied to national security and historically the judiciary afforded extreme deference to the president's emergency powers (Vazquez, 2003, 824). There have been many lawsuits,[29] however, which

[26] As discussed in greater detail in Chapter 4, in recent years, by interpreting the IEEPA's jurisdiction over "US persons" in an expansive manner, OFAC has brought charges of "transaction stripping" against scores of non-US banks, including the German Deutsche Bank, French BNP Paribas and Credit Agricole, Dutch ING Bank, and British Standard Chartered and HSBC. All these banks paid billions of dollars in penalties for making US dollar transactions with banned countries, individuals, and entities by using the US banking system (Breen 2018, 258–259; Emmenegger, 2016).

[27] In the legal challenge brought before an English court in 1987, *Libyan Arab Foreign Bank v. Bankers' Trust Co.*, the court ruled that the Bankers' Trust was obligated to pay the Libyan Arab Foreign Bank $292.5 million in funds that the Libyan bank had deposited with Bankers' Trust, which the US bank froze in accordance with US sanctions on Libya imposed in January 1986. The case originated from the fact that about half of the money was in the London branch of Bankers' Trust and the other half was with a US bank, which the US bank failed to transfer, as directed by the Libyan bank, to its London branch prior to the freeze. In its decision, the court adjudged that the UK law (the law of the place) applied to accounts in the UK, even in the branches of a US bank. Obliging the judgment, the Bankers' Trust paid the Libyan bank $292.5 million, plus $28 million in interest. For further details, see Libyan Arab Foreign Bank v. Bankers Trust Co. (1988) *American Journal of International Law*, 82(1), 132–136.

[28] The instances of lack of procedural protection have indeed increased manifold since 9/11, as the US designated many Muslim American individuals and charitable organizations as "terrorists," and forced many Muslim charities to shut down, and did so without showing any evidence. The 9/11 Commission subsequently acknowledged that "some of the evidentiary foundations for the early designations (of terrorism) were quite weak" (Breen, 2018, 259).

[29] See Casey (2020, 34) for a list of challenges to the IEEPA in US lower courts.

sought to overturn the actions taken pursuant to the IEEPA on various grounds of, for example, exceeding the breadth of congressionally delegated authority or violations of constitutional rights, but almost all of them failed, and those that succeeded also did not seriously undermine the overarching statutory authority embodied in the statute for imposing sanctions (Casey, 2020, 33–35).

Two US Supreme Court decisions, in *US v. Curtiss-Wright Export Corporation* (1936) and *Youngstown Sheet & Tube Company v. Sawyer* (1952), however, have come down as touchstone cases for the presidential power under the IEEPA. In *Curtiss-Wright*, the court held that the president has exclusive power over foreign policy and does not need Congress to delegate power in this area, and that President Roosevelt acted within his constitutional authority when he brought charges against the Curtiss-Wright Export Corporation for selling arms to Paraguay and Bolivia in violation of federal law.[30]

In *Youngstown*, the US Supreme Court took an opposite position – it signaled willingness to address a "political question" and serve as a check on presidential powers.[31] The case was brought by steel companies when President Harry Truman seized control of steel production facilities during the Korean War. The companies challenged the seizure on the grounds that the president lacked the power to seize private property without express authorization from Congress. In its majority opinion, the court agreed with the steel companies.[32]

[30] In *United States v. Curtiss-Wright Export Corp.* [299 U.S. 304 (1936)], Justice George Sutherland held that the US president is "the sole organ of the federal government in the field of international relations … (and)… He, not Congress, has the better opportunity of knowing conditions which prevail in foreign countries and especially is this true in time of war."

[31] See *Youngstown Sheet & Tube Co. v. Sawyer*, 343 U.S. 579 (1952).

[32] *Youngstown*, however, came down as a landmark Supreme Court case because of the three-tiered framework that Justice Robert Jackson used for evaluating the presidential powers vis-à-vis Congress. The framework still serves as the standard for evaluating executive action. Justice Jackson explained the framework as follows:

> First, "[w]hen the President acts pursuant to an express or implied authorization of Congress, his authority is at its maximum, for it includes all that he possesses in his own right plus all that Congress can delegate"; Second, "[w]hen the President acts in absence of either a congressional grant or denial of authority, he can only rely upon his own independent powers, but there is a zone of twilight in which he and Congress may have concurrent authority, or in which its distribution is uncertain." In such a circumstance, Presidential authority can derive support from "congressional inertia, indifference or quiescence." Finally, "[w]hen the President takes measures incompatible with the expressed or implied will of Congress, his power is at its lowest ebb," and the Court can sustain his actions "only by disabling the Congress from acting upon the subject" (Youngstown, 343 U.S. at 635–638).

The "political question" doctrine, however, prevents the US Supreme Court from taking sides on major constitutional issues. In *Goldwater v. Carter* (1979), for example, the court dismissed a lawsuit filed by Senator Barry Goldwater and other members of Congress challenging the right of President Carter to unilaterally nullify the Sino-American Mutual Defense Treaty. The lawmakers claimed that the president could not terminate a defense pact with Taiwan without congressional approval. The Supreme Court dismissed the case after a majority of justices found the underlying issue was a "political question," and thus lay outside the scope of their review: *Goldwater v. Carter*, 444 U.S. 996 (1979).

Some of the other notable challenges to the IEEPA that reached the US Supreme Court include *Dames & Moore v. Regan* and *INS v. Chadha*.[33] In *Dames & Moore*, the petitioners challenged President Carter's EO issued in furtherance of compliance with the terms of the Algiers Accords to bring an end to the Iranian Hostage Crisis. The Algiers Accord obligated the US to terminate all legal proceedings in US courts involving claims of US nationals against Iran, to nullify all attachments and judgments, and to resolve outstanding claims exclusively through binding arbitration by the Iran–US Claims Tribunal set up in the Hague. Subsequent executive orders revoked all licenses that permitted the exercise of any right, power, or privilege with regard to Iranian funds, nullified all non-Iranian interests in assets, and required banks holding Iranian assets to transfer them to the Federal Reserve Bank of New York to be held or transferred as directed by the US Treasury Department (Casey, 2020, 33). But the plaintiffs, Dames and Moore, claimed that the president and the secretary of the Treasury Department had exceeded their statutory and constitutional powers to the extent they adversely affected the judgment against Iran, the execution of that judgment, the prejudgment attachments, and the plaintiffs' ability to continue to litigate against the Iranian banks. The US Supreme Court, citing *Youngstown*, ruled that Congress's implicit approval of the longstanding presidential practice of settling international claims by executive agreement was critical to its holding that the challenged actions were not in conflict with the Acts of Congress (Carter, 1999, 1241–43).[34]

In *INS v. Chadha*, the US Supreme Court struck down legislative vetoes, holding that Congress cannot void the exercise of power by the executive branch through concurrent resolution.[35] Accordingly, in 1985, Congress amended the NEA (1976) requiring termination of national emergencies via a joint resolution by both houses of Congress. That means, Congress can terminate a declared emergency by a joint

[33] See *Dames & Moore*, 453 U.S. at 678–679; *INS v. Chadha*, 462 U.S. at 954–955.

[34] Also see *Dames & Moore*, 453 U.S. at 678–679.

[35] *INS v. Chadha* involved an alien who was lawfully admitted to the US on a non-immigrant student visa, who remained in the US after the expiry of his visa, prompting the INS to seek his deportation. Chadha then applied for suspension of the deportation order. An Immigration Judge, acting pursuant to §244(a)(1) of the Immigration Act, ordered the suspension, and reported the suspension to Congress as required by §244(c)(1) of Act. Thereafter, the House of Representatives passed a resolution pursuant to §244(c)(2) vetoing the suspension, and the Immigration Judge reopened the deportation proceedings. Chadha moved to terminate the proceedings on the ground that §244(c)(2) was unconstitutional, but the judge held that he had no authority to rule on its constitutionality, and ordered that Chadha be deported pursuant to the House Resolution. Chadha then appealed to the Board of Immigration Appeals, but it was dismissed on the ground that the Board had no power to declare §244(c)(2) unconstitutional. Chadha then filed a petition for review of the deportation order in the Court of Appeals, which ruled that §244(c)(2) of the Immigration Act violated the constitutional doctrine of separation of powers, and accordingly directed the Attorney General to cease taking any steps to deport Chadha based upon the House Resolution. See *INS v. Chadha*, 462 U.S. at 954–955.

resolution, but the bill still needs the president's signature to become law, and if the president vetoes it, then Congress would need a supermajority to override it.[36]

III SANCTIONS UNDER NON-EMERGENCY LAWS

In the absence of, and in addition to, a declared national emergency, US presidents can draw upon scores of non-emergency statutes and regulations that grant them extensive authority to impose sanctions with respect to various areas and issues. The discussion here is focused on the presidential sanctioning powers in economic and financial matters involving: (a) foreign assistance and bilateral agreements; (b) export controls; (c) import controls; (d) private financial transactions; and (e) international financial institutions.

A *Foreign Assistance and Bilateral Agreements*

US presidents can exercise extensive powers to impose sanctions on the grounds of foreign policy interests and objectives. Article II of the Constitution grants the president explicit power to appoint and receive ambassadors, and implied powers to recognize foreign governments and conduct diplomacy with the "advice and consent" of the Senate.[37] In addition, as the commander-in-chief, the president enjoys broad constitutional powers to use military force and collect foreign intelligence.[38]

[36] Mustering a supermajority is not always an easy task, however. For example, on February 15, 2019, President Trump invoked emergency powers to fund the Border Wall along the US southern borders by using a statute called the Military Construction Codification Act of 1982, which allows the president to divert funds to military construction projects. But the declaration of national emergency was voted down by the House (248–181) and the Senate (53–36). President Trump vetoed the bill, but Congress failed to muster a veto-proof majority. President Biden terminated the emergency immediately after assuming office. Thus, when it comes to a declaration of emergency, it is the president, not the Congress, who holds the cards in both adopting and terminating them.

[37] The Constitution requires the consent of a simple majority of the Senate for presidential appointments of ambassadors, but treaties with foreign countries or entities require the approval of two-thirds of senators present. The Constitution is, however, silent about the presidential power with respect to ending a treaty. Over the years, the US Senate has approved more than 1,600 treaties, but also rejected or refused to consider many. Based on www.cfr.org/backgrounder/us-foreign-policy-powers-congress-and-president. Famously, Senate rejected the Treaty of Versailles negotiated by President Woodrow Wilson after WWI to establish the League of Nations. More recently, Senate blocked ratification of the UN Convention of the Law of the Sea, which is widely considered as the "constitution of the oceans." The Convention, opened for signature in 1982 and entered into force in 1994, has been ratified by 154 states, including the EU. For greater detail, see legal.un.org/avl/ha/uncls/uncls.html.

[38] The presidential powers over the collection of intelligence, however, have come under serious Congressional scrutiny since the 1970s, particularly with the Church Committee chaired by Idaho Senator Frank Church in 1975. The Committee uncovered serious abuses of privacy (unauthorized surveillance of citizens) committed by various executive agencies, including the Central Intelligence Authority (CIA), the Federal Bureau of Investigation (FBI), and the National Security Agency (NSA). The statutes adopted as result of the inquiry imposed greater oversight to regulate intelligence gathering and supervise the executive branch's activities in these areas as well as covert operations: constitutioncenter.org/blog/looking-back-at-the-church-committee.

The president also enjoys broad constitutional powers to execute federal immigration laws, which allow them to block travels of foreign nationals on the grounds of national security.[39]

Presidents can also draw upon numerous statutory authorities that Congress has passed over the course of time granting them additional powers to act on specific foreign policy issues.[40] At the same time, presidential authority in US foreign policy issues, including foreign assistance, has also changed over the course of time due to changes in Congressional imperatives. Some of the major developments are summarized below.

The National Security Act of 1947

In the aftermath of WWII, the Congress enacted the National Security Act of 1947 (NSA: P.L. 80-253: codified as 50 U.S.C. 3021), empowering the president to integrate domestic, foreign, and military policies relating to national security. It is with this legislation that the US had assumed its position as global superpower in the post–WWII world, and granted the president legislative authority to mold world affairs in the country's security interests (Ginsberg, 2010). Among others, the country's global intelligence gathering agency – the CIA – was created in September 1947 under this Act.[41]

Earlier, the Congress enacted the United Nations Participation Act of 1945 (UNPA: P.L. 79-264), granting the president sweeping powers to set up the necessary executive machinery to comply with international commitments assumed by the US upon its ratification of the UN Charter and apply economic and other sanctions against a target country or its nationals pursuant to mandatory decisions made by the UN Security Council in pursuance of Article 41 of the UN Charter.[42]

On the other hand, in the aftermath of 9/11, Congress hugely expanded the government's surveillance power over citizens by enacting the Patriot Act (2001). For example, §215 of the Act – Records Searches – expands the government's ability to look at records on an individual's activity being held by third parties; §213 of the Act – Secret Searches – expands the government's ability to search private property without notice to the owner; §218 – Intelligence Searches – expands a narrow exception to the Fourth Amendment that had been created for the collection of foreign intelligence information; and §214 – Trap and Trace Searches – expands another Fourth Amendment exception for spying that collects information about the origin and destination of communications: www.aclu.org/documents/surveillance-under-usaPatriot-act.

39 The Constitution, however, grants Congress, not the president, "absolute authority" over immigration laws, and any authority of the president on immigration is thus subject to Congressional statutes or authorizations. More on this below.

40 There are literally hundreds of volumes of such statutes, in many cases each of them containing thousands of pages.

41 The NSA (1947) remained relatively unchanged until the Congress enacted the Intelligence Reform and Terrorism Prevention Act of 2004 (IRTPA: P.L. 108-458), which created the position of the Director of National Intelligence (DNI) for coordination of all US intelligence agencies. The NSA (1947) was amended again in December 2022 through P.L. 117–286.

42 The UNPA (1945), codified as 22 U.S.C. § 287c (1982), went through several amendments, including: the United Nations Reform Act of 1999 (P.L. 106–113), the United Nations Headquarters Agreement

The next major statute was the Economic Cooperation Act of 1948 (the Marshall Plan),[43] which granted the president enormous power to help rebuild the post–WWII war-torn Europe by removing trade barriers, stimulating economic prosperity, and preventing the spread of communism. The Marshall Plan not only helped Europe in avoiding the post-war humanitarian crisis, it also fostered one of the great military alliances in world history – as many as 13 European nations joined the North Atlantic Treaty Organization (NATO) by 1949 largely because of the Plan (McBride, 2018).

In 1951, the Congress passed the Mutual Security Act of 1951 (MSA: P.L. 82-165), which largely replaced the Marshall Plan but granted additional powers to the president to extend military, economic, and technical aid to Western European countries in order to check the former Soviet Union and the spread of communism.

The Foreign Assistance Act of 1961

The MSA (1951) was replaced by the Foreign Assistance Act of 1961 (FAA: P. L. 87-195), which still serves as the legal basis of the presidential powers in matters of US foreign assistance. Framed in the midst of the Cold War, the FAA further extended presidential powers by directing US foreign assistance programs toward much broader foreign policy objectives, such as: (a) to alleviate visible effects of poverty in the world; (b) to assist poor countries to attain equitable economic growth; (c) to encourage economic development along with civil and economic rights; (d) to integrate developing countries into market-oriented global economic system; and (e) to promote good governance through addressing corruption.[44]

The FAA grants the president unusual flexibility with respect to foreign assistance through five special authorities: (a) §506 of the Act – the drawdown authority – enables the president to provide emergency military assistance to a foreign government; (b) §610 of the Act – the transfer authority – enables the president to transfer foreign assistance funds between program accounts; (c) § 614(a) of the Act – the waiver authority – enables the president to waive provisions of a foreign assistance statute; (d) § 614(b) of the Act enabled the president to provide the Economic Support Fund (ESF) to Germany; and (e) § 614(c) of the Act – the cloaking authority – enables the president not to disclose foreign assistance-related actions and their funding sources. Presidents of both the Democratic and Republican parties have invoked such authorities at least 163 times since 1961 (GAO, 1985).[45]

Act (P.L. 80–357), and the U.S. Participation in Certain International Organizations Act (P.L. 81–806). Section 6 of the UNPA authorizes the president to negotiate a special agreement or agreements with the UNSC, but makes them subject to the approval of Congress. The Act does not, however, specifically require the president to obtain Congressional authorization to make available to the UNSC armed forces, facilities, or assistance in support of the UNSC resolutions.

43 Codified as 22 U.S.C. 1501 et seq.

44 The FAA (1961) was amended through P.L. 116-6, enacted on February 15, 2019.

45 Utilization of these special authorities depends on presidential certification known as a Presidential Determination (PD). Records suggest that presidents have used their "waiver authority" frequently – as

The FAA also centralized all US foreign aid efforts under a single agency, named the United States Agency for International Development (USAID), which serves as the president's primary arm of foreign assistance by maintaining a global aid system to bolster the US's geostrategic and security interests (Regilme and Hartmann, 2018). In 2020, USAID was the world's largest international assistance agency, disbursing over $50 billion in that year in about 100 countries.[46]

Congress, however, has modified its mandates for bilateral assistance programs multiple times. During the period between the end of WWII and the enactment of the FAA in 1961, Congressional grants of presidential powers for bilateral assistance were broad-based, expanding both vertically and horizontally, but since the early 1960s such powers were geared more to specific goals, such as food production, rural development, health, and education. Then, from the mid 1970s through the 1980s, US aid programs were more geared to specific countries, such as Vietnam, Korea, India, Israel, Egypt, El Salvador, Guatemala, and Costa Rica, and most of these programs were geared to military assistance largely aimed at curbing the spread of communism (Nephew, 2020).

Since the late 1990s, as the threat of communism largely dissipated, and especially since 9/11, Congress directed the presidential powers of foreign assistance to fight terrorism, which became a greater concern for national security. As a result, countries like Iraq and Afghanistan emerged as the biggest recipients of US foreign aid. Some foreign assistance, however, has also been directed to non-terrorism programs. For example, in 2003, President George Bush created the President's Emergency Plan for AIDS Relief for African countries; in 2004, Congress created the Millennium Challenge Program to assist developing nations in infrastructure and education to sustain economic growth and in raising living standards; and in 2010, President Barack Obama adopted the Presidential Policy Directive on Global Development, directing foreign assistance programs to economic and moral imperatives (Hillard and Schendruk, 2019).

Limits on Presidential Powers

While Congressional mandates often change presidential prerogatives to use bilateral foreign assistance programs as foreign policy tools, presidents themselves can also raise, cut back, and terminate economic and military assistance to other nations, depending on issues such as terrorism, expropriation of US property, money

many as 17 times between 1961 and 1985 involving $1.6 billion in foreign assistance – and about half of these were directed at emergencies or to deal with situations where formal assistance agreements were not available. It is also notable that, over the decades, Congress has revised, relaxed, reinstated, and expanded the president's drawdown authority many times. See GAO (1985) for further details.

46 In 2020, the US also provided $2.6 billion to the World Food Program, and $2.6 billion to the Global Fund to Fight AIDS, Tuberculosis and Malaria (USAID, 2021). The FAA allows the president to grant up to $50 million in foreign assistance to any foreign country without any restriction of aid laws (22 U.S.C. § 2364, 1982 & Supp. III1985) and the ceiling can be higher if the country is a victim of communist or communist-supported aggression (Christopher, 1982; Franck and Weisband, 1979).

laundering, and so on.[47] At the same time, Congress can also thwart the president's efforts to invoke sanctions by opposing presidential decisions not to spend authorized funds, or by authorizing new funds that the president opposes.[48]

One of the lingering issues with respect to the presidential powers centers on the declaration of war. Article I, Section 8, Clause 11 of US Constitution specifically grants the power to declare war to the Congress, but presidents have ordered US forces into hostilities abroad without Congressional authorization numerous times. After prolonged involvement of the US military in the Korean and Vietnam Wars in the 1950s and 1960s without Congressional authorization, toward the end of the Vietnam War, Congress passed the War Powers Resolution of 1973 (P.L. 93-148), over President Nixon's veto, to restrain the presidential power with respect to deploying armed forces abroad. The Resolution requires the president to notify Congress within 48 hours whenever military forces are deployed "into hostilities or into situations where imminent involvement in hostilities is clearly indicated by the circumstances."[49]

Overall, some scholars tend to argue that, over the decades, the president has accumulated considerably more foreign policy powers at the expense of Congress, and the presidential powers tend to overshadow those of Congress especially during times of war or national emergency, as the president enjoys natural advantages over Congress in foreign policy matters.[50]

B *Export Restrictions*

Traditionally, the US restricted exports only in times of war or in special emergency situations, but during both world wars the presidents were empowered to control all exports to all destinations. After the end of WWII, however, sweeping wartime presidential controls over exports continued until the Congress passed the Export Control Act of 1949 (ECA: P.L. 11-127). The ECA, the first comprehensive of export

[47] For example, the US manipulated food and economic aid to the United Arab Emirates (UAE), India, and Chile in the 1960s; and in the 1970s, cut off foreign aid to Allende's Chile, used a carrot-and-stick approach with military aid to Brazil, and curtailed Soviet fishing and landing rights after the 1979 invasion of Afghanistan (Hufbauer, 2007, 46).

[48] For example, in 1975–1978, over the objections of President Ford, Congress cut off most military assistance to Turkey because of its invasion of Cyprus. In 1985, after limiting the president to granting $27 million in humanitarian assistance for the Contras, Congress then appropriated $100 million in 1986 and attached fewer conditions. Similarly, in 1987, Congress cut off most foreign assistance to Haiti unless certain democratic processes were followed there, and conditioned most assistance to Panama to certification by the president that progress was being made toward civilian control of the Panamanian government (Carter, 1999, 1188).

[49] Since the passing of the Resolution in 1973, presidents have submitted over 132 reports of US military involvement abroad to Congress. But there have also been incidents when presidents chose not to report to Congress in a timely manner. For example, President Reagan's deployment of troops to El Salvador in 1981, President Clinton's bombing of Kosovo in 1999, and President Obama's military actions against Libya (2011) and Syria (2014), were not reported to Congress.

[50] See www.cfr.org/backgrounder/us-foreign-policy-powers-congress-and-president.

control legislation ever adopted by the Congress in peace time, however, instead of curtailing presidential powers over exports, granted the president nearly unfettered powers over it. Under the Act, the presidential power over exports was subject only to the vaguest standards of "foreign policy" and "national security and welfare," as the president could cut off the entire export trade, or any part of it, to any country, or deny "export privileges" to any or all persons (Berman and Garson, 1967).

The ECA also granted far-reaching extraterritorial authorities to the president. Under the Act, goods shipped with "general license," issued by the Department of Commerce, could be transshipped to another destination only if the goods were shipped there directly from the US; it was unlawful to divert, trans-ship, or re-export goods in violation of any export control document or prior representation; and the Transaction Controls regulations of the Act made it unlawful for any person situated in the US to ship commodities in the Positive List of the Commerce Department from one foreign country to another if such goods could not have been so shipped directly from the US; and goods moving through the US to the Soviet bloc were treated as goods originating in the US (Silverstone, 1959).

The procedures for implementing export controls were also left almost entirely to the presidential discretion, and violations of any export regulations carried heavy administrative and criminal sanctions. While the Commerce Department administered the ECA export regulations, the TWEA (1917), which the president could also invoke to restrict exports, was administered by the Treasury Department. Meanwhile, the State Department remained responsible for administering the licensing system to regulate exports of arms, ammunition, and other military implements.

The Export Administration Act of 1979

The ECA was renewed every two years until 1979 when the Export Administration Act (EAA) of 1979 replaced it.[51] The EAA provided the president with the principal statutory framework for restricting exports of goods and services and prohibiting any exports not licensed by the Department of Commerce. While a "general license" for exports was easy to obtain, the EAA granted the president the power to impose greater restrictions over certain exports on the statutory grounds of national security, foreign policy, and short supply. To export such restricted items, exporters were required to obtain prior approval, called "validated license," from the Department of Commerce, and violators of such restrictions faced a wide range of penalties, including civil fines, forfeiture, denial of future privileges to export or import, and even criminal charges of felony.

The EAA also contained safeguard measures against "overzealous use and the consequent damage" to US export interests, by enforcing restrictions on: (a) exports

[51] As discussed below, since then presidents have derived their powers to impose sanctions on US exports from numerous statutes, but primarily from the EAA (1979), the Export Administration Amendments Act of 1985 (EAAA: P.L. 99-64), the Arms Export Control Act of 1976, the Atomic Energy Act of 1954 (AEA: P.L. 83-703), and the Nuclear Non-Proliferation Act of 1978 (NNPA: P.L. 95-242).

that amounted to a discriminatory and sector-specific unfair tax to finance foreign policy; (b) sale of goods that were available from foreign competitors or required the cancellation of existing contracts; (c) the most heavily affected firms that suffered lost sales and damaged reputations; and (d) exports of goods that stirred political opposition (Hufbauer, 2007, 109).

Concerns over the presidential powers on export controls began to surface when President Carter used the EAA to impose an agricultural embargo against the then Soviet Union in 1980. Confronting resistance to the move from farmers, Congress in 1981 not only imposed limitations on the presidential authority to restrict exports, but also required that farmers be compensated at a generous rate in the event of any future agricultural embargo against any major foreign purchaser. In 1982, Congress further restricted the presidential powers to curtail exports of any agricultural product under existing sales contracts which required delivery within 270 days of the starting date of any embargo imposed without declaring a national emergency (Carter, 1999, 1194).

Concerns over the presidential powers over exports were also raised in 1982 when President Ronald Reagan imposed export restrictions on the Soviet Union over its pipeline project to export gas to European countries. Reagan prevented foreign subsidiaries of US firms, including those wholly owned by foreigners, from exporting certain equipment and technology, and also restricted independent foreign companies from exporting foreign-origin products that were made with technology acquired through licensing agreements with US companies, although such measures far exceeded the EAA's mandate (Moyer and Mabry, 1983).

The EEA was in force for 15 years, until 1994, with a lapse of one year in 1984–1985, when President Reagan invoked the IEEPA emergency powers to regulate exports. After the expiration of the EEA in 1994, all subsequent presidents also invoked the IEEPA authorities to renew exports regulations annually until 2018 when the ECRA was enacted. In all, the EAA lapsed seven times between 1979 and 2018, with the longest lapse – 17 years – occurring from 2001 to 2018 (Hirschhorn, 2022, 3).

The Export Administration Amendments Act of 1985

The Congress passed the Export Administration Amendments Act of 1985 (EAAA: P.L. 99-64) to address the concerns raised over presidential powers granted by the EAA, but in the end, the legislation both restrained and expanded presidential powers on export restrictions.

First, the EAAA sharply limited presidential powers by imposing a "sunset provision" – a 60-day time limit on any embargo on agricultural goods, which could be extended up to a maximum of one year only by Congress through a joint resolution. This limit was not, however, applicable when the agricultural exports controls were imposed "with respect to a country as part of the prohibition or curtailment of all exports to that country."[52]

[52] See §2406(g)(3)(A) of EAAA.

Second, the EAAA introduced a new provision called "contract sanctity," which allowed the president to impose export controls abrogating existing contracts, while prohibiting them from imposing such controls on the export or re-export of goods or technology under existing contracts or validated licenses, unless the president certified to Congress that: (a) a breach of the peace posed a serious and direct threat to the strategic interest of the US; (b) the prohibition would be instrumental in remedying the situation posing such a direct threat; and (c) the export controls would continue only so long as the direct threat persisted (Carter, 1999, 1194).[53]

Third, the EAAA required the president to determine whether: (a) the proposed export controls were likely to achieve the intended foreign policy purpose; (b) the reaction of other countries was likely to render the controls ineffective; and (c) the US could enforce the proposed controls effectively, that is, whether the goods in question could be available from other foreign sources (Hufbauer, 2007, 111).[54]

Finally, the EAAA granted considerable discretion to the president in asserting extraterritorial jurisdiction in imposing export controls on companies and goods outside US territory. The president had the authority to control exports of any goods and technology subject to the US jurisdiction or exported by any person subject to US jurisdiction. Thus, the president was authorized to expand the reach of exports sanctions to: (a) re-exports by a foreign company of goods or technology of US origin; (b) re-exports of US-origin parts even if included in foreign-made goods; and (c) exports of foreign-origin goods that are the direct products of US-origin technology. Congress however granted such extraterritorial jurisdiction to the president with the expectation that such sanctions would be limited in scope and invoked only on national security concerns (Carter, 1999, 1191–1194).

The Export Control Reform Act of 2018

The Export Control Reform Act of 2018[55] (ECRA: P.L. 115-232)[56] not only thoroughly revamped the entire edifice of US export laws, policy, and administration, but it also granted sweeping powers to the president to restrict: (a) exports and re-exports; (b) transfers of commercial, dual-use, and less sensitive military items to all end users and end uses and all destinations of concern to US national security

[53] Hufbauer (2007, 10) points out that this threshold represented a dilemma. On the one hand, sanctions are likely to be more effective when they are imposed abruptly and with maximum force, which in turn, would require cancelling existing contracts, which may cause domestic dissatisfaction. On the other hand, if existing contracts are honored, domestic costs will be reduced and domestic opposition would be less, but the initial impact on the target will be weakened.

[54] See Section 2405(b) of the EAAA.

[55] The discussion on the ECRA is based on multiple sources, including the original Act; Fergusson (2020, 2021); and the websites of US Congress, the US Departments of Commerce and State, and the EU. Specific sources were not always identified.

[56] The Act was a part of the John S. McCain National Defense Authorization Act (NDAA) of 2019 – the Department of Defense Budget for Fiscal Year 2019. It was, however, made effective retrospectively from August 13, 2018.

interests; and (c) exports of both emerging and foundational technologies that can potentially be used for both civilian and military purposes.

The ECRA consists of two parts: Part I – the Export Controls Act (ECA: 2018) – provides the Bureau of Industry and Security (BIS) under the Department of Commerce with the authority to administer export controls; and Part II – the Anti-Boycott Act (ABC: 2018) – provides the BIS with the authority to control anti-boycott regulations. Since the enactment of the ECRA, the US has two main legal frameworks for regulating exports: the Export Administration Regulations (EAR), administered by the Department of Commerce, and the International Traffic in Arms Regulations (ITAR), administered by the Department of State.

The EAR, under the BIS, regulates exports of dual-use and less sensitive military items by placing them on its Commerce Control List (CCL),[57] while the ITAR (Title 22 C.F.R. parts 120–130), under the Directorate of Defense Trade Controls (DDTC), controls the sale of defense items and defense services. The DDTC maintains a Munitions List (USML) of designated exports and temporary imports of defense articles (pursuant to Title 22 C.F.R. 121.1) that are governed by the Arms Export Control Act (Title 22 U.S.C. 2778).[58]

As mentioned above, the ECRA has replaced most of the EEA (1979), excluding only Sections 11A, 11B, and 11C of the EEA that relate to sanctions on nuclear proliferation.[59] The National Defense Authorization Act (NDAA: 2019), which incorporates the ECRA, also incorporates another act called the Foreign Investment Risk Review Modernization Act (FIRRMA). The passage of both statutes coincided with growing concerns in the US about China's access to critical new technologies, and both of them are aimed at ensuring that the advantages offered by emerging US technologies are not seized by other countries, especially China, upon export, or reaching restricted end users or end uses.

The ECRA has also established an inter-agency process to continuously identify and control emerging and foundational technologies critical to US national security initiatives.[60]

[57] As Hirschhorn (2022, 5–17) explains, the EAR's export controls regimes fall into four general categories: A. Controls in the national security category that cover items that make "a significant contribution to the military potential of any other country or combination of countries that would prove detrimental to the national security of the United States." Such items typically include sophisticated technology or encryption; B. Controls in the category of foreign policy that include exports to terrorist-supporting countries, crime control equipment, items that could affect the stability of geographic regions of concern, and items controlled in fulfillment of international obligations; C. Controls in the non-proliferation category that relate to weapons of mass destruction, such as nuclear weapons, missiles, and chemical and biological weapons; and D. Controls in the "short supply" category – as specified in part 754 of the EAR, they include exports of certain petroleum products, western red cedar, and horses exported by sea, and so on.

[58] Accordingly, the State Department amended the ITAR in September 2022.

[59] The ECRA however largely maintains the regulatory system as codified under the EAR (15 C.F.R. 730 et seq.), which was maintained under the IEEPA (1977) for nearly a quarter-century (Casey, 2021, 1).

[60] Section 1758 of ECRA specifically regulates the development or export of emerging and foundational technologies that are not identified in the EAR or other previous export control regulations.

The responsibility to maintain and establish new controls on such technologies has been vested in multiple agencies under the Departments of Commerce, State, Energy, and Defense, and acquisitions of such technologies by US companies are made subject to stricter national security reviews by the Committee of Foreign Investment in the United States (CFIUS).

The ECRA also significantly expanded the presidential powers with respect to extraterritorial application of exports controls. Under the ECRA, both emerging and foundational technologies selected for control are subject to the same rules as other items currently on the CCL.[61] This means that US-based companies or any companies anywhere in the world that are involved in re-exporting US-made goods or technology, or incorporating technology previously exported from the US, are subject to US jurisdiction. Consequently, even non-US-made products may be subject to the ECRA if their usage of controlled technology or components originating in the US exceeds the threshold determined by the Export Control Classification Numbers (ECCNs) that the BIS assigns to emerging or foundational technologies.

Such extraterritorial application of the presidential powers also extends to exports and re-exports, and in-country transfers of certain military parts and components subject to US jurisdiction, whether involving US persons or foreign persons. The ECRA requires the Department of Commerce to establish and maintain a list of such controlled items, foreign persons, and end uses which may constitute a threat to US national security.[62]

In November 2018, the BIS published an Advanced Notice of Proposed Rule-Making identifying 14 categories of "emerging technologies"[63] and extended its reach to the EAR controlled embargoed countries as well as countries flagged as supporters of international terrorism, and certain restricted end uses or end users. The BIS also announced a list of exports of technologies prohibited by the laws and subject to the ECRA regulations.[64]

[61] Notably, nearly all exports are subject to the EAR, while the CCL establishes controls only on specific items either on a multilateral or unilateral basis. The sanctioned countries or entities are subject to a policy of denial for all products, no matter whether they are on the CCL or not. Pursuant to the EAR (Part 774), the types of items placed on the CCL include: Nuclear Materials, Facilities & Equipment (and Misc. items); Materials, Chemicals, Microorganisms, Toxins; Materials Processing; Electronic Design, Development, and Production; Computers; Telecommunications; Information Security; Sensors and Lasers; Navigation and Avionics; Marine; and Aerospace and Propulsion (Casey, 2021).

[62] The ECRA sanctions individuals up to $1 million or up to 20 years imprisonment, or both, per criminal violation. For civil penalties for each violation, individuals may be fined up to $300,000 or an amount that is twice the value of the transaction that is the basis of the violation. Such penalties may also include revocation of export licenses and prohibitions on the offender's ability to export. The enforcement is carried out by the Office of Export Enforcement (OEE) under the BIS (Fergusson and Kerr, 2021).

[63] The list of emerging technologies includes: artificial intelligence and machine learning, augmented reality, automated machine tools, additive manufacturing, autonomous vehicles, advanced battery technology, "big data," biotechnology, gene editing, high-temperature superconducting technology, hydrogen and fuel cells, integrated circuits, semiconductors and microelectronics, and intelligent mobile terminals. For greater detail, see the ECRA 2018 (P.L. 115-232).

[64] Such transactions include: (a) a finished item with associated technology if the US person that is a party to the transaction generally makes the finished item and associated technology available to its

The Arms Export Control Act of 1976

The AECA was enacted in 1976 to support the defense of countries friendly with the US and to help them participate in activities consistent with the UN Charter and collective measures requested by the UN for maintaining or restoring international peace and security. The Act also provides authority to the president to assist less developed countries to engage in activities helpful for their economic and social development.[65] The ITAR, discussed above, was created under this Act to govern the export of defense articles, services, and technical data as listed in the USML.

The AECA §3(a) specifies the criteria for eligible foreign governments and international organizations to purchase defense articles and services directly from US firms under the Direct Commercial Sales (DCS) provisions, and authorizes the Foreign Military Sales (FMS) program to sell US defense equipment and services and provide training on a government-to-government basis. The AECA §4 restricts the sale of US defense articles and defense services to friendly countries for use solely on internal security and legitimate self-defense, and prohibits the use of US weapons for other purposes, such as aggression, terrorism, smuggling, and so on (Fergusson and Kerr, 2020, 4–5).

Against the backdrop of the War Powers Resolution Act of 1973 and the Hughes-Ryan Amendment (P.L. 93–559)[66] to the FAA (1961), the AECA hugely expanded the Congressional oversight over presidential actions in foreign policy matters, especially with respect to US arms sales. Presidents could bypass such oversights, however, as the law nowhere defined national security interests – it was rather left to presidential interpretation. Moreover, Congress could only disapprove a sale, and had no power to approve. Also, the AECA was rarely used to block any arms deal (Carter, 1999, 1197; Kaiser, 1978, 11–12).

customers, distributors, or re-sellers; (b) a product and the provision of integration services or similar services if the US person that is a party to the transaction generally makes such services available to its customers; (c) transfer of equipment and the provision of associated technology to operate the equipment if the transfer could not result in the foreign person using the equipment to produce critical technologies (as defined in §721(a) of the Defense Production Act of 1950, as amended by §1703); (d) procurement by the US person that is a party to the transaction of goods or services from a foreign person that is a party to the transaction, if the foreign person has no rights to exploit any technology contributed by the US person other than to supply the procured goods or services; and (e) any contribution and associated support by a US person that is a party to the transaction to an industry organization related to a standard or specification, whether in development or declared, including any license of or commitment to license intellectual property in compliance with the rules of any standards organization. For greater detail, see ECRA 2018 (P.L. 115-232).

65 See the AECA, codified at 22 U.S.C. (1982).

66 The Hughes–Ryan Amendment was passed as §32 of the Foreign Assistance Act of 1974 (P.L. 93-559). Among other things, the amendment required the president to report all covert actions of the CIA to relevant Congressional Committees and prohibited the use of appropriated funds for the conduct of any covert action unless and until the president issued an official finding that such operation is important to national security. For greater detail, see Kaiser (1978, 11).

In the end, the AECA clearly grants the president nearly unfettered powers to control exports of defense articles and defense services. There are, however, at least two important provisions of the Act that restrain the presidential powers. First, the Act requires the president to ascertain that the recipient country of arms exports agreed not to transfer the arms to a third country without prior approval of the US and that it would maintain the security of the arms. Second, AECA §36(b) requires the president to formally notify Congress 30 calendar days before taking the final steps to conclude a government-to-government foreign military sale or issue an export license for commercial sales of defense equipment.[67] Such requirements and resultant Congressional oversight have indeed forced several presidents to cancel, revise, or postpone sale of arms to many foreign countries (Fergusson and Kerr, 2020, 5).

The Atomic Energy Act of 1954

Exports of US nuclear materials, equipment, and technology are mainly controlled by the Atomic Energy Act of 1954 (AEA: P.L. 83-703) and its successor, the Nuclear Non-Proliferation Act of 1978 (NNPA: P.L. 95-242). Both statutes grant the president essentially unlimited authority to restrict such exports with the objective of regulating construction of nuclear power plants and the proliferation of nuclear weapons in an effort to maintain the military balance around the world.[68] These statutes also prohibit the president from exporting nuclear fuel and reactors to countries that do not accept the nuclear safeguard standards required by the International Atomic Energy Agency (IAEA),[69] and countries designated for state-sponsored terrorism.[70]

The AEA came as an amendment to the Atomic Energy Act of 1946 (McMahon Act: P.L. 79-585), which granted private companies access to the "Restrictive Data" on technical information on production of nuclear energy and fissile materials for the first time, pursuant to President Dwight D. Eisenhower's "Atoms for Peace" program.[71]

67 Under AECA §36(b), 30 calendar days notification is required for sales of defense equipment valued at $14 million or more, defense articles or services valued at $50 million or more, or design and construction services valued at $200 million or more. In case of arms sales to NATO member states and some other friendly countries like Japan and Australia, the notification requirement is 15 calendar days (Fergusson and Kerr, 2020, 5).

68 See the AEA (1954), codified as 42 U.S.C. §§ 2011-2296, and the NNPA (1978), codified at 22 U.S.C. §§ 3201-3282 (1979).

69 As discussed below, the NNPA imposes stringent nonproliferation requirements for any significant US nuclear exports agreement with any country without comprehensive IAEA safeguards in place, but the president can override this requirement. Congress can, however, override the presidential waiver by a concurrent resolution within 60 days of such an agreement.

70 Section 129b(1) of AEA (1954) forbids the export of nuclear materials and equipment or sensitive nuclear technology to any country designated for state-sponsored terrorism. As mentioned above, the ECRA (2018) repealed most of the provisions of the AEA, except those related to violations of multilateral national security export controls, multilateral missile proliferation controls, and chemical and biological weapons controls. For greater detail, see Hirschhorn (2022, 4–5).

71 "Restricted data" has been defined by AEA (1954) as: "all data concerning (1) design, manufacture, or utilization of atomic weapons; (2) the production of special nuclear material; or (3) the use of special nuclear material in the production of energy."

Under the AEA, all significant US nondefense nuclear cooperation with other countries – including the transfer of US-origin special nuclear material subject to licensing for commercial, medical, and industrial purposes, and the export of reactors and critical parts of reactors – requires a nuclear cooperation agreement. The Act vests licensing authority for all such Section 123 agreements (bilateral agreements) with the Nuclear Regulatory Commission (NRC).

The NNPA (1978), the successor of the AEA, requires nonnuclear-weapon countries to have comprehensive IAEA safeguards as a condition for entering into nuclear cooperation agreements with the US. The Act also tightens the criteria for nuclear cooperation in pursuance of US non-proliferation policy under which importing countries must belong to the Nuclear Non-Proliferation Treaty (NPT) in order to receive US nuclear exports. The Act also requires the US to halt nuclear cooperation if a country tests a nuclear device, violates safeguards agreements, or continues nuclear weapons-related activities.

The NNPA came at a time when US nuclear cooperation policies and programs were embroiled in deep controversy. Until 1971, the US had a near monopoly in nuclear business, when it supplied almost 90 percent of the reactors and the low-enriched uranium (LEU) fuel. The US also set the LEU prices below the cost of production in order to discourage competition from foreign enrichment ventures. But some technically competent European countries, such as France and Germany, soon felt aggrieved by the fact that while they were granted access to unclassified gaseous diffusion technology which required enormous amounts of electricity to run the reactors, US firms ran their own reactors with classified and less expensive centrifuge technology. Then, the Oil Shock of the early 1970s further amplified their need to shift away from oil to reprocessing of plutonium from spent nuclear fuel.

Around the same time, several developing countries also began to display their nuclear ambitions. For example, in 1974 India conducted a successful nuclear test using spent fuel reprocessing, while France signed a contract to provide a nuclear reprocessing plant to South Korea, and in 1975 West Germany signed an agreement with Brazil to provide a full nuclear fuel cycle.[72] Brazil and South Korea, however, abandoned their nuclear ambitions in the face of US sanctions. As several other countries still pursued their nuclear ambitions, in a bid to oppose spent fuel reprocessing because of concerns about nuclear proliferation, the US imposed sanctions against South Africa in 1975, Taiwan in 1976, and Argentina, India, and Libya in 1978.

Given such developments, the NNPA attempted to make the nuclear fuel cycle a less attractive platform from which to develop nuclear weapons by sticking to a

[72] See The United States and South Korea's Nuclear Weapons Program, 1974–1976, Wilson Center, available at www.wilsoncenter.org/article/the-united-states-and-south-koreas-nuclear-weapons-program-1974-1976.

once-through fuel cycle that would avoid using separated plutonium. The Act also sought to defer commercial deployment of breeder reactors, create terminal spent fuel storage facilities, and assure countries that they would have a reliable supply of LEU through the creation of a fuel bank under the International Nuclear Fuel Authority (INFU).

Subsequently, the Comprehensive Iran Sanctions, Accountability, and Divestment Act of 2010 (CISADA: P.L. 111-195) prohibited licensing of nuclear exports to countries that have been sanctioned for conducting certain types of nuclear weapons-related transactions with Iran.[73] Furthermore, §1264 of NDAA (2019) prohibited the president from signing a bilateral agreement with any country that has not signed and implemented the Additional Protocol to IAEA's Safeguards Agreement. The Act, however, exempted the countries with which the US already had Section 123 agreements – as of February 2022, the US had over two dozen such agreements in effect.[74]

The US nuclear exports policy, as well as the policies aimed at preventing proliferation of nuclear weapons around the world, the enforcement of the IAEA's safeguard standards, and preventing supplier states from transferring sensitive nuclear technologies, such as uranium enrichment and spent fuel reprocessing, have largely succeeded, as eventually all other members of the Nuclear Suppliers Group (NSG) also adopted the same strategies by 1992, following Iraq's alleged transgressions for nuclear weapons.

But US presidents have implemented a series of sanctions regimes targeting numerous countries to accomplish specific objectives. Notable instances of such sanctions include measures imposed on South Korea between 1975 and 1976, South Africa from 1975 to 1982, Taiwan during 1976–1977, Brazil from 1978 to 1981, Argentina from 1978 to 1982, India from 1978 to 1982, Libya from 1978 to 2004, Pakistan between 1979 and 2001, China in 1990–1991, North Korea during 1993–1994 (and 2002–), and India from 1998 to 2002.

The US, however, has also signed several nuclear cooperation agreements outside the AEA Process, with countries not signatories to the NPT, or that do not satisfy the IAEA safeguard measures. For example, President Bill Clinton signed an agreement with China in 1998; President George W. Bush signed an agreement with India in 2008; President Obama signed an agreement with Australia in 2010; and President Trump signed an agreement with Norway in 2016.[75]

[73] See §102a.(2)(A) of CISADA (2010).

[74] See Appendix A of Kerr (2022, 14–16) for the list of the countries with which the US has signed such agreements and their expiration dates.

[75] These exceptional agreements often involved long processes. For example, the process of a nuclear deal with China began in 1985 under President Reagan, but eventually it was President Clinton who signed the agreement on January 12, 1998. On the other hand, in the case of India, the process began in 2002, and was finally implemented in October 2008, under the same president. For greater detail, see Kerr (2022, 7–19).

Effectiveness of Exports Restraints

Although Congressional approval and review plays an important role, in the end, as the discussion above indicates, the president enjoys broad discretion to control almost all US exports with respect to a particular country. Even Congressional constraints on the presidential powers to control exports of nuclear materials and equipment have not been insurmountable. Of course, Congress retains the power to disapprove exports agreements signed by the president through concurrent resolutions, but such actions have been very rare. In 1986, for example, Congress passed a joint resolution opposing the sale of $354 million worth of arms to Saudi Arabia, which President Reagan vetoed, but while the House voted to override the veto, the Senate fell short by a single vote (Carter, 1999, 1197).

Historically, US presidents have preferred export sanctions over restrictions on imports as sanctioning measures, and have exercised such powers numerous times since WWII.[76] The presidents do so because Congress has granted them greater flexibility in restraining exports than interrupting imports. They can restrict exports by using export control statutes as well as using the emergency powers granted by the IEEPA. As explained below, the president also has the power to control imports by using IEEPA and §232 of the Trade Expansion Act of 1962 (P.L. 87-794). The presidential use of Section 232, however, may be subject to review under GATT Article XXI.

Another reason for preferring exports over imports is that the US often enjoys a dominant market position as supplier of key exports to target countries. For example, during 1945–2000, the US imposed 66 trade restrictions, of which 50 instances involved exports controls and 16 were control on imports. Also, among the 37 cases of exports restrictions during the period, in 34 cases the US had been the supplier of over 10 percent of key imports of the target countries (Hufbauer, 2007, 90–92).

C *Import Restrictions*

In contrast to exports, presidential powers to restrict imports or use of import as tools for sanctions under non-emergency statutes are very limited.[77] First of all, the president has no general statutory authority to restrict imports on foreign policy grounds, and whatever Congressional authority has been granted to them is scattered among many statutes. Some of those grant authority to restrict imports of critical defense materials, some of those relate to imports from a certain country, or certain products or policy issues, and so on – but all of those are subject to Congressional review.[78]

[76] There are dozens of examples; for greater detail, see Appendix 1A of Hufbauer (2007, 20–33).

[77] The president does have nearly unlimited authority to impose import restrictions or sanctions under the emergency powers of the IEEPA and the TWEA.

[78] Article I, Section 8, of the US Constitution grants the Congress, not the president, the power "To regulate Commerce with foreign Nations" and "To lay and collect Taxes, Duties, Imposts, and Excises."

Second, the president and Congress often have divergent interests when it comes to import restrictions. For example, the president may seek to restrict imports to raise revenues, protect domestic jobs, serve the interests of US industries, or create leverage in negotiations with other countries. Congress, on the other hand, may be reluctant to grant broad discretions to the president to adopt such measures considering their impact on domestic industries, domestic prices, or subsidy policies. And, third, import restrictions may contradict the country's MFN (most favored nation) obligations under the GATT-WTO trade discipline (Hufbauer, 2007, 92–94).

One of the major pieces of non-emergency legislation that grants the president nearly sweeping powers over import controls is the Trade Expansion Act (TEA) of 1962. Section 232 of the TEA authorizes the president with broad powers to impose import restrictions on the grounds of national security interests without Congressional approval.[79] The statute, however, requires that the presidential actions on imports restrictions must be based on an affirmative determination by the Department of Commerce that the targeted products are being imported into the US "in such quantities or under such circumstances as to threaten to impair the national security."[80] As the legislation was enacted in the midst of the Cold War, some scholars believe the rationale behind Section 232 was to limit the imports of critical defense materials in order to protect the domestic production base or to protect against embargo by important foreign suppliers (Carter, 1999, 1201).

Over the decades, Section 232 was amended multiple times. For example, the Trade Act of 1974 (P.L. 93-618) restricted the time limits for the Commerce Department's investigations and actions to one year; the Omnibus Trade and Competitiveness Act of 1988 (P.L. 100-418) shifted the advisory responsibility from the Secretary of Treasury to the Secretary of Commerce; and the Crude Oil Windfall Profit Tax Act of 1980 (P.L. 96-223) restricted the presidential authority on adjustments to petroleum or petroleum product imports. The presidential discretion in the interpretation of "national security," as well as the scope of any investigation, was however left restrained (Fefer, 2021, 58).

Some other non-emergency legislative tools that the president has at their disposal to restrict imports include: (a) Section 201 of the Trade Act of 1974, which allows the

[79] The TEA §232 is a continuation of a similar provisions of the Trade Agreements Extension Act of 1958 (TAEA: P.L. 85-686 §8), which allowed the president to increase trade restrictions when national security was threatened. Earlier, the Trade Agreements Extension Act of 1954 (TAEA: P.L. 83-464 §2) prohibited the president from decreasing duties on any article if the president determined that such a reduction might threaten domestic production needed for national defense (Fefer, 2021, 58).

[80] The Commerce Department's Section 232 investigation considers: (a) the domestic production capacity needed for US national security requirements; (b) the effect of imports on domestic production needed for national security requirements; and (c) the impact of foreign competition on the economic welfare of individual domestic industries. For greater detail, see Section 232 of the TEA, codified as 19 U.S.C. §1862.

president to initiate investigations or actions to address import surges that threaten or pose a substantial and serious injury to a US industry; (b) Section 301 of the Trade Act of 1974, which allows the president to address violations of US trade laws or deny US trade benefits pursuant to trade agreements; (c) Title VII of the Tariff Act of 1930 (the Smoot–Hawley Act), which allows the president to enforce anti-dumping and countervailing duty laws to counter injurious unfair trade practices; and (d) Section 505 of the International Security and Development Cooperation Act, 1985 (ISDCA: P.L. 99-83). Last amended in 2022, the ISDCA authorizes the president to ban imports from countries that support or harbor terrorists or terrorist organizations (Carter, 1999, 1203; Fefer, 2021, 1).

The presidents, however, have used their import restraining authority sparingly, albeit with the major exception of petroleum and petroleum products. President Eisenhower used the TEA (1954) in 1959 to impose a quota system on imports of petroleum and petroleum products, which subsequent presidents – John F. Kennedy, Lyndon Johnson, Richard Nixon, and Gerald Ford – continued. The Nixon Administration also imposed licensing fees and additional supplemental fees on petroleum imports during Great Oil Shock of 1973, which continued until 1978. In 1979, President Carter imposed oil embargoes against Iran. President Reagan imposed an oil embargo against Libya in 1982, and invoked the ISDCA (1985) to ban imports from Iran in 1987 (Carter, 1999, 1201–1203; Hufbauer, 2007, 45).

Overall, between 1962 and 2020, a total of 31 Section 232 investigations were carried out – of which, in 14 cases, the targeted imports were found to have threatened to impair national security, but only in nine cases was presidential action recommended. In 2001, only one Section 232 investigation took place, but no presidential action was taken; and between 2002 and 2017, no Section 232 investigation took place.[81]

But all that changed during the Trump Administration (2016–2020), when eight Section 232 investigations were carried out into the imports of various products.[82] Based on these investigations, President Trump in March 2018 imposed a 25-percent tariff on steel and a 10-percent tariff on aluminum, and in February 2020 further expanded the scope of the products subject to additional tariffs. Trump also negotiated permanent tariff exemptions in exchange for quantitative restrictions (QRS) on imports covering steel for Brazil and South Korea, and both steel and aluminum products for Argentina, while exempting Australia permanently from both tariffs and QRS. Trump also removed tariffs on steel and aluminum imports from Mexico and Canada to secure Congressional support for the United States–Mexico–Canada

81 For the list of these investigations and their outcomes, see Table B-1 of Fefer (2021).

82 The investigated products included: steel; aluminum; automobiles, including sport utility vehicles, vans, and light trucks, and automotive parts; uranium; titanium sponge; electrical transformers; certain grain-oriented electrical steel components; mobile cranes; and vanadium imports.

Agreement (USMCA), and agreed to establish an import monitoring mechanism for USMCA members.[83]

Since his assumption of office in January 2021, President Joe Biden has continued Section 232 tariffs on steel and aluminum imports from several US trading partners, but reached separate agreements with the EU, Japan, and the UK to replace tariffs with tariff-rate quota systems. Under these agreements, the trading partners agreed to remove their retaliatory tariffs[84] and establish joint monitoring teams to restore market-oriented conditions while addressing overcapacity and greenhouse gas emissions issues (Fefer, 2022, 2).

Judicial Interventions

President Trump's Section 232 actions faced several legal challenges, some of which are discussed below.[85] In *Severstal Exp. GmbH v. United States* (2018), for example, Severstal Export GmbH, a US subsidiary of a Russian steel producer, sought a preliminary injunction from the US Court of International Trade (CIT), arguing that the US president acted outside his authority because the tariffs imposed against the company were not truly based on national security purposes. The court declined to grant the injunction, and subsequently both parties settled the matter outside court.[86]

In *American Institute for International Steel, Inc. v. United States* (2019), the American Institute for International Steel (AIIS), a trade association, challenged the constitutionality of the Congress's delegation of authority to the president under Section 232, arguing that "Congress created an unconstitutional regime in section 232, in which there are essentially no limits or guidelines on the trigger or the remedies available to the President, and no alternative protections to assure that the President stays within the law, instead of making the law himself." The court rejected the claim, holding that a 1976 Supreme Court precedent determined that Section 232 did not amount to an unconstitutional delegation because it established an "intelligible principle" to guide presidential action.[87]

83 Trump, however, turned down the Department of Commerce's recommendations in six Section 232 investigations related to imports of automobiles and certain automotive parts. He also did not concur with the Department's finding that imports of uranium ore and related products threatened to impair national security. Trump also refused to restrict imports of titanium sponge from Japan despite the Department's recommendation (Fefer, 2021, 38).

84 In retaliation for President Trump's tariffs on US imports, China, the EU, India, Turkey, the UK, and Russia imposed retaliatory tariffs on US exports, affecting approximately $7.2 billion of US annual exports in 2020.

85 The discussion of these challenges is based on Fefer (2021, 38–41), which provides elaborate discussion on these cases as well as many others. See also US Department of Commerce (2022), which elaborates on dozens of investigations, and criminal and civil penalties awarded to violators.

86 *Severstal Exp. GmbH v. United States*, No. 18-00057 (Ct. Int'l Trade, May 3, 2018).

87 *American Institute for International Steel, Inc. v. United States*, 376 *F. Supp. 3d* 1335–1337 (Ct. Int'l Trade 2019, No. 2019-1727).

In *Transpacific Steel LLC v. United States (2019)*, US importers of Turkish steel alleged that President Trump's increase of the Section 232 steel tariffs from 25 percent to 50 percent on imports from Turkey lacked sufficient national security rationale and violated the plaintiff's Fifth Amendment rights, as it did not follow statutory procedural mandates. The CIT ruled in favor of the plaintiff.[88] Similarly, in *JSW Steel, Inc. v. United States (2020)*, the plaintiff argued that the Department of Commerce's failure to grant the company's products an exclusion from the steel tariffs violated the Administrative Procedure Act.[89] The court remanded the case to the Department of Commerce, and the US then settled the case by agreeing to refund the duties paid on the items that would have benefited from an approved exclusion request.

WTO-Related Challenges

Members of the World Trade Organization (WTO) enjoy MFN status automatically, but WTO Article XXI grants members the right to take sanctioning measures against other members by invoking what is called "national security exception." Historically many targets of US sanctions – such as the former Soviet Union, East Germany, China, former Czechoslovakia, Iran, and Libya – were not members of GATT (1947–1994). These targets also did not have any bilateral agreements with the US, and thus, the US had no MFN obligations toward them. All that changed in recent years, as two of the major targets of US sanctions – China and Russia – became members of the WTO in 2002 and 2012, respectively. Another longstanding target of US sanctions – Iran – however, is still not a member of the WTO.

In April 2018, China brought President Trump's Section 232 actions before the WTO's Dispute Settlement Body. alleging that the US violated its obligations under the WTO agreements with respect to: GATT Article I – the MFN principle – which obligated the US to treat Chinese goods no less favorably than the goods of other WTO members; GATT Article II, which prohibited members from imposing duties on imported goods in excess of upper limits to which they agreed in their Schedules of Concessions and Commitments; and the GATT Agreement on Safeguards.[90] In its defense, the US invoked the "national security exception" of GATT Article

[88] *Transpacific Steel LLC v. United States*, No.19-00009 (Ct. Int'l Trade January 17, 2019).

[89] *JSW Steel, Inc. v. United States*, No. 19-00133 (Ct. Int'l Trade Sept. 21, 2020).

[90] For details of the case, see Request for Consultations by China, *U.S. – Certain Measures on Steel and Aluminum Products*, WT/DS/544/1 (April 9, 2018). For details on the GATT Agreement on Safeguards see www.wto.org/english/docs_e/legal_e/25-safeg.pdf, accessed on September 26, 2022. Briefly, Article 2 of the Agreement provides that a WTO member may apply a safeguard measure to a product only if that member has determined that such product is being imported into its territory in such increased quantities – absolute or relative to domestic production – and under such conditions as to cause or threaten to cause serious injury to the domestic industry that produces similar or directly competitive products. Article 3 of the Agreement further stipulates that a WTO member may apply a safeguard measure only following an investigation by the competent authorities of that member pursuant to procedures previously established and made public in consonance with Article X of GATT 1994.

XXI(b), arguing that this exception is self-judging, and therefore, a WTO Panel may not proceed to the merits of the dispute to evaluate whether the WTO member's use of the exception is proper.[91]

Meanwhile, some important developments essentially paralyzed the WTO dispute settlement system. First, as of December 11, 2019, the WTO's Appellate Body lost its quorum, it failed to assemble three members necessary to decide appeals, and thus failed to issue a final report. Second, several countries affected by US Section 232 actions already imposed retaliatory duties of their own on selected US exports without waiting for the outcome of the WTO proceedings. Third, in July–August 2018, the US filed its own complaints with the WTO over the retaliatory tariffs imposed by Canada, China, the EU, Mexico, Turkey, Russia, and India. Fifth, in May 2019, Canada, Mexico, and the US settled their disputes. Finally, the WTO Appellate Body suspended its operations lacking a quorum.[92]

IV SANCTIONS UNDER THE TRADE POLICY MEASURES

As a signatory to the WTO, the US is obligated to extend MFN status to all WTO members, no matter whether they are allies or enemies. The US is also obligated to extend MFN status to any country with which it has bilateral or regional trade agreements. At the same time, Congress has granted extensive powers to the president to deny or revoke MFN status to any country; grant MFN status to countries that are not entitled to such a status by dint of being a signatory to the GATT/WTO or having bilateral or regional agreements with the US; and grant or withdraw special privileges or preferences to any country for trading with the US.

A *The Trade Act of 1974*

The Trade Act of 1974, enacted in the midst of the Cold War, that granted such sweeping powers to the president, still serves as the foundation of US trade laws through numerous updates and amendments. The Act also grants the president fast-track authority to negotiate trade agreements with other countries and territories, governments, and international organizations which Congress can approve or disapprove but cannot amend or filibuster.[93] Under such fast-track authorities, the

[91] As discussed above, the claim that GATT Article XXI(b) is self-judging and thus not to be adjudged by a WTO panel has been controversial, and in recent decades WTO panels have asserted their jurisdiction in such matters several times.

[92] For greater detail, see Fefer (2022, 41–44), the WTO website, and Hufbauer and Jung (2020).

[93] The fast-track authority, authorized by the 1974 Trade Act, was first granted during the Tokyo Round of GATT negotiations (1973–1979). Such authorities were further extended several times, up to 1993, to enable US negotiations under the subsequent GATT Rounds, which finally culminated in the establishment of the WTO in 1995. The presidential fast-track authority of trade negotiations was restored by the Trade Act of 2000 (P.L. 107-210).

US Office of Trade Representative (USTR) played an instrumental role during the 1970s through the 1990s in shaping global trade rules as the GATT (1947) transitioned into the WTO (1995).[94]

Second, the Trade Act (1974) authorized the president to extend MFN treatment to "non-market economy" countries that did not enjoy MFN status with the US. Thus, the president could deny or suspend MFN rights to any communist country, with the exception of former Yugoslavia, and could deny the benefits of lower tariffs negotiated through trade agreements under the Trade Agreements Extension Act of 1951 (TAEA: P.L. 99-272) and even subject them to higher tariffs under the USTA (1930).[95] In the 1970s and 1980s, US presidents used such powers quite extensively against the former Soviet Union and Eastern European countries.[96] Since the collapse of the Soviet Union and transition of former Soviet Republics and eastern European countries to market-oriented economies in the 1990s, the applicability of such powers has been limited to only a few countries – specifically, to China, Cuba, North Korea, and Vietnam. But all of them, except North Korea, are members of the WTO, and thus any trade measures against them are now subject to WTO review.[97]

Third, Section 301 of the Trade Act (1974) grants the president broad powers to eliminate unfair foreign trade practices that adversely affect US trade and investment in both goods and services, and leaves it with the president to determine such unfair or discriminatory trade practices. The president thus can both determine unfair trade practices and take necessary actions to bring an end to such practices. Most observers agree that Section 301, which has been updated several times, grants probably the most open-ended non-emergency powers to the president.

The use of Section 301 has been very limited, however. Between 1974 and 2022, the USTR conducted 122 investigations in total to determine unfair trade practices – 49 of these, about 40 percent, took place in the 1980s, under just one president,

94 The USTR is a part of the Executive Office of the President and responsible for developing and coordinating US international trade policies with other countries. The head of the USTR – the US Trade Representative – serves as the president's principal trade advisor, negotiator, and spokesperson on trade issues.

95 The USTA, also known as the Smoot–Hawley Act, was signed by President Herbert Hoover. The Act raised hundreds of import tariffs, ranging between 40 and 60 percent, apparently to safeguard US businesses and farmers. Subsequently, President Franklin Roosevelt reduced the tariffs on a reciprocal basis under the authority granted to him by the Reciprocal Trade Agreements Act of 1934 (RTAA: P.L. 73-316).

96 In 1982–1987, President Reagan suspended Poland's MFN status when it outlawed the trade union called Solidarity, although Poland was entitled to MFN status as a signatory to the GATT. Reagan cited Poland's 1967 protocol of accession to GATT, which required it to increase the total value of its imports from GATT Contracting Parties by 7 percent per annum, to argue that Poland had violated the GATT agreement since 1978 by failing to meet this commitment (Carter, 1999, 1186–1187).

97 Cuba was a founding member of the GATT, China became a WTO member in 2002, and Vietnam became a WTO member in 2007.

President Reagan.[98] Since then, such investigations, and consequent actions, nearly disappeared because of the advent of a new system of international trade regulations under the WTO in 1995.

But the Trump Administration in 2017 revived the Section 301 actions vigorously once again, especially focusing on Chinese trade policies with regard to technology transfer, intellectual property rights, which, the Administration believed, had imposed unreasonable or discriminatory burdens or restrictions on US commerce. In August 2017, President Trump imposed 25-percent tariffs on products from China, as a compensation for the $50 billion in estimated annual harm caused by Chinese unfair trade practices with the US. The Department of Treasury also adopted various measures addressing concerns about Chinese investments in certain technology-intensive sectors in the US.

Fourth, Sections 201 and 406 of the Trade Act (1974) grant the president extensive powers to sanction non-market (communist) countries for causing any market disruption in the US. Section 406 deals solely with market disruption caused by communist countries and provides an easier route to impose trade restrictions than Section 201. Section 406 has widely been viewed as "a ready and powerful tool" for limiting imports from communist nations if imports of any article from a communist country increase rapidly in either absolute or relative terms.[99]

In 1979, President Carter sought to invoke Section 406 to limit imports of ammonia from the former Soviet Union, but the move was resisted by the International Trade Commission (ITC), a bipartisan independent body mandated to exercise import controls against unfair trade competition, which found no proof of such market disruption. After the then Soviet Union invaded Afghanistan in December 1979, Carter imposed a partial embargo on agricultural and other exports from Russia by using emergency powers under the IEEPA (Carter, 1999, 1207–1208).

B *Preferential Trade Programs*

The US also offers several preferential trade programs granting special tariff benefits, such as nonreciprocal, duty-free treatment of goods imported from designated developing countries and territories. Such preferential trade programs include the Generalized System of Preferences (GSP), the Caribbean Basin Initiative (CBI), and the African Growth and Opportunity Act (AGOA).[100] All of them grant near-total

[98] President Reagan especially focused on Japan. In 1987 he issued EO 5631 to raise tariffs on a variety of Japanese goods, but mostly on semiconductor chips (Carter, 1999, 1208).

[99] Section 406 even allowed any domestic plaintiff to file a law suit demanding presidential action in this regard. All they need to show to a court is that the imports of any article from a communist country are "increasing rapidly," in either absolute or relative terms. The ITC interpreted "the increasing rapidly test" as both a rapid and a recent rise in the level of imports (Calabrese, 1987).

[100] Such preferential trading programs are compatible with the Special and Differential Treatment (SDT) provisions of the WTO. The EU, Japan, Canada, and some other developed countries also offer similar preferential programs for less developed countries. For greater detail, see Dowlah (2004, 51–76), Dowlah (2011), and Hoekman (2002).

discretionary powers to the president – the president can grant, withdraw, extend, or deny such benefits to any designated country at any time.

The GSP program, mandated by the Trade Act of 1974, was established in 1976, and it is now the oldest and largest US trade preference program that grants preferential trading benefits to thousands of products imported from more than 100 designated beneficiary countries and territories. As of February 2023, as many as 119 countries and territories were designated "beneficiary developing countries" (BDCs) under this program, which has been extended until 2030 by the Consolidated Appropriations Act, 2018 (P.L. 115-141). The GSP program now provides duty-free entry into the US for over 3,500 products (based on eight-digit US Harmonized Tariff Schedule tariff lines) and duty-free status to an additional 1,500 products from 44 GSP beneficiaries designated as "least-developed beneficiary developing countries" (LDBDCs).[101]

In 1983, the US established the CBI under the Caribbean Basin Economic Recovery Act of 1983 (CBERA: P.L. 98-67),[102] granting duty-free access to the US market for most of the goods imported from the Caribbean Basin countries. The CBI was expanded by the Caribbean Basin Trade Partnership Act of 2000 (CBTPA: P.L. 106-200) and by the Trade Act of 2002, which also extended it until 2030. As of February 2022, the CBI had 17 designated beneficiaries under the CBERA. In 2000, the US introduced the AGOA program granting similar preferential access to imports from 36 sub-Saharan countries under the African Growth and Opportunity Act of 2000 (AGOA: P.L. 106-200).[103]

Congressional legislation that underpins these preferential programs grants the president nearly unlimited powers to withdraw, extend, or deny benefits to designated countries on various grounds. Although the purpose of these statutes has been primarily economic, in practice many presidents have often used their discretionary powers to advance US foreign policy goals and national interests.

[101] In 2020, products valued at $16.9 billion (imports for consumption) entered the US duty-free under the program, out of $152.0 billion worth of total imports from GSP-eligible countries. The overall GSP utilization rate, thus, has been around 43 percent. Countries that topped the list of GSP utilization in 2019 were Cambodia (91 percent), Ecuador (90 percent), Indonesia (62 percent), Philippines (56 percent), South Africa (50 percent), Argentina (47 percent), Thailand (44 percent), Brazil (40 percent), Turkey (25 percent) and India (23 percent). The US, however, imports only a small fraction under the GSP program. Of the total US imports of $2.3 trillion in 2020, the share of GSP was only $16.9 billion. For greater detail, see Wong (2022), and ustr.gov/issue-areas/trade-development/preference-programs/generalized-system-preference-gsp.

[102] The countries are: Antigua and Barbuda, Aruba, Bahamas, Barbados, Belize, British Virgin Islands, Curacao, Dominica, Grenada, Guyana, Haiti, Jamaica, Montserrat, St. Kitts and Nevis, St. Lucia, St. Vincent and the Grenadines, Trinidad and Tobago. Eight of these 17 are also beneficiaries under CBTPA: Barbados, Belize, Curacao, Guyana, Haiti, Jamaica, St. Lucia, Trinidad, and Tobago.

[103] Under the AGOA program, the US grants duty-free access to over 1,800 products, in addition to the more than 5,000 products that are eligible for duty-free access under the GSP program. In February 2023, there were 36 countries under the program. In 2015, Congress extended the program to 2025.

For example, under the laws that underpin the GSP program,[104] the president can exclude all communist countries from the GSP benefits, unless they are members of the WTO or the International Monetary Fund (IMF), or they are granted Normal Trade Relations (NTR) status with the US.[105] The president also can exclude countries that: (a) collude with other countries to withhold supplies or resources from international trade or raise the price of goods in a way that could cause serious disruption to the world economy; (b) nationalize or expropriate the property of US citizens (including corporations) or otherwise infringe on US citizens' intellectual property rights (IPR); (c) take steps to repudiate or nullify existing contracts or agreements of US citizens or corporations; (d) impose or enforce taxes or other restrictive conditions or measures on the property of US citizens; (e) sanction countries that fail to act in good faith to recognize as binding or enforce arbitral awards in favor of US citizens or corporations; and (f) grant sanctuary from prosecution to any individual or group that commits acts of international terrorism, or do not take steps to support US efforts against terrorism.

The president can also withdraw, suspend, limit, terminate, or deny GSP benefits to countries that fail to grant internationally recognized worker rights, such as collective bargaining, freedom from compulsory labor, minimum age for employment of children, and occupational safety. In March 2021, for example, the USTR announced that it would consider Myanmar's GSP eligibility with respect to internationally recognized worker rights when it suspended US trade engagement with the country.[106]

The president can also suspend GSP facilities to beneficiary countries on the basis of "competitive need limit" (CNL).[107] Based on CNL review in 2020, Ecuador lost its GSP eligibility for taro, and Brazil lost such facility for gum, wood, or sulfate turpentine and diesel-powered electric generating sets. The president, however, can grant waiver to CNL provision. In 2020, four countries received such waivers: Argentina, Brazil, Ecuador, and Indonesia – for products, including taro, chemicals, plywood, gold jewelry, and engines.

The GSP regulations also authorize the president to grant *de minimis* waivers, which may be applied if the total dollar value of a particular product imported into the US crosses a limit. In 2020, such *de minimis* waivers were granted to 24 products from eight countries, including fresh-cut orchids from Thailand, shelled

[104] The discussion on GSP rules and recent actions is based on Wong (2022, 9–21).

[105] The US grants "permanent normal trade relations" (PNTR) status for free trade with a foreign nation as a synonym for normal trade relations (NTR), pursuant to Section 5003 of the Internal Revenue Service Restructuring and Reform Act of 1998 (RRA98: P.L. 105-206).

[106] See USTR Press Release: "USTR Suspends Trade Engagement with Burma Following Military Coup and Violence against Civilians." March 29, 2021.

[107] The measure called CNL sets in when imports of a product from a single country reach a specified threshold value, which increases by $5 million each calendar year, or when 50 percent or more of total US imports of a product entering under GSP come from a single country.

macadamia nuts from Brazil, and woven rattan from Indonesia. Of course, the president can waive certain mandatory criteria for GSP designation of any country if it is in the national economic interest of the US.[108]

V US FINANCIAL SANCTIONS

Economic and financial sanctioning measures or regimes have undergone two paradigmatic shifts in recent decades. First, since the early 1990s, following the exposure of the devastating effects of comprehensive sanctions on the Iraqi population, both unilateral and multilateral sanctioners have moved to targeted/smart sanctions aimed at specific individuals and entities allegedly involved in wrongful acts under international law, instead of indiscriminately targeting the whole country or population. As a result, economic sanctions are now being increasingly targeted at restricting sector-specific or product-specific imports from or exports to a target country, and financial sanctions are being focused on specific flows of funds and other forms of transactions to and from a target country, individuals, or entities (Carter and Farha, 2013, 910; Gibney, 2022).[109]

Second, since the early 2000s, the US has increasingly been preferring financial sanctions over trade sanctions, particularly focusing on prohibition of transfer of funds and freezing of assets, against individuals, entities, and nations. Apparently, financial sanctions are believed to be relatively easier than trade sanctions to enforce because governments and international financial institutions are important providers or guarantors of financial flows; private financial markets tend to be relatively more regulated than goods markets; and a smaller number of larger players are likely to be involved in international finance than in international trade, which means financial activities can be monitored more easily and penalties for violations of government policy may be levied more readily (Hufbauer, 2007, 46).

Empirical records also indicate greater effectiveness of financial sanctions over trade sanctions. For example, increased US duties on the Dominican Republic's sugar imports in 1961–1962 helped topple the Trujillo regime; US threats to deny MFN status to Romania are believed to have encouraged the regime to relax its emigration restrictions; the freeze on $12 billion in Iranian deposits held in the US

[108] For example, under the GSP statutes, a developing country that enters into a free trade agreement (FTA) with the US generally loses its GSP eligibility. Colombia and Panama lost their GSP status under this provision under the United States–Colombia Trade Promotion Agreement (P.L. 112-42) and the United States–Panama Trade Promotion Implementation Act (P.L. 112-43). But because of presidential waiver, Jordan continues to be eligible for GSP benefits even though it entered into an FTA with the US in 2001.

[109] Financial and economic (trade) sanctions, however, may overlap significantly as freezing of financial assets and restricting financial transactions may also impede trade by making it difficult for the targets to pay for the exports or imports. As discussed in subsequent chapters, many targeted countries, such as Iraq and Venezuela, indeed failed to import essential goods for their population, such as food and medicine, due to financial sanctions.

in 1979–1981 might have had a major impact on the release of the hostage diplomats; private decisions by several US banks not to roll over South Africa's short-term loans might have contributed to a financial crisis in the country in 1985, and several regression analyses show that financial controls have been marginally more effective than trade controls (Carter, 1999, 1179; Hufbauer, 2007, 46).

The US also has a long history of imposing financial sanctions. For example, during WWII, the US blocked Nazi Germany's access to funds of occupied countries held under its jurisdiction. And in recent decades the US has deployed financial pressure campaigns, as stand-alone or along with trade sanctions, targeting many countries, such as Iran, North Korea, and Syria, on the grounds of nuclear proliferation; against many Latin American countries on the grounds of drug trafficking and money laundering; and against corrupt, militant, and kleptocratic regimes of the Democratic Republic of the Congo, Nicaragua, Venezuela, and Myanmar (Goldman and Lindblom, 2021, 134–135; Rosenberg, 2019).

The US has indeed imposed financial sanctions, alone or in combination with trade restrictions, in 153 of 204 sanctions regimes between 1948 and 2000 (Hufbauer, 2007, 46), and since the mid 1990s, especially since 9/11, the US has significantly expanded financial sanctions covering a wide range of countries, sectors, individuals, and transactions (Nephew, 2020). The legislative and executive authority of the president to impose financial sanctions is discussed below in the context of private transactions with sanctioned individuals, entities, and countries, and control/influence over international financial institutions.

A *Sanctions on Private Financial Transactions*

Until the early 1990s, the president had very limited non-emergency statutory authority over private financial transactions of foreigners. Foreigners could deposit in US banks and use US banks for trade and investment – no US law permitted the president to control foreigners' deposits for foreign policy purposes in a non-emergency situation. The US, however, had scores of non-emergency statutes to address private financial transactions of foreigners. For example, the Securities Act of 1933[110] required disclosure of financial and other significant information concerning securities being offered for public sale; the Johnson Act of 1934 (18 U.S.C. §955) provided criminal penalties for American citizens who lent money to foreign countries that had not paid their past war debts; the Securities Exchange Act of 1934 (P.L. 73-291) – that created the Securities and Exchange Commission (SEC) – empowered the SEC with broad authority over all aspects of the securities industry with disciplinary powers, and the Investment Company Act of 1940 (P.L. 110-326) provided regulation for companies engaged in mutual funds to disclose their financial condition and investment policies to investors.

[110] P.L. 117-263, as amended and enacted through December 23, 2022.

Under these statutes, the president obviously had authority to prosecute violators, but had no discretion to alter the rules or regulations. Presidential authority with respect to private financial transactions of foreigners, however, was enhanced by the Bank Secrecy Act of 1970 (BSA: P.L. 91-508), which requires US financial institutions to assist the federal government to detect and prevent money laundering activities. The BSA makes it obligatory for US financial institutions to keep records of cash purchases of negotiable instruments, file suspicious activities reports of cash transactions exceeding $10,000, and report such other suspicious activities that involve money laundering, tax evasion, or such other criminal acts.[111]

Then, in the aftermath of the international debt crisis of 1982, the Congress enacted the International Lending Supervision Act of 1983 (P.L. 98-181), which authorizes the regulators to require strengthened capital and loan-loss reserves to strengthen the banks against potential losses on foreign loans. These changes not only made federal regulation of foreign lending more intensive and uniform, but also granted the president considerable discretion to influence private credit transactions with a foreign country on foreign policy grounds. For example, under the law, the president could influence the categorization of a country so that banks could deny loans to certain countries, and even directly pressure private banks to restrict lending to a certain country regardless of its credit rating (Carter, 1999, 1217).

In 1990, the Treasury Department introduced the Financial Crimes Enforcement Network (FinCEN)[112] to gather intelligence on suspicious international financial transactions. The FinCEN's role, however, expanded massively after 9/11, when President George W. Bush issued EO 13224, granting the Treasury Department the mandate and the means to disrupt the financial support networks of terrorists and terrorist organizations – and their subsidiaries, agents, and associates – which commit, or pose a significant risk of committing, acts of terrorism.

Subsequently, the Patriot Act (2001) provided legislative coverage to FinCEN by empowering the president to impose sanctions on suspicious financial transactions. Specifically, Section 311 of the Patriot Act empowers the president to designate a financial institution as "a money laundering concern" based on numerous jurisdictional and institutional factors, including the extent to which the institution may be involved in facilitating money laundering. The president can also prohibit such concerns in maintaining correspondent accounts with financial institutions in the US, and thus cut off their access to the US dollar-based payment systems (Carter and Farha, 2013, 910).[113]

[111] As the discussion below indicates, the BSA has been amended several times – the latest in 2021.

[112] The FinCEN was initially established administratively in April 1990 under the Department of Treasury Order 105-08. The network gained further strength when the Office of Financial Enforcement of Treasury Department merged with it in 1994, and after the Patriot Act (2001) incorporated and upgraded it.

[113] Section 311 of the Patriot Act also carries additional indirect consequences. For example, in 2005, such a designation of Banco Delta Asia (Macau, China), because of its business with North Korea despite US sanctions against North Korea, triggered a run on the bank by depleting 34 percent of the bank's deposits within days. Eventually, the bank went into receivership, and the Macau government froze accounts that the US Treasury Department had identified as suspected transactions (Gaylord, 2008).

The Sarbanes–Oxley Act of 2002 (P.L. 107-204) then mandated a number of reforms to enhance corporate responsibility, providing for criminal penalties for certain types of misconduct with respect to public corporations' compliance with the law, and the Dodd–Frank Wall Street Reform and Consumer Protection Act of 2010 (P.L. 111-203), that came after the 2008 Great Recession and banking meltdown, almost completely revamped the regulatory system in consumer protection, trading restrictions, credit ratings, regulation of financial products, corporate governance, and disclosure and transparency requirements, and in the process granting the president wider discretionary powers over the banking, securities, and investment activities of individuals and entities at home and abroad.

In January 2021, as a part of the National Defense Authorization Act of 2021 (P.L. 117-81: NDAA), the Congress passed the Anti-Money Laundering Act of 2020 (AML: 2020) and, within the AML Act, included the Corporate Transparency Act (CTA: 2021). The CTA creates a federal beneficial ownership registry requiring certain types of domestic and international corporate entities to file with the FinCEN information about the beneficial ownership of those entities and make disclosures of whether such industries or localities pose any money laundering threats. The Act also brings under its ambit anonymous shell companies that allow criminals and terrorists to launder money, and makes such criminal offenses punishable by a fine of up to $1 million, 10 years' imprisonment, or both.[114]

The CTA also enhances penalties for money laundering violations under the BSA (1970) by providing for a penalty of up to three times the profit gained from the violation, or twice the maximum penalty with respect to the violation to repeat violators. Under the CTA, if an individual partner, director, officer, or employee of a financial institution is convicted of a BSA violation, the individual must repay to the financial institution any bonus received during the calendar year during which or after which the violation occurred, and any individual found to have committed an egregious violation of the BSA may be barred from serving on the board of directors of any US financial institution for 10 years following the conviction or judgment.

As a result of legislative actions since the early 1990s, the president now has wide-ranging discretion to intervene in the private business transactions of individuals and entities. While prior to 1990, private banks headquartered in Western countries were rarely instructed to restrict loans or financial services to target countries, entities or individuals on non-emergency grounds, all that changed in recent decades. For example, in 2010, President Obama instructed Western private banks not to do business with Iraq or Iran, and imposed heavy fines on several European banks for

[114] The Act provides for two types of criminal offense: the first relates to knowingly concealing, falsifying, or misrepresenting a material fact concerning the ownership or control of assets in a monetary transaction involving assets valued at $1 million or more; and the second relates to knowingly concealing the source of funds in a monetary transaction that involves an entity found to be a primary money-laundering concern, or maintaining a correspondent account for such transactions.

evading such instructions, and even cut many of them off from world's financial centers. In 2017, when President Trump withdrew from the Joint Comprehensive Plan of Action (JCPOA) and reimposed sanctions on Iran, to bypass such sanctions, some European countries – France, Germany, and the UK – created a special vehicle called the Instrument in Support of Trade Exchanges (INSTEX) to help EU firms to continue to do business with Iran and facilitate non-US dollar transactions, but many banks refused to defy US sanctions (Beucillon, 2021).[115]

B Sanctions through International Financial Institutions

The global network of international financial institutions (IFIs) consists of the IMF and five multilateral development banks (MDBs): the International Bank for Reconstruction and Development (IBRD/World Bank), the Inter-American Development Bank (IDB), the European Bank for Reconstruction and Development (EBRD), the Asian Development Bank (ADB), and the African Development Bank (AFDB). Among these institutions, the IMF and the World Bank[116] operate globally, while others operate in their respective regions.

Generally, under unwritten laws, the president of the World Bank is a US citizen, the managing directors of the IMF and the president of EBRD are Europeans, the presidents AFDB are Africans, the presidents of ADB are Japanese, and the presidents of IDB are South Americans. Most of the loans of the MDBs are offered at near commercial interest rates, but they also offer low- or no-interest soft loans for the poorest countries.[117] Together the IFIs serve as conduits for channeling billions of dollars around the world each year, and thus, their policies, decisions, and programs play critical roles in the world economy.[118]

[115] The US Federal Reserve also has extensive supervisory and regulatory responsibilities over international operations of member banks, bank holding companies, and related entities, which are routinely involved in lending to and accepting deposits from foreign customers at their US offices, in branch offices abroad, or in their foreign-incorporated subsidiaries. The Federal Reserve is, however, a privately run constitutional entity, independent of presidential control.

[116] The IMF and the World Bank are products of the Bretton Woods Conference, held in July 1944 in New Hampshire in the immediate aftermath of WWII. The Conference, led by the US, was attended by 730 delegates from 44 countries belonging to the Allied Powers. The Conference created the IMF with the purpose of promoting stability of exchange rates and financial flows, and the IBRD for the purpose of assisting in the post-war reconstruction of infrastructure in developing countries. At the time of their creation, the structures, locations, and mandates of both of these institutions were primarily determined by the US, which also had over a third of voting powers in these institutions. For greater detail, see Dowlah (2004, 147–171), Gardner (1980), and Woods (2003).

[117] The largest of the MDBs, the World Bank, opened its soft-loan facility in 1960 under the International Development Association (IDA), which gives loans to developing countries at highly concessional rates. The US has been the largest contributor to the IDA with 20.86 percent of the fund, while the second largest are the UK and France, each contributing 7.3 percent. In general, IDA lending accounts for about 25 percent of IBRD/IDA total lending (Kapur, 1997; Woods, 2003).

[118] For an excellent discussion on the regulatory frameworks, as well as mandates and structures, of these IFIs, as well as other transnational financial institutions, see Bradley (2022, 30–53).

Historically, the US has used the IFIs quite extensively, both directly and indirectly, to advance its foreign policy goals. Both the Congress and the executive branch wield such influence over the IFIs through a number of mechanisms, such as controlling the replenishment of funds, exercising voting power, choosing leaderships, and building alliances with other countries (Wong and Nelson, 2021; Woods, 2003).

The MDBs, however, obtain 80 percent of their funds by tapping world capital markets and the remaining 20 percent by assessing member governments, while the IMF depends solely on quota payments from the member nations. As voting power in the IFIs depends on the levels of contributions of the members, the US holds the largest single voting shares in all of them: 16.77 percent in the IMF, 16.36 percent in the World Bank, 30.01 percent in the IDB, 6.33 percent in the AFB, 12.76 percent in the ADB, and 10.15 percent in the EBRD (US Senate, 2009).

As veto power in the IFIs requires a majority of 86 percent of votes, the US enjoys near veto power in all of them, and thus is capable of exercising major influence on loan requests from these institutions. At the same time, most decisions on loan requests of the IFIs are not decided by a formal vote – they are often reached through informal consensus among the executive board members. Thus, the US does not always succeed in blocking the IFIs from lending to a country which it opposes. For example, in the early 1970s, the US tried to cut off IFI assistance to Chile and Nicaragua for engaging in gross violations of human rights and, between 1977 and 1985, the US voted against seven loans to Nicaragua – two from the World Bank and five from the IDB – but succeeded in blocking the loans only in one instance (Carter, 1999, 1222).

The US, however, maintains very strong influence over two of the largest IFIs – the IMF and the World Bank – by exercising its control over the selection of senior level positions in these institutions,[119] and through regular monitoring of their policies. The Treasury Department formulates and implements all US policies with respect to the IMF, while the State Department does the same with respect to the World Bank. Congress also imposes significant pressures directly and indirectly through these departments and the International Financial Institution Advisory Commission (the Meltzer Commission, established in 1997), which recommends US policy toward these and other multilateral economic organizations (Woods, 2003)

At the same time, the IMF and the World Bank have a very strong track record of accommodating the US in their dealings with and granting of loans to many countries (Hufbauer and Jung, 2020). For example, in 1948, the World Bank geared up its loans for former Yugoslavia after it broke from the Soviet bloc; Nicaragua's US-supported Somoza regime received a disproportionate number of World Bank loans in the 1950s through 1960s; Iran was granted 30 loans, worth $1.2 billion, when

[119] See, among others, Woods (2003) and Kapur (1997) for historical records of hiring practices and biases of the World Bank and the IMF.

it contained Soviet-supported Iraq between 1957 and 1974; the World Bank stepped up its support for Indonesia immediately after the US-backed General Suharto assumed power in 1966, and the Bank also took similar steps toward Turkey and Mexico in the late 1970s (Kapur, 1997, 463–471).

The World Bank and the IMF also need Congressional approval for any increase in resources, and each time an increase in IMF quota or a replenishment of the World Bank's soft-loan window under the International Development Association (IDA) is negotiated, Congress can use the opportunity to reduce or withhold funds and impose special preconditions. In the 1990s, for example, Congress attempted to influence the IMF over the issues of worker rights, the role of the private sector, human rights, and military spending, and so on. Such direct and indirect pressures from Congress have historically enhanced the US's capacity to determine unilaterally many aspects of policy and structure within the IMF and the World Bank (Woods, 2003, 24).

Moreover, scores of US statutes, related to terrorism, drug trafficking, nuclear proliferation, money laundering, and so on, grant direct and indirect powers to the president to influence IFIs from lending to countries subject to US sanctions.[120] Especially, when a country is designated as a "state sponsor of terrorism," such designation requires the president to block lending to the country by any of the IFIs. The Obama Administration, for example, blocked IFI lending to Iran during 2009–2016 due to Iran's attempt to develop nuclear weapons and its support for international terrorism (Goldman and Lindblom, 2021, 130).

VI CONCLUDING REMARKS

Under the US Constitution, both the president and the Congress share responsibilities with respect to foreign affairs and international commerce. Over the course of time, however, the Congress has delegated significant powers and authorities to tilt the powers more in favor of the president in both respects due to historical circumstances, such as the two world wars, the Great Depression, the Cold War, and the 9/11 attacks. As a result, the president now can exert broad authority to limit bilateral trade relations, cut off economic assistance to a foreign country, ban imports or exports, or both, and restrict domestic as well as IFIs from granting credits to a foreign country. A highly intricate and sophisticated legal framework, that rests squarely on weaponization of the legal definition of "US persons" and its extraterritorial applications, enables the president to adopt and impose economic and financial sanctions with extraordinary speed and efficacy around the world by utilizing both emergency and non-emergency powers.

[120] Such statutes, to mention a few, include: the AECA (1976), the Antiterrorism and Effective Death Penalty Act of 1996 (AEDPA: P.L. 104-132), the Patriot Act (2001), the CISADA (2010), the NDAA (2012), the ITRA (2012), and the NDAA (2013).

The US sanctioning measures have undergone significant paradigmatic shifts since the end of the Cold War, however. In recent decades they have increasingly been targeted at sectors, individuals, or entities of a target country, rather than the whole country or population; increasingly they are being geared to financial sanctions over trade sanctions; increasingly both domestic and international financial institutions have been used to advance US foreign policy goals. Export sanctions have increasingly been preferred over import restrictions; and preferential trading arrangements, targeted at developing countries, have increasingly been used to grant, curtail, or deny such facilities depending on their compliance with US foreign policy objectives. The US has also been taking an increasingly aggressive stance to thwart its WTO/GATT obligations with respect to targeted countries by invoking national security exception clauses.

REFERENCES

Beckhy, P. 2018. Sanctions and the Blurred Boundaries of International Economic Law. *Missouri Law Review*, 83(1):1–38.

Berman, H., and J. Garson. 1967. United States Export Controls – Past, Present, and Future. *Columbia Law Review*, 67(5):791–890.

Beucillon, C. (Ed.). 2021. *Research Handbook on Unilateral and Extraterritorial Sanctions*. Cheltenham, UK: Edward Elgar.

Boyle, A., and T. Lau. 2021. *The President's Extraordinary Sanctions Powers*. July 20, 2021. Brenan Center of Justice. July 20. Available at: www.brennancenter.org/our-work/research-reports/presidents-extraordinary-sanctions-powers.

Bradley, C. 2022. International Finance Lectures, Spring 2022. University of Miami. Available at: www.blenderlaw.com/.

Breen, E. 2021. Corporations and US Economic Sanctions: The Dangers of Overcompliance. In C. Beucillon (ed.), *Research Handbook on Unilateral and Extraterritorial Sanctions*, pp. 256–269. Cheltenham, London: Edward Elgar.

Calabrese, J. 1981. Market Disruption Caused by Imports from Communist Countries: Analysis of Section 406 of the Trade Act of 1974. *Cornell International Law Journal*, 14(1):117–133.

Carter, B. 1999. International Economic Sanctions: Improving the Haphazard U.S. Legal Regime. *California Law Review*, 75:1159–1276.

Carter, B., and Farha, R. 2013. Overview and Operation of U.S. Financial Sanctions, Including the Example of Iran. *Georgetown Journal of International Law*, 44(3):903–914.

Casey, C. 2021. *Export Controls: Key Challenges*. Washington, DC: Congressional Research Service, IF11154.

Casey, C et al. 2020. The International Emergency Economic Powers Act: Origins, Evolution, and Use. July update. R45618. Washington, DC: Congressional Research Services.

Christopher, W. 1982. Ceasefire between the Branches: A Compact in Foreign Affairs. *Foreign Affairs*, 60(5):989–1005.

Dowlah, C. 2004. *Backwaters of Global Prosperity: How Globalization and the GATT/WTO Trade Regimes Marginalize the World's Poorest Nations*. New York: Praeger.

Dowlah, C. 2011. Trade Preferences and Development: An Assessment of U.S. GSP Schemes from the Perspective of the Least Developed Countries. In Y. Lee et al. (eds.), *Law and Development Perspective on International Trade Law*, pp. 334–356. New York: Cambridge University Press.

Doxey, M. 2009. Reflections on the Sanctions Decade and Beyond. *International Journal*, 64(2):539–549.

Emmenegger, S. 2016. Extraterritorial Economic Sanctions and Their Foundation in International Law, *Arizona Journal of International and Comparative Law*, 33(3):632–660.

Fefer, R. 2022. Section 232 of the Trade Expansion Act of 1962. Congressional Research Service (CRS), IF10667. Washington, DC.

Fefer, R. et al. 2021. Section 232 Investigations: Overview and Issues for Congress. Congressional Research Service (CRS), R45249. Washington, DC.

Fergusson, I., and P. Kerr. 2020. *The U.S. Export Control System and the Export Control Reform Initiative*. Congressional Research Service, R41916. Washington, DC.

Franck, T., and E. Weisband. 1979. *Foreign Policy by Congress*. New York and Oxford: Oxford University Press.

GAO (General Accounting Office of the United States). 1985. The Comptroller General Report to the Chairman, Subcommittee on Western Hemisphere Affairs, House Committee on Foreign Affairs and Ranking Minority Member, Senate Committee On Foreign Relations of the United States. GAO/NSIAD-85-79, May. Washington, DC.

Gardner, R. 1980. *Sterling-Dollar Diplomacy*. New York: Columbia University Press.

Gaylord, M. 2008. The Banco Delta Asia Affair: The USA PATRIOT Act and Allegations of Money Laundering in Macau. *Crime, Law & Society*, 50(208):293–298.

Gibney, M. 2022. The Historical Development of Extraterritorial Obligations. In M. Gibney et al. (eds.), *The Routledge Handbook on Extraterritorial Human Rights Obligations*, pp. 13–25. London: Routledge.

Gibney, M. et al. (Eds.). 2022. *The Routledge Handbook on Extraterritorial Human Rights Obligations*. London: Routledge.

Ginsberg, B. 2010. Managing Compliance with US Treasury Department: OFAC Obligations. *Global Trade and Customs Journal*, 5(5):183–190.

Goldman, Z., and A. Lindblom. 2021. The US Position and Practice with Regards to Unilateral and Extraterritorial Sanctions: Reimagining the US Sanctions Regime in a World of Advanced Technology. In C. Beucillon (ed.), *Research Handbook on Unilateral and Extraterritorial Sanctions*, pp. 130–148. Cheltenham, UK: Edward Elgar.

Goldsmith, J. 2019. What Is and Isn't a Big Deal in Trump's Executive Actions Related to the Border. *Lawfare*, Feb. 16.

Gordon, R., M. Smyth, and T. Cornell. 2019. *EU, UN and US Sanctions Law*. New York: Bloomberg.

Gottemoeller, R. 2007. The Evolution of Sanctions in Practice and Theory. *Survival*, 49(4):99–110.

Hillard, L., and A. Schendruk. 2019. *Funding the United Nations: What Impact Do U.S. Contributions Have on UN Agencies and Programs?* Council on Foreign Relations. Available at: www.cfr.org/article/funding-united-nations-what-impact-do-us-contributions-have-unagencies-and-programs.

Hirschhorn, E. et al. 2022. *U.S. Export Controls and Economic Sanctions*. Oxford: Oxford University Press.

Hoekman, B. et al. (Eds.). 2002. *Development, Trade and the WTO – A Handbook*. Washington, DC: World Bank.

Hufbauer, G., and E. Jung. 2020. *What's New in Economic Sanctions?* Washington, DC: Peterson Institute for International Economics.

Hufbauer, G. et al. 2007. *Economic Sanctions Reconsidered: History and Current Policy*. Washington, DC: Patterson Institute for International Economics.

Kaiser, F. 1978. *Legislative History of the Senate Select Committee on Intelligence*. Washington, DC: US Library of Congress. Congressional Research Service.

Kapur, D. et al. (Eds.). 1997. *The World Bank – Its First Half Century*. Vol. 1. Washington, DC: Brookings Institution.

Lowenfeld, A. 2002. *International Economic Law*. Oxford and New York: Oxford University Press.

McBride, J. 2018. *How Does the U.S. Spend Its Foreign Aid?* Council on Foreign Relations. Available at: www.cfr.org/backgrounder/how-does-us-spend-its-foreign-aid.

Moyer, H., and L. Mabry. 1983. Export Controls as Instruments of Foreign Policy: The History, Legal Issues, and Policy Lessons of Three Recent Cases. *Law and Policy in International Business: International Journal of Georgetown University Law Center*, 15(1):1–171.

Nephew, R. 2020. Implementation of Sanctions: United States. In M. Asada (ed.), *Economic Sanctions in International Law and Practice*, pp. 93–115. London: Routledge.

Rathbone, M. et al. 2013. Sanctions, Sanctions Everywhere: Forging a Path through Complex Transnational Sanctions Laws. *Georgetown Journal of Law*, 44:1056–1094.

Regilme, S., and H. Hartmann. 2018. Mutual Delegitimization: American and Chinese Development Assistance in Africa. *SAIS Review of International Affairs*. Available at: www.saisreview.org/2018/03/30/china-america-development-assistance/.

Rosenberg, E. 2019. *Assessing the Use of Sanctions in Addressing National Security and Foreign Policy Challenges*. Washington, DC: Center for a New American Security.

Silverstone, P. 1959. The Export Control Act of 1949: Extraterritorial Enforcement. *University of Pennsylvania Law Review*, 107(3):331–362.

US Department of Commerce. 2022. *Actual Investigations of Export Control and Antiboycott Violations*, 2019. Bureau of Industry and Security: Exports Enforcement. Washington, DC.

US Senate. 2009. *Minimizing Potential Threats from Iran: Administration Perspectives on Economic Sanctions and Other U.S. Policy Options: Hearing Before the Senate Banking, House & Urban Affairs Committee.*, 111th Cong. 44. Washington, DC.

USAID (United States International Development Agency). 2021. Foreign Aid Explorer: The Official Record of U.S. Foreign Aid. Available at: foreignassistance.gov/aid-trends.

Vazquez, C. 2003. Trade Sanctions and Human Rights – Past, Present, and Future. *Journal of International Economic Law*, 6(4):797–839.

Wong, L. 2022. *Generalized System of Preferences (GSP): Overview and Issues for Congress*. RL33663. Washington, DC: Congressional Research Services.

Wong, L., and R. Nelson. 2021. *International Financial Messaging Systems*. R46843. Washington, DC: Congressional Research Services.

Woods, N. 2003. The United States and the International Financial Institutions: Power and Influence within the World Bank and the IMF. In R. Foot et al. (eds.), *US Hegemony and International Organizations: The United States and Multilateral Institutions*, pp. 92–114. Online Edition. Oxford: Oxford Academic.

4

Enforcement Infrastructures of US Economic and Financial Sanctions

I INTRODUCTION

The dissolution of the former Soviet Union and the conclusion of the Cold War in December 1991 elevated the United States to the singular status of the world's sole superpower.[1] As military means for confronting foreign policy objectives also became less feasible at the same time, the US invested heavily in the development of a vast economic and financial infrastructure for the enforcement of apparently non-lethal sanctions regimes that can be deployed at any moment, anywhere in the world, to achieve its foreign policy objectives. The resultant intricate infrastructure, that interlinks and interweaves numerous governmental agencies and departments, relies principally on three major instruments: the extraterritorial application of sanctions regimes, the dollar-dominated global payments systems, and the hegemonic influence of the US over global financial institutions and networks.

Over the course of the last three decades, the US enforcement infrastructures for economic and financial sanctions have pivoted around three major paradigmatic shifts. First, since the early 1990s, following the exposure of the devastating effects of comprehensive sanctions on the Iraqi population,[2] along with the world community the US also made a decisive transition to targeted/smart sanctions aimed at specific individuals and entities, instead of a whole country or population. Second, sanctions regimes have increasingly shifted away from economic measures (trade sanctions) toward specific financial measures (to specific flows of funds, credit, dollar transactions, and so on). Third, sanctions regimes have increasingly been reinforced with extraterritorial applications.

This chapter focuses on the US sanctions enforcement infrastructures – the mechanisms and instruments that enforce US economic and financial sanctions

[1] In recent years, however, China has apparently emerged as a peer superpower, and that implies that the US is no longer the only superpower in the world.

[2] The difference between targeted and comprehensive sanctions has been discussed in Chapters 1 and 2, and the devastating effects of comprehensive sanctions on Iraq will be discussed in greater detail in Chapter 7 of this volume.

with breathtaking speed and ferocity across the world. The next section examines the major instruments of this machinery – the extraterritorial nature of US sanctions and their legislative and administrative interpretations. Section III looks into the major US governmental departments and agencies involved in enforcing sanctions; and Section IV concludes the chapter.

II EXTRATERRITORIAL APPLICATION OF SANCTIONS

Extraterritorial application of US sanctions rests on three major tools: (a) aggressively deploying sanctions to force governments, entities, and individuals of third countries to abide by US sanctions; (b) fiercely expanding the definition of "US persons" both legislatively and administratively; and (c) meticulously restricting dollar-denominated international payments systems across the world.

A *Extraterritorialization of Sanctions*

An expansive legal construct of "US persons" serves as a key weapon for extraterritorialization of US sanctions. Most of the US sanctions instruments – Congressional legislation, presidential executive orders, and their official interpretations – designate "US persons" as those who have a "US nexus." This "nexus" includes anybody who presents a sufficient connection with the US through citizenship, residence, business location, tangible and intangible property, use of currency or other financial services, and so on – anything that justifies the legality of US jurisdiction over such persons and entities (Breen, 2021).

Such interpretations of "US persons" thus encompass all US citizens and permanent-resident aliens, regardless of where they are located, as well as all persons and entities located within the US territories – no matter whether they are individuals or corporations, or tourists, or illegal aliens. The definition can even include foreigners if they are acting as a "US person" at the time of their actions. For example, a foreign citizen who is in the US at the time of a violation of US sanctions is considered a "US person" for the purposes of sanctions enforcement, just as a foreign bank is considered a "US person" if it processes any payments using the US financial system (Nephew, 2020).

The legal scope of a "US person" depends, however, on the specific statutory basis of a particular sanction. Under the Trading With the Enemy Act (TWEA: 1917), a "US person" includes a foreign organization owned or controlled by US persons, including foreign subsidiaries of US companies.[3] On the other hand, under the

[3] Since the 1970s, facing criticisms of such a broad assertion of the jurisdiction of "US persons" over foreign-incorporated entities, the Treasury Department began to interpret the term in a much narrower sense by including the jurisdiction over foreign branches of US corporations but excluding separately incorporated subsidiaries. This has, however, been administrative practice; the TWEA was not amended to that effect (Marcuss, 1999).

International Emergency Economic Powers Act (IEEPA, 1977), which is still the main legislation concerning primary sanctions in the US, "US persons" include "all US citizens and permanent resident aliens regardless of where they are located, all persons and entities within the United States, [and] all U.S. incorporated entities and their foreign branches." An amendment to the IEEPA in October 2007 then added the notion of "causing" a US person to violate the Act, which makes it "unlawful" for any person or entity "to attempt to violate, conspire to violate or cause a violation" of the Act. The long arm of the IEEPA thus spills over to non-US persons who may have "caused" a US person or entity to intentionally or inadvertently violate the Act (Casey, 2022, 12).[4]

Some Congressional legislation as well as administrative agencies involved in the implementation of sanctions have either further expanded or contracted the extraterritorial jurisdiction of "US persons." The Iran Sanctions Act (ISA: 2017), for example, not only forbids foreign branches and subsidiaries of US banks from engaging in any business transactions with Iran, but also prohibits US persons employed by foreign companies from involving themselves in any Iranian project. The Act also prohibits foreign companies from selling to Iran any foreign-made products that contain 10 percent or more US-origin content, and makes the prohibition applicable to foreign-incorporated subsidiaries as well.[5] On the other hand, the Burmese Freedom and Democracy Act 2003 (BFDA: P.L. 108-61) prohibits US persons from investing in a third-country company where the company's profits are predominantly derived from Myanmar.[6]

The extraterritorial elements of US sanctions also depend on whether the sanctions regimes are primary or secondary in nature. Ordinarily, primary sanctions are targeted, first and foremost, at US persons, no matter where they are physically located. Such a broad legal construct of "US persons" also implies that when the US imposes primary sanctions on banks located in the US, the sanctions' reach extends

4 Under this term, "causing," most of the US sanctions restrictions may apply to US persons as well as non-US persons in third countries for conspiring with or causing a US person to violate US sanctions, and thus, non-US companies that employ US persons or work with US companies must separate the activities of US persons from business with US-sanctioned parties in order not to violate US sanctions (Hirschhorn, 2022, 202). Such violations, as discussed below, resulted in numerous cases of prosecutions and heavy penalties, especially with respect to "transaction stripping" incidents in which non-US citizens and non-US banks were held accountable, and heavily penalized.

5 For greater detail, see ISA (2017), codified as 31 C.F.R. § 560.204. (2017). Notably, earlier in 2016, pursuant to the Joint Comprehensive Plan of Action (JCPOA), signed in 2015, the US Treasury Department issued a general license authorizing foreign subsidiaries of US companies to engage in certain dealings with Iran which would otherwise constitute illegal facilitation under the ISA (2017) and other sanctions on Iran.

6 In another instance, on January 17, 2017, the OFAC amended the Sudanese Sanctions Regulations, in accordance with presidential EOs 13067 and 13412, to include the processing of transactions involving persons in Sudan; the importation of goods and services from Sudan; the exportation of goods, technology, and services to Sudan; and transactions involving property in which the Government of Sudan has an interest.

to all foreign branches and subsidiaries of the bank, and includes all transactions of that bank that clear through the US, no matter whether the originator or the beneficiary is located inside or outside the US (Goldman and Lindblom, 2021; Nephew, 2020). Thus, although primary sanctions are ordinarily binding on persons subject to US jurisdiction, the nationality link adds an extraterritorial dimension to such sanctions, making them both primary as well as extraterritorial sanctions at the same time.

Secondary sanctions, on the other hand, are generally applicable to individuals and entities located in a third country, other than the country that is subject to the sanctions, and they are fundamentally extraterritorial in nature because they allow the US to impose sanctions on individuals and entities that have no territorial or personal link with the US and normally would not be subject to US law or jurisdiction (Breen, 2021, 260). Such sanctions are thus targeted at foreign countries, entities, and persons who pursue their relationships with individuals, entities or countries sanctioned by the US (Beucillon, 2021), and are designed "for the political end of inducing third states or non-state actors in third states to change their policies or practices concerning economic dealings with the target of the sending state's primary sanctions" (Lowenfeld, 2002, 3).

Thus, both primary as well as secondary sanctions can have extraterritorial jurisdiction. The ISA provides a perfect example of such extraterritorial reach of both primary and secondary sanctions. As mentioned above, it forbids foreign branches and subsidiaries of US banks from engaging in any business transactions with Iran, and also prohibits US persons employed by foreign companies from involving themselves in any Iranian project. Some other sanctioning laws that have similar provisions include the Ukraine Freedom Support Act of 2014 (UFSA: P.L. 113-272) and the Countering Russian Influence in Europe and Eurasia Act of 2017 (CRIEEA: P.L. 115-244).[7]

Such extraterritorial dimensions also functionally transform unilateral sanctions of the US into a form of multilateral sanctions. This occurs through formal mechanisms when the US enters into bilateral or regional agreements with other countries, and through informal mechanisms when the US makes informal arrangements and alliances with other countries to aggravate the impact of its sanctions on the target state, individuals, or entities in order to cut them off from their business partners around the world (Breen, 2021; Mallard and Hanson, 2021).

[7] As discussed in greater detail in Chapters 6 and 7, the Iran Transactions and Sanctions Regulations (ITSR) (31 C.F. R §§ 560.204, 560.205 (2019)), and the Cuban Assets Control Regulations (CACR) prohibit exports of US goods to these countries, but also prohibit "reexports" of US goods from a third country to or transiting through these countries, even if such actions are taken by non-US persons or entities. On the other hand, as discussed in Chapter 5, such extraterritorial sanctions imposed on Russia/Ukraine have dollar thresholds that must be met before any US action is triggered. Overall, the OFAC's actions usually depend on "significant" or "material" assistance or support to the person or activity that is the subject of the US sanctions program, and the OFAC usually provides "a broad list of factors" that constitute such "significant" and "material" assistance with respect to the country concerned (Hirschhorn, 2022, 216–217).

The US also expands the extraterritorial jurisdictions of its sanctions by invoking the effects of a foreign situation on US territory, such as by using any financial transaction denominated in dollars, or stretching the personal nexus of individuals and entities with the target state. In recent decades, the US has also succeeded in doing so through multilateralization of issue-based sanctions, such as sanctions against money laundering, bribery, terrorism, drug trafficking and human rights violations (Beucillon, 2021). Such extraterritorial application of sanctions invariably constrains persons and entities located in or bearing the nationality of a third state to abide by US sanctions although they are otherwise not subject to US jurisdiction (Hirschhorn, 2022, 202).

Scholars, however, differ widely in their interpretation of the legality of such extraterritorial application of sanctions. While the critics deplore such extraterritorialities for crossing the bounds of prescriptive jurisdiction and encroaching on the sovereign rights of other nations on questionable grounds (Clark, 1999, 63; Beckhy, 2018, 9), the proponents argue that such sanctions are perfectly legitimate under international law as long as they have sufficient territorial and nationality ties to the sanctioning state (Knox, 2010; Meyer, 2009).

B *The US Dollar-Denominated Global Payments System*

Another powerful tool that the US has at its disposal to enforce its unilateral sanctions around the world is its legal tender – the US dollar. This mighty green buck, which some describe as "King Dollar" (McDowell, 2023, 20), has literally bestowed upon the nation the largest empire in the entire history of the world. All past empires had geographical limits, but this dollar-denominated empire not only sweeps across all geographical boundaries around the world, but also reigns supreme around the clock by dominating over most of the economic and financial transactions that take place on the surface of the Earth.

The ascendency of the US dollar began with the decisive victory of the US in WWII,[8] and has continued ever since, albeit with some challenges in recent years (Rosenberg et al., 2016). The dominance of the dollar in the global financial system is rooted in its unrivaled fundamentals – its ability to serve as a stable international currency that delivers on the three basic roles of money: as a store of value, as a medium of exchange, and as a unit of account at the global level. No other national currency in the world can make such a claim, no other national currency is more widely used in the world economy, and no other currency can command greater confidence and convenience to investors, traders, governments, and the global marketplace.

8 Prior to that, Great Britain had the mantle when the British pound sterling reigned supreme over the global financial system for several hundred years. The international financial system of the seventeenth and eighteenth centuries was indeed founded on the British pound sterling. For the history of the British pound's dominance, especially prior to WWI, see Mulder (2022, 49–54).

As a result of such "weaponized interdependence" of global financial markets and the US dollar, a vast segment of the contemporary international financial market falls under US jurisdiction in some way or other (Mulder, 2022, 193). It is thus not surprising that, despite major structural shifts in the international monetary system over the past six decades – such as the emergence of digital currencies and new payments ecosystems, the collapse of the Gold Standards that underpinned the Bretton Woods system in the 1970s, and the emergence of new reserve currencies such as the euro and the renminbi in recent decades – for all practical purposes, the US dollar still reigns supreme in global economic and financial transactions.

In 2020, for example, the US dollar was the most dominant reserve currency in the world (with 61-percent share); the most traded currency in the foreign exchange market (with 44-percent share); the most used currency for trade invoicing (with 54-percent share); the largest currency in financial claim denominations (with 51-percent share); and the most stable currency in global foreign exchange turnover since 1989 (Arslanalp, 2020; Gopinath and Stein, 2021). In September 2022, the dollar had an approximately 50-percent share of outstanding international debt securities, and about a 60-percent share of global private credits denominated in foreign currency (BIS, 2022).

Mechanisms of the Dollar Empire

The US dollar-denominated global financial infrastructures have been underpinned by some powerful mechanisms that reach every corner of the world. Such mechanisms include: the Fedwire network of the US Federal Reserve System; CHIPS – the Clearing House Interbank Payments System; and SWIFT – the Society for Worldwide Interbank Financial Transactions.

The Fedwire Network

At the apex of the mammoth US dollar-denominated financial infrastructures under the control of the US government stands the Fedwire – a communication and settlement system, formerly known as the Federal Reserve Wire Network (FRWN), which is owned and operated by the Federal Reserve System. The Fedwire provides a real-time, gross settlement system that processes trillions of dollars worth of wire transfers each day through a highly secure electronic network that provides immediate, final, and irrevocable settlements of funds from across the world.[9]

The Federal Reserve System serves as an intermediary in this process under which US banks maintain "correspondent accounts" through which foreign banks (originator banks) from the around the world wire transfer volumes of funds to

9 A wire transfer involves a transaction in which the transferor or "originator," which may be an individual, a corporation, or a bank, instructs its bank to transfer funds from its account to the account of the recipient or beneficiary. If the originator and beneficiary do not have accounts at the same bank, the originator's bank and the beneficiary's bank can maintain correspondent accounts with each other.

conduct international financial transactions.[10] The Federal Reserve Bank of New York (FRBNY) plays the most important role in this process as most of the Fedwire transactions originate from financial institutions under the FRBNY's jurisdiction.[11]

Clearing House Interbank Payments System (CHIPS)

The US-dollar dominated global currency reserve system is also underpinned by a privately owned clearing system called CHIPS, which is the largest private sector run US dollar clearing system in the world. In 2019, this private sector counterpart to the Fedwire cleared and settled over 470,000 "payment messages" worth an aggregate of $1.6 trillion on any given day (Clearing House, 2020). Unlike the Fedwire system, which is part of a US regulatory body, CHIPS is owned by the financial institutions around the world that use the system for payments that are less time-sensitive in nature. CHIPS is also less expensive than Fedwire, and while Fedwire provides a real-time gross settlement, CHIPS allows the payments to be netted.[12]

A small group of large banks from around the world operate as CHIPS participant correspondent banks. As of February 2023, CHIPS had 43 participant banks, which held a 95 percent share in large-value domestic and international US dollar payments. As not all CHIPS participants are American banks, the foreign institutions associated with CHIPS must have American operations. As a privately owned and operated institution, CHIPS is governed by Article 4A of the Uniform Commercial Code, but all CHIPS transactions are subject to US law.[13]

Society for Worldwide Interbank Financial Communication (SWIFT)

The Brussels-based SWIFT, founded in 1973, is a global financial network that currently serves approximately 11,500 institutions in more than 200 countries and territories around the world. SWIFT is a messaging system, however – it does not wire money from one account to another, it rather requests that money be transferred

[10] For the purposes of the Fedwire, a "correspondent account" is an account established at a US bank by a foreign financial institution to receive deposits from or make payments on behalf of a foreign financial institution, or handle other financial transactions related to such institution. The originator's bank and the beneficiary's bank may both maintain such correspondent accounts at a third intermediary bank as well. Called "payable-through accounts," such accounts refer to those accounts that are established with US banks by foreign financial institutions to enable foreign customers to access the US banking system. Both correspondent accounts and payable-through accounts are subject to American law (Carter and Farha, 2013, 906).

[11] The FRBNY does not actually screen electronic Fedwire transactions as the transactions are processed immediately, in real time. It can, however, screen such transactions for the purposes of US sanctions enforcements but only after the transaction has already taken place.

[12] Under the "Netting" system, CHIPS consolidates all pending payments into a single transaction. For example, if Bank A is to pay Bank B $1 million, and Bank B is to pay Bank A $800,000, the CHIPS system will aggregate this to a single payment of $200,000 from Bank A to Bank B. For the same transaction, the Fedwire system would require two separate payments for the full amounts of $1 million from Bank A and $800,000 from Bank B.

[13] For greater detail on the Uniform Commercial Code (UCC) see: www.uniformlaws.org/acts/catalog/current/ucc, and for CHIPS's organization and operation see: www.theclearinghouse.org/payment-systems/chips.

from one bank account to another through a small number of major currencies designated as the international mediums of exchange. SWIFT thus conducts its payments instructions in both US dollars and some other currencies.

As of April 2022, the US dollar accounted for 41.8 percent of all SWIFT payment instructions by value, while the shares of other currencies were: euro 34.7 percent, British pound 6.3 percent, Japanese yen 3.1 percent, and Chinese renminbi 2.1 percent (Eichengreen, 2021).[14] Between 2009 and 2019, SWIFT's daily messaging services for cross-border debit and credit payments more than doubled, rising from 14.9 million to 33.5 million (Wong and Nelsen, 2021), and in 2020, SWIFT's daily payment orders averaged roughly $5 trillion (McDowell, 2023, 22–30).

Aside from the majority of its transactions being carried in US dollars, the US also enjoys considerable leverage over the SWIFT organization because the US serves as the head of its 25-member governing board; one of the three international data centers of SWIFT is located in the US;[15] and SWIFT depends extensively on the settlement services of Fedwire, CHIPS, and other US payment systems.[16] Moreover, in the aftermath of the September 11, 2001, attacks (9/11), the US reached an agreement with SWIFT and the EU, which allows the Treasury Department to subpoena SWIFT for information on the financial transactions of suspected terrorists or their networks in the course of terrorism investigations (Cipriani, 2023; Koppel, 2011).

Use of Dollar as a Tool of Sanctions

Such a predominant role of the US dollar in global financial system gives the US incomparable coercive power to inflict pain on its sanction targets – no matter whether they are countries, companies, or individuals. Restricting the sanction targets from holding their financial assets in the most important global currency, delinking them from the dollar-denominated cross-border payments systems or global finance and commerce architectures, may cause a so-called "chokepoint effect" on such entities (Cipriani, 2023; Farrell, Newman, 2019, 55–56).

The US has indeed used the incredible power and reach of the dollar quite extensively over the course of time to penalize its adversaries. Even before the dollar became the global currency of the world, during WWII, the US froze assets from occupied countries that were held under US jurisdiction to thwart Nazi Germany (Lowenfeld, 2003). Of course, the usage of the dollar as a tool for sanctions has increased manifold since WWII. For example, during the Korean War in the early

[14] In terms of trade finance, however, in 2020 the US dollar represented 86 percent of the value of SWIFT traffic, whereas the euro represented only 7 percent, and the Chinese renminbi amounted to 2 percent (SWIFT, 2021).

[15] The SWIFT messaging network is run from three data centers – the other two are located in the Netherlands and Switzerland (SWIFT, 2021).

[16] Fedwire is available only to US financial institutions, but a US dollar cross-border fund transfer may involve a Fedwire message if the sending or receiving bank is a Fedwire participant. Thus, financial messages from SWIFT and Fedwire may be used at different stages of the payment chain to complete the transaction (Wong and Nelsen, 2021).

1950s, the US blocked Chinese and North Korean assets subject to US jurisdiction; in the mid 1990s, the US targeted assets of narcotics traffickers in Mexico and Colombia; and since 9/11, such restrictions, prohibitions, and freezing of dollar-based assets have expanded to scores of countries, individuals, entities, sectors, products, and transactions (Goldman and Lindblom, 2021, 134–135).

The US also has a long history of deploying the coercive power of the dollar against adversarial countries that are uniquely dependent on either dollar or dollar-dominated global economic and financial systems. For example, the US imposed sanctions on Cuba in 1959, when 71 percent of its exports and 64 percent of its imports were with the US; Cuba was the ninth largest market for US agricultural exports and the second largest supplier of US agricultural imports (Fandl, 2018). Similarly, the US imposed sanctions against Iran in 1979 when 59 percent of Iranian oil was exported to the US and Western Europe, and 70 percent of Iran's imports came from the same countries, and all such transactions were denominated in dollars. On top of that, Iran had more than $12 billion of assets in US jurisdiction, which the US froze immediately after the Iranian Hostage Crisis (O'Sullivan, 2003, 68–69).

Most recent targets of US sanctions – such as Iraq, Sudan, Iran, Russia, and Venezuela – have also depended predominantly on the export of oil traded in US dollars, and oil exports – the principal source of their foreign exchange and revenues – were denominated in US dollars. US sanctions against these jurisdictions make it more difficult for them to earn, store, and use US dollars, causing significant economic consequences (Goldman and Lindblom, 2021, 137). The pains of such sanctions become even more severe because of the over-compliance by many international banking and finance institutions to monitor and self-report such transactions in order to avoid potentially costly sanctions violations (Beucillon, 2021).[17]

Such over-compliance of international banking and financial institutions has become even fiercer in recent decades, especially since 9/11, as many US sanctions regimes come with built-in statutory extraterritoriality features capitalizing on global dollar dependence and the centrality of the US financial system. Such powers of US sanctions have also been reinforced by the Treasury Department's subpoena powers over SWIFT transactions and its database, aimed at monitoring illicit financial transactions across the world (Cipriani, 2023; Koppel, 2011).[18]

17 At the same time, decades of near-comprehensive sanctions on financial and economic transactions with North Korea in order to prevent the country from developing missile and nuclear technology all but failed. North Korea succeeded in evading US sanctions by relying on technology that is not directly linked to the US-based trade and financial system, such as hacking, cryptocurrency mining, theft, and ransomware, and internet-enabled bank theft. US sanctions also failed to thwart India and Pakistan from acquiring nuclear powers in the 1970s (Hufbauer, 2007, 12–21).

18 SWIFT acknowledges that, under the Terrorist Financing Tracking Program (TFTP), the US Treasury initially subpoenaed its entire database immediately after the 9/11 terrorist attack, but

C *Challenges to the Dollar-Denominated System*

As recent US sanctions regimes against countries like Iran, Russia, and Venezuela demonstrate, the combined outreach of the US dollar – throughFedwire, CHIPS, and SWIFT – is so extensive and inescapable that any country can be thrown out of the global financial system almost instantaneously. It is thus not surprising that attempts are being made to escape from the jurisdiction of US-dollar denominated global payments systems. Apparently, US Treasury officials – since the administration of President Barack Obama – have been cautioning that extensive use of financial sanctions could threaten the central role of the dollar and the US financial system, as many foreign governments targeted by US sanctions and their economic partners have increasingly been exploring and creating ways to reduce their dependence on the US-dollar denominated system (McDowell, 2023; Nelson and Weiss, 2022).

The challenge to the US-dollar denominated global payments system is, however, not limited to adversaries of the US or US-sanctioned countries only – it also emanates from the EU, one of the staunchest allies of the US. Including the EU, major challenges to the US dollar can be identified as: (a) the TARGET, TIPS, and INSTEX of the Eurosystem; (b) the Cross-Border Interbank Payment System (CIPS) of China; (c) the System for Transfer of Financial Messages (SPFS) of Russia; and (d) cryptocurrencies.

The Eurosystem: TARGET and TIPS

The Trans-European Automated Real-Time Gross Settlement Express Transfer (TARGET) system[19], introduced by the Eurosystem in 1999, offers a central bank payment service infrastructure across the national borders within the EU to provide a safe and reliable mechanism for the settlement of euro payments on a real-time gross settlement (RTGS) basis,[20] and to serve the needs of the Eurosystem's monetary policy.

In May 2008, the first-generation system TARGET1 was replaced by the second-generation TARGET2 to settle payments connected with monetary policy operations, as well as interbank payments, customer payments exchanged between banks, and transactions related to other payment and securities settlement systems to act as a catalyst for facilitating the development of the Single Euro Payments Area (SEPA).

subsequently narrowed its subpoena only after the EU expressed concerns about possible violations of the EU's privacy laws. The Treasury's subpoena powers have, however, been narrowed since the EU and the US signed an agreement in June 2007, under which the OFAC's retention of SWIFT data is limited to five years, and the data transfer is subject to monitoring by the EU (Amicelle, 2011; Cipriani, 2023).

[19] The discussion is primarily based on the European Central Bank publication, "TARGET Annual Report 2020," published in May 2021 by the Eurosystem, Brussels.

[20] Under the RTGS payment system, processing and settlement of transactions takes place in real time (continuously), rather than in batch-processing mode, and transactions are settled irrevocably with immediate finality. The system also settles each transfer individually, like the Fedwire network, rather than on a netting basis as under CHIPS. Both the TARGET and its successor TARGET2 use RTGS.

The system is currently available to over 44,000 banks worldwide, including 1,000 credit institutions across Europe, whereby participants can make payments on their own behalf, on behalf of other (indirect) participants, or on their customers' behalf.

In 2020, the TARGET2 system processed over 90 percent of the total value settled by large-value payment systems in euros, serving as one of the largest payment systems worldwide with turnover of €465.8 trillion. This means that less than 10 percent of large-value payment systems, involving transactions among the EU nations, were denominated in the US dollar or other currencies.

The TARGET Instant Payment Settlement (TIPS), an extension of TARGET2 and RTGS, serves as a harmonized and standardized pan-European service for instant settlement of euro-denominated payments in central bank money on an individual basis around the clock. Introduced in November 2018, the functionalities of TIPS include the sending and receiving of instant payments, liquidity transfers, and recalls of settled instant payment transactions in accordance with the SEPA Instant Credit Transfers scheme.

TIPS settles transfers for individuals and firms instantaneously and electronically.[21] Although it still settles transfers in euros only, it is designed with multi-currency capability, and the infrastructure may be expanded to some other European countries.[22] As most of the transactions of individuals and firms in the EU, over 95 percent, take place under TIPS, it indicates that the role of US dollar-denominated transactions across Europe is not significant, and has been in decline.

Instrument in Support of Trade and Exchange (INSTEX)

The INSTEX was created in 2019 as an attempt by three European countries – France, Germany, and the UK – to avoid US sanctions by pursuing non-US dollar-based and non-SWIFT-based trading transactions with Iran. The attempt was made after the administration of President Donald Trump withdrew from the Joint Comprehensive Plan of Action (JCPOA) and reimposed sanctions on Iran. The state-owned company, registered in Paris as a Special Purpose Vehicle (SPV), was designed as a barter system with a goal to facilitate legitimate trade by European market participants who wished to continue trading with Iran. European officials argued that JCPOA was based on the understanding that Iran would limit its civilian nuclear program in exchange for relief from economic sanctions, and European firms' stoppage of trade with Iran would undermine the basic principle of *quid pro quo*.

By July 2021, the INSTEX had enlisted 10 members, as Belgium, Denmark, the Netherlands, Norway, Finland, Spain, and Sweden also joined the system. But the system liquidated itself in January 2023 because of its failure to sustain imports of

21 TIPS, however works, differently than the payment service structure known as the Automated Clearing Houses (ACH). While TIPS provides the settlement of payments instantly, ACH requires another account as a settlement layer to discharge its responsibilities.

22 According to the ECB (European Central Bank)/Eurosystem website, the central banks of Sweden, Denmark, and Norway have been working with TIPS to settle instant payments in their national currencies: www.ecb.europa.eu/paym/target/tips/html/index.en.html.

Iranian oil and manage net monies owed by European importers to Iranian exporters with those owed by Iranian exporters to European importers. During its two years of existence, INSTEX was used on only one occasion to facilitate the export of medical products to Iran during the COVID-19 pandemic (McDowell, 2023, 133). The remarkable failure of INSTEX demonstrates, among other things, that it is extremely difficult to bypass US sanctions, even when such attempts are made by some powerful European nations.

Chinese Cross-Border Interbank Payment System (CIPS)

The Chinese CIPS poses another major challenge to the US-dollar denominated global financial architecture. The People's Bank of China (PBOC) – the Chinese central bank – in 2015 launched the renminbi-based CIPS, which is not only a messaging system, but also offers payment clearing and settlement services for cross-border payments. It is also a RTGS system, as opposed to a netting engine, and as of February 2023, it operated in more than 100 jurisdictions around the world (Cipriani, 2023). The financial institutions that subscribe to the CIPS are categorized as direct participants – those incorporated in China and having an account with the CIPS – and indirect participants – those subscribing to the CIPS service through direct participants.[23]

CIPS, however, operates in close cooperation with SWIFT. In 2019, for example, SWIFT established a wholly foreign-owned unit in Beijing to provide localized services to Chinese users in local languages. Then in 2021, SWIFT and CIPS established a joint venture to establish a digital currency research institute and a clearing center in Beijing. In March 2021, the PBOC established a joint venture with SWIFT to set up a localized data warehouse to monitor and analyze cross-border payment messaging in China (Wong and Nelsen, 2021).

CIPS is thus actively seeking to emerge as an alternative to SWIFT and may well be attempting to replace other Western clearinghouses to ultimately erode the worldwide primacy of the US dollar (Eichengreen, 2021; Wong and Nelsen, 2021). It is not yet a formidable competitor to the dollar-denominated international payments systems, however. Its total transactions in recent years amounted to about 2 percent of the US-based CHIPS clearing system, which, as explained above, transmits and settles an aggregate of $1.6 trillion on any given day, while in March 2022, the daily volume on CIPS was only 385 billion yuan ($45.6 billion) (Yeung and

[23] At the time of launching in 2015, CIPS had 19 direct participants and 176 indirect participants. As of May 2021, the number of total participants of CHIPS rose to a total of 1,189, of which 47 were direct and 1,142 were indirect participants (Wong and Nelson, 2021). By the end of 2022, the number of direct participants of CIPS swelled to 76 and that of indirect participants to 1,304. Most of the direct participants were overseas branches of Chinese banks, and among the indirect participants, about two-fifths were in China and three-fifths were from abroad. Indirect participants from abroad included HSBC and the Standard Chartered Bank of the UK, the Bank of East Asia (Hong Kong), DBS Bank (Singapore), Citi Bank (US), ANZ (Australia), and BNP Paribas (France) (Eichengreen, 2021).

Goh, 2022). CIPS is also not yet a competitor to SWIFT. As mentioned above, the daily average of messages sent through SWIFT amounted to $33.5 million in 2020.[24]

Russian System for Transfer of Financial Messages (SPFS)

The Central Bank of Russia (CBR) in 2014 launched its own international payments system known as the System for Transfer of Financial Messages (SPFS) in response to Western sanctions following the Russian invasion of Crimea the same year. SPFS was introduced as a direct alternative to SWIFT as the system came under increasing pressure from the US as well as the EU to disconnect Russia from its network. SPFS, which transmits messages in the SWIFT format and is thus compatible with the ISO 20022 standard, also has the capability of transmitting free-format messages (Woetzel et al. 2019). As of February 2023, approximately 440 banks were connected to the SPFS – most of them were Russian or from the former Soviet Republics, but some were from other countries, such as Germany, Switzerland, France, Japan, China, Sweden, Turkey, North Korea, Vietnam, and Cuba.[25] Although several Russian banks are connected to China's CIPS as indirect participants, only one Chinese bank is connected to SPFS. Due to its limited scale, SPFS mainly processes financial messages within Russia. In 2021, roughly 20 percent of all Russian domestic transfers were carried out through SPFS (Cipriani, 2023; Shagina, 2021).[26]

As discussed in greater detail in Chapter 5, Russia's efforts to "de-dollarize" its domestic economy due to sanctions resulted in the creation of a domestic bank payment system called Mir, which is run by the National System of Payment of Cards, owned by the Russian Central Bank. Mir was established as an alternative to Visa and Mastercard, which had suspended their operations in Russia in compliance with Western sanctions. By the end of 2020, 84 million Mir cards were issued to Russians, and more than 95 percent of domestic transactions in Russia took place in rubles (Timofeev 2021, 108).[27]

[24] It is, however, notable that nearly 1,200 banks on every major continent are part of the CIPS, and it is increasingly getting footholds in Asia, the Middle East, Europe, and Africa. For greater detail on how China has been gearing up the operational reach of the CIPS both within and outside China, see McDowell (2023, 141–156).

[25] Notably, the CBR does not disclose the names of the participants. News reports suggest that much of the growth, however, took place after the second round of the Russian invasion of Ukraine in February 2022, when Western sanctions were accompanied by military confrontation, and following Russia's demand of foreign transactions in its gas imports in Russian rubles. As a result, 50 new entities joined the SPFS, taking the total number of participants to SPFS to 440. See "Russia's SWIFT Alternative Expanding Quickly this Year, Central Bank Says," Reuters, September 23, 2022.

[26] In October 2019, Russia, China, and India planned to link their respective messaging network systems as an alternative to the dollar-based systems, but its materialization remained uncertain (Wong and Nelson, 2021). India, however, has had its own secure messaging network for financial transactions, called the Structured Financial Messaging System (SFMS) since 2001, which allows inter- and intrabank messaging within India. It is thus a purely domestic messaging system (Cipriani, 2023).

[27] Western sanctions in late 2022, however, prompted some countries like Turkey, Kazakhstan, Vietnam, and Uzbekistan to halt their Mir-based transactions, especially after the US listed the head of NSPC in its List of Specially Designated Nationals and Blocked Persons (SDN List) (Cipriani, 2023).

Since Russia's invasion of Crimea in 2014, in order to withstand Western sanctions, the CBR has implemented a significant reallocation of its reserve portfolio away from the US dollar, mostly into renminbi, which resulted in a sharp decline in the US dollar share in Russian foreign exchange reserves (Iancu et al., 2020, 18–22). The share of Russian exports to Brazil, India, China, and South Africa invoiced in US dollars also declined from 85 percent in the second quarter of 2018 to 36 percent in the fourth quarter of 2022 (Nelson and Weiss, 2022). Since the second round of Western sanctions in February 2022, Russia has been pressuring Western nations to pay for its oil and gas imports in rubles.[28]

Emergence of Cryptocurrencies

In recent years, traditional cross-border transfers and payments systems have come under considerable pressure with the emergence of cryptocurrencies. Based on encrypted algorithms, the cryptocurrencies serve both as units of currency as well as virtual accounting systems; provide a decentralized medium of exchange through a broad distribution among the users via the internet; and unlike traditional currencies, such as dollar or euro, which are controlled and regulated by central banks, these are not issued or controlled by governments or other financial institutions. Cryptocurrencies are rather monitored and organized by a peer-to-peer network called a blockchain, which also serves as a secure ledger of all transactions (buying, selling, and transferring).

Satoshi Nakamoto, a mysterious character to whom the founding of the cryptocurrency has often been attributed, has apparently described this medium as "an electronic payment system based on cryptographic proof instead of trust."[29] Many observers predict that the robust growth of cryptocurrencies may pose significant threats to the supremacy of the dollar-denominated global payments systems that came to dominate the world since WWII (Goldman and Lindblom, 2021, 133).

In recent years, many governments have also been adopting a version of cryptocurrencies called digital currencies. These are issued by the central banks of the countries, thus they are centrally controlled and regulated by a legal governmental entity. Available records suggest that more than 100 central banks have already explored the adoption of digital currencies, and at least 11 of them have already introduced such

[28] McDowell (2023, 79–105) maintains that by the fourth quarter of 2020, currencies other than US dollar were used to settle nearly a quarter of Russian imports from China, down from 90 percent in 2013; in trade with the EU, the dollar's share fell from around 70 percent in 2013 to just over 40 percent in 2020; the dollar's settlement share dropped in Russian exports to India from roughly 95 percent in 2013 to 20 percent in 2019; Russia's dollar-denominated debts dropped from roughly 70 percent in the fourth quarter of 2015 to nearly 50 percent in 2020; and for the banking debts, use of the ruble grew from a low of 10 percent in 2014 to more than a quarter by the end of 2020.

[29] Nakamoto defines it as "an electronic coin" which involves "a chain of digital signatures. Each owner transfers the coin to the next by digitally signing a hash of the previous transaction and the public key of the next owner and adding these to the end of the coin. A payee can verify the signatures to verify the chain of ownership." (bitcoin.org/bitcoin.pdf).

currencies.[30] Although not all digital currencies are aimed at avoiding the dominance of dollar-based payments systems, the 11 countries mentioned above have the professed objective to do so. The discussion below first focuses on the private sector cryptocurrencies, and then moves to the public sector digital currencies.

Private Sector Cryptocurrencies

The very idea of cryptocurrencies emerged only recently, in 2008, when the world underwent a Great Recession. There now exist thousands of cryptocurrencies and blockchains around the world, and market capitalization of such currencies has already grown phenomenally – from less than $100 billion in 2016 to almost $3 trillion in November 2021 (Brainard, 2022).

There are numerous cryptocurrencies in the contemporary world, but two of them are the most well known – bitcoin and stablecoin. While bitcoins are volatile in nature, stablecoins are considered to be less volatile because their digital representation of value is backed by a stable asset, usually the US dollar. Stablecoins have gained greater acceptance because they function as a near-universal unit of account, provide near real-time settlement, and they come with a programmable nature that allows their incorporation into a wide range of financial products and services, such as decentralized lending and cross-border transactions (Hasu, 2020; Hügli, 2020).

Over the past decade, most of the cryptocurrencies have been developed by relatively unknown entities, but in recent years, some large multinational corporations have also joined the bandwagon to create stable digital currencies. For example, in 2018, a consortium of companies led by Facebook introduced a global digital currency called libra, and, in 2019, JP Morgan Chase issued a digital coin (JMP Coin). While JMP Coin is tied to the US dollar, libra, which has since been abandoned, was tied to a basket of currencies, including the US dollar (Nelsen and Weiss, 2022).

Earlier, in 2017, JP Morgan also introduced a blockchain technology-based Interbank Information Network, called Liink, which was rebranded in 2020 as a real-time information sharing system that now links more than 400 financial institutions around the world. Similarly, some private sector financial technology (fintech) companies have also developed blockchain technology-based cross-border payments systems. For example, the California-based Ripple operates a blockchain-based payments network called RippleNet which links hundreds of financial institutions in over 55 countries to facilitate cross-border payments, which is faster and cheaper than legacy systems. In 2020, RippleNet processed approximately three million transactions, five times more than in 2019 (Wong and Nelson, 2021).

The phenomenal rise of the cryptocurrencies, however, has met some serious setbacks in recent years. In the second half of 2022, a major crypto exchange named FTX, and its sister company, Alameda Research, filed for bankruptcy, after it wiped

30 See www.atlanticcouncil.org/cbdctracker.

about $1.3 trillion off the value of crypto tokens.[31] Because of the high interconnectedness of the business, several other major cryptocurrency firms also filed for bankruptcy in 2022, including Genesis, BlockFi, Voyager Digital, and Three Arrows Capital (3AC). In December 2020, the Securities and Exchange Commission (SEC) filed an action against Ripple for selling unregistered securities in the form of its digital asset XRP, which could be used to settle cross-border transactions in lieu of fiat currency.[32]

Despite their phenomenal growth in recent years, cryptocurrencies are still in their infancy, they are not legal tender, and their values are not backed by central banks. Their exchange values are also extremely volatile, their use as a unit of currency and convertibility into physical currency is extremely limited, and they are still far from universal acceptability as an alternative to fiat currency. Still, many believe private sector cryptocurrencies have great potential to provide yet another means by which the targets of US sanctions may evade their effects (Goldman and Lindblom, 2021; Nelson and Weiss, 2022).

Public Sector Digital Currencies

In recent years, governments around the world have also been experimenting with digital forms of currency, often described as Central Bank Digital Currency (CBDC). Such currencies are being issued by the central banks. They are similar to cryptocurrencies but they are regulated and their values are fixed by the central banks, and they are thus equivalent to the issuing country's fiat currency (Georgieva, 2022). The US Federal Reserve Bank defines a CBDC as "a digital liability of a central bank that is widely available to the general public … Like existing forms of money, a CBDC would enable the general public to make digital payments … It would be the safest digital asset available to the general public, with no associated credit or liquidity risk."[33]

As of February 2023, as many as 114 countries, representing over 95 percent of global GDP (gross domestic product), have been exploring CBDCs – about 60 of them are in an advanced stage of such exploration, while 11 have already launched such currencies.[34] The Chinese pilot program on CBDC has already reached 260 million people, and was set to expand to most of the country by the end of 2023. Some other countries, such as Australia, Thailand, Brazil, India, South Korea, Russia, and the EU are also pilot testing such currencies. All the G7 and G20 economies, including the US,[35] have now moved into the

[31] The top executives of the FTX have been indicted for criminal offenses with the Federal Court of Southern District of New York, and at the time of writing this chapter, the trial is ongoing.

[32] See SEC Press Release available at: www.sec.gov/news/press-release/2020-338.

[33] See www.federalreserve.gov/central-bank-digital-currency.htm accessed on February 25, 2023. Also see Federal Reserve Bank (2022).

[34] These countries and territories are: the Bahamas, Antigua and Barbuda, St. Kitts and Nevis, Monserrat, Dominica, Saint Lucia, St. Vincent and the Grenadines, Grenada and Nigeria.

[35] On March 9, 2022, President Biden issued EO 14067, directing the Treasury Department to submit a report on the future of money and payment systems, including the progress of the CBDC program in the US.

development stage of digital currencies, and seven of them have already moved to pilot testing.[36]

Available records suggest that there are at least nine cross-border wholesale CBDC tests and seven cross-border retail projects ongoing now. Although worldwide implementation of CBDC is still far away, a robust development of digital currencies and cross-border payments systems may someday replace the existing forms of physical currency, and may also result in a much diminished role of the US dollar-denominated settlement systems around the world.

One sign in that direction has been coming from the countries affected by US sanctions. In recent years, many of these countries have been making desperate efforts to adopt cryptocurrencies to avoid US dollar-based transactions. North Korea has been found to be using something called crypto-jacking to circumvent US sanctions by gaining access to funds and resources outside the reach of the formal banking system.[37] As discussed in Chapters 5 and 9, Russia and Venezuela have also been adopting elaborate measures to avoid dollar-based settlement systems.[38]

III GOVERNMENTAL MACHINERY FOR SANCTIONS ENFORCEMENT

The US sanctions enforcement process begins with the Executive Office of the President. The National Security Council (NSC), a statutory body created under the National Security Act of 1947 (NSC: P.L. 80-253) that usually comprises the president, the vice president, and the secretaries of the State, Defense, and Energy departments, processes sanctions decisions and coordinates their implementation with various governmental agencies. At the discretion of the president, the NSC also often includes the secretaries of the Treasury and the Homeland Security Departments, the chair of the Joint Chiefs of Staff, the directors of the National Intelligence Agency and the Central Intelligence Agency, the National Security Advisor, and the US Ambassador to the UN (Nephew, 2020, 101).

The sanctions implementation process starts with an Executive Order (EO) of the president – a presidential decree that derives its powers either from the Constitution

36 Based on the Atlantic Tracker available at: www.atlanticcouncil.org/cbdctracker/, accessed on February 27, 2023.

37 For example, in April 2020, the US Treasury Department identified three key cyber tactics that North Korea had allegedly used to target the financial sector and circumvent US sanctions: (a) cyber-enabled financial theft, to gain access to bank computers or infrastructure or hack cryptocurrency exchanges to steal funds; (b) ransomware campaigns, to gain access to an entity's computer network and demand a ransom; and (c) crypto-jacking, to use an entity's computers to mine digital currencies. For greater detail, see: www.treasury.gov/resource-center/sanctions/Programs/Documents/dark_cyber_threat_advisory_20200415.pdf, accessed on February 28, 2023.

38 For greater detail on Russia's and Venezuela's attempts to use cryptocurrencies to avoid US sanctions, see McDowell (2023, 83–103).

or Congressional statutes and governmental regulations.[39] The EO specifies the legislation that grants power to the president; sets out the authorities delegated to the officials, demarcating crucial legal and administrative terms for the enforcement of the decree; and specifies the targets, delineating the associated penalties for any violations. A number of governmental departments and agencies then implement the sanctions regimes, depending on their specific mandates, but three departments play the most critical roles: the Treasury, Commerce, and State departments.

A *The Department of Treasury*

The Department of Treasury has long been at the forefront of both framing and executing economic and financial sanctions regimes, but its mandate has expanded massively since 9/11. Immediately after the terrorist attacks, President George W. Bush issued EO 13224, granting the Treasury the mandate and the means to disrupt financial support networks of terrorists and terrorist organizations – and their subsidiaries, front organizations, agents, and associates around the world – by designating and blocking assets of individuals and entities that commit, or pose a significant risk of committing, acts of terrorism.[40]

The EO significantly widened the mandate that the Treasury already had since 1990 under a program called the Financial Crimes Enforcement Network to gather intelligence on international financial activities, especially suspicious transactions. Among the many agencies that are responsible for tracking international financial transactions on behalf of the Treasury, the most important players are the Office of Foreign Assets Control (OFAC)[41] and the Bureau of Financial Crimes Enforcement Network (FinCEN).[42]

[39] As mentioned before, the US Constitution does not provide any explicit authorization to the president to impose sanctions – the president issues such decrees pursuant to the powers vested in them as the chief executive of the federal government and the powers delegated to them through congressional statutes.

[40] The EO, issued on September 23, 2001, invoked the authorities granted to the president by the IEEPA (50 U.S.C. 1701 et seq.), the National Emergencies Act (50 U.S.C. 1601 et seq.), and the United Nations Participation Act of 1945 (UNPA: 22 U.S.C. 287c). As required by the EEPA, President Bush also declared a national emergency to deal with the unusual and extraordinary threat to US national security and foreign policy.

[41] OFAC owes its origin to the Office of Foreign Funds Control (OFFC) under the Treasury Department that was established in 1940 to prevent Nazi Germany from using the assets of the countries that it invaded. OFFC's mission was to deny the Germans and other Axis powers the ability to profit from their military conquests and use such resources to fuel their military undertakings. In 1950, OFFC was renamed OFAC, when President Harry Truman declared a national emergency with respect to China's entry into the Korean War, and used his authority to freeze assets of China and North Korea subject to US jurisdiction (Nephew, 2020, 96–97).

[42] FinCEN was initially established as an administrative agency by the Treasury Department in April 1990 (Treasury Order 105-08). Subsequently the agency gained strength when it was merged with the Office of Financial Enforcement of Treasury in 1994. Then, the Patriot Act (2001) upgraded the agency to a bureau under the Treasury Department.

Office of Foreign Assets Control

OFAC monitors sanctions regimes primarily under two separate programs: a "country-based" program that targets governments and a "list-based" program that targets specific persons and entities. The country-based program currently targets mainly Cuba, Iran, and Syria, as well as the "Crimea region of Ukraine," and to some extent North Korea. The "list-based" program currently consists of over 20 lists that target a wide variety of sanctioned persons and entities, who are named on OFAC's massive List of Specially Designated Nationals and Blocked Persons (SDN List) or several other lists. Usually, the sanctions on individuals also apply to any entity that is 50 percent or more owned by those persons listed in the SDN or such other lists.[43]

The president can delegate powers to the OFAC through EOs. In order for the OFAC to continue with the authority granted under the IEEPA, the president must renew the IEEPA emergency powers annually. The powers granted under other statutes also depend on the scope of relevant statutes. Most of the sanctions programs that the OFAC monitors are limited to some specific persons or entities in a target country, but some may be as large as a near-total embargo. For example, in response to Russia's second invasion of Ukraine in February 2022, the US imposed numerous "sectoral sanctions" restricting specified dealings with Russia's defense, energy, and finance sectors, and added numerous Russian individuals and entities to the SDN List. The US has also imposed numerous restrictions on both exports to and imports from Russia. The sanctions regimes against Russia thus comprise of both country-based and list-based aspects, and almost resemble comprehensive or near-comprehensive sanctions.[44]

OFAC's Long Arm of Enforcement

Ordinarily, OFAC administers sanctions regimes by using two types of licenses: general licenses and specific licenses. Persons covered by a general license may engage in the licensed conduct without applying for individual permission – however, they must comply with the terms and limits of the licenses, which may include reporting and record-keeping requirements. The specific licenses, which are not published, grant named persons permission to engage in particular conduct under the terms and limits set by OFAC.

[43] OFAC's sanctions programs are listed in 31 C.F.R. Ch. V, and its website, www.ustreas.gov/ofac. OFAC's sanctions lists run into thousands of pages, but it is search-capable. Some sanctions programs may, however, give the impression that they are country-based, while they may actually be targeted at some designated persons or entities. For example, as Beckhy (2018) points out, the Ukraine Related Sanctions Regulations (31 C.F.R. pt. 589), target listed persons, mainly Russians, and are primarily directed against the territory of Russian-occupied Crimea; and the North Korea Sanctions Regulations (31 C.F.R. pt. 510) target mainly sanction-listed persons, but also include an import ban and special export controls against North Korea.

[44] As discussed below, the Commerce Department's Bureau of Industry and Security (BIS) also plays an important role in administering these programs. The US sanctions on Russia are discussed in greater detail in Chapter 5.

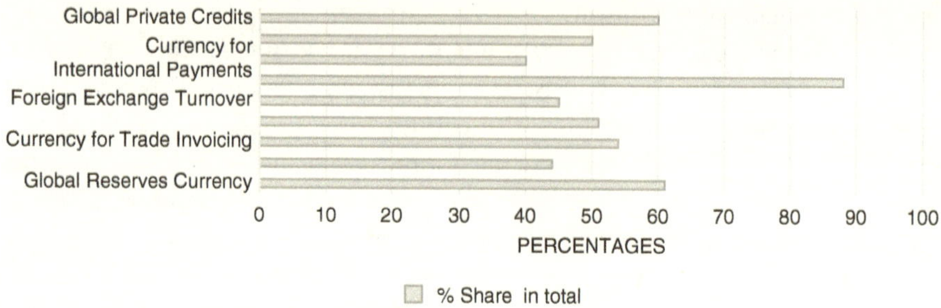

FIGURE 4.1 Share of US dollars in global monetary transactions, 2019 (percent)
Source: Author's compilation based on Bank for International Settlements (BIS, 2020a, 2020b); Goldman and Lindblom (2021); and Iancu et al. (2020).

OFAC's mechanisms of sanctions enforcement largely rest on its interpretation of the legal definition of "US persons." As explained in Chapter 3, under the TWEA (1917), "US persons" included foreign organizations owned or controlled by US persons as well as foreign subsidiaries of US companies. Until the 1970s, the OFAC regulations interpreted the definition in a narrower sense, extending its jurisdiction over the foreign branches of US corporations but excluding separately incorporated subsidiaries. In the 1990s, OFAC moderated the jurisdiction of "US persons" even further by allowing foreign subsidiaries of US corporations to transact business with sanctioned countries, provided they did so without any support by their parent company or other US persons.

After the 2007 IEEPA amendment, which made it unlawful for a person "to violate, attempt to violate, conspire to violate or cause a violation" of the Act, the IEEPA's jurisdiction spilled over to non-US persons as well, who may be held accountable for "attempting," "conspiring," or "causing" a US person to violate the Act. Then, the Comprehensive Iran Sanctions, Accountability, and Divestment Act of 2010 (CISADA: P.L. 111-195) extended sanctions to "US persons" – companies and individuals – who aid Iran's petroleum sector, and the subsequent legislation, the Iran Threat Reduction and Syria Human Rights Act of 2012 (ITRA: P.L. 112-1598) not only makes US firms liable for their foreign subsidiaries' involvement in sanctionable activity in Iran but also subjects non-US firms and their corporate officers to US sanctions.

OFAC, thus, can adopt a broad latitude in its interpretation of "US persons." In 2012, for example, the agency expanded its jurisdiction over foreign subsidiaries of US companies and threatened banks that conducted business with designated Iranian financial institutions, while in 2016, pursuant to the JCPOA, OFAC issued a general license authorizing foreign subsidiaries of US companies to engage in certain dealings with Iran which otherwise would have been considered illegal facilitation (Figure 4.1).

TABLE 4.1 *OFAC settlements with financial institutions*

Year	Institution	Amount of settlement (US$ millions)
2012	HSBC Bank Financial Services	1,256
2012	Standard Chartered Bank Financial Services	667
2012	ING Bank N.V. Financial Services	619
2013	Bank of Tokyo-Mitsubishi UFJ Financial Services	259
2014	BNP Paribas S.A. Financial Services	8,960
2015	Commerzbank AG Financial Services	258
2019	British Arab Commercial Bank	228

Source: OFAC Settlement Agreements 2008–2018 (2018), available at www.visualofac.com/ resources/ settlement-agreements/.

OFAC may consider a foreign citizen who is in the US at the time of a violation of US sanctions to be a "US person," or a foreign bank as a "US person" if it processes payments using the US financial system. In the view of OFAC, foreign banks involved in such "transaction stripping" – conducting illegal transactions using the US financial system – cause violations of US sanctions regimes by concealing key information, such as the names and addresses of the senders and recipients, which could enable US financial institutions to detect such transactions. Based on such an interpretation, in recent years, OFAC has sanctioned many foreign banks and financial institutions (see Table 4.1), and in almost all cases, the institutions involved signed Deferred Prosecution Agreements with OFAC and agreed to pay huge penalties (McDowell, 2023, 26–28; Nephew, 2020).[45]

As OFAC imposes substantial fines even for inadvertent violations or non-compliance with US sanctions, foreign banks and other financial institution now see it as in their best interests to avoid doing business with US-sanctioned persons out of self-deterrence as well as over-abundance of caution and risk avoidance (Beucillon, 2021; Breen, 2021). All domestic and international banks now screen the persons and entities on the US SDN List as part of their normal compliance program. In the case of Iran, the CISADA (2010) specifically threatens banks that do business with designated Iranian financial institutions. To enforce it, OFAC made it obligatory for foreign banks to abide by the SDN List if they wished to do business in the US. This was precisely one reason why INSTEX failed so miserably.

45 In one instance, in 2015, OFAC imposed a hefty $8.9 billion penalty on BNP Paribas – a French bank – for processing 3,897 financial and trade transactions routing them through US banks between 2005 and 2012 in violation of the Sudanese Sanctions Regulations (31 C.F.R. part 538); the Iranian Transactions and Sanctions Regulations (31 C.F.R. part 560); the Cuban Assets Control Regulations (31 C.F.R. part 515); and the Burmese Sanctions Regulations (31 C.F.R. part 537). For greater details on OFAC's other Settlement Agreements during 2008–2018, see www.visualofac.com/ resources/ settlement-agreements/.

OFAC's rather sweeping enforcement powers are not limited to its interpretation of "US persons" alone. For example, existing legislation, such as the Patriot Act (2001), also allows OFAC to adopt a precautionary freeze or other penalties against a suspected individual or entity pending investigation (Savage, 2001). OFAC also has the luxury of operating behind closed doors and can take action based on confidential information and one-sided administrative processes shrouded in secrecy (Petersen 2005, 1391).

Thus, individuals and entities affected by OFAC's designations and freezing orders are largely at the mercy of the agency. Judicial interventions in such matters have also been scarce as the federal courts generally shy away from sanctions matters and are reluctant to enforce due process laws to subject OFAC's decisions to the "arbitrary and capricious" test under the Administrative Procedure Act. The courts have even allowed the government to use undisclosed classified evidence to defend its SDN sanctions (Donohue, 2008; Fabbrini, 2013).[46]

Terrorist Financing Tracking Program

OFAC has another powerful instrument at its disposal since the Treasury Department launched a secret program called the Terrorist Financing Tracking Program (TFTP) in 2001 to track down the monetary flows of terrorist organizations around the world. Over the years, the TFTP has received thousands of valuable leads which helped the OFAC to investigate or prevent violent terrorist attacks or attempted attacks across many countries.[47]

Much of OFAC's enforcement activities under the TFTP are, however, linked with its interface with the Belgian-based SWIFT. As mentioned above, the US enjoys considerable leverage over SWIFT because it is the chair of the organization, and most of SWIFT's messaging transactions are based on US dollar-denominated payments systems. SWIFT also depends extensively on the settlement services of Fedwire, CHIPS, or other US-based international payment systems. Moreover, OFAC can subpoena SWIFT to obtain information on financial transactions of suspected terrorists or their networks for specific terrorism investigations.

OFAC also draws on specific statutes to extend its leverage on SWIFT. For example, OFAC has used the Iran Sanctions, Accountability, and Human Rights Act of 2012 (ISAHRA: H.R. 1905)[48] to delink Iranian financial institutions from the SWIFT network so extensively that even some pharmaceutical companies, wary of risking violation of US sanctions, stopped exporting medicines to Iran, and tens of thousands of Iranian patients died as a result (Prezas, 2021, 389).

[46] See, for example, the court ruling in *Holy Land Foundations for Relief and Development v. Ashcroft*, 333 F.3d 156, 164 (D.C. Cir. 2003).

[47] For greater detail, see: home.treasury.gov/policy-issues/terrorism-and-illicit-finance/terrorist-finance-tracking-program-tftp, accessed on September 12, 2022.

[48] ISAHRA (2012) was enacted to target primarily insurers and shippers that were conducting business with Iran's national oil company and tanker fleet.

SWIFT has a history of resisting political pressures, however. For example, in 2004, it refused to remove Myanmar from its network, despite both the US and EU having imposed sanctions on the country, claiming its neutrality. In 2014, following the Russian invasion of Crimea, it resisted pressure from the EU and the US to delink Russian and Belarussian banking institutions from its network. In the same year, it also resisted pressure from pro-Palestinian groups to disconnect Israeli financial institutions from its network (Prezas, 2021, 389).

On the other hand, following Russia's second invasion of Ukraine in February 2022, SWIFT disconnected many Russian and Belarussian banks and their subsidiaries from its network (Cipriani, 2023, 25). The action was taken in compliance with the EU Council Regulations (2022/345 and 398) – being an organization located in Belgium, an EU territory, SWIFT was obliged to comply with the EU regulations. Similarly, in 2017, SWIFT delinked certain North Korean banks from its network under the instructions of the Belgian government.[49]

Financial Crimes Enforcement Network (FinCEN)

The Treasury Department has yet another powerful instrument called the Financial Crimes Enforcement Network (FinCEN), which is enforced by a bureau that goes by the same name. FinCEN draws its regulatory powers primarily from the Bank Secrecy Act of 1970 (BSA: P.L. 91-58),[50] and enforces anti-money laundering and counter financing of terrorism (AML/CFT) statutes, requiring banks and other financial institutions to safeguard the US financial system from financial crimes, illicit use, and money laundering (FinCen, 2006).

The BSA was amended and updated many times, with a major revision incorporated by Title III of the Patriot Act (2001), which empowers the president to impose restrictions and sanctions on individuals, entities, and foreign countries that harbor terrorists or allow funds for terrorists to pass through their territories. Section 311 of the Act authorizes the president to designate particular jurisdictions as "primary money laundering concerns" requiring "special measures" against such jurisdictions by US financial institutions.

Under such authorities, the Treasury can declare entities as small as individual banks and as large as an entire country as *persona non grata* for the US financial system (Nephew, 2020, 102), and such designations may result in severe consequences, such as prohibition from maintaining correspondent accounts with US financial

[49] The Belgian government took the action in compliance with the UN-imposed sanctions on North Korea. As a result of the SWIFT delinking, the Global Fund to Fight AIDS, Tuberculosis and Malaria, a Geneva-based organization, which supported treatment of nearly 200,000 patients with tuberculosis in North Korea, had to withdraw from that country, expressing concerns of inadvertent violations of sanctions (Prezas, 2021, 389).

[50] Commonly referred to as the BSA, it is also known as the Currency and Financial Transactions Reporting Act of 1970 (31 U.S.C. 310).

institutions, cut off access to US dollar payment systems, or restrictions on doing business in the US (Carter and Farha, 2013, 910).[51]

The Intelligence Reform and Terrorism Prevention Act of 2004 (IRTPA: P.L. 108-458) amended the BSA further to require the president to report on cross-border electronic transmissions of funds in aid of the fight against money laundering and terrorist financing. In 2010 came the Foreign Account Tax Compliance Act of 2010 (FATCA: P.L. 111-147), which enables the Treasury Department to mount regulatory pressures on money laundering practices around the world. Under the Act, the Treasury has concluded agreements with 113 countries and jurisdictions requiring foreign financial institutions to report on the assets held with them by US taxpayers (Morriss and Ku, 2020).

FinCEN takes numerous enforcement actions each year against money service businesses, depository institutions, securities and futures, casinos, and so on for violations of the reporting, record-keeping, or other requirements of the US AML/CFT statutes and regulations, and many such enforcements result in the assessment of civil money penalties.[52] The FinCEN also issues occasional alerts for financial institutions to guard against abridgment of sanctions enforcement. For example, in 2022, FinCEN issued alerts about attempts by some Russian individuals and entities to evade export controls implemented in connection with Russia's invasion of Ukraine, and in January 2023, it issued alerts regarding potential investments in the US commercial real estate (CRE) sector by sanctioned Russian oligarchs and their family members.[53]

FinCEN also monitors AML/CFT activities with its counterpart organizations in other countries and international bodies. One of its principal partners in the task is the Financial Action Task Force (FATF), an inter-governmental body established in 1989 with the purpose of establishing international standards and policies of AML/CFT.[54] The FATF monitors AML/CFT standards around the world, and provides guidance to banks and countries around the world for addressing financial integrity issues.[55] As of February 2023, about 200 countries had adopted AML/CFT legislation.

[51] Even the mere threat of such a designation may result in severe consequences. For example, in 2005, the Treasury issued a threat to Banco Delta Asia, a bank in Macau (China), which conducted business with North Korea despite US sanctions against North Korea. The threat triggered a run on the bank, and depleted 34 percent of its deposits within days (Gaylord, 2008).

[52] For example, FinCEN assesses civil money penalties for record-keeping violations under 31 C.F.R §1010.415; for failing to file a currency transaction report (CTR) (violation of 31 C.F.R. §1010.311); for failure to file a suspicious activity report (SAR) (violation of 31 C.F.R. § 1021.320); for failure to file a report on foreign bank and financial accounts (FBAR) (violation of 31 C.F.R §1010.350); for failure to register with the FinCEN (violation of 31 C.F.R §1022.380).

[53] For greater details see www.fincen.gov/news-room/news, accessed on September 28, 2022.

[54] FATF currently has 32 member countries and territories and two regional organizations. On February 24, 2023, FATF suspended the membership of the Russian Federation, stating that the country's war in Ukraine violated the FTAF's principles.

[55] FATF maintains a "gray list" of "Jurisdictions under Increased Monitoring." The countries in the list are required to address strategic deficiencies in their regulatory frameworks to counter illicit financial transactions in their territories. Being listed in this category carries significant implications for a country's eligibility for US assistance. The March 2022 FATF "gray list" included 24 such countries.

FinCEN and FATF monitor AML/CFT regulations with respect to both onshore and offshore financial centers (OFCs) around the world. Some argue, however, that their success rate in combating money laundering has largely been inconsequential, as the estimated cost of compliance with their regulations is believed to be 100 times more than the funds recovered through their enforcement actions (Pol, 2020a).[56] Some argue that, although OFCs are responsible for only a minuscule share of illicit financial transactions, they face much greater scrutiny for compliance from such regulatory institutions than major onshore centers, located in New York, Miami, Geneva, London, and other metropolitan centers, which are responsible for a much bigger share of illicit financial transactions (Morriss and Hansen, 2013; Morriss and Ku, 2013; Nakajima, 2017).[57]

In addition, as discussed above, the Treasury also uses various international financial institutions (IFIs), such as the World Bank, the International Monetary Fund (IMF), the European Bank for Reconstruction and Development, the Asian Development Bank, and the African Development Bank, and so on, to enforce sanctions by manipulating international monetary system and US developmental assistance.

B *The Department of Commerce*

The Commerce Department's jurisdiction in sanctions enforcement stems primarily from its responsibility for export control enforcement and protection of US national security interests. The department develops, monitors, and enforces US export control policies with respect to most of the goods that may be exported from the US, and maintains public lists of countries, entities, and individuals whose access to various US goods may be restricted or prohibited. It also investigates violations of export controls, levies penalties, and arrests and indicts violators in cooperation with the Justice and State Departments.

56 Some estimates suggest that companies around the world on average spend 3.1 percent of turnover on combating financial crime, or $1.28 trillion globally. On the other hand, the current AML regulations help authorities to intercept about $3 billion of an estimated $3 trillion in criminal funds generated annually (Pol, 2020b). That regulations impose compliance costs far exceeding the benefits is also pointed out by many others, such as Beucillon (2021), Nephew (2020), and Breen (2021). The UN estimates that in 2020 approximately $7 trillion of private wealth, or about 10 percent of world GDP, was hidden in tax haven countries and territories, and in the same year, money laundering flows totaled $1.6 trillion, or 2.7 percent of the world GDP (www.un.org/development/desa/en/news/financing/facti-interim-report.html). Some civil society organizations have released some dramatic reports in recent years, such as the *Pandora Papers* or the *Paradise Papers* – showing that shell companies and illicit financial activities of political leaders seldom result in major criminal prosecutions. See www.icij.org/investigations/pandora-papers/global-investigation-tax-havens-offshore/.

57 The Tax Justice Network (TJN), for example, maintains that the top 10 OFCs, located in the Bahamas, Malta, Cayman Islands, Vanuatu, Antigua and St. Kitts and Nevis, account for less than 1 percent of the global market in illicit financial services (see fsi.taxjustice.net/en/faq/why-include-a-scale-weight). Also see Haberly and Wójcik (2017).

Bureau of Industry and Security

The primary agency of the Commerce Department for export enforcement is the Bureau of Industry and Security (BIS), which administers and enforces export controls on dual-use and certain controlled items through the Export Administration Regulations (EAR) under the authority of the Export Control Reform Act of 2018 (ECRA).[58]

The dual-use items are commodities, software, or technology that have both commercial and military or proliferation applications, such as smoke bombs, spiked batons, certain shotguns, space launch vehicles, turbines for use in nuclear reactors, chemical warfare precursors, biological containment facilities, and radio frequency modules. Controlled items are listed under the 600 series Export Control Classification Numbers (ECCN), and enumerated on the Commerce Control List (CCL). These items, listed on the Wassenaar Arrangement Munitions List (WAML), formerly known as the USML, include commodities, software, and/or technology such as military flight instrument trainers, lightweight turbojet engines, medical facilities for surface or submersible vessels of war, submarine or torpedo nets, telecommunications equipment for a military application, and so on (BIS, 2019, 2).[59]

The export enforcement arm of the BIS investigates violations, interdicts illegal exports, conducts end-use checks, identifies suspicious activities, and evaluates the bona fides of transaction parties. Among the three offices of export enforcement – the Office of Export Enforcement (OEE), the Office of Enforcement Analysis (OEA), and the Office of Antiboycott Compliance (OAC) – the OAC administers and enforces the antiboycott provisions of the EAR by monitoring boycott requests received by US businesses and bringing necessary enforcement actions, and liaising with foreign governments, the Office of the US Trade Representative (USTR), and the Department of State.

[58] The EAR, originally issued pursuant to the Export Administration Act of 2015 (EAA: 50 U.S.C. §§ 4601-4623, Supp. III 2015), and most recently extended on August 14, 2019 (84 Fed. Reg. 41, 881), continued the regulations in effect under the IEEPA (50 U.S.C. § 1701, et seq.; 2012). ECRA §1768 provides that all rules and regulations that were made or issued under the EAA, including as continued in effect pursuant to IEEPA, and were in effect as of ECRA's date of enactment (August 13, 2018), shall continue to be in effect until modified, superseded, set aside, or revoked through action undertaken pursuant to the authority provided under the ECRA (BIS, 2019, 2; Hirschhorn, 2022, 4–17).

[59] As explained in Chapter 3, many defense items, which by definition are not dual-use but solely for military use, are now subject to the Commerce Department's export controls. The Obama Administration, under the Export Control Reform (ECR) initiative, transferred many lower-level defense items from the jurisdiction of the State Department to the Commerce Department (Fergusson and Kerr, 2020). These items are now subject to the EAR and listed in the CCL, and no longer subject to the Arms Export Control Act (AECA) or the International Traffic in Arms Regulations (ITAR) (Hirschhorn, 2022, 4). The State Department, however, still controls the export of defense articles and defense services subject to ITAR, while the Department of Energy controls exports and re-exports of technology related to the production of special nuclear materials, the Nuclear Regulatory Commission controls the export of certain nuclear materials and equipment, and the Treasury Department controls economic sanctions programs (BIS, 2019, 2).

The OEE maintains three major lists: the Entity List, the Unverified List (UVL), and the Denied Persons List (DPL). Of these, the Entity List has evolved into a formidable administrative enforcement tool that prohibits unlicensed exports, re-exports, or transfers of some or all items subject to the EAR to listed foreign entities. Those named on the list pose the risk of diversion of US-origin items to weapons of mass destruction (WMD) programs, destabilizing accumulations of conventional weapons, terrorism, or other activities contrary to US national security or foreign policy interests.

The UVL, on the other hand, maintains the names and addresses of foreign persons that have been parties or intended parties to transactions subject to the EAR whose bona fides could not be confirmed as a result of an end-use check. The persons named on the list face three consequences: They must report all export transactions in the Automated Export System (AES) (§758.1(b)(8) of the EAR); their eligibility for license exception may be suspended (§740.2(a)(17) of the EAR); and for all other EAR transactions not subject to a license requirement, they must obtain a statement from the UVL party agreeing to abide by the EAR (§744.15 of the EAR). A foreign party may be removed from the UVL only after the BIS confirms its bona fides.

The DPL contains the names and addresses of individuals and entities located both within the US and abroad who are subject to a denial of export privileges pursuant to §764.3(a)(2) of the EAR. The BIS may also issue a Temporary Denial Order (TDO) pursuant to §766.24 of the EAR, which typically denies export privileges of a company or individual to prevent an imminent or ongoing export control violation. Such orders are issued ***ex parte*** for a renewable 180-day period and they deny not only the right to export from the US, but also the right to receive or participate in exports from the US.[60]

The BIS thus has the authority and discretion to deny all export privileges under the EAR of a domestic or foreign individual or company. It may impose a denial of export privileges as a sanction in an administrative case, or as a result of a person's criminal conviction under certain statutes. A denial of export privileges prohibits a person from participating in any transactions subject to the EAR. It is also unlawful for other businesses and individuals to participate in an export transaction subject to the EAR with a denied person.[61]

[60] In addition, the BIS also maintains a Military End User List, which identifies foreign parties that are prohibited from receiving items unless the exporter secures a license; and a Consolidated Screening List (CSL), which includes all parties who are restricted for certain exports, re-exports, or transfers of items. These lists are available in a comprehensive screening system managed by the Departments of State, Treasury, and Commerce. See www.export.gov/article?id=Consolidated-Screening-List.

[61] Under §1760(e) of the ECRA, a denial of export privileges may be imposed for up to 10 years from the date of a person's conviction under the EAR, the IEEPA, or §38 of the Arms Export Control Act of 1976 (AECA: P.L. 94-329). Under the ECRA, criminal penalties for the EAR violations may reach up to 20 years imprisonment and $1 million per violation, and administrative monetary penalties can reach up to $300,000 per violation, subject to adjustment in accordance with §701 the Federal Civil Penalties Inflation Adjustment Act Improvements Act of 2015 (P.L. 114-74) or twice the value of the transaction, whichever is greater (BIS, 2019, 6–7).

The Commerce Department's regulations on sanctions violations derive their authority from Congressional legislation as well as presidential EOs and other administrative regulations. Such authorities can be traced to the TWEA (1917) and IEEPA (1977), and numerous other statutes specifically geared to sanctions on different countries, such as Cuba, North Korea, Russia, Venezuela, Iran, and Syria.[62] Many of these statutes also grant the Commerce Department extraterritorial jurisdiction with respect to re-exported and transshipped goods. The department designates any goods that contain more than 10 percent of US content as US goods, and requires a BIS license for any goods that involve US-origin technology manufactured elsewhere. Thus, a large portion of the world's trade, especially involving re-exports and transshipments, is potentially subject to US jurisdiction.[63]

Due to the expansive worldwide presence of US persons and companies, as well as US goods and services, US sanctions constrain many non-US persons, and any violations of US sanctions by non-US persons where a US person or US-origin item is involved may result in significant penalties as they may be considered violations of primary or secondary sanctions. Over the decades, the Commerce Department, in collaboration with the Treasury and the State Departments, has targeted many non-US companies involving transactions of US goods (Hirschhorn, 2022, 202). In fiscal year 2018, for example, BIS investigations led to the criminal conviction of 30 individuals and businesses for export violations with penalties of $618,500 in criminal fines, more than $9.6 million in forfeitures, and 506 months of imprisonment. In addition, the BIS conducted 43 administrative export matters, which resulted in over $1 billion in civil penalties (BIS, 2019, 4).

Some of the major enforcement actions of the BIS in the year 2022 included: (a) indictment of five Russian nationals and two oil traders for sourcing and purchasing sensitive military and dual-use items from US manufacturers, which included advanced semiconductors and microprocessors used in fighter aircraft missile systems; (b) issuance of a record number of TDOs to prevent imminent violations of the EAR against Russia's and Belarus's biggest airlines; (c) listing of nearly 200 aircraft from Russia, Belarus, and Iran that triggered 10 General Prohibition restrictions, which prohibit parties from knowingly taking subsequent actions like refueling, maintenance, and repair;[64] and (d) addition of 519 parties from China, Russia, Pakistan, Iran, and other countries to the Entity List.[65]

[62] For example, the Iran–Libya Sanctions Act, 1996 (ILSA: P.L. 104-172) clearly specifies sanctioning measures, such as denial of export privileges, export–import financing, US government procurement, and visas to corporate executives, in cases of violation of US sanctions and embargoes.

[63] The specific licensing burden attached to re-exports is relatively small, however. For example, out of total US exports of $1.4 trillion in 2020, only $39.4 billion (2.8 percent) required a BIS license.

[64] The EAR identifies 10 General Prohibitions, which, by the way, are not inclusive of all potential violations of the EAR. For a detailed discussion on these prohibitions, see Hirschhorn (2022, 22–25).

[65] See, "Export Enforcement: 2022 Year in Review," US Department of Commerce. More recently, on February 27, 2023, the BIS imposed a $2.77 million penalty on 3D Printing Company for its exports of aerospace and military design documents to China and Germany in violation of the EAR regulations.

C *The Department of State*

The Department of State, as a statutory participant of the NSC, plays a critical role in initiating, adopting, designing, and enforcing sanctions. It is also responsible for negotiating with the US allies, and international organizations, such as the UN, with respect to sanctioning measures and targets, and it plays a critical role in the design, adoption, and implementation of UN Security Council (UNSC) sanctions.

The Department of State derives both broad and specific jurisdictions over sanctions enforcement from scores of Congressional statutes and presidential executive orders. The United Nations Participation Act of 1945 (UNPA: 22 U.S.C. 287c),[66] for example, authorizes the president to act in compliance with the sanctions adopted by the UNSC. The Act makes presidential agreements with the UNSC subject to Congressional approval, and assigns authority to the State Department to negotiate such agreements. The Act also requires the president to make available armed forces, facilities, or other assistance for the enforcement of UNSC resolutions, but the president can do so without any Congressional approval. The president, and thus the State Department, enjoys broad discretion in providing logistical support in the enforcement of sanctions imposed by the UNSC.

The Department of State is also responsible for the enforcement of UN sanctions as they apply to the US as a member of the UN. The US Constitution does not permit implementation of any superseding international obligations of the country unless such obligations are ratified by the Senate. Thus, sanctions adopted by the UNSC cannot be automatically accepted as a legal requirement under US laws. For their implementation in the US, the UNSC sanctions, depending on their nature, must be backed by additional legislative or executive action, or both, and, in implementing UNSC sanctions, the Congress can go beyond what is required by UNSC. For example, in implementing the UNSC sanctions on Iran for nuclear proliferation, the Congress enacted legislation that not only satisfied the US's obligations to UNSC resolutions, but went far beyond them (White, 2018, 2021). The president can implement the UNSC resolutions by invoking the IEEPA and declaring a national emergency. The State Department, exercising the authority of the president, can prohibit visas to those on the UNSC's list of travel bans (Nephew, 2019, 106).

The Department of State is also the most dominant player in sanctions on diplomatic, political, and cultural fronts, such as adopting and enforcing measures aimed at the interruption of diplomatic relations, registering protests and condemnations, expelling or recalling diplomatic representatives, severance of diplomatic relations, restrictions on cultural exchanges, and suspending overflight or transit privileges, tourism, and visa privileges. The State Department also plays a key role in adopting and enforcing US sanctions against aid and assistance to foreign countries. Under

[66] The UNPA (1945) went through several amendments, most recently by the United Nations Reform Act of 1999 (P.L. 106–113), the United Nations Headquarters Agreement Act (P.L. 80–357), and the U.S. Participation in Certain International Organizations Act (P.L. 81–806).

the Foreign Assistance Act of 1961 (FAA: P.L. 87–195, as amended in 2019), the president enjoys broad powers in framing foreign assistance decisions in furtherance of US foreign policy objectives, such as encouraging pro-market economic systems, good governance, and democratization. The State Department routinely uses such broad presidential powers to promote US hegemony around the world.

The key agencies of the State Department that are directly involved in sanctions adoption and implementation are the Bureau of International Security and Non-Proliferation (ISN), and the Directorate of Defense Trade Controls (DDTC) under the Bureau of Political-Military Affairs.

Bureau of International Security and Non-Proliferation

The ISN is specifically responsible for enforcing sanctions related to non-proliferation of nuclear weapons. Thus, it is the ISN's duty to enforce sanctions on individuals, entities, and countries who contribute to the export of nuclear-related goods or technology or help in efforts to illegally acquire unsafeguarded and prohibited nuclear material. The ISN draws its authority from scores of Congressional statutes that authorize the president to take such actions, such as the Iran Freedom and Counter-Proliferation Act of 2012 (IFCA: P.L. 112-239), the Iran Nonproliferation Amendments Act of 2005 (P.L. 109-112), and CAATSA of 2017 (P.L. 115-44).

The ISN also draws its authority directly from presidential EOs issued in furtherance of Congressional legislation. For example, EO 13949 (issued on September 21, 2020) imposes sanctions on persons and entities involved in Iran's conventional arms acquisitions, indigenous manufacturing programs, and support of Iranian paramilitary organizations with arms and materiel; EO 13382 (issued on June 29, 2005) freezes assets of proliferators of WMDs and their supporters, and isolates them financially; and EO 12938 (issued in November 1994, and renewed each year ever since) prohibits US persons and entities from the importation of goods, technology, or services involved in WMD proliferation activities.

Directorate of Defense Trade Controls

The DDTC is responsible for enforcement of US sanctions as they relate to arms control and defense exports. It draws authority from authorization granted to the president by Congressional legislation, especially from the Arms Exports Control Act (AECA: 1976), the Export Administration Act (EAA: 1979), and the Chemical and Biological Weapons Control and Warfare Elimination Act of 1991 (22 U.S.C. 5604-5605) that sanction individuals and entities involved in illegal transfers of missile equipment or technology.

In pursuance of the AECA and the International Traffic in Arms Regulations (ITAR), the DDTC maintains a Debarred List, naming entities and individuals prohibited from participating directly or indirectly in the export of defense articles, including technical data and defense services. The List also includes persons convicted in court of violating or conspiring to violate the AECA and subject to statutory or administrative debarment. Such debarments remain in effect unless the debarred person's application for reinstatement of export privileges is granted by the DDTC.

The DDTC also implements the USML, which controls sales of defense equipment, services, and related manufacturing technologies.[67] Under the ITAR, any US company or individual involved in certain activities involving defense articles described on the USML is required to register with the DDTC. Further, a DDTC license or other approval is required before exporting a defense article (including ITAR-controlled technical data), or providing a defense service to a foreign end user.

The DDTC is also responsible for the enforcement of sanctions imposed under the Lethal Military Equipment to Terrorist States (Section 620H of the FAA and various appropriations acts), which restrict the provision of foreign assistance to any foreign government that provides lethal military equipment to a country whose government is a state sponsor of terrorism; and the Export–Import Bank Act of 1945 (12 U.S.C. 635 et seq.), under which sanctions are imposed on any person who knowingly aids or abets any non-nuclear weapon state to acquire a nuclear explosive device or unsafeguarded special nuclear material.[68]

IV CONCLUDING REMARKS

With the military options for confronting foreign policy objectives becoming less feasible since the end of the Cold War, the US has invested heavily in the development of a vast infrastructure for enforcement of non-lethal sanctions regimes that can be deployed at any moment anywhere in the world with the fierce force and intensity of US military and financial powers. This well-developed enforcement infrastructure rests primarily on three major pillars: extraterritorial application of sanctions, dollar-denominated global payments systems, and hegemonic influence over global financial institutions and networks. Congressional legislation and the presidential executive powers grant broad authority to scores of governmental departments and agencies to enforce the sanctions regimes often with broad discretions. As the presidential decrees that impose sanctions regimes derive their power either from the US Constitution or Congressional legislation, as most of the sanctions are imposed

67 Among others, the DDTC derives its authority from: 22 USC 2752, 2778, 2797; 22USC 2651a: Sec. 1514 (P.L. 105-261); EO 13637, 72 FR 16129.

68 Overall, the DDTC has a very strong record of monitoring and enforcing sanctions violations. Some of the recent examples include: a $20 million settlement with 3D Systems Corporation of South Carolina in February 2023 for unauthorized exports of technical data to Germany and China; a $6.6 million settlement with Keysight Technologies of California in August 2021 for unauthorized export of technical data and software used for testing radar equipment on fixed or mobile platforms; and a $13 million settlement with Honeywell International of North Carolina in May 2021 for unauthorized export and retransfer of technical data that contained engineering prints and layouts for manufacturing castings for multiple aircraft, gas turbine engines, and military electronics. For greater detail, see www.pmddtc.state.gov/ddtc_public.

and enforced in the name of US national security interests and in pursuance of an international order befitting the country's preeminent leadership in the world, they seldom receive judicial scrutiny, although many EOs do provide scope for administrative, legal, and judicial remedies to designated governments, entities, and individuals.

REFERENCES

Amicelle, A. 2011. The Great (Data) Bank Robbery: Terrorist Finance Tracking Program and the SWIFT Affair. Technical Report No. 1047. New York: Federal Reserve Bank of New York.

Arslanalp, S. 2020. Active Diversifiers and the Rise of Nontraditional Reserve Currencies. Washington, DC: International Monetary Fund. WP/22/58 IMF.

Beckhy, P. 2018. Sanctions and the Blurred Boundaries of International Economic Law. *Missouri Law Review*, 83(1):1–38.

Beucillon, C. 2021. An Introduction to Unilateral and Extraterritorial Sanctions: Definitions, State of Practice and Contemporary Challenges. In C. Beucillon (ed.), *Research Handbook on Unilateral and Extraterritorial Sanctions*, pp. 1–18. Cheltenham, UK: Edward Elgar.

BIS (Bank for International Settlements). 2020a. *Statistical Release: BIS Global Liquidity Indicators at End-March 2020* (30 July 2020). Available at: www.bis.org/statistics/ gli2007.pdf.

BIS (Bank for International Settlements). 2020b. *US Dollar Funding: An International Perspective* (June 2020). Available at: www.bis.org/ publ/ cgfs65.pdf.

BIS (Bank for International Settlements). 2022. *Statistical Release: Global Liquidity Indicators. BIS Annual Economic Report, 2022*. Available at: www.bis.org/statistics/gli.htm.

BIS (Bureau of Industry and Security). 2019. *Actual Investigations of Export Control and Antiboycott Violations*. Washington, DC: Department of Commerce. September 2019.

Brainard, L. 2022. Preparing for the Financial System of the Future. Remarks at the 2022 US Monetary Policy Forum. New York. February 18.

Breen, E. 2021. Corporations and US Economic Sanctions: The Dangers of Overcompliance. In C. Beucillon (ed.), *Research Handbook on Unilateral and Extraterritorial Sanctions*, pp. 256–269. Cheltenham, UK: Edward Elgar.

Carter, B., and Farha, R. 2013. Overview and Operation of U.S. Financial Sanctions, Including the Example of Iran. *Georgetown Journal of International Law*, 44(3):903–914.

Casey, C. et al. 2022. The International Emergency Economic Powers Act: Origins, Evolution, and Use. Washington, DC: Congressional Research Service. March 25, 2022. R45618.

Cipriani, M. et al. 2023. Financial Sanctions, SWIFT, and the Architecture of the International Payments System. Federal Reserve Bank of New York Staff Reports, Paper No. 1047.

Clark, H. 1999. Dealing with US Extraterritorial Sanctions and Foreign Countermeasures. *University of Pennsylvania Journal of International Economic Law*, 20(1):61–96.

Clearing House. 2020. *Public Disclosure of Legal, Governance, Risk Management, and Operating Framework*. New York: The Clearing House.

Donohue, L. 2008. Constitutional and Legal Challenges to the Anti-Terrorist Finance Regime. *Wake Forest Law Review*, 43:643–697.

ECB (European Central Bank). 2021. *TARGET Annual Report 2020*. Bonn, Germany.

Eichengreen, B. et al. 2021. Financial Globalization and Inequality: Capital Flows as a Two-Edged Sword. IMF Working Paper WP/21/4. International Monetary Fund, Washington, DC.

Fabbrini, F. 2013. Global Sanctions, State Secrets and Supranational Review: Seeking Due Process in an Interconnected World. In D. Cole, F. Fabbrini, and A. Vedaschi (eds.), *Secrecy, National Security and Vindication of Constitutional Law*, pp. 284–301. ElgarOnline. Available at: www.elgaronline.com/display/9781781953853.00027.xml.

Fandl, K. 2018. Trading with the Enemy: Opening the Door to US Investment in Cuba. *Georgetown Journal of International Law*, 49:563–608.

Farrell, H., and A. Newman. 2019. Weaponized Interdependence. *International Security*, 44(1):42–79.

Federal Reserve Bank. 2022. *Money and Payments: The U.S. Dollar in the Age of Digital Transformation*. Washington, DC: Board of Governors, Federal Reserve Bank.

Fergusson, I., and P. Kerr. 2020. The U.S. Export Control System and the Export Control Reform Initiative. Congressional Research Service (CRS), R41916. Washington, DC.

FinCEN (Financial Crimes Enforcement Network). 2006. Feasibility of a Cross-Border Electronic Funds Transfer Reporting System under the Bank Secrecy Act, 2006.

Gaylord, M. 2008. The Banco Delta Asia Affair: The USA PATRIOT Act and Allegations of Money Laundering in Macau. *Crime, Law & Society*, 50(208):293–298.

Georgieva, K. 2022. The Future of Money: Gearing up for Central Bank Digital Currency. Address to Atlantic Council. February 9, 2022. Available at: www.imf.org/en/News/Articles/2022/02/09/sp020922-the-future-of-money-gearing-up-for-central-bank-digital-currency.

Goldman, Z., and A. Lindblom. 2021. The US Position and Practice with Regards to Unilateral and Extraterritorial Sanctions: Reimagining the US Sanctions Regime in a World of Advanced Technology. In C. Beucillon (ed.), *Research Handbook on Unilateral and Extraterritorial Sanctions*, pp. 130–148. Cheltenham, UK: Edward Elgar.

Gopinath, G., and J. Stein. 2021. Banking, Trade, and the Making of a Dominant Currency. *The Quarterly Journal of Economics*, 136(2):783–830.

Haberly, D., and D. Wójcik. 2017. Culprits or Bystanders? Offshore Jurisdictions and the Global Financial Crisis. *Journal of Financial Regulation*, 3(2):233–261.

Hasu, N. 2020. USD Stablecoins Are Surging, but Zero Interest Rates Complicate Business Model. *CoinDesk* (30 March 2020). Available at: www.coindesk.com/usd-stablecoins-are-surging-but-zero-interest-rates-complicate-business-model.

Hirschhorn, E. et al. 2022. *U.S. Export Controls and Economic Sanctions*. Oxford: Oxford University Press.

Hufbauer, G. et al. 2007. *Economic Sanctions Reconsidered: History and Current Policy*. Washington, DC: Patterson Institute for International Economics.

Hügli, P. 2020. Hyper-Stablecoinization: From Eurodollars to Crypto-Dollars. *CoinDesk* (12 July 2020). Available at: www.coindesk.com/hyper-stablecoinization-from-eurodollars-to-crypto-dollars.

Iancu, A. et al. 2020. *Reserve Currencies in an Evolving International Monetary System*. Washington, DC: International Monetary Fund.

Knox, J. 2010. A Presumption against Extra-Jurisdictionality, *American Journal of International Law*, 104(3):351–396.

Koppel, J. 2011. *The Swift Affair*. Geneva: Graduate Institute Publications.

Lowenfeld, A. 2002. *International Economic Law*. New York: Oxford University Press.

Lowenfeld, A. 2003. Trade Controls for Political Ends: Four Perspectives. *Chicago Journal of International Law*, 4(2):354–369.

Mallard, G., and A. Hanson. 2021. Embedded Extraterritoriality: US Judicial Litigation and the Global Banking Surveillance of Digital Money Flows. In C. Beucillon (ed.), *Research Handbook on Unilateral and Extraterritorial Sanctions*, pp. 270–287. Cheltenham, UK: Edward Elgar.

Marcuss, S. 1999. Grist for the Litigation Mill in U.S. Economic Sanctions Programs. *Law and Policy in International Business*, 30:501.

McDowell, D. 2023. *Bucking the Buck: US Financial Sanctions and the International Backlash against the Dollar*. New York: Online Oxford Academic. Available at: doi-org .access.library.miami.edu/10.1093/oso/9780197679876.001.0001.

Meyer, J. 2009. Second Thoughts on Secondary Sanctions. *University of Pennsylvania Journal of International Economic Law*, 30(3):905–934.

Morriss, A., and C. Hansen. 2013. Regulatory Effectiveness & Offshore Financial Centers. *Virginia Journal of International Law*, 53:418–444.

Morriss, A., and C. Ku. 2020. The Evolution of Offshore: From Tax Havens to IFCs. Texas A&M University School of Law Research Paper No. 21–07.

Mulder, N. 2022. *The Economic Weapon – The Rise of Sanctions as a Tool of Modern War*. New Haven, CT: Yale University Press.

Nakajima, C. 2017. Politics: Offshore Centers, Transparency, and Integrity: The Case of the UK Territories. In D. Masciandro (ed.), *Global Financial Crime, Terrorism, Money laundering and Offshore Centers*, pp. 219–246. New York: Routledge.

Nelson, R., and M. Weiss. 2022. The U.S. Dollar as the World's Dominant Reserve Currency. Washington, DC: Congressional Research Service, IF11707.

Nephew, R. 2019. China and Economic Sanctions: Where Does Washington Have Leverage? Washington, DC: Brookings Institution, September, 2019.

Nephew, R. 2020. Implementation of Sanctions: United States. In M. Asada (ed.), *Economic Sanctions in International Law and Practice*, pp. 93–115. London: Routledge.

O'Sullivan, M. 2003. *Shrewd Sanctions – Statecraft and State Sponsors of Terrorism*. Washington, DC: Brookings Institution Press.

Petersen, N. 2005. Justice for the "Designated": The Process that Is Due to Alleged U.S. Financiers of Terrorism. *Georgetown Law Journal*, 93(2005):1387–1405.

Pol, R. 2020a. Anti-money Laundering: Almost Completely Ineffective. Why it Harms Us All. Available at: medium.com/the-capital/anti-money-laundering-almost-completely-ineffective-why-it-harms-us-all-827d54db7df5.

Pol, R. 2020b. Anti-money Laundering: The World's Least Effective Policy Experiment? Together, We Can Fix It. *Policy Design and Practice*, 3(1):73–94.

Prezas, I. 2021. From Targeted States to Affected Populations: Exploring Accountability for the Negative Impact of Comprehensive Unilateral Sanctions on Human Rights. In C. Beucillon (ed.), *Research Handbook on Unilateral and Extraterritorial Sanctions*, pp. 385–404. Cheltenham, UK: Edward Elgar.

Rosenberg, E. et al. (2016). *The Challenges of Contemporary Sanctions to the United States and on the Global Financial System*. Washington, DC: Center for a New American Security.

Savage, J. 2001. Executive Use of International Emergency Powers Act – Evolution Through the Terrorist and Taliban Sanctions. *Currents: International Trade Law Journal*, 10(28):21–41.

Shagina, M. 2021. How Disastrous Would Disconnection from SWIFT Be for Russia? Washington, DC: Carnegie Endowment for International Peace. Available at carnegiemoscow.org/commentary/84634.

SWIFT. 2021. RMB Tracker: Monthly Reporting and Statistics on Renminbi (RMB) Progress towards Becoming an International Currency. Technical Report, Society for Worldwide Interbank Financial Telecommunication.

Timofeev, I. 2021. Unilateral and Extraterritorial Sanctions Policy: The Russian Dimension. In C. Beucillon (ed.), *Research Handbook on Unilateral and Extraterritorial Sanctions*, pp. 90–110. Cheltenham, UK: Edward Elgar.

White, N. 2018. Autonomous and Collective Sanctions in the International Legal Order. University of Nottingham. Available at: brill.com/abstract/title/54225.

White, N. 2021. Shades of Grey: Autonomous Sanctions in the International Legal Order. In S. Subedi (ed.), *Unilateral Sanctions in International Law*, pp. 61–86. Oxford: Hart Publishing.

Woetzel, J. et al. 2019. China and the World: Inside the Dynamics of a Changing Relationship. New York: McKinsey Global Institute, July, 2019.

Wong, L, and R. Nelson. 2021. International Financial Messaging Systems. Washington, DC: Congressional Research Service, R46843.

Yeung, R., and K. Goh. 2022. Petroyuan Will Not Bring about a Regime Shift Soon. Technical Report, ANZ Research, *China Insight*, April 6.

5

US Economic and Financial Sanctions against the Russian Federation

I INTRODUCTION

The Russian Federation has been the most sanctioned country, as well as the largest economy under sanctions, since WWII, but its saga with sanctions began only recently, in 2012.[1] Most of the sanctions regimes against Russia have been imposed by the US, the country's longstanding geo-political and military rival. The EU, and some others, such as Canada, Japan, Australia, the UK, and Switzerland, have also joined the US in sanctions campaigns against Russia since its annexation of Crimea in 2014, and especially since the invasion of Ukraine in February 2022. All sanctions regimes against Russia have, however, been either unilateral or regional in character – no multilateral sanctions regime by the UNSC is possible as Russia is a permanent member of the UNSC with a veto power.

For about two decades, between 1991, when Russia emerged following the disintegration of the former Union of Soviet Socialist Republics (USSR), which also brought an end to the prolonged Cold War, and 2012, when the US imposed its first rounds of sanctions against Russia, the two countries had rather been close allies in adopting sanctions on other countries under the auspices of the UNSC. During this brief period, the UNSC imposed sanctions regimes against as many as 15 different countries due to lack of hostility between former rivals,

[1] The former Soviet Union – the Union of Soviet Socialist Republics (USSR) – as well as the entire socialist bloc was under broad US sanctions throughout the Cold War period. The discussion here is limited to the Russian Federation, which emerged as a successor of the USSR on December 8, 1991 after the collapse of communism and disintegration of the USSR. The successor of the Russian Empire, founded by Tsar Peter the Great in 1703, Russia is physically the largest country in the world. The country covers 6.6 million square miles (17.1 million square kilometers) and 11 time zones, and is over 6,000 miles (9,656 kilometers) in length, stretching over a vast expanse of eastern Europe and northern Asia. The country is nearly twice the size of Canada, the second largest country in the world with a territory of 3.8 million square miles (9.8 million square kilometers). The current population of Russia is estimated to be around 143.4 million, the majority of whom are ethnic Russians. For greater detail on Russia's past history and transformation, see Bartlett (2003), Blum (1968, 4–62), Dowlah (1992), Dowlah (2022, 116–136), and Kolchin (1997).

while during the entire period of 1945–1990, the UNSC had succeeded in imposing sanctions only twice.[2]

All that has changed in recent years, as the US and its allies – the West – accuse Russia of illegally annexing Crimea and violating Ukrainian sovereignty.[3] The underlying reason for the conflict, however, may lie with a deep disagreement between the West and Russia over the post-Cold War security order in Europe. While Russia wants to preserve its "sphere of influence" over the former Soviet republics, especially over Ukraine, Belarus, Georgia, Moldova, Armenia and Azerbaijan, and Central Asia, the West seeks to bring these countries under the orbit of the US-led international economic and military alliance (Aslund and Sengovaya, 2021).

The conflict deepened further as three former republics of the USSR – Latvia, Lithuania, and Estonia – joined the North Atlantic Treaty Organization (NATO) between 1999 and 2004, and acquired full membership of the EU between 2004 and 2007. Second, when two other former republics of the USSR – Georgia and Ukraine – also pursued a similar goal, Russia staunchly opposed such moves, raising national security concerns. Following a military conflict with Georgia in 2008, Russia created two breakaway republics in Georgian territory – South Ossetia and Abkhazia. Third, after the Georgian war, the EU launched what is called the Eastern Partnership program with the objective to bring Armenia, Azerbaijan, Belarus, Georgia, Moldova, and Ukraine into its orbit. But in response, Russia launched its own Eurasian Customs Union (EACU), which has been joined only by Belarus and Kazakhstan, but Russia seeks to include Armenia, Moldova, and Ukraine as well.

Among all the former republics of the USSR, Ukraine matters the most to Russia, because it is the largest neighbor with which Russia historically shared strong politico-economic and socio-cultural ties.[4] Geo-politically, Ukraine is so

[2] During 1945–1990, the UNSC imposed sanctions twice – against South Rhodesia in 1966 and against South Africa in 1977. For greater detail, see Chapter 1 of this volume, Asada (2020), Gowlland-Debbas (2004), LaRae-Perez (2002), and Reisman and Stevick (1998).

[3] The US allies that have imposed bilateral sanctions on Russia include Japan. Although Japan is an Asian country, in this study, Japan is considered as a Western nation. The country has indeed been considered as part of the West in many studies, mainly because of its historical evolution resembling that of western Europe and its solid alliance with Western countries since WWII. For greater detail, see Coulborn (1956), Dowlah (2022, 155–172).

[4] Close relations between the two countries date back to the fourteenth century, although only an insignificant number of Russians lived in Ukraine at the time. Immediately before the break-up of the USSR, the 1989 Census showed the population of Ukraine comprised 72.7 percent ethnic Ukrainians and 22.1 percent ethnic Russians. The 2001 Census, which is the last one available as no other census has taken place since, showed the share of ethnic Ukrainians at 77.8 percent and that of ethnic Russians at 17.3 percent. The Census also showed that the Russian language was native for 29.6 percent of Ukraine's population, while 67. 5 percent spoke Ukrainian as their native language (Shkolnikov, 2012). As of 2022, it was believed that 81 percent of the country's population spoke the Ukrainian language in their personal life, 34 percent spoke Russian, and 19 percent spoke both languages regularly (Constantin, 2022). The country's population in 2023 was estimated to be 36.7 million, which shows a sharp decline since 2015 when the population was 44.9 million. Ukraine's population has been declining consistently since 1995, when the country had 51 million people. Approximately 11 to 12 million Ukrainians are considered to be ethnically Russian.

tremendously important for Russia's national security that Russia effectively prevented Ukraine from joining NATO or the EU's Eastern Partnership. It was indeed due to Russian pressure that in 2013 Ukrainian President Viktor Yanukovych refused to sign the EU's Eastern Partnership, and instead opted to sign a bilateral agreement with Russia. Eventually, the resultant political crisis and mass protests forced Yanukovych to flee to Russia on February 22, 2015. In turn, Russia not only invaded Ukraine in July 2014, but had also annexed Ukraine's Crimea region to Russia by March 18, 2014 (Oxenstierna and Olsson, 2015).[5]

The rest of this chapter is organized as follows: Section II chronicles the unilateral sanctions regimes imposed on Russia in the post–Cold War era; Section III elaborates on the countersanctions that Russia has imposed on the sanctioner countries including the US; Section IV explores the impacts of the sanction regimes on the Russian economy and population; Section V explores the legal foundations of the sanctions regimes imposed on Russia; and Section VI concludes the chapter.

II CHRONOLOGY OF US SANCTIONS AGAINST RUSSIA

In the post-Cold War era, the US sanctions against Russia began with the Sergei Magnitsky Rule of Law Accountability Act of 2012 (Magnitsky Act: P.L. 112-208),[6] which requires the president to impose sanctions on those who commit human rights abuses against individuals fighting to expose illegal activities of Russian government officials or who seek to exercise or defend internationally recognized human rights and freedoms.[7]

5 The Crimean Peninsula is the only region in Ukraine where ethnic Russians are the majority – about two-thirds of the Crimean population, approximately 1.5 million, are ethnic Russians. Referring to this fact, on April 17, 2014, in his Crimean victory speech, Russian President Vladimir Putin argued:

> The essential issue is how to ensure the legitimate rights and interests of ethnic Russians and Russian speakers in the southeast of Ukraine. I would like to remind you that what was called Novorossiya (New Russia) back in the tsarist days – Kharkov, Lugansk, Donetsk, Kherson, Nikolayev and Odessa – were not part of Ukraine back then. These territories were given to Ukraine in the 1920s by the Soviet government … Russia lost these territories for various reasons, but the people remained (cited in Aslund and Sengovaya, 2021, 11).

6 The Act was named after Sergei Magnitsky, a Russian lawyer who died in a Russian prison in November 2009 after he had uncovered massive tax fraud implicating dozens of Russian government officials.

7 The Magnitsky Act is also a continuation of Title IV of the Trade Act of 1974 (P.L. 93-618, §402), pursuant to which Russia was denied Permanent Normal Trade Relations (PNTR) status with the US because of its socialist economic policies and prohibitive emigration policies. After the collapse of the USSR, the US granted Russia conditional normal trade relations (NTR) beginning in 1992, and then the US facilitated Russia's joining of the World Trade Organization (WTO) in 2012. With Russia joining the WTO, it became automatically entitled to Most Favored Nation (MFN) status, which made the PNTR status redundant. For greater detail on the PNTR, see Baskin and Zagaris (2011) and Welt (2020, 9).

Under the Magnitsky Act, the US sanctioned 55 Russian individuals, of whom 40 were directly associated with the alleged crimes that Sergei Magnitsky uncovered and with his subsequent ill-treatment and death. These individuals were denied entry into the US, and their properties under US jurisdiction were frozen. The US also designated 13 other individuals from Russia's Chechnya region for human rights violations as well as for the 2004 murder of Paul Klebnikov, the American chief editor of the Russian edition of *Forbes*. Two of these individuals were among the suspected killers of former Russian spy Alexander Litvinenko in London in 2006 (Welt, 2020, 8).[8]

The US has, however, vastly expanded its sanctions campaigns against Russia after the Russian annexation of Crimea in 2014. By 2022, the US had imposed numerous sanctions on Russian individuals and entities on scores of grounds, including election interference, malicious cyber-enabled activities, human rights abuses, official corruption, use of a chemical weapon, weapons proliferation, trade with North Korea in violation of UNSC requirements, support for the Syrian and Venezuelan governments, transnational crime, international terrorism, and the second invasion of Ukraine in 2022.

Many other countries have also joined the US in many of these sanctions that targeted Russian government leaders and officials, business entities, and other individuals. Based on sanctions regimes imposed by seven jurisdictions – the US, the UK, the EU, Switzerland, Canada, Australia, and Japan – the Atlantic Council database suggests that, as of November 30, 2022, Russia had been subjected to a total of 11,073 sanctions, of which 8,667 were against individuals, 2,273 were against entities, 116 were against vessels, and 17 were against aircraft. Among these sanctions, 78 percent targeted Russian individuals and around 21 percent targeted Russian entities. Obviously, the US has been the undisputed champion in imposing sanctions on Russia – it has sanctioned 1,097 Russian entities, 1,331 Russian individuals, 116 Russian vessels, and 17 Russian aircraft.[9]

[8] In 2016, US Congress passed the Global Magnitsky Human Rights Accountability Act (P.L. 114-328), a globalized version of the Magnitsky Act, which authorizes the president to apply similar sanctions on government officials around the world; protect whistleblowers and human rights defenders; and deny US visa and freezing of assets of foreign government officials responsible for acts of significant corruption, including the offshore sheltering of ill-gotten gains. On December 20, 2017, President Trump issued Executive Order (EO) 13818, invoking the Global Magnitsky Act and emergency authorities of the National Emergencies Act (NEA; P.L. 94-412) and International Emergency Economic Powers Act (IEEPA; P.L. 95-223). The EO further expanded the scope of the law by making "potentially sanctionable targets" of the law those individuals responsible for "gross violations of internationally recognized human rights." As of 2020, the US had designated 107 individuals and 105 entities from several countries under EO 13818. Countries with five or more individuals designated under the EO included: Saudi Arabia (17 individuals), Uganda (11), Serbia (10), Burma (9), Iraq (8), South Sudan (8), China (7), and Cambodia (6). The designated entities were owned or controlled by these designated individuals. See Weber and Collins-Chase (2020) for greater detail.

[9] The shares of other leading countries in respect to imposing sanctions on Russia were as follows: Canada – 303 entities and 1,539 individuals; Switzerland – 377 entities and 1,223 individuals; the EU – 123 entities and 1,220 individuals (the UK had the same sanctions); and Australia – 118 entities and 1,030 individuals. Based on Atlantic Council Database.

The US sanctions regimes on Russia were imposed in two phases – the first phase began with the Russian invasion of Ukraine in 2014,[10] and the second phase began with the second Russian invasion of Ukraine on February 24, 2022. During the first phase, Russia annexed Crimea, and Russian-backed paramilitaries seized parts of the Donbas region, the Luhansk and Donetsk oblasts of Ukraine. During the second phase, Russia extended recognition to the Donetsk People's Republic and the Luhansk People's Republic as self-proclaimed breakaway states in the Donbas region. The second invasion represented a major escalation of the Russo-Ukraine War, which Russian president Putin described as a "special military operation" aimed at demilitarization and denazification of Ukraine and ending the alleged genocide of Russians in Ukrainian territory.

A *Sanctions during the First Phase*

The US sanctions in the first phase, launched following the Russian invasion of Ukraine in 2014, were based on national emergency authorities granted to the president by the National Emergencies Act (NEA: 1976) and the International Emergency Economic Powers Act (IEEPA: 1977), and scores of non-emergency statutes including: the Magnitsky Act (2012); the Support for the Sovereignty, Integrity, Democracy, and Economic Stability of Ukraine Act of 2014 (SSIDES: P.L. 113-95); the Ukraine Freedom Support Act of 2014 (UFSA: P.L. 113-272); the Countering Russian Influence in Europe and Eurasia Act of 2017 (CRIEEA: P.L. 115-44); and the Countering America's Adversaries Through Sanctions Act of 2017 (CAATSA: P.L. 115-44).

These statutes, especially CRIEEA and CAATSA, codified Ukraine-related and cyber-related presidential executive orders (EOs), identified several new targets for sanctions, and established Congressional review of any action the president can take to ease or lift sanctions imposed on Russia. The sanctions regimes were imposed through a series of EOs issued by President Barack Obama (EOs 13660, 13661, 13662, and 13685) and President Donald Trump (EOs 13818, 13848, and 13883).[11] Under those EOs, the US Treasury Department imposed sanctions on more than 680 Russian individuals, entities, vessels, and aircraft between 2014 and 2019 (Welt, 2020).

[10] Russia invaded Ukraine on February 28, 2014. The next day, the Russian Parliament (the Duma) authorized the use of force on the territory of Ukraine. On March 2, 2014, the G7 countries – the US, Canada, the UK, France, Italy, Germany, and Japan – condemned Russia's "clear violation of the sovereignty and territorial integrity of Ukraine, in contravention of Russia's obligations under the UN Charter and its 1997 basing agreement with Ukraine," and suspended its participation in the G8 summit scheduled to take place in Sotchi, Russia. On March 17, 2014, the EU imposed travel bans and asset freezes on a range of Russian officials and other individuals deemed responsible for the destabilization of Ukraine, which included Russian deputy prime minister Dmitry Rogozin. Such actions, some scholars believe, constituted acts of retorsion (Dawidowicz, 2017, 231).

[11] In adopting the EOs, the presidents invoked the IEEPA (50 U.S.C. 1701 et seq.), the NEA (50 U.S.C. 1601 et seq.), Section 212(f) of the Immigration and Nationality Act of 1952 (8 U.S.C. 1182(f)), and Section 301 of title 3 United States Code.

Presidential Executive Orders

President Obama's EOs targeted numerous individuals and entities who undermined Ukraine's democratic processes, institutions, sovereignty, or territorial integrity, including scores of government and military officials and entities operating in key sectors of the Russian economy; and prohibited business, trade, or investment in occupied Crimea.

Under EO 13660 – blocking the property of certain persons contributing to the situation in Ukraine – issued on March 6, 2014, the Office of Foreign Asset Control (OFAC) of the Treasury Department designated many individuals and entities in the Specially Designated Nationals List (SDN) for their involvement in the destabilization and invasion of Ukraine, which included former Ukrainian president Viktor Yanukovych, Ukrainian separatist officials in Crimea and eastern Ukraine, and several associated entities.

Under EO 13661 – blocking the property of additional persons contributing to the situation in Ukraine – issued on March 16, 2014, and EO 13662 – blocking the property of additional persons contributing to the situation in Ukraine – issued on March 20, 2014, OFAC designated a wider circle of Russian government officials and entities, including prominent businesspeople and associates considered to be part of Russian president Putin's "inner circle." Among those designated were Russia's minister of internal affairs, security council secretary, directors of the Russian Foreign Intelligence Service (SVR) and National Guard Troops; the chairs of both houses of parliament; and the chief executive officers of the state-owned oil company Rosneft, gas company Gazprom, defense and technology conglomerate Rostec, prominent banks VTB and Gazprombank, and several politically connected Russian oligarchs, including Yevgeny Prigozhin, who allegedly backed private military companies operating in Ukraine, Syria, and other countries, and interfered in elections in the US and elsewhere.

Later, under EO 13685 – blocking property of certain persons and prohibiting certain transactions with respect to the Crimea Region of Ukraine – issued on December 19, 2014, OFAC designated several other Russian or Crimea-based companies and subsidiaries, vessels, and individuals for their illicit business operations in occupied Crimea.

As of January 2020, OFAC had placed more than 390 individuals, entities, vessels, and aircraft on the four Ukraine-related SDN lists.[12] The entities designated included holdings owned or controlled by individuals listed in SDNs, such as Bank Rossiya; privately held banks and financial services companies, such as SMP Bank and the Volga Group; gas pipeline construction company Stroygazmontazh; construction company Stroytransgaz; vehicle manufacturer GAZ Group; private

[12] See Table 1 and Table B-1 in Welt (2020) for the sanctioned individuals, entities, vessels, and aircraft. Including those sanctioned in the Sectoral Sanctions Identification List (SSI) of OFAC, the total number of sanctions exceeded 680.

aluminum company Rusal; electric company EuroSibEnergo; several defense and arms firms, such as the state-owned United Shipbuilding Corporation, Almaz-Antey (air defense systems and missiles), Uralvagonzavod (tanks and other military equipment), NPO Mashinostroyenia (missiles and rockets) and several subsidiaries of the state-owned defense and hi-tech conglomerate Rostec, including the Kalashnikov Group (firearms) (Welt, 2020, 10–11).

Election Interference and Cyber-Enabled Activities

Two presidential EOs: EO 13694 – blocking the property of certain persons engaging in significant malicious cyber-enabled activities, issued on April 1, 2015, and EO 13757 – taking additional steps to address the national emergency with respect to significant malicious cyber-enabled activities, issued on December 28, 2016, were directed at election interference and malicious cyber-enabled activities. EO 13694 targeted those engaged in cyberattacks against critical infrastructure for financial or commercial gain, or to significantly disrupt the availability of a computer or network by expanding the scope of cyber-related activities subject to sanctions as mandated by CRIEEA (2017). EO 13757, which came as an amendment to EO 13694, established sanctions against individuals and entities engaged in misinformation campaigns with the purpose of interfering with or undermining election processes or institutions.

By March 2018, OFAC had designated more than one dozen Russian individuals and at least eight entities for election-related malicious cyber activities under these EOs, including "NotPetya," a ransomware entity which conducted one of the "the most destructive and costly cyberattacks in history"; Russia's Federal Security Service (FSB); Russian's military intelligence agency (GRU); and Russian Internet Research Agency (IRA) (Welt, 2020, 19–20).

In 2018, President Trump issued two EOs; EO 13848 – imposing certain sanctions in the event of foreign interference in a US election – issued on September 12, 2018; and EO 13849 – EO authorizing the implementation of certain sanctions set forth in CAATSA, issued on September 20, 2018. Both of these EOs were targeted at foreign individuals and entities located outside the US, who had directly or indirectly engaged in or sponsored foreign interference in a US election by engaging in such activities through the proliferation of digital devices and internet-based communications. In addition, EO 13849 also established the means to implement certain sanctions mandated by the CRIEEA (2017) and the UFSA (2014), as amended.

As of January 2020, OFAC had designated at least 49 Russian individuals and related entities, vessels, and aircraft for election-related interference under these EOs, including a Russian cybercriminal organization called "Evil Corp" and 23 related individuals and entities.

Proliferation of Weapons of Mass Destruction

The US sanctions against suspected Russian individuals and entities with respect to proliferation of weapons of mass destruction began long before the Russian annexation of Crimea in 2014. In October 2012, the Bureau of Industry and Security (BIS) of the Department of Commerce imposed restrictions on 119 Russian individuals and entities (along with 45 others from 11 other countries), for their involvement in the procurement and delivery of military-related items to Russia in violation of the US Export Administration Regulations (EAR) and the International Traffic in Arms Regulations (ITAR).

In December 2017, the BIS imposed export-licensing restrictions on two Russian entities for producing a ground-launched cruise missile system and associated launcher in violation of the Intermediate Range Nuclear Forces Treaty (INF Treaty).[13] Then, in August 2018, the State Department determined that Russia had used a chemical weapon in the UK in March 2018, in contravention of the Chemical and Biological Weapons Control and Warfare Elimination Act of 1991 (CBW: P.L. 102-182).[14] In response, the Trump Administration issued EO 13883 in August 2019 ordering mandatory sanctioning measures against Russia.

In March 2021, in response to the Russian opposition leader Alexei Navalny's poisoning and imprisonment, the US terminated all assistance to Russia under the Foreign Assistance Act (FAA: 1961), except for urgent humanitarian assistance; all sales under the Arms Export Control Act (AECA: 1976) of any defense articles or services on the USML; and prohibited any export to Russia of any goods or technology (Welt, 2020, 31).

At the same time, the State Department added six Russian defense and intelligence entities to its List of Specified Persons, invoking CAATSA Section 211, and OFAC designated seven top officials of the Russian government including two deputy ministers of the Ministry of Defense, two first deputy chiefs of staff of President Putin's executive office; the director of the Russian FSB, and the prosecutor general of the Russian Federation.

North Korea Related Sanctions

North Korea has been under sanctions imposed by both the UN and the US since the 1990s for its nuclear tests and heavy weaponry and missile technology programs, but the sanctions imposed by the US have been far wider than those imposed by the UN. Also, in recent years, the US further expanded its sanctions against North Korea. For example, in 2014, the US imposed sanctions against North Korea in response to its breach of Sony computer systems; in 2017, the US imposed sanctions for North Korea's WannaCry ransomware attack as well as for human rights violations and money laundering. The US has also sanctioned several Chinese and Russian banks, entities, and individuals for their support of North Korea's weapons programs in violation of US export controls.

[13] Also, due to Russia's failure to return to compliance with the INF Treaty, in August 2019 the US withdrew from the treaty.

[14] The CBW Act had been invoked only twice before: in August 2013, against Syria under the national security waiver authority; and in February 2018, against North Korea for its nerve agent attack on Kim Jong Nam, half-brother of North Korean leader Kim Jong-un, in Malaysia in 2017.

In 2017, President Trump also issued a series of EOs to freeze North Korean assets, to restrict its trade and financial transactions and the travel of designated North Korean officials, and to penalize foreign individuals and entities engaged in supporting the country's economic and trading activities.[15] Implementing the EOs, the OFAC designated at least 22 Russia-related individuals, entities, and vessels for evading US sanctions by engaging in restricted trade and financial transactions with North Korea (Welt, 2020, 31).

Syria Related Sanctions

The US designated Syria as a state sponsor of terrorism back in 1979, but sanctions against the country intensified after the enactment of the Iran Nonproliferation Act of 2000 (INA: P.L. 106-178); the Syria Accountability and Lebanese Sovereignty Restoration Act of 2003 (SAA: P.L. 108-175); and the Iran, North Korea, Syria Nonproliferation Act of 2013 (INKSNA: H.R. 893).

Beginning in 2004, a series of EOs (nos. 13338, 13572, 13573, 13582, and 13685) were directed at imposing sanctions on Syrian as well as foreign government officials, entities, and individuals in response to the country's occupation of Lebanon, support of international terrorism, pursuit of weapons of mass destruction, and undermining international efforts to stabilize Iraq. They aimed to force the Assad regime to allow for a democratic transition and stop human rights abuses.

Many of these Syria related sanctions were directed at dozens of Russian individuals, entities, and vessels which provided material support and services to Syria, bolstered the Assad regime by illicitly moving oil from Iran to Syria, and funneled funds to the Islamic Revolutionary Guard Corps-Quds Force, Hamas, and Hezbollah, and assisted Syria by evading US sanctions on Ukraine and Venezuela.[16]

Energy Export Pipelines

The recent US sanctions campaign in relation to Russian pipelines to export gas to European countries came against the backdrop of several developments. First, in 2013–2014, Russia and China struck a deal to build the "Power of Siberia" pipeline from eastern Siberia to China under which Russia agreed to export 38 billion cubic meters (bcm) of gas per year to China beginning in 2018. Second, in May 2015, Russia signed a deal with Turkey to build the "Turk Stream" pipeline across the Black Sea to deliver 16 bcm of gas per year to Turkey beginning in 2016, and to extend the pipeline to deliver another 47 bcm per year to the Greek–Turkish border. Third, in 2017, Russia's state-owned Gazprom signed agreements with several

[15] In issuing his first EO (13810) against North Korea on September 21, 2017, President Trump invoked IEEPA (1977), UNPA (1945), INA (1952), and UNSC Resolutions (nos. 2321, 2356, 2371, and 2375). The subsequent EOs were mandated by the North Korea Sanctions and Policy Enhancement Act of 2016 (P.L. 114-122), as amended by the Korean Interdiction and Modernization of Sanctions Act (Title III of CAATSA, 2017).

[16] For greater detail, see Welt (2020, 32) and www.state.gov/syria-sanctions/, accessed on January 24, 2023.

European companies for construction of the Nord Stream 2 natural gas pipeline to increase Russian gas exports to Germany and other parts of Europe via the Baltic Sea. And, finally, in December 2019, Russia concluded an agreement with Ukraine to continue transiting Russian natural gas through Ukraine (Welt, 2020, 33–47).

The US Congress passed two major pieces of legislation providing statutory authority to the president to impose sanctions in relation to Russian energy export pipelines: CRIEEA (2017) and the Protecting Europe's Energy Security Act of 2019 (PEESA: 22 U.S.C. 9526).[17] Section 232 of CRIEEA specifically authorizes the president to impose sanctions on individuals and entities that engage in trading and in the construction of Russian energy export pipelines, and PEESA requires the president to impose sanctions on foreign persons and entities who sell, lease, or provide subsea pipe-laying vessels for the construction of Nord Stream 2 and Turk Stream, or any successor Russian pipelines.

Pursuant to CRIEEA (2017), PEESA (2019), and IEEPA (1977), three EOs were issued between April 2021 and March 2022 (EO 14024, EO 14039, and EO 14066) to impose sanctions against scores of Russian individuals, entities, and vessels for violations of US restrictions with respect to Russian energy export pipelines. These EOs also forbid any investment and any otherwise involvement of any US individuals, companies, and their subsidiaries and any transaction in US dollars in any activities involving Russian pipelines.

In the meantime, the Turk Stream's subsea pipelines were completed in November 2018, and the Nord Stream 2 pipeline was completed in September 2021.[18] The pipeline was expected to enter service in 2022 to deliver gas to European consumers for 50 years. In February 2022, following Russia's invasion of Ukraine, however, Germany halted the certification of the pipeline. To be operational, the pipeline also needed to be certified by the EU. But in the meantime, on September 26, 2022, a series of clandestine bombings and subsequent underwater gas leakages rendered both Nord Stream 1 and Nord Stream 2 unoperational. At the time of writing this chapter in June 2023, it remains controversial as to who actually carried out the explosion.

Transnational Crime and Terrorism

The US sanctions against Russian groups in the category of Specially Designated Global Terrorists (SDGTs) and Transnational Criminal Organizations (TCOs)

[17] PEESA was enacted as Title LXXV of the National Defense Authorization Act for Fiscal Year 2020 (NDAA: P.L. No. 116-92).

[18] Nord Stream 2 is a 1,200 kilometer-long offshore natural gas pipeline that connects Europe to the world's largest reserves in northern Russia. Its design and route follow that of the Nord Stream pipeline which entered service in 2011, and had delivered 400 bcm of Russian gas to Europe as of April 2021. Originating from eastern Russia, Nord Stream 2 passes through Finnish, Swedish, and Danish waters to terminate near the German coast of the Baltic Sea. As an expansion of the existing Nord Stream pipeline, Nord Stream 2 is expected to supply energy to approximately 26 million households a year, with a capacity of 55 bcm. Russia's state-owned Gazprom invested over half of the $11 billion pipeline, while the remainder was invested jointly by companies including Engie (French), OMV (Austrian), Royal Dutch Shell (Anglo-Dutch), Uniper (German), and Wintershall (German).

date back to 2010, when Doku Umarov, the founder of the Caucasus Emirate, a terrorist and insurgent group in Russia's North Caucasus region, was designated. Subsequently, the Caucasus Emirate itself was designated in 2011; an Islamic State affiliate named the Caucasus Province (Vilayet) was placed on the SDGTs list in 2015. The Wagner Group was designated in 2017 for threatening the sovereignty and territorial integrity of Ukraine; the same year, a TCO named "Thieves-in-Law," a Eurasian crime syndicate and 12 affiliated individuals, were designated as SDGTs; and in 2018, two Russian individuals belonging to the Wagner Group were designated for their involvement in training military and security forces of the Central African Republic and for illicit control of gold and diamond mines in that country.

B *Sanctions during the Second Phase*

During the second phase, Russian troops crossed into Ukraine under what was called the "Special Military Operation" on February 24, 2022. The US sanctions on Russia, however, began three days before, on February 21, 2022 with EO 14065 – blocking property of certain persons and prohibiting certain transactions with respect to continued Russian efforts to undermine the sovereignty and territorial integrity of Ukraine – issued in response to Russian president, Vladimir Putin's, recognition of the independence and sovereignty of the Luhansk People's Republic (LNR) and the Donetsk People's Republic (DNR), and for his orders to send Russian troops to defend those territories. The EO, built on a series of EOs issued since 2014, among others, blocked new US investment in, US exports to, or US imports from, the Ukrainian regions.[19]

In its implementation of the EOs, on February 22, 2022, OFAC sanctioned two major Russian state-owned financial institutions (VEB and PSB) and their subsidiaries, as well as five Kremlin-connected oligarchs, and imposed additional restrictions on Russian sovereign debt. On February 24, 2022, on the day the Russian troops crossed into Ukraine, the US sanctioned over 20 Russian state-owned and private banking entities as well as several Russian oligarchs, and further circumscribed Russian access to technology, including semiconductors, computers, telecommunications, and information security equipment by further restricting US exports or reexports from third countries to Russia.

Since then, OFAC has designated numerous Russian officials and entities as well as oligarchs and other private individuals to isolate Russia from the global financial system and cripple its military power over Ukraine. The sanctions often seemed like torrential rain as they kept on coming, piling on existing sanctions, and often reinforced by close US allies. In the last week of February 2022, all US property interests involving Russia's president, foreign minister, and 11 members of the Russian

[19] The EOs incorporated into EO 14065 include: EOs 13660, 13661, 13662, and 13685 of 2014; EO 13849 of 2018; and EO 14024 and EO 14039 of 2021.

Security Council were frozen; several Russian banks were delinked from the SWIFT financial messaging system; the Russian Central Bank was brought under sanction; and all transactions with Russia's National Wealth Fund, Direct Investment Fund, and the Ministry of Finance were blocked.

In the first week of March 2022, US sanctions blocked Russian aircraft and airlines from entering US airspace; imposed additional sanctions against several oligarchs and their family members tied to the Russian defense industry;[20] further restricted US exports destined for the Russian oil refining industry and other entities that supported Russian military operations; and further restricted US exports or exports from third countries that use US inputs destined for Belarus's defense, aerospace, and maritime industries.

In the second week of March 2022, President Joe Biden issued two EOs (nos. 14066 and 14068) banning imports of Russian oil, liquefied natural gas, and coal into the US; imposing sweeping new prohibitions on trade with and investment in Russia; raising import tariffs to eliminate MFN benefits of Russia; denying Russia's borrowing privileges at the World Bank and the International Monetary Fund (IMF); directing sanctions on exports of luxury goods to Russia and Belarus; enlarging the net of sanctions on more Russian oligarchs, business executives, and politicians; and warning against sanction evasion through cryptocurrencies or other virtual currencies.[21]

In the last week of March 2022, the US sanctioned dozens of Russian defense companies, more than 300 members of the Russian parliament (the Duma), the Central Bank of Russia, and over a dozen individuals, including the CEO of Sberbank – Russia's largest financial institution; and expanded the reach of sanctions to Russian aerospace, marine, and electronics sectors. Also, in March 2022, the US Justice Department announced the launch of Task Force KleptoCapture, an interagency law enforcement task force dedicated to enforcing the sanctions, export restrictions, and economic countermeasures that the US and its allies had adopted against Russia.[22]

In the first week of April 2022, the US expanded export controls to Russia by adding 120 Russian and Belarusian firms in the Commerce Department's Entity List for their support to the Russian and Belarusian militaries; and issued temporary denial orders (TDOs) revoking export privileges of three Russian airlines (Aeroflot,

[20] The list of sanctioned elites included Yevgeniy Prigozhin, the financier of the Internet Research Agency, and Alisher Usmanov, who had significant interests in Russian telecom and IT sectors through a 49-percent ownership of USM Holdings Ltd., along with information outlets controlled by Russian intelligence services.

[21] EO 14068, issued on March 11, 2022, also prohibited the importation of fish, seafood, alcoholic beverages, and non-industrial diamonds from Russia.

[22] The Task Force, equipped with cutting-edge investigative techniques – including data analytics, cryptocurrency tracing, foreign intelligence sources, and information from financial regulators and private sector partners – was tasked with identifying sanctions evasion and related criminal misconduct.

Azur Air, and Utair), and Alrosa (the largest diamond mining company of Russia) and the United Shipbuilding Corporation – a major Russian company responsible for building Russian navy warships. The same week, the US also sanctioned Hydra – the world's largest darknet market, and Garantex – a ransomware-enabling virtual currency exchange; imposed financial sanctions on Sberbank, Alfa-Bank, and top Russian officials and their family members, including President Putin's adult children and Foreign Minister Lavrov's wife and daughter.

Meanwhile, in April 2022, the US Congress enacted the Ending Importation of Russian Oil Act of 2022 (P.L. 117-109) prohibiting energy imports from Russia, and the Suspending Normal Trade Relations with Russia and Belarus Act of 2022 (P.L. 117-110) raising US tariffs toward both Russia and Belarus. The same month, the US prohibited Russian-affiliated vessels from entering US ports, and imposed sanctions on several Russian entities and individuals for their attempts to evade US sanctions, including Transkapitalbank, Bitriver, and some other companies involved in Russia's virtual currency mining industry, and a network led by Russian oligarch Konstantin Malofeyev.

In May 2022, the US imposed new visa restrictions on scores of Russian bank executives and other individuals, defense companies, and state-owned television stations.[23] In June 2022, the US banned imports of Russian gold, and imposed financial sanctions on an additional 70 Russian entities and 29 Russian individuals,[24] and in August 2022, the US sanctioned Kremlin-connected elites, including President Putin's alleged girlfriend Alina Maratovna Kabaeva, a major multinational company, and a sanctions evasion operation.

In September 2022, the US imposed further export controls on industrial and commercial items that could support Russian and Belarusian military aggression against Ukraine; brought dozens of more individuals associated with Russia's military-industrial complex under sanctions, including two international suppliers, and 278 members of Russia's legislature under sanctions. In addition, 57 entities in Russia and the Crimea region of Ukraine were added to the Entity List to restrict exports of technologies.

In October 2022, the US issued a TDO against Russia's Ural Airlines for violation of US export controls on Russia, and sanctioned a Russian network that procured

[23] The sanctions, among others, targeted executive board members of the Sberbank and the members of Gazprombank JSC's board of directors, and the JSC Bank Moscow Industrial Bank. In addition, three of Russia's top state-owned/controlled television networks were added to the sanctions list: JSC Channel One Russia, television station Russia-1, and JSC NTV Broadcasting. The sanctions also blocked the sale of equipment to the broadcasters, and cut off any US-originated advertising revenue.

[24] These sanctions included entities tied to Russia's defense industry, including state defense entity Rostec, as well as 29 Russian individuals. These sanctions also included an additional 45 entities, including Russian Federation military units and Russia's Federal Security Service. The sanctions also imposed visa restrictions on more than 500 Russian Federation military officers and Russian Federation officials.

military and sensitive dual-use technologies from US manufacturers and supplied them to Russian end users. The Justice Department also indicted five Russian nationals and two oil traders on charges of global sanctions evasion and money laundering schemes.

In November 2022, the US sanctioned 14 new individuals and 28 new entities engaged in a transnational network procuring technology that supported the Russian military-industrial complex,[25] and several entities and individuals for their involvement in the production or ongoing transfer to Russia of Iranian unmanned aerial vehicles (UAVs) used for attacking Ukraine.

In December 2022, three new entities were added in the list of sanctions on Iranian-made UAVs; and four new individuals were sanctioned for their involvement in Russia's filtration operations in Ukraine, and 10 Russian naval entities and the PJSC Rosbank and its subsidiaries were brought under sanctions.[26]

Continuing the sanctions campaign, in January 2023, the US designated scores of new entities and individuals, including JSC Aviacon Zitotrans – a Russian cargo airline that handles cargo shipments for Russia's defense entities; the Ural Civil Aviation Factory (UCAF), which supplies UAVs to Russia's defense ministry; the National Aviation Service Company (NASC) – a state-owned enterprise that repairs aircraft and electronic equipment; the Research & Production Enterprise Prima – that produces communication equipment for Russian helicopters and airplanes; and the Scientific and Production Enterprise Gamma – a technology entity that works for the Russian Federal Security Service (FSB).

On February 24, 2023, on the occasion of the first anniversary of Russia's second invasion of Ukraine, further US sanctions targeted scores of banking and financial institutions, scientific and military establishments, as well as the metals and mining sectors. These sanctions designated 22 individuals and 83 entities, including over 30 third-country individuals and companies connected to Russia's sanctions evasion efforts, arms trafficking, and illicit financial transactions (see Appendix 5.1). Some of these firms were accused of producing or importing specialized, high-technology equipment for Russian defense entities for manufacturing of advanced Russian weapons systems.

25 These sanctions included the Wagner Group and its associates across several continents for operating the defense and related materiel sector of the Russian Federation economy. The Wagner Group associates brought under sanctions included: Joint Stock Company Terra Tech (Terra Tech) – a Russia-based technology firm that supplies space imagery acquired by commercially active satellites; Changsha Tianyi Space Science and Technology Research Institute Co. LTD (Spacety China) – that provided Terra Tech synthetic aperture radar satellite imagery orders over locations in Ukraine; Spacety Luxembourg, Spacety China's Luxembourg-based subsidiary; and BARL – a Russian space company supporting Russia's military activities in Ukraine. For greater detail, see Nelson et al. (2023).

26 On January 6, 2023, the US also sanctioned six executives and board members of a key Iranian defense manufacturer of UAVs, as well as the director of an organization responsible for overseeing Iran's ballistic missile programs, for supporting Russia's attacks on Ukraine.

By end-February 24, 2023, the US had implemented more than 2,500 sanctioning measures against Russia since the Russian invasion of Ukraine on February 24, 2022.[27] As Appendix 5.1 indicates, the sanctions regimes targeted countless Russian government officials, including Russian president Putin and foreign minister Lavrov; private citizens, state and non-state entities, and encompassed almost all sectors of the Russian economy, and also targeted numerous third-country individuals and entities.[28]

The US sanction regimes thus have effectively brought more than 80 percent of Russia's banking sector assets under sanctions; frozen Russia's central bank's assets under US jurisdiction; delinked all major banks, including the Russian Central Bank, from the SWIFT network; restricted all Russian sovereign wealth funds and Russian debts; and banned all exports and reexports of high-tech products such as computers and semiconductors to Russia. The world has never seen such a magnitude of unilateral sanctions before, except perhaps with respect to Iraq.

Coordination with Allies

The US and its allies have often imposed sanctioning measures against Russia in a coordinated manner. Especially during the second phase of the Russian invasion of Ukraine, military support for Ukraine has been conducted in close cooperation and coordination among the US, the G7, and NATO members.[29]

During the first phase of Russian invasion, both the US and the EU pursued largely similar policies, and their sanctions aimed at restoring Ukraine's territorial integrity, supporting domestic political reforms, denying visas and freezing assets of Russian and Ukrainian government officials and pro-Russian separatists. But differences surfaced when the US imposed its first round of sectoral sanctions against Russia on July 16, 2014, while many EU members held back considering their extensive trade and investment relations with Russia and their heavy dependence on Russian oil and gas supplies.

While the US sanctions extensively targeted Russian individuals and entities on scores of grounds, such as human rights violations, malicious cyber activities, corruption, transnational crime, and so on, the EU initially refrained itself from imposing such widespread sanctions. But the EU's political calculus changed dramatically after separatist fighters in eastern Ukraine downed Malaysia Airlines flight MH17 in July 2014 by using a Russian missile, which killed all 298 passengers and

27 See home.treasury.gov/news/press-releases/jy1296.

28 The chronology of sanctions on Russia, as discussed above, is based on numerous websites, including those of the White House; the US Departments of Treasury, State, and Commerce; the US embassy in Moscow, and the EU, and the Radio Free Europe. Notably, only a few heads of state have been placed under US sanctions – the small club of US-sanctioned heads of state include Russian president Putin, North Korean leader Kim Jong-un, Syrian president Bashar al-Assad, and Venezuelan president Nicolas Maduro.

29 Established in 1949 with 12 members, NATO currently has 31 members including the US, all EU countries, the UK, and Canada.

crew, of whom over 200 were EU citizens.[30] The EU then joined the US in sanctioning many Russian individuals and entities in financial, defense, and energy sectors, and the EU also agreed to impose sanctions targeting Russian individuals and entities following the Skripal attack in March 2018.[31]

The EU, however, faced significant internal resistance in imposing sanctions on the Russian energy sector, especially on Russian export pipelines to European countries. Such concerns flared up in early 2017 when US Congress and the Trump Administration began tightening sanctions on Russia's energy export and Nord Stream 2 pipeline (explained above). Germany and some other EU member states, which depended heavily on Russian gas supplies, persuaded the EU to impose lending and investment restrictions only on the oil sector, not on Gazprom or other companies involved in Russian gas sector. Aside from such differences, as Appendix 5.2 shows, most of the US sanctions against Russia have been implemented in tandem with the EU and other allies.[32]

As mentioned above, no multilateral sanctions could be adopted against Russia as the country is one of the permanent members of the UNSC. But during the first round of the Russian invasion of Ukraine, the UN General Assembly adopted Resolution 68/262 on March 17, 2014, upholding Ukraine's territorial integrity, declaring the March 16, 2014 referendum on Crimea administered by Russia invalid, and denouncing Russian annexation of Crimea. Similarly, on the occasion of the first anniversary of the second invasion of Ukraine, the UN General Assembly, on February 23, 2023, adopted a resolution calling for an end to Ukraine war and affirming the international community's commitment to the sovereignty and territorial integrity of Ukraine.[33]

30 The Malaysian flight (MH17) was shot down on July 17, 2014. The Netherlands and Austria, two of the countries which had largest number of victims, believed that it was hit by a Russian missile and they held Russia responsible for the incident. Russia denied any responsibility, however. Eventually, in early September 2014, a ceasefire agreement was reached in the Belarus capital, Minsk. For greater detail, see the Council of the European Union, "Statement of the Heads of State or Government on Ukraine" (March 6, 2014) and EU Council Decision 2014/145/CFSP (March 17, 2014).

31 The Skripal incident involved an attempted murder of two Russian nationals, Sergei Skripal, a former double-agent of a British intelligence agency, and his daughter Yulia, in March 2018. Both of them survived the attack, which took place in the English town of Salisbury, echoing the assassination of another Russian operative named Alexander Litvinenko about a decade before. British authorities believed that two Russian GRU officials – Alexander Petrov and Ruslan Boshirov – were directly involved in the assassination attempt. The British claim was supported by 28 other countries, including the US. In March 2018, the Trump Administration expelled 153 Russian diplomats in retaliation for this incident.

32 The UK, as a non-member of the EU, also adopted largely similar sanctions, although the country has been a haven for wealthy Russians for several decades. Other US allies, including Switzerland, Australia, and Japan, have also done the same.

33 The resolution was approved by 141 countries, with seven votes against – the Belarus, North Korea, Eritrea, Mali, Nicaragua, Russia, and Syria, and 32 abstentions, including China, India, and Pakistan. An attempt was also made to adopt a UNSC Resolution on February 25, 2023, but failed because of Russian veto.

III RUSSIAN COUNTERSANCTIONS

Russia responded to unilateral sanctioning measures imposed by the US and other countries through a variety of retaliatory measures or countersanctions. In response to the Sergei Magnitsky Act 2012 of the US, Russia imposed restrictions on beef, pork, and poultry imports from the US, banned US adoptions of Russian children, and imposed visa restrictions on US citizens involved in human rights violations or crimes against and persecution of Russian citizens.

After the US issued the first list of designations under the Sergei Magnitsky Act in April 2013, Russia also designated a list of US citizens prohibiting their entry in Russia. Russia also implemented a series of countersanctions in response to sanctions imposed by the US and the EU following Russia annexation of Crimea in 2014. Such measures included additional travel prohibitions and a ban on the import of agricultural products from the countries that imposed sanctions on Russia.

Immediately after the US Congress passed CRIEEA in July 2017, Russia ordered a reduction of US mission personnel in Russia to 455, equal to Russian diplomatic personnel in the US. This measure also reflected Russian response to the Obama Administration's declaration of certain Russian diplomatic personnel as *persona non grata* and denial of access to two Russian government-owned compounds in the US in December 2016.

In August 2017, the Trump Administration closed the Russian Consulate General office in San Francisco, a chancery annex in Washington, DC, and a consular annex that functioned as a trade office in New York City. In March 2018, the Trump Administration expelled 60 Russian diplomats and closed down the Russian consulate in Seattle in response to the Skripal incident discussed above. In response, Russia also expelled 60 US diplomats and closed down the US Consulate office in St. Petersburg.

After the US imposed new designations of Russian government officials and politically connected oligarchs and their holdings in April 2018, the Russian Duma enacted a law authorizing restrictions on trade with the US and other unfriendly states, as well as blocking foreign access to Russian public procurement and privatization.[34]

After the US and its allies imposed sanctions on Russia following its second invasion of Ukraine in February 2022, Russia reacted by imposing a series of "countersanctions" against "unfriendly" states, individuals, and entities that complied with those sanctions.[35] As of April 2022, such countersanctions included: (a) allowing

[34] The chronology of US sanctions and Russian responses and countersanctions, explained in five paragraphs above, is primarily based on Welt (2020, 36–37), which provides a compilation of news reports on these developments.

[35] Such "unfriendly states" included the US, all EU member states, Albania, Andorra, Australia, Canada, Iceland, Japan, Liechtenstein, Micronesia, Monaco, Montenegro, New Zealand, North Macedonia, Norway, San Marino, Singapore, South Korea, Switzerland, Taiwan, Ukraine, and the UK.

Russian debtors to pay off their large debts (exceeding 10 million rubles) to non-Russian creditors in Russian rubles; (b) obliging buyers of Russian natural gas to pay for gas in Russian rubles; (c) prohibiting Russian residents from providing loans in rubles and transferring of ownership of securities or real estate; (c) suspending any money transfers from Russian accounts of nonresidents (companies or individuals) to their accounts outside of Russia for six months; (d) prohibiting companies from "unfriendly states" from buying any non-ruble currency in Russia; (e) allowing Russian state companies subject to sanctions to refrain from publishing information on their public procurements and suppliers; (f) allowing Russian banks and financial institutions to refrain from publishing information regarding their ownership and management bodies; (g) prohibiting Russian insurance companies from entering into contracts with foreign insurance and reinsurance companies and insurance brokers; and (h) banning several top officials of unfriendly countries from entering Russia.[36]

Russia also took a number of measures to mitigate the effects of sanctions on its economy by redesigning the Russian food industry, reorienting trade relations, restricting dollar-based transactions, bolstering government support for domestic production, and penalizing sanctioning countries (Pospieszna et al., 2020). Some of the key measures included: Professional brokers were prohibited from selling securities on behalf of any non-Russian companies or individuals; prohibition on issuance and trading outside Russia of depositary receipts representing shares of Russian companies; prohibition on transferring of money using non-Russian electronic payment services without opening an account and transferring non-ruble currency to any nonresidents under loan agreements; obligating Russian residents participating in foreign trade to sell 80 percent of non-ruble currency received through foreign trade contracts; and prohibiting cash exports of non-ruble currency from Russia exceeding $10,000 in value.[37]

IV IMPACTS OF SANCTIONS ON RUSSIAN ECONOMY

Russia is the largest economy ever brought under widespread unilateral sanctions (Gould-Davies, 2018). It is obviously premature to assess overall impacts of the sanctions on Russian economy and population. Only the near- and immediate-term impacts of the sanctions have been examined below in the context of: (a) the effectiveness of the import substitution and other measures undertaken by the Russian government to withstand or combat the impacts of sanctions; (b) Russia's trade and

36 Based on www.gibsondunn.com.

37 For resident companies and individual entrepreneurs, this threshold was set at $5,000, while for nonresident companies and individual entrepreneurs, cash withdrawals in American, Japanese, German, and European currencies were completely banned. For greater detail, see Table 1 and Figure 1 in Nelson (2015).

investment relations with the US and the EU; (c) the magnitude of the sanctions regimes imposed on Russia; and (d) the macroeconomic performance of Russia in terms of gross domestic product (GDP) growth, balance of payments, budget deficits, foreign currency reserves, inflation rate, and the stability of the ruble.

A *Russia's Import Substitution Strategies*

After the first round of sanctions imposed against the country in 2014, Russia restricted imports of food and food products from West European countries and took measures to cut back domestic consumption of such products (Korhonen et al., 2018). Some of these preventive groundworks were put in place even before, in 2010, under what was called the Food Security Doctrine. The scheme set the minimum targets for domestic production, defined as a share of domestic production in total consumption, for basic foodstuffs such as potatoes, dairy products, grains, meat and meat products. For some essential products, such as milk and dairy products, and meat and meat products, the domestic production target was set between 85 and 90 percent (Vassilieva and Smith, 2010).

In 2012, Russia also adopted the Development Program for Agriculture 2013–2020, which was aimed at increasing production volumes and raising quality in the agriculture and food industries and substituting agricultural imports with domestic production. Then in 2014, Russia adopted a policy called Government Program on Industries and Competitiveness, which was aimed at increasing domestic production in almost all industries with government-supported research. The program specially emphasized production of fish, fresh milk and dairy products, and fruit and vegetables, and banned imports of some of these products (Simola, 2014).

B *De-dollarization Measures*

As a consequence of expanding sanctions and increased prohibition on exports to Russia of arms and dual-use goods as well as advanced equipment for oil exploration, Russian domestic banks' and companies' increasingly found it difficult to raise credits on international capital markets. At the same time, factors like capital flights, currency depreciation, and decline in productivity keep the economy bleeding. To combat such trends, the Russian government made significant efforts to "de-dollarize" the Russian economy by converting dollar settlements into other currencies, and entering trade agreements denominated in Russian rubles.

As explained above, by April 2022, the Russian government had taken a number of measures, such as Russian debtors being allowed to pay off their large debts (exceeding 10 million rubles) to non-Russian creditors in Russian rubles; buyers of Russian natural gas were obligated to pay for gas in Russian rubles; Russian residents were prohibited from providing loans in rubles and transferring of ownership of securities or real estate; and Russian companies were prohibited from buying any non-ruble currency from unfriendly countries; and Russian banks and financial institutions were allowed to refrain from publishing information regarding their ownership and management bodies.

Also, to move away from US dollar-based transactions, in 2018 the Central Bank of Russia (CBR) launched a domestic bank payment system called Mir, which is run by the National System of Payment of Cards (NSPC) owned by the CBR. Mir came as an alternative to Visa and MasterCard, both of which suspended their operations in Russia in March 2022 in compliance with Western sanctions. By the end of 2020, the NSPC had issued approximately 84 million Mir cards to Russians, and the same year more than 95 percent of domestic transactions in Russia took place in rubles (Timofeev, 2021, 108).[38]

Since the Russian invasion of Crimea in 2014, the CBR has also implemented a significant reallocation of its reserve portfolio away from the US dollar, mostly using Chinese renminbi, which resulted in a sharp decline in the US dollar share in Russian foreign exchange reserves (Iancu et al., 2020, 18–22). Also, as a result of this transition, the share of Russian exports, invoiced in US dollars, to countries like Brazil, India, China, and South Africa declined from 85 percent in the second quarter of 2018 to 36 percent in the fourth quarter of 2022 (Nelson and Weiss, 2022). Also, since the second round of Western sanctions began in February 2022, Russia has been pressuring Western nations to pay for its oil and gas imports from Russia in rubles.

McDowell (2023, 79–105) maintains that by the fourth quarter of 2020, currencies other than US dollars were used to settle nearly a quarter of Russian imports from China, down from 90 percent in 2013; in trade with the EU, the dollar's share fell from around 70 percent in 2013 to just over 40 percent in 2020; the dollar's settlement share dropped in Russian exports to India from roughly 95 percent in 2013 to 20 percent in 2019; Russia's dollar-denominated debts dropped from roughly 70 percent in the fourth quarter of 2015 to nearly 50 percent in 2020; and for the banking debts, the use of the ruble grew from a low of 10 percent in 2014 to more than a quarter by the end of 2020.

C *Oil and Gas Sector Strategies*

The Russian oil and gas sector came under US sanctions in March 2014 as EO 13660, issued in response to the Russian occupation of Crimea, prohibited US entities from engaging in debt financing transactions with specified Russian oil companies and restricted access of such companies to US technology, goods, and services, for deep water as well as offshore oil exploration and production.

38 Western sanctions in late 2022, however, prompted some countries like Turkey, Kazakhstan, Vietnam, and Uzbekistan to halt their Mir-based transactions, especially after the US listed the head of the NSPC in its SDN list (Cipriani, 2023).

Despite the sanctions as well as the decline in gas prices, Russian oil and gas production had rather increased during the 2014–2018 period. On a monthly basis, production increased by approximately one million barrels per day (bpd) between July 2014 (10.4 million bpd) and December 2018 (11.45 million bpd).[39] Apparently, three factors – the availability of alternative financing, currency devaluation, and oil tax and export duty policies of the government – helped in boosting oil and gas production (Brown, 2020, 10–16).

First, Russian oil companies could withstand the US sanctions as they had access to the country's strong international currency reserves, partly owed to high oil prices during the 2011–2014 period. Also, Russia's main oil exporter, state-owned Rosneft, was able to borrow money from the domestic bond market to manage its debt obligations and fund its business operations. Rosneft also arranged financing by selling minority ownership positions to several Chinese and Indian companies, and through equity sales – the company sold a 19.5-percent ownership position to the Qatari Investment Authority and Swiss multinational Glencore for $11.3 billion in 2016.

Second, the devaluation of the ruble also helped Russian oil production and exports. In June 2014, in the immediate aftermath of the Russian annexation of Crimea, the exchange rate for a US dollar was approximately 34 rubles, reaching 59 rubles in December 2014, and then as high as 75 rubles in January 2016. The currency devaluation had a negative effect on the Russian economy overall, but it actually raised profits and cash flows for Russian oil companies. This occurred because Russian oil export sales were primarily denominated in US dollars, while most of their expenses were denominated in rubles.

Thus, at a specified level of oil pricing, the depreciation of the currency amplified the number of rubles obtained from the sale of oil denominated in dollars, with the exchange rate exerting no direct impact on ruble-denominated expenditures. Consequently, the profitability denominated in rubles experienced an increase, even in circumstances where oil prices were comparatively modest. The reduction in oil prices observed from 2014 to early 2016 also contributed to a downward pressure on the prices of oilfield equipment and services, benefiting producers in this sector.

Third, governmental oil tax policy incentivized Russian oil companies to maintain and increase oil production, even when the benchmark oil prices reached levels as low as $20 per barrel. The governmental oil tax framework consisted of two basic elements – a mineral extraction tax (MET), and an export duty (ED) – and both

[39] Russia's oil production began to decline in December 2018, however, and by May 2019, it had dropped to 11.1 million bpd. The decline was attributed to two main factors: implementation of a voluntary OPEC+ oil production agreement (agreement with the OPEC and other non-OPEC oil-producing countries) and oil contamination in Russia's Druzhba pipeline that temporarily disrupted oil shipments to Europe (Brown, 2020, 14).

were linked to the benchmark oil prices and calculated by using formulas aimed at incentivizing oil production. Under the framework, the government assumed most of the financial risk from low oil prices and received most of the benefits from high oil prices so that oil companies could increase production without paying much attention to the fluctuation of oil prices on global markets.[40]

D *Russia's Trade and Investment Relations with the US*

Russia has long been one of the largest oil and natural gas producers and exporters in the world. In 2018, the country had 106 billion barrels of oil reserves – the sixth largest in the world, and its crude oil and condensate production was approximately 11.2 million bpd – the largest in the world (British Petroleum, 2019).[41]

Russia, however, had relatively little direct trade and investment relations with the US. In 2013, prior to the Russian occupation of Crimea, only 5.6 percent of Russian imports came from the US, and 2.7 percent of Russian exports were destined for the US. Also, of approximately $550 billion in foreign direct investment that Russia received in 2013, less than 3 percent came from the US. The US also had relatively low direct financial exposures to Russia – US banks accounted for less than 13 percent of foreign bank loans to Russia in the second quarter of 2014. Likewise, in 2013, less than 0.4 percent of US overseas investment went to Russia, and in the second quarter of 2014, Russia accounted for 0.8 percent of outstanding US bank loans overseas (Nelson, 2015).

The US–Russian relationship at the firm and sector level has been quite substantial, however, at least in some respects. For example, in 2011, ExxonMobil signed an agreement worth billions of dollars with Rosneft to drill in the Russian Arctic; PepsiCo was the largest food and beverage company in Russia; Ford had a partnership with Russian car company Sollers; General Electric had joint ventures with several Russian firms to manufacture gas turbines; Boeing was among the top US exporters to Russia; Visa and MasterCard provided payment services for up to 90 percent of market transactions in Russia; United Launch Alliance, a Lockheed Martin and Boeing joint venture, imported Russian rocket engines; Russia was an important market for Philip Morris and Avon Products, and about 230 US companies had registered businesses in Russia (Nelson, 2015).

40 For example, if the government fixes no tax at the price of $10 per barrel, and the oil price actually drops to $10 per barrel, then the government's tax and duty receipts would be zero. But if oil price jumps to $70 per barrel, then government receipts could be $50 per barrel. Thus, oil companies' cash flows fluctuated, but to a much lesser extent as they were insulated to some extent from the oil prices in global markets.

41 The US (with 11 million bpd) and Saudi Arabia (with 10.5 million bpd) were second and third respectively. Back in 1987, the former Soviet Union was the largest oil producer in the world at nearly 12.5 million bpd, but its oil production declined to 10.3 million bpd in 1991, the year the Soviet Union collapsed and the Russian Federation came into being. At the time of its birth, Russia had almost 90 percent share in the Soviet oil production (Yergin, 1991, 261).

Russia was also a major supplier for some US imports. For example, the US imported Russian rocket engine for its civilian and military space launch programs; Boeing bought about 35 percent of the titanium for its commercial jetliners from Russian titanium producer VSMPO; and Russian palladium, used in catalytic converters in cars, accounted for a third of US imports of palladium. The US also imported Russian iron and steel, enriched uranium, fertilizers, fish and crustaceans, and certain synthetic rubbers.[42]

As the US had a very small share in trade, investment, bank loans, and credits with Russia, negative effects of US sanctions on Russia emanated primarily from two other sources. The first is from the multilateralization of US sanction regimes through enlisting the European nations with which Russia had substantial trade and investment relations. In 2013, prior to Russian occupation of Crimea, more than 50 percent of Russian exports went to the European countries, about a third of EU's total imports of oil and natural gas came from Russia, and 46 percent of Russia's imports came from the EU. Also, European banks accounted for about 75 percent of Russia's total foreign bank loans in the second quarter of 2014. The US sanctions disrupted all such trade and investment relations. Second, from the delinking of the Russian economy from the US-dollar denominated global financial system, which occurred through both secondary and extraterritorial sanctions, and as the discussion above indicates, had disastrous effects on the Russian economy.

E *Magnitude of Sanctions*

As mentioned above, as of November 30, 2022, Russia had been subjected to a total of 11,073 sanctioning measures, and many more sanctions have been added since then. In just one year, between February 2022 and February 2023, the US had added over 2,500 Russia-related targets to its SDN List, which included 2,400 individuals and entities, 115 vessels, and 19 aircraft. These designations included Russian president Putin and his family members, all members of the Duma (450), all members of the Russian Federation Council (170), all provincial governors (47), and over 600 individuals tied to Russia's military-industrial complex and major military manufacturing firms of the country.[43]

The sanctions regimes targeted nearly a dozen revenue generating sectors of the Russian economy, including metals and mining, trust and corporate formation, aerospace, marine, electronics, financial services, technology, and defense and related materiel.[44] Over 80 percent of Russia's banking sector by assets was brought

[42] For greater detail, see Table 1 and Figure 1 in Nelson (2015).

[43] Based on US Treasury Department's Fact Sheet: home.treasury.gov/news/press-releases/jy1298.

[44] To minimize unintended negative consequences of sanctions, OFAC has however issued 68 new and 40 amended general licenses to protect and preserve agricultural, humanitarian, and energy transactions. For greater detail, see IMF (2022).

under the jurisdiction of US sanctions, including the country's central bank, RCB, and the top 10 state-owned banks of the country.[45]

More than half of Russia's $580 billion of currency reserves have been frozen and most of its big banks are cut off from the SWIFT global payments system.[46] Over 200 targets associated with Russian sanctions evasion, spanning across several continents, have been brought under the sanctions net.[47] More than 1,000 foreign companies and multinationals have either ceased or curtailed their operations in Russia since February 2022, and in December 2022, the EU and the G7 countries adopted a cap of $60 per barrel for crude oil of Russian origin, severely curtailing Russia's main source of foreign exchange. Meanwhile, as mentioned above, the September 2022 blasts rendered all four pipelines of Nord Stream unoperational.

F *Russia's Macroeconomic Performance*

During the first phase of the Russian invasion of Ukraine, the sanctions regimes hardly entailed any significant adverse effects on the Russian economy or population. The impact was rather mild because the sanctioners feared that greater economic pain could alienate the Russian population. They also refrained from pursuing the destabilization of the Russian economy, being apprehensive that excessively stringent sanctions might precipitate a crisis akin to the Lehman Brothers collapse in the US in 2008. Instead, they made a deliberate choice to exempt Russian Central Bank reserves and the SWIFT payments system from the scope of the sanctions (Giumelli, 2016).

Still, because of the sanctions, during the first phase, Russia's per capita GDP on average was 1.5 percent lower than what it could have been during 2014–2017 in the absence of sanctions (Aslund and Sengovaya, 2021, 18). During this period, the Russian economy also suffered because of Russia's own countersanctions – studies suggest that such measures reduced the welfare level of the average Russian household by raising the prices of many goods; they reduced the country's GDP by 0.2 percent and real incomes by 2–3 percent between 2014 and 2018 (Korhonen, 2019).

The economic consequences of the second phase of sanctions on the Russian economy and population have been disastrous. During the first phase, the EU sanctions were mild at best, but the EU ramped up its sanctions regimes against Russia after the Minsk agreement, signed in 2017, holding Russia responsible for the downing of the Malaysian passenger plane over Ukraine in 2014. The EU further accelerated its sanctions after Russia invaded Ukraine in 2022. Since then, sanctions of both the US and the EU have been relentless – no stone was left unturned to cripple the Russian economy through comprehensive trade embargoes as well as investment and banking restrictions.

45 By February 2023, the US, along with its allies, had immobilized about $300 billion worth of RCB assets, limiting its ability to aid Russian war efforts and mitigate sanctions impacts. See US State Department Press Release: www.state.gov/the-impact-of-sanctions-and-export-controls-on-the-russian-federation/.

46 Based on *The Economist*, August 25, 2022.

47 In addition, over 60 family members of Russian elites were designated.

The IMF (2022) reports that during 2014–2018, Russian GDP growth averaged 0.7 percent per annum, and overall, between 2014 and 2020, GDP declined by 35 percent, while the real disposable income of the population fell by about 10.5 percent. The World Bank (2023) reports that Russian GDP fell from $2.29 trillion in 2013 to $1.78 trillion in 2021, reflecting a 23 percent drop in nominal terms since the invasion of Ukraine in 2014. During the same period, the exchange rate for a US dollar ranged between 59 and 74.6 Russian rubles (see Table 5.1).

Much of the economic decline of Russia may well be attributed to sanctions-induced factors, such as: withdrawal of foreign investment;[48] inability of Russian banks and businesses to raise funds in international capital markets;[49] the RCB's inability to provide adequate liquidity and foreign reserves; Russia's inability to bypass sanctions by turning to the banking systems of America's adversaries, such as China and the Persian Gulf; strong capital outflows;[50] sharp fall in the ruble's exchange rate;[51] falling real wages and erosion in consumer spending; fall in the exports of oil and gas, and sale of oil and gas at discounted prices.

In 2020, however, Russia's government debt was only 18 percent of its GDP, which compared favorably with the government debts in many Western countries which far exceeded their annual GDP. Of Russia's total foreign debt of $470 billion in 2020, only $66 billion was government debt, of which $21 billion was in foreign currencies and $43.8 billion in ruble-denominated bonds. Of the rest, $72.5 billion was held mostly by state-owned banks, and $318.5 billion was held by other corporations (Aslund and Sengovaya, 2021, 10). But such a dramatic decline in Russian government debt had occurred because Russia's banking sector, especially large Russian state-owned banks, such as Sberbank and VTB, were unable to arrange long-term financing in international capital markets due to the sanctions regimes (Korhonen, 2018).[52]

48 Between 2014 and 2019, Russia's annual net inflows of foreign direct investment averaged only 1.39 percent of its GDP, compared with 3.05 percent in the preceding six-year period. The IMF (2022) asserts that Western sanctions compelled Russia to forego international credits up to $479 billion, or about one third of the country's 2020 GDP.

49 The IMF (2022) asserts that Russia's total foreign debt shrank from $729 billion at the end of 2013 to $470 billion at the end of 2020, and the decline might have contributed to reduction in Russia's economic growth by 2.5 to 3.0 percent per year, that is, about $50 billion per year.

50 Between 2014 and 2018, gross external outflows from Russia averaged 2 percent of the country's GDP per year (IMF, 2022), but Russian private money held abroad was estimated to be no less than $1 trillion, of which about one quarter was reportedly held by Putin and his close aides (Aslund and Sengovaya, 2021; Korhonen, 2018; Novokmet et al., 2017).

51 As mentioned above, the exchange rate of the ruble plummeted from an average of 30.73 rubles per dollar in 2013 to 73.84 rubles per dollar in 2021.

52 Studies suggest that the foreign debt of Russian banks peaked in March 2014 at $214 billion, and then declined to $80 billion in June 2019, reflecting a 62 percent reduction. On average, net capital flows from the sanctioning countries' banks to Russia declined by $700 million per quarter after the March 2014 international sanctions, and much of the decline can be attributed to the dominant position of two state-owned banks – Sberbank and VTB (Korhonen, 2019).

TABLE 5.1 *Macroeconomic performance of the Russian Federation, 2014–2022*

Indicators	2014	2015	2016	2017	2018	2019	2020	2021	2022
GDP growth (annual, %)[1]	0.7	−2	0.2	1.8	2.8	2.2	2.7	4.7	
Inflation rate (annual, %)[2]	7.82	15.33	7.04	3.68	2.88	4.47	3.38	6.69	13.7
Budget deficit (annual, %)[3]	−1.07	−3.39	3.67	−1.47	2.92	1.93	−4	0.80	−2.0
Exchange rate (rubles per dollar)[4]	36.05	62.34	75.25	58.30	56.34	65.66	66.70	74.16	101.04

Notes:
1 Based on World Bank Database. Available at data.worldbank.org/indicator/NY.GDP.MKTP.KD.ZG?locations=RU, accessed on March 6, 2023.
2 Based on Statista, available at www.statista.com/statistics/, accessed on March 6, 2023.
3 Based on data available at countryeconomy.com/deficit/russia, accessed on March 6, 2023.
4 Based on Statista. Exchange rates are monthly averages in the month of February each year. Available at www.statista.com/statistics/376232/usd-rub-exchange-rate-monthly/, accessed on March 6, 2023.

Russia's macroeconomic scenario since 2014, as Table 5.1 shows, provides a mixed picture of the country's endurance to the sanctions regimes. Annual budget deficits of the country have rather been stable – the worst occurred in 2022, when it increased to 2 percent of GDP.[53] The exchange rate of the national currency, however, shot up from around 36 rubles in 2014 to 101 rubles in 2022, reflecting almost three-fold depreciation of the ruble during the period. But the inflation rate ranged between 7.8 percent and 13.7 percent – which is far from hyperinflation. During the same period, many Western countries, including the US, had experienced double-digit inflation rates.

The impact on Russian oil and gas exports has also been insignificant. The International Energy Agency (IEA) reports that, by the end of August 2022, total Russian oil exports were 7.6 million bpd – down just 390,000 bpd from the levels before the Russian invasion of Ukraine in 2022.[54]

Mahlstein (2022), however, suggests that the effects of the comprehensive trade embargo on both imports and exports, foreign direct investment, and increased trade costs between Russia and non-Western countries, might result in a reduction

53 Much of the budget deficits stem from a sharp drop in oil and gas revenues, while the country experienced a massive increase in its defense spending due to the invasion of Ukraine. The US Treasury Department claims that, as a result of sanctions, in January 2023, Russian oil and gas revenues declined by 46 percent and military spending outlays increased by 59 percent, compared with January 2021 levels. See IMF (2022).

54 For greater detail, see: www.energypolicy.columbia.edu/, and www.iea.org/reports/oil-market-report-september-2022.

in Russia's real GDP of up to 14 percent, and non-Western economies may benefit from Russian trade diversion caused by sanctions. Another study (Nguyen and Do, 2021), based on data from 49 trading partners of Russia during 2011 to 2018, shows that sanctioning measures may cause a decline of 25.25 percent of Russian export values, while Russian countersanctions may cause a decline of 25.92 percent of Russia's import values from the sanctioning countries.

V LEGAL INTERPRETATIONS OF SANCTIONS REGIMES

All the sanctions imposed on Russia are unilateral in nature, and they came in two phases. In the first phase, following the Russian invasion of Ukraine in 2014, the US, the principal sanctioner, principally targeted Russian individuals and entities, prohibited "US persons" from engaging in any transactions with such individuals and entities, and restricted exports of oil-related and dual-use technology and other specific exports. The restrictive measures of the EU, the second biggest sanctioner, also comprised a ban on imports into the EU of goods originating in Crimea or Sevastopol, and exports of armaments and dual-use goods, and equipment and services for the Russian oil industry (see Appendix 5.2).

The stated aims of these sanctions regimes were rather limited – they sought to impose costs on the Russian leadership for violating Ukraine's territorial and sovereign integrity and undermining the sovereignty of other eastern European countries, in a material breach of Article 2(4) of the UN Charter. The sanctioners wanted to force the cessation of these violations by keeping up pressure on Russia without further escalating tension or alienating the Russian population by imposing heavy costs to the Russian economy and causing isolation of Russia from the global community.[55]

In sharp contrast, the sanctions regimes of the second phase, launched following the second invasion of Ukraine in February 2022, have been much more antagonistic, aggressive, and comprehensive. These sanctions targeted almost all sectors and spheres of Russian society and economy, and many of those measures were equipped with secondary and extraterritorial enforcement requirements. These sanctioning measures must have been driven by a rather clear realization on the part of the sanctioners that stand-alone economic and financial sanctions are inadequate to deter Russia from its geo-political ambitions, and the country and its population must be isolated from the rest of the global community through military offensives as well.

Moreover, the unilateral sanctions regimes against Russia were largely designed and enforced autonomously – although they often resembled multilateral sanctions,

[55] Numerous scholars and observers have maintained such a position. See, for example, Giumelli (2016), Hayashi (2020, 231), Hofer (2017), Ilieva et al. (2018), Oxenstierna and Olsson (2015), Nephew (2020, 111), and Prezas (2021).

there was no formal coordination among the sanctioners, and the sanctioning measures have been carried out entirely outside the UN framework. The sanctioning measures against Russia have also been very distinct from those imposed on Iran, Iraq, Cuba, North Korea or Venezuela – there have been no UNSC resolutions, no UN Sanctions Committee or UN Panel of Experts to monitor the adoption or implementation of the sanctions (Hayashi, 2020).

The applicable standards for examining the legality and legitimacy of unilateral sanctions rest with the UN Charter, the ILC Articles on Responsibility of States for Internationally Wrongful Acts (ARSIWA), the international law on countermeasures, and the GATT Article XXI. As international law standards applicable to unilateral sanctions have been discussed extensively in Chapter 2, here the discussion will be brief.

A *The UN Charter, ARSIWA and International Law of Countermeasures*

Articles 39 and 41 of the UN Charter grant exclusive rights to the UNSC alone to impose collective, multilateral, sanctions "ranging from individualized asset freezes to embargoes" on any member state on the grounds of "threat to the peace," "breach of the peace," "act of aggression," or "internationally wrongful act," in order to maintain or restore international peace and security.[56] But when Russia invaded Ukraine in 2014, and then again in 2022, and thus committed "an internationally wrongful act" by threatening the territorial integrity of a sovereign nation and breached international peace and security, the UNSC could not adopt any such measure against Russia because it is a permanent member of the UNSC with a veto power to reject any such proposal.[57]

Thus, the only option left to Ukraine was to resort to countermeasures or countersanctions against Russia. The UN Charter grants an "injured State" the right to take countermeasures against another state that "breaches its sovereignty or commits an internationally wrongful act against it" (ILC, 2001). But the state adopting unilateral sanctions must establish that it was indeed an "injured State" of the alleged "internationally wrongful act," and such acts were actually committed against it. Ukraine, being a directly injured state, thus has every right to adopt countermeasures against Russia for breaching its sovereignty and threatening its integrity.

But questions may arise how the US, or the EU, or other sanctioning states, can assert that they are also "injured States" by the alleged "internationally wrongful act" of Russia by dint of its invasion of Ukraine. Under the UN Charter, a third state, not

[56] For greater detail, see Chapter 2 of this volume.

[57] Russia indeed turned down such a proposal placed before the UNSC immediately after its first invasion of Ukraine in 2014. The UN General Assembly, as explained above, however, adopted some resolutions condemning Russia for its invasion of Ukraine, but such resolutions have no teeth. As discussed in Chapter 2, only the UNSC-adopted resolutions under Chapter VII of the UN Charter are mandatory for all members of the UN.

injured directly by an "internationally wrongful act" by another state, can legally and legitimately adopt countermeasures against an alleged violator of international peace and security only under a UNSC resolution. Thus, it can be argued that as the sanctioning states have imposed unilateral sanctions on Russia in accordance with their own foreign policy goals and objectives, which were neither authorized nor endorsed by the UNSC, they themselves might have violated the international principle of nonintervention/noninterference while trying to prevent such violations by another state (Krause, 2016; Ronzitti, 2016).

On the other hand, as Russia's annexation of Crimea – a part of a territory of another sovereign state – constitutes a *prima facie* violation of international law, and Russia's second invasion aimed at further disintegration and destabilization of Ukraine further reinforces such violations, the international community may well construe such actions as *prima facie* violations of the prohibition on the use of force, a peremptory norm of international law, and thus such actions may be construed as an *erga omnes* violation – a violation of the obligations of a state toward the international community as a whole in a matter that concerns all states and in which all states might have a legal interest. Such an interpretation would justify unilateral sanctions of the US and others against Russia as a response to an *erga omnes* violation (Burke, 2015; White, 2018).

ARSIWA (2001) also authorizes third-party countermeasures against an "internationally wrongful act," under which a third state not directly attacked or injured by the initial wrongful act can impose sanctions on the violators of the UN prohibition on the use of force (Hayashi, 2020, 231–232). Article 54 of ARSIWA entitles states not directly injured by the wrongdoer to take "lawful measures" (and not countermeasures) against the wrongdoer. ARSIWA uses the expression "lawful measures" as no agreement exists establishing whether a state or a group of states not directly injured are entitled to take countermeasures, while a clear guideline exists that the UNSC is the only competent authority in such matters. At the same time, in numerous instances individual states or group of states not directly affected by an "internationally wrongful act" have resorted to countermeasures (Thouvenin, 2020, 83–92).

Ronzitti (2016, 29), however, maintains that, under international law, a state not directly injured may resort to countermeasures only if there is a serious violation of obligations owed toward the international community. But such measures must be subject to several conditions, such as: They must not cross the bounds of legal jurisdiction; must not encroach on the sovereign rights of other nations; and must not involve extreme economic or political coercion that may endanger the territorial integrity of the target country.

Also, as discussed in Chapter 2, unilateral sanctioning measures must satisfy the requirements of necessity and proportionality doctrines as envisaged by international law on countermeasures (Dawidowicz, 2017), and the requirements of the International Covenant on Economic, Social and Cultural Rights (ICESCR) that such measures be taken through negotiations with the international community and states, must be monitored effectively, and the sanctioning party must refrain from inflicting any disproportionate pain on vulnerable groups in the target country (Gestri, 2016; Ronzitti, 2016, 14–15).

B The Russian Stance

On its part, Russia has questioned all three elements of unilateral countermeasures: legitimacy, necessity, and proportionality. Russia repeatedly claimed that the sanctioning measures were "invented and illegitimate," that they violate the WTO rules and contradict international law because sanctions can only be imposed within the framework of the UNSC (Dawidowicz, 2017, 237). In a joint declaration, both Russia and China, two permanent members of the UNSC, in June 2016 categorically declared that "unilateral coercive measures," are "examples of double standards," that reflect the "imposition by some States of their will on other States," which contradict the "generally recognized principles and rules of international law."[58]

Russia also raised questions of the legitimacy of unilateral sanctions on the grounds of free flow of goods and services under the WTO trading system, but failed to initiate a formal process of dispute settlement within the WTO framework against any of the sanctioners (Chercheneff, 2021). Russia further raised questions of the legitimacy and legality of the unilateral sanctions on the grounds of other treaties. Russia's state-owned oil company, Rosneft, for example, sought to use the EU–Russia Cooperation and Partnership Agreement (CPA), which facilitates EU–Russia trade relations, by alleging that several of the restrictive measures adopted by the EU in 2014[59] were incompatible with the CPA. The European Court of Justice, however, rejected Rosneft's claim, holding that the CPA provisions allowed such exceptions (Hayashi, 2020, 236).

Russia's position on unilateral countermeasures is duplicitous, however, as it has itself adopted such measures against other countries numerous times. For example, Russia banned imports of agro-food products from Poland in 2010; imposed travel bans and food embargoes on Ukraine in response to Ukraine's decision to expand its own list of prohibited imports from Russia in 2014 (Bychkov and Efremov,

[58] See "The Declaration of the Russian Federation and the People's Republic of China on the Promotion of International Law." June 25, 2016.

[59] The dispute referred to EU Council Decision 2014/512 and EU Council Regulation 833/2014. EU Council Decision 2014/512 urged Russia to stop the flow of weapons, equipment, and militants across the border in order to achieve rapid and tangible results in de-escalation, and to withdraw its additional troops from the border area; prohibited the sale, supply, transfer, or export of dual-use items for military use or to military end users in Russia; and prohibited the sale, supply, transfer, or export of certain sensitive goods and technologies when they are destined for deep water oil exploration and production, Arctic oil exploration and production, or shale oil projects. EU Council Regulation 833/2014 prohibited the sale, supply, transfer, or export, directly or indirectly, of aircraft, to any natural or legal person, entity, or body in Russia or for use in Russia.

2019); banned imports of agro-food products from the EU, the US, Japan, Canada, and Australia, in response to their sanctions on the country in 2014 (Hayashi, 2020, 232); and imposed unilateral financial sanctions on more than 322 members of the Ukrainian elite and 68 business entities in 2018 (Early and Cilizoglu, 2020, 442).

C *The Ukrainian Stance*

Since the second phase of the Russian invasion of Ukraine in 2022, the nature of the conflict between the two countries has changed dramatically. The countries are now in the midst of a full-scale military offensive that indirectly involves almost all sanctioning countries, especially the US and the EU. Article 51 of the UN Charter allows military offensive as self-defense if an armed attack has occurred on a sovereign state. Thus, it has been within Ukraine's right to respond militarily on both occasions of Russian invasion of the country. However, questions can be raised whether other states can legally and legitimately be involved in such a military conflict, especially in the absence of any UNSC resolution. This treatise is not about military conflicts, however, the discussion here is rather limited to economic and financial sanctions.

As mentioned above, as far as non-military but coercive economic and financial sanctions or countermeasures are concerned, there is no dispute that a state directly injured by an internationally wrongful act may resort to such measures against the state that has committed such an act. As long as Ukraine's actions are limited to countermeasures, questions may arise only on the grounds of the legitimacy, necessity, and proportionality of these measures, and their conformity to the UN Charter and other international laws and conventions. Ukraine's economic and financial might is, however, no match for that of Russia to proportional countermeasures.

Ukraine invoked the GATT XXI(b) "security exception" in 2016. As discussed in Chapter 2, in Russi*a: Measures Concerning Traffic in Transit*,[60] Ukraine alleged that Russia restricted transit by road and rail from Ukraine through the Russian Federation to third countries.[61] In response, Russia maintained that the dispute involved "obvious and serious national security matters," which the WTO is "not designed or equipped to handle," and thus, the WTO Panel should decline jurisdiction over such "self-judging" matters (Chercheneff, 2021; Watson, 2021).

The WTO Panel determined that Russia's invocation of Article XXI(b)(iii) was within the terms of reference of the Panel for the purposes of the WTO's dispute settlement mechanism, but concluded that Russia had satisfied the conditions of the chapeau of GATT Article XXI(b), and met all the requirements for invoking the

60 See WTO, *Russia: Measures Concerning Traffic in Transit – Report of the Panel* (April 5, 2019) WT/DS512/R.

61 In May 2018, four years after the annexation of Crimea, Russia succeeded in building a bridge that connected the Crimean Peninsula to the Russian mainland. Until then, the only land route to Crimea was via Ukraine (Hayashi, 2020, 223).

national security provision.[62] Neither Russia nor Ukraine proceeded further with their claims of non-WTO compatibility of their unilateral sanctions (Watson, 2021; Hofer, 2021).

Ukraine has also initiated several other proceedings against the Russian invasions with other international forums. Examples are: (a) invoking the compulsory dispute settlement procedure under Annex VII to the UN Convention on the Law of the Sea (UNCLOS), Ukraine instituted a case against Russia in the Permanent Court of Arbitration, concerning its coastal rights in the Black Sea, Sea of Azov, and Kerch Strait; (b) citing Article 13(2) of the Rome Statute of the International Criminal Court (ICC), Ukraine claimed ICC jurisdiction over the incidents and events since February 2014; (c) using the interstate complaint system within the European Convention on Human Rights, Ukraine lodged multiple complaints against Russia regarding incidents in Eastern Ukraine and Crimea since 2014; and finally, (d) Ukraine filed a case against Russia with the International Court of Justice (ICJ) in 2017 (Hayashi, 2020, 223).

VI CONCLUDING REMARKS

The history of sanctions against the Russian Federation has been extraordinary in many respects. First, they have been unilateral, none mandated by the UNSC. Second, the sanctioning measures were steered by the US – Russia's longstanding geo-political and military rival. Third, the underlying reason for the conflict lies with the rivalry about the post-Cold War security order in Europe. While Russia wants to preserve its sphere of influence over Ukraine – its next-door neighbor with longstanding economic and political ties – by preventing the country from joining NATO or the EU, the US and EU seek to delink Ukraine from Russia. Fourth, since Russia's second invasion of Ukraine in 2022, the sanctions regimes literally turned into a comprehensive trade and investment embargo, which has nearly isolated Russia from the rest of the global economy. Fifth, the professed goals of economic and financial sanctions, such as the cessation of Russian violation of Ukraine's sovereignty and integrity, have not yet been achieved despite literally one third of Russia's GDP having been wiped out. And sixth, in the second phase of Russia's invasion, the West has mounted massive military support for Ukraine, exposing the futility of stand-alone economic and financial sanctions as a means to confront violation of international legal norms.

62 As discussed in Chapter 2, in *Russia: Traffic in Transit*, the WTO Panel introduced a novel framework on the distinction between objective and subjective elements of the national security clause. The Panel interpreted GATT Article XXI's prerequisite, "taken in time of war or other emergency in international relations," as an objective element for a "limitative qualifying clause;" and ruled that the subjective element – a determination of "essential security interests" and the necessity of such measures ("necessary for the protection") – should be reviewed against the background of the principle of good faith. For greater detail on the interpretation, see Bogdanova (2021).

From the legal standpoint, there can be little dispute that the Russian invasion of Ukraine in 2014 as well as in 2022 constituted "an internationally wrongful act" that threatened Ukraine's sovereignty and integrity, and thus called for a Chapter VII resolution of UNSC to restore international peace and security. As the UNSC was unable to adopt such measures because Russia is a permanent member of the UNSC with a veto power, the US and others were left with no choice but autonomous unilateral sanctions. As the UN Charter grants an "injured State" the right to take countermeasures against another state if it "breaches its sovereignty," Ukraine's right to adopt such measures against Russia cannot be challenged. But questions may be raised whether the US and other unilateral sanctioners can also legitimately claim to be states "injured" by the internationally wrongful acts of Russia, and whether the unilateral sanctions themselves might be violating the international principle of nonintervention/noninterference.

At the same time, under international law, unilateral sanctions of the sanctioning states may well be deemed legitimate if they are construed as measures in response to an *erga omnes* violation of Russia toward the international community as a whole in a matter that concerns all states and in which all states have a legal interest. Also, the international law of countermeasures and ARSIWA grant third parties, not directly attacked or injured by the initial wrongful act of the target state, the legitimate right to adopt sanctioning measures under certain conditions.

Appendix 5.1

RUSSIAN INDIVIDUALS AND ENTITIES BROUGHT UNDER US SANCTIONS ON FEBRUARY 24, 2023

The newly designated banking and financial institutions included: Credit Bank of Moscow, a non-state bank that is also one of the 10 largest banks in Russia; Lanta Bank (Moscow); Metallurgical Investment Bank (Moscow); MTS Bank (Moscow); Novosibirsk Social Commercial Bank (Novosibirsk); Bank Saint-Petersburg (St. Petersburg); Primorye (Vladivostok); SDM-Bank (Moscow); Ural Bank for Reconstruction and Development (Yekaterinburg); Bank Uralsib (Moscow); Bank Zenit (Moscow); and financial institutions Zenit Finance, Zenit Leasing, and Zenit Factoring MSP, CONFIDERI. and IC Veles Capital.

The newly designated scientific and armament facilities included: UMATEX, Russia's largest producer of a wide range of carbon fibers and fiber-based items; Argon, which produces carbon fiber materials used by aircraft-building companies; Zavod, which produces carbon fiber used in the aerospace industry; and UVICOM LTD, which develops technologies for and produces carbon fiber materials. The newly designated aerospace companies included: Prepreg Advanced Composite Materials, which produces an assortment of materials used in aircraft engineering;

Alabuga-Fibre, which produces various types of carbon fibers used in aerospace and aircraft engineering; Prepreg-Dubna, which produces an assortment of materials used in aircraft engineering; Research Institute of Graphite-Based Materials (NIIGRAFIT), a research institution that develops special types of carbon materials and products; and the Urals Scientific Research Institute of Composite Materials, which specializes in fabrication of composite goods for rocket and space hardware.

The newly designated defense and related materiel sector companies included: Perm Scientific Research Technological Institute, a research institute that provides solutions related to the development and application of modern equipment including artillery mounts and missile systems; and Military-Industrial Corporation NPO Mashinostroyenia, which develops and fabricates weapons and military hardware (this company was also sanctioned previously in 2014).

The newly sanctioned technology and electronics companies included: ODay Technologies, Iteranet, OKB Spektr, Maxtech, Eshstru, Novilab Mobile, Promtekhekspert, PSV Technologies, Tamimed, Russian High Technologies, Forward Systems, R&DC, ZAO Akuta, Vakuum.ru, ByTrade, Lavina Puls, Inforus, Elara, and UVICOM.

The new entities sanctioned for collaborating with the Russian defense ministry included: TsNII EISU, which performs a system-forming role in the development of the command-and-control systems of the Russian armed forces; Independent Insurance Group (IIG), which provides insurance services to companies in Russia's defense sector; and PMC Redut, a Russian mercenary force fighting in Ukraine.

The new metals and mining sector entities brought under sanctions for supporting Russian armaments included: Burevestnik Central Scientific Research Institute, an arms and artillery manufacturer; Metallurg-Tulamash, which manufactures armaments for Russia's navy; TPZ-Rondol, a subsidiary of one of Russia's leading ammunition manufacturers; and Mtsenskprokat, which produces unique metal alloys and products for Russia's aviation and defense industries.

For greater detail see: home.treasury.gov/news/press-releases/jy1296, accessed on March 5, 2023.

Appendix 5.2

CHRONOLOGY OF SANCTIONS IMPOSED BY THE UNITED STATES AND THE EUROPEAN UNION AGAINST RUSSIA IN 2022

United States	European Union
Feb. 21. In response to Russian president Putin's recognition of the independence and sovereignty of Luhansk People's Republic (LNR) and Donetsk People's Republic (DNR) and orders to send Russian troops to those territories, President Biden issued EO 14065, banning new US investment in, exports to, or imports from the regions. Feb. 22. Per EO 14065, US Treasury Department sanctioned Russian state-owned financial institutions (VEB and PSB) and their subsidiaries, and five Kremlin-connected oligarchs, and imposed additional restrictions on Russian sovereign debt.	Feb. 23. In response to Russia's recognition of the Donetsk and Luhansk oblasts in Ukraine as independent entities, and the ensuing decision to send Russian troops into these areas, the European Council adopted targeted sanctions against 351 members of the Russian State Duma and an additional 27 individuals; restrictions on economic relations with the Donetsk and Luhansk oblasts, and Russia's access the EU's capital and financial markets and services.
Feb. 24. In response to Russian troops crossing the border into Ukraine as a "Special military operation," the Treasury Department sanctioned Sberbank of Russia; froze assets of Russian VTB Bank, Otkritie, Novikom, and Sovcom; and sanctioned 13 Russian state-owned and private entities as well as other Russian oligarchs. The Department of Commerce restricted Russian access to technology, including semiconductors, computers, telecommunications, information security equipment, lasers, and sensors, by controlling US exports or exports from third countries that use US inputs, such as equipment, software, and blueprints. Feb. 25–28. The Treasury Department sanctioned all US property interests involving Russian president Putin, foreign minister Lavrov, and 11 members of the Russian Security Council; banned selected Russian banks from the SWIFT financial messaging system and imposed restrictive measures on the Central Bank of Russia (CBR) and blocked transactions with the CBR, and prohibited transactions with Russian National Wealth Fund, Ministry of Finance, and Direct Investment Fund.	Feb. 25. The EU froze the assets of Russian president Vladimir Putin, and Russian foreign minister Sergey Lavrov, and also imposed restrictive measures on the members of the Russian National Security Council and the remaining members of the Russian State Duma. The EU also adopted a further package of individual and economic measures covering the finance, energy, transport and technology sectors, as well as visa policy. Feb. 28. The EU adopted further measures which included a ban on transactions with the CBR; € 500 million support package to finance equipment and supplies to the Ukrainian armed forces; a ban on the overflight of EU airspace and access to EU airports by Russian carriers; and new sanctions on additional 26 persons and one entity.

March 2. The Department of Commerce imposed controls on US exports or exports from third countries that use US inputs destined for Belarus's defense, aerospace, and maritime industries, and the Department of Transportation and the Federal Aviation Administration blocked Russian aircraft and airlines from entering American airspace.

March 3. The Treasury and State Departments imposed additional financial sanctions against a number of Russian oligarchs and their family members as well as those tied to the Russian defense industry, and the Department of Commerce imposed controls on exports destined for the Russian oil refining industry and other entities supporting Russian military operations. The list of sanctioned elites included Yevgeniy Prigozhin, the financier of the Internet Research Agency, and Alisher Usmanov, who holds significant interests in the telecom and IT sectors, along with information outlets controlled by Russian intelligence services.

March 8–11. President Biden issued EO 14066 banning imports of Russian oil, liquefied natural gas, and coal into the US. On March 11, the Biden Administration issued EO 14068 imposing sweeping new prohibitions on certain trade with and investment in Russia, raising import tariffs to eliminate the WTO membership benefits of Russia, and took measures to deny Russia's borrowing privileges at the World Bank and IMF. The Department of Commerce restricted exports of luxury goods to Russia and Belarus, and the Treasury Department sanctioned more Russian oligarchs, business executives, and politicians, and issued guidance to protect against sanction evasion through cryptocurrencies or other virtual currencies.

March 2–9. The EU suspended broadcasting activities in the EU of Russian state-controlled outlet Sputnik and its associated outlets to stop disinformation and information manipulation actions against the EU and its member states. The EU also excluded seven Russian banks from SWIFT: Bank Otkritie, Novikombank, Promsvyazbank, Rossiya Bank, Sovcombank, Vnesheconombank (VEB), and VTB Bank. The EU also imposed bans on: investing, participating or otherwise contributing to future projects co-financed by the Russian Direct Investment Fund; and selling, supplying, transferring or exporting euro banknotes to Russia or to any natural or legal person or entity in Russia. The EU also imposed restrictive measures on an additional 160 individuals, which included 14 oligarchs and prominent businesspeople, and 146 members of the Russian Federation Council.

March 15. The EU imposed a fourth package of economic and individual sanctions, which included a ban on: all transactions with certain state-owned enterprises; the provision of credit rating services to any Russian person or entity; and new investments in the Russian energy sector. The EU also expanded the list of persons connected to Russia's defense and industrial base, dual-use goods, and goods and technology which might contribute to Russia's technological enhancement of its defense and security sector. The EU also imposed trade restrictions for iron, steel and luxury goods; and sanctioned additional 15 individuals and 9 entities.

(continued)

United States	European Union
March 23. The export credit agencies of the US, the UK and Canada jointly withdrew any new export finance supports for Russia and Belarus – the agencies were the US Export–Import Bank (EXIM), the UK Export Finance (UKEF), and the Export Development Canada (EDC). March 24–31. The Treasury Department sanctioned dozens of Russian defense companies, more than 300 members of the Russian Duma, and other Russian individuals, expanded financial sanctions on 21 entities and 13 individuals to prevent Russia from evading earlier sanctions and acquiring foreign technology, and expanded sanctions under EO 14024 to include aerospace, marine, and electronics sectors.	
April 1. The Department of Commerce expanded export controls by adding to the Entity List 120 Russian and Belarusian firms allegedly involved in supporting the two countries' militaries. April 5. The Treasury Department sanctioned two Russian entities: Hydra, the world's largest darknet market, and Garantex, a ransomware-enabling virtual currency exchange. April 6. President Biden issued EO 14071, banning new outbound US foreign investment into Russia as well as exports of services, and the Treasury Department imposed financial sanctions on Sberbank, Alfa-Bank, and family members of Putin, Lavrov, and Russian Security Council members. The sanctions froze assets of Sberbank and Alfa-Bank, and prohibited US persons from doing any business with them. The US also banned new investment in Russia and imposed full blocking sanctions on key companies owned by the Russian state, and against top Russian officials and their family members, including President Putin's adult children and Foreign Minister Lavrov's wife and daughter.	April 8. The EU adopted a fifth package of sanctions against Russia, which included bans on imports from Russia of coal and other solid fossil fuels; all Russian vessels from accessing EU ports; Russian and Belarusian road transport operators from entering the EU; imports of other goods such as wood, cement, seafood and liquor; exports to Russia of jet fuel and other goods; and deposits to crypto-wallets. The EU also adopted sanctions against 217 individuals and 18 entities. These include a full transaction ban on four key **Russian banks**, representing a 23 percent market share in the Russian banking sector.

April 7. The Department of Commerce issued temporary denial orders (TDOs) revoking the export privileges of 3 Russian airlines, Aeroflot, Azur Air, and Utair, for alleged violations of earlier US export controls. The Treasury Department sanctioned Alrosa, Russia's largest diamond mining company, and the State Department sanctioned United Shipbuilding Corporation, a major Russian company responsible for building Russian navy warships. April 8–21. The US enacted the Ending Importation of Russian Oil Act (H.R. 6968) prohibiting energy imports from Russia, and the Suspending Normal Trade Relations with Russia and Belarus Act (H.R. 7108), raising US tariffs toward these countries. The Treasury Department sanctioned several entities and individuals involved in attempts to evade US sanctions, including Transkapitalbank, Bitriver, and other companies in Russia's virtual currency mining industry, and a network led by Russian oligarch Konstantin Malofeyev. The State Department announced visa restrictions on hundreds of individuals. The US prohibited Russian-affiliated vessels from entering US ports.	
May 8. The Treasury and State Departments imposed new sanctions – including a ban on exports of accounting, trust, and corporate formation, and management consulting services –, financial sanctions and visa restrictions on Russian bank executives and other individuals, defense companies, and state-owned television stations. The sanctions targeted executive board members of Sberbank and members of	June 3. the EU adopted its sixth package of sanctions, which included a ban on imports from Russia of crude oil and refined petroleum products; a SWIFT ban for an additional three Russian banks and one Belarusian bank; suspension of broadcasting in the EU for three more Russian state-owned outlets; sanctions against an additional 65 individuals and 18 entities.

(continued)

(continued)

United States	European Union
Gazprombank JSC's board of directors, JSC Bank Moscow Industrial Bank, among other entities. In addition, three of Russia's top state-owned and/or controlled TV networks were added to the sanctions list: JSC Channel One Russia, television station Russia-1 and JSC NTV Broadcasting Co. The sanctions also blocked the sale of equipment to the broadcasters and cut off any US-originated advertising revenue.	June 20. The EU renewed sanctions introduced in response to the Russian annexation of Crimea and Sevastopol for another year until June 2023. Those restrictive measures included: prohibitions targeting the imports of products originating from illegally annexed Crimea or Sevastopol into the EU; infrastructural or financial investments and tourism services from illegally annexed Crimea or Sevastopol; the exports of certain goods and technologies to Crimean companies or for use in illegally annexed Crimea in the transport, telecommunications and energy sectors; and the prospection for and exploration and production of oil, gas and mineral resources
June 28. The Treasury Department banned imports of Russian gold, and imposed financial sanctions on an additional 70 Russian entities and 29 Russian individuals. These sanctions included entities which were tied to Russia's defense industry, including state defense entity Rostec, as well as 29 Russian individuals. Sanctions also included an additional 45 entities and 29 individuals; including Russian Federation military units and Russia's Federal Security Service. The sanctions also imposed visa restrictions, including on more than 500 Russian Federation military officers and on Russian Federation officials.	July 21. The EU adopted new measures intended to tighten existing economic sanctions targeting Russia. The measures, known as the "maintenance and alignment" package, prohibited purchase, import, or transfer of Russian-origin gold, including jewelry; reinforced export controls of dual-use goods; extended the existing ban on port access to locks; clarified existing measures in the fields of public procurement, aviation and justice; sanctioned an additional 54 individuals and 10 entities, including the mayor of Moscow and Sberbank, a major financial institution.
Aug. 2. The Treasury Department sanctioned Kremlin-connected elites, including President Putin's alleged girlfriend Alina Maratovna Kabaeva, a major multinational company, and a sanctions evasion operation.	Oct. 6. The EU adopted new sanctions which included a price cap related to the maritime transport of Russian oil for third countries; added new items to the list of restricted items which might contribute to Russia's military and technological enhancement; imposed additional restrictions on trade and services with Russia; and sanctioned an additional 30 individuals and 7 entities.

Sept. 15. The Department of Commerce imposed further export controls on industrial and commercial items that could support Russian and Belarusian military aggression against Ukraine. Treasury Department sanctioned an additional 22 individuals and 2 entities, including Russians and others operating on behalf of Russia in Russian-occupied territories.

Sept. 30. The Treasury Department sanctioned 14 persons in Russia's military-industrial complex, including two international suppliers, three key leaders of Russia's financial infrastructure (including Elvira Nabiullina, the governor of Russia's central bank), immediate family members of senior Russian officials, and 278 members of Russia's legislature. The Department of Commerce expanded export controls by adding 57 firms in Russia and the Crimea region of Ukraine to the Entity List, and issued a new warning to third countries that might be seeking to replenish ("backfill") technologies subject to US export controls.

Oct. 17. Department of Commerce issued a temporary denial order against Russia's Ural Airlines for operating in apparent violation of US export controls on Russia. Treasury Department sanctioned a Russian network that procured military and sensitive dual-use technologies from US manufacturers and supplied them to Russian end users. In a concurrent action, Department of Justice unsealed an indictment charging 5 Russian nationals and 2 oil traders in a global sanctions evasion and money laundering scheme.

Oct. 20. The EU added three Iranian individuals and one Iranian entity to the list of those subject to restrictive measures for undermining or threatening the territorial integrity, sovereignty and independence of Ukraine. These individuals and entity were held accountable for the development and delivery of unmanned aerial vehicles (UAVs) used by Russia in its war against Ukraine. Those designated were subject to an asset freeze and EU citizens and companies were forbidden from making funds available to them. Natural persons are additionally subject to a travel ban, which prevents them from entering or transiting through EU territories.

(continued)

(continued)

United States	European Union
Nov. 14–15. The Treasury and State Departments sanctioned 14 individuals and 28 entities engaged in a transnational network procuring technology that supported the Russian military-industrial complex. Treasury Department sanctioned several firms and individuals involved in the production or ongoing transfer to Russia of Iranian UAVs used to attack Ukraine. Dec. 9–12. Treasury Department sanctioned four individuals who were directly involved in Russia's filtration operations, whereby Ukraine's civilians were subjected to interrogations and searches, and the State Department sanctioned 3 Russian entities involved in a deal with Iran to acquire UAVs to potentially deploy in the war with Ukraine. The State Department sanctioned 10 Russian naval entities. Dec. 15. The US imposed sanctions on Russian businessman Vladimir Potanin, three members of his immediate family and his company, Interros Co. The new sanctions also targeted Russian lender PJSC Rosbank, which Potanin acquired earlier in 2022, and 17 subsidiaries of VTB Bank PJSC.	Nov. 28. The EU adopted a decision to add violation of restrictive measures to the list of "EU crimes" in the Treaty on the Functioning of the EU to ensure a similar degree of sanctions enforcement throughout the EU and deter attempts to circumvent or violate its sanctions Dec. 3. The EU set an oil price cap for crude oil and petroleum oils and oils obtained from bituminous minerals which originate in or are exported from Russia, at $60 per barrel. The price cap limited price surges driven by extraordinary market conditions and drastically reduced the revenues Russia earned from oil after it unleashed its illegal war of aggression against Ukraine Dec. 16. The EU adopted a ninth package of sanctions against Russia. The new measures included bans on exports of drone engines, exports of dual-use goods and technology, investments in the mining sector, transactions with the Russian Regional Development Bank, and the provision of advertising, market research, and public opinion polling services. The EU also suspended the broadcasting licenses of 4 additional Russian outlets and sanctioned an additional 141 individuals and 49 entities.

Source: Author's compilation based on official websites of the White House and various departments of US government, and those of the EU and the EU Council.

REFERENCES

Asada, M. 2020. Definition and Legal Justification of Sanctions. In M. Asada (ed.), *Economic Sanctions in International Law and Practice*, pp. 3–23. London: Routledge.

Aslund A., and M. Sengovaya. 2021. The Impact of Western Sanctions on Russia and How They Can Be Made Even More Effective. Report: Atlantic Council, Washington, DC, May.

Bartlett, R. 2003. Serfdom and State Power in Imperial Russia. *European History Quarterly*, 33(1):29–64

Baskin, A., and B. Zagaris. 2011. U.S. Blacklists Russian Officials Linked to Human Rights Violations. *International Enforcement Law Reporter*, 27(10):918.

Blum, J. 1968. *Lord and Peasant in Russia from the Ninth through the Nineteenth Century*. Princeton, NJ: Princeton University Press.

Bogdanova, I. 2021. Targeted Economic Sanctions and WTO Law: Examining the Adequacy of the National Security Exception. *Legal Issues of Economic Integration*, 48:171–200. doi .org/10.54648/ LEIE2021010.

British Petroleum (BP). 2019. BP Statistical Review of World Energy, 2019. 68th ed. Available at: www.readkong.com/page/bp-statistical-review-of-world-energy-5676813.

Brown, P. 2020. *Oil Market Effects from U.S. Economic Sanctions: Iran, Russia and Venezuela*. Washington, DC: Congressional Research Service, R46213.

Burke, J. 2015. Economic Sanctions against the Russian Federation are Illegal under Public International Law. *Russian Law Journal*, 3(3):126.

Bychkov, A., and V. Efremov. 2019. Russia Expands Sanctions against Ukraine. *Sanction News*, April 23. Available at: sanctionsnews.bakermckenzie.com/russia-expands-sanctions-against-ukraine/.

Chercheneff, L. 2021. Challenging Unilateral and Extraterritorial Sanctions under International Economic Law: Exploring Leads at the WTO and the OECD. In C. Beucillon (ed.), *Research Handbook on Unilateral and Extraterritorial Sanctions*, pp. 239–256. Cheltenham, UK: Edward Elgar.

Cipriani, M. et al. 2023. Financial Sanctions, SWIFT, and the Architecture of the International Payments System. Federal Reserve Bank of New York Staff Reports, Paper No. 1047.

Constantin, S. 2022. Ethnic and Linguistic Identity in Ukraine? It's Complicated. EURAC Research. Available at: www.eurac.edu/en/blogs/mobile-people-and-diverse-societies/ethnic-and-linguistic-identity-in-ukraine-it-s-complicated.

Coulborn, R. (Ed.). 1956. *Feudalism in History*. Princeton, NJ: Princeton University Press.

Dawidowicz, M. 2017. *Third-Party Countermeasures in International Law*. Cambridge: Cambridge University Press.

Dowlah, A. 1992. *Soviet Political Economy in Transition: From Lenin to Gorbachev*. Westport, CT: Greenwood Press.

Dowlah, C. 2022. The Russian Serfdom. In C. Dowlah (ed.), *Foundations of Modern Slavery: Profiles of Unfree and Coerced Labor through the Ages*, pp. 116–136. London and New York: Routledge.

Early, B., and M. Cilizoglu. 2020. Economic Sanctions in Flux: Enduring Challenges, New Policies, and Defining the Future Research Agenda. *International Studies Perspectives*, 21:438–477.

Gestri, M. 2016. Sanctions Imposed by the European Union – Legal and Institutional Aspects. In N. Ronzitti (ed.), *Coercive Diplomacy, Sanctions and International Law*, pp. 70–102. Leiden: Brill.

Giumelli, F. 2016. From Effective to Useful Sanctions: Lessons Learned from the Experience of the European Union. Coercive Diplomacy, Sanctions and International Law. In N. Ronzitti (ed.), *Coercive Diplomacy, Sanctions and International Law*, pp. 246–269. Leiden: Brill.

Gould-Davies, N. 2018. Economic Effects and Political Impacts: Assessing Western Sanctions on Russia. BOFIT Policy Brief 8/2018. Bank of Finland, Institute for Economies in Transition (BOFIT), Helsinki. Available at: nbn-resolving.de/urn:nbn:fi:bof-201808091970.

Gowlland-Debbas, V. 2004. Sanctions Regimes under Article 41 of the UN Charter. In V. Gowlland-Debbas (ed.), *National Implementation of United Nations Sanction: A Comparative Study*, pp. 3–31. Boston, MA: Brill/Nijhoff.

Hayashi, M. 2020. Russia: The Crimea Question and Autonomous Sanctions. In M. Asada (ed.), *Economic Sanctions in International Law and Practice*, pp. 223–243. London: Routledge.

Hofer, A. 2017. The Developed/Developing Divide on Unilateral Coercive Measures: Legitimate Enforcement or Illegitimate Intervention. *Chinese Journal of International Law*, 16(2):175–214.

Hofer, A. 2021. Unilateral Sanctions as a Challenge to the Law of State Responsibility. In C. Beucillon (ed.), *Research Handbook on Unilateral and Extraterritorial Sanctions*, pp. 186–204. Cheltenham, UK: Edward Elgar.

Iancu, A. et al. 2020. *Reserve Currencies in an Evolving International Monetary System*. Washington, DC: International Monetary Fund.

ILC (International Law Commission). 2001. *Articles on the Responsibility of States for Internationally Wrongful Acts (ARSIWA)*. New York: United Nations.

Ilieva, J., A. Dashtevski, and F. Kokotovic. 2018. Economic Sanctions in International Law. *UTMS Journal of Economics*, 9(2):201–211.

IMF (International Monetary Fund). 2022. *World Economic Outlook*, 2022. Washington, DC: International Monetary Fund.

Kolchin, P. 1997. *Unfree Labor: American Slavery and Russian Serfdom*. Cambridge, MA: Harvard University Press.

Korhonen, I. 2019. Sanctions and Counter-Sanctions – What Are Their Economic Effects in Russia and Elsewhere? Helsinki: Bank of Finland. BOFIT Policy Brief 2/2019. September 2019.

Korhonen, I., H. Simola, and L. Solanko. 2018. Sanctions, Countersanctions and Russia: Effects on Economy, Trade and Finance. Helsinki: Bank of Finland. BOFIT Policy Brief, No. 4/2018.

Krause, K. 2016. Western Economic and Political Sanctions as Instruments of Strategic Competition with Russia – Opportunities and Risks. In N. Ronzitti (ed.), *Coercive Diplomacy, Sanctions and International Law*, pp. 270–286. Leiden: Brill.

LaRae-Perez, C. 2002. Economic Sanctions as Use of Force: Re-evaluating the Legality of Sanctions from an Effects-based Prspective. *Boston University International Law Journal*, 20(1):161–188.

Mahlstein, K. et al. 2022. Estimating the Economic Effects of Sanctions on Russia: An Allied Trade Embargo. *World Economy*, 45(11):3344–3383.

McDowell, D. 2023. *Bucking the Buck*. Oxford: Oxford University Press.

Nelson, R. 2015. U.S. Sanctions on Russia: Economic Implications. Washington, DC: Congressional Research Service, R43895.

Nelson, R. et al. 2023. Russia's War on Ukraine: Financial and Trade Sanctions. Washington, DC: Congressional Research Service, IF12062.

Nelson, R., and M. Weiss. 2022. The U.S. Dollar as the World's Dominant Reserve Currency. Congressional Research Service (CRS), IF 11707. Washington, DC.

Nephew, R. 2020. Implementation of Sanctions: United States. In M. Asada (ed.), *Economic Sanctions in International Law and Practice*, pp. 93–115. London: Routledge.

Nguyen, T., and M. Do. 2021. Impact of Economic Sanctions and Counter-Sanctions on the Russian Federation's Trade. *Economic Analysis and Policy*, 71(September):267–278.

Novokmet, F., T. Piketty, and G. Zucman. 2017. From Soviets to Oligarchs: Inequality and Property in Russia, 1905–2016. Washington, DC: National Bureau of Economic Research. Working Paper no. 23712.

Oxenstierna, S., and P. Olsson. 2015. The Economic Sanctions against Russia: Impacts and Prospects of Success. Swedish Ministry of Foreign Affairs. FOI-R-4097-SE.

Pospieszna, P., J. Skrzypczyńska, and B. Stępień. 2020. Hitting Two Birds with One Stone: How Russian Countersanctions Intertwined Political and Economic Goals. *PS: Political Science & Politics*, 53(2):243–247.

Prezas, I. 2021. From Targeted States to Affected Populations: Exploring Accountability for the Negative Impact of Comprehensive Unilateral Sanctions on Human Rights. In C. Beucillon (ed.), *Research Handbook on Unilateral and Extraterritorial Sanctions*, pp. 385–404. Cheltenham, UK: Edward Elgar.

Reisman, W., and D. Stevick. 1998. The Applicability of International Law Standards to United Nations Economic Sanctions Programs. *European Journal of International Law*, 9:86–141.

Ronzitti, N. 2016. Sanctions as Instruments of Coercive Diplomacy: An International Law Perspective. In N. Ronzitti (ed.), *Coercive Diplomacy, Sanctions and International Law*, pp. 1–32. Leiden: Brill.

Shkolnikov, V. 2012. Ukrainians and Russians in Ukraine and in Russia. In F. Meslé, and J. Vallin (eds.), *Mortality and Causes of Death in 20th-Century Ukraine*, Demographic Research Monographs, pp. 103–107. London: Springer Science and Business Media.

Simola, H. 2014. Russia's Restrictions on Food Imports. Helsinki: Bank of Finland. BOFIT Policy Brief 8/2014.

Thouvenin, J. 2020. History of Implementation of Sanctions. In M. Asada (ed.), *Economic Sanctions in International Law and Practice*, pp. 83–92. London: Routledge.

Timofeev, I. 2021. Unilateral and Extraterritorial Sanctions Policy: The Russian Dimension. In C. Beucillon (ed.), *Research Handbook on Unilateral and Extraterritorial Sanctions*, pp. 90–110. Cheltenham, UK: Edward Elgar.

Vassilieva, Y., and M. Smith. 2010. Russian Federation: Food Security Doctrine Adopted. Global Agricultural Information Network Report RS1008. Available at: apps.fas.usda .gov/newgainapi/api/report/downloadreportbyfilename?filename=Food%20Security%20 Doctrine%20Adopted%20_Moscow_Russian%20Federation_2-11-2010.pdf.

Watson, J. 2021. The World Trade Organization and Unilateral Sanctions: Prohibited or Possible? In S. Subedi (ed.), *Unilateral Sanctions in International Law*, pp. 185–206. Oxford: Hart Publishing.

Weber, M., and E. Collins-Chase. 2020. The Global Magnitsky Human Rights Accountability Act. Congressional Research Service (CRS), IF 10576. Washington, DC.

Welt, C. et al. 2020. U.S. Sanctions on Russia. Washington, DC: Congressional Research Service, R45415.

White, N. 2018. Autonomous and Collective Sanctions in the International Legal Order. *The Italian Yearbook of International Law Online*, 27(1):1–32.

Yergin, D. 1991. *The Prize: The Epic Quest for Oil, Money, & Power*. New York: Simon & Schuster.

6

US Economic and Financial Sanctions against the Islamic Republic of Iran

I INTRODUCTION

The Islamic Republic of Iran[1] has experienced an extended duration of economic sanctions, ranking among the most protracted instances globally since the end of WWII. The country came under a myriad of both unilateral and multilateral sanctioning measures adopted by the UN, the US, the EU, and several other Western countries ever since the Iranian Islamic Revolution overthrew the monarchic regime of Mohammad Reza Shah Pahlavi (1919–1980) and installed a cleric named Ayatollah Ruhollah Khomeini (1902–1989) as the country's Supreme Leader on February 11, 1979. The US commenced its sanctioning measures against Iran on November 12, 1979, in response to what became known as the Iranian Hostage Crisis, when several thousand Iranian revolutionaries, mainly students, captured the US Embassy in Tehran and took 90 people hostage, including 60 US diplomats and staff.

More than four decades later, in the 2020s, the saga still continues – among others, the severance of diplomatic relations between the two countries that occurred in 1979 still continues. President Jimmy Carter's Executive Order (EO) 12170 of 1979, which imposed sanctions against Iran in response to the hostage crisis, froze $12 billion of Iranian assets, and suspended imports of Iranian oil and exports of all military equipment to Iran, was last renewed by President Joe Biden in November 2022.[2]

[1] Historically known as Persia, this West Asian nation is the heir to one of the world's oldest civilizations, established by the Elamite kingdoms in the fourth millennium BC. With a landmass of 1.64 million square kilometers, and a population of 87.92 million (2021), the country shares its borders with Iraq and Turkey to the west, Azerbaijan and Armenia to the northwest, the Caspian Sea and Turkmenistan to the north, Afghanistan and Pakistan to the east, and the Gulf of Oman and the Persian Gulf to the south. Iran is also the 17th largest country in the world, geographically and by population size, and the second largest in the Middle East.

[2] The renewal came with President Biden's solemn declaration, "the national emergency declared on November 14, 1979, and the measures adopted on that date to deal with that emergency, must continue in effect beyond November 14, 2022." See www.whitehouse.gov/briefing-room/presidential-actions/2022/11/08.

Over the course of the decades since 1979, the goals and objectives of the US sanction regimes against Iran have changed: from the release of hostages to combatting terrorism and drug trafficking, from preventing nuclear proliferation to prohibiting human rights, and so on. The sanctions regimes also took a variety of forms, ranging from targeting Iran's energy, investment, and oil sectors to almost comprehensive embargoes.[3] At times the severity of sanctions was marked by a brief respite, but they quickly reverted (Cilizoglu and Bapat, 2020; Brown, 2020; Suzuki, 2020).

This chapter explores the US sanctions regimes against Iran, but as many of those measures are also interlinked and intertwined with those of the UNSC and the EU, the discussion has been explored in those contexts as well. The rest of the chapter progresses as follows: Section II provides a historical background of sanctions against Iran; Section III looks into the impact of the sanctions regimes on the Iranian economy and population; Section IV provides a legal interpretation of the sanctions regimes; and Section V concludes the chapter.

II THE HISTORICAL CONTEXT

Bad-blood between the US and Iran dates back to 1953 and the historic overthrow of the government of Mohammad Mossadegh by a US-aided military coup which restored the shah, Mohammad Reza Shah Pahlavi, to power in Iran.[4] Mossadegh's cardinal sin was that he nationalized the Iranian oil industry, ending almost 50 years of British monopoly over the sector.[5] The nationalist fervor that Mossadegh sowed in the early 1950s eventually culminated in the Iranian Islamic Revolution in 1979, which forced the shah to take refuge in exile, while catapulting the exiled cleric Ayatollah Khomeini to power as Iran's Supreme Leader.[6] When the revolution was

3 See Appendix 6.1 for the timeline of US sanctions against Iran, and summary of the major presidential EOs and congressional legislation under which those sanctions were imposed.

4 During his brief interregnum as prime minister of Iran, in March 1951, Mossadegh, a lawyer by training, nationalized the Anglo-Iranian Oil Company, a British-owned monopoly of the Iranian oil industry, which led to the displacement of Mohammad Reza Shah Pahlavi from power. Mossadegh's regime collapsed in August 1953, however, when a US-sponsored coup restored Pahlavi to power. A grateful Pahlavi then signed the Treaty of Amity, Economic Relations, and Consular Rights with the US on August 15, 1955. For greater detail see Aldrich (1996, 3–4); Christopher and Mosk (2007); and Pepe (1997).

5 Declassified records in recent decades show that the US Central Intelligence Agency (CIA) financed and directed the coup against Mossadegh (Allen-Ebrahimian, 2017). The US Secretary of State Madeline Albright in April 2000 also acknowledged the role of the US in the overthrow of the Mossadegh government but described the US policy as "regrettably shortsighted." Cited in www.cfr.org/timeline/us-relations-iran-1953-2022, accessed on January 11, 2023.

6 Mohammad Reza Shah Pahlavi, who replaced his father Reza Shah Pahlavi at the age of 22, ruled Iran from 1941 to 1979, albeit excepting the period of Mossadegh interregnum, apparently left the country on an "extended vacation." He first went to Egypt, later to Morocco, Mexico, Panama, and the US, and finally returned to Egypt, which granted him asylum. One year later, in 1980, he died of cancer in Egypt. He was buried in Cairo: Aldrich (1996); Christopher and Mosk (2007).

barely in its ninth month, several thousand revolutionaries stormed the US Embassy in Tehran and took hostage all the diplomats and staff.

A *The Tehran Hostage Crisis*

President Jimmy Carter responded to the hostage crisis a week later, on November 12, 1979, by suspending all oil imports from Iran into the US, and then two days later, by issuing EO 12170,[7] which effectively froze all Iranian assets under the US jurisdiction and suspended all defense exports ordered during the Pahlavi regime. Soon the US expanded the sanctions to prohibit all commerce and travel between the two countries, and severing diplomatic relations with Tehran. The US also made efforts to convince the UNSC to impose sanctions on Iran, but failed to do so.[8]

The European Community (EC), and scores of Western European countries, Canada, Australia, and Japan (which was the largest single importer of Iranian oil at the time) also joined the US by imposing unilateral sanctions banning export of arms to Iran, curtailing imports of Iranian oil, denying extension of new credits to Iran, and reducing economic and financial relations with Iran. Some countries, such as Denmark, the UK, Norway and Australia, recalled their ambassadors as well (Dawidowicz, 2017).

The unilateral sanctions of the US and its allies against Iran came at a time when the country's economy was heavily dependent on trade with them. In 1978, immediately before the revolution, 19 percent of Iranian oil exports entered the US, while 40 percent went to Western Europe; 21 percent of Iranian imports were from the US while 49 percent came from Western Europe; and US military sales and assistance to Iran amounted to $2.5 billion – the highest level for the country in the 1970s.[9]

Because of the embargo against Iran, between 1980 and 1981, US exports to Iran plummeted from $3.7 billion to $23 million, while US imports from Iran dropped from $2.9 billion to $458 million, and the total economic cost to Iran during the period was estimated to be around $3.3 billion (Hewitt and Nephew, 2019).

Court Intervention

On November 29, 1979, the US brought proceedings before the International Court of Justice (ICJ) against Iran, alleging grave violations of diplomatic and consular law arising from the seizure and holding of the US diplomatic and consular staff

7 President Carter issued EO 12170 on November 14, 1979 (44 F.R. 65729), invoking the authority of the International Emergency Economic Powers Act of 1977 (IEEPA: 50 U.S.C. 1702). It was the first use of IEEPA to invoke a presidential EO.

8 The UNSC adopted two resolutions under the UN Charter, Chapter VI, urgently calling on Iran to release the hostages (UNSC Resolution 457, Dec. 4, 1979; UNSC Resolution 461, Dec. 31, 1979). Such resolutions, however, do not require mandatory enforcement. A draft UNSC resolution calling for the adoption of non-military sanctions against Iran under Chapter VII of the Charter, which could be mandatory, was however vetoed by the former Soviet Union (UN Doc. S/13735, 10 Jan. 1980).

9 See Figures 3.3, 3.4, and 3.5 in O'Sullivan (2003, 68–69).

as hostages. The ICJ[10] held Iran responsible for "egregious violations" of the basic principles of diplomatic and consular by stressing the "imperative character of the legal obligations incumbent upon the Iranian Government."[11]

The ICJ's "guidance" remains controversial, however. Some scholars interpret the "guidance" as affirmation of Iran's *erga omnes* obligations as envisaged by the *Barcelona Traction dictum* (*Barcelona Traction, Light and Power Company, Limited (Belgium v. Spain)*. 1970 ICJ 3 (Judgment of Feb. 5)), while others contend that the "guidance" rather emphasized treaty-based mechanisms of enforcement by pointing out that, prior to the institution of the ICJ proceedings, the US had responded to the hostage crisis by placing the matter before the UNSC, by adopting several unilateral coercive measures (such as issuing several EOs) against Iran, and even a month before the Court could render its judgment, the US made an unsuccessful military offensive against Iran (Operation Rice Bowl) to rescue the hostages.[12]

The Algiers Accord

With the Western allies also joining the US in restricting trade relations and freezing large amounts of Iranian assets, and President Carter issuing a series of new sanctions through EOs,[13] the US gained significant leverage for negotiating the release of the hostages.

By then, the freezing of Iranian assets had already had a significant effect – it deprived Iran of access to over $14 billion of assets and properties; the sanctions closed down the US financial markets to Iran, and being denied access to international transactions in US dollars, Iran was forced to pay in cash to its trading counterparts. On top of that, Iran also faced an unprecedented legal battle in the US and

[10] The ICJ, established in 1945 under Articles 92–96 of the UN Charter, serves as the "principal judicial organ" of the UN. To some scholars, the ICJ mainly provides non-binding advisory opinions, and as of May 2013, in its then 68 years of history, the ICJ had received only 23 requests for its opinion from the UN General Assembly, only one request from the UNSC, and only two requests from the UN Economic and Social Council (ECOSOC) (Dawidowicz, 2017, 43; Sloan and Hernández, 2013, 197–198). During her review of the draft of this chapter, Professor Lori Damrosch from Columbia Law School highlighted that the ICJ exercises two distinct forms of jurisdiction: contentious jurisdiction, applicable to cases involving disputes between sovereign states, and advisory jurisdiction, invoked when UN organs seek legal guidance from the ICJ. This delineation is codified in Articles 92–94 of the UN Charter and Article 59 of the ICJ Statute. Notably, in cases falling under contentious jurisdiction, the states parties are not only legally bound by the ICJ's judgments but are also obligated to adhere to and implement them under the aforementioned legal provisions.

[11] For greater detail, see *Case Concerning the United States Diplomatic and Consular Staff in Tehran (United States of America v. Iran)*. [1980] ICJ Re 3. Decided on November 29, 1979.

[12] President Carter launched a military operation to rescue the hostages on April 24–25, 1980. The ill-fated operation was, however, aborted in the Iranian desert after the breakdown of several helicopters and a collision between two aircraft, which resulted in eight deaths (Christopher and Mosk, 2007, 167). For greater detail on the controversy over the ICJ's "guidance," see Annacker (1994, 21–22); Dawidowicz (2017); Katzman (2016); and Sicilianos (2010, 152).

[13] For example, EO 12170 blocked all Iranian government property under US jurisdiction; EO 12205 (issued on April 7, 1980) and EO 12211 (issued on April 17, 1980) banned virtually all US trade with Iran. As explained above, the results of these bans were catastrophic for the Iranian economy.

Europe – over 450 US banks and giant corporations held the Iranian government responsible for expropriation without compensation (Alerassool, 1993; Christopher and Mosk, 2007; Massaroni, 1982).

Iran was thus forced to come to the negotiating table, and the protracted negotiations resulted in the Algiers Accord on January 19, 1981, just one day before the end of President Carter's term of office. Under the terms of the Accord, brokered by the Algerian government and signed in Algiers, Iran agreed to release the hostages, and in exchange, the US agreed to lift all economic sanctions on Iran, freeze all the assets of Mohammad Reza Shah Pahlavi, unfreeze most of the Iranian assets held with American banks and their subsidiaries, and prohibit US firms from making expropriation claims against Iran, and committed itself not to interfere in the internal affairs of Iran (Christopher and Mosk, 2007; Mosk, 1987).[14]

Some of the experts who were involved in the negotiations maintain that these agreements closely reflect what Iran had demanded on September 2, 1980 as conditions for releasing the hostages: return Mohammad Reza Shah Pahlavi's wealth, cancel US claims against Iran, unfreeze Iranian funds in the US, and guarantee non-interference in Iran (Christopher and Mosk, 2007, 165). Under the Accord, the US indeed agreed to release nearly $8 billion of Iranian assets held in escrow by the US after the Iranian revolution, and transfer an additional $1 billion in Iranian securities and deposits with the US banks in six months.

Professor Lori Damrosch, on the other hand, maintains that Iran actually achieved very few of its September 1980 demands, as the US claims against Iran were not canceled, only the hostage claims were barred, and apart from the claims of the hostages themselves, all other claims were sent to the newly established Iran–US Claims Tribunal which paid out billions of dollars from Iranian funds to US claimants. Also, the US declined to make any commitment to freeze or turn over any assets belonging to Pahlavi by not acceding to Iranian demands.[15]

President Carter implemented the Algiers Accord by issuing EO 12283.[16] The EO prohibited any person subject to US jurisdiction from prosecuting in any court within the US or elsewhere any claim against the government of Iran arising out of events related to the seizure of the hostages on November 4, 1979; their subsequent detention; any injury to US property or property of US nationals within the US embassy compound in Tehran after November 3, 1979; or any injury to US nationals

[14] Disputes over the return of many Iranian assets and expropriation claims were placed under the jurisdiction of a third-party arbitration called the US–Iran Claims Tribunal, established in The Hague (Alerassool, 1993). For in-depth discussion of the US-Iran Claims Tribunal's proceedings, the website *Jus Mundi* of Georgetown University Law School provides electronic access to nearly 1,100 decisions and awards issued by the Tribunal: guides.ll.georgetown.edu/c.php?g=371540&p=4196086.

[15] Professor Damrosch of Columbia University Law School made this remark while reviewing this chapter before its publication.

[16] The EO was issued in pursuance of Section 203 of the IIEPA of 1977, Section 301 of Title 3 of the United States Code (U.S.C.), Section 1732 of Title 22 of U.S.C. and Section 301 of the National Emergencies Act of 1976 (NEA: 50 U.S.C. 1631).

or their property as a result of the Islamic Revolution in Iran. The EO further prohibited any person not a US national from prosecuting any such claim in any court within the US; ordered the termination of any previously instituted judicial proceedings based upon such claims; and prohibited the enforcement of any judicial order issued in the course of such proceedings. On January 20, 1981, just minutes after President Ronald Reagan was sworn in, Iran released all 52 hostages under its captivity, but the US Embassy in Tehran still remained under the control of Iranian revolutionaries.

The US–Iran Claims Tribunal

The property disputes between the two countries and numerous private businesses and US nationals were left with the US–Iran Claims Tribunal set up in The Hague. The Algiers Accord granted the Tribunal jurisdiction over the "expropriations or other measures affecting property rights" encompassing claims for property nationalized by decree as well as property seized *de facto* (Brower, 1987, 640).[17]

The private property disputes mainly involved claims of expropriations, breaches of contract, default on loans, tortious injury, and so on, that resulted from the nationalization of all banks and insurance companies as well as certain heavy industries by the Iranian government immediately after the revolution, and the Iranian parliament's adoption of the Single Article Act on January 8, 1980, which nullified all oil contracts and nationalized the country's oil industry. As many of these businesses and commercial operations were owned by American as well as Iranian nationals who held dual citizenships with the US, they sought compensation for expropriations.[18]

To deal with government-to-government claims, the Tribunal established a special court, the Iran–US Arbitration Court, which addressed matters involving the Iranian government's claims for compensation for hundreds of foreign military sales agreements signed during the Shah's regime. The court took decades to make any significant progress, however. Finally, in January 2016, it announced a major settlement between the US and Iran under which the US paid Iran $1.7 billion for the frozen account of Mohammad Reza Shah Pahlavi's purchase of military equipment

17 For the Tribunal to have jurisdiction over an American expropriation claim, the claimant was required to show that the dispute was "outstanding" as of January 19, 1981; that the claimant was a "US national" (a US citizen) or a corporation in which the US citizen had at least a 50 percent share, and the corporation was formed under the laws of a US jurisdiction; and that the respondent was the government of Iran, including any agency, political subdivision, instrumentality, or controlled entity thereof: Alerassool (1993); Brower (1987, 640). See also Claims Settlement Declaration, IRAN-US. C.T.R. 3 (1981–1982), 20 I.L.M. 223 (1981).

18 The Tribunal comprised nine arbitrators – three appointed by Iran, three by the US, and three by the members acting jointly. The members were mandated to conduct business in accordance with the arbitration rules of the United Nations Commission on International Trade Law (UNCITRAL) (Massaroni, 1982, 158). The Tribunal succeeded in resolving approximately 4,700 private US claims filed against Iranian government, resulting in more than $2.5 billion in awards to US nationals and entities in the first 20 years of its existence.

and services before the Iranian revolution, of which $1.3 billion was accrued interest. Some of the cases before the court are still pending, however.

Post-Hostage Crisis Developments

The hostilities between Iran and the US have continued ever since. Even before the release of the hostages, when Saddam Hussain invaded Iran, fearing a Shiite revolt against his regime in Iraq, the US provided economic aid, training, and dual-use technology to Iraq in 1980. Then, after the release of hostages and in the midst of Iraq–Iran war, the Reagan Administration under the "Operation Staunch" program sought to orchestrate an international arms embargo against Iran in 1983.[19]

The same year, Hezbollah – an Iran-backed international terrorist group – drove two trucks loaded with explosives into a US military barracks in Lebanon, killing 241 US military personnel and causing the largest single-day casualties for the US Armed Forces since the Tet Offensive of the Vietnam War. As a result, the State Department designated Iran as a "state sponsor of terrorism" in 1984. The designation came at a time when Iran was already under a ban for exports of defense and dual-use items, and this measure further restricted any foreign assistance to Iran as well as any lending to Iran by international finance institutions (IFIs).[20]

In 1987, President Reagan further intensified pressure on the Iranian regime by designating it a major narcotic-trafficking country, and prohibiting nearly all imports into the US from Iran.[21] Then, in 1988, following an Iranian attempt to sink an American frigate in the Strait of Hormuz, the US Navy destroyed two Iranian oil platforms, sunk a frigate, and shot down an Iranian passenger flight, killing all 290 people on board, including 66 children.[22]

[19] Under "Operation Staunch," the US sought to dissuade its allies as well as many Arab countries from selling American arms to Iran. But between 1981 and 1986, the US also secretly facilitated the sale of arms to Iran under what came to be known as the Iran–Contra Affair. The Iran–Contra affair involved secretly selling arms to Iran in violation of: the Boland Amendments (1982–1984) that prohibited the sale of arms to the Contras, rebel forces in Nicaragua; the International Security and Development Cooperation Act of 1985 (P.L. 99-83) that prohibited arms sales to the Contras; and the Intelligence Oversight Act of 1980, which led to the conviction of almost a dozen officials by an independent counsel in one of the biggest scandals that rocked President Reagan's presidency. For greater detail, see US Congress (1987) and Wilbur (1990).

[20] As explained in Chapter 3, the US designates a country as a "state sponsor of terrorism" in accordance with Section 40 of the Arms Export Control Act of 1976 (AECA: P.L. 94-329), and Section 620A of the Foreign Assistance Act of 1961 (FAA: P.L. 87-195). Such designations automatically result in restrictions on foreign assistance and exports of dual-use items; bans on defense exports and sales; and miscellaneous financial restrictions, including blocking lending to the country by IFIs.

[21] The ban, however, exempted Iranian crude oil refined in a third country and allowed American oil companies to continue purchasing Iranian oil and selling it to non-US markets (O'Sullivan, 2003, 49; Brown, 2020).

[22] For the shooting down of the Iran Air flight 655, the US paid Iran $61.8 million in compensation ($300,000 per wage-earning victim, $150,000 per non-wage earner) for the 248 Iranians killed, and also provided a used aircraft to Iran instead of paying for the Iranian Airbus (Katzman, 2016, 2–3).

B *Post-Khomeini Era*

In the late 1980s, three major developments contributed to a phase of moderation of hostilities between the countries: the UN-brokered ceasefire of Iran–Iraq war in 1988; Ayatollah Ruhollah Khomeini, the revolutionary leader, died in June 1989; and Ali Akbar Hashemi Rafsanjani, a moderate leader, was elected president of Iran in July 1989. These developments prompted some European countries to revive their longstanding trade and investment relations with Iran, while Iran's tacit support of the US-led Desert Storm coalition prompted President George H. W. Bush to signal a possible improvement of relations with Iran.[23]

Both sides still had many contentious issues to grapple with, however. The US had major concerns over the Iranian efforts to obstruct US peace efforts in the Middle East; Iran's support of terrorist groups, such as Hezbollah; Iran's efforts to acquire nuclear weapons; and Iran's post-revolutionary hostility toward the US. On the other hand, Iran's prime concerns were US policies in the wider Middle East, especially unwavering US support for Israel; US meddling in the internal affairs of Iran and its support for Iraq during the Iran–Iraq war; and the shooting down of the Iranian passenger airliner in 1988 (O'Sullivan, 2003, 52–54).

Although Iran's tacit support for the US during the Gulf War somewhat softened the relationship between the countries, the truce did not last long. In October 1992, Congress passed the Iran–Iraq Arms Nonproliferation Act of 1992 (P.L. 102-484) authorizing the president to apply sanctions and controls with respect to Iran, Iraq, and other nations and persons who assist them in acquiring weapons of mass destruction (WMD).[24] The Act further tightened trade restraints with Iran by banning all sales of military items, dual-use items, and products on the US Commerce Department's Export Control List.[25] This legislation also granted extraterritorial jurisdiction over foreign individuals and entities in prohibiting the supply of "advanced conventional weapons" to Iran (Weed, 2001, 21).

The Clinton Administration

The administration of President Bill Clinton differed widely from the Bush Administration in its foreign policy strategies toward Iran. To begin with, while President Bush played Iran and Iraq against one another, President Clinton adopted

[23] Coincidentally, at about the same time, the US–Iran Claims Tribunal in The Hague ruled that the US must compensate Iran for the advance payments it made for arms purchases under the Shah's regime, leading the US to return $278 million to Iran in November 1991.

[24] The Act also empowered the president to take all actions necessary in accordance with the Foreign Assistance Act of 1961, the Nuclear Non-Proliferation Act of 1978, the Chemical and Biological Weapons Control and Warfare Elimination Act of 1991, chapter 7 of the Arms Export Control Act, and other relevant statutes, regarding the non-proliferation of WMDs and the means of their delivery.

[25] As discussed in Chapter 4, the US Department of Commerce maintains a Commerce Control List (CCL), which determines whether an export license is needed from the Department for exporting any product that has a specific Export Control Classification Number (ECCN). The alpha-numeric ECCN describes the item and indicates the licensing requirements.

a "dual containment policy" to isolate both countries from major developments in the region (Ehteshami, 2022). Also, after the collapse of the Soviet Union, Bush sought to establish relations with the Caspian and Central Asian countries, counting on their huge oil reserves to diversify US oil suppliers, Clinton, instead, supported the construction of a pipeline running from Baku (Azerbaijan) to Ceyhan (Turkey) in 1995 (O'Sullivan, 2003, 53).

Clinton also further tightened sanctions against Iran by persuading US allies to restrict arms exports to Iran and to impose a moratorium on the extension or rescheduling of new export credits to the country. As a result, France and Germany prohibited the sale of light-water reactors to Iran, which prompted Iran to sign a deal with Russia in February 1995 for the completion of its nuclear reactor at Bushehr (O'Sullivan, 2003, 53).

In response, Clinton issued EO 12957 on March 15, 1995 banning all US trade and investment relations with Iran, barring Iran's energy sector, but the subsequent EO 12959, issued on May 6, 1995, banned all US trade and investment relations with Iran[26] aiming at curbing Iran's pursuit of nuclear power, support for international terrorism, and opposition to the US-led Middle East peace process.[27]

Congressional Legislation

In 1996, the US Congress passed three major statutes further tightening sanctions against Iran. In February, the National Defense Authorization Act of 1996 (NDAA: P.L. 104-106) further widened the scope of US restrictions on Iran on "advanced conventional weapons," including chemical, biological, and nuclear weapons-related technologies. By then, Iran was already under the restrictions put in place by the Iran–Iraq Arms Nonproliferation Act of 1992.

Then in April, the Congress enacted the Antiterrorism and Effective Death Penalty Act of 1996 (AEDPA: P.L. 104-132), requiring the president to withhold foreign aid from any country that provides financial assistance or arms to any country in the US terrorism list. The Act made it a criminal offense for US persons to conduct financial transactions with the governments on the terrorism list, and stripped Iran and other state sponsors of terrorism of their sovereign immunity in cases in which US plaintiffs sue them for damages.

The Congress then passed the Iran–Libya Sanctions Act of 1996 (ILSA: P.L. 108-21), supplementing the presidential executive orders with measures to force foreign companies to end their involvement in Iran. The Act required the president to impose at least two of the six specified sanctioning measures against any foreign

[26] The EO 12959 invoked not only IEEPA (1977) and NEA (1976), but also Section 505 of the International Security and Development Cooperation Act of 1985 (ISDCA: P.L. 99-83), and United States Code Section 560 of Federal Regulations (Iranian Transactions Regulations – ITRs).

[27] Apparently, Newt Gingrich, then Speaker of the US House of Representatives, recommended the overthrow of the Iranian regime, and proposed to allocate $20 million for the purpose (O'Sullivan, 2003, 56).

entity that invested more than $20 million a year in the Iranian or Libyan energy industry. The legislation also subjected foreign firms involved in the construction of energy transit routes through Iran in the Caspian region to abide by US sanctions.[28] The EU, however, fiercely opposed ILSA by forbidding its companies from complying with it on the ground that it violated international trade agreements that bar extraterritorial application of national laws (O'Sullivan, 2003, 53).

In 1997, Iran elected a new president named Mohammad Khatami, who famously called for a "dialogue of civilizations" in an effort to rebuild relations with Western powers.[29] The next year, in 1998, US Secretary of State Madeleine Albright met with Iran's deputy foreign minister, Javad Zarif, at an eight-nation meeting convened by UN Secretary General Kofi Annan in New York to discuss the ongoing civil war in Afghanistan. The meeting provided an opportunity for the first high-level talks between the US and Iran since 1979, but nothing significant was accomplished as the US believed that Khatami preached dialogue while secretly making rapid progress toward building Iran's nuclear program (Ehteshami, 2022).

Such suspicions led the US Congress to pass the Iran Nonproliferation Act of 2000, which later expanded into the Iran–North Korea–Syria Nonproliferation Act of 2000 (INKSNA: P.L. 106-178). The Act authorized the president to impose extraterritorial sanctions on foreign persons (individuals or companies in third countries) for assisting in any way or transferring any technology to Iran for developing WMD programs. Such sanctions included a prohibition on US exportation of arms and dual-use items to the sanctioned entity; and a ban on US government procurement and imports to the US from the sanctioned entity under EO 12938 (issued on November 14, 1994).[30]

The Bush Administration

The terrorist attacks of September 11, 2001 (9/11) brought a temporary respite in the US–Iran relationship. As most of the hijackers hailed from Iran's major regional rival, Saudi Arabia, and as the country's Shiite Muslims historically opposed the Sunni-Muslim-led Taliban and Al-Qaeda, after 9/11, Iran could extend its support to the US efforts to root out the Taliban and Al-Qaeda,[31] and cooperate with the

[28] The ILSA, however, granted two sorts of presidential waiver in regard to Iran – a national interest waiver, which allowed the president to waive the stipulated sanctions on a specific company on the grounds of US national interest; and a country waiver, which the presidents could use when a parent country of the company making the investment agrees to impose economic sanctions on Iran (O'Sullivan, 2003, 51).

[29] Mohammad Khatami, the fifth president of Iran (1997–2005) made a call for a "dialogue of civilizations" in an interview with CNN in January 1998. Apparently, his election platform also pledged greater democratization, social moderation, and respect for freedom and human rights in Iran, and he enjoyed strong support among Iranian women and young people (Ehteshami, 2022).

[30] The INKSNA also banned US extraordinary payments to the Russian Aviation and Space Agency for transferring WMD or missile technology to Iran.

[31] Following the 9/11 attack, apparently the Bush Administration established a back channel with Iran for its help with the US fight against Al-Qaeda and the Taliban. The back channel worked until President

UN-sponsored six-plus-two talks[32] and the Bonn Conference on the Afghan crisis.[33] But the pause in hostilities between the countries proved to be momentary once again – it lasted until President George W. Bush, in his State of the Union address in 2002, famously included Iran in the "axis of evil," specifically holding the country responsible for state-sponsored terrorism and for secretly pursuing the acquisition of WMD.

In June 2005, President Bush issued EO 13382, blocking assets of proliferators of WMD and their supporters including numerous Iranian banks and financial institutions as well as defense-related entities and individuals, such as the Islamic Revolutionary Guard Corps (IRGC), Karaj Nuclear Research Center, the Atomic Energy Organization of Iran (AEOI), and the Iranian Ministry of Defense and Armed Forces Logistics.[34]

Then, in September 2006, the US Congress passed the Iran Freedom Support Act of 2006 (P.L. 109-293), authorizing the president to sanction firms or persons who sold to Iran chemical, biological, or nuclear weapons or related technologies, including ballistic or cruise missiles, and other destabilizing advanced conventional weapons. The Act also authorized the president to fund Iranian civil society and promote democracy.[35]

The Obama Administration

The Obama Administration's period (2009–2016) largely coincided with that of a more hardline regime in Iran under President Ahmadinejad (2005–2013). The US pursued two-prong sanctions policies toward Iran during this period: Numerous new and stringent sanctioning measures were adopted against Iran in response to the country's efforts to develop nuclear weapons programs and its support for

Bush branded Iran a member of the "axis of evil" in 2002. After the declaration, Iran stopped the secret meetings with US diplomats that had previously helped the US in capturing some Al-Qaeda operatives and combating the Taliban.

32 The six-plus-two group on Afghanistan consisted of six bordering countries of Afghanistan – China, Iran, Pakistan, Tajikistan, Turkmenistan, and Uzbekistan – plus the US and Russia. Organized by the UN, the group worked during 1997–2001 to find a peaceful solution to the Afghanistan issue.

33 The Bonn Conference on Afghanistan, organized by the UN in December 2001, was aimed at creating the Islamic Republic of Afghanistan following the US invasion of Afghanistan. As Afghanistan had had no nationally agreed-upon government since 1979, prominent Afghan warlords were invited to join the conference. The conference resulted in an agreement on Provisional Arrangements for creating a national government in Afghanistan, under which the Afghan Interim Authority (AIA) was created on December 22, 2001 with a six-month mandate, to be followed by a two-year Transitional Authority (TA). The Agreement also led to UNSC Resolution 1386, adopted on December 20, 2001, which established the International Security Assistance Force (ISAF) for Afghanistan.

34 Also, in June 2006, the US sanctioned four Chinese entities for assisting in Iranian WMD efforts: Beijing Alite Technologies, LIMMT Economic and Trading Company, China Great Wall Industry Corp, and China National Precision Machinery Import/Export Corp (Katzman, 2016, 71–72).

35 Meanwhile, Iran elected Ahmadinejad as the country's president in 2005. In 2006, he sent a personal letter to President Bush – the first from an Iranian leader since 1979 – seeking to ease US–Iran nuclear tensions. Ahmadinejad was largely viewed as a hardliner, however, and not much progress was achieved during his tenure (2005–2013).

international terrorism, and at the same time, significant efforts were made to stabilize relations with Iran in pursuance of President Obama's campaign pledges.

Between 2011 and 2013, the US Congress passed several laws further tightening sanctions against Iran, such as: (a) the Comprehensive Iran Sanctions, Accountability, and Divestment Act of 2010 (CISADA: P.L. 111-195); (b) the National Defense Authorization Act of 2012 (NDAA: P.L. 112-81); (c) the Iran Threat Reduction and Syria Human Rights Act of 2012 (ITRA: P.L. 112-158); and (d) the National Defense Authorization Act of 2013 (P.L. 112-239), which included the Iran Freedom and Counter-Proliferation Act (IFCPA) of 2013.

Among this legislation, Section 303 of CISADA authorizes the president to designate a country as a "Destination of Diversion Concern" if the country allows substantial diversion of goods, services, or technologies to Iranian end-users or intermediaries. The targeted technologies include any goods that could contribute to Iran's nuclear or WMD programs, as well as goods listed on the Control List of the Department of Commerce or the Munitions List of the State Department.[36] Any country designated as such is subject to denial of licenses for US exports to that country of the goods that are being re-exported or diverted to Iran.

Section 104 of CISADA significantly restricts Iran's access to the international financial system to obtain "letters of credit" to buy or sell goods in international markets, and prohibits US banks from opening new "correspondent accounts" or "payable-through accounts" to any foreign bank that conducts significant financial transactions with any entity sanctioned by EO 13224 (issued on September 23, 2001) or EO 13382 (issued on June 29, 2005).

The CISADA also designates any foreign bank that facilitates Iran's efforts to acquire WMD or delivery systems as a "Foreign Terrorist Organization" (FTO). Such restrictions on Iran's access to the international financial system came on the back of the Obama Administration's determination in November 2011 that Iran was a "jurisdiction of primary money laundering concern" under Section 311 of the USA Patriot Act (31 U.S.C. 5318A). Scores of foreign banks, including Credit Suisse (Switzerland), ING (the Netherlands), Standard Chartered (UK), Clearstream (Luxembourg), BNP Paribas (France), Bank of Moscow (Russia), Bank of Kunlun (China), and Elaf Islamic Bank (Iraq) were penalized millions of dollars for violations of such sanctions between 2009 and 2014.[37]

Overall, the sanctioning measures imposed against Iran in pursuance of the statutes mentioned above were so severe that it was practically impossible for US financial institutions or US persons to engage in transactions with almost any Iranian bank

[36] As discussed in Chapter 4, the State Department manages the USML through the International Traffic in Arms Regulations (ITAR), which categorize various firearms, weapons, and other armament ammunition/ordnance, which provide critical military or intelligence advantage or other military functions.

[37] For greater detail, see Chapter 4 and Table 4.1 of this volume; Table 2 of Katzman (2016, 26–27); and Goldman and Lindblom (2021).

or other financial institution. Iran's access to the international trade and financial systems was so restrained that the country was barely able to earn revenue through oil sales and to spend that revenue to obtain goods and services in international markets; and it was also barely able to earn, store, and use US dollars (Carter and Farha, 2013, 911; Goldman and Lindblom, 2021, 130).

The Joint Comprehensive Plan of Action

In September 2013, the election of Hasan Rouhani (2013–2021) as president of Iran brought a positive phase in the Iran–US negotiations.[38] In November 2013, President Obama made a call to Rouhani to discuss Iran's nuclear program – it was the first direct contact between the heads of the two countries since 1979.[39] Two months later, Iran and the P5+1 – the five permanent members of the UN Security Council plus Germany – signed an initial nuclear agreement, providing Iran with some sanctions relief.

Finally, on July 14, 2015, Iran, P5+1, and the EU signed the Joint Comprehensive Plan of Action (JCPOA), under which Iran agreed, among others, to dismantle and redesign its nuclear reactor in Arak, allow more intrusive verification of its nuclear programs by the International Atomic Energy Association (IAEA), and limit its uranium enrichment program for at least 15 years.

C *Sanctions Imposed by the UN and the EU*

Iran started its nuclear program back in the 1950s, albeit with the assistance of the US, during the reign of Mohammad Reza Shah Pahlavi. As a signatory to the Nuclear Non-Proliferation Treaty (NPT), Iran also concluded several nuclear-related contracts, including construction of the Bushehr nuclear reactor, prior to 1979. After the Iran–Iraq war (1980–1988), Iran revived its nuclear program with clandestine cooperation from Pakistani nuclear scientist A. Q. Khan, and in 1995, signed a contract with Russia to complete its Bushehr nuclear reactor and develop three new reactors. These agreements, alongside the country's efforts to acquire sensitive nuclear technology, brought international attention to Iran's nuclear activities in 2002 when an opposition political group named Mujaheddin-e-Khaliq (MEK) revealed the country's secretive nuclear activities (Suzuki, 2020).

[38] Hasan Rouhani won the presidential election in 2013 largely because of support from the middle class and young people who, being adversely affected by the sanctions, longed for improving relationship with the West. At the time of his election, the Iranian economy was at its lowest ebb since the end of the Iran–Iraq war in 1988. The country was plagued with stagflation – year-on-year the inflation rate exceeded 40 percent, and the unemployment rate was around 20 percent (Bazoobandi, 2015; Bergeijk, 2015).

[39] Apparently, the Obama Administration had opened a secret channel with Iran and a wider P5+1 discussion group for a pragmatic solution of the Iran issue in 2012, and with the election of centrist leader Rouhani, the discussion came to a fruition in 2013 (Suzuki, 2020).

Following this revelation, Iranian president Khatami began negotiations with the UK, France, and Germany (the EU3), which culminated in the Paris Agreement in 2004 under which Iran agreed to allow IAEA inspection of its nuclear facilities and uranium enrichment capability, pursuant to the Additional Protocol (AP) of the IAEA Comprehensive Safeguard Agreement.

In June 2006, however, the IAEA reported noncompliance of Iran in taking the agreed steps to halt its nuclear activities.[40] At the same time, Iranian president Ahmadinejad rejected the agreement with the EU3, and reinforced nuclear activities, including the construction of the Arak heavy water reactor and an increase in the number of centrifuges at the Fordow and Natanz nuclear facilities (Suzuki, 2020).

As Iran repeatedly ignored the IAEA requests to halt its nuclear programs, on July 31, 2006, the UNSC adopted Resolution 1696, expressing serious concerns at Iran's continued suspension of cooperation with the IAEA under the Additional Protocol, and demanded that Iran suspend all enrichment-related and reprocessing activities, including research and development, and subject them to IAEA verification. Since then, the UNSC has adopted as many as eight resolutions aiming at thwarting Iran's nuclear ambitions.

UNSC Resolution 1737, issued in December 2006, imposed a worldwide ban on Iranian export and import of goods and technologies relating or potentially relating to its nuclear program, froze the assets and property of Iranian WMD-related entities, and imposed financial sanctions against numerous Iranian persons and entities involved in Iran's nuclear program.

In March 2007, the UNSC adopted Resolution 1747, imposing a conventional arms embargo on Iran, and urging all UN member states and international financial institutions to refrain from making grants or loans to Iran, except for development and humanitarian purposes. Then, in June 2010, the UNSC adopted Resolution 1929, authorizing UN member states to impose sanctions on key sectors of the Iranian oil and gas industry.[41]

The EU started its unilateral sanctions against Iran in 2010, but with a much wider scope than the UN. Like the US, the sanctions regimes imposed by the EU not only encompassed trade, banking, and other financial transactions against Iranians, but

[40] The member states of the IAEA voted in favor of the transfer of the Iranian file to the UNSC through the IAEA Board of Governors. The IAEA Statute requires the IAEA to report noncompliance to IAEA members, to the UNSC, and to the UN General Assembly, to adopt any of the following measures: curtailment or suspension of assistance by the IAEA to the country, call for the return of materials and equipment made available to the recipient member by the IAEA, or suspension of the country from the IAEA (Dupont, 2016, 60).

[41] Notably, UNSC Resolution 1929 specifically drew a connection between Iran's energy exports revenues and the funding of Iran's nuclear activities. Immediately after the passing of the Resolution, in 2011, the EU banned almost all dealings with Iran's energy sector, while the US already had such ban in force.

also extended to the nationals and secondary entities of other states which maintained economic and financial ties with Iranian nationals and entities.[42]

As a result of combined sanctions by the US, the EU, and the UN, Iran was effectively cut off from international financial markets; Iran's petroleum industry, from which the country derived most of its revenues, was effectively placed under embargo; almost all banking transactions involving Iranian banks including the Iranian Central Bank were prohibited; insurers were prohibited from dealings with Iran's shipping industry; and the overseas assets of a large number of Iranian individuals and public and private entities were effectively frozen. Thus, Iran had little choice but to accept the JCPOA's limitations on its nuclear program (Cilizoglu and Bapat, 2020; Joyner, 2017).

Implementation of JCPOA

The JCPOA prohibited Iran from production of either highly enriched uranium or plutonium that could be used in a nuclear weapon and sought to ensure that the country's Fordow, Natanz, and Arak nuclear facilities pursued only civilian work, which may include medical and industrial research. The Accord also imposed limits on the numbers and types of centrifuges Iran could operate, the level of enrichment, as well as the size of its stockpile of enriched uranium.[43]

Under the agreement, Iran also allowed the IAEA inspectors unfettered access to carry out monitoring and verification of its nuclear facilities. The agreement set forth multiple sunset provisions, such as: (a) the number of advanced centrifuges would be gradually relaxed by 2024; (b) restrictions on centrifuge production would be lifted in 2026; and (c) constraints on Iran's stockpile of enriched uranium would last until 2030. The agreement mandated IAEA to continue its enhanced monitoring of Iran's nuclear facilities until 2040, and the country's implementation of IAEA's Additional Protocol indefinitely.

The JCPOA mandated the IAEA to submit quarterly reports to its board as well as to the UNSC on Iran's implementation commitments. A Joint Commission, with representatives of all negotiating parties, was also put in place to monitor the implementation processes. In exchange, the EU, the UN, and the US committed themselves to lifting their nuclear-related sanctions on Iran, and to withdraw bans on Iran's transfer of conventional weapons and ballistic missiles after five years, subject to the IAEA certification to the effect that Iran has only been engaged in civilian nuclear activities.

[42] The EU sanctions on Iran is not subject of this volume. For greater detail on the EU sanctions on Iran, see Cordesman et al. (2014), Dreyer and Luengo-Cabrera (2015), Dupont (2016), and Solingen (2012).

[43] There are three naturally occurring isotopes of uranium: uranium-238, uranium-235, and uranium-234. Among those, uranium-235 is the only isotope that undergoes fission. Uranium enriched to 5 percent is used in nuclear power plants, and at 20 percent it can be used in research reactors or for medical purposes, but only highly enriched uranium, at 90 percent or so, can be used for nuclear weapons.

The UNSC Resolution 2231, adopted on July 20, 2015, approved the JCPOA by terminating the relevant provisions of previous UNSC resolutions on the Iranian nuclear issue, and setting up a procurement network for the P5+1 to approve of all purchases for Iran's ongoing nuclear program.[44]

The agreement came into effect in January 2016. As required by the agreement, Iran consented to the redesign of its Arak reactor to guard against future production of weapons-grade plutonium and to export spent fuel from all its reactors to IAEA designated destinations. As a result, in early 2016, the IAEA certified that Iran had met its preliminary pledges, and accordingly, the US, the EU, and the UN repealed or suspended some of their sanctions.

As a part of the agreement, the US committed itself to lift its sanctions on Iranian oil exports, but not to lift its sanctions on financial transactions that deterred international trade with Iran, and its sanctions on Iran's ballistic missile program, support for terrorist groups, and human rights abuses. Following the IAEA's certification, the Obama Administration in 2016 lifted sanctions on the Iranian oil sector, which allowed Iran to quickly ramp up oil exports to nearly pre-sanctions levels. Subsequently, both the US and EU also unfroze about $100 billion worth of Iranian assets.

Criticisms of JCPOA

The JCPOA drew criticisms from many circles, but as the agreement was signed by President Obama, a Democrat, most of the criticisms came from the Republicans. The critics broadly argued that: (a) the lifting of the sanctions would bolster the revolutionary elements in the Iranian government, enabling them to destabilize the region; (b) as many of the essential restrictions on Iran's nuclear ambitions were slated to expire soon, Iran would soon be able to resume its uranium enrichment programs; (c) the sunset provisions of the deal would only delay the day when Iran would acquire nuclear power, while the sanctions relief would allow Iran to underwrite its terrorism activities in the region; and (d) the inspection regimes put in place would be incapable of preventing Iran from acquiring nuclear power (Gerecht, 2018).

Also, because of opposition from the Republicans, the JCPOA could not be granted a treaty status, which requires two-thirds of Senate votes. Instead, the US Congress approved the JCPOA as a part of the Iran Nuclear Agreement Review Act of 2015 (INARA: P.L. 114-17), which required the president to confirm Iranian compliance with the JCPOA provisions to the Congress every three months. The agreement thus remained vulnerable to US domestic politics.

Then, in August 2017, the Congress enacted the Countering America's Adversaries Through Sanctions Act of 2017 (CAATSA: P.L. 115–44), further tightening the

[44] The Preamble of JCPOA states that it provides for "comprehensive lifting of all UN Security Council sanctions as well as multilateral and national sanctions related to Iran's nuclear program, including steps on access in areas of trade, technology, finance, and energy" (cited in Dupont, 2016, 37).

existing sanctions on Iran on multiple grounds. CAATSA, among other provisions, incorporated an amendment to the Iran Sanctions Act of 1996, which authorized the president to impose severe sanctions on third states and their businesses that engaged in certain economic dealings with Iran;[45] expanded Section 105 of CISADA by bringing scores of new human rights abuses in Iran, such as extrajudicial killings, torture, and the exposure of illegal activities by Iranian officials under the ambit of US sanctions; and made it mandatory for the president to impose sanctions on the entities that materially contributed to Iran's ballistic missile program. Subsequently, the NDAA of 2017 required the president to submit quarterly reports to Congress on Iran's missile launches, and authorized sanctions on Iran's ballistic missile launches until December 31, 2019.[46]

D *Sanctions under the Trump Administration*

President Donald Trump, who derided JCPOA as "one of the worst deals ever" during his election campaign, pulled out of the accord in May 2018 by reinstating many of the banking and oil sanctions that were relaxed or waived by the Obama Administration. Then, on November 5, 2018, in a single day, the Trump Administration relisted all of the EO 13599-designated entities under the Office of Foreign Assets Control (OFAC) SDN list, including the Atomic Energy Organization of Iran (AEOI) and its 23 subsidiaries (Katzman, 2022, 3).

In withdrawing from the JCPOA and reinstating the sanctions on Iran, Trump reiterated the same Republican arguments, that the deal failed to address Iran's ballistic missile program, its proxy warfare in the region, and the sunset provisions of the deal were inadequate to prevent Iran from pursuing nuclear weapons.[47] While announcing the US withdrawal from the deal, however, Trump pledged to seek a more comprehensive deal with Iran and proposed "twelve requirements" to do so, but the Iranian Supreme Leader Ali Khamenei responded by proposing seven conditions for remaining in the JCPOA.[48]

The JCPOA provided that if any signatory of the agreement suspected Iran of violating the agreement, the UNSC would decide whether to continue the sanctions relief

[45] As discussed above, the ISA is a classic example of secondary and extraterritorial sanctions – it imposes US sanctions on third states and their businesses that engage in certain economic dealings with Iran in an effort to induce them to curtail those dealings. Such sanctions, as discussed in Chapter 2, are allowed under international law as long as the sanctioner has sufficient territorial and nationality ties to the target state, and it is deemed that the ISA largely passes this test (Cilizoglu and Bapat, 2020; Meyer, 2009).

[46] Subsequently, in the 2018 financial year, the NDAA (P.L. 115-91) extended this requirement until December 31, 2022, adding entities that assisted in Iranian missile launches (Katzman, 2016, 58–59).

[47] Notably, Iran's traditional rivals in the Middle East – Israel and Saudi Arabia – also raised similar concerns that JCPOA failed to address Iran's ballistic missile program or constrain the country's support for terrorist groups such as Hamas and Hezbollah.

[48] The resultant negotiations lasted for more than a year but ended in failure (Carl, 2021).

to Iran. The Trump Administration, however, pulled out of the deal unilaterally without UNSC approval, and by April 2020, had snapped back most of the sanctions on Iran, while the other members of the Accord – France, Germany, and the UK – not only remained steadfast with the deal, but also developed an alternative international payment system – called the Instrument in Support of Trade Exchange (INSTEX) – to continue trade relations with Iran by avoiding US dollar-based transactions.[49]

The Trump Administration used a number of past EOs to reimpose sanctions on Iran, such as: (a) in October 2017, EO 13533 (issued on March 1, 2010) was used to impose sanctions on Iran for human rights abuses; (b) in November 2018, EO 13382 (issued on June 29, 2005) was used to impose sanctions on entities assisting Iran's ballistic missile program or any system capable of delivering WMD, or sold or transferred to or from Iran, any major combat systems, including tanks, armored vehicles, warships, missiles, combat aircraft, and attack helicopters; and in September 2019, EO 13224 (issued on September 23, 2001) was used to impose sanctions on Iranian economic entities that furnished funds for the IRGC and its regional activities, and extended sanctions on the already sanctioned Central Bank of Iran.[50]

President Trump also issued scores of new EOs to impose new sanctions on Iran, such as:

(a) EO 13871 (issued on May 8, 2019) sanctioned transactions involving Iran's minerals and industrial commodities, a sector that had about 10 percent share in Iran's total exports revenues, and blocked US-based property of persons and entities who conducted significant transactions with Iran's iron, steel, aluminum, or copper sectors;

(b) EO 13876 (issued on June 24, 2019) blocked the US-based property of Iranian Supreme Leader Ali Khamenei and his top associates, and several other senior officials, including Iran's Foreign Minister Mohammad Javad Zarif;

(c) EO 13902 (issued on January 10, 2020), issued in response to the Iranian missile strikes on an Iraqi air base following the killing of IRGC commander Qasem Soleimani, barred from the US financial system any foreign bank that conducted transactions regarding the construction, mining, manufacturing, or textiles sectors of Iran, and with any persons that supplied goods or services to those sectors;

(d) EO 13902 (issued on January 10, 2020) comprehensively shut Iran's banking system out of the international financial system by designating Iran's remaining unsanctioned banks for sanctions. A provision was made, however, to grant general licenses in order to make purely humanitarian transactions.[51]

49 As explained in detail in Chapter 4, the INSTEX was a futile attempt.

50 Earlier, on September 4, 2019, the State Department announced a $15 million reward to any person who could help the US in disrupting the financial operations of the IRGC and its Qods Force, the IRGC unit that assisted Iran-linked forces and factions in the region.

51 EO 13902 was issued in the midst of the COVID-19 pandemic. In early 2020, the Trump Administration offered humanitarian assistance to Iran, via the World Health Organization, to help battle the COVID-19 outbreak, but Iran refused to accept the aid.

(e) EO 13949 (issued on September 21, 2020) came in response to UNSC's refusal to extend its Resolution 2231, which banned arms transfers to and from Iran with an expiration date of October 18, 2020. The EO blocked any entity that materially contributed to the supply, sale, or transfer, directly or indirectly, to or from Iran, of arms or related material, including spare parts, or facilitated or financed such transactions.[52]

III IMPACT ON IRANIAN ECONOMY AND POPULATION

Iran has been under a volley of sanctions for more than four decades. The saga that began with the hostage crisis of 1979 has continued ever since, albeit with increasingly severe sanctions and widening sanction objectives, with respites few and far-between. The UN joined the sanctions campaign in 2006, following the revelation of Iran's secret underground nuclear program, and largely at the behest of the US. The same year the EU also joined the sanctions campaign against Iran, largely aligning its sanctioning measures with those of the US. Both the US and the EU – the two largest economies in the world – enforced their unilateral sanctions against Iran, many of them came with extraterritorial jurisdictions.

The sanctions regimes against Iran, that were imposed up to the adoption of UNSC Resolution 1929 in 2010, as Gal and Minzili (2011) put it, created four concentric circles: (a) a central circle imposed by the UNSC Resolutions that provided legitimacy for the whole structure of international sanctions; (b) a second circle comprised of unilateral sanctions by the US and the EU that not only encompassed almost all major sectors of the Iranian economy but also pressured other governments to join the sanctions campaign; (c) a third circle forced enforcement of the UN, the US, and the EU sanctions by important trade partners of Iran; and (d) a fourth circle forced business sectors – banks, insurance companies, international businesses and financial institutions – to be wary of engaging in trade and investment relations with Iran.

By 2014, as a consequence of the CISADA (2010), the ITRA (2012), and the NDAA (2012 and 2013), Iran was effectively cut-off from the global financial messaging system SWIFT;[53] its banking and finance system, including the Iranian Central Bank,

[52] For a comprehensive list of sanctions imposed on Iran by the UN, the EU, and the US, and for the entities sanctioned, see Appendix A to D in Katzman (2016, 61–90). Also, see Askari (2003) for US statutes and executive orders, and how these affected the Iranian as well as the US economy during 1979–1997. This study covers the US sanctions on Iran up to the year 2020, the end of the Trump Administration. In January 2021, the Biden Administration announced that the US would return to JCPOA if Iran came back into compliance with the JCPOA.

[53] Iran was cut-off from SWIFT on March 15, 2012, in compliance with EU instructions to discontinue its communications services to Iranian financial institutions that are subject to European sanctions. Prior to the ban, Iran's dependence on SWIFT for worldwide financial communication and transaction was substantial. In just one year in 2010, reportedly 19 Iranian banks and 25 Iranian financial

were delinked from the global financial system, and virtually the entire Iranian banking sector was declared as money laundering entities; the country's petrochemical industry, that brought more than 90 percent of the country's hard currency, was completely paralyzed (Arnold, 2015; Cordesman et al., 2014).

Then with the Trump Administration's "maximum pressure campaigns," during 2016–2020 (withdrawal from JCPOA, the enactment of CAATSA (2017), and a series of EOs), the sanctions regimes against Iran became so aggressive and so comprehensive that almost all sectors of the economy, including energy, shipping, transportation, insurance, finance, military and so on, as well as almost all the top leaders of the country, including the country's supreme leader and foreign minister, were brought under US sanctions. Some observers argue that Iran has thus been effectively placed under comprehensive sanctions, although apparently the global community had abandoned comprehensive sanctions since the Iraqi debacle of the 1990s (Jazairy, 2019). The resultant impacts on the Iranian economy and population are elucidated below.

Structural Changes of Iranian Economy

First, the Iranian economy has been through major structural changes. Largely due to the sanctions regimes, Iran's economic structure has changed dramatically over the decades. In 1979, the oil sector had an overwhelming 75 percent share in the economy, while the services sector had a share of 13 percent, and industry and agriculture had 9 and 2 percent shares, respectively. In 2019, four decades later, the structure had reversed almost completely – the services sector came to dominate the economy with a 50 percent share, while the share of industry and mining rose to 32 percent, the share of agriculture rose to 13 percent, and that of oil declined to just about 5 percent (Rome, 2022).[54]

Second, the country's international trade pattern changed drastically. In 1978, almost 80 percent of Iranian exports were destined to the US and other Western countries, while less than 1 percent went to China. By 2001, the share of Western countries dropped to 47 percent, while that of China and other developing countries increased to 10 percent and 43 percent, respectively (see Table 6.1). Iran's import patterns also changed dramatically. While in 1978 over 77 percent of Iranian imports originated from the West, by 2001, the share dropped to less than 50 percent, while more than 40 percent of imports originated from developing countries.

Over the years, such diversification of trade helped Iran to minimize the effects of sanctions on its economy. For example, in 1987, the US banned imports of Iranian carpets and pistachios, affecting almost one-fifth of the country's total non-oil

institutions used the network over two million times. This ban still affects all banking transactions with Iran, including Iranian oil transportation, and all transactions with Iran's state-owned oil company and its main tanker fleet (Cordesman et al., 2014).

54 Such a large-scale drop in the share of the oil sector resulted from sanctions which rendered Iran unable to export oil freely. More on this below.

TABLE 6.1 *Transformation of Iran's trade relations, 1978–2022 (shares as percent of total)*

Year	United States	Western Europe	Other industrial countries	China	Japan	Rest of developing world	Rest of Asia
				(a) Imports			
1978	21	49	2	<1	15	9	3
1994	3	51	5	1	8	24	8
2001	<1	43	5	5	5	27	14
				(b) Exports			
1978	19	40	3	<1	17	12	7
1986	7	37	2	0	16	16	17
2001	<1	25	<1	10	22	16	27

Source: Author's compilation based on Figures 3.3 and 3.4 in O'Sullivan (2003, 68–69).

exports, but Iran managed to sell those non-oil products to other countries, and could even sell in the US market through third country exports up to 1995. As a result, the actual costs borne by Iran as a result of the import ban were far less than the approximately $8 billion in non-oil imports that Iran could earn from exporting these products to the US up to the year 2000 (O'Sullivan, 2003, 65–66).

Since the early 2000s, the sanctions regimes of the US and the EU on Iranian trade have been more far-reaching and intense than before because they extensively affected Iran's transport and shipping, banking and insurance sectors. As a result, the UAE emerged as one of the most important trading partners of Iran – a substantial part of Iran's imports come through the huge free-trade zones of Dubai and others in the UAE. The trade with the UAE, however, has been curtailed in recent years as the UAE has also come under Western sanctions (Gal and Minzili, 2011).

Diversification of Iranian trade has continued. In 2018, Iran's major export destinations were China (21 percent), Iraq (21 percent), UAE (14 percent), Afghanistan (6.8 percent), South Korea (5.9 percent), Turkey (5.5 percent), and India (4.7 percent). As a result, the shares of the US and other Western nations dwindled to one percent or less. Similarly, Iran's imports also mainly came from developing countries. In 2018, the shares were as follows: China (25 percent), UAE (14 percent), India (6.3 percent), Turkey (6.3 percent), Germany (6.0 percent), Switzerland (5.1 percent), South Korea (5.0 percent).[55] In 2019, the five largest trade partners of Iran were: China (36 percent), UAE (14 percent), India (12 percent), Turkey (7 percent), and Brazil (4 percent), while Western countries, including the US, had a share of less than 3 percent.[56]

55 Based on COMTRADE database, accessed on January 3, 2023. comtradeplus.un.org/.

56 In addition to export diversification, Iran also adopted a policy of reallocating investment funds and import substitution to increase domestic production of manufactured goods under what is called a

Oil and Gas Sector

The oil and gas sector has been the most critical sector for Iran's foreign exchange earnings – historically, over 80 percent of the country's export revenue came from this sector. This sector was also the most important source of revenue in the state budget. Iran has the fourth largest oil reserves in the world, and it has been one of the largest oil producers and exporters in the world.[57] It is thus not surprising that this sector had been the prime target of Western sanctions.

In 1974, Iran produced six million barrels of oil per day (bpd), but due to sanctions and the devastation that occurred during the war with Iraq (1980–1988), the country has so far failed to recover its pre-revolutionary levels of oil production (Rome, 2022). The US ban on imports of Iranian oil, imposed in 1987, however, had limited effect on Iranian economy because the ban affected approximately 600,000 bpd of Iranian oil that the US imported at the time, and Iran was able to direct its oil exports to non-US destinations. This loophole in the US sanctions also allowed major US oil companies – Exxon, Texaco, and Mobil – to resell $4 billion worth of Iranian oil each year to third markets up to 1994.

Even after the closing of the loophole in 1995, Iran experienced only short-term costs for up to 20 to 25 percent of its crude oil exports, as Asian liftings increased from 790,000 bpd in 1995 to one million bpd in 1996, and the European lifting increased from 389,000 bpd to 495,000 bpd in 1996. Thus, although Iranian oil exports dipped to 2.62 million bpd in 1995, down from 2.65 million bpd in 1994, by 1996 the export volume had recovered to 2.63 million bpd (O'Sullivan, 2003, 65–66).

Iranian crude oil exports came under the full force of the combined sanctions in 2010, when the EU also joined the international oil embargo against Iran, and as a result, crude oil production of Iran fell to about 2.2 million bpd. The next year there was a little bump upward, but ever since the country's oil production has declined, and in recent years, it has produced less than one million bpd. Export revenues declined commensurately – ranging between $38 billion and $64 billion between 2013 and 2021 (see Table 6.2). Some studies suggest that Iran lost between $300 billion and $450 billion in oil revenues in a decade because of the Western sanctions (Rome, 2022).

"resistance economy," aimed at reducing dependence on imports and foreign investment. Moreover, since 2010, some of the country's state-owned enterprises have been transferred to the control of quasi-governmental entities, including cleric-run foundations, holding companies, and investment groups. Also, since 2005, state subsidies were reduced and gasoline prices raised to levels similar to those in other countries in the region (Katzman, 2016, 54–55).

57 Iran has also witnessed a significant augmentation in its natural gas production, escalating from a nominal volume during the Iranian Revolution to an excess of 18 trillion cubic meters in recent years. However, more than 90 percent of this formidable natural gas reservoir is domestically utilized, with the remaining portion earmarked for export, predominantly directed towards Iraq and Turkey through established pipeline networks. In December 2022, Iran's natural gas exports reached 18,793.981 million cubic meters, compared with 18,425.471 million cubic meters in December 2021. The average natural gas exports of Iran during 1960–2022 amounted to 864.000 million cubic meters. For greater detail, see the CEIC Database: www.ceicdata.com/en/indicator/iran/natural-gas-exports.

TABLE 6.2 *Key indicators of Iranian economic performance, 2010–2021*

Year	GDP (billion US$)	Annual GDP growth rate (%)	Per capita GDP (US$, in purchasing power parity)	Annual inflation rate (%)	Iran's population (in millions)	Annual population growth rate (%)	Exchange rate (Rials equal to 1 US$)	Crude oil exports (1,000 barrels per day)	Crude oil export revenues (US$ in billions)
2010	486.81	5.80	4,091	10.9	75.37	1.41	10,254.18	2,247	
2011	626.13	2.65	2,746	26.29	76.34	1.29	10,166.31	2,537	
2012	644.04	−3.75	3,278	27.26	77.32	1.29	12,175.55	2.102	
2013	492.78	−1.52	3,874	36.60	78.46	1.47	18,414.45	1,215	64.54
2014	460.38	4.98	5,759	16.61	79.96	1.92	25,941.66	1,109	55.41
2015	408.21	−1.42	5,497	12.18	81.79	2.29	29,011.49	811	31.85
2016	457.95	8.82	4,991	7.25	83.31	1.85	30,914.55	1.921	55.75
2017	486.63	2.76	5,758	8.04	84.50	1.44	33,226.30	2.125	65.82
2018	331.68	−2.25	6,281	18.01	85.62	1.32	40,864.33	1,849	60.73
2019	283.75	−2.66	8,329	39.91	86.56	1.11	42,000.00	651	29.03
2020	239.74	3.33	8,202	30.59	87.92	0.84	42,000.00	404	21.04
2021	359.71	4.72	6,459	43.39	88.55	0.73	42,000.00	734	38.72

Source: GDP (gross domestic product) figures, population, and exchange rates are based on World Bank database, Microtrends (www.macrotrends.net/countries/IRN/iran/gdp-gross-domestic-product), and Bank of Iran. Figures of oil exports and revenues are based on www.ceicdata.com/en/indicator/iran/crude-oil-exports and tradingeconomics.com/iran/oil-exports.

As a result of the reimposition of US sanctions in 2018, Iran's oil production dropped to less than one million bpd with a commensurate decline in export revenues. With the US oil embargo in place, Iran can export to only a few countries by circumventing sanctions, such as India and China. Japan, a long-time importer of Iranian oil, discontinued its import of Iranian oil after the reimposition of US sanctions, and India also drastically curtailed its oil imports from Iran as the US Treasury Department geared up its actions against illicit trading of Iranian petroleum and petroleum products.[58]

Macroeconomic Performance

The Iranian economy has obviously struggled over the decades to withstand international sanctions as it has been plagued with soaring inflation and unemployment, massive decline in the standard of living, and lack of foreign credits and investments.[59] Often the economy experienced stagflation, as negative economic growth was accompanied by inflation as well as high unemployment, which affected women and young people the most (Bazoobandi, 2015; Bergeijk, 2015, 61). To most of the Iranian population, economic sanctions were economic warfare against them, as tens of millions lacked access to food and basic medicine (Jazairy, 2019).

In the early to mid 1970s, Iran was one of the wealthiest countries outside the Western world, as high oil prices in global market brought in hefty revenues. All that changed with the Iranian revolution and international sanctions since 1979. One study suggests that trade sanctions alone cost Iran in the range between $700 million and $1.4 billion per year, while financial sanctions cost the country between $800 million and $1.3 billion per year, and thus, the combined cost of international sanctions on the Iranian economy ranged between $1.5 billion and $2.6 billion per year (Preeg, 1999). Another study estimates the cost of international sanctions on Iranian trade between $1.16 billion and $1.3 billion per year (Haidar, 2016).

By all indications, the Iranian economy continues to suffer due to sanctions. Between 2010 and 2020, Iranian GDP (gross domestic product) more than halved – declining from $487 billion in 2010 to $240 billion in 2020, and for almost half of the period, GDP growth was negative (see Table 6.2). Per capita income, measured in purchasing power parity, showed some improvements, but the inflation rate ranged between 7 percent and 43 percent.

58 In November 2022, for example, OFAC sanctioned 13 companies – based in Dubai, Hong Kong, and China – for illicit trading of hundreds of millions of dollars' worth of Iranian petrochemicals and petroleum products to buyers in East Asia on behalf of US-sanctioned Iranian petrochemical companies Gulf Petrochemical Industry Commercial Co. (PGPICC) and Triliance Petrochemical Co. Ltd. (Triliance), as well as the National Iranian Oil Company (NIOC) and its marketing arm, Naftiran Intertrade Company Ltd (NICO).

59 Even many international financial institutions could not lend money to Iran. For example, due to American pressure the World Bank in 1991 suspended $847 million in loans in support of six development projects in Iran (O'Sullivan, 2003, 67).

Because of the international sanctions campaigns, Iran was unable to access its hard currency accounts abroad during 2011–2016, which stood at about $115 billion. During 2016–2018, because of the easing of sanctions under the JCPOA, Iran regained access to its funds abroad, but then with the reimposition of US sanctions in 2018, the country's access to its hard currency abroad dwindled to about $85 billion.

The reimposition of US sanctions also took a serious toll on Iran's foreign exchange rate. At the time of US withdrawal from the JCPOA, 35,000 Iranian *rial* equaled one US dollar, but with the reimposition of sanctions, the *rial*'s market value plummeted to 150,000 to the dollar by the November 5, 2018, and to 265,000 to the dollar in September 2020, and then to about 300,000 *rials* to the dollar in early December 2021. While the inflation rate in Iran shot to about 60 percent during 2011–2013, the rate fell to single digits by June 2016 due to the easing of sanctions, but then with the reimposition of US sanctions, the inflation rate soared to about 45 percent in 2021. At the time of the Iranian revolution in 1979, one US dollar equaled 79 Iranian *rials*.

IV LEGAL PERSPECTIVES

Iran has been one of the most sanctioned states in the world, having been subjected to both unilateral and multilateral sanctions for a very long time. This discussion on the legality of the prolonged sanctions regimes against Iran first focuses on the unilateral sanctions regimes, and then moves to multilateral sanctions.

Unilateral Sanctions

As elaborated in previous chapters, international law provides a wide variety of unilateral measures, such as sanctions, retorsion, reprisals, reciprocity, countermeasures, termination and suspension of treaties, and so on, from which an aggrieved or injured state can choose the course of action that best secures the "fulfilment of the obligations deriving from, or otherwise react to, the commission of an internationally wrongful act" (Arangio-Ruiz, 1991, 2; Dupont, 2016, 41).

With respect to Iran, leading unilateral sanctioners – the US and the EU – opted for non-forcible economic sanctions as countermeasures.[60] Such countermeasures derive their legal standing from the customary international law of self-defense (Reisman and Stevick, 1998), and such self-defense triggers whenever Article 2

[60] It is notable that a distinction is often made between the legal regimes established by countermeasures and those established by sanctions. While non-forcible measures taken by states constitute countermeasures, such measures taken by international organizations, such as the UN, are dubbed as sanctions. Such an understanding implies a hierarchical relationship between the UN and the implementing states, which, in turn, implies that injured states are entitled to take certain non-forcible actions within a bilateral context against a state responsible for a breach of international law, but they are also bound in hierarchical relationship with the sanctions imposed by the UN and such other international organizations (Crozet and Hinz. 2020; Gowland-Debbas, 2001, 2; White and Abass, 2018, 521–523).

(4) of UN Charter actually occurs (Ronzitti, 2016, 14–15).[61] The Articles on State Responsibility (ARISWA, 2001) endorses such sanctions as long as the sanctioning states can establish that the measures are aimed at inducing the target state to comply with its international obligations, and the measures are necessary and proportionate to the injury suffered, do not affect fundamental human rights, and are terminated when the wrongful act has ceased (Hovell, 2019; Joyner, 2015).

As the discussion above indicates, the first set of US sanctions[62] against Iran was imposed in 1979 when President Carter froze Iranian assets as a countermeasure to the seizure of the US Embassy in Tehran and taking hostage of US diplomats and staff by the Iranian revolutionaries. Those measures largely conform to the requirements of countermeasures as set forth in customary international law, the UN Charter, and the ARSIWA. These measures were prompted by a violation of international law, to compel the targeted state to adhere to its international legal responsibilities. The measures were also intended to establish a possibility for the state to rectify the situation by isolating funds that could potentially be used for reparations to address any incurred injuries (Damrosch, 2019). The sanctioning measures were also temporary, as required by international law – President Reagan withdrew the sanctions following the release of the hostages in January 1981.

The second set of sanctions against Iran came after the US designated the country as a state-sponsor of terrorism following a massive suicide attack on US Marine barracks in Lebanon in 1983. Carried out by Hezbollah, a terrorist group associated with Iran, the attack left 241 American soldiers dead. Such military action could prompt legitimate military offensive action in self-defense. Article 51 of the UN Charter allows a state to resort to armed self-defense if an armed attack occurs (Ronzitti, 2016, 14–15). Instead, the US imposed a complete ban on Iranian imports, and a near complete ban on Iranian exports. Such sanctions can hardly be considered disproportionate to the injury that the US had actually suffered.[63] At the same time, the

61 Article 2 (4) of UN Charter prohibits the threat or use of force and calls on all UN members to respect the sovereignty, territorial integrity and political independence of other states, but Article 51 of the UN Charter allows a state, under armed attack, to resort to armed response in self-defense. Article 51 of UN Charter states:

> Nothing in the present Charter shall impair the inherent right of individual or collective self-defense if an armed attack occurs against a Member of the United Nations, until the Security Council has taken measures necessary to maintain international peace and security. Measures taken by Members in the exercise of this right of self-defense shall be immediately reported to the Security Council and shall not in any way affect the authority and responsibility of the Security Council under the present Charter to take at any time such action as it deems necessary in order to maintain or restore international peace and security.

62 Unilateral sanctions against Iran have been discussed here in the context of the US sanctions only. As discussed above, the EU joined the Iran sanctions campaign as unilateral sanctioner in 2010, and its restrictive measures were largely aligned to that of the US until 2017, when the Trump Administration withdrew from the JCPOA.

63 The US took several military actions against such armed attacks. For example, in response to the bombing of a West Berlin nightclub on April 5, 1986, that killed three people, including a US

Hezbollah attack was made in the midst of the Iraq–Iran war in which the US sided with Iraq, and it could be deemed as an act of retaliation to US support for Iraq.

The third set of US sanctions was adopted during 1984–1987, in response to Iran's alleged role in international terrorism and narcotics trafficking. By 1987, such measures culminated in a complete ban on imports from Iran, and strict restrictions on most forms of international assistance, arms-related exports and sales, exports of dual-use items to Iran, and opposition to loans to Iran from international financial institutions.

Most of these sanctions, however, emanated from pre-existing US statutes – many of which came with built-in extraterritorial legal effect or applicability to foreign countries, nationals, and entities. Even when these measures were officially deemed as primary sanctions, many of them embodied threats of secondary or extraterritorial sanctions, and thus might have violated the international principles of legal equality of states, national sovereignty, and nonintervention in the internal affairs of another state (Breen, 2021; Mallard and Hanson, 2021; Prezas, 2021).

Scholars widely differ on the issue of the legality of extraterritorial application of sanctions, however. While some deplore such sanctions for crossing the bounds of prescriptive jurisdiction and encroaching on the sovereign rights of other nations on questionable grounds or self-determined foreign policy goals (Beckhy, 2018, 9; Clark, 1999, 63; Ronzitti, 2016), there are others who argue that such sanctions may be justified under international law as long as they have sufficient territorial and nationality ties to the sanctioning state, and various circumstances may well provide rights to a sanctioning state to lawfully assert jurisdiction over conduct beyond its territory (Knox, 2010; Mayer, 2009).

The fourth phase of US sanctions against Iran began in the 1990s with the passage of the Iran–Iraq Non-proliferation Act of 1992, which was aimed at preventing Iran from acquiring WMD. The Act was reinforced by several other statutes, including the Iran Sanctions Act (ISA, 1996), ITRA (2012), and CAATSA (2017) – all of which came with extraterritorial features in order to impose sanctions on third states, businesses, and individuals that engage in certain economic, financial, and military dealings with Iran. As discussed previously, some of these statutes even extend the jurisdiction over "US persons" to include foreign subsidiaries of US-based companies.

serviceman, and injured 229 more, President Reagan, on April 14, 1986, ordered a midnight aerial campaign, code-named "Operation El Dorado Canyon," against Libyan leader Muammar Gaddafi. The attack lasted just about 12 minutes and dropped about 60 tons of munitions on Gaddafi's official residence. Being tipped off by the Italian prime minister, Gaddafi survived the attack, but many people were injured. Ramsey Clark, a former US Attorney General, later sued the US and the UK in the US District Court in Washington DC, claiming damages for the injured Libyans. The case, *Saltany v. Reagan*, was dismissed in 1988. Also, in 2001, following the 9/11 terrorist attack, the US relied on the principle of self-defense to declare war against Afghanistan, although the US was not attacked by Afghanistan – it was rather attacked by a terrorist group called Al Qaeda, albeit with indirect support of the Taliban regime (Asada, 2020, 36).

Such extraterritorial reach of US legislation that seeks to cut off foreign parties from access to the US financial and commercial markets for conducting business with the targets of US primary sanctions has come under criticism from the perspective of legal principles as well as other grounds (Bechky, 2018; Meyer, 2009; Ryngaret, 2008). Several countries, as discussed in Chapters 3 and 4, have indeed refused to recognize the extraterritorial reach embodied in such legislation by adopting "blocking statutes" (Rathbone et al., 2013, 1071–1075; Ruys, 2019). The EU, for example, prohibited companies and nationals in its member states from complying with some of these laws (Meyer, 2009; Ruys, 2019).[64]

Moreover, while international law allows countermeasures, an injured state cannot resort to extreme economic or political coercion designed to endanger the territorial integrity or political independence of the target state which has allegedly committed an internationally wrongful act. Countermeasures or sanctions cannot turn into "economic warfare," such as "belligerent blockade" and the "strategic bombing of factory infrastructure" (Lowe and Tzanakopoulos, 2012). Some scholars even maintain that economic and political countermeasures may be illegal if they are aimed at coercing a target state to subordinate the exercise of its sovereign rights or its independence (Dupont, 2016; Gowland-Debbas, 2001; Pellett, 2024).

Some of the unilateral sanctions imposed by the US and the EU against Iran may indeed be questionable under the guidelines of the UN Charter and other international law conventions.[65] For example, as Dupont (2016, 49–65) points out, UNSC Resolution 1929 (adopted in 2010) on the "potential connection" between Iran's revenues derived from its energy sector and the funding of its "proliferation-sensitive nuclear activities" can hardly be used as a legal basis for imposing unilateral sanctions on the sector. But both the US and the EU imposed unilateral sanctions on this sector by using UNSC Resolution 1919. Articles 31 and 32 of the Vienna Convention on the Law of Treaties (1969) also do not grant states the right to auto-interpret UNSC resolutions in order to take liberties in their execution (Orakhelashvili, 2010; Sicilianos, 2010; Wood, 1998).

Second, the sanctioning measures taken against the Iranian Central Bank contradict the rules of governing immunities and privileges of foreign states under the UN Convention on Jurisdictional Immunities of States and their Property (2004), which provides for the immunity of the property of a central bank or other monetary

[64] See EU Council Regulations 2271/1996 and 267/2012. As discussed before, similar blocking legislation was also adopted by Canada and Mexico. Earlier, in 1982, a Dutch court also declined to allow the enforcement of US sanctions against a Dutch subsidiary of a US company. There have also been occasions when resistance of third countries forced the US to revoke certain sanctions or to agree to suspend their enforcement as secondary sanctions (Ruys, 2019).

[65] The EU, like the US, also implemented the UN sanctions against Iran with its own additional extraterritorial measures. For greater detail on EU sanctions, see Cilizoglu and Bapat (2020), Dawidowicz (2017), Katzman (2016, 61–63), Nevill (2016), Subedi (2021), and White and Abass (2018); O'Connell (2005)

authority from execution (Dupont, 2016, 44; Mouri, 1994).[66] In recent years, the US has also sanctioned the central banks of Russia and Venezuela as well. But sanctions against a country's central bank violate Article VIII(2)(a) of the IMF Agreement, which provides that no IMF member "shall, without the approval of the Fund, impose restrictions on the making of payments and transfers for current international transactions."[67]

Third, as Dupont (2016, 65) points out, whether the US or the EU qualifies as an "injured" state or international organization, entitled to take countermeasures against Iran, may be dubious, and the sanctioning measures undertaken by such unilateral sanctioners against Iran also may not *prima facie* comply with the requirement of proportionality as envisaged by the principle of countermeasures. Moreover, the availability of a recourse by states (or a regional organization) to countermeasures in situations in which the UNSC has already taken action under Chapter VII may be questionable, as such unilateral countermeasures may have a negative impact on the coherence of the collective security system and performance in good faith of international treaty provisions.[68]

Multilateral Sanctions

Lastly, multilateral sanctions against Iran were first adopted by UNSC Resolution 1737, which imposed a worldwide trade embargo against Iran for its alleged pursuance of nuclear programs. It is not disputable that Article 41 of the UN Charter (Chapter VII) grants monopoly rights to the UNSC to adopt and enforce such multilateral sanctions in order to maintain international peace and security.[69] Also,

[66] See UN Convention on Jurisdictional Immunities of States and their Property, UNGA Resolution 59/38 (December 2, 2004). UN Doc A/RES/59/38, Art 21(1)(c). As of April 2019, the Convention was ratified by 22, while 30 ratifications are needed for the Convention to enter into force per Article 30 of the Convention. But nonetheless the Convention has proved to be influential on the development of the law of state immunity, and some of its provisions have already been codified as customary international law by international and national courts. Also, reference to the Convention has become routine in proceedings involving issues of state immunity.

[67] See the Articles of Agreement of the International Monetary Fund, adopted at the United Nations Monetary and Financial Conference, Bretton Woods, New Hampshire, on July 22, 1944. Also see Crozet and Hinz (2020).

[68] Also, referring to the EU's freezing of the assets of Iran's Central Bank in January 2012, in response to Iran's apparent failure of compliance with its obligations under the IAEA-Iran Safeguards Agreement, Dawidowicz (2017) maintains that it was doubtful whether Iran actually committed any breach, and thus, the EU lacked standing to take such countermeasures; and even in the case that any such violation had actually occurred, only a bilateral countermeasure, based on Article 42(b)(ii) ARSIWA, could be justified. See also ILC (2001) and Treves (2005).

[69] Article 41 of UN Charter states:

> The Security Council may decide what measures not involving the use of armed force are to be employed to give effect to its decisions, and it may call upon the Members of the United Nations to apply such measures. These may include complete or partial interruption of economic relations and of rail, sea, air, postal, telegraphic, radio, and other means of communication, and the severance of diplomatic relations.

Article 25 of the UN Charter makes it obligatory for all member states to implement UNSC resolutions, adopted under Chapter VII, in domestic jurisdictions. The world community granted the UNSC such monopoly rights because it can induce cooperation among the sanctioners to exert greater coercive power on the target (Drezner, 2011, 75).

While the UNSC's right and responsibility to adopt and enforce multilateral sanctions cannot be questioned, questions however can be raised when the multilateral sanctions imposed by the UNSC contradict and impede the rights and privileges granted to the member states by the UN Charter, international human rights laws, international humanitarian laws, and other international customs and conventions.[70]

V CONCLUDING REMARKS

Iran has been under US sanctions for more than four decades, and the measures have been much wider and deeper than those of the UN and the EU. Barring a brief respite under the JCPOA during 2015–2017, when some but not all restrictions were relaxed, the US sanctions regime covers almost all sectors of the Iranian economy: banking and finance, investment and credit, oil and petroleum, shipping and transportation, and arms and military equipment. The range and scope of US sanctions against Iran has thus been very aggressive as well as comprehensive, despite the global community apparently having abandoned comprehensive sanctions since the Iraqi debacle in the 1990s.

There have been divergent views and analyses whether the sanctions against Iran have been effective. Some claim that the sanctions imposed in the aftermath of the 1980 hostage crisis, such as freezing of assets, were effective as they forced Iran to release the hostages (Hufbauer, 2007, 48; Lowenfeld, 2003; Smith et al., 2019); some believe that the goals of the sanctions regimes were achieved as they succeeded in changing, weakening, or containing the Iranian regime (O'Sullivan, 2003, 75);[71] and there are others who claim that the sanctions campaigns, especially those targeted to Iran's oil and financial sectors, were effective as they made Iran come to the negotiating table and eventually agree to the terms of JCPOA (Bazoobandi, 2015; Cilizoglu and Bopat, 2020; Van Bergeijk, 2015).

The Trump Administration, obviously, viewed the sanctions against Iran as having failed to achieve the intended goals. While withdrawing from the JCPOA in 2017, President Trump claimed that the deal was inadequate to force Iran to abandon its nuclear ambitions and prevent it from supporting international terrorism. This implies

[70] The theoretical implications of these laws and conventions have been explored in Chapters 1 and 2, and their empirical implications are explored in the context of sanctions on Iraq (Chapter 7), Cuba (Chapter 8), and Venezuela (Chapter 9).

[71] O'Sullivan (2003, 75) maintains that at any time since the Iranian revolution, the US would have been pleased to see the end of the Islamic regime in Tehran, but overthrowing the Iranian government, or regime change in Iran, was never an explicit goal of US sanctions.

that the US goals of sanctions regimes against Iran have not yet been achieved. On the other hand, Secretary of State Mike Pompeo asserted in 2018 that with "the maximum pressure campaign" of the Trump Administration, Iran would "be battling to keep its economy alive." Thus, if the success of the sanctions is measured in terms of deliberately inflicting pain on the Iranian population, there is no dearth of evidence that the sanctions have inflicted huge pain on the Iranian population.

The sanctions regimes have indeed inflicted devastating and debilitating pain on the Iranian economy and population. Over the decades, economic growth faltered, unemployment and inflation soared, severe economic and financial isolation bred inefficiency and corruption, and an extremely unhealthy domestic economic environment, such as overwhelming reliance on oil revenues for foreign exchange, insufficient economic diversification, uncompetitive subsidized industries, regressive tax regimes, marginalization of the private sector, the prioritization of Shia ideology over national economic interests all but crippled the economy (Ghadar and Sobhani, 2011; Kirkham, 2022).

Finally, from the legal perspective, international law allows an injured state to adopt unilateral countermeasures against a state for committing an internationally wrongful act, but questions can be raised whether the US and the EU can legitimately claim to be states "injured" by the alleged wrongful act of Iran; whether unilateral sanctioning measures adopted against Iran comply with the requirements of necessity and proportionality doctrines as envisaged by the international law of countermeasures; whether the built-in extraterritorial application of many of the unilateral sanctions crosses the bounds of legal jurisdiction and encroaches upon the sovereign rights of other nations; whether the unilateral sanctions involve extreme economic or political coercion that endangers the territorial integrity or political independence of Iran and whether they subordinate Iran's sovereign rights or independence; whether such unilateral sanctions undermine UNSC, when it has already taken Chapter VII actions addressing the same wrongful act; and whether the unilateral sanctions conform to the UN Charter, and other international laws and conventions pertaining to human rights, humanitarian rights, right to development, and safety of women and children. Similarly, questions may also be raised whether multilateral sanctions imposed by the UNSC contradict or impede the rights and privileges of Iranians granted by the UN Charter, international human rights laws, international humanitarian laws, and other international laws and conventions.

Appendix 6.1

MAJOR LEGISLATION AND PRESIDENTIAL EXECUTIVE ORDERS PERTAINING TO SANCTIONS AGAINST IRAN, 1979–2023

The US has designated numerous Iranian individuals and government and non-government entities for their involvement in nuclear proliferation, ballistic missile development, support for terrorist groups, and human rights abuses. This time-line summarizes the major presidential Executive Orders (EOs) and Congressional legislation under which those sanctions were imposed.

Nov. 14, 1979. EO-12170 froze $12 billion in Iranian assets and imposed an import ban, in response to the seizure of the US Embassy in Tehran.

April, 1980. President Carter banned all commerce and travel between Iran and the US, except for humanitarian aid.

Jan. 19, 1981. As a result of the Algiers Accord, the US lifted sanctions on Iran by unblocking most Iranian assets under US jurisdiction and lifting the trade embargo.

Jan. 1984. The US designated Iran a state sponsor of terrorism, prohibited arms-related exports and sales, restricted export of dual-use items, and banned most forms of economic assistance to Iran.

1987. The US designated Iran a major narcotics-trafficking country.

Oct. 29, 1987. The US prohibited nearly all imports from Iran in response to its support for terrorism.

1992. The Congress passed the Iran–Iraq Non-Proliferation Act, which tightened exports to Iran, banned the sale of items on the USML, suspended dual-use technical exchange agreements, and ended any economic aid to Iran. The 1996 amendment of the Act requires mandatory sanctions against any government helping Iran to acquire weapons of mass destruction.

March 15, 1995. EO 12957 prohibited any US involvement in the development of the Iranian petroleum industry.

May 6, 1995. The US banned virtually all economic transactions with Iran.

April, 1996. The Congress enacted the Antiterrorism and Effective Death Penalty Act, which prohibits financial dealings with Iran and prohibits aid to countries providing Iran with military assistance.

Aug. 5, 1996. The Congress passed the Iran–Libya Sanctions Act, which imposed penalties against foreign firms making substantial investments (more than $20 million) in Iranian oil and gas development.

Aug. 19, 1997. EO 13059 further restricted US exports to third countries when the goods are destined for reexport to Iran, and bans virtually all trade and investment activities with Iran.

July, 1998. The US imposed sanctions on 10 Russian entities for their alleged involvement in Iran's missile development.

Dec. 1998. Iran was removed from the US list of major narcotic-producing countries.

April, 1999. The US allowed exports of food and medicine to Iran, Libya, and Sudan.

Sept. 1999. The State Department designated Iran as a serious violator of religious freedom.

March 14, 2000. The Congress passed the Iran Nonproliferation Act, which tightened controls on Iran's ability to acquire weapons technology by prohibiting the export of goods on the banned list to any foreign entity.

March 17, 2000. The US announced the lifting of US sanctions on some of Iran's non-oil exports, including carpets, caviar, and pistachios.

Jan. 2001. The US imposed sanctions on a North Korean company for providing Iran with missile parts.

June, 2001. The US imposed sanctions on a North Korean company and two Chinese companies for providing Iran with missile parts and chemical weapons components.

Aug. 3, 2001. The US Congress reauthorized the Iran–Libya Sanctions Act for another five years.

Sept. 23, 2001. EO 13224 imposed sanctions on entities accused of supporting Iran's acts of terrorism.

Jan. 29, 2002. President Bush, in his State of the Union address, branded Iran, Iraq, and North Korea as the "axis of evil."

May 9, 2002. The US imposed sanctions on several firms from Moldova, Armenia, and China for selling weapons-related goods to Iran.

June 28, 2005. EO 13382 imposed sanctions on entities accused of supporting Iran's nuclear proliferation and missile-related activities.

July 1, 2010. The Congress passed the Comprehensive Iran Sanctions, Accountability, and Divestment Act and amended the Iran Sanctions Act of 1996.

Sept. 29, 2010. EO 13553 imposed sanctions on Iranian officials responsible for serious human rights abuses.

May 23, 2011. EO 13574 imposed further sanctions on entities under the Iran Sanctions Act of 1996.

Nov. 21, 2011. EO 13590 imposed sanctions on persons involved in certain activities in Iran's energy and petrochemical sectors.

Dec. 31, 2011. Section 1245 of the National Defense Authorization Act for fiscal year 2012 imposed unilateral sanctions against the Central Bank of Iran.

Feb. 6, 2012. EO 13599 blocked the property of the Government of Iran and all Iranian financial institutions.

April 23, 2012. EO 13606 blocked the property and suspended the entry into the US of certain persons involved in grave human rights abuses via information technology.

May 1, 2012. EO 13608 prohibited certain transactions with and suspended entry into the US of Iran sanctions evaders.

July 30, 2012. EO 13622 and the Iran Threat Reduction and Syria Human Rights Act, that builds on Section 1245 of the National Defense Authorization Act for fiscal year 2012, imposed sanctions on private or public entities for knowingly conducting transactions for the acquisition of Iranian oil.

Aug. 1, 2012. The Congress passed the Iran Sanctions, Accountability, and Human Rights Act of 2012 (H.R. 1905), targeting companies conducting business with Iran's national oil company and tanker fleet, such as insurers and shippers.

Oct. 9, 2012. EO 13628 imposed certain sanctions set forth in EO 13622 and added additional sanctions on Iran.

June 3, 2013. EO 13645 prohibited certain transactions related to the Iranian currency (*rial*), automotive sector, and persons that materially assist Iranian persons on the list of Specially Designated Nationals and Blocked Persons as well as certain persons whose property and interests in property were blocked.

Aug. 6, 2018. EO 13846 reimposed sanctions lifted as part of the 2015 nuclear deal or Joint Comprehensive Plan of Action (JCPOA).

May 8, 2019. EO 13871 blocked transactions with Iran's iron, steel, aluminum, and copper sectors.

June 24, 2019. EO 13876 imposed sanctions on Supreme Leader Ayatollah Ali Khamenei and his office.

Jan. 10, 2020. EO 13902 blocked transactions with and barred entry to the US financial system for any individual or entity operating in the construction, manufacturing, textiles, or mining sectors of the Iranian economy.

Sept. 21, 2020. EO 13949 imposed secondary sanctions on individuals supporting Iran's nuclear, missile and conventional arms-related activities.

Sources: Author's compilation from various sources, principally from the websites of the White House, and the US Departments of State, Commerce and Treasury.

REFERENCES

Aldrich, G. 1996. *The Jurisprudence of the Iran-United States Claims Tribunal: An Analysis of the Decisions of the Tribunal*. 1st ed. Oxford: Clarendon Press.

Alerassool, M. 1993. The Algiers Accords: The Way the Crisis Was Resolved. In *Freezing Assets. International Political Economy Series*, pp. 105–123. London: Palgrave Macmillan.

Allen-Ebrahimian, B. 2017. 64 Years Later, CIA Finally Releases Details of Iranian Coup. *Foreign Affairs*, June 20. Available at: foreignpolicy.com/2017/06/20/64-years-later-cia-finally-releases-details-of-iranian-coup-iran-tehran-oil/.

Annacker, S. 1994. The Legal Régime of "Erga Omnes" Obligations in International Law, *Austrian Journal of Public International Law*, 46 (1994):131–154.

Arangio-Ruiz, G. 1991. Third Report on State Responsibility. UN Doc A/CN.4/440 and Add 1, II(1) *ILC Year Book*.

Arnold, A. 2015. *Current State of Global Sanctions against Iran*. Harvard University: Harvard Belfer Center. It is online publication. Available at: www.belfercenter.org/publication/current-state-global-sanctions-against-iran-0.

Asada, M. 2020. Definition and Legal Justification of Sanctions. In M. Asada (ed.), *Economic Sanctions in International Law and Practice*, pp. 3–23. London: Routledge.

Askari, H. et al. 2003. *Case Studies of U.S. Economic Sanctions: The Chinese, Cuban, and Iranian Experience*. Westport, CT: Praeger.

Bazoobandi, S. 2015. Sanctions against Iran: Winners and Losers. In I. Dreyer, and J. Luengo-Cabrera (eds.), *On Target? EU Sanctions as Security Policy Tools*, pp. 57–66. Paris: EU Institute for Security Studies.

Beckhy, P. 2018. Sanctions and the Blurred Boundaries of International Economic Law. *Missouri Law Review*, 83(1):1–38.

Bergeijk, P. 2015. Sanctions against Iran – A Preliminary Economic Assessment. In I. Dreyer, and J. Luengo-Cabrera (eds.), *On Target? EU Sanctions as Security Policy Tools*, pp. 49–56. Paris: EU Institute for Security Studies.

Breen, E. 2021. Corporations and US Economic Sanctions: the Dangers of Overcompliance. In C. Beucillon (ed.), *Research Handbook on Unilateral and Extraterritorial Sanctions*, pp. 256–269. Cheltenham, UK: Edward Elgar.

Brower, C. 1987. Current Developments in the Law of Expropriation and Compensation: A Preliminary Survey of Awards of the Iran-United States Claims Tribunal. *The International Lawyer*, 21(3):639–669.

Brown, P. 2020. *Oil Market Effects from U.S. Economic Sanctions: Iran, Russia, Venezuela*. Washington, DC: Congressional Research Service.

Carl, N. 2021. Whatever It Takes to End It: Iran's Shift toward More Oppressive Governance. American Enterprise Institute. December 16, 2021. Available at: www.aei.org/research-products/report/whatever-it-takes-to-end-it-irans-shift-toward-more-oppressive-governance/.

Carter, B., and R. Farha. 2013. Overview and Operation of U.S. Financial Sanctions, Including the Example of Iran. *Georgetown Journal of International Law*, 44(3):903–914.

Christopher, W., and R. Mosk. 2007. The Iranian Hostage Crisis and the Iran-U.S. Claims Tribunal: Implications for International Dispute Resolution and Diplomacy. *Pepperdine Dispute Resolution Law Journal*, 7(2):165–175.

Cilizoglu, M., and N. Bapat. 2020. Economic Coercion and the Problem of Sanctions-Proofing. *Conflict Management and Peace Science*, 37(4):385–408.

Clark, H. 1999. Dealing with US Extraterritorial Sanctions and Foreign Countermeasures. *University of Pennsylvania Journal of International Economic Law*, 20(1):61–96.

Clifton, M., N. Bapat, and Y. Kobayashi. 2014. Threat and Imposition of Economic Sanctions 1945–2005: Updating the TIES Dataset. *Conflict Management and Peace Science*, 31(5):541–558.

Cordesman, A., B. Gold, and C. Coughlin-Schulte. 2014. *Iran: Sanctions, Energy, Arms Control, and Regime Change*. Washington, DC: Center for Strategic & International Studies (CSIS).

Crozet, M., and J. Hinz. 2016. Collateral Damage: The Impact of the Russia Sanctions on Sanctioning Countries' Exports. CEPII Working Paper. Available at: www.cepii.fr/PDF_PUB/wp/2016/wp2016-16.pdf.

Crozet, M., and J. Hinz. 2020. Friendly Fire: The Trade Impact of the Russia Sanctions and Counter-Sanctions. *Economic Policy*, 35(101):97–146.

Damrosch, L. 2019. The Legitimacy of Economic Sanctions as Countermeasures for Wrongful Acts. *Ecology Law Quarterly*, 46:95–111.

Dawidowicz, M. 2017. *Third-Party Countermeasures in International Law*. Cambridge: Cambridge University Press.

Dreyer, I., and J. Luengo-Cabrera (Eds.). 2015. *On Target? EU Sanctions as Security Policy Tools*, pp. 57–66. Paris: EU Institute for Security Studies.

Drezner, D. 2011. Sanctions Sometimes Smart: Targeted Sanctions in Theory and Practice. *International Studies Review*, 13(1):96–108.

Dupont, P. 2016. Unilateral European Sanctions as Countermeasures: The Case of the EU Measures against Iran. In M. Happold, and P. Eden (eds.), *Economic Sanctions and International Law: Law and Practice*, pp. 37–65. Oxford: Bloomsbury Publishing.

Ehteshami, A. 2022. Iran and the United States: Four Decades of Tension and Missed Opportunities. Available at: www.iemed.org/publication/iran-and-the-united-states-four-decades-of-tension-and-missed-opportunities/.

Gal, Y., and Y. Minzili. 2011. The Economic Impact of International Sanctions on Iran. Lauder School of Government, Diplomacy & Strategy: Herzliya, Israel.

Gerecht, R. 2018. The Iran Deal Is Strategically and Morally Absurd. *Atlantic Council*, May 4, 2018.

Ghadar, F., and R. Sobhani. 2011. "It's the Economy, Stupid." Trials and Tribulations of the Iranian Economy. *Harvard International Review*, 33(1):22–26.

Goldman, Z., and A. Lindblom. 2021. The US Position and Practice with Regards to Unilateral and Extraterritorial Sanctions: Reimagining the US Sanctions Regime in a World of Advanced Technology. In C. Beucillon (ed.), *Research Handbook on Unilateral and Extraterritorial Sanctions*, pp. 130–148. Cheltenham, UK: Edward Elgar.

Gowlland-Debbas, V. (Ed.). 2001. *United Nations Sanctions and International Law*. London, Boston: Kluwer Law International.

Haidar, J. 2016. Are Export Sanctions Effective? ERF Policy Brief 18. *Economic Research Forum*. Available at: erf.org.eg/app/uploads/2016/09/PB18.pdf.

Hewitt, K., and R. Nephew. 2019. How the Iran Hostage Crisis Shaped the US Approach to Sanctions. Washington, DC: Brookings Institution, Brookings Papers. March 12, 2019.

Hovell, D. 2019. Unfinished Business of International Law: The Questionable Legality of Autonomous Sanctions. *American Journal of International Law*, 113:140–145.

Hufbauer, G. et al. 2007. *Economic Sanctions Reconsidered: History and Current Policy*. Washington, DC: Patterson Institute for International Economics.

ILC (International Law Commission). 2001. *Articles on the Responsibility of States for Internationally Wrongful Acts (ARSIWA)*. New York: United Nations.

Jazairy, I. 2019. Unilateral Economic Sanctions, International Law, and Human Rights. *Ethics & International Affairs*, 33(3):291–302.

Joyner, D. 2012. *Arms Control Law, EU Courts, and Iran Sanctions*. London: Routledge.

Joyner, D. 2015. International Legal Limits on the Ability of States to Lawfully Impose International Economic/Financial Sanctions. In A. Marossi, and M. Bassett (eds.), *Economic Sanctions under International Law: Unilateralism, Multilateralism, Legitimacy and Consequences*, pp. 83–93. London: Springer.

Joyner, D. 2017. UN Counter-Proliferation Sanctions and International Law. In L. Herik (ed.), *Research Handbook on UN Sanctions and International Law*, pp. 110–121. Cheltenham, UK: Edward Elgar.

Katzman, K. 2016. *Iran Sanctions*. Report RS20871. Washington, DC: Congressional Research Services.

Katzman, K. 2022. Iran Sanctions. Congressional Research Services. Report No. RS20871. Washington, DC.

Kirkham, K. 2022. *The Political Economy of Sanctions: Resilience and Transformation in Russia and Iran*. London: Springer.

Knox, J. 2010. A Presumption against Extra-Jurisdictionality. *American Journal of International Law*, 104(3):351–396.

Lowe, V., and A. Tzanakopoulos. 2012. Economic Warfare. In R. Wolfrum (ed.), *Max Planck Encyclopedia of Public International Law*. Oxford: Oxford University Press. Available at: opil.ouplaw.com/display/10.1093/law:epil/9780199231690/law-9780199231690-e292.

Lowenfeld, A. 2003. Trade Controls for Political Ends: Four Perspectives. *Chicago Journal of International Law*, 4(2):354–369.

Mallard, G., and A. Hanson. 2021. Embedded Extraterritoriality: US Judicial Litigation and the Global Banking Surveillance of Digital Money Flows. In C. Beucillon (ed.), *Research*

Handbook on Unilateral and Extraterritorial Sanctions, pp. 270–287. Cheltenham, UK: Edward Elgar.

Massaroni, C. 1982. The United States-Iran Hostage Agreement: A Study in Presidential Powers. *Cornell International Law Journal*, 15(1):150–200.

Meyer, J. 2009. Second Thoughts on Secondary Sanctions. *University of Pennsylvania Journal of International Economic Law*, 30(3):905–934.

Mosk, R. 1987. Lessons from The Hague – An Update on the Iran-United States Claims Tribunal. *Pepperdine Law Review*, 4.

Mouri, A. 1994. Treatment of the Rules of the International Law of Money by the Iran-U.S. Claims Tribunal. *Asian Yearbook of International Law*, 3:71–110.

Nevill, P. 2016. Sanctions and Commercial Law. In M. Happold, and P. Eden (eds.), *Economic Sanctions and International Law: Law and Practice*, pp. 227–254. London: Bloomsbury.

O'Connell, M. 2005. Controlling Countermeasures. In M. Ragazzi (ed.), *International Responsibility Today. Essays in Memory of Oscar Schachter*, pp. 49–62. Leiden: Martinus Nijhoff.

O'Sullivan, M. 2003. *Shrewd Sanctions – Statecraft and State Sponsors of Terrorism.* Washington, DC: Brookings Institution Press.

Orakhelashvili. 2010. Unilateral Interpretation of Security Council Resolutions: UK Practice. *Göttingen Journal of International Law*, 2:823–842.

Pellet, A., and A. Miron. 2024. Sanctions. In R. Wolfrum (ed.), *The Max Planck Encyclopedia of Public International Law, Vol. IX.* Oxford: Oxford University Press. Available at: opil .ouplaw.com/display/10.1093/law:epil/9780199231690/law-9780199231690-e984.

Preeg, E. 1999. Feeling Good or Doing Good with Sanctions. Working Paper. Center for Strategic and International Studies (CSIS), Washington, DC.

Prezas, I. 2021. From Targeted States to Affected Populations: Exploring Accountability for the Negative Impact of Comprehensive gunilateraanctions on Human Rights. In C. Beucillon (ed.), *Research Handbook on Unilateral and Extraterritorial Sanctions*, pp. 385–404. Cheltenham, UK: Edward Elgar.

Rathbone, M. et al. 2013. Sanctions, Sanctions Everywhere: Forging a Path through Complex Transnational Sanctions Laws. *Georgetown Journal of Law*, 44:1056–1094.

Reisman, W., and D. Stevick. 1998. The Applicability of International Law Standards to United Nations Economic Sanctions Programs. *European Journal of International Law* 9:86–141.

Rome, H. 2022. *Iran's Revolution at 43: The Economy*. Washington, DC: United States Institute of Peace.

Ronzitti, N. 2016. Sanctions as Instruments of Coercive Diplomacy: An International Law Perspective. In N. Ronzitti (ed.), *Coercive Diplomacy, Sanctions and International Law*, pp. 1–32. Leiden: Brill.

Ruys, T. 2019. Immunity, Inviolability and Countermeasures – A Closer Look at Non-UN Targeted Sanctions. In T. Ruys, N. Angelet, and L. Ferro (eds.), *The Cambridge Handbook on Immunities and International Law*, pp. 670–710. Cambridge: Cambridge University Press.

Ryngaert, C. 2008. Extraterritorial Export Controls (Secondary Boycotts). *Chinese Journal of International Law*, 7(3):625–658.

Sicilianos, L.-A. 2010. Countermeasures in Response to Grave Violations of Obligations Owed to the International Community. In J. Crawford, A. Pellet, and S. Olleson (eds.), *The Law of International Responsibility*, pp. 1137–1141. Oxford: Oxford University Press.

Sloan, J., and G. Hernández. 2013. The Role of the International Court of Justice in the Development of the Institutional Law of the United Nations. In C. Tams, and J. Sloan (eds.), *The Development of International Law by the International Court of Justice*, pp. 197–333. Oxford: Oxford University Press.

Smith, A., S. Connor, and R. Roeder. 2019. *U.S., EU, and UN Sanctions: Navigating the Divide for International Business*. Arlington, VA: Bloomberg Law.

Solingen, E. (Ed.). 2012. *Sanctions, Statecraft, and Nuclear Proliferation: Sanctions, Inducements, and Collective Action*. Cambridge: Cambridge University Press.

Subedi, S. 2021. The Status of Unilateral Sanctions in International Law. In S. Subedi (ed.), *Unilateral Sanctions in International Law*, pp. 19–60. Oxford: Hart Publishing.

Suzuki, K. 2020. The Role and Effectiveness of UN Sanctions. In M. Asada (ed.), *Economic Sanctions in International Law and Practice*, pp. 178–199. London: Routledge.

Treves, T. 2005. The International Law Commission's Articles on State Responsibility and the Settlement of Disputes. In M. Ragazzi (ed.), *International Responsibility Today. Essays in Memory of Oscar Schachter*, pp. 223–234. Leiden: Martinus Nijhoff.

US Congress. 1987. *Report of the Congressional Committees Investigating the Iran-Contra Affair: With Supplemental, Minority, and Additional Views*. Washington, DC: US Congress, Congressional Historical Documents and Reports. November, 1987.

Weed, M. 2001. Authorization for Use of Military Force: Issues Concerning Its Continued Application. CRS Report R43983. Congressional Research Services, Washington, DC.

White, N. and A. Abass. 2018. Countermeasures and Sanctions. In M. Evans (ed.), *International Law*. 5th ed., pp. 521–547. Oxford: Oxford University Press.

Wilbur, R. 1990. The Iran-Iraq War: An Analysis of the Cease-Fire. *The Fletcher Forum of World Affairs*, 14(1):111–127.

Wood, M. 1998. The Interpretation of Security Council Resolutions. *Max Planck Yearbook of United Nations Law*, 2(73):86–87.

7

US and Multilateral Sanctions Regimes against the Republic of Iraq

I INTRODUCTION

Immediately after Saddam Hossain invaded the neighboring sovereign state of Kuwait on August 2, 1990 and annexed it as a province of Iraq,[1] the UNSC adopted a series of sweeping resolutions condemning Iraq's aggression, demanding immediate withdrawal of Iraqi troops from the territory of Kuwait, and prohibiting UN members from engaging in any trade and financial transactions with Iraq.[2] Over the course of the next 12 years (1990–2002), the UNSC adopted more than 50 resolutions,[3] while scores of countries, including the US, the UK, the then European Community, Japan, and Australia also joined the campaign with their own additional unilateral sanctions. Iraq thus came under both multilateral and unilateral sanctions regimes simultaneously, and bore the brunt of vastly institutionalized comprehensive sanctions regimes for more than a decade. The resultant humanitarian disaster and physical destruction made the Iraqi sanctions episodes the most devastating of all in modern history.

1 Saddam invaded Kuwait in July 1990, apparently due to a conflict over oil exports. Available records suggest that as the falling price of oil exacerbated Iraq's economic plight, Iraq accused Kuwait and the UAE of deliberately exceeding their OPEC production quotas, thereby creating a glut in the global oil market. Iraq also accused Kuwait of establishing military and police posts and oil installations inside Iraqi territory and siphoning oil from the Rumaila oil field along the borders. After diplomatic negotiations failed to end the standoff, Iraq annexed Kuwait on August 2, 1990, declaring it the 19th province of Iraq (Ismael and Ismael, 2015, 151; Juster, 2000, 59; Scherrer, 2011, 27).

2 Iraq was the third country to be placed under comprehensive sanctions by the UN. Previously, the UNSC imposed comprehensive sanctions against Rhodesia in 1966 and South Africa in 1977 (Dodge, 2010; Reisman and Stevick, 1998).

3 The major UNSC Resolutions on Iraq were UNSC Res. 660 (August 2, 1990); 661 (August 9, 1990); 665 (August 18, 1990); 666 (September 13, 1990); 678 (November 29, 1990); 686 (March 2, 1991); 687 (April 3, 1991); 688 (April 5, 1991); 706 (August 15, 1991); 712 (September 19, 1991); 715 (October 11, 1991); 778 (October 2, 1992); 986 (April 14, 1995); 1051 (Match 27, 1996); 1137 (November 12, 1997); 1284 (December 17, 1999); 1302 (June 8, 2000); 1441 (November 8, 2002); 1443 (November 25, 2002); 1483 (May 22, 2003); and 1518 (November 24, 2003). Source: Based on UNSC website: www.un.org/securitycouncil/sanctions/information.

Throughout the 1990s, and up to April 9, 2003, when Saddam's regime collapsed, the US Congress also passed half-a-dozen statutes, and US presidents issued scores of Executive Orders (EOs), to force Iraq to withdraw from Kuwait, to secure reparation of injuries unlawfully inflicted by Iraq, to ensure the elimination of Iraq's chemical, biological, and non-existent nuclear weapons of mass destruction (WMD), and to bring the country into compliance with both multilateral and unilateral sanctions.[4] Throughout the period, as explained below, the US not only played the most crucial role in enforcing UNSC the mandated sanctions regime against Iraq, but also actively manipulated the UNSC in adopting increasingly aggressive sanctions regimes against Iraq to suit its own foreign policy objectives, which also included overthrowing the regime of Saddam Hossain.

Numerous studies indicate that the comprehensive sanctions regimes against Iraq were enforced ruthlessly, with not much consideration given to human lives, human suffering, or human rights. The country was almost totally isolated from the rest of the world; cut off from the global credit and financial systems; its infrastructure reduced to rubble; at least one million people, mostly children and infants, lost their lives; and many described the resultant horrors as a "humanitarian disaster," a "genocide," mandated by global community (Biehler, 2003, 16; Gordon, 2010; Joyner, 2017, 3; Mulder, 2022).

The sanctions regimes against Iraq were so devastating that not only the UN but also many unilateral sanctioners have since resolved not to impose such comprehensive sanctions ever again on any nation, and have switched to what is called smart or targeted sanctions (Brzoska, 2003, 2015; Drezner, 2011). Over the years, the Iraqi debacle has also received widespread scrutiny – the literature on the ferocity and magnitude, human costs and human rights, and the legitimacy and legality of the sanctions regimes has indeed been monumental.[5]

This chapter examines the sanctions regimes imposed against Iraq during 1990–2003 with a brief reference to post-invasion Iraq up to March 2023.[6] The chapter is organized as follows: Section II explains the evolution of multilateral sanctions regimes under the auspices of the UN; Section III focuses on unilateral sanctions

[4] Major EOs issued by US presidents against Iraq included: EO 13668 (May 27, 2014); 13438 (July 17, 2007); 13364 (November 29, 2004); 13350 (July 30, 2004); 13315 (August 29, 2003); 13303 (May 22, 2003), and 13290 (March 20, 2003). Source: US Department of Treasury website: ofac.treasury.gov/sanctions-programs-and-country-information/iraq-related-sanctions.

[5] Some of the important works include: Alnasrawi (2001); Ballard (2010); Biehler (2003); Brozska (2003, 2015); Butt and Butt (2014); Drezner (2011); Falk (2003); Garfield (1999, 2011); Gordon (2010); Hoskins (1997); Hufbauer (2007); Ismael and Ismael (2004, 2015); Joyner (2003, 2017); Juster (2000); Lopez and Cortright (2004); Marr (2004); Mulder (2022); O'Sullivan (2003); Pellett (2011); Reisman and Stevick (1998); Scherrer (2011); Sponeck (2006); UNICEF (1995, 1998, 1999).

[6] Iraq had been under US sanctions previously – in 1979, the Carter Administration designated Iraq as a "state sponsor of terrorism" for its support of the Palestine Liberation Organization. The designation was lifted three years later, in 1982, during the Iran–Iraq war, when the US found it in its strategic interest to side with Iraq, apparently to prevent neighboring Iran from gaining regional influence and expand Soviet dominance in the region (Sciolino, 1991, 142).

regimes adopted by the US and the eventual toppling of the regime of Saddam Hossain in 2003; Section IV examines the governance of post-Saddam Iraq by the Coalition Provisional Authority; Section V examines the overall impact of the multilateral and unilateral sanctions regimes on the Iraqi economy and population during the phase of sanctions and post-invasion Iraq; Section VI examines the Iraqi episode of sanctions from legal perspectives; and Section VII concludes the chapter.

II UN SANCTIONS AGAINST IRAQ

Sanctions against Iraq began immediately after Saddam Hossain annexed Kuwait, and then progressed swiftly and decisively. On August 2, 1990, within hours of Iraq's annexation of Kuwait, acting under Articles 39 and 40 of the UN Charter, the UNSC adopted Resolution 660, condemning the occupation as a serious "breach of international peace and security," demanding immediate and unconditional withdrawal of Iraqi forces from Kuwait,[7] and at the same time, emphasizing "intensive negotiations" between Iraq and Kuwait for immediate resolution of their differences under the auspices of the Arab League.[8]

Iraq's non-compliance with the resolution set the UNSC on a course of imposing dozens of sanctions regimes against the country in a matter of one decade. On August 9, 1990, the UNSC adopted Resolution 661 urging all UN members to prevent imports and exports of commodities and products to and from Iraq and Kuwait, and urged them not to recognize any regime set up in Kuwait by Iraq, demanding again "immediate and unconditional withdrawal of the Iraqi army from the Kuwaiti territorial space" in accordance with Resolution 660. Resolution 661 also established the 661 Committee to monitor progress and implementation of the sanctions imposed on Iraq by the UN.

As Iraq still failed to comply with the UN demands, the UNSC adopted Resolution 665 on August 18, 1990 authorizing a naval blockade to enforce the trade embargo against Iraq imposed by Resolution 661. The resolution authorized all UN members to halt all inward and outward maritime shipping (to and from Iraq and Kuwait) in order to inspect and verify their cargoes and destinations, and to ensure compliance with the provisions of Resolution 661, "with maximum use of political and diplomatic measures."[9]

7 UNSC Resolution 660 was adopted by 14 votes – one non-permanent member of the UNSC, Yemen, abstained.

8 Formerly known as the League of Arab States (LAS), it was founded in Cairo in 1945 with six members – Egypt, Iraq, Transjordan (renamed Jordan in 1949), Lebanon, Saudi Arabia, and Syria. Yemen joined the Arab League later in the same year. The League currently has 22 members from northern, western, and eastern Africa, and western Asia.

9 The embargo imposed by UNSC Resolution 661, however, exempted imports for "strictly medical or humanitarian purposes, and, in humanitarian circumstances, foodstuffs." Subsequently, UNSC Resolution 666, adopted on September 13, 1990, addressed the "urgent humanitarian needs" to provide foodstuffs to Iraq in association with the International Committee of the Red Cross (ICRC) or

Following Iraq's refusal to withdraw from Kuwait's territory and to comply with other demands envisaged by previous resolutions, the UNSC adopted Resolution 678 on November 29, 1990, as an ultimatum to Iraq – "one final opportunity, as a pause of goodwill" – to withdraw from Kuwait by January 15, 1991. The Resolution also authorized UN members to "use all necessary means" to uphold and implement Resolution 660 and all subsequent resolutions to restore international peace and security in the area.[10] Resolution 678 was supported by 122 of 159 UN members (O'Sullivan, 2003, 107), but some UN members interpreted it as a clear authorization by the UNSC to resort to a military campaign against Iraq, something sanctions were supposed to avert (Lowenfeld, 2003).

Accordingly, on January 17, 1991, the US led a massive military attack against Iraq named "Desert Storm." The campaign marshaled 750,000 troops, of which 540,000 were US personnel, and the rest came from other countries including the UK, France, Germany, the former Soviet Union, Japan, Egypt, and Saudi Arabia. Under the 1,100-hour military campaign, over 250,000 sorties were flown and hundreds of Iraqi targets were bombed, including Iraq's military establishments and civilian infrastructure. The destruction was so massive that a UN envoy described it as a "near-apocalyptic" operation which relegated Iraq to a "pre-industrial age" (Alnasrawi, 2001; Chesterman and Malone, 2016).[11]

After the restoration of Kuwait's independence, on March 2, 1991, the UNSC adopted Resolution 686, demanding Iraq's immediate rescindment of actions purporting to the annexation of Kuwait, cessation of all hostilities toward coalition members, release of all detainees and prisoners, return of all Kuwaiti property seized, acceptance of liability for Kuwaiti damages, and implementation of all 12 UNSC resolutions that had been adopted against Iraq.[12]

The UNSC adopted Resolution 687 on April 3, 1991, imposing a series of stringent conditions to lift its sanctions against Iraq, which included: (a) formal recognition of the inviolability of the international boundaries of Kuwait; (b) stationing of a UN Observer Unit to monitor the borders and the establishment of a demilitarized zone; (c) destruction of deadly weapons capability, reaffirmation of the Geneva Protocol for the prohibition of chemical weapons, and the Treaty on Non-Proliferation of Nuclear Weapons; (d) return of all Kuwaiti property; (e) establishment of a Compensation Fund and a Commission to pay

other appropriate humanitarian agencies, and exports and delivery of medical supplies under the strict supervision of the government of the exporting state or by appropriate humanitarian agencies.

[10] Cuba, a member of the UNSC at the time, opposed the Resolution by stating, "We are asked to approve specific sanctions that have already been implemented unilaterally by the principal developed Powers of the world": UN Doc. S/PV.2933 (August 6, 1990), 38 (Cuba).

[11] It was indeed one of the most destructive bombing campaigns since WWII, with more explosives discharged than were dropped on Europe during the entire period of that war (Ismael and Ismael, 2004, 93–94). For greater detail on the destruction, see also Gordon (2002, 2010), Hindawi (2017), Joyner (2017), and White (2018).

[12] See UNSC Resolution 686, UN Doc. S/RES/686 (1991).

compensation for losses, damages, and injuries to foreign governments and nationals; (f) the destruction of Iraqi ballistic missiles with a range greater than 150 kilometers; and (h) prohibiting Iraqi support of international terrorism or harboring terrorists within Iraq.[13]

Resolution 687 also signified several far-reaching stipulations and assumptions about the Iraqi sanctions episode. First, the legal basis for the UN sanctions regime against Iraq shifted away from wrongful international behavior or a breach of international peace to the presence of persistence threat to international peace and security due to Iraq's wrongly alleged possession of WMD (Farrall and Rubenstein, 2009, 262–263).[14] Among the three countries against which the UNSC adopted sanctions on the grounds of proliferation of WMD since WWII – North Korea had nuclear power, Iran attempted to own nuclear power, Libya planned to build nuclear capability – but Iraq never had nuclear power (Joyner, 2015).[15]

Second, Resolution 687 warned Iraq that a full trade embargo against the country would remain in place until all UNSC demands were fully satisfied, and that the embargo on the purchase of Iraqi oil would be lifted only after the country had completed all actions required by the cease-fire resolution. Resolution 687, however, exempted Iraqi imports of goods for humanitarian purposes from the embargo, and placed no specific limitations on Iraq's conventional army, except in respect to missiles of certain range, as described above.

UNSC Resolution 688, adopted on April 5, 1991, was targeted at the alleged repression by the regime of Saddam Hossain of the civilian population in the Kurdish-populated areas in northern Iraq. Describing such repression as "a threat to peace and security in the region," the resolution demanded immediate cessation of such repression and access to international humanitarian organizations to observe the situation. The resolution also appealed to UN members and humanitarian organizations to contribute to humanitarian relief efforts in Iraq, and asked the UN Secretary General to report on the plight of the Iraqi civilian population suffering from the repression.[16]

The subsequent UNSC Resolution 715, adopted in October 1991, created the UN Special Commission (UNSCOM) and entrusted it, as well as the International Atomic Energy Agency (IAEA), to monitor the implementation of Resolution 687, which called for elimination of Iraq's weapon facilities. Specifically, UNSCOM's

[13] See UNSC Resolution 687, UN Doc. S/RES/687 (1991).

[14] Among other conditions, UNSC Resolution 687 specifically mandated that Iraq must "unconditionally agree not to acquire/develop nuclear weapons or nuclear-weapons-usable material or any subsystems or components or any related research, development, support, or manufacturing facilities."

[15] Iraq, however, had a nuclear program in the 1970s when France helped the country to build the Osirak nuclear reactor outside Baghdad and trained Iraqi scientists and technicians to run it. But in 1981, before the plant could become operational, Israeli jets bombed and destroyed it. Subsequently, Saddam Hossain apparently made some clandestine efforts to purchase components for a nuclear program from France, the UK, Germany, Brazil, and Pakistan (Juster, 2000, 53; Sciolino, 1991, 152).

[16] See UNSC Resolution 688, UN Doc. S/RES/688 (1991).

mandate was "to carry out immediate on-site inspections of Iraq's biological, chemical and missile capabilities."[17] Resolution 715 was further reinforced by UNSC Resolution 1051, adopted in March 1996, which demanded Iraq's unconditional cooperation with UNSCOM and the IAEA, in addition to creating a special maritime observation force called the Multinational Interception Force (MIF) to check Iraq's international trade.[18]

Together, UNSC Resolutions 687, 688, 715, and 1051 established a demilitarized zone in Iraq; held Iraq responsible for reparations for the war (including compensation for losses and injuries to foreign governments and nationals during the war); forced Iraq to destroy its defense capabilities; required Iraq to allow the UN and other international humanitarian organizations to monitor its internal law and order; mandated UNSCOM and the IAEA to eliminate Iraq's non-existent nuclear weapon facilities and capabilities; authorized the MIF to monitor Iraq's international trade; and required Iraq to submit to all such international controls, regulations, and mechanisms absolutely unconditionally.

These resolutions thus established an unprecedented international jurisdiction over the domestic spheres of Iraq, tantamount to a "functional occupation and invasion" of the country (Doxey, 1996, 37). Between 1991 and 1995, the UN inspectors apparently uncovered a massive Iraqi program to develop biological and nuclear weapons. In July 1995, Rolf Ekeus, chief of the UN Special Commission for Weapons Inspection, confirmed the elimination of Iraq's chemical and ballistic missile capacity (Doxey, 1996, 39). Thus, the goals of disarming of Iraq, "a high-speed destruction of biological weapons," went so well that by 1997 a large part of Iraq's unauthorized weapons capacity was destroyed (Wallensteen and Staibano, 2005, 7–8).

By then, however, it also became obvious that Iraq possessed no nuclear capabilities (Wallensteen and Staibano, 2005, 7–8). Still, Hans Blix, the chief of the UN Monitoring, Verification and Inspection Commission (UNMOVIC), which replaced UNSCOM in 1999,[19] suspended UN weapons inspections of Iraq, citing Saddam's refusal to cooperate with such efforts.[20] Later, however, Blix admitted that Iraq never had nuclear weapons to begin with. He told the press:

17 UNSCOM was directed by Rolf Ekeus, a Swedish diplomat, during 1991–1997. His successor, Richard Butler, an Australian public servant, held the position until it was dissolved in 1999.

18 See UNSC Resolution 715, UN Doc. S/RES/715 (1996).

19 UNSC Resolution 1284, adopted in December 1999, replaced UNSCOM with UNMOVIC to monitor the elimination of WMD in Iraq. The resolution was adopted with Russia, France, and China abstaining from voting, which prompted Iraq to reject it (Tripp, 2008, 269).

20 Throughout the existence of UNSCOM (1991–1999), the organization accused Iraq of evading and denying access to its unauthorized weapons, while Iraq maintained that UNSCOM was used for espionage purposes and to harass and humiliate the Iraqi government (Falk, 2003, 19). In November 1997, the UNSC adopted Resolution 1137, which imposed travel restrictions on several Iraqi civil and military officials for their alleged non-compliance with the UN inspection team's efforts to uncover Iraq's nuclear and other WMDs. See UNSC Resolution 1137, UN Doc. S/RES/1137 (1997).

"There were about 700 inspections, and in no case did we find weapons of mass destruction … it was like hanging a sign on the door saying 'Beware of the dog' when you don't have a dog."[21]

Oil for Food Program

The Iraqi Oil for Food Program (OFFP) proved to be one of the most controversial parts of the comprehensive sanctions regimes enforced by the UN against Iraq. The program was adopted in the backdrop of one of the most profound human tragedies that occurred in modern times squarely because of the indiscriminate and ill-thought-out sanctions regimes. Numerous studies have documented how, within just two years, the sanctions regimes created massive malnutrition among the children, which led to extremely high rates of infant mortality, and how lack of clean drinking water along with acute shortage of medical supplies gripped the Iraqi population (FAO-WFP, 1993; Gordon, 2010; Joyner, 2015).

The health situation of the Iraqi population became so alarming that as early as 1993 a report by the Food and Agriculture Organization (FAO-WFP, 1993) warned the world community that "a grave humanitarian tragedy" was unfolding in Iraq because of "the recent war and subsequent civil strife, but above all by the continued sanctions since August 1990." The report also noted that the sanctions had already caused "persistent deprivation, severe hunger and malnutrition for a vast majority of the Iraqi population, particularly the vulnerable groups." Similarly, noting chronic hunger, endemic undernutrition, and widespread human suffering, a UNICEF (1995) report claimed that more than one million Iraqis had died, of which 567,000 were children, as a direct consequence of the economic sanctions, and among them were 4,500 children under the age of five who had died each month from hunger and disease alone.

Responding to the global outcry to the humanitarian disaster in Iraq, on April 14, 1995, the UNSC adopted Resolution 986 authorizing "exports of small amounts of Iraqi oil … sufficient to produce a sum not exceeding a total of one billion United States dollars every 90 days," under the supervision of UNSCOM to allow Iraq to import essential foods, medicine, and other primary goods to meet emergency humanitarian needs. Resolution 986 directed UNSCOM to monitor the sale of petroleum and petroleum products via the Kirkuk-Yumurtalik pipeline from Iraq to Turkey, and from the Mina al-Bahr oil terminal, with the assistance of independent inspection agents.[22]

Accordingly, the OFFP was launched in December 1996 to sell $2 billion worth of Iraqi petroleum in six months, and deposit the fund in an escrow account in an international bank chosen by the UN Secretary General. The funds in the escrow

[21] A Swedish diplomat, Hans Blix served as the UN chief weapons inspector for Iraq during 2000–2003. Previously he was head of the IAEA from 1981 to 1997. His interview is available at: newsarchive.berkeley.edu/news/media/releases/2004/03/18_blix.shtml, accessed on March 18, 2023.

[22] See UNSC Resolution 986, UN Doc. S/RES/986 (1995).

account were then spent to finance the export to Iraq of medicine, health supplies, foodstuffs, and materials and supplies for essential civilian needs.[23]

Not all the proceeds of the sale of oil, however, were directed to relieving the suffering of the Iraqi population. Under the formula adopted for the distribution of the proceeds, 30 percent was earmarked for the Gulf War reparations; about 66 percent was allocated to medical supplies and foodstuffs for civilian needs (of which about 15 percent was set aside for the UN Inter-Agency Humanitarian Program operating in Iraq's Kurdish north); and the rest of the proceeds were earmarked for covering the cost of the UN operation and supervision of the oil sale (Bearman, 1996, 163).[24]

In December 1999, UNSC Resolution 1284, which extended the OFFP for another 180 days, lifted the limit on oil sales proceeds, and transferred the approval of the lists of necessary goods for import to the newly created Office of Iraq Program (OIP). As the oil proceeds failed to mitigate the profound human tragedy that the Iraqi population confronted, albeit except in the US-controlled Kurdish area in northern Iraq, the UNSC then adopted Resolution 1302 in June 2000, further extending the OFFP for another 180 days. The resolution also called for an independent expert report on the current humanitarian situation in Iraq (Gowlland-Debbas, 2004).

The OFFP has often been described, falsely, as a humanitarian assistance program, but it has never been so – no food or medical supplies were donated by any relief agency or any country to the Iraqi people. Iraq itself paid for all the food and medicine it obtained with the proceeds from the sale of oil. Between 1996 and 2002, Iraq earned a total of $55.4 billion from oil sales under the program, of which nearly 33 percent went for the payments to UN weapons inspectors and other UN expenses and war reparations to Kuwait. Of the remaining proceeds, $35.8 billion was paid in contracts to support the program; $23.5 billion spent for food and medicine delivered to Iraq; and the remaining $10 billion was held up by the UNSC for disputes involving the oil sales (Ballard, 2010, 89–90).

The OFFP was also plagued with scandals from the very beginning. The procedures and policies put in place by the UN itself opened many avenues of corruption. Apparently, to address those loopholes, the UNSC in 2001 introduced a policy of

[23] Notably, earlier UNSC resolutions – Resolution 706 (adopted in August 1991) and Resolution 712 (adopted in September 1991) – had proposed partial lifting of UN sanctions to enable Iraq to sell up to $1.6 billion worth of oil for purchasing humanitarian supplies under strict UN monitoring of the contracts and distribution of such supplies. The program failed to materialize due to Iraq's rejection to the terms of the deal as well as the UN Inspector Hans Blix's complaint that Iraq was not complying with its obligations to Resolution 687, which mandated destruction of Iraq's non-existent WMD facilities (Ismael and Ismael, 2015; FAO, 1995; Kondoch, 2001, 278).

[24] Resolution 986 specifically directed between 130 and 150 million dollars to the UN Inter-Agency Humanitarian Program, which served the Kurds in northern Iraq and the Shiites in southern Iraq, who had sided with the American-led military campaign since the 1991 Gulf War and against whom Saddam Hossain sought revenge (Falk, 2003, 18–19).

"retroactive oil pricing" for oil sales (Stauffer, 2001). Under the policy, purchasers were required to sign oil contracts blindly, without knowing the price and the UN committee overseeing the Iraq sanctions (UNSCOM) set the price retroactively in the following month. But purchasers showed little interest in such a policy, and as a result, Iraqi oil sales collapsed, and due to shortage of funds, contracts worth billions of dollars for humanitarian purchases were cancelled, further contributing to the food insecurity and widespread malnutrition in the country (Ballard, 2010; Gordon, 2010; Volcker et al., 2006).

The OFFD was credited with some positive effects as well. This program indeed reconnected the Iraqi economy and population with the outside world, after five gruesome years of comprehensive sanctions. Also, because of this program, between 1997 and 2001 the supply of food and medicine in Iraq increased remarkably, and inflation also came down significantly. The International Law Commission (IIC, 2005) noted that the food supplies provided through the program succeeded in reversing a serious and deteriorating food crisis, preventing widespread hunger, and reducing deaths due to malnutrition. The Volcker Committee, which was appointed to inquire about corruption of the program, also acknowledged that the OFFP "served as the main source of sustenance for 60 percent of Iraq's estimated 27 million people, reducing malnutrition amongst Iraqi children by 50 percent" (Muller and Muller, 1999, 3; Volker, 2005, 179).

The opening up of Iraq to the rest of the world through the OFFD program also had some positive effects on the Iraqi economy. For example, in 1997 Iraq's GDP (gross domestic product) expanded by 40 percent, and the next year, by another 35 percent, compared with 1990. Iraqi oil production also almost tripled and exports increased more than 17-fold between 1997 and 1998, compared with 1990. In 1999, Iraq produced oil at the level of 1989, and in 2000, Iraq's oil production exceeded its 1989 level both in terms of revenues and production capacity. With the OFFD in place, US imports of petroleum and petroleum products from Iraq also increased significantly. While in 1999, the US imported more than 600,000 barrels per day (bpd), accounting for 44 percent in dollar value of all Iraqi exports, and in 2000, the US bought even more Iraqi oil than before the Gulf War (O'Sullivan, 2003, 130–152). In the end, the OFFP provided about $177 annually to each Iraqi citizen, roughly 50 cents a day, to pay for their health care, food, electricity, sewage, and other essential services (Ballard, 2010, 90).

III US SANCTIONS AND THE OVERTHROW OF SADDAM

Overthrowing the regime of Saddam Hossain was never an objective of the sanctions regimes imposed by the UNSC against Iraq, but it was the paramount aim of the US from the very beginning of the conflict (Drury, 2001, 247; Lowenfeld, 2003). President George H. W. Bush implied this as early as August 5, 1990, when he famously declared from the White House lawn, "This will not stand," in response to Saddam's annexation of Kuwait.[25] As Saddam failed to comply with the UNSC demand for immediate withdrawal from Kuwait, on February 15, 1991, Bush asserted, "There's another way for the bloodshed to stop, and that is for the Iraqi military and the Iraqi people to take matters into their own hands and force Saddam Hussein, the dictator, to step aside and then comply with the United Nation's resolution."[26]

The US Congress also aggressively sought the removal of Saddam from power. The Congress passed the Iraq Liberation Act, 1998 (P.L. 105-338) on August 5, 1998, which not only authorized the president to undertake aggressive strategies against Iraq, but also allocated up to $97 million to pursue Saddam's ouster, and even provided for the creation of a war crimes tribunal for Saddam (O'Sullivan, 2003, 119).[27] Then, on August 14, 1998, Congress passed a joint resolution finding the Government of Iraq in unacceptable and material breach of its international obligations (P.L. 105-235), urging the president "to take appropriate action, in accordance with the Constitution and relevant laws of the United States, to bring Iraq into compliance with its international obligations" (Ballard, 2010, 92).

The Congress also passed two other major pieces of legislation in the 1990s that impacted sanctions against Iraq: the Iran–Iraq Arms Non-Proliferation Act, 1992 (Iran–Iraq Act: P.L. 102-484), which required the president to deny exports of all dual-use items to Iraq and Iran, and mandated sanctions against all foreign entities that transferred conventional weaponry to these countries; and the Anti-Terrorism and Effective Death Penalty Act, 1996 (AEDPA: P.L. 104-132), which required the president to withhold foreign assistance to any country that provided aid or military assistance to any country on the US anti-terrorism list.

Prior to the invasion of Kuwait, however, Saddam was a close ally of the US. Some even claim that Saddam was used as a tool by the US Central Intelligence Agency (CIA) and Defense Intelligence Agency (DIA) for 40 years until July 1990, before he invaded Kuwait (Scherrer, 2011, 27). In the 1980s, during the Iran–Iraq war (1980–88), the US had not only sided with Iraq, but also significantly strengthened its diplomatic and trade relations with the country. In 1982, the US removed Iraq from the list of state sponsors of terrorism, and in 1984, the US restored diplomatic relations with Iraq. Between 1985 and 1990, the US approved sales of military equipment and technology to Iraq worth over $1 billion, and annual trade

25 President Bush's statement cited from: bushlibrary.tamu.edu/research/papers/1990/90080502.html.

26 Excerpts from: Two Statements by Bush on Iraq's Proposal for Ending Conflict. *New York Times*, February 16, 1991, cited in Ballard (2010, 80).

27 Earlier, in 1992, Congress passed the Iran–Iraq Arms Nonproliferation Act of 1992 (P.L. 102-484) authorizing the president to apply sanctions and controls with respect to Iran, Iraq, and those nations and persons who assist them in acquiring weapons of mass destruction. The Act also empowered the presidents to take actions in accordance with the Foreign Assistance Act of 1961; the Nuclear Non-Proliferation Act of 1978; the Chemical and Biological Weapons Control and Warfare Elimination Act of 1991; chapter 7 of the Arms Export Control Act, 1976; and other relevant statutes, regarding the non-proliferation of WMD and the means of their delivery.

between the countries had increased from $500 million to $3.5 billion by 1990 (Graham-Brown, 1999, 2–3).

Apparently, Saddam's annexation of Kuwait came as a surprise to the US, and it posed a threat to US policy to preserve regional stability in the Gulf region by resisting the emergence of a dominant power hostile to US interests; prevent the proliferation of WMD and ensure the security of Israel; and ensure a secure and unfettered flow of oil and gas to the US from the region (Juster, 2000, 52; Sciolino, 1991, 140–142).[28] Some observers, however, suggest that the US strategies toward Iraq began to change even earlier, coinciding with end of the Iran–Iraq war, when Iraq emerged as a militarily powerful state in the Gulf region, while the US viewed the rise of Iraq as a regional power as a threat to the Gulf oil reserves as well as Israel's security (Falk, 2003, 24).[29]

In the end, it was the US-led military offensive – Operation Desert Storm – that drove Saddam out of Kuwait, and brought an end to Iraq's regional aspirations. But the US kept on aggressively manipulating the UNSC, taking full advantage of its sweeping victory in the Cold War and the end of hostility with the Russian Federation, not only to adopt increasingly coercive sanctions regimes against Iraq, but also to establish dominance over Iraq's internal affairs. It was at the behest of the US and its principal ally, the UK, that the UNSC adopted more than 50 resolutions during a short span of 12 years (1990–2002) against Iraq in three sequential stages – weapons inspection, inspections with humanitarian aid, and aid without inspections – which institutionalized and entrenched sanctions on Iraqi life (Ismael and Ismael, 2004, 95).

Although initially, in the early 1990s, all UNSC permanent members displayed a united stand for adopting sanctioning measures against Iraq, by the late 1990s, three of the five permanent members – China, France, and Russia – increasingly expressed concern with the aggressive character of the sanctions regime, and indeed repeatedly urged either termination or substantial easing of the sanctions regime against Iraq. These three UNSC permanent members also opposed attempts to bring down the regime of Saddam Hossain and to cause further damage to the Iraqi civilian population, but the US and the UK brushed aside such arguments stoutly,

[28] Dennis Halliday, a top UN official in Iraq at the time, maintained that the enforcement of US sanctions against Saddam Hossain was primarily driven by Israel, which led the UN inspectors to destroy over 100 Iraqi long-range missiles (not just Scud missiles) that could reach Israel. Israel was also critical of Saddam's pro-Palestine stance (Scherrer, 2011, Part I:7).

[29] Evidently, after the Iran–Iraq war, Saddam himself began to portray Iraq as a regional power. At the summit of the Arab Cooperation Council in February 1990, for example, Saddam asserted that Iraq had accumulated a foreign debt of approximately $80 billion during its war with Iran, but as Iraq fought the war on behalf of the entire Arab world, it had no obligation to pay back the loans received from other Arab countries (Baram, 1993, 9–10). Moreover, during the Iran–Iraq war, in addition to bolstering diplomatic and trade relations with the US, Iraq also acquired more than $50 billion worth of conventional arms, primarily from the former Soviet Union, China, and France (Juster, 2000, 53; Sciolino, 1991, 140–142).

blaming the regime of Saddam Hossain for the sufferings of the Iraqi population (Drezner, 2011; Gordon, 2010; Lowenfeld, 2003).

There had been divergent interpretations of the developments at the operational levels as well. For example, on December 15, 1998, two key IAEA weapons inspectors submitted starkly different reports to the UNSC for its consideration. One of the inspectors, Mohamed El Baradei, maintained that Iraq had "provided the necessary level of cooperation to enable … [our] activities to be completed efficiently and effectively," but Richard Butler, the other inspector, deplored the Iraqi authorities for their "lack of disclosure, and concealment." Butler, however, also acknowledged that "the majority of the inspections of facilities and sites under the ongoing monitoring system were carried out with Iraq's cooperation" (Tripp, 2008, 252).

The US, however, took a hardened approach. In October 2002, US Congress passed a joint resolution – the Iraq War Resolution, 2002 (P.L. 107-243) – authorizing the president to "use any means necessary" to handle the Iraqi situation in order to "defend the national security of the United States," and enforce all relevant UNSC resolutions regarding Iraq. The Congressional Resolution accused Iraq, among others, of violating the UN-imposed cease-fire after the liberation of Kuwait and other UNSC resolutions, pursuing WMD programs that threatened US interests, and harboring of al Qaida members.

The next month, in November 2002, at the behest of the US, the UNSC adopted Resolution 1441, holding Iraq in "material breach" of its obligations under several UNSC resolutions, especially for its failure to cooperate with the UN and the IAEA in their inspection of WMDs in Iraq, pursuant to Resolution 687 (1991). Resolution 1441 explicitly warned Iraq of severe consequences for its failure to grant "immediate, unimpeded, unconditional, and unrestricted access to any and all, including underground" areas and facilities, to the country's chemical, biological, and nuclear weapons. The Resolution granted Iraq "a final opportunity" to comply with its disarmament obligations and for a "full and verified completion" of the disarmament process established by previous UNSC resolutions.

Although UNSC Resolution 1441 did not explicitly authorize armed intervention to overthrow the regime of Saddam Hossain, citing the authority granted under the Resolution as well as the US Congressional Resolution of 2002, President George W. Bush, in January 2003, declared war against Iraq, vowing to destroy Iraqi WMD and bring an end to the dictatorial rule of Saddam Hossain. The US invasion of Iraq – known as the Second Gulf War – was launched on March 19, 2003 along with some forces from the UK and some other countries.[30] The war lasted just three weeks, ending on April 9, 2003, when Saddam's regime

30 The North Atlantic Treaty Organization (NATO), as an organization, however, had no role in the campaign against Iraq. Some of the members of the coalition of forces that attacked Iraq were NATO members, but some were not.

collapsed, and he went into hiding.[31] The invasion of Iraq and the toppling of the regime was thus carried out with the explicit approval of the US Congress, but without the clear authorization of the UNSC (Gowlland-Debbas, 2004).

IV IRAQ UNDER OCCUPATION FORCES

Following the collapse of the regime of Saddam Hossain, the Coalition Provisional Authority (CPA) headed by L. Paul Bremer, a US diplomat, was installed in Iraq in May 2003.[32] As the overarching reason for the invasion of Iraq and more than a decade of comprehensive sanctions against Iraq – nuclear power and WMDs – had already been found to be a complete hoax, the US policy objectives then shifted toward the stabilization and reconstruction of Iraq (Tripp, 2008, 282). The CPA immediately took two major steps: (a) de-Baathification of the Iraqi government, under which more than 30,000 government servants and 300,000 military personnel of the Iraqi army were thrown out of their jobs; and (b) a 25-member Iraqi Governing Council (IGC) was set up to help the CPA to establish liberal democratic institutions in Iraq.

Immediately after the CPA established its control over Iraq, President Bush ordered the transfer of frozen Iraqi assets held with the Federal Reserve Bank of New York in pursuance of the UNSC Resolution 778, and EO 12722 (1990) and EO 12817 (1992),[33] and issued a series of EOs to remove longstanding US economic sanctions against Iraq, including those imposed on the grounds of terrorism.[34]

31 Saddam Hossain was captured on December 14, 2003, and on December 30, 2006, his court-mandated execution by hanging was carried out in a globally televised event. Saddam (1937–2006) was seen walking into the gallows clutching a Quran.

32 The Ba'ath Party, which played a pivotal role in catapulting Saddam Hossain to Iraq's presidency in 1979, and ultimately solidified his dictatorship through ruthless suppression of dissent, professed nationalist and socialist ideology. The party also emphasized Arab nationalism, which facilitated Saddam's rise to regional prominence. Immediately after the US-led Coalition invaded Iraq, the US sought to rule Iraq directly under the Office of Reconstruction and Humanitarian Assistance (ORHA), set up in mid April, 2003. In mid May the same year, however, the US replaced the ORHA with the Coalition Provisional Authority (CPA) under Paul Bremer, who carried out de-Baathification of the Iraqi government by disbanding the Iraqi army and intelligence services. For greater detail, see Holden (2012, 336); Tripp (2008, 282); and Timmerman (1991). UNSC Resolution 1483, adopted on May 22, 2003 also gave the US and the UK a mandate to "occupy" Iraq and rebuild it. The resolution also assigned the responsibilities to "rebuild" Iraq to the UN, the IMF, the World Bank, and the Arab Fund for Social and Economic Development, but their roles were essentially marginalized by the CPA. See also Ismael and Ismael (2004, 120).

33 The fund was originally created to provide humanitarian relief, and finance the UN Compensation Commission, which adjudicated claims against Iraq arising from its invasion of Kuwait (Bettauer, 1994, 35).

34 For example, EO 13350 (issued on July 30, 2004) terminated EO 12722 and modified EO 13290 (issued on March 20, 2003). Earlier, the US Congress authorized the president to waive all sanctions against Iraq. A divided panel of the US Court of Appeals for the District of Columbia Circuit, however, later concluded that the authority conferred by the Congress to the president did not extend to restoration of the sovereign immunity that Iraq had been denied during the period of its designation as a state sponsor of terrorism (Lowenfeld, 2003).

On January 24, 2004, the Bush Administration finally conceded that its claims of extensive stockpiles of chemical, biological, and nuclear weaponry in Saddam's Iraq was absolutely false. David Kay, a top US weapons inspector, told US Congress directly, "We are almost all wrong." In March 2005, a presidential WMD Commission, established by EO 13328 on February 6, 2004, reached an astonishing conclusion that "not one bit" of the intelligence on Iraqi WMD was true.[35]

As of March 2004, the CPA had spent $1.67 billion for "emergency needs, including salaries for civil servants and pensions, and for ministry operations," and approximately $900 million in assets seized by the US military in Iraq for humanitarian and reconstruction activities.[36] The CPA was never welcomed by the Iraqi population, however. Instead of being greeted as liberators, as the Bush Administration expected, the Iraqi people, "physically, economically, morally, spiritually" exhausted, rather mounted massive insurgency movements that cost hundreds and thousands of additional deaths (Ballard, 2010, 97).[37]

Peter Monsoor, an executive officer to General David Petraeus, who served as the first commander of the multinational security transition command of Iraq, identified three major sources for the abysmal failure of the CPA: (a) the de-Baathification measures, by heavily targeting Sunnis, caused fear of loss of Sunni power and ultimately created a political base for insurgency; (b) the disbanding of the Iraqi Army left many Iraqi soldiers unemployed and ostracized, and drove them into the arms of the insurgency; and (c) the CPA policies empowered sectarian politics in Iraq, intensifying detrimental effects on the future of Iraq and the region (Bremer, 2014; Ismael and Ismael, 2015, 2).

The US combat operation in Iraq, however, continued until August 31, 2010, and the war officially ended on October 21, 2011 with a declaration to that effect made by the Obama Administration. The Iraq War thus lasted nearly nine years, during which more than one million air force personnel, soldiers, sailors, and Marines were deployed in Iraq. The war cost the US over $800 billion, nearly 4,500 American deaths, and approximately 150,000 Iraqi fatalities. The occupation of Iraq continued until 2011 as the last US soldier left Iraq on December 18, 2011.

Removal of UN Sanctions

The UN, on its part, also removed all its sanctions regimes against Iraq following the end of the Second Gulf War in 2003. UNSC Resolution 1483, adopted on May 22, 2003,[38] recalled all previous resolutions on the situation between Iraq and Kuwait; lifted all trade sanctions against Iraq except the arms embargo that was put in place

[35] The report is available at: irp.fas.org/offdocs/wmdcomm.html.

[36] See GAO-04-579T Recovering Iraq's Assets (March 18, 2004).

[37] By October 2004, civilian deaths in Iraq at the hands of the Coalition forces ranged from a conservative estimate of 30,000 up to 100,000, and on top of that, there were casualties resulting from combat and violence, and deteriorating conditions of daily life (Bremer, 2003; Trips, 2008, 295–337).

[38] See UNSC Resolution 1483 (May 22, 2003), UN Doc. S/RES/1483.

to ensure Iraq's compliance with the demands of disarmament; extended the OFFP for another six months; and slated a review of the mandates of UNMOVIC and the IAEA in respect to Iraq within 12 months (Joyner, 2015; Lauro, 2020).

Resolution 1483 also established a Development Fund for Iraq (DFI) with the Central Bank of Iraq but vested its supervisory authority with the International Advisory and Monitoring Board (IAMB) comprised of representatives from the UN Secretary General, the International Monetary Fund (IMF), the World Bank, and the Arab Fund for Social and Economic Development. The resolution also authorized a transfer of $1 billion to the DFI from the OFFD, and granted immunity to the sale of petroleum, petroleum products, and natural gas originating in Iraq from legal proceedings (Gowlland-Debbas, 2004). The DFI disbursed its resources in consultation with the CPA for humanitarian, reconstruction, disarmament, and civilian administration purposes.[39]

Finally, Resolution 1483 brought an end to the UN sanctions regime on Iraq, putting in place a process of gradual transfer of the Iraqi administration onto the transitional authority CPA and authorized the appointment of a UN Special Representative for Iraq to report to the UNSC on post-conflict events and developments in Iraq.[40] Later, in November 2003, UNSC Resolution 1518 launched a new monitoring administrative committee, replacing the 661 Sanctions Committee, to monitor developments in Iraq.[41]

V IMPACT OF SANCTIONS ON THE IRAQI ECONOMY AND POPULATION

Iraq came under the "Mount Everest of sanctions in the post-Cold War era" (Hufbauer, 2007, 132) in 1990, imposed multilaterally by the UN and unilaterally by the US and its allies, and the ominous saga continued for 13 years, until 2003, when the regime of Saddam Hossain was overthrown by a US-led military offensive. During this excruciating period, on top of a relentless barrage of both multilateral and unilateral sanctions, the Iraqi economy and population also experienced massive military offensives twice. Although all sanctions regimes were disbanded after the fall of Saddam, post-Saddam Iraq was under foreign occupation until October 2011.

The impact of the sanctions regimes on the Iraqi economy and population has been explored in two phases – the first phase focuses on the 1990–2003 period, when

39 See OHCHR Press Release, available at www.ohchr.org/en/press-releases/2009/10/.

40 Resolution 1483 also called upon all UN member states to take appropriate steps to facilitate the safe return to Iraqi institutions of Iraqi cultural property and other items of archaeological, historical, cultural, rare scientific, and religious importance illegally removed from the Iraq National Museum, the National Library, and other locations in Iraq since the adoption of UNSC Resolution 661 (1990), and called upon UNESCO, Interpol, and other international organizations to assist in the implementation of this provision.

41 See UNSC Resolution 1518 (November 24, 2003), UN Doc. S/RES/1518.

the sanctions regimes were in place, and the second phase focuses on the 2003–2011 period, when Iraq was under foreign occupation.

First Phase – Before Saddam's Fall

Macroeconomic Performance

Prior to the sanctions, Iraq was a prosperous country in the Gulf region. Between 1974 and 1980, the country registered an average growth rate of 10.4 percent, and in 1988, the final year of the Iran–Iraq war, the per capita GDP of the country was estimated to be $3,510. In 1989, a year before the sanctions, despite more than 250,000 deaths[42] and significant damage to civilian infrastructure due to the war, the UN categorized Iraq as a high–middle-income country with a modern social infrastructure, which had a GDP of $75.5 billion with per capita income at $3,510. Although Iraq's oil production declined precipitously during the war, in July 1990, the country's oil production reached 3.5 million bpd, almost matching the level of production prior to the war (Ismael and Ismael, 2015, 151; UN, 1999).

But immediately after the sanctions campaign began, in just one year, by 1991, Iraq's economy shrank by five-sixths as its oil production and exports, which traditionally earned more than 95 percent of the country's foreign exchange, declined by more than 85 percent, and the country's oil-refining capacity declined from 3.5 million bpd to 460,000 bpd (O'Sullivan, 2003, 359). The decline continued to 1996, when Iraq was completely cut off from the rest of the world under the most severe comprehensive sanctions ever imposed on any country since WWII.[43]

The 1990–1996 period was thus extremely paralyzing for the Iraqi economy and population. The country had almost no access to international trade, credit, investment, or bilateral assistance, and as a result, the population endured the disastrous collapse of the economy all alone. Over $4.5 billion of Iraqi foreign assets were frozen due to the sanctions, which made it impossible for the country to meet its debt obligations to Western nations, which at the time stood at over $13.7 billion, or import essential food and medicine. Moreover, Iraq lost $175 to $250 billion in possible oil revenues because of the sanctions as its oil exports came to a grinding halt (O'Sullivan, 2003, 125–128).

This period was also marked by hyperinflation and high unemployment. The annual inflation rate of the country ranged between 2,000 percent and 5,000 percent during 1990–1995, when at least one-fourth of Iraq's labor force was unemployed (Butt and Butt, 2014) and the monthly food expense of families rose 250-fold (Hoskins, 1997, 112). In 1989, the official rate for one Iraqi dinar was $3.2, but by the mid-1990s, the value declined to 3,000 dinars per US dollar (Pellett, 2011, 6).

[42] Actual casualties of the Iran–Iraq war remain controversial. Some estimates suggest that the war cost more than 1.5 million casualties to both sides, and forced millions to take refuge in other countries due to incessant fighting (Ballard, 2010, 27).

[43] As discussed above, Iraq was opened to the rest of the world when the OFFP was launched in 1996.

During 1996–2002, Iraqi economy recovered slightly – due to the limited opening through the OFFP, adopted in 1996. Iraq's GDP increased from $10.8 billion in 1996 to $31.8 billion in 2002 – it was, however, still less than half the country's GDP level of 1989 (Sanford, 2003, 11). By then, years of sanctions had reduced the per capita GDP of Iraqis to less than $500, making it one of the poorest countries in the world (Pellett, 2011, 6).

Overall, the decade-long economic blockade resulted in declining GDP, soaring inflation, high unemployment rates, massive capital flights, currency depreciation, serious shortages of basic food and medicine – all these hurt all sections of the Iraqi population, but the poorest were the hardest hit (Sanford, 2003, 11).

Humanitarian Disaster

The humanitarian effects of international sanctions regimes against Iraq have been almost universally condemned as one of the worst and most disastrous incidents since WWII. Hundreds of thousands of infants and children suffered from massive malnutrition, long-term health problems, and cognitive deficits (Gordon, 2010; Ismael, 2007), and the infant mortality rate in Iraq more than doubled in the first nine years after the sanctions began (UNICEF, 1996). While Iraq's under-five mortality rate declined steadily between 1974 and 1990, reaching about 63 per thousand live births during 1986–1990, the rate rose dramatically to 118 per thousand in 1991, and then the number of excess deaths of under-fives ranged between 400,000 and 500,000 during 1991–1998 (Ali et al., 2011).

UNICEF reports (1996, 1999a and 1999b) attributed 4,500–6,000 excess deaths per month to embargo-related causes, and put excess deaths among under-five-year-olds at 560,000 in 1995 and 750,000 in 1998. Similarly, Garfield (1999) noted that the sanctions caused a minimum of 100,000 and up to 227,000 excess deaths among young Iraqi children between August 1991 and March 1998. Zurbrigg (2007) suggests that Iraq suffered "slow famine" and an estimated 1.5 million excess deaths because of a catastrophic undermining of civilian livelihood triggered by the embargo.

In 2000, UNICEF reported to the UNSC that 25 percent of children in the south and central provinces of Iraq suffered from chronic malnutrition, most of which was irreversible, and 9 percent of the victims suffered from acute malnutrition.[44] Baram (2000) blamed the embargo for 1.4 million Iraqi deaths, while Muller and Muller (1999, 51) concluded that economic sanctions caused more deaths in Iraq than the so-called WMD throughout history. The UN Secretary General's team, headed by Marti Ahtisaari, reported in March 1991 that the conditions in Iraq were "near apocalyptic," with scant medicines and humanitarian supplies getting through to those in need (Chesterman and Malone, 2016, 376).

Some studies suggest that the humanitarian catastrophe resulted from the US-led military offensive against Iraq during the first Gulf War, when in the process of

[44] See UN Resolution 661, Summary Record, Meeting 195, S/AC.25/SR.195, March 20, 2000.

driving the Iraqi forces out of Kuwait, much of the of the civilian infrastructure of the country, including factories, electric power stations, water treatment plants, and sewage plants were either destroyed or disabled (Pellett, 2011, 1). Some studies suggest that failing to obtain spare parts due to sanctions, Iraqi authorities cut off about 2.5 million people from the pre-war levels of water supply, and the remaining 14.5 million who received water were allowed to receive only one-quarter of the pre-war level of water supply (Butt and Butt, 2014). Some studies accuse the US and the UK of intentionally targeting Iraqi water purification systems (Falk, 2003, 24; Nagy, 2001).[45]

The catastrophe caused by the sanctions was indeed enormous and inhumane by any measure. Leon Eisenberg (1997), a Harvard medical professor wrote, "The Cuban and Iraqi instances make it abundantly clear that economic sanctions are, at their core, a war against public health." Dennis Halliday, who served as UN Humanitarian Coordinator for Iraq during 1997–1998, resigned in protest at the disaster, asserting, "We are in the process of destroying an entire society. It is as simple and terrifying as that … I don't want to administer a program that satisfies the definition of genocide." Halliday's successor, Hans-Christof von Sponeck, who served in Iraq from 1998 to 2000, also resigned in protest at the "genocide" (Biehler, 2003, 16; Joyner, 2015, 3; Sponeck, 2006).[46]

Subsequently, when the humanitarian disaster caused by the comprehensive UN sanctions on Iraq drew global condemnation, the UNSC adopted Resolution 1302 in June 2000, directing the UN Secretary General to appoint independent experts to assess the humanitarian situation in Iraq (Gowlland-Debbas, 2004).

Some studies however point to some factors aside from sanctions for the humanitarian catastrophe in Iraq. These include: (a) eight years of the Iran–Iraq war, which apparently cost the nation around $130 billion; (b) the militarization of the Iraqi economy, the invasion of Kuwait, and the ensuing Gulf War, left the country heavily

[45] This issue remains highly controversial, however. Some studies suggest that declassified documents of the DIA later confirmed that the US deliberately targeted civilian infrastructure of Iraq, especially water treatment plants, considering their effects on Iraqi civilian life (Falk, 2003, 24; Nagy, 2001). Some studies claim that the US and the UK were aware of the fact that chemicals necessary for water purification were blocked by sanctions, but still went ahead with the bombing and damaging water treatment facilities (Barrett, 2002; Haass and O'Sullivan, 2000; Ismael and Ismael, 2015, 152).

[46] Both Halliday and von Sponeck expressed concern that "the current policy of economic sanctions has destroyed society in Iraq and caused the death of thousands, young and old," on the grounds of the alleged existence of WMD in Iraq (Biehler, 2003, 17). In 2006, they described the human tragedy of sanctions against Iraq as:

> What we have done to you in the name of freedom and democracy has no parallel in history. We have trampled the truth concerning your suffering, we endeavored to solicit allies through bribery and ruthlessly marginalized those who objected to our imperial intentions. Brute force became the substitute for the promise of 1945 "to save future generations from the scourge of war." It was you who paid the price … Your museums are empty, your libraries burnt, your universities destroyed. Only your pride is still there […] and our guilt. *Will you ever forgive us?* (cited in Ismael and Ismael, 2015, 5).

indebted to some Gulf States and western financial institutions; and (c) even prior to the sanctions of the 1990s, the country suffered from hyperinflation, sporadic food shortages, and large-scale unemployment (Butt and Butt, 2014; O'Sullivan, 2003, 123). And there are some also who claim that "the deleterious impact of sanctions upon the Iraqi population has been grossly exaggerated" (Rubin, 2001).

Most scholars, however, broadly agree that although such non-sanctions factors might have played a role, it was rather the force, the intensity, and the open-endedness of the international sanctions regimes which must bear major responsibility for the human catastrophe that the Iraqi population endured in the 1990s (Alnasrawi, 2001).

Spread of Corruption

The comprehensive trade embargo imposed on Iraq distorted markets by creating strong incentives for businesses to resort to black markets, and also contributed to widespread corruption and lawlessness not only in Iraq but also among the neighboring countries and the UN monitoring organizations that operated in the country (Andreas, 2005; Drezner, 2011). Especially, corrupt practices in the operations of OFFP became so pervasive that in 2004 the UN Secretary General appointed an independent inquiry committee under Paul Volcker, a former head of the US Federal Reserve Board.

The Volcker Committee, in its three-volume report, identified as many as 2,200 companies, mostly based in France and Russia, which paid $1.8 billion in kickbacks to the Iraqi regime during the period of OFFP operation.[47] The report also incriminated scores of UN personnel in such corrupt practices (Doxey, 2009, 544; Volker, 2005).[48]

The Volcker Committee also reported that, between 1990 and 2003, while comprehensive UN trade sanctions were in place, the Iraqi regime managed to smuggle about $11 billion worth of oil to neighboring countries.[49] One of the most notorious and verifiable smuggling activities involved Iraq's construction and operation of an oil pipeline from its northern oil fields near Kirkuk to Syria (Meyer, 2009). Apparently, traders paid 25–45 cents in kickbacks per barrel of oil to Iraqi authorities (Ballard, 2010, 90).

47 The Volker Report also found that Russian and Chinese companies received more than $19.3 billion and $4.9 billion of oil sales, respectively, amounting to more than one-third of the total of $64.2 billion of oil that Iraq was allowed to sell under the OFFP. The Russian state-owned oil company was the largest single purchaser of oil under the program – with payments funneled through the Iraqi embassy in Moscow. Russian, Chinese, and French companies also paid approximately $1.8 billion in kickbacks fo the Saddam regime (Meyer, 2009; Volker et al., 2006).

48 Among others, the Committee faulted improper procedures and policies set forth by the UN for prompting corrupt practices. One of the UN managers of the program, a Cypriot named Benon Sevan, was indicted for taking $160,000 in bribes. Also, in 2006, a South Korean businessman, named Tongsun Park, was convicted in New York of conspiracy to launder money and acting as an unregistered agent of Saddam Hossain (Ballard, 2010, 90).

49 The US Government Accountability Office (GAO, 2014) however maintains that Iraq earned $6.6 billion in illicit revenues from oil smuggling and surcharges during 1997–2001.

Such a scale of corruption occurred despite the UN-sponsored MIF stopping and checking over 10,000 Iraqi shipments in 10 years (Wallensteen and Staibano, 2005, 8).

The Volker Committee also held three UNSC permanent members – Russia, China and France – responsible for routinely blocking efforts to investigate widespread reports of smuggling activity in Iraq, and pointed out that, under the OFFP program, Iraq sold more oil to Russian and Chinese state-owned companies than all other companies around the world combined (Volker, 2005, 179; Muller and Muller, 1999, 3).[50]

Second Phase – Post-Invasion Iraq

Approximately 4,600 US troops and 3,650 US contractors were killed in the Iraq war, and countless others were maimed. The war also cost the lives of approximately 45,000 Iraqi military and police personnel and 35,000 Iraqi insurgents, and injured tens of thousands more.[51] On top of that, more than one million Iraqis, mostly infants and children, lost their lives during the period when international sanctions against Iran were in place (1990–2003).

Moreover, the sanctions and military invasion also displaced approximately two million Iraqis internally, about 1.4 million externally as refugees, over 80 percent of whom were women and children.[52] Such a massive scale of displacement of Iraqis occurred mainly because of massive destruction of public infrastructure, degradation of services, siege warfare, and sectarian violence (IDMC, 2012; Ismael and Ismael, 2015, 60; MIT, 2013).[53]

At the time of writing this chapter, the US-led military invasion that toppled the Saddam regime on March 20, 2003 was marking its 20th anniversary. The invasion, as mentioned above, actually ended in October 2011. Nearly half of Iraq's 2023 population of 45 million was born after 2000, and thus neither experienced the regime of Saddam Hossain nor witnessed the insurgencies and other atrocities that cost an estimated 300,000 Iraqi deaths between 2003 and 2019.[54]

The economic performance of post-invasion Iraq has not yet reached its pre-sanctions level. Between 2012 and 2021, as Table 7.1 indicates, the country's GDP ranged between $43 billion and $66 billion, whereas, more than three decades ago

[50] These countries also abstained from voting for UNSC Resolution 1284 in December 1999, when UNSCOM was replaced by UNMOVIC to monitor the OFFP.

[51] Based on Watson Institute of Brown University. watson.brown.edu/costsofwar/figures/2021/WarDeathToll accessed on March 20, 2023.

[52] A study by Massachusetts Institute of Technology (MIT) estimated the number of displaced persons, both internal (within Iraq) and external (refugees, mainly in Jordan and Syria) to be between 3.5 million and 5 million, directly attributable to the war, and virtually all first-hand accounts blamed violence as the cause of moving, or threats of ethnic or sectarian cleansing of neighborhoods. The report is available at: web.mit.edu/humancostiraq/.

[53] In 2010, Iraqi official sources claimed that five million Iraqi children were orphans, of whom about 500,000 lived on the streets. The Iraqi Children Foundation reported, for the same year, that one in six Iraqi children under the age of 18 was an orphan (Ismael and Ismael, 2015, 161).

[54] Based on watson.brown.edu/costsofwar/figures/2021/WarDeathToll, accessed on March 20, 2023.

TABLE 7.1 *Macroeconomic performance of Iraq*, 2012–2021

Year	GDP US$ billion (in nominal dollars)	Annual GDP growth rate (%)	Per capita GDP (in nominal dollars)	Debt to GDP ratio	Unemployment rate (%)	Inflation rate (%)	Exports in US$ billions (Nominal dollars)	Trade as % of GDP
2012	64.38	12.21	6,437.5	–	7.96	6.09	97.03	15.41
2013	66.13	2.72	6,216.0	–	9.26	1.88	93.07	11.92
2014	62.16	−6.0	6,216.0	–	10.59	2.24	88.95	8.90
2015	44.17	−28.94	4,416.9	27.39	10.73	1.34	57.56	0.56
2016	43.85	−2.53	4,305.2	29.48	10.82	0.56	46.83	1.63
2017	47.25	9.76	4,725.2	35.56	13.02	0.18	63.45	8.05
2018	56.01	18.84	5,601.5	27.44	12.97	0.37	92.77	15.80
2019	56.21	0.35	5,621.0	–	12.06	−0.20	88.90	7.11
2020	43.32	−22.93	4,332.3	–	14.09	0.57	50.19	−2.21
2021	47.75	10.23	4,775.4	–	14.19	6.04	78.26	13.47

Source: World Bank Database

TABLE 7.2 *Economic performance of Iraq – periodic estimates, 2005–2019*

Year	Unemployment rate (%)	Poverty rate (%)	Annual inflation rate (%)	Oil exports (million bpd)	Share of oil revenues in government budget (%)	Sectoral share		
						Oil	Industry	Agriculture
2005	17	20	37	0.20	92	61.3	2.2	6.6
2010	18	15	2.5	1.46	81.3	43.8	2.9	5.0
2015	19	30	1.4	2.51	83.6	58.8	2.2	4.2
2019	23	23	1.2	3.63	88.8	65.0	1.6	1.7

Source: Fakir and Farhan (2019).
Notes: Source of data attributed to the Ministry of Planning of the Iraqi government and IMF. Poverty rate is based on $3 per day.

in 1989, prior to international sanctions, Iraq's GDP was $75 billion. Also, Iraq experienced negative growth rate three times between 2012 and 2021 – and in 2020, when the GDP dipped by almost one-quarter (23 percent). Per capita income of the population during the period ranged between $4,305 and $6,437, whereas in 1989 it was $3,774.2, which was equivalent to $9,156.70 in 2022.[55]

Iraq is still the second-largest crude oil producer in the OPEC after Saudi Arabia, and holds the world's fifth-largest proven crude oil reserves – which is 17 percent of proven reserves in the Middle East and 8 percent of global reserves.[56] But, as Table 7.2 indicates, although Iraqi crude oil exports increased to 3.63 million bpd in 2019, the production had been much more lackluster in previous years. Moreover, revenues from oil exports hovered between $50 billion and $97 billion between 2012 and 2021 (Table 7.1), while in the late 1990s, the country's annual oil revenue exceeded $100 billion.

Oil is still the most dominant sector of the Iraqi economy – its share ranged between 43 percent and 61 percent during 2005 and 2019, while the combined share of agriculture and industry ranged between 3 percent and 8 percent (Table 7.2). At the same time, most of the oil export revenues end up in the government budget, which ranged between 81 percent and 92 percent during 2005–2019. Corruption remained predominant in Iraq – in 2015, Iraq was ranked at 161 place among 168 countries listed in the corruption percent index of Amnesty International (Fakir and Farhan, 2019).

The World Bank database indicates that, during 2012–2021, the unemployment rate in Iraq ranged between 8 percent and 14 percent, and the inflation rate ranged between minus 2 percent and 6 percent (Table 7.1). This means at least one-tenth of the labor force remained out of work. An alternative macroeconomic scenario, as depicted in Table 7.2 which is based primarily on Iraqi government sources, however, indicates that unemployment rates in Iraq ranged between 17 percent and 23 percent during 2005–2019, reflecting that about one-fifth of the country's workforce had been unemployed. Also, between one-fifth and one-third of the population lived below the poverty line during the period.

VI LEGAL PERSPECTIVES ON SANCTIONS AGAINST IRAQ

The discussion above indicates that the sanctions episode against Iraq was not only the "mount Everest of all sanctions" (Hufbauer, 2007), but they were also "certainly the most severe of all sanctions" imposed by UNSC in its entire history (Scherrer, 2011, 7).[57] It is also clear that the sanctions regimes against Iraq involved

[55] The US dollar had an average annual inflation rate of 2.64 percent between 1989 and 2022, which translates into a cumulative price increase of 142.61 percent.

[56] For greater detail, see www.eia.gov/international/analysis/country/IRQ, accessed on March 21, 2023.

[57] Examples of UNSC sanctions that involved the use of armed offensives have been few and far between. The most recent examples include sanctions against Sudan (due to the genocide in Darfur) in 2005 and Côte d'Ivoire in 2004.

both multilateral and unilateral sanctions, reinforced by massive military offensives, lasted more than a decade, and resulted in over one million ascertainable deaths, of whom over 80 percent were women and children.[58] The sanctions regimes also led to the demolition of the infrastructure of a relatively prosperous country, reducing it to the level of a "pre-industrial age" (Halliday, 2000; IAC, 1996).

Most importantly, the sanctions regimes were imposed absolutely baselessly, and they succeeded in accomplishing none of their stated objectives. For example: (a) the sanctioning measures did not lead to the removal of Iraq's WMD, which never even existed. Top US weapons inspector David Kay and the Congressional Commission on WMD confirmed that the claim of nuclear weapons was a total hoax, while Iraq's biological and chemical weapons were insignificant; (b) the sanctions regimes obviously did not succeed in overthrowing the regime of Saddam Hossain – the regime was toppled by a US-led military offensive, not by the pressures of a population distressed by sanctions; and (c) the sanctions regimes did not result in ending Iraqi support for international terrorism – Saddam's Iraq was never a sanctuary for terrorists; rather, it became so after his fall (Gowlland-Debbas, 2004; Lowenfeld, 2003; O'Sullivan, 2003).

Numerous scholars, observers, and practitioners from around the world rather agree that 13 years of sanctions campaigns had reduced Iraq to one of the poorest countries in the world by crippling its infrastructure and causing havoc to the lives of the ordinary population. The consequences of the sanctions had indeed been so disastrous that in the late 1990s the global community moved away from comprehensive sanctions once and for all by adopting something called "smart" or targeted sanctions (Brzoska, 2003, 1345–1346; Haass, 2009; Drezner, 2011). Some of the inescapable conclusions of the sanctions saga against Iraq can be enumerated as follows.

A. The sanctions episodes were mandated by the UNSC, which, under Article 41 of the UN Charter, had the legal right to adopt and enforce such sanctions, but two of the permanent members of the UNSC, the US and the UK, overtly manipulated the UNSC into adopting and enforcing such measures. The remaining three UNSC permanent members – China, France, and Russia – often abstained from voting for some of the crucial UNSC resolutions. And, right from the start, and ever increasingly so in the following years, the sanctions regimes were enforced in outright violation of the UN Charter and many other instruments of international law (Ballard, 2010; Cordon, 2010; Halliday, 1999a; Sponeck, 2006).

[58] Analyses conducted by many organizations, including the Iraq Body Count (IBC), found that, of the Iraqis killed from air raids, 39 percent were children; and among all Iraqi fatalities resulting from mortar attacks by invasion forces, 42 percent were children. Also, according to the Iraqi Children Foundation and UN General Assembly, approximately one in six Iraqi children under the age of 18 became an orphan due to the sanctions and invasion. See Ismael and Ismael (2015, 159–161).

B. The 43-day military offensive and aerial bombardments – launched in 1991 as Operation Desert Storm to liberate Kuwait – devastated not only Iraq's military forces in Kuwait but also Iraqi civilian infrastructure across the entire country, when more explosives were dumped on Iraq than were dropped on Europe in the whole of WWII (Gordon, 2002; Ismael and Ismael, 2004, 93–94).

C. Under the UNSC mandate to destroy Iraq's WMD, almost all Iraqi manufacturing plants that were even remotely linked to chemical and biological weapons were destroyed. Such acts of destruction were often carried out with the aim to inflict pain on the Iraqi civilian population under the presumption that ordinary people would rise up against the regime of Saddam Hossain. At the same time, the sanctioning bodies were aware that the vulnerable groups, afflicted by sanctions, had little legitimate means of exerting pressure on their political leaders (CESR, 1996). Even the CIA warned that the behavior of Saddam or his regime was unlikely to change through sanctions-induced pain.[59]

D. The UNSC and other sanctioners continued to adopt and enforce ever more aggressive and intrusive sanctions against Iraq despite numerous reports – by UN agencies and other institutions, as well as independent authors – pointing out the disastrous humanitarian effects of the sanctions regimes on the Iraqi civilian population, especially on infants, children, women, and elderly people, as early as 1991; that lack of food and medicines, starvation and malnutrition, and preventable mass death had became rampant; and it was known that the physical destruction of the country had already caused the potential for thousands more civilian deaths in the future (Scherrer, 2011, Part I:8; Bossuyt, 2000).[60]

E. Some key US officials of the Bush Administration – who were architects and enforcers of the sanctions regimes against Iraq – bluntly justified the disastrous effects of the sanctions on the Iraqi civilian population. Madeleine Albright,

59 In his testimony to the US Congress in 1990, the CIA chief, William Webster, stated: "Our judgement has been and continues to be that there is no assurance or guarantee that economic hardships will compel Saddam to change his policies or lead to internal unrest that would threaten his regime" (cited in Pellett, 2011, 2). Also, in 1995, lamenting the humanitarian effects of sanctions on Iraq, UN Secretary General Boutros Boutros-Ghali stated that it raises "the ethical question of whether suffering inflicted on vulnerable groups in the targeted country is a legitimate means of exerting pressure on political leaders whose behavior is unlikely to be affected by the plight of their subjects" (cited in Ballard, 2010).

60 The UNSC also ignored calls from many UN member states that expressed concern over the impact of the sanctions; such countries included Brazil, China, Egypt, South Korea, Kenya, France, Russia, Slovenia, and almost the whole Arab world, where Saddam's popularity increased almost proportionally with the sanctioning measures (Ballard, 2010, 96; Ismael and Ismael, 2004, 2015; Scherrer, 2011, II:134). Gordon (2002, 58) argues that although there was initially considerable international support for the sanctions, at least within the UNSC, by 2002, the US was nearly alone in its continued support for comprehensive sanctions against Iraq.

then US ambassador to the UN, in her interview with the CBS *60 Minutes* television program on May 12, 1996, famously went on record to describe the horrific deaths of Iraqi children and babies during 1991–1995 as "worth it."[61] Similarly, US Secretary of State at the time, Colin Powell, infamously stated, "We don't count the civilian loss of life, it's not important."

F. The sanctions regimes literally wiped out any semblance of Iraq's sovereignty – the country was totally under siege. The enforcement of no-fly zones as well as other military incursions was literally military warfare by conventional means. Working under questionable authority, the US, the UK,[62] and France (until 1996) enforced no-fly zones ultimately covering over 40 percent of Iraqi territory, and they conducted over 250,000 sorties, bombing hundreds of targets (Hindawi, 2017). Then, during the second phase of military offensives, under Operation Desert Fox in 1998, the US and the UK struck nearly 100 sites in Iraq, dropping over 1,000 bombs and cruise missiles. Such airstrikes escalated considerably in the run-up to the final military offensive against Iraq – the US-led invasion in 2003 (Gordon, 2010).

UNSC Resolution 1441, adopted on November 8, 2002, also literally denied Iraq's sovereignty by ordering the country to comply with the UNMOVIC and IAEA inspections unconditionally, to provide a complete list of all WMD programs and dual-use items within 24 hours, and granting the inspectors complete authority to access even the most sensitive of Iraqi sites, and interrogate any Iraqi officials without advance notice. The resolution was also drafted under the threat of an impending US invasion of Iraq (Ismael and Ismael, 2004, 117–118).[63]

G. The invasion of Iraq in 2003 was driven by baseless claims that Iraq had developed WMD (Gordon, 2010). Ultimately, the UNSC, the US and the world community at large acknowledged that Iraq had no WMD. Iraq, however, had long ago had a nuclear plant– the Osirak nuclear reactor plant – which was blown away by Israel in 1981 before it could become operational, and subsequent clandestine efforts of Iraq to purchase components for a nuclear program never succeeded (Juster, 2000, 53; Sciolino, 1991, 152).

[61] Lesley Stahl, *60 Minutes* correspondent, asked, "We have heard that half a million children have died. I mean, that is more children than died in Hiroshima. And, you know, is the price worth it?" Albright responded, "I think that is a very hard choice, but the price, we think, the price is worth it." See archive.globalpolicy.org/security/sanction/iraq1/2004/01sanctionsworth.htm. accessed in January 14, 2023.

[62] No-fly zones were authorized by UNSC Resolution 688 for northern and southern Iraq in order to protect minorities in those regions. But the US used the authorization as a way of challenging the Iraqi regime militarily, on a daily basis impinging on Iraqi sovereignty.

[63] Referring to the 30-day deadline imposed on Iraq to declare not only its weapons program, but also all chemical, biological, and nuclear programs unrelated to weapons production, even Hans Blix, chief of UNMOVIC, told the UNSC that the deadline was unrealistic (Ismael and Ismael, 2004, 119).

Another pretext used for imposing sanctions against Iraq – its support for Al-Qaeda and international terrorism – was also ultimately found to be untrue (Ballard, 2010, 98).[64]

H. At the end of the sanctions saga, Iraq's economy was a shambles – the country's per capita GDP fell from more than $3,000 in 1989 to less than $500 in 2003 (ILC, 2005); billions of dollars, earned through the sale of Iraqi oil and earmarked for the country's reconstruction, simply disappeared (Gordon, 2010); and the Iraqi people were "physically, economically, morally, spiritually" exhausted (Ballard, 2010, 97). All because of some made-up excuses and a worldwide mass deception campaign – it defies common sense to believe that the US and the UK did not know from the very outset that Iraq never had WMD.

Given such facts and developments, many legal scholars and practitioners, both Western and non-Western, argue that the sanctioning measures adopted against Iraq, both by the UNSC as well as unilateral sanctioners, had violated many legal norms and standards enshrined in international law, international human rights law, and international humanitarian law. The literature, deservingly, is indeed voluminous. The discussion here, however, is limited to some of the enduring questions, such as: (a) whether the humanitarian disaster that occurred in Iraq due to the sanctions constituted war crimes or genocide; (b) whether the UNSC overstepped its legal authority in adopting and enforcing multilateral sanctions against Iraq; (c) whether the UNSC had violated other international legal norms and standards, including those of the UN Charter itself, in pursuing sanctioning measures against Iraq; and finally, (d) whether the US and its allies violated customary international law on state sovereignty and non-interference in the internal affairs of another state by knowingly orchestrating worldwide mass deception to mislead the global community.

A *The Question of Genocide*

Numerous scholars, practitioners, and observers have claimed that the Iraqi sanctions episode indeed constitutes "genocide" pursuant to Article II of the UN Convention on the Prevention and Punishment of the Crime of Genocide, which entered into force on January 12, 1951. Article II identifies three essential elements of genocide as follows:

[64] The then US Secretary of State, Colin Powell, in a lengthy address to the UN on February 5, 2003, presented "evidence" – intelligence materials, including a slideshow – showing alleged links between Al-Qaeda and the Ba'ath Party to prove Iraq's failure to comply with UNSC Resolution 1441 and to justify military invasion against Iraq, on top of showing that Iraq had stockpiles of chemical, biological, and nuclear arms. The speech is available at: press.un.org/en/2003/sc7658.doc.htm, accessed on January 21, 2023.

> Any of the following acts committed with intent to destroy, in whole or in part, a national, ethnical, racial, or religious group, as such: i) Killing members of the group; ii) Causing serious bodily harm or mental harm to members of the group; iii) Deliberately inflicting on the group conditions of life calculated to bring about its physical destruction in whole or in part.[65]

Denis Halliday, who observed the tragedy in Iraq first hand as UN Humanitarian Coordinator, has argued that the systematic, highly planned and coordinated sanctioning measures against Iraq, which were enforced with devastating effects, and the magnitude of the deaths and of the suffering of the population from widespread malnutrition, epidemics of disease, and lack of treatment for many illnesses, clearly fits the definition of "genocide."[66] As mentioned above, Halliday had resigned from his position in protest against "genocide" in Iraq – he asserted, "I don't want to administer a program that satisfies the definition of genocide." His successor, Hans-Christof von Sponeck, who served in Iraq during 1998–2000, also resigned, protesting the "genocide" (Biehler, 2003, 16; Joyner, 2015, 3; Sponeck, 2003).

Marc Bossuyt (2000), a UN human rights expert, also concluded that the sanctions regime against Iraq was "unequivocally illegal under existing international humanitarian law and human rights law. Some would go as far as making a charge of genocide." Bossuyt also concluded that "the question of legality, especially in terms of human rights and humanitarian law, has been at best peripheral to the international dialogue on sanctions," and the sanctioners cannot be absolved from having the intent to destroy the Iraqis, especially when Madeleine Albright, the US ambassador to the UN, openly acknowledged that half a million Iraqi children's deaths were worth it.

Elias Davidsson (2011), a close observer of the unfolding events, not only claimed that the human disaster caused by the sanctions against Iraq satisfies "genocidal intent," but squarely blames it on the US. He argues that "the acts committed, the degree of premeditation available to the defendants, the foreseeability of the consequences, the feedback received regularly by the defendants regarding the consequences of their deeds and the span of time in terms of months or years of the act" are sufficient to constitute a *prima facie* case of genocide (cited in Scherrer, 2011, Part II:4–5).

To Christian Scherrer (2011, Part II:4–5), another observer of the Iraqi sanctions episode, there is "abundant [and] unquestionable evidence" to indicate that the sanctioning measures were intentionally directed at inflicting inhumane suffering on the Iraqis as a national group, which satisfies the applicable Rome Statute of the

[65] Available at: www.ohchr.org/en/instruments-mechanisms/instruments/convention-prevention-and-punishment-crime-genocide, accessed on January 21, 2023.

[66] Halliday claimed, on September 30, 1999, that by 1999 between one million and 1.5 million Iraqis had died from malnutrition or inadequate health care resulting from economic sanctions. "For me what is tragic, in addition to the tragedy of Iraq itself, is the fact that the United Nations Security Council member states ... are maintaining a program of economic sanctions deliberately, knowingly killing thousands of Iraqis each month. And that definition fits genocide." See news.cornell.edu/stories/1999/09/former-un-official-says-sanctions-against-iraq-amount-genocide, accessed on January 18, 2023.

International Criminal Court (Part 2, Article 7b), which lists "extermination" as one of 11 crimes against humanity. The Rome Statute defines "extermination" as "intentional infliction of conditions of life, inter alia, the deprivation of access to food and medicine, calculated to bring about the destruction of part of a population."[67]

There are some others, however, who reject the claims of genocide in Iraq. Joy Gordon (2002), for example, has argued that, although the planning of the Iraqi sanction regimes was deliberate and thorough, although they were maintained systematically and deliberately for more than a decade, the human disaster in Iraq may not fit the "intent" element of the Genocide Convention. Although the Convention effectively places no limit on the amount of damage that may be indirectly intended, it may still be problematic to show that the Iraqi population was targeted as an ethnic or racial group, or the sanctions regimes explicitly targeted or anticipated the extermination of the Iraqis.[68]

B *Violations of International Humanitarian Laws*

Some scholars argue that the Iraqi sanctions episode must be interpreted in the light of established armed conflict laws because the sanctions were first imposed in 1990 in response to Iraq's military invasion of Kuwait, then maintained during the Gulf War, extended after the first phase of military hostilities, and continued through aerial strikes until the final invasion of Iraq in 2003. Thus, the strict measures stipulated in international humanitarian law – the Geneva Convention of 1949 – for the protection of civilians in armed conflict should be applicable to the Iraqi situation, and the sanctions regimes as well as their sponsors should be prosecuted for war crimes (Bossuyt, 2000).

As discussed in Chapter 2, the Geneva Convention (Protocol 1, Article 54), provides for the exemption of medical supplies and essential goods for the survival of the civilian population, prohibits the starvation of civilians as a method of warfare, and protects women and children from military warfare. Viewed from the vantage point of the Geneva Convention, the sanctions regimes imposed by the UNSC may well be viewed as illegal, as they clearly caused mass starvation and malnutrition, and mass death of Iraqi infants and children. Some even claim that the US and the UK should also be blamed for the "infanticide" that occurred in Iraq under vicious and calculated manipulation of UNSC-imposed sanctions by these

[67] See the Rome Statute of the International Criminal Court, available at www.icc-cpi.int/sites/default/files/RS-Eng.pdf.

[68] As mentioned above, the US defense agency DIA acknowledged that US bombers deliberately targeted the civilian infrastructure of Iraq, including water treatment facilities, with the intention of disrupting civilian life. Thus, the impact was not only foreseeable, it was in fact foreseen. The "intent" element of genocide, as stipulated by the UN, is highly controversial, however. Even the uprooting of the Latin American Indian population, which wiped out millions of aboriginals, never received the UN stamp as a genocide. See Dowlah (2022, 56, fn. 11); Rosenbaum (1996); and Resendez (2016).

countries (Scherrer, 2011, Part II:135). Sponeck (2006), who resigned from his UN position in Iraq protesting the "genocide," also accused the UNSC of engaging in "punitive and destructive" sanctions policies toward the country.

There exists no international treaty or convention that explicitly deals with or imposes legal limits on economic sanctions, except that the UN has officially abandoned comprehensive sanctions by adopting targeted sanctions since the late 1990s following the Iraqi debacle (Brzoska, 2003, 1345–1346). Article 41 of UN Charter, which empowers the UNSC to impose sanctions, is also silent on the questions of the precise scope and duration of economic sanctions (Kondoch, 2001, 285). As explained in Chapter 2, some scholarly consensus exists, however, that emphasizes *jus cogens* rules, non-derogable provisions of human rights law, and the Geneva Convention to demarcate the limits of the permissibility of economic sanctions when it comes to the civilian population (Normand, 2001).

Under international humanitarian law, as laid out in the Geneva Convention (1949), civilians enjoy a right to humanitarian assistance, although different rules apply to international and non-international armed conflicts. But the Geneva Convention strictly forbids starvation as a method of warfare, which in turn, implies that humanitarian laws should be binding with respect to the regulation of relief actions aimed at preventing starvation during wartime. That hundreds of thousands of Iraqi infants, children, and women died of starvation and malnutrition due to lack of essential food and medicine should thus qualify as violations of international humanitarian laws (Kondoch, 2001, 285).

C *Violations of Other UN Charters and International Conventions*

As discussed in Chapter 2, Article 24 of the UN Charter requires the UNSC to act in accordance with the purposes and principles of the UN in its authority to maintain peace and security in the world. Article 1 of the Charter also requires the promotion of human rights as among the most fundamental purposes and principles of the UN. That makes it highly questionable whether the UNSC itself is entitled to violate such principles in the name of enforcing global peace and security. It is also questionable whether Iraq's failure to comply with the UNSC resolutions gives the UNSC license to disavow its independent obligation with respect to the human rights of the civilian population of Iraq. A report by the Center for Economic and Social Rights (CESR, 1996) asserts that, by disavowing its own obligation to human rights with respect to Iraq, the UNSC "has placed itself beyond legal accountability, in violation of its minimal procedural duties under the UN Charter and international law"(cited in Pellett, 2011, 18).[69]

69 In contrast, the sanction regimes against Iraq were imposed prior to the 1991 Gulf War were largely consistent with international law and morality – they did enjoy virtually unanimous backing of the membership of the UN, even most of the Middle Eastern countries supported those measures (Falk, 2003, 23).

Many of the sanctions imposed against Iraq clearly violated civilian rights to health and adequate standard of living, which are well recognized by the Universal Declaration of Human Rights (UDHR), and the International Covenant on Economic, Social and Cultural Rights (ICESCR), which were discussed in great detail in Chapter 2. Comprehensive economic sanctions – wholesale restrictions on both imports from and exports to Iraq – that prevented imports of basic food and medicines, which was also compounded by lack of foreign exchange and bilateral assistance, clearly stood in the way of the Iraqi population's realization of the rights guaranteed, for example, by the UDHR and the ICESCR.

By adopting comprehensive sanctions against Iraq, which led to indiscriminate death and illness among the civilian population, while exempting the Iraqi military and political leadership from harm, involves the unescapable moral and legal responsibility of the UNSC as well as those countries that supported Iraqi sanctions (Falk, 2003, 25). Moreover, the UN charters as well as many other treaties grant special rights and protections to children as they are uniquely vulnerable to conflicts. As children rather died in hundreds of thousands in Iraq does not suggest that their rights and protections had received any serious consideration. Many of the sanctioning measures also violated the UN Declaration of the Right to Development, which has been ratified by a number of conventions since its adoption in 1986 (Pellett, 2011, 18; Subedi, 2021).

D *Irrational Exuberance of the US and the UK*

There is no dispute that the US and the UK actively manipulated the UNSC into adopting comprehensive sanctions regimes against Iraq, and that they also adopted their own unilateral sanctions often far exceeding those mandated by the UNSC. For example, the removal of Saddam Hossain from power or regime change in Iraq was never a stated objective in any of the UNSC resolutions, but the US and UK pursued such a policy from the very beginning (Ballard, 2010, 80).

Second, although the US Congress passed a Joint Resolution (P.L. 107-243) on October 16, 2002, authorizing President Bush to invade Iraq and topple Saddam Hossain, UNSC Resolution 1441, adopted on November 8, 2002, did not authorize the invasion of Iraq or overthrow of the regime. The UNSC also rebuffed the US's efforts to obtain another resolution, with specific authorization for invading Iraq on February 5, 2003, when Secretary of State Powell made a presentation at the UN with fake intelligence to substantiate the US claim that Iraq had WMD and presented a threat to world peace and security. President Bush then went ahead in declaring war against Iraq on March 19, 2003 under what is known as the "shock and awe" bombing campaign, which led to the collapse of the regime of Saddam Hossain on April 9, 2003.[70] Thus, the invasion of Iraq and the toppling of the regime

[70] Two days later, on April 11, 2003, President Bush declared US victory in the Iraq war.

was carried out with the explicit approval of the US Congress, but without clear authorization by the UNSC, which led some to conclude that it was "illegal military action against Iraq" (Gowlland-Debbas, 2004).

Third, during 1991–1997, UNSCOM carried out on-site inspections of Iraq's biological, chemical, and missile capabilities under UNSC Resolution 688. Although the resolution established no-fly zones for surveillance operations at the 32nd parallel, the US and British planes not only patrolled the no-fly zones but also challenged Iraq militarily on a daily basis (Falk, 2003, 18–19). These countries were thus engaged in active war with Iraq without declaring war and without any UNSC resolution to that effect.

And, fourth, it is also evident that in imposing sanctions against Iraq, the primary interest of the US was not to maintain global peace and security, as it claimed, but to secure an unfettered flow of oil and gas from the Gulf region, and protect its close ally Israel from the threat of any dominant power in the region (Juster, 2000, 52). Moreover, by the time the US invaded Iraq in March 2003, the country was totally and utterly disarmed (Ismael and Ismael, 2015, 164).

VII CONCLUDING REMARKS

Numerous scholars, practitioners, and observers, from both the western and eastern hemispheres, have characterized the sanctions regimes against Iraq as the "Mount Everest of sanctions," the "mother of all sanctions," the "severest sanctions ever," "war crimes," "genocide," and so on. It is indeed hard to see how any rigorous analysis of the facts and developments of the saga can avoid such inescapable characterizations. The sanctions regimes against Iraq were comprehensive and all pervasive, multilateral and unilateral, involved the largest sanctions operation in the history of UN, requiring on-site inspections and monitoring, encompassed both economic sanctions and military offensives, and lasted unremittingly for 13 gruesome years.

The humanitarian cost of the saga has been catastrophic: More explosives were dumped on Iraq than were dropped on Europe during WWII; the entire infrastructure of a middle-income country was turned into rubble; at least two million Iraqis, 80 percent of whom were children and women, lost their lives; starvation and malnutrition, lack of clean drinking water and essential medicine, and interference with civilian lives and access to food and essentials were rampant. A relatively prosperous country before sanctions is now, after three decades, one of the poorest countries in the world.

Most of the sanctioning measures against Iraq were carried out under the auspices of the UN, in clear violation of public international law, international human rights law, international humanitarian laws, the UN Charter, the Geneva Convention, and a whole range of international conventions and agreements involving human rights, and this collective body, which subjects all its members to abide by such laws, clearly abdicated its own responsibility to abide by such norms and standards.

Some scholars contend that the sanctions regimes against Iraq fail the "Martens Clause test," which, in its contemporary applications, assesses the consequences of sanctions in the context of international human rights law and international humanitarian law, as well as the UN Charter.[71]

Most importantly, the whole sanctions saga was driven by absolutely baseless claims cooked up by the US and the UK that Iraq had WMD. Worse still, these countries also carried out such a massive worldwide mass deception with full knowledge that Iraq never had any nuclear power. The evidence is available in plain sight – North Korea, despite creating a much bigger nuisance and threat to the world peace and security, was never attacked militarily. The deception has indeed been gruesome, and inexcusable.

The Iraqi saga also defied the conventional wisdom that if sanctions cause enough suffering within the society, then popular discontent would eventually force the ruling elite to change the policies that are deemed to be in breach of international law.[72] But neither the Iraqi population nor the Iraqi army toppled Saddam from power, despite many years of inhumane suffering. Instead, Saddam succeeded in shifting the blame to the UN and the US for the disastrous humanitarian crisis in the country. Saddam Hossain was eventually toppled from power not by economic sanctions, but by massive military offensives. Rather than being welcomed as liberators, the provisional authority (CPA) which replaced Saddam was greeted by massive insurgency and sectarian violence, which caused the internal and external displacement of millions of Iraqis.

REFERENCES

Ali, M., J. Blacker, and G. Jones. 2011. Annual Mortality Rates and Excess Deaths of Children Under-Five in Iraq, 1991–1998. In C. Scherrer (ed.), *Iraq: Genocide by Sanctions*. Part II. Penang, Malaysia: Penerbit USM.

Alnasrawi, A. 2001. Iraq: Economic Sanctions and Consequences, 1990–2000. *Third World Quarterly*, 22(2):205–218.

[71] Originally proposed by Fyodor Fyodorovich Martens –a Russian diplomat – at the First Hague International Peace Conference of 1899 (the Hague Convention on the Laws and Customs of War on Land), the Martens Clause has become a central principle of contemporary international military and humanitarian law to ensure humanization of warfare. The Clause has been adopted by international humanitarian law to protect human rights in time of war, and has acquired the status of customary international law to regulate military situations occurring in the course of hostilities between conflicting parties that are not covered by existing international and national legal standards. The test, in essence, underlines that, in cases not covered by international humanitarian law treaties, persons affected by armed conflict will never find themselves completely deprived of protection, and they would rather be protected by the laws of nations, the laws of humanity, and from the dictates of public conscience. Based on internet sources.

[72] Bossuyt (2000), a close observer of the Iraqi episode, contends that the sanctions regimes against Iraq failed on all counts of a six-point test: Are the sanctions imposed for valid reasons? Do the sanctions target the proper parties? Do the sanctions target the proper goods or objects? Are the sanctions reasonably time-limited? Are the sanctions effective? Are the sanctions free from protest arising from violations of the principles of humanity and the dictates of the public conscience?

Andreas, P. 2005. Criminalizing Consequences of Sanctions: Embargo Busting and Its Legacy. *International Studies Quarterly*, 49(2):335–360.
Ballard, J. 2010. *From Storm to Freedom: America's Long War with Iraq*, pp. 79–88. Annapolis, MD: US Naval Institute Press.
Baram, A. 1993. The Iraqi Invasion of Kuwait: Decision-Making in Baghdad. In A. Baram, and B. Rubin (eds.), *Iraq's Road to War*. New York: St. Martin's Press.
Baram, A. 2000. The Effect of Iraqi Sanctions: Statistical Pitfalls and Responsibility. *The Middle East Journal*, 54(2):194–223.
Bearman, S. (Ed.). 1996. *Strategic Survey 1995/96*. London: Oxford University Press.
Biehler, G. 2003. Legal Limits to International Sanctions. *Hibernian Law Journal*, 4:15–24.
Bossuyt, M. 2000a. The Bossuyt Report to UN Economic and Social Council. UN Sub-Commission on the Promotion and Protection of Human Rights. Fifty-second session. June 21. E/CN.4/Sub.2/2000/33.
Bossuyt. M. 2000b. The Adverse Consequences of Economic Sanctions on the Enjoyment of Human Rights: Working Paper. Geneva: United Nations, 21 June. Available at: digitallibrary.un.org/record/419880.
Bremer, L. P. 2014. Only America Can Prevent a Disaster in Iraq. *Wall Street Journal*, June 15. Available at: www.wsj.com/articles/l-paul-bremer-only-america-can-prevent-a-disaster-in-iraq-1402869886.
Bremer, P. 2003. *Salam Pax: The Clandestine Diary of an Ordinary Iraqi*. New York: Grove Press.
Brzoska, M. (Ed.). 2001. *Design and Implementation of Arms Embargoes and Travel and Aviation Related Sanctions: Results of the "Bonn-Berlin Process."* Bonn, Germany: Bonn International Center for Conversion.
Brzoska, M. 2003. From Dumb to Smart? Recent Reforms of UN Sanctions. *Global Governance*, 9(4):519–535.
Brzoska, M. 2015. International Sanctions before and beyond UN Sanctions. *International Affairs*, 91(6):1339–1349.
Butt, K., and A. Butt. 2014. UN Sanctions against Iraq: From Ailment to Chronic. *Journal of Political Studies*, 21(2):271–295.
CESR. 1996. *Unsanctioned Suffering: A Human Rights Assessment on the United Nations Sanctions on Iraq*. New York: Center for Economic and Social Rights.
Chesterman, F., and D. Malone. 2016. *Law and Practice of the United Nations: Documents and Commentary*. 2nd ed. Oxford: Oxford University Press.
Dodge, T. 2010. The Failure of Sanctions and the Evolution of International Policy towards Iraq, 1990–2003. *Contemporary Arab Affairs*, 3(1):83–91.
Dowlah. C. 2022. Slaveries of Amerindians and Native Americans. In C. Dowlah (ed.), *Foundations of Modern Slavery*, pp. 49–64. London and New York: Routledge.
Doxey, M. 1996. *International Sanctions in Contemporary Perspective*. 2nd ed. New York: St. Martins.
Doxey, M. 2009. Reflections on the Sanctions Decade and Beyond. *International Journal*, 64(2):539–549.
Drezner, D. 2011. Sanctions Sometimes Smart: Targeted Sanctions in Theory and Practice. *International Studies Review*, 13(1):96–108.
Drury, A. 2001. Sanctions as Coercive Diplomacy: The U.S. President's Decision to Initiate Economic Sanctions. *Political Research Quarterly*, 54(3):485–508.
Eisenberg, L. 1997. The Sleep of Reason Produces Monsters? Human Costs of Economic Sanctions. *New England Journal of Medicine* (24 April 1997), 336(17):1248–1250.
Fakir, M., and A. Farhan. 2019. Features of the Iraqi Economy: Comparative Study to Some Economic Elements for the Years 1990–2019. *International E-Journal of Advances in Social Sciences*, 5(15):1414–1422.

Falk, R. 2003. Iraq, the United States, and International Law: Beyond the Sanctions. In T. Ismael, and W. Haddad (eds.), *Iraq: The Human Cost of History*, pp. 16–33. New York: Pluto Press.

FAO (Food and Agricultural Organization). 1995. *Evaluation of the Food and Nutrition Situation in Iraq*. Technical Cooperation Program TCP/IRQ/4552. Rome, Italy: Food and Agricultural Organization.

FAO/WFP (Food and Agricultural Organization and World Food Program). 2000. *Evaluation of the Food and Nutrition Situation in Iraq*. Technical Report TCP/IRQ/8924. Rome, Italy: Food and Agriculture Organization.

Farrall, J., and K. Rubenstein (Eds.). 2009. *Sanctions, Accountability and Governance in a Globalized World*. Cambridge: Cambridge University Press.

GAO (Government Accountability Office). 2014. Weapons of Mass Destruction: U.N. Confronts Significant Challenges in Implementing Sanctions against Iraq. Washington, DC: GAO. Available at: digital.library.unt.edu/ark:/67531/metadc294523/.

GAO (US General Accounting Office). 2004. Recovering Iraq's Assets. GAO-04-579T. March 18, 2004. Washington, DC: US General Accounting Office.

Garfield, R. 2011. Excess Mortality in Iraq during Sanctions. In C. Scherrer (ed.), *Iraq: Genocide by Sanctions*. Penang, Malaysia: Penerbit USM.

Garfield, R., and S. Santana. 1997. The Impact of the Economic Crisis and the US Embargo on Health in Cuba. *American Journal of Public Health*, 87(1):15–20.

Gordon, J. 2002. When Intent Makes All the Difference in the World: Economic Sanctions on Iraq and the Accusation of Genocide. *Yale Human Rights & Development Law Journal*, 5:57–85. Available at: law.yale.edu/sites/default/files/documents/pdf/LawJournals/Joy_Gordon_YHRDLJ.pdf.

Gordon, J. 2010. *Invisible War: The United States and the Iraq Sanctions*. Cambridge, MA: Harvard University Press.

Gowlland-Debbas, V. 2004. Sanctions Regimes under Article 41 of the UN Charter. In V. Gowlland-Debbas (ed.), *National Implementation of United Nations Sanction: A Comparative Study*, pp. 3–31. Boston, MA: Brill/Nijhoff.

Graham-Brown, S. 1999. *Sanctioning Saddam: The Politics of Intervention in Iraq*. New York: St. Martins.

Haass, R. 2009. *War of Necessity, War of Choice: A Memoir of Two Iraq Wars*. New York.

Haass, R., and M. O'Sullivan. (Eds.). 2000. *Honey and Vinegar: Incentives, Sanctions, and Foreign Policy*. Washington, DC: Brookings Institution Press.

Halliday, D. 1999a. The Impact of the UN Sanctions on the People of Iraq. *Journal of Palestine Studies*, 28(2):29–37.

Halliday, D. 1999b. Former UN Official Says Sanctions against Iraq Amount to "Genocide." September 30, 1999. Available at: news.cornell.edu/stories/1999/09/former-un-official-says-sanctions-against-iraq-amount-genocide.

Halliday, D. 2000. The Deadly and Illegal Consequences of the Economic Sanctions on the People of Iraq. *Brown Journal of World Affairs*, 7(1):229–233.

Hindawi, C. 2017. Twenty Years in the Shadow of Chapter VII. In K. Makdisi, and V. Prashad (eds.), *Land of Blue Helmets: The United Nations and the Arab World*, pp. 194–211. Berkeley: University of California Press.

Holden, S. 2012. *A Documentary History of Modern Iraq*. Gainesville: University Press of Florida.

Hoskins, E. 1997. The Humanitarian Impacts of Economic Sanctions and War in Iraq. In T. Weiss et al. (eds.), *Political Gain and Civilian Pain*, pp. 91–149. Lanham, MD: Rowman and Littlefield.

Hufbauer, G. et al. 2007. *Economic Sanctions Reconsidered: History and Current Policy*. Washington, DC: Patterson Institute for International Economics.

IAC. 1996. *The Children Are Dying: The Impact of Sanctions on Iraq*. New York: International Action Center and World View Forum.

IDMC (Internal Displacement Monitoring Centre). 2012. Internally Displaced Persons in Iraq. Available at: www.internal-displacement.org/middle-east-and-north-africa/iraq/figures-analysis.

IIC (Independent Inquiry Committee). 2005. The Impact of the Oil-for-Food Program on the Iraqi People. Report of an independent Working Group established by the Independent Inquiry Committee. New York, September 7, 2005. Available at: www.iic-OFFP.org/Impact_Report.htm.

Ismael, S. 2007. The Cost of War: The Children of Iraq. *Journal of Comparative Family Studies*. 38(2):337–357.

Ismael, T., and J. Ismael. 2004. The Iraqi Predicament: People in the Quagmire of Power Politics. In T. Ismael, and J. Ismael (eds.), *UN Sanctions: Tools of Domination and Oppression*, pp. 90–125. London: Pluto Press.

Ismael, T., and J. Ismael. 2015a. Introduction: Iraqi Ruination – The Humanitarian Cost of an Imposed State. In T. Ismael, and J. Ismael (eds.), *Iraq in the Twenty-First Century: Regime Change and the Making of a Failed State*, pp. 1–10. London: Routledge.

Ismael, T., and J. Ismael. 2015b. Children of the Occupation: A Decade after the Invasion. In The Humanitarian Cost of an Imposed State. In *Iraq in the Twenty-First Century: Regime Change and the Making of a Failed State*, pp. 149–169. London: Routledge.

Joyner, C. 2003. United Nations Sanctions after Iraq. *Chicago Journal of International Law*, 4 (2): Article 7.

Joyner, D. 2015. International Legal Limits on the Ability of States to Lawfully Impose International Economic/Financial Sanctions. In A. Marossi, and M. Bassett (eds.), *Economic Sanctions under International Law: Unilateralism, Multilateralism, Legitimacy and Consequences*, pp. 83–93. London: Springer.

Joyner, D. 2017. UN Counter-Proliferation Sanctions and International Law. In L. Herik (ed.), *Research Handbook on UN Sanctions and International Law*, pp. 110–121. Cheltenham, UK: Edward Elgar.

Juster, K. 2000. The United States and Iraq: Perils of Engagement. In R. Haass, and M. O'Sullivan (eds.), *Honey and Vinegar: Incentives, Sanctions, and Foreign Policy*, pp. 51–69. Washington, DC: Brookings Institution Press.

Kondoch, B. 2001. The Limits of Economic Sanctions under International Law: The Case of Iraq. *Journal of International Peacekeeping*, 7(2001):267–294.

Lauro, A. 2020. The UN Sanctions Regime. Working Paper No. 9/2018-2019. Rome, Italy: LUISS Academy.

Lopez, G., and D. Cortright. 2004. Containing Iraq: Sanctions Worked. *Foreign Affairs*, 83(4):90–103.

Lowenfeld, A. 2003. Trade Controls for Political Ends: Four Perspectives. *Chicago Journal of International Law*, 4(2):354369.

Marr, P. 2004. *The Modern History of Iraq*. Boulder, CO: Westview Press.

Meyer, J. 2009. Second Thoughts on Secondary Sanctions. *University of Pennsylvania Journal of International Economic Law*, 30(3):905–934.

MIT Center for International Studies. 2013. *The Human Cost of the War in Iraq*. Available at: web.mit.edu/humancostiraq.

Mulder, N. 2022. *The Economic Weapon: The Rise of Sanctions as a Tool of Modern War*. New Haven, CT: Yale University Press.

Muller, J., and K. Muller, 1999. Sanctions of Mass Destruction. *Foreign Affairs*, 78(3):43–53.

Nagy, T. 2001. The Secret behind the Sanctions: How the US Intentionally Destroyed Iraq's Water Supply. Available at: progressive.org/mag/nagy0901.html.

Normand, R., and C. Wilcke. 2001. Human Rights, Sanctions, and Terrorist Threats: The United Nations Sanctions against Iraq. *Transnational Law & Contemporary Problems*, 11(2):299–343.

O'Sullivan, M. 2003. *Shrewd Sanctions – Statecraft and State Sponsors of Terrorism*. Washington, DC: Brookings Institution Press.

Pellett, P. 2011. Sanctions and Nutritional Health in Iraq. In C. Scherrer (ed.), *Iraq: Genocide by Sanctions*. Part II. Penang, Malaysia: Penerbit USM.

Reisman, W., and D. Stevick. 1998. The Applicability of International Law Standards to United Nations Economic Sanctions Programs. *European Journal of International Law* 9:86–141.

Resendez, A. 2016. *The Other Slavery: Uncovered Story of Indian Enslavement in America*. Boston: Mariner Books.

Rosenbaum, A. (Ed.). 1996. *Is the Holocaust Unique? Perspectives on Comparative Genocide*. Boulder, CO: Westview Press.

Rubin, M. 2001. Sanctions on Iraq: A Valid Anti-American Grievance? *Middle East Review of International Affairs*, 5(4):100–115.

Sanford, J. 2003. *Iraq's Economy: Past, Present, Future*. Washington, DC: Congressional Research Service.

Scherrer, C. (Ed.). 2011. *Iraq: Genocide by Sanctions*. 2 vols. Penang, Malaysia: Penerbit USM.

Sciolino, E. 1991. *The Outlaw State: Saddam Hussein's Quest for Power and the Gulf Crisis*. New York: John Wiley and Sons.

Sponeck, H. C. von 2003. *To an Unknown Iraqi*. The Translators Network for Linguistic Diversity. Available at: blog.transnational.org/2013/01/to-an-unknown-iraqi/.

Sponeck, H. C. von 2006. *A Different Kind of War: The UN Sanctions Regime in Iraq*. Bonn, Germany: Berghahn Books.

Stauffer, T. 2001. Critical Review of UNCC Award for Lost Production and Lost Revenues. *MMN (Media Monitors Network)*. September 10, 2001. Available at: mediamonitors.net/critical-review-of-uncc-award-for-lost-production-and-lost-reserves/.

Subedi, S. 2021. *Declaration on the Right to Development. United Nations Audiovisual Library of International Law*. New York: United Nations.

Timmerman, K. 1991. *The Death Lobby: How the West Armed Iraq*. Boston: Houghton Mifflin.

Tripp, C. 2008. *A History of Iraq*. 2nd ed. Cambridge: Cambridge University Press.

UN (United Nations). 1999. Report of the Second Panel Established Pursuant to the Note by the President of the Security Council of 30 January 1999 (S/1999/100), Concerning the Current Humanitarian Situation in Iraq. Available at: www.casi.org.uk/info/panelrep.html.

UNDP (United Nations Development Program). 1998. Integrating Human Rights with Sustainable Human Development – A UNDP Policy Document. Available at: magnet.undp.org/Docs/policy5.html.

UNHCHR (United Nations High Commission on Human Rights). 1998. Declaration on the Right to Development. New York: United Nations. Available at: www.unhchr.ch/html/menu2/10/e.

UNICEF (United Nations Children's Emergency Fund). 1995. *The Status of Children and Women in Iraq: A Situation Report*. Baghdad (Iraq): UNICEF, September 1995.

UNICEF (United Nations Children's Emergency Fund). 1996. Promotion and Protection of the Rights of Children: Impact of Armed Conflict on Children. New York: UNICEF. Available at: www.unicef.org/graca/a51-306_en.pdf.

UNICEF (United Nations Children's Emergency Fund). 1999a. *Iraq Child and Maternal Mortality Survey 1999*. New York: UNICEF.

UNICEF (United Nations Children's Emergency Fund). 1999b. Iraq Child and Maternal Mortality Survey, 1999: Preliminary Report. New York: UNICEF. Available at: www.childinfo.org/cmr/Irq/irqrptsc3.pdf.

United Nations. 1999. Report of the Second Panel Established Pursuant to the Note by the President of the Security Council of 30 January 1999 (S/1999/100), Concerning the Current Humanitarian Situation in Iraq. Available at: www.casi.org.uk/info/panelrep.html.

UNMOVIC (United Nations Monitoring, Verification and Inspection Commission). Compendium of Iraq's Proscribed Weapons Programs in the Chemical, Biological, and Missile Areas. Available at: onlinebooks.library.upenn.edu/webbin/book/lookupid?key=olbp60650.

Volcker, G. 2005. Independent Inquiry Committee into the United Nations Oil-for-Food Program (Final Report). September 7. New York: United Nations.

Volcker, P., J. Meyer, and M. Califano. 2006. *Good Intentions Corrupted: The Oil-for-Food Scandal and the Threat to the UN*. New York: Public Affairs.

Wallensteen, P., and C. Staibano. 2005. *International Sanctions: Between Wars and Words in Global System*. New York: Frank Cass.

White, N. 2018. Autonomous and Collective Sanctions in the International Legal Order. *The Italian Yearbook of International Law Online*, 27(1):1–32. Available at: www.researchgate.net/publication/348833316_Autonomous_and_Collective_Sanctions_in_the_International_Legal_Order.

Wilbur, R. 1990. The Iran-Iraq War: An Analysis of the Cease-Fire. *The Fletcher Forum of World Affairs*, 14(1):111–127.

Zurbrigg, S. 2007. Economic Sanctions on Iraq: Tool for Peace, or Travesty? *Muslim World Journal of Human Rights*, 4(2). Available at: doi.org/10.2202/1554-4419.1108.

8

US Economic and Financial Sanctions against the Republic of Cuba

I INTRODUCTION

The US had sanctions regimes in place against its southern neighbor – a small island nation called the Republic of Cuba – long before Fidel Castro overthrew the regime of Fulgencio Batista in January 1959 through a violent communist revolution.[1] Even the overthrow of the Batista regime was largely facilitated by US sanctions, and the US was also among the first nations in the world to extend recognition to the Castro regime.[2] But the relationship between the two countries began to sour soon after Fidel Castro began to undertake measures aimed at expropriating Cuban property owned by US investors, raising taxes on Cuban exports to the US, and establishing trade relations with the then Soviet Union.[3]

At the time of Castro's assumption of power, most of Cuban businesses were owned by US investors. For example, the Cuban Telephone and Telegraph Corporation was an affiliate of US-based AT&T; almost all the casinos, ranches, and farms were owned by US investors; the US-based United Fruit Company owned Cuban companies named United Brands and Chiquita Brands; US-owned oil refineries – Esso/Standard Oil and Texaco – owned all the oil and petroleum establishments in Cuba; and almost all Cuban banking businesses were owned by a few

[1] The largest and westernmost island in the West Indies, Cuba is located about 150 kilometers south of Key West (Florida), the southernmost point of the US. With a land surface of 110,860 square kilometers, it is about the size of the US State of Pennsylvania, and has an estimated population of 11 million. A former Spanish colony, Cuba had a long, checkered, and troublesome history with its northern neighbor, the US. Following the Spanish–American War, which the Spanish Empire lost, Cuba came under the control of the US in 1899, and remained a US protectorate until 1902, when it became a Republic. For greater detail, see Hudson (2001) and Suchlicki (1986, 2001).

[2] Batista ruled Cuba as a military dictator for seven years, when the US served as a staunch ally due to the regime's anticommunist stance. Following Castro's revolution, Batista fled to Portugal, but he died in Guadalmina (Spain) in 1973. The US extended recognition to the Castro regime on January 7, 1959 – within a week of Castro's assumption of power. See Bain and Walker (2021); LeoGrande (2021); Sullivan (1999); USITC (2001, 1–9).

[3] Some of the important sources on the troubled relationship between the US and Cuba include: Horowitz and Suchlicki (2001); LeoGrande (2021); Rathbone (2013); and USITC (2001).

US-based banks, such as the First National Bank of Boston, the City Bank of New York, and the Chase Manhattan Bank. By October 1960, in less than two years in power, Castro nationalized all these businesses, denying any compensation.[4]

Prior to the communist revolution, the US was also the largest trading partner of Cuba – in 1958, the US accounted for 67 percent of Cuba's exports and 70 percent of its imports (ECLAC, 1965, 273), and in 1959, Cuba exported 2.9 million metric tons of sugar to the US – 35 percent of US total sugar imports (ECLAC, 1963, 259–273). The same year, 2.5 percent of US exports were destined for Cuba, while 3.0 percent of US imports came from that country (USITC, 2001, 2–13).

In February 1960, within just one year of the revolution, Castro drastically cut back trade relations with the US by signing a major trade and economic assistance agreement with the then Soviet Union, under which Cuban sugar, which earned over 80 percent of the country's export revenues, was slated for importing Soviet crude oil and petroleum products.

The US response to Cuba's action was sweeping and immediate. By the fall of 1959, President Dwight D. Eisenhower adopted a policy aimed at removing Fidel Castro from power through a combination of measures encompassing economic sanctions, covert aid to Castro's opponents, assassination attempts, and a paramilitary invasion of Cuba (LeoGrande and Kornbluh, 2015).[5] In July 1960, Eisenhower canceled all sugar imports from Cuba, and in October the same year, a complete ban was imposed on US exports to Cuba except for nonsubsidized foodstuffs and medical supplies (USITC, 2001, 2–13).

Continuing the hardline policy, President John F. Kennedy in January 1961 broke off diplomatic relations with Cuba, and denied any US foreign assistance to Cuba pursuant to the Foreign Assistance Act of 1961 (FAA: P.L. 87-195). The next year, in February 1962, Kennedy imposed a full-scale trade embargo against Cuba,[6] and two months later, in May 1962, the US also suspended both preferential and Most-Favored Nation tariff treatment of Cuban goods, invoking Section 401 of the Tariff Classification Act of 1962 (TCA: P.L. 87-456).

4 By June 1959, Castro had nationalized the Cuban Telephone and Telegraph Corporation, and expropriated all the casinos, ranches, and farms owned by US investors; the United Brands and Chiquita Brands were nationalized in January, 1960; all US-owned oil refineries and petroleum product businesses were expropriated by February, 1960; the US-owned Esso/Standard Oil and Texaco were nationalized in June–July, 1960; all the US owned banks in Cuba – the First National Bank of Boston, the First National City Bank of New York, and Chase Manhattan Bank – were nationalized in August–September 1960; and most of the remaining US-owned properties were nationalized by October 24, 1960. For greater detail, see, Franklin (1997, 18–33); Horowitz and Suchlicki (2001); and USITC (2001, 1–9).

5 The CIA's covert operations against Cuba, approved by Eisenhower on March 17, 1960, evolved into the Bay of Pigs invasion in 1961 (LeoGrande, 2015, 234).

6 President Kennedy issued Executive Order (EO) 3347 – Embargo on All Trade with Cuba – on February 3, 1962, enforcing the FAA 1961 which prohibited "the importation into the United States of all goods of Cuban origin and all goods imported from or through Cuba."

In the meantime, in April 1961, in pursuance of the Bay of Pigs Invasion plan developed earlier by Eisenhower, Kennedy deployed a 1,400-man invasion brigade consisting of Cuban exiles to overthrow the Castro regime. The Cuban military, however, thwarted the invasion in three days.[7] Eventually, in the fortnight of October 14–28, 1963, the tension between the two countries spilled over to a global superpower conflict when US spy satellites discovered a Soviet nuclear missile base on the Cuban island. Following the discovery, Kennedy ordered a naval quarantine around Cuba, demanding the immediate removal of Soviet weapons.

The resultant 13-day standoff – known as the "Cuban Missile Crisis" – brought the world to the edge of a nuclear war, which was eventually averted when the Soviet Union agreed to withdraw its missiles from Cuba in exchange for a US pledge not to invade Cuba and to withdraw its nuclear missiles from Turkey.[8] The relationship between the two countries has remained highly tense and problematic ever since, throughout the last six decades, when the US maintained its longest-running sanctions measures against Cuba (Bain and Walker, 2021; LeoGrande and Kornbluh, 2015).

The rest of the chapter is organized as follows: Section II examines the progression of the US economic and financial sanctions regimes against Cuba along with their legal underpinnings; Section III examines the economic impact of US sanctions on the Cuban economy and population; and Section IV concludes the chapter.

II SIX DECADES OF SANCTIONS

The US has maintained near-comprehensive sanctions regimes against Cuba since 1963 – for exactly six decades by now. No other country in the world has been subjected to such a prolonged and sustained campaign of sanctions since WWII. Given the fact that prior to the communist revolution that brought Fidel Castro to power, the US was the largest source of foreign investment for Cuba and the country's largest trading partner, and the US sanctions regimes on the country have been in place ever since, it is rather obvious that the sanctions regimes would have far-reaching and devastating effects on the country's economy and population (Rathbone, 2013, 1075).

7 Almost 1,200 members of the brigade surrendered, and more than 100 were killed. The prisoners remained in captivity for 20 months, until a deal was struck with Fidel Castro. After the disaster at the Bay of Pigs, President Kennedy initiated another plan, called Operation Mongoose, to sabotage and destabilize the Castro government and economy, including the assassination of Fidel Castro. For greater detail, see John F. Kennedy, Presidential Library and Museum: www.jfklibrary.org/search?search=operation%20mongoose&sort_by=search_api_relevance&sort_order=DESC. See also Howard (2008); Mallett (2013).

8 The body of scholarly work on the Cuban Missile Crisis is voluminous. Some of the important works include: Chang and Kornbluh (1999); Elliston (1999); Mollinedo (2021); Scott and Hughes (2015); and Stern (2005). For important documents, see George Washington University's National Security Archive, available at nsarchive2.gwu.edu/nsa/cuba_mis_cri/index.htm.

The legal foundations of such protracted sanctions regimes against Cuba rest mainly on the following statues and regulations: the Trading with the Enemy Act, 1917 (TWEA: P.L. 65-91); the FAA; the International Emergency Economic Powers Act, 1977 (IEEPA: P.L. 95-223); the Cuban Democracy Act, 1992 (CDA: P.L. 102-484); the Cuban Liberty and Democratic Solidarity Act, 1996 (Helms–Burton Act: P.L. 104-114); the Trade Sanctions Reform and Export Enhancement Act, 2000 (TSRA: P.L. 106-387); and the Cuban Asset Control Regulations, 1963/2004 (CACR: C.F.R. Part 515). Such a linear progression of sanctions regimes against Cuba indicates that both the presidents and the Congressional leaders moved hand-in-hand when it came to Cuba.

Kennedy to Johnson Administrations

In July 1963, under the authority of Section 620(a) of the FAA and Section 5(b) of the TWEA, the Office of Foreign Assets Control (OFAC) issued the CACR of 1963, prohibiting all unlicensed financial and commercial transactions by US persons with Cuba or its citizens and banning all direct or indirect exports and imports of all products and services to and from Cuba.[9] The CACR also froze all Cuban government and private assets under US jurisdiction, and prohibited all US nationals from traveling to Cuba, and any trade and business by any foreign-incorporated entities owned or controlled by US persons (Mollinedo, 2021, 84–85; Varona, 1994, 7). The CACR thus enforced a total embargo on trade and business with Cuba and imposed sweeping restrictions targeting virtually any US person and Cuban citizen anywhere in the world (Sullivan and York, 1999, 3; USITC, 2001, 2–5).

President Lyndon B. Johnson further expanded the US embargo by making the sanctions against Cuba multilateral. In 1964, the Johnson Administration succeeded in convincing the OAS, a US-led regional body, to suspend its diplomatic and trade relations with Cuba on the grounds of Cuba's close economic, political, and military ties with the Soviet Union. Johnson also convinced several South American countries to break-off diplomatic and economic relations with Cuba for allegedly sponsoring communist movements in those countries (DeMelfi, 2006; Schoultz, 2011).[10]

In 1966, President Johnson opened the door for Cubans to seek political asylum and citizenship in the US for the first time, in pursuance of the Cuban Adjustment Act, 1966 (CAA: P.L. 89-732). The CAA empowered the president to grant preferential treatment to Cubans who fled the island to seek permanent residency in the

[9] The CACR, however, granted exception from the embargo for up to $100 worth of Cuban merchandise, in case those were accompanied by returning pre-authorized travelers.

[10] For greater detail, see OAS Resolution I, Sixth Meeting of Consultation of Ministers of Foreign Affairs, Final Act, San Jose, 16–21 August, 1960. For similar efforts under the Johnson Administration, see OAS Resolution I, Ninth Meeting of Consultation of Ministers of Foreign Affairs, Final Act, Washington, DC, 22–26 July, 1966. Notably, earlier, in March 1961, the Kennedy Administration released a "White Paper" accusing Cuba of posing a danger to the western hemisphere due to its links with the international communist movement and the Soviet Union, and authorized "Operation Mongoose" to sabotage the Castro regime.

US provided that they: (a) were inspected and admitted or paroled into the US after January 1, 1959; (b) were physically present in the US for one year; and (c) had family ties to US citizens or residents. Available estimates suggest that approximately 270,000 Cubans took advantage of this legislation (Sullivan, 1999, 3).

Nixon to Carter Administrations

Apparently, President Richard M. Nixon also adopted a similar soft approach toward Cuba. In February 1973, Nixon signed an anti-hijacking agreement with Cuba under which both countries agreed to prosecute hijackers or return them to each other's country for prosecution. The agreement came against the backdrop of a meteoric rise in plane hijacking incidents in the 1960s – between 1961 and 1967, as many as 325 plane hijackings took place around the world, of which 17 landed in Cuba alone (LeoGrande and Kornbluh, 2015, 123).[11] At the same time, the Nixon Administration also carried out a large number of terrorist activities against the Castro regime, including attacks on fishing boats and Cuban missions abroad, as well as spreading African swine fever in Cuba (Mollinedo, 2021, 87).

Under President Gerald Ford, the relationship between the countries improved remarkably. In January 1975, under an agreement reached in New York, the US agreed to ease its embargo by allowing ships trading with Cuba to resupply in US ports, and the US subsidiaries were allowed to export to Cuba products that contained less than 20 percent of US-made content. The same year, the OAS also lifted its multilateral trade ban on Cuba completely, and quickly restored trade relations with Cuba. The process of easing the US embargo, however, faded soon, when Cuba sent troops to aid the communist movement in Angola in October 1975 (LeoGrande and Kornbluh, 2015; Mollinedo, 2021, 88).

The US relationship with Cuba improved robustly under President Jimmy Carter, however. In 1977, the Carter Administration relaxed travel restrictions on Cubans and Americans, and opened diplomatic relations between the two countries by establishing diplomatic "Interests Sections" – under which Cuba set up an interests section in the Czech Embassy in Washington, DC, while the US set up its interests section at the Swiss Embassy in Havana. President Carter also established special flight links between Havana and Miami, authorized transactions in dollars between the financial entities of both countries, suspended US spy flights over Cuba, and signed several agreements with Cuba on maritime boundaries, fishing exploitation, and air piracy (Franklin, 1997, 119–121; Mollinedo, 2021, 887).

The Carter Administration also admitted 125,000 Cubans into the US on the grounds of economic and political hardships during April–October, 1980 (Sullivan, 1999, 4). The operation was, however, marred by some ill-fated diplomatic incidents

[11] Cuba, however, suspended the anti-hijacking agreement with the US in October 1976 after a bomb exploded on a *Cubana* airlines flight as it took off from the southern Caribbean port city of Barbados, which killed all 73 people on board (Sullivan, 1999, 3).

in April 1980, often described as the Mariel Boatlift,[12] when more than 10,000 Cubans crowded at the gates of the Peruvian Embassy in Havana seeking asylum in the US in response to Fidel Castro's announcement that anyone wishing to leave Cuba for the US could do so from Mariel Harbor over the course of the next six months. Castro also encouraged criminals and mental patients to leave the country by taking this opportunity. Between the time that Castro opened the port of Mariel in April and its closure in September, hundreds of small boats ferried thousands of Cuban emigrants to the US in "utterly uncontrolled, unregulated, and essentially illegal migration" (LeoGrande, 2015, 236).

The Carter Administration's normalization efforts also faltered when Cuba sent troops to Ethiopia in 1979, in collaboration with the Soviet Union, and in response, President Carter resumed spy flights over Cuban territory and military maneuvers in the Caribbean Sea. He issued Presidential Directive 52 on October 4, 1979, abandoning constructive engagement with Cuba and directing the US government agencies to contain a source of "violent revolutionary change" by removing Cuban military forces stationed abroad, undercut Cuba's drive for Third World leadership, and inhibit the Soviet build-up of Cuba's armed forces (LeoGrande, 2021, 35).[13]

The Reagan Administration

President Ronald Reagan entered office with the "intent on reversing the tide of Soviet-Cuban advancements throughout the Third World" (Varona, 1994, 9). Reagan not only reinvigorated Carter's Presidential Directive 52, which was set in motion in October, 1979, but also tightened sanctions against Cuba by reversing many of the normalizing policies adopted by Carter toward Cuba. Such a reversal was prompted by several developments, such as: In August 1979, the US became aware of the presence of a Soviet combat brigade of 2,000–3,000 soldiers in Cuba (Kaplowitz, 1998); Castro used the Mariel Boatlift to force normalization of relations with the US (Mollinedo, 2021); Castro continued his support for revolutionary movements and subversive activities in many Central and Latin American countries, such as Colombia, Chile, Ecuador, Nicaragua, Peru, Colombia, Costa Rica, and Venezuela, and Grenada; and domestically, anti-Cuban sentiments spread throughout the US (Alzugaray, 2006; Hudson, 2001, 52–53).

Some of the major sanctioning measures adopted by the Reagan Administration against Cuba included: (a) in 1982, a partial ban on travel of US persons to Cuba was re-imposed, and subsidiaries of US corporations were warned not to exceed the limits established on trade content eligible for exports to Cuba; (b) the same

[12] The Mariel fiasco, which led to Castro opening up for free emigration from Cuba, President Carter later claimed in his memoir, played a key role in his electoral defeat in 1980. The incident is also notable for the fact that during the turmoil, on September 11, 1980, an official of Cuba's Mission to the UN in New York was assassinated by anti-Castro terrorist groups. For greater detail, see Alzugaray (2006, 18–19); Mollinedo (2021, 88); Sullivan (1999, 4); and Varona (1994).

[13] For greater detail, see Presidential Directive/ NSC-52, available at jimmycarterlibrary.gov.

year, Cuba was designated a state sponsor of terrorism and the Castro regime was warned against providing support to militant communist groups in African and Latin American countries; (c) in 1983, the US conducted a military intervention in Grenada to protect US lives and to end Cuban influence on the island; and (d) in 1985, Radio Martí, a propaganda station modeled on Radio Free Europe and named after José Martí, the father of Cuban independence, was introduced as a mouthpiece of the newly formed Cuban American National Foundation (CANF), composed of wealthy Miami exiles who pressed for hardline policies against Castro's Cuba (LeoGrande, 2015, 236–237; Sullivan, 1999, 4; Varona, 1994).

In 1984, however, President Reagan signed an immigration agreement with Cuba under which the US agreed to issue up to 20,000 preference immigration visas each year and grant immigrant visas to Cuban residents who were close relations of US citizens. In exchange, Cuba agreed to take back 2,700 unwanted Cuban refugees who had migrated to the US during the Mariel Boatlift incident. But only 23 of these refugees had actually returned to Cuba by 1985, when Castro suspended all immigration proceedings with the US in response to the Radio Martí program in Cuba. The radio station, however, continued throughout the 1980s and 1990s and served as the most powerful domestic political voice on US–Cuban relations (Allison, 2012; Hudson, 2001, 27; LeoGrande, 2015).

The George H. W. Bush Administration

The 1990s began with the collapse of the Soviet Union, the end of the Cold War, and the disappearance of the Soviet socialist bloc named the Council for Mutual Economic Assistance (COMECON). All these developments had very profound and far-reaching impacts on Cuba's economic and political survival. For Cuba, just the collapse of the Soviet Union meant an annual loss of around $4.5 billion in foreign assistance and subsidies.[14] Moreover, the drying up of subsidized imports of fertilizer, pesticides, petroleum, and machinery from the former Soviet Union, on which the Cuban economy depended so heavily for many decades, proved to be catastrophic (USITC, 2001, 3–7).

The resultant hardship not only forced the Castro regime to implement drastic austerity measures at home, but also forced it to terminate its support networks for insurgencies in Latin American and African countries (Mollinedo, 2021, 90–91; Sullivan, 1999, 5). Then, in March 1992, the UN Commission on Human Rights approved a resolution requesting the appointment of a UN special representative to examine the human rights situation in Cuba,[15] and six months later, in October

[14] The CIA World Fact Book (2000, 34), however, suggests that Cuba received an estimated $4 billion to $5 billion annually from the former Soviet Union – $5 billion in economic assistance, $1 billion in military assistance, and 10 million tons of petroleum. Estimates by LeoGrande and Thomas (2002, 342) show that the Soviet Union's assistance to Cuba totaled $65 billion between 1960 and 1990.

[15] The resolution – E/1992/22-E/CN.4/1992/84 – was adopted at the 52nd meeting of UN Commission on Human Rights, 27 January–6 March 1992. Also see Vazquez (2003).

1992, the US Congress passed the Cuban Democracy Act (CDA-Torricelli Act), requiring the president to further tighten the embargo against Cuba in order to force the Castro regime to introduce democratic reforms, address human rights violations, and discourage countries that received US foreign aid from providing any assistance to the Castro regime (Kaplowitz, 1998, 9–10; Vazquez, 2003).

The CDA was a major reversal of the US policy direction of the 1970s. For example, Title XVII of the CDA required the president: (a) to maintain strict limits on remittances to Cuba from the US; (b) restrict the amount of US currency traded with Cuba; (c) bar vessels that had exchanged goods with Cuba in the previous 180 days from docking at US ports; (d) prohibit foreign subsidiaries of US businesses from trading with Cuba; (e) require onsite verification of exports of medicines or medical supplies to Cuba; and (f) levy civil fines and property forfeitures on those found to be in violation of the sanctions against Cuba (Teegen et al., 2002; USITC, 2001, 2–7).

Among other goals, the CDA emphasized: (a) a peaceful transition to democracy and a resumption of economic growth in Cuba through careful application of sanctions directed at the Castro government and support for the Cuban people; (b) speedy termination of any remaining military or technical assistance, subsidies, or other forms of assistance to Cuba from the independent states of the former Soviet Union; (c) maintaining sanctions on the Castro regime so long as it continued to refuse to move toward democratization and greater respect for human rights; (d) reducing the sanctions in carefully calibrated ways in response to positive developments in Cuba; (e) encouraging free and fair elections to determine Cuba's political future; and (f) the development of a comprehensive US policy toward Cuba in a post-Castro era.[16]

The CDA also sought a regime change in Cuba through a "peaceful transition" supported by the development of a "civil society," to be developed through "people-to-people" contacts, which would eventually erode Castro's grip on society through the diffusion of democratic ideas (LeoGrande, 2015, 240; Mollinedo, 2021, 90–91). The Act also offered a path to the Castro regime for normalizing its relations with the US, provided it undertook significant economic and political reforms to build a democratic Cuba.

The Clinton Administration

At the outset of his tenure, President William Clinton signed two immigration agreements with Cuba in 1994–95. The first sought to keep all rescued Cubans at the US naval base at Guantánamo Bay and limit the entry of Cubans into the US to 20,000 persons per year, excluding immediate relatives of US citizens. The second agreement, called "wet foot, dry foot," was aimed at sending Cubans intercepted by US authorities at sea back home, while allowing others who made landfall in the US

[16] Based on United States Code title 22. Foreign Relations and Intercourse. Chapter 69.

to remain in the US and pursue permanent residency after one year.[17] These agreements also allowed more than 30,000 Cubans detained at Guantánamo Bay at the time to enter into the US on parole (Dominguez, 2001; Marino, 2002).

These agreements were prompted by a serious migratory crisis that brewed in Cuba following the steep decline in the country's trade with the former Soviet Union. Between 1989 and 1993, for example, Cuba's real GDP (gross domestic product) fell by 40 percent in official estimates and by more than 50 percent in unofficial estimates; production of industrial plant declined by 70 percent, agricultural production declined by more than 60 percent, exports declined by two-thirds, imports fell by three-fifths, and unemployment and underemployment soared (USITC, 2001, 3–10). Confronting such a dire situation, Cuba adopted wartime strategies to control and limit consumption, reduce expenditures, and strengthen domestic food production, but by 1993, the situation became so dreadful that tens of thousands of Cubans took to rafts to reach the US shore (LeoGrande and Thomas, 2002, 343).

During the first six months of 1993, the US Coast Guard picked up about 1,300 Cubans from rafts, and by 1994, the number had soared to 4,700 (GAO, 1995). Also, in June–August 1994, violence by both the Cuban authorities and asylum seekers escalated when at least 37 asylum seekers and two Cuban officials were killed, and over 200 US military personnel were injured in riots by more than 1,000 Cuban refugees at US camps in Panama (Sullivan, 1999, 11). The agreements signed by the Clinton Administration restored some normalcy in US–Cuban immigration relations, but the policy that Cuban immigrants intercepted at sea or placed at the Guantánamo naval base must return home reversed a three-decade old US policy of welcoming Cuban refugees into the US.[18]

Flickers of a Softening Stance

In the mid 1990s, American business and political establishments somewhat softened their stance toward the Castro regime. During 1994–1995, over 200 executives representing over 170 US companies traveled to Cuba to explore business opportunities in the event of the possible lifting of the US embargo. In 1995, Cuban officials met with 1,300 US executives who proposed billions of dollars of foreign investment in Cuba.[19] In June 1995, a delegation of the Inter-American Dialogue, sponsored by Atlanta-based Carter Center, traveled to Havana, and on their return, proposed lifting of US sanctions on travel and remittances to Cuba while keeping the embargo as a bargaining chip (Falk, 1996; Jones and Rich, 1998).

[17] Under the agreements, the US accepted almost all Cubans who had emigrated illegally in 1994, excepting a few criminals who were returned to Cuba (Dominguez, 2001, 278).

[18] As a result of the policy, approximately 33,000 Cubans were picked up at sea and sheltered at Guantánamo Bay (GAO, 1995, 3–4).

[19] These executives represented scores of high-level companies, such as Eli Lilly, Merck, Marriott, Hyatt, Radisson, Johnson and Johnson, AT&T, ESSO, AMOCO, Chiquita, Nabisco, Chase Manhattan, Carlson Companies, Revlon, Consolidated Cigar Aficionado, General Motors, Dow Chemical, Texaco, Sears, JCPenney, Kmart, and Radio Shack (Marino, 2002, 59).

Also, in October 1995, 60 top American business executives flew to Cuba on a private fact-finding mission on the business possibilities in Cuba, and met with Fidel Castro. Many of these business executives also met Fidel Castro when he visited New York in the fall of 1995 to attend the 50th anniversary of the UN (Marino, 2002, 56–59).

The Helms–Burton Act, 1996

All that changed quickly, however, following the downing of two airplanes operated by a Cuban exile group – named Brothers to the Rescue – over international waters by the Cuban military on February 24, 1996, resulting in the death of all four crew members (Dominguez, 2001, 278). Cuba claimed that the incident occurred inside Cuban airspace, between five and eight miles off the Cuban coast, and that the pilots received warnings from Cuban air controllers prior to entering Cuban airspace. The US, however, asserted that the incident occurred over international waters, a claim that was later found to be true (Sullivan, 1999, 22–23).[20]

Following the downing incident, in March 1996, the US Congress passed the Cuban Liberty and Democratic Solidarity Act, 1996 (P.L. 104-114)[21] further consolidating and expanding long-running US sanctions against Cuba. The Act comprises of four titles: Title I codified the US embargo on trade and financial transactions which had been in effect since 1962, requiring the president to oppose Cuban membership in any international financial institutions (IFIs), and restrict US payments to any IFI that provide assistance to Cuba over US objections; Title II required the president to produce a plan for providing economic assistance to a transition government in Cuba, and remove all sanctions on Cuba contingent on the settlement of all outstanding claims on US property expropriated by Cuba; Title III created a private cause of action authorizing US nationals with claims to confiscated property in Cuba to file suit in US courts against persons who might be "trafficking" in such properties; and Title IV required the president to deny visas to and exclude from the US persons who "traffic" in confiscated property in Cuba.

The Helms–Burton Act also provided funds for opposition movements in Cuba along with a framework for a post-Castro transitional government, and prevented the US president from normalizing relations with Cuba without the explicit approval of the Congress. It also underlined that any transitional government of Cuba must exclude Fidel Castro and his brother Raúl Castro, and stipulated that the sanctions regimes on Cuba could only be lifted after Fidel Castro and his brother Raúl were no longer in office, and only after Cuba moved toward free elections and a free press, and released political prisoners.[22]

20 On June 27, 1996, the International Civil Aviation Organization (ICAO) confirmed that the downing of the planes occurred in international waters.

21 The Act, also known as LIBETAD, was sponsored by Senator Jesse Helms of North Carolina and Representative Dan Burton of Indiana.

22 For greater detail on the Helms–Burton Act, see Dominguez (2001); Fisk (2000); Kaplowitiz (1998); Kerbrat (2021); LeoGrande (1997); Teezen (2002); and Vasquez and Rodriguez (1996).

Trafficking in Expropriated Property

The Helms–Burton Act thus enforced nearly comprehensive sanctions regimes on Cuba as long as Fidel or Raúl Castro remained part of the Cuban government. One of the distinctive features of the Act has been that it not only crossed the usual yardsticks of necessary and appropriate countermeasures, but also adopted an innovative term, "trafficking in expropriated property," extraordinarily expanding its extraterritorial reach.

For example, Title III of the Helms–Burton Act creates a civil penalty for "any person that ... traffics in property which was confiscated by the Cuban government on or after January 1, 1959," and makes such a person "liable to any United States national who owns the claim to such property for money damages." Title IV of the Act defines and sets the legal scope of the term "trafficking of expropriated property" in the context of Cuba.

While previous US legislation used the word "trafficking" principally in the context of the narcotics trade, the Helms–Burton Act uses the term to refer "not only to selling, transferring, buying, or leasing the property in question, but also in engaging in a commercial activity arising or otherwise benefiting from confiscated property" (Lowenfeld, 2003, 3). The legislation's reach also extends to family members as it provides for denial of a US visa to any person who confiscated property as well as to their spouse and minor children (Meyer, 2009, 907).

Second, to deter foreign investment in Cuba, the Helms–Burton Act makes foreign corporations subject to lawsuits in US courts if they "traffic" in property confiscated from US citizens, including naturalized Cuban-Americans. The legislation thus: (a) encompasses all properties confiscated by Cuba since Fidel Castro took power in 1959 and allows law suits with US domestic courts to recover damages;[23] (b) allows Cuban expatriates the right to sue foreign companies for profits made on expropriated Cuban land; (c) bars anyone who trafficks or participates in trafficking such confiscated property from entering the US; (d) threatens sanctions against third countries for doing business with Cuba; (e) sanctions foreign persons/corporations investing in properties expropriated from US persons by the Cuban government, and (f) provides that any US person claiming a property title to the confiscated goods is entitled to compensation amounting at least to its value with added damages (Beucillon, 2021, 122; Fisk, 2000).[24]

[23] Since virtually all commercial enterprises were taken over by the Castro regime, no matter whether they were owned by US nationals, Cuban nationals, or third-country nationals, any enterprise that could be regarded as a successor to such properties stood exposed to litigation in the US because of the Helms–Burton Act. Lowenfeld (2003), however, maintains that the principal purpose of the Act was not to stimulate litigation in the US, but to deter nationals of third countries from doing business with and investing in Cuba.

[24] Earlier, the CDA (1992) provided for deterring vessels from entering a port or place in Cuba to engage in the trade of goods or services from loading or unloading any freight at any place in the US, without a license from the Department of Treasury. The Helms–Burton Act goes even further by imposing penalties for importing into the US any goods of Cuban origin, in whole or in part, without a license from the department (White, 2021).

For Cuba, such a sweeping regime of US sanctions came on the heels of the drying up of its long-running Soviet assistance, and at a moment when the country lost 75 to 80 percent of its international trade, its GDP had shrunk by more than one-third, and the population was already teetering from the sanctions imposed by the CDA (Gordon, 2016a, 474; LeoGrande, 1997, 211).[25] Studies suggest that such a steep tightening of US sanctions on Cuba resulted from pressures mounted by some anti-Castro segments of the Cuban-American community who sought to prevent the Clinton Administration from relaxing the embargo in response to Castro's reforms aimed at boosting private investment and tourism (Jones and Rich, 1998; O'Sullivan, 2003).

There are others, however, who point out that a major impetus for tightening the sanctions against Cuba came from concern among the US political leadership that foreign investors, especially from France, Italy, Spain, and Canada, could take over and refurbish properties that had belonged to American interests or to former Cubans who had become American citizens (Aronson and Roger, 1999; Lowenfeld, 2003). Also, President Clinton, relying on a provision of the Helms–Burton Act that authorized such action, suspended the enforcement of Title III of the Act, which authorized US citizens and firms to sue in US courts those firms from other countries that trafficked properties with Cuba (Dominguez, 2001, 276).

Extraterritorial Nature of the Helms–Burton Act

Another major controversial aspect of the Helms–Burton Act's extraordinary extraterritorial nature lies with its interpretation of "US persons." Under the Act, the scope of a "person subject to the jurisdiction of the United States" not only embraces all US citizens and residents, all persons in the US, and all corporations incorporated under US law, but it also includes any "corporation, partnership, or association, wherever organized or doing business, that is owned or controlled" by such person(s).

Thus, a bank operating in and organized under the laws of another country is prohibited from extending or guaranteeing a loan to a Cuban individual or firm if the bank is owned or controlled by US person(s). Under customary international law, on the other hand, a company is ordinarily considered to be a national of the state under the laws of which it is registered and the place of business where it operates (Clark, 1999, 64).

Second, both Title III and Title IV of the Helms–Burton Act explicitly entail extraterritorial jurisdiction of US legislation as, although the sanctions are imposed on US territory by the US authorities and subject to the jurisdiction of US courts, the conduct of the sanctioned "trafficking" actually takes place abroad. The sanctions instituted by the Act imply the existence of an obligation on the part of anyone,

25 The effects of this legislation on Cuba – on starvation, on life expectancy, on the weight of the average Cuban, on the impact on newborn babies – were detailed in a report produced by the American Association for World Health in 1997, titled "Denial of Food and Medicine: the Impact of the U.S. Embargo on Health and Nutrition in Cuba."

including foreigners, who invest in properties that had been expropriated by the Cuban government since 1959, and thus, enforces US domestic law extraterritorially to investments in a foreign country by a foreign person or entity incorporated abroad (Kerbrat, 2021, 176).

Third, as the embargo imposed by the Helms–Burton Act precludes foreign companies that are owned or controlled by US persons from conducting business with Cuba, and forbids foreign persons from exporting to the embargoed country most goods that are of US origin or that contain a certain amount of US content, a subsidiary of a US company cannot engage in "reexports" or third-country transactions to do business with embargoed individuals and entities in Cuba (Clark, 1999, 64).[26]

Finally, the secondary sanction measures of the Helms–Burton Act broadened the impact of existing primary sanctions against Cuba. The Act deters foreign citizens and companies from economic relations with Cuba involving any property the Cuban government had previously expropriated from US citizens,[27] and deeming such acts as wrongful "trafficking" in expropriation of property, the Act not only denies "traffickers" visas to enter the US, but also authorizes the US victims of expropriation to file suit in US courts for damages of up to three times the original value of the property (Gordon, 2016b; Meyer, 2009).[28]

Foreign Reactions to the Helms–Burton Act

The extraterritorial nature of the Helms–Burton Act generated widespread controversy worldwide, even some of the staunch allies of the US challenged the attempt to expand the reach of US legislation beyond its borders in violation of international law. The European Commission, for example, filed a formal complaint with the World Trade Organization (WTO), asserting that the Act violated several provisions of the General Agreement on Tariff and Trade (GATT) as well as the General Agreement on Trade in Services (GATS). As a consequence, in May 1998, the EU and the US reached an understanding under which the EU agreed to develop its own rules regarding investment projects dealing with illegally expropriated properties,

[26] Incorporating President Kennedy's EO 3347 (issued in February 1962), Section 110(a) of the Helms–Burton Act prohibits "the importation into the United States of all goods of Cuban origin and all goods imported from or through Cuba."

[27] The Act does so despite the US having a long history of condemning secondary boycott laws when they involved other nations. For example, the US repeatedly condemned the Arab League – an umbrella organization of 22 Middle Eastern and African countries and entities – which required US companies not to do business with Israel. The League's boycott of Israeli companies and Israeli-made goods, imposed in 1948, is still largely in force. The US has adopted multiple legislative actions in opposition to the boycott since 1959, and in 1977, the Congress made it illegal for US companies to cooperate with the boycott and authorized the imposition of civil and criminal penalties against US violators (Meyer, 2009, 907; Sullivan, 2017).

[28] A major concern was that the Helms–Burton Act provides for denial of entry not only to persons directly involved in "trafficking" but also, for any "trafficking" transaction conducted in the name of a foreign corporation, including any "corporate officer, principal, or shareholder with a controlling interest" in the corporation, as well as to the "spouse, minor child or agent" of such individuals (Meyer, 2009).

while the Clinton Administration sought to ask Congress to grant authority to waive restrictions under Titles III and IV of the Act (Lowenfeld, 2003; Sullivan, 1999, 28).[29]

Canada and Mexico passed their own legislation in response to the Helms–Burton Act's extraterritorial overreach. Canada amended its Foreign Extraterritorial Measures Act (FEMA) of 1992 requiring Canadian companies, including US subsidiaries in Canada, to ignore any instruction not to trade with Cuba, declaring the Helms–Burton Act illegal in Canada. Under FEMA, Canadian companies were also prohibited from complying with the CDA (1992) on the grounds that it exceeded the limits of US jurisdiction under international law (Kerbrat, 2021, 174).[30]

Mexico passed its own version of blocking legislation, levying fines on Mexican companies for complying with the Helms–Burton Act (Teegen, 2002, 8). The uncertainty and dilemma created by such blocking legislation came to full display with the saga of a Mexican company named Grupo Domos.[31]

Cuba, on its part, also reacted sharply to the Helms–Burton Act. In 1996, the Cuban National Assembly passed the Law for the Reaffirmation of Cuban Dignity and Sovereignty (Law No. 80) criminalizing any cooperation, whether direct or indirect, with the provisions of the Helms–Burton Act, penalizing any dissident activity by Cubans supported by the US, and offering Cuban government support to foreign companies that wanted to hide their investments in Cuba to avoid potential US sanctions (LeoGrande, 2015, 243; Sullivan, 1999, 27).

Also, in 1999, Cuba adopted the Law for the Protection of Cuban National Independence and the Economy (Law No. 88), which made it illegal to disseminate subversive material from the US, collaborate with foreign mass media for such purposes, receiving of any material resources from the US government, and any involvement of Cubans with the US Agency for International Development's (USAID) program for the promotion of democracy in Cuba (Garcia, 2001, 280–285).

[29] As Title III of the Helms–Burton Act authorizes the president to suspend its application for up to six months, the Clinton Administration initially sought to apply the provision to the EU in response to the blocking actions. But the EU asserted that such temporary suspension was inadequate because "the threat of suits hanged like the sword of Damocles" (Lowenfeld, 2003). Following an agreement reached at the Blair–Clinton summit in May 1998, the EU suspended its request to the WTO for a dispute settlement panel over the extraterritorial reach of the Helms–Burton Act (Sullivan, 1999, 28).

[30] Ireland also objected to the CDA by observing that: "The United States has no basis in international law to claim the right to license non-United States transactions with Cuba by companies incorporated outside the United States, whatever their ownership or control" (Beucillon, 2021, 121).

[31] In 1994, Grupo Domos purchased a 49-percent share of *Empresa de Telecomunicaciones de Cuba* (Emtel) in a highly publicized debt-for-equity swap. But being unable to meet its payment schedule in the wake of the Mexican pesos crisis, Grupo Domos sold 25 percent of its share of Emtel at a large discount to STET, an Italian telecommunications concern. Subsequently, when US regulators notified them of possible violation of US sanctions, STET agreed to pay $25 million to International Telephone and Telegraph (ITT) for the right to use its property in Cuba. For greater detail, see LeoGrande and Thomas (2002, 346).

The UN General Assembly also adopted a resolution in June 2021 expressing concern over the Helms–Burton Act's "extraterritorial effects" on "the sovereignty of other States" from the standpoint of the UN Charter as well as international law.[32]

The George W. Bush Administration

By the end of the Clinton Administration, the US had made some friendly gestures toward Cuba. In 1998, coinciding with Pope John Paul II's visit to Cuba, President Clinton resumed regular air links to Cuba and restored Cuban American remittances that had been cut off since the 1994 rafts migration crisis, and in October 2000, the Congress passed the Trade Sanction Reform and Export Enhancement Act, 2000 (P.L. 106-387), which, among others, allowed the direct sale of food and agricultural products to Cuba on a cash payments basis or with financing from a third-country entity (Mollinedo, 2021, 92).[33]

But, in a radical shift away such friendly gestures, President George W. Bush instituted a series of measures against Cuba during 2002–2004 aiming at tougher enforcement of travel bans, limiting remittances, restricting humanitarian assistance, and abolishing educational and cultural exchanges with Cuba. As a result, travel to Cuba by US residents was cut by half, annual humanitarian assistance decreased from some $10 million to $4 million, and annual remittance flows to Cuba dropped from $1.25 billion to about $1 billion.[34]

President Bush further made it a condition that any easing of strict sanctions against Cuba would depend on Cuba's adoption of democratic reforms, such as holding democratic elections; giving opposition parties the freedom to organize and speak, thereby allowing non-communist candidates to participate in the 2003 legislative elections; freeing of all political prisoners; and allowing the development of independent trade unions (Hudson, 2001).

In 2004, OFAC issued the amended CACR prohibiting virtually all business between the US and Cuba except those specifically licensed by OFAC, and made the amended regulations applicable to virtually any Cuban citizen located anywhere in the world, as well as all US persons and any foreign-incorporated entities owned or controlled by US persons.[35] The amended CACR prohibits any person

[32] The Resolution was approved by 180 members of the UN. See "UN General Assembly Resolution to end Cuban Embargo," available at: news.un.org/en/story/2021/06/1094612.

[33] Section 2009, Subsection (a) of the Trade Sanction Reform and Export Enhancement Act, 2000, amended the travel-related transactions listed in subsection (c) of Section 515.560 of title 31, Code of Federal Regulations, to authorize on a case-by-case basis specific licenses for travel to, from, or within Cuba for the commercial export sale of agricultural commodities pursuant to the provisions of this Act.

[34] Visits by Cubans to the US were virtually eliminated. Cuban officials seeking to meet with US businessmen to legally buy food and medicine were denied US entry, and visas for Cuban musicians were held up so long that 22 of them missed the Grammy Awards ceremony in 2002. One reason for imposing such coercive sanctions on Cuba was that the country was still on the State Department's list of state sponsors of terrorism (LeoGrande, 2015, 241–242).

[35] See the amended CACR (31 C.F.R. Part 515). The original CACR (31 CFR part 515), was issued on July 8, 1963, under the TWEA (50 U.S.C. App. 5 et seq.). It has been modified and updated frequently

subject to US jurisdiction from engaging in any trade in services, which included providing banking, insurance, legal, transportation, telecommunication, construction services, and so forth to Cuba or Cubans. It also prohibits any direct or indirect investment in Cuba, lending money to a Cuban person or a third-country person for the purpose of financing that person's business dealings in Cuba. In the end, the regulations were so severe that simply eating or staying at a Cuban hotel could make a US person liable for "dealing" in Cuban property.[36]

The amended CACR also prohibits any shipping and cruises involving Cuba by denying entry into US ports to any vessel carrying goods or passengers to or from Cuba and extended such denial for up to 180 days after the vessel leaves Cuba. The new regulations also require the US government to use its "voice and vote" against Cuba's admission to any IFIs, and cut off US contributions to any IFI that extends assistance to Cuba over US objections (Beckhy, 2018).

Hirschhorn (2022, 216) maintains that although the CACR applies to all US-owned or controlled foreign affiliates (pursuant to 31 C.F.R. § 515.329 (2019)), it does not provide any definition of the terms "own" and "control," and OFAC's interpretation of the concepts extends to ownership of 50 percent or more or a firm's common stock and a lesser percentage of shares if the stockholder has "working control."[37] Parties designated under the CACR are added to OFAC's Specially Designated Nationals (SDN) List, which also means that the property and interests in property of persons on the list are blocked or frozen, and US persons are prohibited from engaging in any business transactions with them.

OFAC has also been very aggressive in enforcing such regulations. For example, in 2003, OFAC insisted a Sheraton Hotel in Mexico, which was owned by a Mexican subsidiary of a US hotel company, had to evict a Cuban delegation that stayed at the hotel for meetings with the Mexican government, although Mexican law prohibits discrimination against hotel guests based on their nationality (Bechky, 2018, 21). Similarly, in 2016, OFAC brought an enforcement action against a company for engaging in transactions with a joint venture that was only 5 percent owned by a Cuban state-owned oil company (Hirschhorn, 2022, 222).[38]

since then; 2004 is just one of those occasions. The CACR (2004) was published in Federal Register (Vol. 69, No. 242) on December 17, 2004.

[36] The amended CACR (2004) provides that "a person who accepts goods or services in Cuba without paying for them is in fact engaging in a prohibited dealing in property in which Cuba or a Cuban national has an interest."

[37] Hirschhorn (2022, 216–220) maintains that OFAC still uses the 1964 interpretation of ownership and control made by OFAC's legal review paper (Sommerfeld, 1964), which extends "control" and "ownership" to corporations and affiliates wholly or partially owned by a US person(s); "controlled in fact" by a US person(s) in day-to-day operations; subject to some form of US control over major corporate decisions; or there are other indications of "control," as set forth, for example, in the antiboycott provisions of the Commerce Department's Export Administration Regulations (EAR).

[38] See OFAC Enforcement Information, February 25, 2016, available at www.treasury.gov/ resource-center/sanctions/ CivPen/ Documents/20160225.

The Obama Administration

President Barack Obama came to office with a pledge to adopt a softer approach toward Cuba.[39] Accordingly, in 2009, the Obama Administration lifted travel restrictions on both Cubans and Americans for educational and religious purposes, and allowed US telecommunication companies to pursue business opportunities in Cuba. By then, after over 50 years in power, on February 9, 2008, Fidel Castro had handed over the country's presidency to his younger brother Raúl Castro, who previously served as second-in-command of the government and as a general of Cuban armed forces.

During his second term, on December 17, 2014, President Obama reached a historic agreement to restore diplomatic relations with Cuba after the country fulfilled its promise to release political prisoners.[40] Apparently, the agreement was reached following secret negotiations that began in mid 2012 with the mediation of Pope Francis and the Canadian government (LeoGrande, 2015, 246–248; Mollinedo, 2021, 95).

In 2015, President Obama lifted certain trade and travel restrictions against Cuba by using executive authorities,[41] and also met with Cuban leader Raúl Castro in Panama – the first such meeting since 1956. The same year, in May 2015, the US removed Cuba from its list of state sponsors of terrorism – a position that had stigmatized Cuba since 1982 – which paved the way to easing of economic sanctions and allowing Cuba to access US banking services. The Obama Administration also eased restrictions on trade, telecommunications, and financial services. As a part of these measures, the US Treasury Department raised the allowable amount of funds that Cuban-Americans could send to Cuba from $2,000 to $8,000, and also allowed them to use US-issued credit and debit cards in Cuba (LeoGrande, 2015; Sullivan, 2022).

In July 2015, in a major shift in US-Cuba relations, the countries resumed diplomatic relations after 54 years by reopening embassies in their respective capitals, and permitting US citizens to travel to Cuba for religious and educational purposes. On March 21, 2016, President Obama became the first sitting US president in nearly 90

[39] Obama signaled for a softening relationship with Cuba back in 2004 when as a senator he spoke against continuing the embargo on Cuba (Mollinedo, 2021, 241). Also, restoring diplomatic relations with Cuba was one of his campaign promises for the US presidency. In 2008, while campaigning for the presidency, Obama asserted: "If the Cuban leadership begins opening Cuba to meaningful democratic change, the United States must be prepared to begin taking steps to normalize relations and to ease the embargo of the last five decades." See: www.cfr.org/timeline/us-cuba-relations.

[40] It was indeed a prisoner swap under which Cuba released a US intelligence officer in exchange for three Cuban counterintelligence officers. These Cuban officers were charged in 1998, during the Clinton Administration, with conspiracy to commit espionage for allegedly infiltrating Cuban-American exile groups in Miami. Found guilty in 2001, two of them were released at the end of their terms in 2011 and 2014, and the remaining three were released on December 17, 2014 as part of the prisoner swap.

[41] Earlier, Obama also enlarged the number and scope of general licenses in the CACR as a part of his efforts to normalize relations with Cuba, but could not go further to ease or lift the embargo because of the constraints imposed by the statutory codification of aspects of the embargo in the Helms–Burton Act, and easing of the embargo required Congressional action (Hirschhorn, 2022, 247).

years to visit Cuba.[42] The trip came just a month after the countries signed an agreement to allow commercial flights between their capitals after more than 50 years.[43] Also, for the first time, on October 26, 2016, the US government abstained from voting against a UN resolution condemning the embargo on Cuba (LeoGrande and Kornbluh, 2015, 453; Mollinedo, 2021, 96).

At the end of his term, on October 14, 2016, Obama signed Presidential Directive No. 43, directing all US government agencies to advance the process of normalization with Cuba, and on January 12, 2017 – just three days before the expiry of his presidency – Obama made a joint statement ending the "wet foot dry foot" policy and the special "parole" visa program that had been in place since the mid 1990s (Mollinedo, 2021).

The Trump Administration

President Donald J. Trump imposed a series of increasingly coercive economic sanctions regimes against Cuba, effectively reversing most of the Obama policies of engagement and normalization of relations with the country[44]. On June 16, 2017, the Trump Administration reinstated almost all travel and business restrictions on Cuba, leaving in place direct flights from the US, cruise ship routes, and some hotel ventures, and warned that sanctions regimes against the country would be tightened further unless Cuba freed its political prisoners, respected freedoms of assembly and expression, legalized opposition parties, and scheduled free and fair elections (Bain and Walker, 2021).[45]

Continuing its hardline policies toward Cuba, in September 2017, the Trump Administration added 231 hotels and businesses belonging to the Cuban military, intelligence, and security services to the State Department's "Cuba Restricted List." Most US diplomats and staff were withdrawn from the US Embassy in Havana after many of them developed mysterious health problems, and 15 Cuban diplomats were expelled from the US.[46]

[42] The last and only American sitting president ever to visit Cuba was Calvin Coolidge, in January 1928. President Jimmy Carter also visited Cuba in March 2011, but he did so as a former president.

[43] Fidel Castro was alive when President Obama visited Cuba, but he died soon after, on November 25, 2016, at the age of 90.

[44] This section is largely based on US State Department's Cuba Sanctions Archive, 2009–2017, US Treasury Department website, and news reports.

[45] These measures were adopted in accordance with President Trump's national security memorandum on Cuba issued in June 2017 to roll back the Obama Administration's efforts to normalize relations, and impose new sanctions on Cuba. Accordingly, the CACR (31 C.F.R. Part 515) and the Export Administration Regulations (15 C.F.R. Parts 740 and 746) were amended in November 2017.

[46] Meanwhile, on April 19, 2018, a significant political transition occurred in Cuba as Raúl Castro relinquished his position as the Cuban president after the electoral endorsement by the Cuban National Assembly of Miguel Diaz-Canel, the first vice president of the Cuban Communist Party and a designated successor chosen by Castro. This transition marked the conclusion of over six decades of governance by the Castro siblings. Notwithstanding his withdrawal from the presidential role, Raúl Castro continued to serve as the leader of the Cuban Communist Party until 2021, and under his leadership, Cuba underwent constitutional reforms in 2019, introducing certain changes while upholding the state's predominant role in the economy and maintaining the Cuban Communist Party's overarching influence in the nation's political landscape.

On October 20, 2017, President Trump issued a National Security Policy Memorandum (NSPM-5) directing his administration, among others, to: (a) tighten or remove some of the general licenses previously issued under the CACR; (b) end economic practices disproportionately benefiting the Cuban government; (c) support the Helms–Burton Act and oppose the ending of the embargo; (d) extend support to the Cuban people through the expansion of internet services, free press, free enterprise, free association, and lawful travel; and (e) advance human rights in Cuba, encourage the growth of a private sector and understanding of scientific and environmental challenges, and facilitate safe civil aviation.[47]

In November 2018, US National Security Advisor John Bolton labeled Cuba, Nicaragua, and Venezuela as the "Troika of Tyranny," accusing them of human rights abuses, causing regional instability, and embracing communism (Bolton, 2018; Sullivan, 2022). Soon after, the Trump Administration announced a wave of sanctions against Cuba. In April–May 2019, EO 13850 (related to US sanctions on Venezuela) imposed financial sanctions on eight shipping companies and seven vessels involved in transporting Venezuelan oil to Cuba.

On April 30, 2019, President Trump threatened a "full and complete embargo" on Cuba and the "highest-level sanctions" unless Cuba ceased its military support for the Maduro regime of Venezuela.[48] In May 2019, Trump permitted US nationals to file lawsuits against those trafficking in confiscated property in Cuba pursuant to Title III of the Helms–Burton Act (1996), citing Cuba's support for the Maduro regime as the reason for the implementation of Title III.[49]

In April 2019, the Trump Administration also tightened rules for non-family travel to Cuba and restricted remittances to Cuba to $1,000 per person per quarter and discontinued so-called "U-turn transactions" – which allowed processing of commercial transactions of Cuba and Cuban nationals in US dollars through US financial institutions and correspondent banks. In June 2019, the US eliminated the travel category of "people-to-people educational travel" altogether and prohibited cruise ships, private and corporate aircraft, sailboats, and fishing boats from going to Cuba.

47 Based on NSPM-5, "Strengthening the Policy of the United States toward Cuba," issued on October 20, 2017. Available at: www.federalregister.gov/documents/2017/10/20/2017-22928/strengthening-the-policy-of-the-united-states-toward-cuba.

48 President Trump's threat came after his National Security Advisor John Bolton in April 2019 publicly claimed that Cuba had security forces of 20,000 to 25,000 personnel in Venezuela. Cuban officials, however, asserted that the vast majority of those were medical workers. In May 2019, Secretary of State Mike Pompeo claimed that about 2,300 of them were Cuban security personnel (Sullivan, 2022).

49 News reports suggest that by the end of 2019, lawsuits had been filed against the Miami-based Carnival Corporation by descendants of two families who owned port facilities in Cuba confiscated in 1960 and against Cuba's state-owned oil company and a state-owned holding company by Exxon Mobil Corporation (formerly Standard Oil) for the expropriation of an oil refinery, product terminals, and service stations in 1960 (Sullivan, 2022).

Continuing coercive sanctions against Cuba, the Trump Administration in 2020 prohibited the processing of remittances for entities on the "Cuba Restricted List," a measure that prompted the Western Union corporation to terminate its business in Cuba. The same year, Trump also prohibited US travelers from staying at over 400 hotels and private residences identified as owned or controlled by the Cuban government. Then, in May 2020, the Trump Administration branded Cuba as a country "not cooperating fully" with US anti-terrorism efforts, and in January 2021, just a week before leaving office, Trump designated Cuba as a state sponsor of international terrorism for allegedly harboring several US fugitives and members of Colombia's National Liberation Army, and supporting the Maduro regime of Venezuela.

Also, under the Trump Administration, since 2017, the State Department had maintained the abovementioned "Cuba Restricted List" of entities or sub-entities under the control of, or acting for or on behalf of, the Cuban military, intelligence, or security services with which direct financial transactions were prohibited. Such entities included Cuban government ministries, holding companies, hotels, tourist agencies, marinas, commercial stores, and others. In addition, the revised CACR effectively prohibited US persons from traveling to or from Cuba unless authorized by OFAC, and restrictions were placed on any financial transactions related to travel to Cuba, or the receipt of any goods or services in Cuba, unless licensed by OFAC. The property of Cuba and Cuban nationals was blocked, "essentially treating Cuba and all Cuban nationals as persons on the SDN List" (Hirschhorn, 2022, 247–250).[50]

The US policy toward Cuba has not changed much since President Joe Biden assumed power in January 2021. In May 2022, Biden eased some of the restrictions on Cuba, which included expansion of flights to Cuba, reestablishment of the family reunification program, increased visa processing, and lifting of the remittance cap for families.

III IMPACT OF SANCTIONS ON CUBAN ECONOMY AND POPULATION

Cuba has been under US sanctions, including embargoes, for more than six decades, and the country's economic performance has always been conditioned by such sanctioning measures throughout the period. Still, Cuba was a relatively well-off southern neighbor of the US for decades until the collapse of the Soviet Union and the resultant disappearance of billions of dollars in aid, which had a debilitating effect on its economy. The Cuban economy has struggled ever since, with no appreciable recovery, and only deteriorated further with the tightening of US sanctions under the CDA (1992), the Helms–Burton Act (1996), and other coercive measures

[50] The revised CACR, however, unblocked the property of Cuban nationals who had taken up lawful permanent residence in the US or in third countries and who were not prohibited officials associated with the Cuban government or the Cuban Communist Party.

taken by the Bush and Trump Administrations. The toll was excruciating for Cuba's import capability, export revenues, foreign investment, remittance flows, and the overall living standards of the Cuban people.

With the Obama Administration's easing of sanctions, as Table 8.1 indicates, the country's economic performance improved slightly. The GDP growth rate improved between 2014 and 2018, and then, of course, with the reimposition of sanctions by the Trump Administration, the growth rate plummeted by almost 11 percent in 2020. Cuba's export earnings also declined precipitously coinciding with the Trump Administration's tightening of sanctions – while the country received $4.85 billion in exports in 2014, the revenue fell to $2.37 billion in 2018 and $1.7 billion in 2020.[51]

In 2021 Cuba was the 158th economy out of 226 in the world, in terms of total exports and the 154th in total imports. The top exports of Cuba were rolled tobacco, nickel mattes, raw sugar, hard liquor, and zinc ore. Major imports were poultry meat, wheat, concentrated milk, crude petroleum, and rice. In 2021, Cuba's export revenue totaled $1.09 billion, and the major export destinations were China (18.6%), Spain (10.8%), Germany (6.5%), Belgium (5.4%), Switzerland (4.3%) and Portugal (4.1%). In 2021, the total imports of Cuba stood at $3.4 billion, and imports came from Spain (21.5%), China (16.7%), the US (8.9%), Canada (6.5%), Italy (5.4%), Brazil (5.2%), France (4.6%), and Germany (3.9%).[52]

Historically, Cuba maintained a full-employment economy. But during 2014–2018, according to Cuban official sources, the country's unemployment rate hovered around 3 percent, while the inflation rate ranged between 4.2 percent and 6.9 percent. According to the Economic Commission for Latin America and the Caribbean (ECLAC, 2021), the Cuban inflation rate jumped to 18.5 percent between December 2019 and December 2020 as a result of supply-side constraints generated by foreign exchange shortages.[53]

The steepest decline of Cuban GDP in nearly two decades, and the third-sharpest decline since the country began keeping records, however, occurred during the

[51] Compilation from: Tradingeconomics.com, and oec.world/en/profile/country/cub. The Observatory of Economic Complexity (OEC) reported that in 2020, Cuba ranked 151st in the world in exports and 149th in imports, among 226 countries surveyed by OEC. The report is available at oec.world/en/profile/country/cub, accessed on March 24, 2023.

[52] OEC report at oec.world/en/profile/country/cub, accessed on January 3, 2024. In contrast, in 2013, Cuba mainly imported from Venezuela (37.1%), the EU (20.7%), China (12.1%), Brazil (4.7%), Canada (4.0 %), Mexico (3.3%) and the US (3.2%), and Cuba's main export destinations were the EU (26.7%), Canada (16%), China (15.1%), Venezuela (14.1%), Guyana (3.4%), Belize (3.3%) and Brazil (3.2%). Based on www.cepal.org/en/presentations/economic-survey-latin-america-and-caribbean-2021, accessed on March 17, 2023.

[53] ECLAC maintains that inflation soared in 2020 mainly because of an increase in agricultural prices. In December 2020, the agricultural consumer price index (CPI) registered a 44.7-percent year-on-year increase. Overall CPI for the non-state sector also increased, it accounted for 11.6 percent of the rise in the inflation rate. For greater detail, see *Economic Survey of Latin America and the Caribbean, 2021*, available at: www.cepal.org/en/presentations/economic-survey-latin-america-and-caribbean-2021, accessed on March 24, 2023.

TABLE 8.1 *Economic performance of Cuba, 2014–2021*

Year	GDP (US$ in billions)	Annual GDP growth rate (%)	Debt-to-GDP ratio (%)	Per capita income ($)	Annual unemployment rate (%)	Annual inflation rate (%)	Annual export revenues (US$ in billions)
2014	80.7	1.0	18.9	7,362	2.7	6.0	4.85
2015	87.1	3.0	18.2	7,684	2.4	5.3	3.35
2016	91.4	0.5	19.9	7,722	2.0	4.2	2.32
2017	96.9	1.8	18.3	7,865	1.7	4.5	2.40
2018	100.1	2.2	18.4	8,048	1.7	5.5	2.37
2019	103.4	−0.2	19.0	8,049	1.7	6.9	2.06
2020	107.4	−10.9	50.0	7,172	2.6	5.6	1.70
2021	–	1.3	117	7,291	2.8	4.2	1.96

Sources: GDP, GDP Growth Rates, and per capita GDP compiled from World Bank Database, others are based on National Office of Statistics of Cuba as available at Tradingeconomics.com, accessed on March 24, 2023; and Economic Commission for Latin America and the Caribbean (ECLAC), available at www.cepal.org/en/presentations/economic-survey-latin-america-and-caribbean-2021, accessed on March 24, 2023.

COVID-19 pandemic. As a result of the pandemic, the country's debt-to-GDP ratio jumped to 50 percent in 2020, while previously, during 2014–2018, the ratio had ranged between 18 and 19 percent (ECLAC, 2021). In 2021, the Cuban economy grew by 1.3 percent, but the Cuban government in November 2022 cut its forecast for 2022 to 2 percent, due to slow recovery of the tourism sector, global supply chain constraints, damage to Cuba's main oil storage facility in August 2022, and Hurricane Ian, which caused severe damage to western Cuba in late September 2022.[54]

IV CONCLUDING REMARKS

The US has maintained sanctions regimes against its small southern neighbor Cuba ever since Fidel Castro took power through a communist revolution more than six decades ago, in January 1959. Throughout this prolonged and unbroken chain of campaigns, the objectives, rationales, and modalities of the sanctions policies were obviously packaged and repackaged depending on domestic politics and presidential transitions, but a broad generalization can be made that most of the Democratic presidents preferred easing of sanctions as well as constructive engagement and normalization of relations with Cuba, while most of the Republican presidents pursued coercive sanctioning measures, even often reversing and further tightening sanctions against Cuba.

54 The US Congressional Research Service estimates that Cuban inflation rates ranged between 150 percent and 500 percent in 2021, while the Economist Intelligence Unit (EIU) estimates that Cuban inflation rates averaged at 60 percent in 2022 and may decline to 37 percent in 2023 (Sullivan, 2022).

During the Cold War, when the former Soviet Union provided billions of dollars in subsidies and assistance to Cuba, the US remained steadfast in its economic embargo against the country, demonstrating its firm resolve to punish and penalize Cuba for spreading communism in its backyard and around the word. In the aftermath of the Cold War, the US Congress also demonstrated its firm stance against Cuba by enacting the CDA (1992) and the Helms–Burton Act (1996). Such legislative measures not only further tightened sanctions against Cuba, but also extended their reach through secondary and extraterritorial sanctions to anybody, anywhere in the world, who directly or indirectly assisted or intended to assist Cuba.

During the Obama Administration, the US established diplomatic relations with Cuba and made considerable progress in easing sanctions after many decades, but it was short-lived as the Trump Administration reversed almost all those normalization measures. The Biden Administration has eased some of those sanctions, but for all practical purposes, Cuba, its economy, and population still remain subject to a near-comprehensive US economic embargo.

REFERENCES

Allison, G. 2012. The Cuban Missile Crisis at 50: Lessons for U.S. Foreign Policy Today. *Foreign Affairs*, 91(4):11–16.

Alzugaray, C. 2006. The US Blockade and the Development of Self-Reliance in Cuba. In R. Ramsaran (ed.), *Size, Power & Development in the Emerging World Order: Caribbean Perspectives*, pp. 131–157. San Juan, Trinidad & Tobago: Lexicon Trinidad Ltd.

Aronson, B., and W. Roger. 1999. U.S.-Cuba Relations in the 21st Century. Council on Foreign Relations Independent Task Force. Washington, DC.

Bain, M., and C. Walker (Eds.). 2021. *Cuban International Relations at 60: Reflections on Global Connections*. Blue Ridge Summit, PA: Lexington Books.

Bechky, P. 2018. Sanctions and the Blurred Boundaries of International Economic Law. *Missouri Law Review*, 83(1):1–38.

Beucillon, C. (Ed.). 2021. *Research Handbook on Unilateral and Extraterritorial Sanctions*. Cheltenham, UK: Edward Elgar.

Bolton, J. 2018. *Remarks by National Security Advisor Ambassador John R. Bolton on the Administration's Policies in Latin America*. The White House, May 10, 2020.

Chang, L., and P. Kornbluh (Eds.). 1999. *The Cuban Missile Crisis, 1962*. New York: New Press.

CIA (Central Intelligence Agency). 2000. CIA World Fact Book. Washington, DC: Central Intelligence Agency.

Clark, H. 1999. Dealing with US Extraterritorial Sanctions and Foreign Countermeasures. *University of Pennsylvania Journal of International Economic Law*, 20(1):61–96.

DeMelfi, C. 2006. Nothing but the Facts: An In-Depth Analysis of the Effects of Economic Sanctions against Cuba. *Journal of International Business and Law* 5(1):137–173.

Dominguez, J. 2001. Chapter 4: Government and Politics. In R. Hudson (ed.), *Cuba: A Country Study*, pp. 229–279. Washington, DC: Library of Congress Library, Federal Research Division.

ECLAC (UN Economic Commission for Latin America and the Caribbean). 1963. *Economic Survey of Latin America*. Mexico City: UN Economic Commission for Latin America and the Caribbean.

ECLAC (UN Economic Commission for Latin America and the Caribbean). 1965. *Economic Survey of Latin America*. Mexico City: UN Economic Commission for Latin America and the Caribbean. Available at: www.un-ilibrary.org/content/books/9789210583503.

ECLAC (UN Economic Commission for Latin America and the Caribbean). 2021. *Cuba: Economic Survey of Latin America and the Caribbean*. Mexico City: Economic Commission for Latin America and the Caribbean.

Ellison, J. (Ed.). 1999. *Psywar on Cuba: The Declassified History of U.S. Anti-Castro Propaganda*. New York: Ocean Press.

Falk, P. 1996. Eyes on Cuba: U.S. Business and the Embargo. *Foreign Affairs*, 75(2):16.

Fisk, D. 2000. Economic Sanctions: The Cuba Embargo Revisited. In S. Chan, and A. Drury (eds.), *Sanctions as Economic Statecraft: Theory and Practice*, pp. 65–85. London: Macmillan.

Franklin, J. 1997. *Cuba and the United States: A Chronological History*. New York: Ocean Press.

GAO. 1995. U.S. Response to the 1994 Cuban Migration Crisis. GAO/NSIAD-95-211. Washington, DC: General Accounting Office of the United States.

Garcia, J. (Ed.). 2001. *Cuban Revolution Reader: A Documentary History*. Melbourne: Ocean Press.

Gordon, J. 2016a. Economic Sanctions as Negative Development. *Journal of International Development*, 28(4):473–484.

Gordon, J. 2016b. Extraterritoriality: Issues of Overbreadth and the Chilling Effect in the Cases of Cuba and Iran. *Harvard International Law Journal Online* 57:1–12.

Hirschhorn, E. et al. 2022. *U.S. Export Controls and Economic Sanctions*. Oxford: Oxford University Press.

Horowitz, I., and J. Suchlicki (Eds.). 2001. *Cuban Communism*. 10th ed. New Brunswick, NJ: Transaction.

Howard, J. 2008. *The Bay of Pigs: Pivotal Moments in American History*. Oxford: Oxford University Press.

Hudson, R. 2001. Introduction. In R. Hudson (ed.), *Cuba: A Country Study*, pp. xlvi–lxxxii. Washington, DC: Library of Congress Library, Federal Research Division.

Jones, K., and D. Rich. 1998. Opportunities for U.S.-Cuba Trade: A Study by the Cuban Studies Program of the Johns Hopkins University, School of Advanced International Studies. Washington, DC: Johns Hopkins University.

Kaplowitz, D. 1998. *Anatomy of a Failed Embargo: U.S. Sanctions against Cuba*. Boulder, CO: Lynne Rienner Publishers.

Kerbrat, Y. 2021. Unilateral/Extraterritorial Sanctions as a Challenge to the Theory of Jurisdiction. In C. Beucillon (ed.), *Research Handbook on Unilateral and Extraterritorial Sanctions*, pp. 165–185. Cheltenham, UK: Edward Elgar.

Lecuona, R. 1997. International Law, Cuba, and the United States of America. *International Journal on World Peace*, 14(1):37–49.

LeoGrande, W. 1997. Enemies Evermore: US Policy toward Cuba after Helms-Burton. *Journal of Latin American Studies*, 29(1):211–221.

LeoGrande, W. 2015. Epilogue: Cutting the Shackles of the Past. In W. LeoGrande, and P. Kornbluh (eds.), *Back Channel to Cuba: The Hidden History of Negotiations between Washington and Havana*, pp. 418–453. Chapel Hill, NC: University of North Carolina Press.

LeoGrande, W. 2021. Coercive Diplomacy or Constructive Engagement: Sixty Years of U.S. Policy toward Cuba. In M. Bain, and C. Walker (eds.), *Cuban International Relations at 60: Reflections on Global Connections*, pp. 33–48. Lexington Books.

LeoGrande, W., and P. Kornbluh. 2015. *Back Channel to Cuba: The Hidden History of Negotiations between Washington and Havana*. Chapel Hill: University of North Carolina Press.

LeoGrande, W., and J. Thomas. 2002. Cuba's Quest for Economic Independence. *Journal of Latin American Studies*, 34(2):325–363.

Lowenfeld, A. 2003. Trade Controls for Political Ends: Four Perspectives. *Chicago Journal of International Law*, 4(2):354–369.

Mallet, M. 2013. Bay of Pigs Invasion. In C. Cortes, and G. Geoffrey (eds.), *Multicultural America: A Multimedia Encyclopedia*. Boston: Sage Publications. Available at: scholar .harvard.edu/files/marielauremallet/files/mallet_bay_of_pigs_sage.pdf.

Marino, C. 2002. U.S.-Cuban Relations during the Clinton Administration. *Latin American Perspectives*, 29(4):47–76.

Meyer, J. 2009. Second Thoughts on Secondary Sanctions. *University of Pennsylvania Journal of International Economic Law*, 30(3):905–934.

Mollinedo, L. 2021. From Eisenhower to Trump: A Historical Summary of the U.S.-Cuba Conflict (1959–2020). In M. Bain, and C. Walker (eds.), *Cuban International Relations at 60: Reflections on Global Connections*, pp. 81–100. Lanham, MD: Lexington Books.

O'Sullivan, M. 2003. *Shrewd Sanctions – Statecraft and State Sponsors of Terrorism*. Washington, DC: Brookings Institution Press.

Rathbone, M. et al. 2013. Sanctions, Sanctions Everywhere: Forging a Path through Complex Transnational Sanctions Laws. *Georgetown Journal of Law*, 44:1056–1094.

Schoultz, L. 2011. *That Infernal Little Cuban Republic: The United States and the Cuban Revolution*. Chapel Hill: University of North Carolina Press.

Scott, L. and R. Hughes (Ed.). 2015. *The Cuban Missile Crisis: A Critical Reappraisal*. London: Routledge.

Sommerfeld, S. 1964. Treasury Regulations Affecting Trade with the Sino-Soviet Bloc and Cuba. *The Business Lawyer*, 19(4):861–974.

Stern, S. 2005. *The Week the World Stood Still: Inside the Secret Cuban Missile Crisis*. Stanford, CA: Stanford University Press.

Suchlicki, J. 1986. *Cuba: From Columbus to Castro*. 2nd ed. New York: Pergamon-Brassey's.

Suchlicki. J. 2001. Chapter 1: Historical Setting. In R. Hudson (ed.), *Cuba: A Country Study*, pp. 1–85. Washington, DC: Library of Congress Library, Federal Research Division.

Sullivan, M. 2017. Cuba: Issues and Actions in the 114th Congress. Congressional Research Service, RL43926. Washington, DC.

Sullivan, M. 2022. Cuba: U.S. Policy Overview. Congressional Research Service, IF10045. Washington, DC.

Sullivan, M., and S. York. 1999. Cuba-U.S Relations: Chronology of Key Events since 1959. Congressional Research Service, RL30386. Washington, DC.

Teegen, H. et al. 2002. Economic and Strategic Impacts of U.S. Economic Sanctions on Cuba. The Center for Latin American Issues. George Washington University, Washington, DC.

USITC. 2001. *The Economic Impact of U.S. Sanctions with Respect to Cuba*. Investigation No. 332–413. Washington, DC: US International Trade Commission.

Varona, A. 1994. *Propaganda and Reality: A Look at the U.S. Embargo against Castro's Cuba*. Miami, FL: Cuban American National Foundation.

Vasquez, I., and L. Rodriguez. 1996. Trade Embargo in and Castro Out. *Cato Institute*. December 12, 1996. Washington, DC. Available at: www.cato.org/commentary/ trade-embargo-castro-out.

Vazquez, C. 2003. Trade Sanctions and Human Rights–Past, Present, and Future. *Journal of International Economic Law*, 6(4):797–839.

White, N. 2021. Shades of Grey: Autonomous Sanctions in the International Legal Order. In S. Subedi (ed.), *Unilateral Sanctions in International Law*, pp. 61–86. Oxford: Hart Publishing.

9

US Economic and Financial Sanctions against the Bolivarian Republic of Venezuela

I INTRODUCTION

The Bolivarian Republic of Venezuela[1] – a South American country bordering the Caribbean Sea and the North Atlantic Ocean – had rather sound relations with the US, its North American neighbor, from the late eighteenth century when both nations fought for independence from the European colonial powers (Gill, 2019). The country, which holds the largest proven oil reserves in the world,[2] began commercial oil production in 1914 (Gallegos, 2016, 57; Yergin, 1991, 234), and US investors had been involved in the country's oil exploration, production, and exports since 1919 (Di-John, 2009; Rivas, 2002). Even during the Cold War, the two nations had friendly relations as Venezuela consistently maintained a pro-American, pro-private sector, and anticommunist stance, and US investors continued their dominance in the country's oil exploration and production (Grandin, 2006; Tinker, 2005).

Venezuela was among the fastest-growing economies in Latin America and one of the of richest countries in the world until the 1980s, when it produced more than 10 percent of the world's crude oil and had a per capita gross domestic product (GDP)

[1] Before Hugo Chavez (1998–2013) established the Fifth Republic of Venezuela, renaming the country as the Bolivian Republic of Venezuela in 1999 in honor of the country's founding father Simon Bolivar through a constitutional referendum, Venezuela was officially known Estado de Venezuela during 1830–1856, as República de Venezuela during 1856–1864, as Estados Unidos de Venezuela during 1864–1953, and República de Venezuela during 1953–1999. Originally a Spanish colony, the country gained its independence in 1811. Currently it has a landmass estimated to be around 912,050 square kilometers, which is larger than Alaska – the largest state of the US, and more than double the size of California. In 2022, Venezuela had a population of about 30 million (Bull and Rosales, 2020; Ellner and Hellinger, 2003; López, 2016; Polga-Hecimovich, 2019).

[2] Venezuela is endowed with huge reserves of petroleum and natural gas. The country's oil reserve was discovered in 1914 by the Caribbean Development Corporation, a subsidiary of the Anglo-Dutch Shell Oil Company (Salazar-Carrillo and West, 2004, 262). In 2021, the country had approximately 300 billion barrels of proven oil reserves. The largest oil reserve area of the country – the Orinoco Oil Belt – alone had an estimated capacity of more than 200 billion barrels. For greater detail, see www.worldatlas.com/articles/the-world-s-largest-oil-reserves-by-country.html. Another estimate suggests that the Orinoco Oil Belt, which encompasses approximately 50,000 km of the East Venezuela Basin Province, is underlain by more than one trillion barrels of heavy oil-in-place (USGA, 2009).

many times bigger than that of its next-door neighbors – Brazil and Colombia – and was not far behind that of the US, when petroleum provided more than 90 percent of the country's export revenues and foreign exchange.[3] From 1920 to 1980, Venezuela achieved a spectacular average GDP growth rate of 6.4 percent per annum, the highest in any Latin American country during the period (Di-John, 2009, 17), and also maintained rapid manufacturing growth until the mid 1960s, and relatively high levels of physical and human capital investment in a moderately democratic polity (Salazar-Carrilo and West, 2004, 251–267).

Historically, oil revenues served as the golden goose by contributing to the growth of other sectors of the economy. The sector financed the public sector provision of services; supplied bulk of foreign exchange earnings; expanded the economic wealth and productive capacity of the nation; strengthened the country's capital goods industry; and served as the multiplier-accelerator for the country's aggregate demand, volume of savings, and human resource development (Salazar-Carrillo and West, 2004, 252).[4]

But since the 1970s, Venezuela's "rentier economy," which depended on rents from foreign-led[5] trade of a single commodity rather than from diversified domestic productive resources, suffered from what is often called the "Dutch Disease" – a resource curse – an economic condition when the productive apparatus could no longer absorb rents to increase productivity, and instead, the dependence on oil brewed social dynamics of dependence on the distributive state, fueling corruption, nepotism, crony-capitalism, and authoritarian practices, which increasingly diverted investment abroad and protected largely inefficient sectors (Bull and Rosales, 2020; Buxton, 2020; Hellinger, 2017; Ross, 2015).[6]

As a result, despite decades of relatively stable oil revenues, albeit with windfall gains from oil exports in the early 1970s when the country refused to join the OPEC sponsored oil embargo and continued oil supply to Western countries including the US,[7] Venezuela entered one of the worst growth implosions in Latin America

[3] See: www.opec.org/opec_web/en/about_us/171.htm, accessed on December 3, 2022.

[4] During 1940–1960, Venezuela was among the recipients of the highest levels of European immigration, the majority of whom were classified as educated and/or skilled. In the 1970s and early 1980s, Venezuela also drew substantial numbers of highly skilled immigrants from other South American countries, such as Argentina, Uruguay, and Chile (Di-John, 2009, 29).

[5] In roughly two decades since the discovery of oil, Venezuela rose from an obscure agricultural backwater in the Andes to the world's largest oil exporter and the second-largest oil producer after the US, but the oil industry remained firmly in the hands of foreign oil companies, especially those from the US. Although a 1943 Venezuela law mandated a fifty-fifty principle, under which Venezuela would earn the same amount of money as the oil companies' net profits, by 1970, foreign oil companies retained 78 percent of oil business profits (Gallegos, 2016, 57–68; Karl, 1997).

[6] This so-called "resource curse" is not unique to Venezuela, however. It applies to scores of countries that depend on petroleum resources as the mainstay of their economy, such as Algeria, Cameroon, Chad, Ecuador, Indonesia, Iran, Libya, Russia, Saudi Arabia, and the UAE.

[7] Venezuela was a founding member of the OPEC (Organization of Petroleum Exporting Countries), but refrained from joining the Oil Embargo of the early 1970s. Between 1972 and 1974, the average

between 1980 and 1998, when the country's annual average GDP grew only by 1.5 percent. While in 1970, middle-class Venezuelans amounted to 58 percent of the population, during the prolonged period of stagnation, the country experienced a sustained increase in the incidence of poverty – the share of Venezuelan households below the poverty line increased from 20 percent in 1980/81 to 36 percent in 1985/86, to 42 percent in 1989/90, and to 51 percent in 1994/95 (Di-John, 2009, 17–19; Wiestbrot, 2009).

Thus, in the late 1990s, a dramatically altered economic, social, and political landscape of Venezuela provided a fertile ground for the emergence of a staunchly nationalist and socialist voice to emerge as a national leader, and in 1998, Hugo Chavez was elected the country's president with 56 percent of the vote – the highest popular vote in the nation's history in four decades (Tinker, 2015, 140). Chavez, who had maintained close ties with Cuban leader Fidel Castro since the early 1990s, was also propelled to power by a fierce tide of anti-US and anti-colonial and pro-socialist sentiments, which the country had never experienced before (Baburkin, 1999).

Chavez indeed built his populist platform by openly championing socialism and establishing a coalition of lower middle-class and working-class people with a vow to evict neo-liberal capitalists who "squandered Venezuela's oil resources" at the expense of working people (Sylvia and Danopoulos, 2003).[8] Much of the bad blood between the US and Venezuela, and the consequent flurries of US unilateral sanctions against the country, began with the Chavez regime, largely because of the regime's expulsion of international capital as well as its avowed socialist agenda.

This chapter focuses on the unilateral sanctions regimes that the US has imposed against Venezuela, and their impact on the Venezuelan economy and population from legal and economic perspectives. The discussion also sheds light on the sanctions imposed by the EU and Canada, who joined the sanctions campaign against Venezuela in 2017. The next section explains the evolution of sanctions regimes against the country; Section III focuses on the economic impact of the sanctions regimes; Section IV examines the sanctions regimes from international law perspectives; and Section V concludes the chapter.

II EVOLUTION OF US SANCTIONS REGIMES AGAINST VENEZUELA

Before Hugo Chavez, a former lieutenant colonel in the Venezuelan military, emerged as a prominent political figure, Venezuela was a principal ally of the US

price of Venezuelan crude oil rose from $2.50 to $10.50 a barrel, and this extraordinary increase in oil prices ushered in a prolonged period of historically high earnings from the export of oil, which amounted to $247 billion between 1974 and 1985 (Di-John, 2009, 17–18).

8 In 1995, Castro gave Chavez a hero's welcome in Havana following his release from prison for a 1992 coup attempt against Venezuelan President Carlos Andres Perez. The coup was staged by the Chávez-led Revolutionary Bolivarian Movement-200 (MBR-200), and he served two years for his role in the coup (Seelke, 2020, 2).

in Latin America. Venezuela provided petroleum to the US in times of heightened hostility and military warfare in the Middle East, during the OPEC embargo in 1973, and during the periods of US sanctions against Iraq and Iran in the 1990s and 2000s. Venezuela was also a major player for the US hegemony in Latin America during the Cold War – it helped the US to isolate and undermine Castro's communist revolution, expel Cuba from the OAS in 1961, to disarm the guerillas in El Salvador and Guatemala in the 1990s, and successive Venezuelan regimes played a strategic role in policing the Central American-Caribbean region, an important regional market for US exports and multinational business.[9]

The longstanding friendly relations between the US and Venezuela began to sour with Chavez's assumption of the Venezuelan presidency in 1998. His campaign for the expulsion of international capital, however, began in earnest in 2001–02 with re-nationalization of the state-run oil monopoly, Petróleos de Venezuela, S.A. (PdVSA). The nationalization decree that originally established the company in 1976 under the then Venezuelan president Carlos Andrés Pérez was fraught with loopholes that allowed foreign companies to operate in Venezuela through service contracts or in advisory roles. And, although a 1943 law required foreign companies to share net profits on a fifty-fifty principle, they paid less than 20 percent to the Venezuelan government, citing the needs for international initiatives and reinvesting profits into the company (Tinker, 2015, 146–150).

Chavez sought to eliminate those loopholes by reasserting full state control over the country's petroleum industry,[10] and bring the oil conglomerate PdVSA under full control of the government under a new hydrocarbon law enacted in 2001. The law also brought oil production under the Apertura Petrolera (Oil Opening) project, which had increased foreign presence in the country's oil industry in the Orinoco basin to meet the OPEC-mandated output.[11] Between 2005 and 2007, Chavez forced all foreign oil companies involved in the country's oil exploration and production

[9] For greater detail, see Gill (2019); Grandin (2006); Corrales and Romero (2012, 1–10); Karl (1977); and Petras (2010).

[10] To the Chavistas, the dominance of foreign oil companies was the real reason for Venezuela's economic backwardness, and the country could develop only if and when Venezuelans controlled and ran the oil business. Some studies, however, suggest that, at the time of Chavez's assumption of power, the Venezuelan government received more than half the profits from oil produced, and that portion surpassed 80 percent as Chavez raised taxes and royalties on foreign oil companies by retroactively using the 1999 oil law to give them a choice to accept minority stakes in all oil ventures, with the state holding majority control, or face nationalization (Gates, 2023; Gellagos, 2016, 83–84).

[11] Chavez viewed the Apertura Petrolera as a process of disguised privatization by the PdVSA, under which it offered generous deals to foreign firms in exchange for a fee for every oil barrel produced but agreed to cover their costs and investments. Under the initiative, however, Venezuelan oil production rose above three million barrels per day (bpd) – the highest levels in many years (Gallegos, 2016, 80–81). At the same time, with the inclusion of the Orinoco basin – which included the States of Guárico, Anzoátegui, Monagas, and Delta Amacuro – OPEC-certified Venezuelan reserves reached 296 billion barrels of oil, making the country the world's largest exporter of oil, surpassing Saudi Arabia (Tinker, 2015, 148–149).

to sign joint ventures (operating agreements) with the PdVSA by granting the company 60-percent share or face nationalization.

Almost all – 30 out of 32 – foreign oil companies involved in Venezuelan oil exploration and production at the time signed such "operating agreements," which included Chevron and Texaco (USA), Statoil (Norway), Total (France), BP (UK), and some Chinese, Indian, and Russian energy companies. But two US-based companies – ExxonMobil and ConocoPhillips – refused to sign such agreements, and eventually left Venezuela, filing lawsuits accusing the Chavez regime of actions tantamount to nationalization without compensation (Victor et al., 2012; Tinker, 2015, 148–150).[12]

By 2008–09, Chavez had hugely expanded his nationalization and socialization spree by taking over thousands of private companies and industries in sectors ranging from petroleum and oil to steel and mining, banking to telecommunications, and tourism and travel to transportation.[13] Chavez also offered tax and financing benefits to companies to run their businesses by worker cooperatives – numbers of such cooperatives swelled to 280,000 in 2009 from 820 in 1999 when Chavez took office (Gellagos, 2016, 84). As a result of Chavez's massive nationalization drive, the number of private companies in Venezuela dropped from 14,000 in 1998 to 9,000 in 2011 (Brown, 2018, 2). From the early 2000s, Chavez also vastly increased his social programs and services to help reduce poverty, improve literacy, and increase access to health care among the poor (Hellinger and Spanakos, 2017).[14]

Chavez also attempted to salvage Cuba from the financial ruins caused by the discontinuation of Soviet financial assistance since the end of Cold War (Hufbauer et al., 2007, 13). In October 2000, Chavez signed the *Convenio Integral de Cooperación* (Oil for Services Agreement) with the Castro regime, under which Venezuela supplied 53,000 barrels per day (bpd), one-third of Cuba's energy needs, worth approximately $400 million – one-sixth of Cuba's total imports. As a result, by early 2004, Cuba's debt to PdVSA reached $752 million (Erikson, 2005, 411).[15]

[12] See also: foreignpolicy.com/2018/07/16/how-venezuela-struck-it-poor-oil-energy-chavez/, accessed on January 11, 2023.

[13] The Chavez regime in 2009 took over a 60-percent stake in Venezuela's largest steel producer, Ternium SA; nationalized food giant Cargill and Fertintro, the country's largest fertilizer producer, which was partially owned by Koch Brothers (US); seized 494,000 acres of land from British meat company Vestey Foods; seized Venezuelan gold mine company, Gold Reserve Inc., and two years later nationalized all the gold mines. Earlier, in 2007, Chavez nationalized CANTV, in which Verizon (US) had 28.5-percent share; in 2010, he took over Banco Federal (and also arrested 16 bankers); and in 2011, he nationalized Conferry, the country's largest commercial shipping company (Miltimore, 2020)

[14] Studies suggest that the Chavez regime spent more than $23 billion on social programs between 2003 and 2008, which succeeded in reducing the number of poor households in the country by approximately 50 percent and extremely poor households by 72 percent (Weisbrot, 2009). Overall, the programs succeeded in driving down poverty rates in Venezuela from 37 percent in 2005 to 25 percent in 2012 (see Table 1 in ECLAC, 2014).

[15] Chavez indeed provided crucial financial support to Cuba during his entire tenure (1998–2013). His successor, Nicolas Maduro, also continued the support. In 2013–2014, Maduro supplied Cuba with

Chavez also significantly expanded Venezuela's ties with China. When he came to power, Venezuela did not sell any oil to China, but in 2012 Venezuela sold over 600,000 bpd, and by April 2014 China and India jointly received 959,000 bpd – making the Asian countries the leading market for Venezuelan oil (Tinker, 2015, 150–151). Chavez also invited Chinese investors to invest in the Venezuelan oil industry (Erikson, 2005, 415–417). In September 2009, in response to the US arms embargo of 2006 against Venezuela, Chavez signed a $2.2 billion arms purchase deal with Russia, further strengthening the Russian presence in Venezuela. By then, Russian-owned Petromonagas already had a sizeable share in the Orinoco belt (Bull and Rosales, 2020; Corrales and Penfold, 2011, 100–101).[16]

Sanctions against the Chavez Regime

The US geared up sanctions against the Chavez regime in 2005 under President George W. Bush. Using the Foreign Relations Authorization Act of FY2004–2005 (P.L. 107-228), the Bush Administration in 2005 determined that Venezuela had failed to adhere to its obligations under international narcotics agreements. The next year, the US imposed an arms embargo against Venezuela by prohibiting all commercial arms sales and retransfers to the country, pursuant to Section 40A of the Arms Export Control Act, 1976 (P.L. 94-329), for its failure to cooperate with the narcotics agreements.[17]

In 2008, the US Treasury Department used Executive Order (EO) 13224, originally issued in 2001 in response to the September 11 attack, to impose financial sanctions on two individuals and two travel agencies in Venezuela for their support for a Lebanon-based Shiite group named Hezbollah (Seelke, 2022, 1). Then, on September 11, 2008, Chavez gave Patrick Duddy, the US ambassador to Venezuela, 72 hours to leave the country, accusing him of instigating violent protests in Venezuela. In response, the Bush Administration expelled Venezuela's top envoy from Washington.[18]

Subsequently, in 2009, the US Government Accountability Office (GAO) in 2009 determined that the Chavez regime had contributed to an increase in narcotics trafficking in the Latin American region by not cooperating with US counternarcotics efforts, and by allowing the Revolutionary Armed Forces of Colombia (FARC), a

80,000 bpd, although Venezuela's oil exports fell by 20 to 30 percent during the period (Riggirozzi, 2011, 15). Also see Erickson (2005).

16 Corrales and Romero (2012, 8–9), however, maintain that the US ban on arms sales to Venezuela might have driven the Chavez regime to seek closer relations with Russia and Iran, but the arms deal with Russia actually did not result in a "colossal and disproportionate expansion" of Venezuelan arms spending.

17 Apparently, President George Bush's sanction on Venezuela was also prompted by the public spectacle of Hugo Chavez. On September 20, 2006, while addressing the UN General Assembly session in New York, Chavez called Bush "the devil."

18 For greater detail, see: www.cfr.org/timeline/venezuelas-chavez-era, accessed on January 6, 2023.

Colombian leftist paramilitary group, to carry on drug production and trafficking through the Venezuelan territory.[19]

Sanctions against the Maduro Regime

The US sanctions campaign against Venezuela scaled up momentously after Nicolas Maduro, Chavez's handpicked successor, became president of the country in 2013, following Chavez's death.[20] A staunch political and ideological lieutenant of Chavez,[21] Maduro himself was elected in the next presidential election held on April 14, 2013, within five weeks of Chavez's death.[22] Immediately after assuming power, Maduro went on the offensive against the US, expelled three US diplomats accusing them of facilitating acts of sabotage against his government and assisting opposition movements against his regime.[23]

In December 2014, the US Congress passed the Venezuela Defense of Human Rights and Civil Society Act, 2014 (P.L. 113-278) requiring the president to impose sanctions against those responsible for significant acts of violence, serious human rights abuses, and antidemocratic actions in Venezuela. Pursuant to this Act, in March 2015, the Obama Administration issued EO 13692 blocking assets and imposing visa restrictions against those persons or entities who, currently or formerly, engaged in undermining democratic processes or institutions, human rights abuses, penalizing freedom of expression and peaceful assembly, and public corruption in Venezuela.

These sanctions had immediate effect on the Venezuelan economy and polity. In 2015, the country's oil exports declined sharply, when global oil prices also fell to $30 per barrel, and consequently, the country's predominantly oil-dependent GDP shrunk by 16 percent, and inflation rate soared to 68.5 percent. As a result, in the Venezuelan National Assembly election held in 2015, Maduro's political party –the United Socialist Party (PSUV, *Partido Socialista Unido de Venezuela*) – suffered its largest electoral loss in 16 years, when the US-backed opposition coalition – the Democratic Unity Roundtable (MUD, *Mesa de la Unidad Democrática*) – won a two-thirds supermajority.

19 Report number GAO-09-806. July 20, 2009.

20 Chavez was Venezuelan president for 14 years (1998–2013). He won the country's presidential elections four times: in 1998 with 56 percent of the vote; in 2000, with 59.7 percent (in 2002, he was overthrown by a military coup, but reinstalled in power within two days); in 2006, with 63 percent, and in 2012, with 54 percent. Venezuelan presidents were originally elected for a five-year term without the possibility of immediate reelection, but in 1999, Chavez changed the term to six years and eliminated term limits. Chavez's constitutional reform allowed all elected political officials, not just the president, to seek indefinite reelection. Chavez also reshaped the country's Supreme Court with judges of his own choice (Bull and Rosales, 2020; Gellagos, 2016; Tinker, 2015).

21 Maduro served as a member of Venezuelan National Assembly, as foreign minister, and as vice president during the Chavez regime. In 2012, after revealing that he suffered from cancer, Chavez asked his party to support Maduro in the future presidential election.

22 Maduro, however, won with a narrow margin of just 1.5 percent over his challenger, in contrast with his mentor Chavez, who managed to win decisively, defeating opposition candidates in most cases by double digits (Tinker, 2015, 210).

23 U.S. Expels Three Venezuelan Diplomats in Tit-for-Tat Move. *Reuters News*, October 2, 2013.

Venezuelan economic conditions deteriorated even further the next year as inflation skyrocketed, the government's import capabilities withered, and widespread shortages of staples and medicines hit the general population. In January 2016, Maduro declared a state of economic emergency as crude oil exports, which accounted for around 90 percent of the country' total exports, descended from $88 a barrel in 2015 to $34 in 2016, more than halving national income in just one year, and the country's inflation rate jumped to 720 percent, with food inflation peaking at 1,400 percent (Cannon and Brown, 2016, 615–616; Santos, 2017, 61). Capitalizing on the rapidly deteriorating political situation, in March 2016 the opposition-controlled National Assembly passed legislation recalling Maduro from office (Bisson, 2019; Gill, 2017).

Sanctions under the Trump Administration

President Donald Trump issued six EOs in four years, imposing the harshest ever financial sanctions on Venezuela, citing, among others, the Maduro government's abuse of human rights, antidemocratic actions, and corruption.[24] EO 13808, issued in August 2017 following the July 2017 Venezuelan parliamentary election in which Maduro declared victory while the opposition alleged widespread vote rigging,[25] restricted the Maduro government's access to US financial markets and prohibited US persons, companies, and anyone financially related to US persons from purchasing or trading new Venezuelan government debt, including PdVSA bonds, with certain maturity dates.[26]

In 2017, the EU and Canada also joined the US in imposing unilateral sanctions against the Maduro government. In its first sanctioning measures, the EU urged Venezuelan political actors and institutions to reach a constructive solution by fully respecting the rule of law and human rights, democratic institutions, and the separation of power (Beucillon, 2016, 113).[27] Canada, in its turn, imposed targeted asset freezes and prohibitions on some named individuals within the Maduro government, blaming it for "systemic erosion of Venezuela's democratic institutions and its grave human rights abuses."[28] In response, the Maduro government expelled the Canadian top diplomat in Venezuela (Hofer, 2018, 164).

[24] The EOs were: EO 13808 (issued on August 24, 2017), 13827 (issued on March 19, 2018), 13835 (issued on May 21, 2018), 13850 (issued on November 1, 2018), 13857 (issued on January 25, 2019), and 13884 (issued on August 5, 2019).

[25] The election was marked by numerous clashes between government security forces and protesters that left more than 130 dead and hundreds injured (OHCHR, 2017).

[26] Some news reports suggest that President Trump in August 2017 considered a "military option" on Venezuela, a proposition rejected by many Latin American leaders. Apparently to quell such speculation, Vice President Mike Pence later that year visited several Latin American countries (Ramsey and Smilde, 2020, 15–16).

[27] See European Council Decision concerning restrictive measures in view of the situation in Venezuela (2017/2074/CFSP).

[28] See: www.international.gc.ca/world-monde/international_relations- relations internationales/sanctions/venezuela.aspx?lang=en.

By early 2018, under the pressures of Western sanctions, the Venezuelan economy was in free fall: The country's GDP had fallen by almost 50 percent since 2013; although oil prices recovered in early 2016, reaching more than double the lowest point in 2014, the country's oil production dropped from roughly three million bpd in 1999 to about 1.25 million bpd in 2016. Due to the balance-of-payments crisis, the Maduro government had to cut its imports by more than 70 percent, which led to a severe scarcity of food, medicines, and basic staples in the country; 87 percent of the country's households fell below the national poverty line; the infant mortality rate increased by at least 30 percent while maternal mortality went up 65 percent, compared with 2015. The worsening humanitarian situation resulted in the largest migration and refugee crisis the western hemisphere in modern history – over 2.3 million Venezuelans fled the country, mostly since 2015, and neighboring Colombia alone received at least one million (Bahar, 2018; Cheatham and Roy, 2023).

To bypass the disastrous effects of sanctions, in February 2018, the cash-strapped Maduro government lunched a Bitcoin-like cryptocurrency called the "*petro*," linking its value to Venezuelan crude oil and other commodities, and claimed that the *petro* had already raised $3.3 billion. But it was actually issued as a debt instrument, not as a cryptocurrency, and its operational viability remained highly questionable as it was neither circulated widely within Venezuela nor sold on any major cryptocurrency exchange (Seelke, 2019, 14). Also, Venezuelan law explicitly prevents the use of oil reserves for backing any financial instruments (Hernandez, 2018, 10).

In response, the Trump Administration issued three Executive Orders in quick succession between March and November 2018: EO 13827, issued in March, prohibited US persons and businesses from any transactions involving Venezuelan digital currency, coin, or token; EO 13835, issued in May, prohibited any transactions of Venezuelan debt, effectively cutting off the Maduro government, including the state monopoly PdVSA, from any kind of debt financing or raising funds in international markets; and EO 13850, issued in November, set forth a framework to block the assets of, and prohibit certain transactions with, any person who engaged in illicit transactions with the PdVSA, the Central Bank of Venezuela (*El Banco Central de Venezuela*), the state gold mining company Minerven, and such other entities. The EO also designated 26 Venezuelan officials, including Maduro and seven justices of the Venezuelan Supreme Court (Camilleri, 2021, 91; Seelke and Nelson, 2018).[29]

In December 2018, when the country was almost totally paralyzed by severe economic sanctions and domestic political turmoil, Maduro was reelected for the second term with 68 percent of the vote. But over 50 countries, including the US, Canada, the EU, and many Latin American neighbors of Venezuela, labeled the election as illegitimate and unacceptable. Immediately after Maduro was sworn in for his second term on January 10, 2019, the National Assembly leader Juan Guaidó

[29] Maduro was the fourth head of state brought directly under US sanctions – the others were Libyan leader Kaddafi, Iranian leader Khomeini, and Russian president Putin.

claimed himself as the president of the country, declaring that the illegal election disqualified Maduro and entitled him to the presidency.[30] Guaidó received instant recognition from many countries, including the US and the EU, as well as the OAS. Maduro, on the other hand, backed by a few countries, such as Cuba, Mexico, and Russia, dismissed Guaidó's actions as a coup, and ordered the expulsion of all US diplomats from Venezuela within 72 hours (Ramsey and Smilde, 2020; Seelke, 2020, 19).

The US response was sharp and immediate. In January 2019, President Trump issued EO 13857, blocking all property and interests of PdVSA subject to US jurisdiction and prohibiting US persons and companies from engaging in any transactions with the company, and restricting the financial and visa transactions of non-US persons, including foreign energy companies, that assisted or supported the Maduro government or the PdVSA. Then, in August 2019, Trump issued EO 13884, freezing the property and interests of the Maduro government in the US and within the control of US persons, and imposing sanctions on several Venezuelan vessels and aircraft.[31]

In December 2019, the US Congress passed two important statutes in relation to Venezuelan sanctions: the Venezuela Emergency Relief, Democracy Assistance, and Development Act, 2019 (VERDAD: P.L. 116-94) and the Humanitarian Assistance to the Venezuelan People Act, 2019 (H.R. 854). The VERDAD, among others, recognized Guaidó as interim president of Venezuela, acknowledged the Guaidó-led National Assembly as the country's only legitimate legislative body, extended sanctions against Venezuela on the grounds of corruption and undemocratic actions through 2023, and directed the president to seek diplomatic engagement and negotiated settlement to pave the way for free and fair elections in Venezuela.[32]

By June 2020, the Office of Foreign Assets Control (OFAC) had imposed sanctions on, and frozen the assets of, at least 144 Venezuelan or Venezuelan-connected individuals, including seven Venezuelan law makers, and the State Department revoked the visas of hundreds of individuals and their families, including Venezuela's top political leaders, and the officials of state oil company PdVSA and the Venezuelan Central Bank (Seelke, 2022, 2).

[30] In December 2022, the Venezuelan National Assembly removed Guaidó from office, and replaced him with Dinorah Figuera.

[31] The EO however authorized the Office of Foreign Assets Control (OFAC), under the Treasury Department, to issue licenses for transactions involving delivery of food, agricultural commodities, medicine, and remittances; and to allow certain transactions and activities related to PdVSA and its US subsidiaries, such as PDV Holding Inc. (PDVH) and CITGO Holding, and to grant licenses to some US companies, such as Chevron, to work in Venezuela with PdVSA up to July 2019 (Seelke, 2022).

[32] The VERDAD also restricted export of defense articles to Venezuela, and required related government agencies to adopt strategies to counter any Russian influence in Venezuela (Seelke, 2020).

Measures against Evasion of Sanctions

The Trump Administration also took a variety of measures to prevent the evasion of sanctions by the Maduro government[33]. In 2019, the US sanctioned 24 Venezuelan-owned shell companies based in Florida and New York for their links to sanctioned Venezuelan individuals who allegedly controlled a $2.4 billion foreign exchange network to conceal illicit ownership of luxury goods, aircraft, and yachts in violation of US sanctions. The same year, the US also sanctioned 21 Colombia-related designations for money laundering and other illicit transactions in favor of sanctioned Venezuelan individuals and entities, and imposed maritime sanctions on Panama, the Marshall Islands, and Liberia for serving as flags of convenience for illicit maritime activity aimed at helping Venezuela in evading US sanctions.

In 2020, the US targeted Venezuela's air transport and maritime industries, including state-owned flag carrier Conviasa and its fleet of 40 planes, and pressured international ship certification companies to withdraw certifications for Venezuelan tankers involved in exports of oil and other sanctioned materials.

The US also accused several of its traditional adversaries, including Russia, China, Iran, and Cuba, of helping Venezuela evade sanctions. For example, the US accused Russia of helping Venezuela by sending military personnel and equipment and helping illicit shipment of Venezuelan oil; China of supplying advanced technology to the Maduro government for surveillance of Venezuelan citizens; Cuba of providing military and intelligence support to the Maduro government in exchange for subsidized oil;[34] and Iran of using Iranian tankers for illicit deliveries and transport of Venezuelan gasoline and oil.[35]

The US also sanctioned two subsidiaries of Russian state-controlled oil company Rosneft and four other Russian shipping companies for transporting Venezuelan oil;[36] Moscow-based Evrofinance Mosnarbank for financing Venezuela's failed cryptocurrency, the *petro*; several Russian individuals and entities, including Switzerland-based subsidiaries of Rosneft for facilitating Venezuelan oil shipments, in addition to four maritime firms and vessels for illegally transporting Venezuelan oil to Cuba.[37]

33 This section is primarily based on Regilme (2022).

34 As discussed in Chapter 8, in 2019, US Secretary of State Mike Pompeo alleged that more than 2,000 Cuban security personnel provided military and intelligence support and trained Venezuelan security forces in exchange for subsidized oil.

35 The US authorities reportedly detected that, in May 2020, five Iranian vessels delivered gasoline and other petroleum products to Venezuela and Iran provided Venezuela with equipment, supplies, and technical expertise to support PdVSA refinery operations (Seelke, 2022, 28).

36 Rosneft had long been involved in Venezuela's oil exports and it also provided the PdVSA with diluent cargos as an alternative supplier to US exporters and participated in multiple joint venture oil production projects in Venezuela. Rosneft maintained, however, that its trading with PdVSA did not constitute a violation of US sanctions. As of February 2020, no sanction was imposed directly on Rosneft for its trading with PdVSA (Brown, 2020, 33).

37 No sanction was, however, imposed on the Iranian oil tanker company, the National Iranian Tanker Company (NITC), which was found to be involved in illicit deliveries and transport of Venezuelan

The US also sanctioned a Chinese company, the China National Electronics Import and Export Corporation (CEIEC), in 2017 for supplying advanced technology for surveillance of Venezuelan citizens.

Sanctions under the Biden Administration

President Joe Biden continued the US sanction regimes against Venezuela. On March 1, 2023, Biden renewed EO 13692 – originally issued by President Obama in 2015 – describing the situation in Venezuela as an "unusual and extraordinary threat" to US national security and foreign policy. The EO, which has been renewed every year since 2015, provides an expansive basis for the US to continue its unilateral sanctioning measures against Venezuela and the Maduro regime.

In April 2020, the Biden Administration also opposed the IMF's emergency financial relief to Venezuela,[38] and in March 2021, a US delegation to the World Trade Organization (WTO) blocked Venezuela's request to the WTO Panel to review US sanctions, arguing that the Venezuelan delegation lacked legitimacy to represent the Venezuelan people (Akande et al., 2021).

As of July 2023, the Biden Administration had not imposed any new sanctions on Venezuela, except that in June 2021 it pledged over $400 million in humanitarian assistance to Venezuelans and authorized certain COVID-19 related transactions, and on November 26, 2022, OFAC eased some oil sanctions on Venezuela in an effort to allow US oil company Chevron and some others to resume a "limited" amount of oil production in Venezuela under the condition that the profits from the sale would be directed to paying down debt owed to Chevron, rather than to the coffers of the state-owned PdVSA. The concession was also prompted by a severe gas shortage and sky-rocketing gas prices in the US at the time, as well as newly started negotiations between the Maduro government and the country's opposition leaders.[39]

III IMPACT OF SANCTIONS ON VENEZUELAN ECONOMY AND POPULATION

By the end of 2022, Venezuela had come under near-comprehensive economic and financial sanctions regimes imposed primarily by the US, that encompassed an arms embargo, a ban on oil and petroleum exports, designation of key individuals and entities under sanctions lists, and the freezing and capture of assets of important individuals and businesses. The sanctions regimes covered more than 100 key Venezuelan officials, including the country's head of state,[40] key business entities,

gasoline and oil, as by then the company was already under sanctions under the Iran Threat Reduction and Syria Human Rights Act, 2012 (P.L. 112-158) (Brown, 2020, 6).

[38] US to Block Iran's Request to IMF for $5 Billion Loan to Fight Coronavirus. *Wall Street Journal*. April 7, 2020.

[39] President Joe Biden Starts to Lift Sanctions on Venezuela. *The Economist*. November 27, 2022.

[40] The targeted individuals included Venezuelan President Maduro, his wife and son; Vice President Delcy Rodríguez, Diosdado Cabello (Socialist Party president); eight Supreme Court judges; the

including in the petroleum, gold, mining, food, and banking sectors, including Venezuela's central bank and PdVSA, the country's largest foreign exchange earner.

The sanctions regimes, which became increasingly severe from 2014, coinciding with Maduro's assumption of power, have already had debilitating effects on the Venezuelan economy and population. The economy is literally in shambles, inflation and poverty rates skyrocketed, outward migration of the people has already created one of the largest refugee crises in the western hemisphere in modern times, the law and order situation has deteriorated, and human rights violations have become rampant (Rodriguez, 2019; Weisbrot and Sachs, 2019).

Economic Depression

Available records indicate that Venezuela's GDP (in 2010 US dollars) declined from about $450 billion in 2013 to less than one-quarter of that, $100 billion, in 2020.[41] A decline of more than 80 percent of GDP in six years, which is more than twice the magnitude of decline that the US endured during the Great Depression in the 1930s, signifies "the single largest economic collapse outside of war in at least 45 years" (Seelke, 2020, 11). Such a catastrophic plunging of the economy may be attributed to many factors, such as political turmoil, economic mismanagement, fluctuations of global oil prices, and so on, but the single-most important factor must be the near-comprehensive sanctions imposed by the US and other Western countries.

Crude Oil Production and Exports

As mentioned above, historically the petroleum and oil sector accounted for over 95 percent of Venezuela's export revenues and foreign exchange earnings. In 1970, the country produced 3.7 million bpd, which declined to the range of 1.6 to 2.1 million bpd during the 1970s and 1980s, and then increased to 3.4 million bpd in 1998. During the Chavez regime (1998–2013), the country's oil production stabilized in the range of 2.5 to 3.3 million bpd (Brown, 2020, 18–19).[42]

After the imposition of the first round of US sanctions targeted at the oil sector and the PdVSA in 2017, Venezuela's oil production nose-dived. By April 2018, crude oil production declined to 1.4 million bpd, the lowest since 1949 (Hernandez, 2018), and by 2020, it declined further to less than 0.5 million bpd (Seelke, 2020, 47). The

leaders of Venezuela's army, national guard, and national police; governors; the director of the central bank; and the foreign minister. In May 2019, OFAC lifted sanctions against the former head of Venezuela's intelligence service, General Manuel Cristopher Figuera, who broke ranks with Maduro, and in June 2022, sanctions on Carlos Malpica Flores, a nephew of Maduro's wife, were lifted (Seelke, 2022).

41 The Economic Intelligence Unit (EIU)'s Country Report on Venezuela 2020 forecasted a further contraction of the Venezuelan economy by another 30 percent in the year 2020. The World Bank website provides Venezuelan GDP data up to the year 2014 only (accessed on May 12, 2023). Trading Economics (Tradingeconomics.com, accessed on May 12, 2023) suggests that Venezuelan GDP has shrunk by double digits annually since 2015, and by 35 percent in the year of 2019 alone.

42 See also Giusti (1999); Johnson (2018); and Rentner (2004).

country's oil production, however, recovered somewhat from its historical low in 2020 to 636,000 bpd in 2021, and to 788,000 bpd in February, 2022.[43]

Such a catastrophic decline in Venezuela's oil production and exports was caused mainly because the country lost its biggest oil importer – the US. Between 2014 and 2020, the country's crude oil exports to the US fell from approximately 0.07 million bpd to 0.01 million bpd.[44] Also, the US sanctions prohibited US refineries from processing of Venezuelan petroleum products and crude oil. Moreover, the US sanctions regimes not only seek to eliminate US–Venezuela petroleum trade, they also aim to make it challenging for Venezuela to secure alternative buyers (Brown, 2020, 2–3).[45]

Venezuela, however, managed to export considerable amounts of crude oil to China, India, Cuba, and some other countries, but exports to Cuba suffered a setback after the US imposed secondary sanctions in 2018 on the subsidiaries of Russian oil company Rosneft, which had been helping PdVSA to evade the sanctions (Seelke, 2020, 2).[46] Available records indicate that Venezuelan crude oil exports to India and China increased by 49 percent and 34 percent, respectively, in early 2019, which was within the range of export volumes to these countries since 2017.

Since April 2019, however, the OFAC has imposed additional restrictions on non-US entities from oil and petroleum transactions with the PdVSA involving the US financial system, pursuant to EO 13884. As a result, importers of Venezuelan oil must find alternatives to US dollar and the US banking and finance systems to continue to import Venezuelan oil (Brown, 2020, 19–20).

43 See OPEC *Monthly Oil Market Report* of March, 2022; and Palacios and Monaldi (2022). According to the US Energy Information Administration's International Energy Statistics, in 2021, Venezuela was no longer among the top 10 crude oil producers or exporters in the world: www.eia.gov/tools/faqs/faq.php?id=709&t=6.

44 Some contend, however, that the declining oil production of Venezuela cannot be attributed to the sanctions alone as production had been trending lower since 2014 (Rodriguez, 2019). For greater detail on Venezuelan production and exports of crude oil in recent years, see Brown (2020); Hernandez and Monaldi (2016); Ramsey and Smilde (2020); and Seelke (2020, 47).

45 The US economic sanctions against Venezuela do not explicitly prohibit non-US entities from trading in Venezuelan oil and petroleum products, although US sanctions frameworks make it difficult for the PdVSA to secure alternative buyers and suppliers. As mentioned above, Russian oil company Rosneft facilitated Venezuelan crude oil trade with independent oil refiners in China and provided Venezuela with petroleum products. The Further Consolidated Appropriation Act, 2020 (P.L. 116-94) of the US Congress raised concerns about Rosneft's cooperation with Venezuela and required the president to coordinate sanctions on Venezuela with international partners. Also, EO 13884, issued in August 2019, makes non-US entities that transact with PdVSA potentially subject to US sanctions (Brown, 2020, 20–21).

46 Some US and Russian oil companies still operate in Venezuela under general licenses issued and renewed periodically by OFAC. For example, American Chevron, Halliburton, Schlumberger, Baker Hughes, and Weatherford International, and Russian Petromonagas have been allowed to produce crude oil in Venezuela, albeit in joint ventures with state-run monopoly PdVSA. Russian joint venture Petromonagas produces about 120,000 bpd, or 15 percent of Venezuela's total oil production (Seelke, 2020, 2). As mentioned above, due to a sharp rise in gas prices in the US following the Russian invasion of Ukraine, the Biden Administration in November 2022 allowed Chevron to produce and export Venezuelan oil to the US.

Acute Shortages of Essentials

An inevitable result of the steep decline in exports commensurately affected the Venezuelan government's capacity to import essential food, medicine, and other necessities of life – goods for which Venezuela has little or no domestic production capacity, and has traditionally depended on imports. Since 2017, the government's revenue has been in free fall due to loss of export earnings as well as lack of domestic revenue generation activities, but by 2021, the government's revenue had contracted by almost 99 percent.[47]

Consequently, average monthly imports into Venezuela declined by 46 percent in 2019 compared with 2018, and by another 50 percent in 2020 (Ramsey and Smilde, 2020, 14). On top of that, some estimates suggest that consumer prices increased by more than 17,000 percent in 2019, critically depleting the value of salaries and savings of ordinary people (Palacios and Monaldi, 2022).[48]

In August 2018, a UN team reported that sanctions regimes were responsible for both directly and indirectly aggravating the shortages in medicines, such as insulin and anti-retroviral drugs, in Venezuela (Ashley, 2021; OHCHR, 2017). The Venezuelan population has indeed been gripped with massive shortages of essential food and medicine at least since 2019.

Massive Spread of Poverty

Several indicators suggest that the sanctions have phenomenally increased poverty and starvation in Venezuela, and that as many as 40,000 deaths that occurred during 2017–2018 can be attributed to the burgeoning humanitarian catastrophe unleashed by the sanctions regimes (Weisbrot and Sachs, 2019). Studies indicate that the percentage of Venezuelans living in poverty had increased from 48.4 percent in 2014 to 96 percent in 2019 – and 80 percent of them were considered to be in extreme poverty (UNOCHA, 2020). The World Food Program (WFP) estimates that as of mid 2019, more than 9.3 million Venezuelans were food insecure, of which 7 million (24.4 percent) were moderately food insecure, and 2.3 million people (8 percent) were severely food insecure (Seelke, 2022, 14). The report also noted that 25 percent of Venezuelan households surveyed lacked reliable access to potable water, electricity, and gas supplies (UNOCHA, 2020).

Mass Exodus

Another inevitable consequence of near-comprehensive sanctions against Venezuela has been a massive exodus of the population abroad. Available reports indicate that, as of August 2020, more than 5.1 million, more than 15 percent of the country's population, fled the country. Roughly 4.3 million (about 85 percent) moved to Latin

47 See "Preliminary Findings of UN Special Rapporteur Alena Douhan on the Negative Impact of Unilateral Coercive Measures on Venezuela." February 21, 2021. Available at www.ohchr.org.

48 Some other useful references include: Cannon and Brown (2016); Cheatham and Roy (2023); Santos (2017); and Seelke (2020).

American and Caribbean countries, such as Colombia (more than 1.8 million), Peru (829,708), Chile (455,494), Ecuador (362,857), Argentina (179,069), Brazil (264,617), and Panama (121,123), and many thousands also moved to the US (Seelke, 2022, 15; UN, 2019; UNOCHA, 2020).

A report of February 2023 suggests that the number of Venezuelan refugees had swelled to more than 7.17 million – about one-quarter of the population – making the exodus one of the largest refugee crises in the contemporary world. More than 80 percent of these refugees (nearly six million) settled in 17 countries in the Caribbean and Latin America. The recipients of the largest numbers of refugees were Colombia (2.48 million), Peru (1.51 million), Ecuador (502,200), Chile (444,400), and Brazil (414,500).[49]

Some studies, however, suggest that the exodus of Venezuelans began in the late 1990s, coinciding with the advent of the Chavez regime, and that an estimated 1.5 million Venezuelans moved to neighboring Colombia and Brazil, as well as the nearby Caribbean islands of Trinidad and Tobago, Aruba, and Curaçao, as well as the US, during the Chavez regime (1998–2013) (Ellis, 2017).

IV LEGAL INTERPRETATION OF SANCTIONS AGAINST VENEZUELA

The discussion above indicates that in the mid-to-late 2000s, US sanctions against Venezuela were directed primarily at the country's lack of cooperation in US efforts to combat international terrorism, money laundering, and drug trafficking, and that, since 2014, coinciding with Maduro's assumption of power, the US has targeted the Maduro regime's antidemocratic actions, human rights violations, corruption, and so on, with an overarching goal of a regime change.[50] The discussion above also indicates that the near-comprehensive sanctions regimes imposed against Venezuela may well be responsible for economic depression, numerous deaths, severe shortage of food and medicine, massive poverty and starvation, and mass exodus of Venezuelans from their homeland.

It is also clear that almost all the sanctions regimes imposed by the US and some other countries against Venezuela have been unilateral and extraterritorial in nature – no multilateral sanctions have been imposed by the UN. On the face of it, the grounds of unilateral sanctions, such as lack of cooperation with respect to terrorism, money laundering, and drug trafficking, may well constitute a breach of the

[49] The report, produced by the Center for Disaster Philanthropy in May 2023, indicates that there are human movements in both directions across Venezuelan borders. However, the number of people who have returned is believed to be low. For greater detail, see: disasterphilanthropy.org/disasters/venezuelan-refugee-crisis/.

[50] Among others, President Trump's EO 13808, issued on August 24, 2017, clearly stipulates that the objectives of US sanctions include the removal of Maduro from office on the grounds of "human rights abuses, including arbitrary or unlawful arrest and detention of Venezuelan citizens, interference with freedom of expression …."

international rights of another state because of the international nature of such activities. On the other hand, the grounds like the Maduro regime's violations of the political and civil rights of its own citizens may constitute egregious violations of international human rights norms and customs, as envisaged, for example, by the UN Human Charter, the International Covenant on Civil and Political Rights (ICCPR), and the International Covenant on Economic, Social, and Cultural Rights (ICESCR), but they may not constitute a breach in international law *per se* (Ashley, 2021, 194).

The legality and legitimacy of unilateral sanctions, including those with extraterritorial character, were explained in great detail in Chapter 2. Here the discussion will be limited to some of the useful international law principles, pertaining to the tests of necessity, proportionality, distinction, non-intervention, and the legal theory of *erga omnes*.

Necessity and Proportionality Tests

Available reports suggest that the human rights violations allegedly committed by the Maduro regime were investigated by various international bodies, including the International Labor Organization (ILO), the International Criminal Court (ICC), and the UN Human Rights Council (UNHRC), focusing on the principles of necessity and appropriateness for potential intervention by the international community.[51] The US and some other countries, on the other hand, have imposed unilateral sanctions on Venezuela either prior to, or during, such investigations, and, thus, determined the necessity of the sanctions in accordance with their own political preferences, clearly undermining the international community (Ashley, 2021, 241).[52]

Second, unilateral sanctions regimes imposed against Venezuela can also be questioned on the grounds of proportionality and distinction. The country's central bank's access to the global financial system has been blocked, its entire flag carrier has been sanctioned, most of its ships have been delicensed, and even third countries have largely been barred from trading with it. Venezuela is thus effectively left with no means to handle its exports and imports to ensure the availability of essential food or medicine for its population. The sanctions have thus reverberated through the lives of the entire population (Beucillon, 2021, 268). Also, the sanctions regimes have effectively blocked all property of the state-run petroleum monopoly

[51] See, for example, the call made by Michelle Bachelet, UN High Commissioner for Human Rights, on March 24, 2020, to urgently re-evaluate assistance to countries facing the coronavirus pandemic. Available at: www.ohchr.org/en/2020/03/bachelet-calls-easing-sanctions-enable-medical-systems-fight-covid-19-and-limit-global.

[52] As explained above, it is not only in respect to Venezuela, but unilateral sanctions episodes against countries like Cuba, Russia, Iran, Syria, Myanmar, Sudan, or Zimbabwe demonstrate that the sanctions regimes and consequent stigmatization of targeted states depend primarily on the targeted state's historical interactions with the sanctioning states. See also Davis and Ness (2021); Hofer (2018); and Nossal (1989).

PdVSA – the largest employer and the life-line of the country which earns more than 95 percent of the nation's exports revenue and foreign exchange – and thus, the sanctions have been indiscriminate, and most certainly impacted the whole population without any distinction (Prezas, 2021).

Third, the sanctions regimes in Venezuela have been likened to "medieval sieges of towns" (UN, 2018, 13–14),[53] that plunged the country into a "devasting humanitarian crisis" (Galbraith, 2019, 13–14), which has already resulted in a massive exodus of more than one-quarter of the country's population due to lack of access to food, medicine, and other essentials.[54] Thus, the sanctions must have violated the principle of proportionality. Although many of the sanctioning measures targeted specific companies and individuals, they have actually impacted the most vulnerable populations much more severely, as they have been left at the mercy of the black market for medical and other essential supplies (Ashley, 2021, 242).[55]

Fourth, in the midst of the Covid-19 pandemic, in April 2020, the US prevented the IMF from granting emergency financial relief to Venezuela. Such actions also violate the principle of proportionality because the suffering of the population is in no way responsible for the policies being pursued by the targeted regime, and more importantly, the loan was intended to prevent the devasting effect of a global pandemic on a population that had already been living in inhumane conditions for a prolonged period (Bachelet, 2020).[56]

Principle of Non-Intervention

The unilateral sanctions regimes imposed on Venezuela, and for that matter on any other country, can also be questioned on the ground of the principle of non-intervention. As discussed in Chapter 2, the *Declaration on Principles of International Law concerning Friendly Relations and Cooperation among States*, adopted by the UN General Assembly on October 24, 1970, and codified as customary international law, explicitly prohibits unilateral economic sanctions, and makes

[53] Following his mission to Ecuador and Venezuela in 2018, the UN Independent Expert on the Promotion of a Democratic and Equitable International Order, Alfred-Maurice de Zayas reported that economic "sanctions kill" and, likening sanctions to "medieval sieges of towns" that cause "many deaths," Mr. de Zayas remarked that "sanctions contravene the human rights obligations of the countries imposing them" (UNGA 2018, 13–15 (A/HRC/39/47/Add.1). Also see Liou et al. 2021, 808).

[54] A late 2023 update from the Brookings Institution suggests that, since 2014, nearly eight million Venezuelan refugees fled to neighboring countries and beyond, but more than 300,000 returned home since September 2020 (Cheatham and Roy, 2023).

[55] Notably, pointing to "a multifaceted economic war waged against Venezuela" by "discouraging foreign investments and shutting down the country's ability to access financial markets and crippling the country's economy," UN representative Idris Jaziary (2019) concluded that such sanctions cannot withstand the tests of necessity or proportionality under international law.

[56] Apparently, the sanctions against Venezuela have also been driven by the same old mistaken approach of "more pain for more gain" – just like Cuba, Iran, Russia, North Korea, Syria – on the presumption that devastating a target country's economy and inflicting pain on the civilian population would lead to concessions on the part of the target regime. See Chapter 1 of this volume, Gutmann (2018); and Peksen (2019) for greater detail.

it a rather duty of states to refrain from "military, political, economic or any other form of coercion aimed against the political independence or territorial integrity of any State."[57] Similarly, the 1993 *Vienna Declaration and Program of Action* (Vienna Declaration)[58] also requires states to refrain from any unilateral measure which is not in accordance with international law and which impedes the full realization of the human rights as set forth in the Universal Declaration of Human Rights, and such other international human rights instruments.[59]

Principle of *erga omnes*

Most importantly, despite massive violation of human rights domestically, Venezuela may not be held accountable for breaching international law. It is plainly obvious that no foreign state can claim to be a victim, or injured party, of a breach of international law by the actions of the Maduro regime. The situation of Venezuela rather reflects a case where the injured party is the civilian population of the state itself, who are also targeted by the sanctions imposed by the US and some other states. The Maduro regime is thus in violation of the human rights of its own population that are enshrined in the UN Charters as well as other international covenants, which have been ratified by Venezuela and incorporated in the country's law and constitution. Thus. the sanctioning states are entitled to enforce *erga omnes partes* obligation, under which third states could hold the Maduro regime accountable for committing unconstitutional acts in violation of fundamental democratic principles to its own population, in which the "international wrongful act," arguably, could be the violation of Venezuelan constitutional law (Beucillon, 2016, 194).

International Judicial Interventions

On September 26, 2018, six American states – Argentina, Canada, Colombia, Chile, Paraguay, and Peru – referredVenezuela to the ICC, accusing the Maduro government of committing human rights abuses amounting to crimes against humanity, pursuant to Article 14 of the Rome Statute of the International Criminal Court (ICC Statute).[60] The alleged crimes were based on the May 29, 2018 Report of the OAS General Secretariat and the Panel of Independent Experts on the Possible Commission of Crimes against Humanity in Venezuela (Akande et al., 2021).[61] In framing the charges against the Maduro government, the OAS Secretariate took into cognizance its own investigations as well as scores of UN reports, such as OHCHR (2017), United Nations Rapporteur (2017 and 2018), UNGA (2018), Rapporteur

57 See UNGA Resolution 2625 (XXV), Supp. No. 18, UN Doc A/RES/2625(XXV) (1970).

58 See UNGA Resolution 48/121, No. 49 UN Doc. A/CONF.157/23 (1993).

59 Many such measures may even qualify as crimes against humanity (Akande et al., 2021; Tzanakopoulos, 2015). For greater detail, see also Damrosch (2019); Dawidowicz (2017); Dupont (2012); Hofer (2017); Ruys (2017); and UNHRC (2014).

60 See the Rome Statute of the International Criminal Court, July 17, 1998, 2187 UNTS 3, art. 53(1)(a) (entered into force July 1, 2002).

61 The report, OEA/Ser.D/XV.19 (2018), is available at www.oas.org.

(2017), and UNHCHR (2019). In response, on February 13, 2020, the Maduro government submitted a competing referral, with the ICC alleging that unilateral economic sanctions regimes imposed by the US and other states against the country were rather crimes against humanity, pursuant to Article 14 of the ICC Statute.[62]

As of writing this chapter in May 2023, the case is still pending. Some experts and scholars who have joined the debate appear to be unconvinced that the Venezuelan case will hold in the ICC (Beucillon, 2016, 195; Wynter, 2020). Among other issues, they point out that, even if it is considered that unilateral sanctions are not permitted under international law, Venezuela must show proof that the sanctions regimes indeed constituted an attack directed primarily against the Venezuelan civilian population within the meaning of Article 53(1)(a) of the ICC Statute (Akande et al., 2021, 24).

Earlier, in December 2018, the Maduro government brought a complaint before the WTO (we have to keep it if not mentioned before) arguing that the US sanctions were inconsistent with the free trade principles enshrined in the General Agreement on Tariff and Trade (GATT, 1947) and the General Agreement on Trade in Services (GATS, 1994), and contributed to the economic and humanitarian crises in Venezuela (Rendon and Price, 2019).[63] As explained in Chapter 2, Venezuela eventually withdrew the complaint as the US claimed that the Maduro government lacked the legitimacy to represent Venezuela. The US also refused to approve the agenda of the WTO Dispute Settlement Body's meeting involving the Venezuelan complaint (Bogdanova, 2021).

V CONCLUDING REMARKS

Historically, Venezuela has been one of the most prosperous nations in the Americas, and one of the staunchest allies of the US in the western hemisphere. But all that changed, and quite dramatically, in the last two decades, coinciding with two phenomenal developments in the nation's history. The first was the socialist path trodden by Hugo Chavez and his heir Nicolas Maduro, which led to wholesale nationalization of almost all industrial and commercial enterprises, including the nation's bread and butter, the oil and petroleum industry, between 2005 and 2008. The second was near-comprehensive sanctions regimes imposed by the US,

[62] The Venezuelan referral – *Situation in the Bolivarian Republic of Venezuela II*, ICC-01/20 – is available at www.icc-cpi.int.

[63] The complaint alleges that the US laws and regulations, on the basis of which individual sanctions as well as trade-restrictive measures have been adopted against Venezuela, constituted a breach of GATT provisions (Art. I:1, II:1, III:4, V:2, X:3, XI:1, XIII:1) and GATS provisions (Art. II:1, XVI:2, XVII:1, XXIII:3). See United States-Measures Relating to Trade in Goods and Services – Request for consultations by Venezuela. December 28, 2018. WT/DS574/1. Previously, the former Czechoslovakia, Nicaragua, and Cuba brought such charges during the 1947–1994 GATT era, but all failed. Venezuela, however, has been the only targeted member of the WTO which has brought such a complaint since the establishment of the WTO in 1995 (Bogdanova, 2021; Chercheneff, 2021, 247–248).

especially since 2014, cutting off the country's state-run oil monopoly PdVSA as well as its central bank from the global financial system, and effectively embargoing all Venezuelan trade by sanctioning its airlines and shipping lines, and imposing a wide net of extraterritorial sanctions on third-country individuals and entities, prohibiting any cooperation with Venezuelan authorities, individuals, and companies.

Mounting evidence suggests that the unilateral sanctions regimes imposed by the US and some other countries have already had devastating effects on the Venezuelan economy and population. The economy has literally plunged into a Great Depression; the government lacks revenue, including foreign currency, to import essential food and medicine; production and export of crude oil has bottomed; hyperinflation and lack of employment and income has pushed more than two-thirds of the population below the poverty line; more than one-quarter of the population left home for abroad; and a fly-away humanitarian catastrophe has been exacerbating the situation every day as the Maduro regime tries to cling to power despite massive international resistance.

Meanwhile, the main goal of the sanctions regimes, to overthrow the Maduro regime, has so far failed miserably – even in the midst of massive sanctions, he was reelected with huge margin of the popular vote in 2017 (although the integrity of the election remains questionable). The legal standing of unilateral sanctions on Venezuela remains highly questionable because there has been no injured state; the sanctioning measures are not based on authorization of the UNSC; none of the states that have imposed unilateral sanctions against Venezuela can claim to be an "injured state"; and the actual party injured by the actions of the Maduro regime – the people of Venezuela – whose fundamental human rights and constitutional rights are being violated – are in double jeopardy under an oppressive regime as well as near-comprehensive economic and financial sanctions imposed by other nations.

REFERENCES

Akande, D., A. Payam., and E. Bjorge. 2021. Economic Sanctions, International Law, and Crimes against Humanity: Venezuela's Referral to the International Criminal Court. *American Journal of International Law*. doi.org/10.1017/ ajil.2021.20.

Ashley, L. 2021. Unilateral Coercive Measures: Towards International Humanitarian Law and International Human Rights. In S. Subedi (ed.), *Unilateral Sanctions in International Law*, pp. 233–254. Oxford: Hart Publishing.

Baburkin, S. et al. 1999. The 1992 Coup Attempts in Venezuela: Causes and Failure. *Journal of Political & Military Sociology*, 27(1):141–154.

Bachelet, M. 2020. Urgent Call for Re-evaluating Assistance to Countries Facing the Coronavirus Pandemic. Statement of UN High Commissioner for Human Rights, March 24, 2020. Available at: www.ohchr.org/en/2020/03/bachelet-calls-easing-sanctions-enable-medical-systems-fight-covid-19-and-limit-global, accessed on December 22, 2022.

Bahar, D. et al. 2018. *Venezuela: A Path Out of Misery. Policy Brief.* Washington, DC: Brookings Institution.

Beucillon, C. 2016. Practice Makes Perfect, Eventually? Unilateral State Sanctions and the Extraterritorial Effects of State Legislation. In N. Ronzitti (ed.), *Coercive Diplomacy, Sanctions and International Law*, pp. 103–126. Boston: Brill.

Beucillon, C. (Ed.). 2021. *Research Handbook on Unilateral and Extraterritorial Sanctions*. Cheltenham, UK: Edward Elgar.

Bisson, M. (Ed.). 2019. *Venezuela in Focus: Economic, Political and Social Issues*. Hauppauge, NY: Nova Science Publishers.

Bogdanova, I. 2021. Targeted Economic Sanctions and WTO Law: Examining the Adequacy of the National Security Exception. *Legal Issues of Economic Integration*. May Issue. doi.org/10.54648/LEIE2021010.

Brown, P. 2018. Venezuela Oil Sector Sanctions: Market and Trade Impacts. Congressional Research Service (CRS). IN11037. Washington, DC.

Brown, P. 2020. Oil Market Effects from U.S. Economic Sanctions: Iran, Russia, Venezuela. Congressional Research Service (CRS). R46213. Washington, DC.

Bull, B., and A. Rosales. 2020. The Crisis in Venezuela: Drivers, Transitions, and Pathways. *European Review of Latin American and Caribbean Studies*, 109(2020):107–133.

Buxton, J. 2020. Continuity and Change in Venezuela's Bolivarian Revolution. *Third World Quarterly*, 41(8):1371–1387.

Camilleri. 2021. Evolution or Revolution? U.S. Policy on Venezuela from Obama to Trump. *The Dialogue*. Available at: www.thedialogue.org/analysis/evolution-or-revolution-u-s-policy-on-venezuela-from-obama-to-trump/.

Cannon, B., and J. Brown. 2016. Venezuela 2016: The Year of Living Dangerously. *Revista de Ciencia Política*, 37(2):613–633. Maynooth University, Ireland. Available at: www.redalyc.org/articulo.oa?id=32453264017.

Cheatham, A., and D. Roy. 2023. Venezuela: The Rise and Fall of a Petrostate. Council on Foreign Relations, Washington, DC. Accessible at www.cfr.org/backgrounder/venezuela-crisis.

Chercheneff, L. 2021. Challenging Unilateral and Extraterritorial Sanctions under International Economic Law: Exploring Leads at the WTO and the OECD. In C. Beucillon (ed.), *Research Handbook on Unilateral and Extraterritorial Sanctions*, pp. 239–256. Cheltenham, UK: Edward Elgar.

Corrales, J., and M. Penfold. 2011. *Dragon in the Tropics*. Washington, DC: Brookings Institution Press.

Corrales, J., and C. Romero. 2012. *U.S.-Venezuela Relations since the 1990s: Coping with Midlevel Security Threats*. London: Routledge.

Cheatham, A., and D. Roy. 2023. Venezuela: The Rise and Fall of a Petrostate. Council on Foreign Relations, Washington, DC. Available at: www.cfr.org/backgrounder/venezuela-crisis.

Damrosch, L. 2019. The Legitimacy of Economic Sanctions as Countermeasures for Wrongful Acts. *Ecology Law Quarterly*, 46:95–111.

Davis, S., and I. Ness. 2021. Introduction: Why Are Economic Sanctions a Form of War? In S. Davis, and I. Ness (eds.), *Sanctions as War: Anti-imperialist Perspectives on American Geo-economic Strategy*, pp. 1–24. Leiden and Boston: Brill.

Dawidowicz, M. 2017. *Third-Party Countermeasures in International Law*. Cambridge: Cambridge University Press.

Di-John, J. 2009. *From Windfall to Curse?: Oil and Industrialization in Venezuela, 1920 to the Present*. University Park: Pennsylvania State University Press.

Dupont, P. 2012. Countermeasures and Collective Security. The Case of EU Sanctions against Iran. *Journal of Conflict and Security Law*, 17(3):301–336.

ECLAC. 2014. *Social Panorama of Latin America*. Mexico: Economic Commission for Latin America and the Caribbean.

Ellis, R. 2017. The Collapse of Venezuela and Its Impact on the Region. Military Review, July-August issue.

Ellner, S., and D.Hellinger. 2003. *Venezuelan Politics in the Chavez Era: Class, Polarization, and Conflict*. Boulder, CO, and London: Lynne Rienner.

Erikson, D. 2005. *Cuba, China, Venezuela: New Developments. The 2005 Annual Proceedings of the Association for the Study of the Cuban Economy*. Available at: www.ascecuba.org/c/wp-content/uploads/2014/09/v15-erikson.pdf.

Galbraith, J. 2019. Contemporary Practice of the United States. *American Journal of International Law*, 113:601–608.

Gallegos, R. 2016. *Crude Nation: How Oil Riches Ruined Venezuela*. Washington, DC: Potomac Books.

Gates, L. 2023. *Capitalist Outsiders: Oil's Legacy in Mexico and Venezuela*. Pittsburgh: University of Pittsburgh Press.

Gill, T. 2017, Embattled Venezuela Can Still Count on International Lifelines, From Russia to China. *World Politics Review*, January 12. Available at: www.worldpoliticsreview.com/embattled-venezuela-can-still-count-on-international-lifelines-from-russia-to-china/.

Gill, T. 2019. Shifting Imperial Strategies in Contemporary Latin America: The U.S. Empire and Venezuela under Hugo Chávez. *Journal of Historical Sociology*, 32(3):294–310.

Giusti, L. 1999. La Apertura: The Opening of Venezuela's Oil Industry. *Journal of International Affairs*, 53(1):117–128.

Grandin, G. 2006. *Empire's Workshop: Latin America, the United States, and the Rise of the New Imperialism*. New York: Owl Book.

Gutmann, J. et al. 2018. Economic Sanctions and Human Rights: Quantifying the Legal Proportionality Principle. Research Papers in Economics, No. 2/18. Universität Trier, Germany.

Hellinger, D. 2017. Oil and the Chávez Legacy. *Latin American Perspectives*, 44(1):54–77.

Hellinger, D., and A. Spanakos. 2017. The Legacy of Hugo Chávez. *Latin American Perspectives*, 44(1):4–15.

Hernandez, I. 2018. Venezuela and U.S. Sanctions: Some Considerations. IAEE Energy Forum. Third Quarter.

Hernandez, I., and F. Monaldi. 2016. Weathering Collapse: An Assessment of the Financial and Operational Situation of the Venezuelan Oil Industry. *Center for International Development at Harvard University*, Nov. 2016.

Hofer, A. 2017. The Developed/Developing Divide on Unilateral Coercive Measures: Legitimate Enforcement or Illegitimate Intervention. *Chinese Journal of International Law*, 16(2):175–214.

Hofer, A. 2018. The Curiouser and Curiouser: Legal Nature of Non-UN Sanctions: The Case of the US Sanctions against Russia. *Journal of Conflict & Security Law*, 23(1):75–104.

Hufbauer, G. et al. 2007. *Economic Sanctions Reconsidered: History and Current Policy*. Washington, DC: Patterson Institute for International Economics.

Johnson, K. 2018. How Venezuela Struck It Poor. *Foreign Policy*, July 16.

Karl, T. 1977. *The Paradox of Plenty: Oil Booms and Petro-States*. Berkeley, CA: University of California Press.

Liou, R., Amanda M., and D. Peksen. 2021. Revisiting the Causal Links between Economic Sanctions and Human Rights Violations. *Political Research Quarterly*, 74(4):808–821.

Miltimore, J. 2020. 8 Venezuelan Industries Hugo Chavez Nationalized (Besides Oil). *FEE Stories*, January 10, 2020. Available at: fee.org/articles/8-industries-hugo-chavez-nationalized-besides-oil-on-venezuelas-road-to-serfdom/.

Nossal, K. 1989. International Sanctions as International Punishment. *International Organization*, 43(2):301–322.

OHCHR (Office of the United Nations High Commissioner for Human Rights). 2017. *Human Rights Violations and Abuses in the Context of Protests in the Bolivarian Republic of Venezuela from 1 April to 31 July 2017, August 30, 2017*. Geneva: United Nations.

Palacios, L., and F. Monaldi. 2022. *Venezuela Oil Sanctions: Not an Easy Fix*. New York: Center for Global Energy, Columbia University School of International and Public Affairs.

Peksen, D. 2019. When Do Imposed Economic Sanctions Work? A Critical Review of the Sanctions Effectiveness Literature. *Defense and Peace Economics*, 30(6):635–647.

Petras, J. 2010. U.S. Venezuelan Relations: Imperialism and Revolution. *Voltaire Net*. Available at: www.voltairenet.org/article163455.html, accessed on May 9, 2023.

Polga-Hecimovich, J. 2019. Bureaucratic Politicization, Partisan Attachments, and the Limits of Public Agency Legitimacy: The Venezuelan Armed Forces under Chavismo. *Latin American Research Review*, 54(2):476–498.

Prezas, I. 2021. From Targeted States to Affected Populations: Exploring Accountability for the Negative Impact of Comprehensive Unilateral Sanctions on Human Rights. In C. Beucillon (ed.), *Research Handbook on Unilateral and Extraterritorial Sanctions*, pp. 385–404. Cheltenham, UK: Edward Elgar.

Ramsey, G., and D. Smilde. 2020. Recalibrating U.S. Policy in Venezuela: Learning from Failure and Seizing Opportunities. Washington, DC: Washington Office on Latin America (WOLA).

Regilme, S. 2022. United States Foreign Aid and Multilateralism under the Trump Presidency. *New Global Studies*. Available at: doi.org/10.1515/ngs-2021-0030.

Rendon, M., and M. Price. 2019. *Are Sanctions Working in Venezuela? Center for Strategic and International Studies (September 3, 2019)*. Available at: www.csis.org/analysis/are-sanctions-working-venezuela.

Rentner, S. 2004. Venezuela: How a Hydrocarbons Law Crippled an Oil Giant. *Hastings International and Comparative Law Review*, 27(2):351–362.

Riggirozzi, P. 2011. Region, Regionness and Regionalism in Latin America: Towards a New Synthesis. *New Political Economy*, 17(4):421–443.

Rivas, D. 2002. *Missionary Capitalist: Nelson Rockefeller in Venezuela*. Chapel Hill: University of North Carolina Press.

Rodríguez, F. 2019. Sanctions and the Venezuelan Economy: What the Data Say. Torino Economics, June 19. Available at: sanctionsplatform.ohchr.org/record/4734.

Ross, M. 2015. What Have We Learned about the Resource Curse? *Annual Review of Political Science*, 18(1):239–259.

Ruys, T. 2017. Sanctions, Retortions and Countermeasures: Concepts and International Legal Framework. In L. Herik (ed.), *Research Handbook on UN Sanctions and International Law*, pp. 19–51. Cheltenham, UK: Edward Elgar.

Salazar-Carrillo, J., and B. West. 2004. *Oil and Development in Venezuela during the 20th Century*. Santa Barbara, CA: ABC-CLIO.

Santos, M. 2017. Venezuela: Running on Empty. *LASA Forum*, XLVIII(1):58–62.

Seelke, C. 2020. *Venezuela: Background and U.S. Relations*. Washington, DC: Congressional Research Services.

Seelke, C. 2022. Venezuela: Overview of U.S. Sanctions. Congressional Research Service. IF10715. Washington, DC.

Seelke, C., and R. Nelson. 2018. *Venezuela: Background and U.S. Relations*. Washington, DC: Congressional Research Service.

Seelke, C. et al. 2019. Venezuela: Background and U.S. Relations. Congressional Research Service. R44841. Washington, DC.

Sylvia, R., and C. Danopoulos. 2003. The Chávez Phenomenon: Political Change in Venezuela. *Third World Quarterly*, 24(1):63–76.

Tinker, M. 2005. Staying the Course: United States Oil Companies in Venezuela, 1945–1958. *Latin American Perspectives*, 32(2):147–170.

Tinker, M. 2015. *Venezuela: What Everyone Needs to Know*. Oxford: Oxford University Press.

Tzanakopoulos, A. 2015. The Right To Be Free from Economic Coercion. *Cambridge Journal of International and Comparative Law*.

UN Rapporteur. 2018. UN Special Rapporteur on the Negative Impact of Unilateral Coercive Measures on the Enjoyment of Human Rights, 'Report of the Special Rapporteur', 17 July 2018, A/73/175.

UNGA (United Nations General Assembly). 2018. Report of the Independent Expert on the Promotion of a Democratic and Equitable International Order on His Mission to the Bolivarian Republic of Venezuela and Ecuador. A/HRC/39/47/Add. 1, September 10–28. New York: United Nations. Available at: reliefweb.int/report/venezuela-bolivarian-republic/reportindependent-expert-promotion-democratic-and-equitable.

UNHCHR. 2019. *Report of the United Nations High Commissioner for Human Rights on the Situation of Human Rights in the Bolivarian Republic of Venezuela*. Retrieved from United Nations. Available at: www.ohchr.org/EN/HRBodies/HRC/RegularSessions/Session41/Documents/A_HRC_41_18.do cx.

UNHRC (United Nations Human Rights Council). 2014. Human Rights and Unilateral Coercive Measures. UNHRC Res. (03 October 2014). A/HRC/RES/27/21.

United Nations. 2019. *Refugee and Migrant Response Plan 2020*. U.N. Coordination Platform for Refugees and Migrants from Venezuela, Response for Venezuelans (RV4), *Refugee and Migrant Response Plan 2020: January – December 2020*, December 2019.

United Nations Rapporteur. 2017. Report of the Special Rapporteur on the Negative Impact of Unilateral Coercive Measures on the Enjoyment of Human Rights, A/72/370 of 29 August 2017.

UNOCHA (UN Office for the Coordination of Humanitarian Affairs). 2020. Venezuela: Humanitarian Response Aims to Assist 4.5 million people in 2020. August 3, 2020.

USGA (United States Geological Survey). 2009. An Estimate of Recoverable Heavy Oil Resources of the Orinoco Oil Belt, Venezuela. Fact Sheet 2009-3028. Washington, DC: US Department of the Interior.

Victor, D., D. Hults., and M. Thurber. 2012. *Oil and Governance: State-Owned Enterprises and the World Energy Supply*. Cambridge: Cambridge University Press.

Weisbrot, M., and R. Ray. 2010. Update on the Venezuelan Economy. Center for Economic and Policy Research. Washington, DC. Available at: www.cepr.net/documents/publications/venezuela-2010-09.pdf.

Weisbrot, M., and J. Sachs. 2019. *Economic Sanctions as Collective Punishment: The Case of Venezuela*. Washington, DC: Center for Economic and Policy Research. Available at: www.cepr.net/images/stories/reports/venezuelasanctions-2019-04.pdf.

Weisbrot, M. et al. 2009. The Chavez Administration at 10 Years: The Economy and Social Indicators. Center for Economic and Policy Research, Washington, DC. Available at: www.cepr.net/documents/publications/venezuela-2009-02.pdf.

Wynter, F. 2020. US Sanctions in Venezuela: Economic Crimes against Humanity? *Opinio Juris*, May 23.

Yergin, D. 1991. *The Prize: The Epic Quest for Oil, Money, & Power*. New York: Simon & Schuster.

Index

www.ingramcontent.com/pod-product-compliance
Lightning Source LLC
LaVergne TN
LVHW091524200926
848483LV00002B/296
* 9 7 8 1 0 0 9 4 7 1 3 4 3 *